OXFORD PAPERBACK REFERENCE

A Dictionary of

Critical Theory

SEE WEB LINKS

Many entries in this dictionary have recommended web links. When you see the above symbol at the end of an entry go to the dictionary's web page at www.oup.com/uk/reference/resources/criticaltheory, click on **Web links** in the Resources section and locate the entry in the alphabetical list, then click straight through to the relevant websites. Additional web links are available in an appendix.

Professor Ian Buchanan is Chair of Critical and Cultural Theory at Cardiff University. He is the author of *A Reader's Guide to Deleuze and Guattari* (2007), *Fredric Jameson: Live Theory* (2006), *Deleuzism: A Metacommentary* (2000), and *Michel de Certeau* (2000). He has also edited a dozen books and special issues of journals, as well as founding the journal *Deleuze Studies*.

A Dictionary of

Critical Theory

FIRST EDITION

IAN BUCHANAN

OXFORD
UNIVERSITY PRESS

OXFORD
UNIVERSITY PRESS

Great Clarendon Street, Oxford OX2 6DP

Oxford University Press is a department of the University of Oxford. It furthers the University's objective of excellence in research, scholarship, and education by publishing worldwide in

Oxford New York

Auckland Cape Town Dar es Salaam Hong Kong Karachi
Kuala Lumpur Madrid Melbourne Mexico City Nairobi
New Delhi Shanghai Taipei Toronto

With offices in

Argentina Austria Brazil Chile Czech Republic France Greece
Guatemala Hungary Italy Japan Poland Portugal Singapore
South Korea Switzerland Thailand Turkey Ukraine Vietnam

Published in the United States
by Oxford University Press Inc., New York

First published 2010

British Library Cataloguing in Publication Data
Data available

Library of Congress Cataloging in Publication Data
Library of Congress Control Number: 2010923323

Typeset by SPI Publisher Services, Pondicherry, India
Printed in Great Britain
on acid-free paper by
Clays Ltd, St Ives plc

ISBN 978–0–19–953291–9

1 3 5 7 9 10 8 6 4 2

Contents

Introduction

Writing a dictionary is a strange and complicated task. It is strange because as a form of writing it is governed by criteria not of the writer's own making. It is complicated because deciding just what terms it should define isn't always as straightforward as one might expect. I suspect critical theory has leakier borders than most disciplines, not least because at its origins it is a hybrid of history, philosophy, psychoanalysis, and sociology. Its interdisciplinary beginning has led only to more not less interdisciplinarity as the field has grown, which is of course one of the reasons why a dictionary like this is necessary.

Somewhat arbitrarily I have set the borders in such a way as to limit the overlap between the *Oxford Dictionary of Critical Theory* and its stablemates, the *Oxford Dictionary of Literary Terms* and the *Oxford Dictionary of Philosophy.* There are cases though where I have felt it necessary to include some of the same terms these other two dictionaries cover either because critical theory has borrowed from these disciplines and used the terms in a new or expanded way, or because critical theory was in fact the point of origin of the terms.

In writing the individual entries I have tried as far as possible to anticipate the inevitable question of 'what does a particular concept do?' by giving examples of it in action. Although I have tried to be as comprehensive as possible in all entries, I have also tried to keep them simple and straight to the point. I hope the inevitable loss of detail this sometimes entails is worth it in terms of enhanced usability. There seemed to me no point in providing entries that were so dense they left the reader in need of still another dictionary to decode them. My hope is that this dictionary will serve as a stimulating starting point (not an end point!) for its readers.

Lastly, I must thank my family Tanya, Courtney and Sebastian for enduring the writing of this dictionary for over two years. No family should have to put up with that much grumpy reclusiveness.

Ian Buchanan
Cardiff, October 2009

abject That which disturbs the self, by provoking either disgust, fear, loathing or repulsion. Belonging to the realm of the psychic, the abject is the excessive dimension of either a subject or an object that cannot be assimilated. As such, it is simultaneously outside or beyond the subject and inside and of the subject. Our own bodily fluids are for the most part loathsome to us, but the intensity of that loathing owes precisely to the fact that they come from us. Thus human faeces are more disgusting to us than dog faeces, despite the fact that there is no real difference between them. The abject is not therefore an intrinsic quality of a thing, a being, or a state of affairs. It is rather a peculiar type of response, the strange power of which seems to suggest we are drawn to that which repels us. According to Julia *Kristeva, the Paris-based Bulgarian linguist and psychoanalyst, this is because it recalls—psychically—the moment of our separation from the womb, an occasion that is simultaneously bloody, painful, traumatizing, liberating and beautiful. For this reason, too, the abject tends to be associated more with the feminine than the masculine. For obvious reasons, the concept of the abject has been particularly important in cinema studies, where it is used to explain the appeal of gory horror films and slimy SF films. *See also* KHŌRA.

Further Reading: B. Creed *The Monstrous Feminine: Film, Feminism, Psychoanalysis* (1993).
J. Kristeva *Powers of Horror: An Essay on Abjection* (1982).

aboriginality A term coined by Indigenous Australian anthropologist and activist Marcia Langton to conceptualize the disparity between representations of Indigenous Australians in film and media and their actual life circumstances. Aboriginality, like Edward *Said's term *Orientalism, on which it is modelled, seeks to expose the underlying assumptions and prejudices guiding the depictions of Indigenous Australians made by white Australians. Moreover it is concerned to show the 'real world' effects these depictions have in shaping policy and hence the daily lives of Indigenous Australians.

Further Reading: C. Healy *Forgetting Aborigines* (2008).

absent cause *See* STRUCTURAL CAUSALITY.

Abstractionism In art, a movement away from *representation and *mimesis towards a kind of imagery that aims to provoke a response for what it is rather than what it looks like. For this reason, it is also known as non-figurative art. Abstractionism can take a variety of forms—in the 20th century, the major forms of Abstractionism (to a greater or lesser degree) were: *Avant-garde, *Dadaism, *Expressionism, *Futurism and *Surrealism. Artistic movements such as *socialist realism rejected Abstractionism as unworthy of the goal of celebrating the achievements of socialism. Outside of the visual arts there were attempts at Abstractionism in writing (e.g. Gertrude Stein) and music (e.g. Anton Webern).

Absurdism A term created by theatre critic Martin Esslin in his 1961 book, *The Theatre of the Absurd*, to encompass a wide range of works produced in the two decades after World War II which seem to dramatize Albert Camus' philosophical position in *Le Mythe de Sisyphe* (1942), translated as *The Myth of Sisyphus* (2005), that life is inherently absurd. Esslin identified Samuel Beckett, Eugene Ionesco, Jean Genet, and Arthur Adamov, later adding Harold Pinter to the list, as authors whose work typifies what he means by absurd. Although the work of these authors varies quite widely, it shares in common the creation of impossible situations, wordplay, a pervasive but indefinable sense of menace coupled with seemingly random explosions of violence. The absurd is closely related to the work of the *Dadaists and *Surrealists; it also claims Alfred Jarry's notion of *'pataphysics and Antonin *Artaud's *theatre of cruelty as its precursors. Although the term was originally conceived to describe theatrical productions, its use has grown more general to encompass a wide range of texts sharing the same qualities. Outside of the theatre, the work of Czech writer Franz Kafka would certainly qualify as Absurdist as would the work of Polish author Witold Gombrowicz. But it is not just a literary or 'high art' phenomenon. Today, one could point to *The Simpsons* and *South Park* as continuing examples of what Absurdism might mean. Certainly, Homer Simpson's great line 'it's funny because it's true' is utterly Absurdist in spirit.

actant A logical category in the narrative grammar devised by the Paris-based, Lithuanian linguist Algirdas Julien *Greimas.

The actant is in Greimas's language an isotope of the action. This means narrative analysis occurs at a level below that of character and indeed of character type. Thus to take one very restricted example, if detective fiction can be understood as a battle between doing good and doing evil then good and evil actants are required by the narrative structure. The obvious implication of this insight is that the detective can be a man, woman, child, alien, good or bad, all without altering the formal structure of the narrative. Moreover, multiple characters may fulfil the various actants each narrative type requires. For Greimas, the actual detective is an *actor, not an actant: the actant operates at a level below character, and tends to coincide more with what is usually known as *ideology. The redemption of the good is the actual narrative enacted through the detective bringing a killer to justice. This deep structural approach enables the inner tensions in narratives, which make them interesting to us, to be articulated. Along the same lines, Greimas proposed a *semiotic square as a means of mapping out these tensions and showing how they interact with one another.

Further Reading: A.J. Greimas *On Meaning: Selected Writings in Semiotic Theory* (1987).

active and reactive German philosopher Friedrich *Nietzsche (and after him French philosopher Gilles *Deleuze) used these categories to describe two different ways of acting and—by extension—being in the world. An action (which may be a thought, feeling, or practice) is active when it takes something as its object; conversely, it becomes reactive when it is made the object of someone or something else. Thus, if we feel sad (or happy) and we do not know why we feel this way, then we are reactive; if, however, we can discover the reason we are feeling this way, we can convert reactive forces into active forces. Reactive is not the same as negative and should not be thought of as intrinsically bad; it is, rather, the usual state of things. It is, however, a limiting state of things, because it separates us from what we can do—if we are sad for no apparent reason, and we do not seek out the cause, then we are prevented from forming an appropriate response to that cause, and our power to act is reduced. We are reacting when we could be acting, and more problematically still we are using our reaction to excuse our lack of action. Nietzsche generally refers to this state as **ressentiment*. Therefore, the challenge for both philosophy and life, according to Nietzsche, is to overcome the reactive state of things and become active, thereby constantly enhancing our power to act.

Further Reading: G. Deleuze *Nietzsche and Philosophy* (1983).

actor Any agent, perceptible at the level of *discourse, who plays a part in a narrative. In contrast to the *actant, the actor always refers to a specific individual person or thing—fate, for example, can be an actor.

actor-network theory A material-semiotic theory of social action. Developed by the sociologists Bruno Latour, Michel Callon, and John Law at the Centre de Sociologie de l'Innovation at the École Nationale Supérieure des Mines de Paris in the early 1980s as a means of explaining the conditions for the emergence of innovation. It is characterized by its treatment of people, things, and ideas as *actants, recognizing that all three are capable of initiating and sustaining an action; it also emphasizes that actants are incapable of performing most actions by themselves, but require the support of a network of other actants; similarly, actants are needed to keep networks going. Perhaps the most striking use of this type of thinking is Dutch architect Rem Koolhaas' *Delirious New York* (1994) which, in apparent ignorance of actor-network theory, produced a striking account of the development of New York which claimed just three things were crucial to its present-day look: the laying out of the city grid, the invention of the elevator, and the building code restrictions with regard to the casting of shadows. Actor-network theory is particularly useful for identifying the critical components of a particular business enterprise or a whole sector, but finds it difficult to deal with more open-ended institutions such as *culture and *society.

actual and virtual A modal distinction proposed by French philosopher Gilles *Deleuze as a replacement for the problematic real-possible distinction more commonly used in philosophy. The possible is a bad concept according to Deleuze because it presupposes that everything that is real must also be possible (which rules out a great number of conceptual inventions, consigning them to the ontologically lesser category of the unreal, or impossible), and it is unable to explain why that which is possible has not already come into being. For Deleuze, both the actual and the virtual are fully real—the former has concrete existence, while the latter does not, but it is no less real for that fact. The importance of this distinction can readily be seen by giving thought to the state of being of an idea: it may only exist in our heads, or on paper, but its effects are fully real and may also be fully actual too. Initially treated as an esoteric distinction of interest only to specialists in the field of *ontology, since the advent of computer games, and more especially the Internet, this distinction has become very important because it allows that what is seen or experienced on screen is still real, even if it isn't actual.

Adorno, Theodor (1903–69) See overleaf.

affect That which the body and mind suffers (in the classical philosophical sense), which means simply that it is something we experience passively rather than *actively. One may be affected both by internal stimulus, from the imagination, the *instincts, or more generally the *unconscious (*psychoanalysis as a whole is premised on this idea), or external stimulus, which may take a huge variety of forms, from simple physical or sensorial stimuli to complex and cognitive stimuli. Affect is sometimes treated as a synonym for emotion, but as Brian Massumi argues in *Parables for the Virtual* (2002) it differs from emotion in that it is beyond our voluntary control. For example, we may be able to discipline ourselves to ignore pain in the course of physical training, but we will still feel that pain. Pain, then, belongs to the order of affect and it is autonomous from the circuit of emotion, which is effectively our psychological response to it. In *cultural studies, in part because of work by Massumi, and also Lauren Berlant, Lawrence Grossberg, Meaghan Morris, and Elspeth Probyn, affect has become a key term for rethinking *ideology. It is generally used to explain why ideology has the hold it does. To some degree this interest in affect is sparked by an interest in the work of Gilles *Deleuze, but it also marks a strong turn toward cognitive psychology. In philosophy, affect is central to the work of Baruch de Spinoza and Henri *Bergson, authors from whom Deleuze drew a great deal of inspiration.

Further Reading: J. Halley *The Affective Turn* (2007).

affective fallacy A core idea of *New Criticism. In a famous paper, entitled 'The Affective Fallacy' (1954), W.K. Wimsatt and Monroe Beardsley, argue that the way a work affects its reader—whether it makes us laugh, cry, bored, etc.—is not a valid source of critical judgement about a text's relative worth as literature. Rather one must concentrate on its formal properties because these and these alone are sufficient to distinguish good literature from bad.
See also INTENTIONAL FALLACY.

ADORNO, THEODOR (1903–69)

German cultural critic, philosopher and key member of the *Frankfurt School. A refined critic with an incredible range of interests, Adorno wrote influential essays on music, literature, philosophy, sociology and contemporary mass culture. He belongs to a handful of thinkers who can truly be said to have been key thinkers of the 20th century.

An only child, Adorno was born in Frankfurt am Main. Comfortably middle class, his Jewish father ran a successful wine-exporting business, while his devoutly Catholic mother was (before marriage) an opera singer of some note. Adorno attended the Kaiser-Wilhelm Gymnasium, graduating at the precocious age of 17. On the advice of his friend (despite the 14 years that separated them) and tutor Siegfried *Kracauer, he studied philosophy, psychology and sociology at the Johann Wolfgang Goethe University in Frankfurt. He then completed a doctorate on *Husserl's *phenomenology in 1924. In the same year he heard fragments of Alban Berg's (as yet unfinished) opera *Wozzeck* and resolved that he would become a composer. He moved to Vienna in order to study composition with Berg and Schoenberg, but it didn't work out as he had hoped and he returned to Frankfurt in 1925. He continued to write about music for the rest of his life, but decided at this point to make philosophy his profession.

His initial attempt at producing a habilitation thesis, the passport to professorial appointment in the German system, came unstuck at the hands of the same thesis examiners who had failed his friend Walter *Benjamin. Supported by an allowance from his father, Adorno then tried unsuccessfully to follow Benjamin's footsteps and make a career as a critic, focusing primarily on music. Travelling frequently to Berlin, he mixed with theatre and music luminaries Bertolt *Brecht, Kurt Weill, and Lotte Lenya. Unlike Benjamin, Adorno was given a second chance. In 1929, a new professor was appointed at Frankfurt University, giving Adorno another opportunity to complete his habilitation, which he succeeded in doing in 1931 with a dissertation on Kierkegaard.

Now, on the threshold of his academic career, history intervened to unseat his plans. When the Nazis came into power in 1933 they immediately cracked down on what Jewish people were able to do and in 1934 Adorno's licence to teach was revoked. He moved to Oxford where he was advised to complete another doctorate under the supervision of Gilbert Ryle so as to enable him to have a career in Britain. But this proved unsatisfactory and in 1937 he accepted an invitation from Max *Horkheimer to join him in New York, where he had re-established his Institute for Social Research at Columbia University. While based in New York he also contributed to the Princeton Radio Project, which was interested in the ideological influence of radio.

In 1941, again at the instigation of Horkheimer, he relocated to Los Angeles, where he joined a large expatriate community that included Schoenberg, Brecht, and the Nobel Prize winning author Thomas Mann, whom he advised on musical matters for his anti-Nazi allegory *Doktor Faustus. Das Leben des deutschen Tonsetzers Adrian Leverkühn erzählt von einem Freunde* (1947), translated as *Doctor Faustus: The Life of the German Composer Adrian Leverkühn, as Told by a Friend* (1948). He arrived in LA with a completed manuscript of *Philosophie der neuen Musik* (1949), translated as *Philosophy of Modern Music* (1973), in his suitcase. He shared this with Horkheimer, who immediately warmed to its attack on the fragmentary nature of contemporary life and it confirmed their desire to work together, which they did over the next couple of years, producing one of the most important books of the period, *Dialektik der Aufklärung* (1944), translated as *Dialectic of Enlightenment* (1972).

Written as it was by two exiles from the Holocaust, *Dialectic of Enlightenment* does not have a particularly cheerful message, but it was in consonance with the times. Two themes stood out in particular: first, its critique of the media, or what it labelled the *culture industry; second, its critique of western rationality. Adorno and Horkheimer make the essential point that rationality, by which they mean both science and philosophy, had not prevented the genocide perpetrated against the Jews of Europe, therefore salvation for the future could not lie in that direction. The mass media, they argue, has contributed to the problem by disseminating works that are too easy, with the result that our critical faculties have become enfeebled. These themes were to be made even more explicit in what is probably Adorno's best known work *Negative Dialektik* (1966), translated as *Negative Dialectics* (1973), which famously pronounced that a new categorical imperative has been imposed, namely to arrange one's thoughts and actions so that Auschwitz will not be repeated.

Although his letters indicate that life in Santa Monica was anything but unpleasant, Adorno's writings during his seven years in America were far from sunny in disposition. Indeed, his next book *Minima Moralia*, begun in 1942 but not published until 1951, was later appended with the telling subtitle 'Reflexionen aus dem beschädigten Leben' (Reflections from a Damaged Life). But then as a German examining his home nation's collective guilt for the catastrophe that had befallen Europe there was very little to be cheerful about. Composed of short aphorisms, *Minima Moralia* tries to explain both the ideological appeal of Nazism and why Germany's defeat did not necessarily spell the end to fascism. On publication, the book rapidly became a bestseller and crossover critical success.

Despite his many misgivings about Germany, he leapt at the chance to return there definitively in 1953 as Professor of Philosophy and Sociology at the University of Frankfurt. He had made tentative steps in this direction in 1949, but it took a couple of years to sort out a proper position for him. In the intervening years he completed two further works on mass media: a study of horoscopes (published in 2001 in English as *The Stars down to Earth: And Other Essays on the Irrational Culture*) and a study of what he called the pseudo-culture of television (a collection of essays on this theme was published in 1991 in English as *The Culture Industry*). But perhaps most importantly, he saw to publication the great collective work of *The Authoritarian Personality* (Adorno et al., 1950), which sought to dissect the very character of the modern American.

Adorno's return to Germany brought with it some incredible highs, but it saw some terrible lows as well. He officially took over the directorship of the Institute for Social Research from Horkheimer who retired in 1958, though in practice he had effectively been its director since the Institute's return to Germany in 1950. He completed his thoughts on culture after Auschwitz, published in the monumental *Negative Dialectics*, which for many set the agenda for ethical discussions in the wake of the Holocaust. Adorno conceived the concept of *negative dialectics as a defence of *metaphysics. Philosophy, he argued, has missed its moment to realize itself. Alongside this project, he also developed a powerful critique of

Heidegger in *Jargon der Eigentlichkeit: Zur deutschen Ideologie* (1964), translated as *The Jargon of Authenticity* (1973), which provided a counterweight to the latter's near hegemonic hold over western philosophy. Lastly, he tried to bring together his thoughts on aesthetics, but was unable to complete this project. Drafts in various states of completion were published posthumously as *Ästhetische Theorie* (1970), translated (twice) as *Aesthetic Theory* (1984 and 1998). In this work Adorno explored the invidious position of the artwork that critiqued society from within a position of capture by the market.

In the late 1960s, Adorno was drawn into and in some respects became a target of student activism. Dismayed by the state's authoritarian response to the students' protests Adorno was willing to express solidarity with their anti-war position (he saw the Vietnam War as a continuation of the state of terror he associated with the Holocaust), but he did not share their anti-Americanism, nor could he sympathize with what he saw as their anti-intellectual posture. In January 1969, following months of student protests, strikes and sit-ins, a group of students approached the Institute for Social Research with the intent of engaging its directors in their initiatives. For some unknown reason, Adorno panicked, and fearing that the students might damage or destroy the Institute's premises called the police and asked them to intervene.

In August 1969, exhausted by several intimidating encounters with student activists, Adorno decided to vacation in Zermatt in the Swiss Alps, where against the advice of doctors he climbed a 3,000 metre high mountain. On reaching the summit, he immediately began experiencing severe chest pain. At his wife's insistence, he went to the hospital in Visp, as a precaution, and died that evening.

Further Reading: D. Claussen *Theodor W. Adorno: One Last Genius* (2008).
L. Jäger *Adorno: A Political Biography* (2004).
F. Jameson *Late Marxism: Adorno, or, The Persistence of the Dialectic* (1990).
S. Jarvis *Adorno: A Critical Introduction* (1998).
M. Jay *The Dialectical Imagination* (1973).
S. Müller-Doohm *Adorno: A Biography* (2005).
A. Thomson, *Adorno: A Guide for the Perplexed* (2006).
R. Wiggershaus *The Frankfurt School* (1994).

a

Agamben, Giorgio (1942–) Italian philosopher best known for his concept of **homo sacer*. Agamben studied at the University of Rome, completing a doctorate on the political thought of Simone Weil. In 1966 and 1968 he participated in Martin *Heidegger's seminars on Heraclitus and *Hegel. He was close friends with Pier Paolo Pasolini (who gave him a bit part in one of his films) and Italo *Calvino, two of Italy's most prominent intellectuals of the period. Passionate about Walter *Benjamin's work, which he researched extensively in the archives at the Bibliothèque Nationale de France where he discovered several important manuscripts, Agamben also edited the translation into Italian of his complete works. More recently, his work has focused on Carl Schmitt and Michel *Foucault. A highly erudite *philologist, Agamben reads contemporary works through the lens of Classical Philosophy. Probably the most well-known instance of this is his observation that the distinction between *bios* and *zoē*—which Classical Philosophy uses to distinguish between political life (*bios*), i.e. a form of life regulated by notions of the good and the proper, and the simple fact of life itself (*zoē*), i.e. that which animals and humans have in common—does not exist in most modern European languages. Following Foucault, he shows that the effect of this collapsing of the distinction between *bios* and *zoē* has been the creation of a kind of politics of *bare life, or *biopolitics. Agamben finds this development disturbing. He sees it as the genesis of fascism because it enables a politics that puts the biological before the social, regulating bodies not people. Agamben's later work follows the thread from this starting point to the paradoxes of democratic constitutions, which allow that to 'save' democracy, democracy itself may be suspended by the declaration of martial law. Agamben describes this as a 'state of exception' and his work traces the way this paradoxical process of excluding to include features in a wide variety of social mechanisms.

Further Reading: M. Calarco and S. Decaroli *On Agamben: Sovereignty and Life* (2007).

L. De la Durantaye *Giorgio Agamben: A Critical Introduction* (2009).

C. Mills *The Philosophy of Agamben* (2008).

SEE WEB LINKS

- A comprehensive overview of Giorgio Agamben's work, with references and further reading.

agency In sociology and philosophy, the degree to which a *subject is able to determine the course of their own actions. The concept is generally used in the context of discussions about the factors that shape *everyday life and place a limit on agency.

For instance, relative levels of wealth clearly impact on the degree of agency someone might have. As Karl *Marx famously put it, people make history, but not in conditions of their own choosing.

alienation (*Entfremdung*) Karl *Marx used this term to describe the changes in the economic and social conditions of *modernity which separated (i.e., *alienated*) workers from the product of their labour, the process of their labour, the reason for their labour, and finally each other. A factory worker in a car manufacturing plant is responsible for only one small part of the final product, and that may even be invisible in the finished item; the workers do not control the flow of work, but have to adapt themselves to the demands of the production line (Henry Ford famously didn't allow toilet breaks!); moreover, whether there is in fact any work at all is completely beyond their control, it all depending on the global market; from this point of view, the workers in one plant benefit when workers in plants elsewhere fail. Compare this to the peasant farmer who is responsible for planting, tending and harvesting his or her crop and works as much or as little as his or her needs dictate. Marx develops this concept in the posthumously published 'Economic and Philosophical Manuscripts' (1844) by reworking *Hegel's concept of *Geist* (spirit).

alienation-effect A translation of German *Verfremdung*; however *estrangement-effect is the preferred English term.

allegory A form of artwork whose outward appearance is contrived to suggest a hidden meaning. This is usually achieved by means of symbols. For example, readers of C.S. Lewis's Narnia books or J.R.R. Tolkien's Ring Trilogy are bombarded by images that point to a deeper significance, or meaning beyond the surface of the text. In the case of Narnia, self-sacrificing characters like the great lion Aslan cannot but be figures of Christ, while it is difficult not to think of the Hobbits as personifications of that mythic place known as 'middle England'. For the most part allegories are creative re-writings or re-imaginings of a pre-existing text such as the Bible. But as Fredric *Jameson shows in *The Political Unconscious* (1981), history itself can be used as a prior text for the purpose of constructing allegory. In his later work he develops a notion of *national allegory to describe artworks that use the nation itself as their prior text. Allegory is important to the work of Northrop *Frye and Walter *Benjamin, both of whom devise multi-layered models of allegory.

Further Reading: M. Warner *Monuments and Maidens: The Allegory of the Female Form* (1996).

alterity The otherness of the other. Alterity refers to both the quality of strangeness inherent in the other and the fact of their strangeness. Strangeness here means simply that neither our prior knowledge nor our prior experience prepares us for the encounter with *this* other. For Emmanuel *Levinas, the Paris-based Lithuanian philosopher and ethicist who established the concept, the only being capable of fully satisfying these conditions is God. His notion of ethics revolves around the idea that one should open oneself to an encounter with the divine Mystery, that is, the alterity, of God as other. This notion has also been used in anthropology, particularly by Michael Taussig in *Mimesis and Alterity* (1993), as a way of thinking about the relationship between the colonizers and the colonized. It has also been used in *psychoanalysis to describe the relationship between the self and the other, namely that part of ourselves (such as the *abject) that we disavow.

alternate modernity The theory in development studies and *Postcolonialism that different parts of the world experienced *modernity in their own fashion and at their own time. This theory is especially prominent in China and Brazil, where it is argued that modernity means something quite specific and different from modernity as experienced elsewhere. Fredric *Jameson argues very strongly against this viewpoint in *A Singular Modernity* (2002), suggesting that modernity is in reality a codeword for the advent of capitalism and that this was a global phenomenon.

Althusser, Louis (1918–90) French Marxist philosopher and one of the most influential thinkers of the 20th century. His work fused the insights of *Marxism, *structuralism and *psychoanalysis to create a powerful critique of contemporary capitalist society, focusing particularly on the function of *ideology. His aim was to revive the revolutionary dimension of Marxism and construct a theory that could make a real and practical difference in the world.

Althusser was born in Birmandries in Algeria, but raised in France. His family were middle-class Catholics. He passed the exam to gain entrance to the prestigious Parisian institution, the École Normale Supérieure (ENS), in 1939. But he was drafted into the army and mobilized immediately. He was captured by the Germans and spent five years in a prisoner of war camp in Schleswig-Holstein. He resumed his education at the ENS after the war, passing the *agrégation* exam enabling him to become a tutor in 1948. He obtained his *Doctorat d'Etat* from the University of Picardy in 1975. His physical and mental health were always quite uncertain. He was hospitalized several times and even received electro-shock therapy.

Althusser's academic career was unconventional. In spite of his renown, he never held a prestigious chair at a university. He worked as a tutor at the ENS for his entire career, where his students included such future luminaries as Michel *Foucault and Jacques *Derrida, among many others. Although a prolific and ambitious author (his goal was nothing less than a complete re-interpretation of *Marx), he never produced a full account of his theory. His publications consist of a series of fragmentary interventions (several written in collaboration with students) into a variety of philosophical and political debates as well as a number of autocritiques or self criticisms, frequently as damning as any of those produced by his detractors. He also left behind a substantial corpus of unpublished work, including a number of book-length manuscripts, a full assessment of which has yet to be made. His most important works, *Pour Marx* (1965) translated as *For Marx* (1969), *Lire le capital* (1968), translated as *Reading Capital* (1970), and *Lenin and Philosophy* (1971) continue to be read and studied.

In his highly combative account of Althusser's work *Arguments within English Marxism* (1980), Perry *Anderson argues that Althusser's thought took shape in response to the Sino-Soviet dispute which erupted in response to Khrushchev's denunciation of Stalin in 1956. Contrary to E.P. *Thompson, whose *Poverty of Theory* (1978) provided the immediate occasion for Anderson's remarks, Anderson argues that Althusser was sympathetic to Khrushchev's anti-Stalinist position, but unsympathetic to his reformist proposals, which he felt betrayed the revolutionary spirit of Marx. He called instead for a 'Left critique' of Stalin, which in effect meant trying to get back to an understanding of Marx's thought before the Stalinist re-interpretation of it. Althusser used the slogan 'return to Marx' to rally support for this program at the same time that his friend Jacques *Lacan was calling for a 'return to Freud'. This put him out of favour with the French Communist Party, of which he was a staunch member for most of his life, because it implies a higher authority than the party itself.

In the sympathetic but exacting work, *Althusser: The Detour of Theory* (1987), for many the definitive account of Althusser and Althusserianism, Gregory Elliott argues that Althusser's philosophical position is best defined in terms of what he was against: he was anti-Hegel, anti-*historicism, and anti-*humanism. He rejected the young Marx, who was an avid reader of *Hegel and consequently still a humanist and a historicist, in favour of the mature

Marx, who claimed to have stood Hegel back on his feet. The mature Marx was in Althusser's view the founder of a science, namely *historical materialism, with all the attendant connotations of objective rigour that term implies. Marx, he argued, had established a science of the general laws of the development of *society, but for that very reason his work remained incomplete and it was the task of contemporary Marxism to continue his project. In political terms, Althusser's reasoning was that if society could be understood scientifically (in the same way humans understand the natural world), then that would enable a program of change to be implemented. History, for Althusser, is a process without a *subject. He maintained that it is the masses who make history (not individuals) and that class struggle is the motor of history.

Spinoza, from whom he adopted the idea of *structural causality, rather than Hegel was Althusser's surprising choice of philosophical predecessor, because it allowed him to conceive of society and culture as so many manifestations of an otherwise invisible omnipotent force. In doing so, Althusser renovated Marx's famous spatial metaphor, which separated society into an economic *base (infrastructure), determinant in the last instance, and a subordinate but semi-autonomous politico-legal and ideological *superstructure, by creating the analytic apparatus to explain how the two levels interact. Comprised of two interrelated but distinct systems, the Repressive State Apparatus (RSA) and the *Ideological State Apparatus (ISA), the superstructure provides the conditions needed for the infrastructure to operate by facilitating the reproduction of the social relations inherent to capitalist production. Control of the RSAs (e.g., police, army, courts, prisons) is not sufficient by itself to maintain power, the state must also achieve *hegemony over and in the ISAs (e.g., churches, schools, family media, trade unions, cultural forms). Ideology was, in turn, redefined by Althusser as the imaginary relationship we have to the real conditions of our existence; this relationship is fostered by a process Althusser referred to as *interpellation.

As a leading spokesperson for the revolutionary spirit of Marx's thought, Althusser was expected by his students and followers to be at the forefront of the events of *May 1968, but illness prevented him from participating fully. Many saw this as a betrayal and it is now part of the Althusser legend that his stock as a theorist went into decline at this precise moment, but the truth is more complicated than that. Indeed, in the Anglophone world, Althusser's peak period of influence came after *May '68 in the 1970s when the authors behind the seminal British film studies journal *Screen* championed his thought. Similarly, it was not until the 1970s that Althusser's thought took effect in literary studies, the path having been blazed by the pioneering work of Pierre *Macherey in France and Terry *Eagleton in Britain. It was rather his inadequate responses to two other historical events, the discrediting of the Cultural Revolution in Communist China and Alexander Solzhenitsyn's revelation of the existence of gulags in the USSR, which brought his star down to earth.

For most of his life Althusser lived in the tutor's hall of residence at the ENS on the Rue d'Ulm. There, in 1980, he strangled to death his partner of 34 years, Hélène Rytman. The exact circumstances are not known, but Althusser was never charged with murder. He was found to be of diminished capacity and he was committed to the Sainte-Anne psychiatric hospital, where he remained for three years. He wrote two autobiographical works *L'avenir dure longtemps* (1992), translated as *The Future Lasts a Long Time* (1993) and *Les faits* (1992), translated as *The Facts* (1993), which sought to explain what happened. Althusser died of a heart attack in 1990 at the age of 72.

Althusser's legacy is difficult to assess. His work no longer has the influence it did at its peak—there are very few, if any scholars remaining who would consider themselves to be Althusserian. In part, this is no doubt a reaction to the tragic events in Althusser's own life, but it is also attributable to a general decline in the influence of Marxist thought. Yet, having said that, many of Althusser's former students and collaborators (e.g. Alain *Badiou, Étienne *Balibar, Régis *Debray, Pierre *Macherey, Michel *Pêcheux, Nicos *Poulantzas, and even Jacques *Rancière, who effectively renounced his connection to Althusser in the rather stern critique *La Leçon d'Althusser* (1974) (The Lesson of Althusser)) have gone on to become significant theorists in their own right, and in their own way they continue his project of developing Marxism as a problematic. And in that sense one can say he achieved his goal of renewing Marxism by invigorating debate within Marxism.

Further Reading: L. Althusser *L'avenir dure longtemps* (1992), translated. as *The Future Lasts a Long Time* (1993).
P. Anderson *Arguments within English Marxism* (1980).
F. Boutang *Louis Althusser: Une Biographie 1: La Formation du myth* (1992).
A. Callinicos *Althusser's Marxism* (1976).
G. Elliott *Althusser: The Detour of Theory* (1987).
E.P. Thompson *The Poverty of Theory and Other Essays* (1978).

ambivalence The co-existence of contradictory feelings or impulses toward the same *object. Sigmund *Freud adapted the term from Eugen Bleuler's groundbreaking work on schizophrenia, *Dementia praecox oder der Gruppe der Schizophrenien* (1911), translated as *Dementia praecox or the group of schizophrenias* (1950), to account for a commonly experienced problem in the *transference process known as resistance. Freud noted that in some cases, the analysand's affection for their analyst is also the reason they do not trust them and are unable to establish a proper therapeutic relationship. Ambivalence is also exhibited in those stages of sexual development when the libidinal and destructive tendencies toward an object operate side by side, as in the sadistic phases. *Object relations theorists, especially child psychoanalyst Melanie *Klein, make extensive use of the concept to theorize the genesis of the mature *ego. Klein theorizes that the child perceives every object ambivalently because this is what their experience teaches—the breast does not always produce milk, so it is at once a good object and a bad object. How the child deals with this will determine what kind of an adult they turn out to be. In *Postcolonial Studies ambivalence has been used by critics like Homi *Bhabha to account for the difficult situation of the *subaltern subject torn between the material benefits colonization sometimes brings (e.g., jobs in colonial administration) and the crushing weight of the loss of national sovereignty.

anaclisis Derived from the Greek word meaning to rest upon or lean on, it is used in *psychoanalysis to designate the relationship between the sexual instincts and the self-preservation instincts (or life-drive). Sigmund *Freud uses anaclisis in two main ways: first, to explain the genesis of sexuality; and, second, to explain *object choice. According to Freud, sexual instincts lean on the life instincts because the body provides the erotic zones and specific pleasures or affects that it detaches and develops into sexual pleasures. For example, the breast-feeding baby obtains pleasure from suckling that is over and above—'bonus pleasure' Freud calls it—the simple satisfaction of hunger. This affect and its object, the breast, become in turn the foundations of sexual pleasure. Similarly, the choice moves beyond auto-eroticism by attaching itself to an *object initially favoured by the *ego.

analysand The term used in *psychoanalysis for anyone undergoing analysis. It is used in preference to 'patient' because not all analysands undertake treatment for medical or psychiatric conditions. Many do so simply to clarify feelings and emotions.

analytic philosophy A catch-all phrase designating a variety of different types of work that have in common their opposition to continental philosophy, *metaphysics, and all *post-Kantian thought (including *critical theory). Often known as Anglo-American philosophy because it originated in Britain at the turn of the 20th century with the work of Bertrand Russell, Alfred North Whitehead, and G.E. Moore (all of whom were influenced in this direction by the work of the German logician Gottlob *Frege), and because its practice tends to be confined to Anglophone countries, analytic philosophy is primarily interested in logic. It is suspicious of language's ability to mislead and misdirect via *rhetoric, so it aims to find a logical core to its operations and thereby eliminate its power to obfuscate. It does this by converting all statements into their propositional form; where this proves impossible, it detects fuzzy thinking and falsehood. *See also* EMPIRICISM; LOGICAL POSITIVISM.

anamorphosis A device used in art, particularly in Europe in the 16th and 17th centuries, whereby an image is constructed in such a way that it can only be seen by viewing the painting from a specific angle. Today one most often sees it in sport—corporate logos are painted onto the pitch at slightly distorted angles so as to improve their visibility on TV. French *psychoanalyst Jacques *Lacan uses the example of Holbein's *The Ambassadors* (1533), which contains an image of a skull concealed in its foreground, to explain *desire's inability to perceive what it wants. The *object of desire, or more particularly the object of the drive, cannot be perceived head-on. Slavoj *Žižek makes extensive use of this concept in his account of *ideology in order to explain how it is possible for ideological statements to appear non-ideological.

anaphora A means of linking two sentences, paragraphs, or indeed thoughts, by means of a repetition of a part of the previous utterance. In the example, 'John came into the room. He picked up his coat.' the pronoun 'he' functions anaphorically to inform us who picked up the coat. This point can perhaps be seen more clearly when compared to the passive formulation of the same example: 'John came into the room. The coat was picked up.' There isn't anything in the second sentence to connect it to the first, so we have no idea whether or not there is any relationship between John entering the room and the coat being picked up. *See also* CATAPHORA.

anarchy A state of lawlessness owing to the absence or non-recognition of any sovereign authority.

Anderson, Benedict (1936–) British Marxist scholar specializing in South East Asian studies who came into prominence for his groundbreaking work on the origins of nationalism, *Imagined Communities* (1983). A regular contributor to *New Left Review*, he is also the author of *The Spectre of Comparisons* (1998) and *Under Three Flags* (2005). *See also* IMAGINED COMMUNITY; NATION; NATIONALISM.

Anderson, Perry (1938–) British Marxist historian specializing in the history of political thought. He is described by his contemporary Terry *Eagleton as Britain's most brilliant intellectual. His work has been described by Scott Malcomson as a synoptic oeuvre stretching from 800 BC to last week. Few (if any) scholars display a comparable grasp of both the broad sweep of world history and its finer nation-specific details, and fewer still have his command of the vast literature—in several European languages—devoted to the subject. For much of his career, Anderson's work has been distinctive for its interest in strategy, the need as Marx famously put it not merely to understand society but to try to change it as well.

Anderson was born in London, but his family moved to Shanghai shortly after his birth, and then to the US (when the Japanese invaded China), where he spent the remainder of war. He has produced his own account of this period of his life, which can be found in *Spectrum: From Right to Left in the World of Ideas* (2005). After the war, his family returned to Ireland, his ancestral home. He was schooled at Eton and then Worcester College, Oxford, where he met Isaac Deutscher, the formidable Marxist intellectual and biographer of Leon Trotsky who was to have such a formative influence on his career.

In 1962, in controversial circumstances that have never been fully explained, Anderson took over the editorship of *New Left Review*, bringing onto the editorial committee such stalwarts of the *new* New Left as Tom Nairn, Robin Blackburn, Juliet Mitchell, Gareth Stedman Jones, Alexander Cockburn and Peter Wollen. Under his stewardship *New Left Review* became what it is today, one of the most important forums for critical writing on art, history, politics, literature and film. The journal took a broad international focus, exploring in detail the specific historical situations of a wide range of countries; in particular, it focused on the situation in the Third World, perceiving there to be greater scope for radical change at the periphery; it also sought to explore and interrogate the new theories being produced by Left-oriented scholars such Louis *Althusser, Jean *Baudrillard, and Jacques *Lacan, but pointedly not Gilles *Deleuze, Jacques *Derrida, and Michel *Foucault. In 1970, Anderson founded New Left Books (later known as Verso) to extend the project begun with *New Left Review* in book form.

A prolific author of short essays, many of them published anonymously as editorials in *New Left Review*, or under a variety of pseudonyms, Anderson is surprisingly reticent about republishing these in book form. Indeed he has consistently refused to republish several of his most famous essays and in some cases has actively repudiated his previous work.

It was his essays on British national culture which became part of what is now known as the Nairn-Anderson theses that propelled him into mainstream attention. These essays, particularly 'Origins of the Present Crisis' (1964) and 'Components of a National Culture' (1968), both since republished in *English Questions* (1992), are Anderson at his uncompromising best. Treating the UK as a foreign country, they lacerate their subject matter with the incisiveness of a scalpel.

Anderson's first book-length publications were instalments in a projected but never completed multi-volume work on the origins of capitalism: *Passages from Antiquity to Feudalism* (1974) and *Lineages of the Absolutist State* (1974). His inability to complete the project can perhaps be read as symptomatic of an intellectual change of heart—as his later work demonstrates, Anderson lost faith with the Marxist dictum that one form of society must necessarily give way to another and that capitalism will inevitably be succeeded by socialism. *Considerations on Western Marxism* (1976), *Arguments within English Marxism* (1980), a book length defence of Althusser, and especially *In the Tracks of Historical Materialism* (1983), are all resolutely negative in tone and outlook, gone is the conviction that a radical transition to socialism is just a matter of time. It would be wrong to describe him as defeatist at this point, but the defeat of the Left is a topic that weighs heavily on him.

In the early 1980s, Anderson stepped down as editor of *New Left Review* and took up a professorial position in history at UCLA. His work since then is every bit as searching as it used to be, but the tone has mellowed. To the shock of many, he has taken to writing even-handedly about such right-wing theorists as Michael Oakeshott, Leo *Strauss and Friedrich von Hayek—see the essays republished in *Spectrum*. But those who worry he is losing his fire will doubtless be reassured by *The New Old World* (2009), which provides a typically incisive and merciless account of the history of the formation of the European Union.

Further Reading: P. Blackledge *Perry Anderson: Marxism and the New Left* (2004).
G. Elliott *Perry Anderson: The Merciless Laboratory of History* (1998).
G. Elliott *Ends in Sight: Marx, Fukuyama, Hobsbawm, Anderson* (2008).

a

androcentrism 19th-century American Charlotte Perkins Gilman used this term in *The Man-made World or Our Androcentric Culture* (1911) to characterize what she saw as western thought's orientation around a male point of view, with the result that what was treated as common sense or universal was in fact a reflection of male identity and values. In this system of thought, the feminine perspective is treated as aberrant, a deviation from the male-centred norm. Feminist linguists like Dale Spender have shown how this male-centred outlook is ingrained in language, particularly in the use of the masculine pronoun as the universal term.

androgyny A neologism constructed from the Greek words for male (andro-) and female (-gyny) to describe a state of unity or ambiguity with respect to gender assignment arising from the presence in one body of sex characteristics from both genders. The androgyne has a central position in Swiss psychoanalyst Carl Jung's theory because in his view the androgyne represents the resolution of the anxieties and tensions of sexual difference in favour of complementarity. His theorization of the place of the androgyne in culture reflects the widespread presence of such figures in myth. And although Christianity is surprisingly free of such figures, Jung detected in Christ an androgyne quality he saw as essential. For similar reasons, though arrived at quite independently, English writer Virginia Woolf gives prominence to the androgyne as well. She famously argued in *A Room of One's Own* (1929) that an androgynous consciousness was an essential precondition to becoming an artist. Her viewpoint is not, however, widely shared in feminist theory.

***Annales* School** A loosely-knit group of French historians associated with the journal *Annales d'histoire économique et sociale*, which was first published in 1929. Founded by Lucien Febvre and Marc Bloch, a 16th century specialist and medievalist respectively, the journal was intended to promote a new kind of history that would shift the focus of historiography from narrative to analysis, and in doing so give attention to the full range of human activities, making space for collaboration with other disciplines (geography, sociology, psychology, anthropology, linguistics and economics) in order to produce what would come to be called 'total history'. It dismissed narrowly empirical approaches to history, or what it called *histoire évenementielle* (factual history), in favour of a much broader approach, which came to be codified by Fernand *Braudel as the three-tiered model, generally known by the first of its levels the *longue durée*, which refers to human interaction with the physical environment and a timescale almost imperceptible to the human eye. It addressed itself to 'problems' in history—for example, Febvre's *Le problème de l'incroyance au 16e siècle: la religion de Rabelais* (1942), translated as *The Problem of Unbelief in the Sixteenth Century* (1983), attempted to explain why 'unbelief' was impossible in the 16th century. From its rebellious and small beginning, the *Annales* School rapidly rose to a position of hegemony in the French academy, expanding enough to fracture back into small rebellious factions all over again. It is customary to treat the history of the *Annales* School in terms of generations: the first generation was Bloch and Febvre, but Bloch who was active in the Resistance during World War II was executed by the Gestapo in 1944, so it was left to Febvre to keep the movement going; the second generation was dominated by the towering figure of Febvre's student, Braudel; the third generation was led by Braudel's students Jacques Le Goff, Emmanuel le Roy Ladurie, and Marc Ferro. Although never part of the *Annales* School, historians like Michel de *Certeau, Michel *Foucault and Henri *Lefebvre were also influenced by its approach to history.

Further Reading: P. Burke *The French Historical Revolution: The Annales School 1929–89* (1990).

anomie The absence of social norms, regulations or laws. Not to be confused with *anarchy, anomie is an *existential condition rather than a specific state of affairs. Anomie can arise even within a very well regulated society if those norms, regulations or laws lose their legitimacy and aren't replaced by an alternative vision of how things should be. Derived from the Greek word 'nomos', meaning law, the term was first used by French philosopher Jean-Marie Guyau, but its most well-known formulation is that of French sociologist Émile *Durkheim, who used it in his book *Suicide* (1897) to describe a situation in which social changes—particularly those relating to employment prospects—bring about a situation in which people begin to feel hopeless and without a future because of the discrepancy between public discourse (what the government proclaims to be true) and the evidence on the ground, which belies that rhetoric.

anti-foundationalism A philosophical position which rejects *foundationalism, i.e. it rejects the need to ground philosophy. Anti-foundationalist philosophers are often accused of being *nihilists or moral *relativists because their position cannot claim any absolute ground on which to base itself. This is exacerbated, too, by its refusal of *metaphysical categories such as truth, which might be used in place of absolute grounds. However, while it is true that anti-foundationalism is susceptible to these charges, that does not mean the position is an empty one. Noted anti-foundationalist philosophers include Richard *Rorty and Stanley *Fish.

anti-psychiatry A highly politicized group of psychiatrists and psychotherapists active in London in the 1960s and 1970s who rejected traditional definitions of madness as well as the (then) standard treatments for mental illness (e.g. electro-convulsive therapy, lobotomy, anti-psychotic drugs). It viewed madness as a social construct, or more strongly as an effect of the pressures society places on certain people. It saw psychosis as a shamanistic journey by means of which people tried to express the oppressive effects of socialization. The term itself was coined by David *Cooper, a South African psychiatrist who collaborated with R.D. *Laing and others in the establishment of Kingsley Hall, an experiment in community-psychiatry started in 1965 in East London. *Mary Barnes: Two Accounts of a Journey through Madness* (1971) written by one of the patients at Kingsley Hall in collaboration with her psychiatrist Joseph Berke offers a keen, but not altogether flattering insight into what anti-psychiatry meant in practice. In fact, the book did the movement a lot of damage by exposing what many of its critics saw as its unethical practices. French philosopher, Michel *Foucault is often associated with the anti-psychiatry movement, but although his first book *Folie et Déraison: Histoire de la Folie à l'âge classique* (1961), translated in abridged form as *Madness and Civilization* (1965) and in complete form as *History of Madness* (2006), was a powerful influence on Laing and Cooper in particular, he did not consider himself a part of the movement. Similarly, anti-psychoanalyst Félix *Guattari was influenced by some of the tenets of anti-psychiatry, but ultimately he rejected the movement as a failed experiment because in his eyes it did nothing to alleviate the suffering of schizophrenics.

Further Reading: Z. Kotowicz *R.D. Laing and the Paths of Anti-psychiatry* (1997).

anxiety (*angst*) In *psychoanalysis, the mental and physical manifestation—or symptom—of either (i) a heightened amount of stimulation (specifically, sexual stimulation), or (ii) the absence or insufficiency of the processes of 'working through' or expelling excess excitation. Anxiety is ideational inasmuch as it is always bound to an idea (i.e. a particular image or thought), but the idea is usually impossible to decipher or decode as a sign or substitute for another repressed idea. Anxiety differs from *hysteria, which presents in a very similar manner, in that nervous tension is deflected onto a physical object, rather than the psyche. The two pathways are by no means mutually exclusive and they are often seen occurring together. In *existentialism, particularly in the work of the Danish theologian Søren Kierkegaard, anxiety is an unfocused, or objectless fear, such as the fear provoked by freedom—being free to do what one pleases creates the anxiety of not-knowing what one wants to do or indeed should do. This theme, the anxiety caused by freedom, is further developed in the work of Martin *Heidegger and Jean-Paul *Sartre.

anxiety of influence Harold *Bloom's theory of poetic influence and succession. First outlined in detail in *The Anxiety of Influence* (1973), but central to all his subsequent work, Bloom's thesis is that all poets must confront their precursors in a quasi-*Oedipal struggle in order to create an imaginative space for themselves. The strong poets are able to digest, or sublimate their precursors via a process Bloom refers to as creative misreading. That is, these strong poets find their own truth in the work of their precursors and use that as their source of inspiration. In contrast, weak poets are only able to idealize and imitate their precursors. Bloom extended this idea to all forms of creative writing in *The Western Canon: The Books and the School of the Ages* (1994).

Anzaldúa, Gloria (1942–2004) Mexican-American, radical lesbian cultural critic and writer. Born in the Rio Grande Valley in Southern Texas, she received her BA from the Pan American University and her MA from the University of Texas at Austin. Anzaldúa was an early critic of what she saw as the colour and class blindness of feminist theory and through collective works like *This Bridge Called My Back: Writings by Radical Women of Colour* (1981), co-edited with Cherríe Moraga, sought to raise awareness of the implications of this blindness. Her most famous work, *Borderlands/La Frontera: The New Mestiza* (1987), is a poetic attack on the binaries that shape everyday life—black/white, male/female, and so on—and a powerful celebration of diversity. Anzaldúa advocated a vision of life she referred to as 'mestiza', which means 'mixed', but should also be understood as a refusal of binary logic, extending it to every sphere of existence from biology to ideology.

aphanisis Ernest Jones, Sigmund *Freud's biographer, adopted this word, which in Greek means 'disappearance', to describe the loss of sexual desire. In Jones's view, Freud's theory of castration does not go far enough—it is not the fear of castration that motivates the resolution of the *Oedipal complex he argues, but the far greater fear of the loss of desire itself. By this means he sought to find a common denominator in the sexual development of boys and girls that did not centre on the presence or absence of the penis. Jacques *Lacan also uses this term, though not in exactly the same way. For Lacan it means the loss of subjectivity. The *neurotic, Lacan argues, is not afraid of losing desire; on the contrary, losing desire is precisely what they want to achieve. Aphanisis is in this latter regard a mechanism of defence.

aphasia A language disorder that manifests itself as either an inability to speak or an inability to comprehend speech, or both. The disorder can vary in degrees of severity up to and including complete loss of language. It may affect written language comprehension as well. Sigmund *Freud and more especially Roman *Jakobson were interested in aphasia, both seeing it as a key to understanding language more generally.

aporia In classical philosophy, it is a point of perplexity, where a combination of axioms and/or propositions (each true in their own right) are found to be incompatible. Contemporary ethics is constantly faced by such situations: consider the conundrum posed by the notions of the 'right to life' and the 'freedom to choose' in the case of abortions. Taken on their own, most people would support the notion that everyone has a right to life and a right to the freedom to choose how they live that life. In the case of abortion, the proper allocation of these rights is difficult to determine with any precision. Faced with such vexed issues as this, many commentators find themselves resorting to the second meaning of aporia, which in *rhetoric refers to figures of speech in which the speaker expresses self doubt, e.g. 'I really don't know how to decide between these two rights, but I will nonetheless endeavour to do so'. In the work of Jacques *Derrida aporia is a central concern: it is a basic point of the *deconstruction method that any text, indeed any statement, can be shown to consist of a multiplicity of aporias.

Appadurai, Arjun (1949–) Indian-born, US-based cultural anthropologist and co-founder of the important *postcolonial theory journal *Public Culture*. Born and educated in Mumbai, Appadurai moved to the US in 1967, completing a BA at Brandeis, followed by a PhD at the University of Chicago. He now works at The New School, New York. In 1988 he edited a collection of essays entitled *The Social Life of Things: Commodities in Cultural Perspective*, which set out to chart (on a global scale) the creation and regulation of and variation in taste, asking why one kind of thing is valued in one place and not another and just as importantly at one time and not another. His introductory essay to this collection is a landmark in the field of cultural anthropology. Perhaps his most important work, at least from the perspective of critical theory, is *Modernity at Large: Cultural Dimensions of Globalization* (1996), which offers a fivefold theory of global cultural flows, or *scapes, that taken together comprise the contemporary social *imaginary. His most recent work, *Fear of Small Numbers: An Essay on the Geography of Anger* (2006), has concentrated on *affect, particularly anger.

apperception A term invented by Leibniz to describe the mind's apprehension of its own inner state. Immanuel *Kant distinguishes between two types of apperception: empirical and transcendental. The former is the changing consciousness of the *everyday self, while the latter is the unchangeable consciousness that provides the unity of experience necessary to the existence of the *subject.

archaeology French historian Michel *Foucault uses this term to describe his research methodology. It is characterized by the suspension of all established conventions for thinking and doing history and the supposition that those very conventions for thinking and doing history should themselves be subjected to historical inquiry. Outlined in extensive detail in *L'Archéologie du savoir* (1969), translated as *The Archaeology of Knowledge* (1972), archaeology takes shape as a series of injunctions against the perceived unities of author, discipline, genre, and a corresponding call to recognize the significance of dispersion, recurrence, and transformation. Foucault wanted to shift the objective of history away from what has been said and done to the set of conditions (which he referred to as the *discursive formation) enabling those things to be said and done. For example, for Foucault what is important is not the fact that the mentally ill are locked up, but the diverse ways by which the very classification 'mentally ill' came into being in such a way as to render 'normal' the incarceration of those people so classified.

Further Reading: J. Bernauer *Michel Foucault's Force of Flight* (1990). C. O'Farrell *Michel Foucault* (2005).

archetype The inherited dimension of the *psyche according to the analytical psychology of Carl *Jung. Archetypes are ways of thinking and acting that derive from the most primitive aspects of our psyche, which for Jung means that dimension of the psyche we have in common with our most distant ancestors. There is a large variety of archetypes, each one pointing to a different mode of action such as caring for another or defending oneself from attack.

Taken together they form a dynamic preconscious system which is actively seeking actualization in the form of an association, *complex, idea, or at the negative extreme a symptom. The most well-known example is the binary pair animus/anima—the former is the archetypal image woman has of man and the latter the archetypal image man has of woman. Archetypes can usefully be compared with the structure referred to in *ethology as innate releasing mechanisms. They are powerful forces compelling action, which is why the conscious has to engage them and bring them under control.

archive The general horizon or frame of what French historian Michel *Foucault called *archaeological analysis. The archive is a generic term for the limit of what can be known about a particular moment or period in history. In itself it consists of *discursive practices, by which Foucault means the anonymous rules of language, economics, history, society that taken together enable a culture to function. By its nature, however, it is never fully available for inspection. Indeed, Foucault quite categorically states that the archive of one's own time is unknowable. Thus, both our knowledge of it and our ability to describe it will only ever be fragmentary at best. In *Mal d'archive: une impression freudienne* (1995) translated as *Archive Fever: A Freudian Impression* (1998), Jacques *Derrida explores the limits of the knowability of the archive that is our personal history.

Further Reading: J. Bernauer *Michel Foucault's Force of Flight* (1990).

Arendt, Hannah (1906–75) German-Jewish political philosopher best known for her thesis that evil is ultimately banal. Born in Hanover, she grew up in Königsberg (birthplace of Immanuel *Kant), and studied philosophy in Marburg under Martin *Heidegger, with whom she famously had an affair. After breaking up with him, she moved to Heidelberg and completed her doctorate under the supervision of Karl *Jaspers. She fled Germany in 1933, first to Paris where she met Walter *Benjamin, and then to the US. She returned to Germany after the war, but soon returned to the US. In 1959 she became the first woman to be appointed full professor at Princeton University. Her reputation was established with *The Origins of Totalitarianism* (1951), which sought to set Nazism and Stalinism in historical context and show how genocidal political systems are able to gain traction in the public sphere. Her particular concern was to make apparent the fate of stateless peoples: she had in mind those people, like the Jews in Germany, who have had their citizenship revoked by the state; but also those displaced persons who find they cannot return to their state because it has been destroyed or somehow rendered closed to them. The Italian philosopher Giorgio *Agamben has developed this aspect of Arendt's work in his analyses of what he calls the **homo sacer*. Probably her most influential work, *The Human Condition* (1958) pursued the problems raised in the previous work by examining political action, specifically the establishment of rights. She gained public notoriety in 1963 when she reported on the Eichmann war crimes trials in Jerusalem for the *New Yorker* (later in the same year published in book form as *Eichmann in Jerusalem*). Eichmann was responsible for a large proportion of the logistical side of the Holocaust, such as the sourcing, routing, and timetabling of trains that transported millions of Jews to the death camps. Her observation that Eichmann was a perfectly ordinary man who perpetrated monstrous deeds via perfectly ordinary bureaucratic processes inspired her famous phrase 'the banality of evil'. She followed this up with the books *On Revolution* (1963) and *On Violence* (1970).

Further Reading: S. Swift *Hannah Arendt* (2008).

Artaud, Antonin (1896–1948) French poet and playwright. His notion of a *theatre of cruelty had an enormous influence on 20th-century experimental theatre. Owing to illness, both mental and physical, Artaud spent a considerable portion of his childhood in hospital. This set a trend that was to continue for the rest of his life. He was conscripted into the army in 1916, but was soon discharged on medical grounds. It was during one of his rest cures, as they were known, in a sanatorium that he was prescribed laudanum as a mental relaxant, with the result that he became an addict of opiates.

Artaud never had a proper career. He lurched from one thing to another, seemingly at random, but apparently with the constant aim of challenging the perception of reality. At the age of 27, Artaud sent poems to the journal *La Nouvelle Revue Française*, which were rejected by its editor Jacques Rivière, who was nonetheless intrigued enough by what he read to start a correspondence with Artaud. These letters in turn became Artaud's first major book. He was also able to pick up work as an actor in a few silent films, gaining minor roles in films directed by Germaine Dulac and Carl Dreyer.

Artaud was involved with the *Surrealist movement at this time too, but he was expelled by the so-called Pope of Surrealism André *Breton, though not before he formed an association with Roger Vitrac, who was also expelled from the movement. Together they ran the Alfred *Jarry Theatre, named after the creator of *'pataphysics, from 1926–28. They directed works by Vitrac, Claudel, and

a

Strindberg, to great critical success. Despite the fact that productions were attended by the leading intellectuals of the period, including André Gide and Paul Valéry, the venture failed commercially and was forced to fold.

In 1931 Artaud witnessed a performance of Balinese dance at the Colonial Exposition in Paris and though he didn't understand it fully, it proved utterly transformative of his thinking about what theatre can and should be. Its influence can clearly be seen in the 'First Manifesto for a Theatre of Cruelty', which was published in *La Nouvelle Revue Française* in the same year. A few years later, in 1935, Artaud travelled to Mexico where he had a second transformative experience in an encounter with the Tarahumaran people (his experiments with peyote were no doubt a factor too). He returned to France in 1937. His most important work *The Theatre and its Double*, bearing the traces of both these encounters, was published in 1938. It proved to be one of the most influential theatrical manifestos of the 20th century.

The last ten years of Artaud's life were spent in mental asylums. He continued to write prolifically, however, and produced some of his most challenging works in these years. It is highly likely that Artaud was a schizophrenic and it is as an authentic voice of 'madness' that his work, outside of the theatre, is celebrated and examined, particularly by Michel *Foucault and Gilles *Deleuze.

Further Reading: M. Esslin *Antonin Artaud* (1976).

art worlds Sociologist Howard S. Becker's concept for the milieu that artists create and require in order to produce art. Like that of Pierre *Bourdieu, Becker's ultimate goal is to show that art is not the product of the isolated genius, but is rather the product of a cooperative community. An art world consists of the institutions and people necessary to the production and consumption of artistic works.

Further Reading: H. Becker *Art Worlds* (1982).

Auerbach, Eric (1892–1957) German literary critic and philologist. Along with Ernst Robert Curtius and Leo Spitzer he is generally regarded as one of the greatest exponents of *philology of the 20th century. He is best known for his magisterial survey of *realism in western literature, *Mimesis* (1946), which he wrote—famously—in exile in Istanbul without access to a library equipped for the study of European literature. Although his first degree was in law, he decided to pursue a career in literature and completed a doctorate in 1921 on Romance literatures. In 1929 he was appointed professor of philology at Marburg University and in the same year published his first book, a study of the Italian poet Dante entitled *Dante als Dichter* *der irdischen Welt*, translated as *Dante: Poet of the Secular World* (2007). As a Jew he was obliged to give up his post as a professor in 1935 and then for safety's sake to leave Germany in 1936. He relocated to Istanbul, where he remained until 1947; then he moved to the US, where he held positions at Pennsylvania State University, Princeton, and Yale. Auerbach was primarily a medievalist and it is in that field where his work has been the most influential. He was not a literary theorist and as a result since the advent of *structuralism his work has fallen into a state of relative neglect.

Further Reading: E. Said *The World, the Text, and the Critic* (1983).

Augé, Marc (1935–) A French anthropologist, Augé belongs to the generation of scholars who were trained in the 1960s in Paris, for whom the likes of Louis *Althusser, Michel de *Certeau, Gilles *Deleuze and Michel *Foucault can be counted as teachers and crucial influences or antagonists as the case may be. A prolific, witty, and complex author, Augé considers himself to be an anthropologist; but his lifelong project has been one of reinventing what it means to do anthropology in the rapidly changing times he refers to as *supermodernity (*surmodernité*).

Marc Augé's career can be divided into three stages, reflecting shifts in both his geographical focus and theoretical development: early (African), middle (European) and late (Global). These successive stages do not involve a broadening of interest or focus as such, but rather the development of a theoretical apparatus able to meet the demands of the growing conviction that the local can no longer be understood except as a part of the complicated global whole.

Augé's career began with a series of extended field trips to West Africa, where he researched the Alladian peoples situated on the edge of a large lagoon, west of Abidjan on the Ivory Coast. The culmination of this endeavour is the masterly *Le Rivage alladian: Organisation et évolution des villages alladian* (1969) (The Alladian Riparian Peoples: Organization and Evolution of Alladian Villages). The sequel, *Théorie des pouvoirs et Idéologie: Études de cas en Côte d'Ivoire* (1975) (Theory of Powers and Ideology: Case Study in the Ivory Coast), followed a series of three further field excursions to the Ivory Coast between 1968 and 1971. Augé coined the term ideo-logic to describe his research object, which he defined as the inner logic of the representations a society makes of itself to itself. A third and final instalment in this series of studies of the Alladian peoples was added in 1977, *Pouvoirs de vie, Pouvoirs de mort* (Powers of Life, Powers of Death).

The second or European stage, consists of a sequence of three interrelated books: *La Traversée du Luxembourg* (1985) (Traversing Luxembourg Gardens); *Un ethnologue dans le métro* (1986); translated as *In the Metro* (2002); and *Domaines et Châteaux* (1989) (Homes and Palaces). In this period of his career, Augé took the novel approach of applying methods developed in the course of fieldwork in Africa to his local Parisian context. Augé focused on four key aspects of contemporary Parisian society: (i) the paradoxical increase in the intensity of solitude brought about by the expansion of communications technologies; (ii) the strange recognition that the other is also an 'I'; (iii) the *non-place, the ambivalent space that has none of the familiar attributes of place—for instance, it incites no sense of belonging; (iv) the oblivion and aberration of memory. The work in this period emphasizes the anthropologist's own experience in a way that neither the earlier nor later work does. Augé does this by comparing his own impressions of these places with those produced by some of French literature's greatest writers. What this comparison illustrates is the apparent insuperability of the gap between language and experience. Yet it is that very gap, he argues, that his anthropology must be able to close if it is to be of continuing relevance in contemporary society.

The third or global stage has so far yielded four books: *Non-Lieux, Introduction à une anthropologie de la surmodernité* (1992) translated as *Non-Places: Introduction to an Anthropology of Supermodernity* (1995); *Le Sens des autres: Actualité de l'anthropologie* (1994) translated as *A Sense for the Other: The Timeliness and Relevance of Anthropology* (1998); *Pour une anthropologie des mondes contemporains* (1994) translated as *An Anthropology for Contemporaneous Worlds* (1998); and *Le Guerre des rêves: exercises d'ethno-fiction* (1997) translated as *The War of Dreams: Exercises in Ethno-fiction* (1999). Taken together these works comprise an extended meditation on the disparity between observations made in the course of anthropological fieldwork in the first and the second stages of his career. The third stage of Augé's career has a twofold aim: on one hand, it is an attempt to theorize *globalization as it is lived in properly global terms; on the other hand it is an attempt to reinvigorate the discipline of anthropology as a whole. To that end he deploys a number of innovative writing techniques, describing the synthetic results as 'ethno-novels'.

See also POSTMODERNISM.

Further Reading: I. Buchanan 'Non-Places: Space in the Age of Supermodernity' in R. Barcan and I. Buchanan (eds.) *Imagining Australian Space* (1999).

J. Frow *Time and Commodity Culture* (1997).

aura The intrinsically unreproducible aspect of a work of art, namely its original presence in time and space. It is, in effect, the quality of uniqueness that separates the original from its copy and can be compared to the specificity to the eye of a particular mountain range or some other natural wonder. But more than that, it is what cannot be copied, regardless of technological capacity. Walter *Benjamin proposed this term in what is probably his most famous essay, 'Das Kunstwerk im Zeitalter seiner technischen Reproduzierbarkeit' (1936), translated as 'The Work of Art in the Age of Mechanical Reproduction' (1968), as a means of explaining his larger thesis that the nature of perception itself is subject to change in the course of history. New types of artwork, especially film, came into being at the end of the 19th century, which could no longer be said to be reproductions of originals. The original in such a context is always already a copy. What Benjamin wanted to explain is this difference between a painting and a film and he argued that the aura of the former was no longer to be found in the latter and therefore the very idea of aura itself was in decay. Although he doesn't use this term, Umberto *Eco's account of *postmodernity, or what he tends to refer as *hyperreality, is based on precisely this thesis.

Austin, John Langshaw (1911–60) British philosopher of language, best known as the originator of *speech act theory and the concept of the *performative. Born in Lancaster, but raised in St Andrews in Scotland, Austin was educated at Balliol College, Oxford. During World War II he served with MI6. After the war he was appointed to a professorship at Oxford. Austin was very far from prolific; he published only seven papers in his lifetime. His most influential work, *How to Do Things with Words: The William James Lectures delivered at Harvard University in 1955* (1962), was published posthumously. Austin's decisive and lasting contribution to language philosophy was to challenge the accepted view of his own time that the principle function of sentences is to state facts (real or imagined). Austin argued persuasively that there are whole classes of sentences which either do more than simply state facts, or do not state facts at all, but rather perform actions. These types of sentences, such as declarations like 'I name this ship *Enterprise*', he called performative utterances because the very act of saying them can in certain conditions perform an action. Similarly, by saying 'it is cold' we may induce someone to close a window or switch on a heater, so again the utterance has a performative dimension. Austin died before he could develop his ideas into a full-blown theory (which he seemed to lack the taste for in any case), so it has been left to others, particularly John *Searle and (in very different, much more speculative ways) Judith *Butler and Gilles *Deleuze, to explore all its implications. Austin's work is not without its critics, the two most prominent being Ernst *Gellner and Jacques *Derrida. The latter wrote a short critique of Austin's theory in *Marges de la philosophie* (1962), translated as *Margins of Philosophy* (1982), which prompted a reply from Searle, and thereby sparked one of the most spectacular ripostes in philosophical history from Derrida.

***auteur* theory (author theory)** A theory of film which not only ascribes the director with an authorial-like control over the final look of the film, but also dismisses as worthless those films in which no such unity of vision is discernible. Following this model, any film by Alfred Hitchcock, even the half-baked late ones like *Torn Curtain* (1966) and *Topaz* (1969), will always be more highly regarded than any film by Michael Bay, including his blockbusters like *Bad Boys* (1995) and *Armageddon* (1998), even though Bay's thrillers are more thrilling than Hitchcock's to the majority of today's viewers. *Auteur* theory is generally associated with the French film journal *Cahiers du cinéma,* which was launched in 1951, particularly the 1954 article 'Une certaine tendance du cinéma' by critic and director François Truffaut which became a kind of manifesto for the *French New Wave or *Nouvelle Vague. The actual phrase '*auteur* theory' originates with American film critic Andrew Sarris, who transformed the debate in the pages of *Cahiers du cinéma* referred to as the *politique des auteurs* into a distinctive methodological programme. This debate began when, impressed by the Hollywood films imported into France following the end of the Second World War after several years absence, the *Cahiers du cinéma* authors re-evaluated their view of American film, which they had previously dismissed as commercial schlock. They noted that while American directors like Howard Hawks and John Ford (two favourites) had little control over the production of their films because of the way the studio and star systems worked, they nonetheless managed to exercise considerable control over the style of the movie. The authors of *Cahiers du cinéma* conceived of a new way of thinking about authorship, focusing on the finished style of a film rather than its actual process of production. In this respect, *auteur* theory is paradoxical at its core because while it acknowledges that films are not created by individuals, but in fact require a veritable army of creative people—ranging from cost accountants to script writers and camera operators—to realize them, it nevertheless upholds the idea that the final look of a film can be attributed to a single individual. In the end, this position proved untenable and film theory has since taken a much more 'multiple' approach to film.

Further Reading: P. Wollen *Signs and Meaning in the Cinema* (1972).

authenticity The term used in *existentialist philosophy to describe what it considers the ideal mode of living. It is characterized by high levels of self-awareness, self-direction, and self-reflection. That is to say, someone whose life may be considered authentic is always fully aware of both what they are doing and why they are doing it. Attaining this level of self-knowledge effectively means overcoming the power of the *unconscious to compel us to act without fully knowing why, therefore most theorists of authenticity treat it as project, something one aspires to or works towards. In philosophy, Jean-Paul *Sartre and Martin *Heidegger wrote extensively on the problematic authenticity, while Theodor *Adorno attacked it as obfuscating. Outside of philosophy, authenticity has been a topic of interest for both literary studies and *cultural studies—in the case of the former it generally refers to life in the pre-industrial era (e.g. F.R. *Leavis, Raymond *Williams), while in the latter it is used as a synonym for artistic or cultural production that is 'independent' or anti-commercial (e.g. 'grunge' music and Dogme cinema have at different times been claimed as authentic).

Further Reading: C. Taylor *The Ethics of Authenticity* (1992).

authority In political theory and sociology it refers to the legitimacy (or not) of the use of power. If a particular power is perceived as legitimate and it has authority, then we accede to its demands without the need of coercion or threat. The analysis of authority was developed by the German sociologist Max Weber, who was principally interested in the issue of how authority is obtained. Weber identified three kinds of authority: (i) rational-legal—government depends for its authority on the fact that laws have the appearance of necessity (e.g., it is rational to ban murder and so on); (ii) traditional authority—authority derives from long established customs, laws and practices, the sense that things have always been thus and should remain thus; (iii) charismatic authority—the authority an individual claims or derives from a higher power, such as destiny or God. Michel de *Certeau, in his analysis of *May '68, argued that what the street protests indicated was that the government of the day had lost its authority, even though it had retained power. More recently Slavoj *Žižek has argued, with regard to the events in Iran in 2009 and earlier in the so-called 'Spring Awakening' in the Czech Republic, that the loss of authority was a precursor to the loss of power.

autopoiesis Self creation or self organization. The term was introduced by the evolutionary biologists Humberto Maturana and Francisco Varela in their groundbreaking book, *Autopoiesis and Cognition: The Realization of the Living* (1972). The autopoietic system is one that produces itself. It is perhaps best understood in contrast to an allopoietic system, such as a factory, which takes in materials and uses them to produce something other than itself.

Avant-garde A military term referring to a group of soldiers who attack in advance of the main body, used as a metaphor for any form of art that challenges artistic conventions and is, as it were, ahead of its time. It first came into vogue in the latter part of the 19th century in France. It is sometimes used as a synonym for *modernism, but while there is an element of truth in this it is misleading too, inasmuch that Avant-garde does not imply either a particular period or style. More generally, though, Avant-garde is used in *critical theory as a codeword for the problem of the new, which in the era of *postmodernism is considered especially acute because it is thought all possible forms of artistic experimentation have been tried. The notion of the Avant-garde is therefore an *ontological as well as artistic or historical problematic in that it contains the question of its own possibility: what does it take to be absolutely new? For this reason, books about the Avant-garde tend to focus on its theory, rather than its *praxis.

Further Reading: P. Bürger *Theory of the Avant-Garde* (1984).
M. Calinescu *Five Faces of Modernity* (1987).
R. Poggioli *The Theory of the Avant-Garde* (1968).

axiomatic (*L'axiomatique*) Gilles *Deleuze and Félix *Guattari's term for the capitalist *mode of production. An axiom is a proposition which cannot be proven true or false and from which one is able to construct a system of rules. Sport offers plenty of examples of axioms —for example, rugby is built on the axiom that the ball can never go forward from the hands, while soccer is built on the axiom that no player (except the goalkeeper) may touch the ball with their hands. There is no justification for these rules; they serve only to construct the necessary conditions for the game. The shape of the pitch, the type of ball used, the number of players on each side, are also axioms for the same reason. In contrast, the offside rule both rugby and soccer have instituted (in different forms of course) is designed to alter the playing conditions of the game as it is already constructed.

You could remove the offside rule and it wouldn't substantially alter the game, it would still be rugby or soccer. In *Mille Plateaux* (1980), translated as *A Thousand Plateaus* (1987), Deleuze and Guattari utilize this logic to describe the operation of the state as a form of government. *Globalization is probably the clearest example of what they mean by axiomatic—e.g., the World Trade Organization enjoins countries to set aside their specific national agenda and abide by rules that facilitate the profit-making of corporations.

Bachelard, Gaston (1884–1962) French philosopher of science. Born in Bar-sur-Aube, in the Champagne region of France, Bachelard's academic career was very slow to start. He spent several years working in a post office before even commencing university study. And it was not until after the First World War, in which he served with distinction (earning the Croix de Guerre), that he finally attained an academic post. His first job was a professor of physics and chemistry at a College in Bar-sur-Aube. He remained there from 1919 until 1930, during which time he began to focus more and more on the philosophy of science. And it was in this area that he eventually made his mark, becoming professor of the philosophy of science at the Sorbonne in 1940. There are two main trajectories in Bachelard's work, reflecting his conviction that there are two types of thought: scientific and poetic. With respect to science, Bachelard was one of the first thinkers to emphasize discontinuity in the history of thought. Knowledge does not progress according to a logical, linear set of steps moving from partial to complete understanding; rather it progresses unevenly from one misconception to another until understanding is finally attained. On this view, the previous attempts at understanding a particular phenomenon cannot be used as a reliable guide as to how knowledge was attained in the final instance. Bachelard introduced the concept of the *epistemological break to characterize the gap between past ignorance and present understanding. This concept was widely influential and was developed further by Georges *Canguilhem (in his account of medical science) and Michel *Foucault (in his histories of the clinic, prison, and madness). It also had enormous impact on Louis *Althusser, who used it to articulate his claim that *Marx broke with both *Hegel and Feuerbach. The other trajectory in Bachelard's work, reflecting strongly the influence of Carl *Jung, concerns the poetic image, which for Bachelard is not the same thing as a metaphor. It is rather an opening toward the future. In a series of studies on elemental themes—air, water, fire, and space—Bachelard produced a powerful account of the daydream or reverie, arguing that it enables us to get in touch with the deeper reserves of our imagination. The best known of these studies is *La Poétique de*

l'espace (1958) translated as *The Poetics of Space* (1964), which was a worldwide bestseller. Other books in the series include: *La psychanalyse du feu* (1938) translated as *The Psychoanalysis of Fire* (1977); *L'eau et les rêves* (1942) translated as *Water and Dreams: An Essay on the Imagination of Matter* (1994); and *La poétique de la rêverie* (1960) translated as *The Poetics of Reverie: Childood, Language, and the Cosmos* (1992).

Further Reading: D. Lecourt *Marxism and Epistemology: Bachelard, Canguilhem and Foucault* (1975).
M. McAllester *Gaston Bachelard: Subversive Humanist* (1991).
M. Tiles *Bachelard: Science and Objectivity* (1984).

bad faith (*mauvaise foi*) A form of self-deception and avoidance of one's freedom. French *existentialist philosophers Jean-Paul *Sartre and Simone de *Beauvoir used this term (in subtly differing ways) to account for what they saw as the inauthenticity inherent in modern life, by which they meant the individual subject's failure to grasp the truth of their situation in *late capitalism. That is to say, if bad faith can be thought of as a lie to oneself, it should not be thought of as a form of lying because the liar in this case is not in possession of the truth. Indeed, as Sartre argues in *L'Être et le néant* (1943), translated as *Being and Nothingness* (1958) the real liar, the one who knows the truth and intends to deceive, does not in fact act in bad faith at all. The point is that bad faith as Sartre wants it understood refers to the way one acts with regard to one's own self and not with regard to others. For Sartre, offering the two by now 'classic' case examples of the waiter and the seduced woman, all social roles contain within them the demand that we act in bad faith—we can play the part of the waiter, but we cannot be the waiter in our being; the seduced woman is constrained from acknowledging both her own desires and that of her suitor by social conventions. Toril Moi offers a brilliant feminist critique of this latter argument in her intellectual biography of Beauvoir: *Simone de Beauvoir: The Making of an Intellectual Woman* (1994). Erving *Goffman's theory of performance in *The Presentation of Self in Everyday Life* (1959) takes this situation of a divided consciousness, which for Sartre was what was problematic about modern life, as the normal condition.

Badiou, Alain (1937–) French Marxist philosopher, novelist and playwright. Born in Rabat, Morocco, Badiou completed high school in Toulouse before moving to Paris for undergraduate studies at the prestigious École Normale Supérieure (ENS), where he worked closely with Louis *Althusser, but was never one of the select group of disciples who came to be known as Althusserians. After completing his obligatory military service, Badiou taught in Reims, first at a lycée, then at the university. In 1968 he was invited by Michel *Foucault to join the department of philosophy at Vincennes (University of Paris VIII), where his colleagues included Hélène *Cixous, Gilles *Deleuze, and Jean-François *Lyotard. After spending 30 years at Vincennes, Badiou left in 1998 to return to his alma mater ENS.

Badiou is an austere, uncompromising thinker of great originality and range, whose magnum opus *L'Ětre et l'événement* (1988), translated as *Being and Event* (2005), is premised on the conviction that mathematics is an ontology—his conception of being is non-representational, but schematic: it presents structures of situations, with a view towards identifying what he calls evental sites, i.e. places where a political praxis might develop. Badiou's philosophy is primarily interested in the event, which for him is a moment of rupture in history's continuum, a shift in the very condition of things after which there is no turning back. Very few so-called events satisfy this condition in Badiou's eyes and, by the same token, history has overlooked several events it lacked the conceptual model to see. A reader-friendly example of how this notion of philosophy works in relation to history can be found in *Le Siècle* (2005), translated as *The Century* (2007).

Badiou's model of praxis is usually described as subtractive because it operates on the premise that political action can only work if it subtracts itself from the power and processes of the state. Slavoj *Žižek adopts this model in his self-styled political manifesto *In Defence of Lost Causes* (2008). Throughout his career, Badiou has been actively involved in politics. During the events of *May '68 he was a member of highly vocal Maoist groups. In more recent times he has been involved with L'Organisation Politique, a politicized group he helped found. Because of its powerfully political texture, Badiou's philosophy is increasingly widely read today, a measure both of the volatility of the times and the lucidity of his thought.

Further Reading: J. Barker *Alain Badiou: A Critical Introduction* (2001).
O. Feltham *Alain Badiou: Live Theory* (2008).
P. Hallward *Badiou: A Subject to Truth* (2003).

Bakhtin, Mikhail (1895–1975) A Russian linguist and literary critic, Bakhtin was a prodigious author who worked under difficult circumstances for most of his life—two World Wars as well as a revolution—and he was one of the most influential literary theorists of the 20th century. An instinctively anti-systemic yet utterly rigorous thinker, his concepts of the *carnivalesque, *chronotope, *dialogism, *heteroglossia and *polyphony have had enormous resonance in almost every domain of contemporary aesthetics, but especially film and literature. He is often associated with the *Russian Formalists, but in reality his work was always quite distinct in its goals and ambitions.

Bakhtin was born in Orel to a landless but noble family. His father was a mid-level bank official who moved the family from Orel to Vilnius and finally to Odessa as Bakhtin was growing up. He began his university studies in Odessa but soon transferred to St Petersburg University. From there he moved to Nevel, where he taught for two years. It was here that the members of the first 'Bakhtin circle' came together. Among them was V. N. Vološinov, under whose name it is alleged Bakhtin published one of his most famous books, *Marxism and the Philosophy of Language* (1973). He published a second book, *Freudianism* (1927) under his name too, as well as another, *The Formal Method in Literary Scholarship* (1928) under the name of another close colleague P. N. Medvedev. Opinion is divided as to the status of these texts and it is not really known why Bakhtin might have decided to do it. In 1920 he moved to Vitebsk, where the great modernist artists El Lisitsky, Malevich, and Marc Chagall were taking refuge from the revolution.

In 1924 he moved back to St Petersburg, which had by then been renamed Leningrad, and finally began to publish some of his work, which until then had only circulated amongst a closed group of friends and admirers. But in a pattern that was to recur throughout his life, many of these manuscripts he attempted to publish were either suppressed or lost. Some survived to be published decades later, but many vanished altogether. There is a famous story that during World War II Bakhtin, an inveterate smoker, used the completed manuscript of a book to make his cigarettes because paper was in short supply. His first major book, translated as *Problems of Dostoevsky's Poetics* (1984), which introduced the concepts of dialogism, heteroglossia and polyphony wasn't published until 1929.

He submitted his doctorate in 1940, but owing to the war it could not be defended until 1946. The thesis, which would eventually be published in 1965, translated as *Rabelais and his World* (1968), divided the academic community and he was denied his doctorate. In contrast to the strict philological expectations of the time, Bakhtin's thesis ranged widely over history and sociology and tried to situate Rabelais in the context of his own culture. For this reason, he didn't shy away from or politely ignore the crudity of Rabelais' prose and interests as might have been prudent, at least from the point of view of establishing his career. His friends nonetheless managed to secure an appointment for him and he was able to teach at university level for many years until ill health forced him to retire in 1969.

Well known in Russia from the early 1920s, it wasn't until the 1970s that Bakhtin became known in the West, but as soon as the translations began to appear in English (as well as French and German) it was immediately obvious that his was a great voice in literary theory. His work provides one of the few truly original theories of the novel.

Further Reading: K. Clark and M. Holquist *Mikhail Bakhtin* (1984).
M. Holquist *Dialogism* (2002).
D. Lodge *After Bakhtin* (1990).
P. Stallybrass and A. White *The Politics and Poetics of Transgression* (1986).
R. Stam, *Subversive Pleasures: Bakhtin, Cultural Criticism and Film* (1989).

Balibar, Étienne (1942–) French *Marxist philosopher and social theorist. Born in Bourgogne, Balibar studied at the École Normale Supérieure, where he met Louis *Althusser, who became his mentor. Balibar rose to prominence as an 'Althusserian', one of a select group of Althusser's students and colleagues, that included Pierre *Macherey, Michel *Pêcheux, Nicos *Poulantzas, and Jacques *Rancière, among others, who worked together to advance Althusser's structuralist rewriting of Marxist doctrine. Balibar collaborated with Althusser, Macherey and Rancière to write *Lire le capital* (1968), partially translated as *Reading Capital* (1970), which is a close reading of several key sections of Karl *Marx's *Das Kapital.* Although Balibar's contribution to this work tends to be conflated with Althusser's (Macherey and Rancière have fared much worse as their contributions were deleted from subsequent editions and are not even included in the English translation), it is significant for the way it lays out the basic principles of *historical materialism, formulating it as a general theory of social formations. In the 1970s, when Marxism came under increasingly heavy attack because of the revelations about the existence of Gulags in the USSR, Balibar did not renounce Marxism altogether, but he did quit the Communist Party, of which he had been a member for some twenty years. In the 1980s and 1990s, still working within a Marxist framework, but now outside of the shadow of Althusser, Balibar turned to more 'practical' questions, such as the problems posed by the transformation of nations under the aegis of global capitalism and the continuing problems of racism. In a book co-written with Immanuel Wallerstein, *Race, nation, classe: les identités ambiguës* (1988), translated as *Race, Nation, Class: Ambiguous Identities* (1991), Balibar proposes the concept of *neo-racism to explain the perpetuation of this phenomenon in the postcolonial era. More recently, his thoughts have turned to the problem of the emergence and development of the European Union: *Nous, citoyens d'Europe? Les frontiers, l'État, le people* (2001), translated as *We, the People of Europe? Reflections on Transnational Citizenship* (2004), and *Europe, Constitution, Frontière* (2005).

Further Reading: N. Hewlet, *Badiou, Balibar, Rancière: Re-thinking Emancipation* (2007).

J. Lezra (ed.) *Depositions: Althusser, Balibar, Macherey and the Labor of Reading* (1996).

Balint, Michael (1896–1970) Hungarian psychoanalyst. Born in Budapest, the son of a Jewish physician, Balint initially studied medicine, but while he was at university he became interested in the work of Sigmund *Freud and began attending the lectures of Sándor Ferenczi (at that time Freud's close friend). In 1920 he moved to Berlin to work on a doctorate in biochemistry, but he kept up his interest in *psychoanalysis. He returned to Hungary in 1924, but the political situation there soon compelled him to leave again and he moved to Britain, where he remained for the rest of his life. In the UK he became influenced by the work of Melanie Klein, and is generally regarded as an *object relations theorist like her. There, too, he was able to further his interest in psychoanalysis, eventually developing it into a full-time practice devoted to marital problems. His major works are *Primary Love and Psycho-analytic Technique* (1956) and *Basic Fault* (1967).

Further Reading: A. Elder et al. *Michael Balint: Object Relations, Pure and Applied* (1996).

bare life (*nuda vita*) Italian philosopher Giorgio *Agamben's concept for life that has been exposed to what he terms the structure of exception that constitutes contemporary *biopower. The term originates in Agamben's observation that the Ancient Greeks had two different words for what in contemporary European languages is simply referred to as 'life': *bios* (the form or manner in which life is lived) and *zoē* (the biological fact of life). His argument is that the loss of this distinction obscures the fact that in a political context, the word 'life' refers more or less exclusively to the biological dimension or *zoē* and implies no guarantees about the quality of the life lived. Bare life refers then to a conception of life in which the sheer biological fact of life is given priority over the way a life is lived, by which Agamben means its possibilities and potentialities. Suggestions made in 2008 by Scotland Yard and the Institute for Public Policy Research in Britain that children as young as five should be DNA typed and their details placed in a database if they exhibit behavioural signs indicating future criminal activity is a perfect example of what Agamben means by bare life. It reduces the prospects of the life of a particular child to their biology and takes no interest in or account of the actual circumstances of their life. *See also* HOMO SACER.

Further Reading: G. Agamben *Means without End* (2000).

Barthes, Roland (1915–80) French literary and cultural critic and leading light of both the *structuralist and *post-structuralist movements. His career was slow-moving to begin with, but at his death he was one of the most influential intellectuals in the world.

Born in Cherbourg, in north-west France, in lowly circumstances (his father was a naval officer and his mother a homemaker) Barthes grew up in Bayonne, near the Spanish border. His childhood was uneventful and he would later remember it as punctuated by prolonged and intense periods of boredom. In 1924 he moved to Paris, going to school at the Lycée Montaigne in the sixth arrondissement behind the Luxembourg Gardens until he was 14 and then the Lycée Louis-le-Grand near the Sorbonne. In 1934 Barthes contracted tuberculosis, which required his removal to a mountain sanatorium, severely interrupting his academic career for the next ten years. Exempted from military service because of his illness, he spent the Second World War—when not in a sanatorium—working as a secondary school teacher, first in Biarritz, then in Paris.

After the war Maurice Nadeau invited Barthes to contribute to the cultural pages of the prestigious underground publication *Combat*, founded by the Resistance and edited by an illustrious team of authors that included Albert Camus and Jean-Paul *Sartre. The essays Barthes submitted, which dealt with the ethico-political responsibility of writers, would become his first book *Le Degré zéro de l'écriture* (1953), translated as *Writing Degree Zero* (1967). Although this book spoke in favour of a politically engaged form of writing of the kind Sartre advocated (*littérature engagé* or committed writing), Barthes rarely if ever involved himself directly in political struggles. Indeed, in 1960 he fell out with his friend Nadeau because he refused to put his name to the 'Manifesto of the 121' declaring the right of insubordination in response to the Algerian War. Again in *May 1968, Barthes kept his distance from the events of the student protest. Similarly in 1971 he joined neither the **Groupe d'Information sur les Prisons* (Group for Information on Prisons) nor the *Front Homosexuel d'Action Révolutionnaire* (Homosexual Revolutionary Action).

Barthes career path was chequered to say the least. Before he took his first academic job in the sixth section of the École Pratique des Hautes Études in 1960 (at the advanced age of 45), he worked for a number of years in the French Foreign Office. His first posting was to the French Institute in Romania, where he gave lectures on popular culture, developing the style he would perfect with *Mythologies* (1957), translated as *Mythologies* (1972). When the Romanian authorities decided to expel the Institute in 1949, Barthes was reassigned to Alexandria in Egypt, where he spent a great deal of his free time with the semiotician Algirdas *Greimas who introduced him to the work of Ferdinand de *Saussure. In 1950 he returned to Paris, still without an academic job. He soon quit his job at the Foreign Office, finding it unbearably tedious, choosing instead to make ends meet by combining a series of untenured research assistant posts with cultural journalism.

In 1953, again at the invitation of Maurice Nadeau, Barthes started writing a monthly column for the newly-established cultural journal, *Les Lettres nouvelles*. These essays looked through a critical lens at the minutiae of *everyday life in all its banality, covering everything from soap bubbles, to striptease and pasta advertisements. When these essays were collected and published in book form as *Mythologies* in 1957 they were an immediate sensation. In this period, Barthes also contributed reviews to *Théâtre populaire*. The work of *Brecht's Berliner Ensemble, which regularly brought its productions to Paris, made a particularly big impression on Barthes. According to Fredric *Jameson, Brecht's influence can readily be seen in *Mythologies*, which in his view is a profound instance of the *estrangement-effect at work. The concept of *myth that emerged from this work had a significant effect on the development of *cultural studies.

In 1958, Barthes asked Claude *Lévi-Strauss to supervise a doctoral dissertation on fashion, but the latter turned him down, though not without offering the invaluable advice that he should read Vladimir Propp's *Morfologija skázki* (1928), translated as *Morphology of the Folktale* (1958). He eventually found a supervisor in linguist André Martinet, but never got around to actually finishing his PhD. His proposed project on fashion was however completed and published as *Système de la mode* (1967), translated as *The Fashion System* (1985). In 1963 he met Philippe *Sollers, the flamboyant novelist and editor of the newly established journal *Tel Quel*, with which Barthes' name would become inextricably linked in the early 1970s in spite of the overtly Maoist orientation it adopted.

In 1976, at Michel *Foucault's instigation, Barthes was elected to the chair of literary semiology at the illustrious Collège de France, an incredible achievement for someone with such an unorthodox academic pedigree. His final book, written as a work of mourning for his mother, who died in 1977, *La Chambre claire* (1980) translated as *Camera Lucida* (1982), was a meditation on photography, a subject that had interested him his entire life. Now at the peak of his fame, largely thanks to the bestseller status of his previous book, the charming semi-autobiographical *Fragments d'un discourse amoureux* (1977), translated as *A Lover's Discourse* (1979), Barthes was even interviewed by *Playboy.* Then tragedy struck. On February 25, 1980, while crossing the road, Barthes was knocked down by a delivery van. He was taken to the Hôpital Pitié-Salpêtrière and although the doctors did not think he'd been seriously injured he never regained his health and died a few weeks later on March 26. *See also* READERLY AND WRITERLY; WORK AND TEXT.

Further Reading: R. Bensmaïa *The Barthes Effect: The Essay as Reflective Text* (1987).
J. Calvet *Roland Barthes: A Biography* (1994).
J. Culler *Barthes* (1983).
F. Jameson *Brecht and Method* (1998).
A. Lavers *Roland Barthes: Structuralism and After* (1982).
M. Moriarty *Roland Barthes* (1991).
A. Stafford *Roland Barthes, Phenomenon and Myth: An Intellectual Biography* (1998).

base and superstructure Analogy proposed by Karl *Marx to characterize modern society as a dual system consisting of two semi-autonomous (as Louis *Althusser would later characterize them) types of operations: the base is the economy, the forces and relations of production, while the superstructure is the non-economic support apparatus comprising the judiciary, government, police, but also culture itself. Marx's most explicit articulation of this concept is in his 1859 'Preface' to *A Contribution to the Critique of the Political Economy,* but his meaning is much disputed. At issue is whether or not the 'base' should be regarded as the cause of the 'superstructure' in some direct or indirect way. So-called 'vulgar' Marxists generally take the view that the base is causal, whereas 'historical' or 'cultural' Marxists tend to take the view that the two systems are mutually reinforcing.

Bataille, Georges (1897–1962) French religious historian, philosopher and novelist. For most of his professional life he worked as a librarian, which not only gave him access to vast collections of arcane texts and items but also plenty of free time to trawl through them, as his various works amply evidence. Contradicting the stereotypical image of the librarian as an anti-social type who prefers books to people, Bataille was a great organizer: he was one of the founding members of the Collège de Sociologie (along with Roger Caillois and Michel Leiris) and its journal *Documents*;

he was co-founder of the journal *Acéphale* and its associated secret society; and he was the founding editor of *Critique*. He also was affiliated with the *Surrealists and helped establish the off-shoot anti-fascist group Contre-Attaque.

Born in Billom in the Auvergne district of France, Bataille initially wanted to be a priest, but abandoned these plans in his late teens and instead studied medieval history, particularly religious history, focusing on working with books and manuscripts. His first job was at the Bibliothèque Nationale in Paris, where he remained for over twenty years. Then following a seven-month spell of medical leave, convalescing with tuberculosis, he worked at libraries in Carpentras and Orleans. Fittingly, it was to Bataille that the German Jewish writer and philosopher Walter *Benjamin entrusted his manuscripts when he fled Paris in 1940 after the German Army occupied the city.

Bataille's name is inexorably tied to the concept of transgression. His entire career can be seen as an investigation into both the actual ontology of transgression and the anthropology of its apparent necessity. For Bataille transgression is inherent in any and every system, no matter how rigorously it seems to be excluded. His exploration of transgression takes two main forms. First, and probably best known, is his fiction—part essay, part treatise; his erotic novels *Histoire de l'oeil* (1928), translated as *Story of the Eye* (1967), and *Madame Edwarda* (1941) have been admired in print by Yukio Mishima, Susan *Sontag and Roland *Barthes and are a staple part of any course on experimental fiction (that André Breton attacked him for being an 'excremental' writer hasn't hurt his reputation in this respect). Second is his philosophical and historical accounts of the centrality of transgression to social life, the best known work being *La Part maudite* (1949), translated as *The Accursed Share* (1988).

Bataille's theory of transgression is this: every 'restricted economy', his word for any putatively closed system or self-contained idea or concept, always produces more than it can contain and is fractured by this unacknowledged excess. Thus a notion like chastity only has meaning insofar as it is acknowledged that it is the negative of carnality; the fact that being chaste means choosing not to have sex means that the idea of actually having sex is never far from the surface. By the same token, the pleasure of transgression depends upon such restrictions being imposed in the first place (this is what theorists like Michel *Foucault and Gilles *Deleuze mean when they say power is productive).

Outside of philosophy, Bataille's most enduring influence has been in the field of art history, particularly the group surrounding the journal *October* which is interested primarily in modern and contemporary art.

Further Reading: F. Botting and S. Wilson *Bataille* (2001).
M. Surya *Georges Bataille, la mort à l'oeuvre* (1992), translated as *Georges Bataille: An Intellectual Biography* (2002).

Baudrillard, Jean (1929–2007) French cultural critic and semiotician. Born in Reims, Baudrillard developed an early interest in German language and culture. He taught German at secondary-school level from 1956–66, and translated plays by the German authors Bertolt *Brecht and Peter *Weiss, while undertaking his university education at Paris X – Nanterre. He completed his doctoral thesis in 1966 and it was published two years later as *Le système des objets* (1968), translated as *The System of Objects* (1996). This was followed in quick succession by *La Société de consummation* (1970), translated as *The Consumer Society* (1998); *Pour une critique de l'economie politique du signe* (1972), translated as *For a Critique of the Political Economy of the Sign* (1981); and *Le Miroir de la production* (1973), translated as *The Mirror of Production* (1975). These three books not only established Baudrillard as one of the most significant thinkers of the second half of the 20th century, they also helped initiate the global re-evaluation of the state of society in the era of *late capitalism that would subsequently be known as *postmodernism.

While Baudrillard himself rejected the term postmodernism, his work has always been—however unjustly—associated with that concept because the main thrust of his writing is congruent with its *anti-foundational impulse. He has also been described as a post-Marxist because although his work contains many quite powerful critiques of Marx, it is neither anti-Marx nor right-wing. More recently critics have pointed up his debts to *Situationism and Alfred Jarry's *'pataphysics as a means of sidestepping debates about his politics, arguing that his goal was always to provoke thought rather than propound a particular doctrine. On balance, there is probably no need to choose between these classifications since each is partly true.

Baudrillard's theory, which took shape in his very first publication and was maintained throughout his life, combines George *Bataille's theory of the sacred and Freudian *psychoanalysis and applies it to the contemporary *situation. What Baudrillard refers to as the real is in effect the equivalent of what Bataille calls the sacred, it is that which serves as the ultimate anchor and support of meaning. Secularization effectively destroys this point of reference with the result that meaning becomes unmoored and 'free-floating'. To compensate, contemporary society has constructed numerous simulacra of the sacred, such as the media, which superficially, and in a highly artificial manner, serve the purpose of grounding meaning. But of course the manifold simulations of the real which western society has conjured can never truly replace the sacred so for all intents and purposes the real has disappeared. Baudrillard's argument is not that there is no reality any more as he has sometimes been taken to mean. It is rather that there is nothing that can guarantee the meaning of reality.

What is of particular interest in Baudrillard's work, then, is his explanation of how we cope with the loss of the real. Baudrillard developed an elaborate system of symbolic meaning that seeks to account for the apparent addiction western society has for commodities. Instead of simply blaming this on a deterioration of national character as conservative cultural critics like Allan *Bloom did in *The Closing of the American Mind* (1987) and Christopher Lasch did in *The Culture of Narcissism* (1979), Baudrillard argues that consumption is the new form of the sacred. But a sacralized commodity is also a dematerialized commodity because its value is no longer intrinsic, but attaches to it as a function of belief. Consequently, our longing for a commodity object is, symbolically speaking, more important to us than its actual possession. In effect, no matter what we have it is bound to be a disappointment, and it is this paradox that according to Baudrillard drives western culture.

In the 1970s and 1980s he travelled extensively and wrote several aphoristic and elegiac books observing in minute and often hilarious detail the diverse manifestations of this paradox, which he aptly termed the 'impossible exchange', e.g. *Cool Memories* vols I–V (1987–2007), *America* (1988), and *The Transparency of Evil* (1993).

Unconventional in his outlook and always willing to be controversial as well, Baudrillard attained true notoriety in 1991 when he pronounced that the Gulf War would not take place despite the fact that the UN Security Council had already authorized the use of force. Then, after the invasion had already commenced, he asked if the war was actually taking place. And finally, after the hostilities were over, he questioned whether the Gulf War had in fact taken place. First published in a series of articles for the French journal *Libération* and shortly thereafter published in book form as *La Guerre du Golfe n'a pas eu lieu* (1991), translated as *The Gulf War did not take Place* (1995), these essays were for many the height of postmodern folly. Given that the whole world had been able to watch the war live on CNN, Baudrillard's questioning of it seemed to defy sense and it

b

provoked more than a few sceptical commentators to write him off as a crank (e.g. Christopher Norris's *Uncritical Theory: Postmodernism, Intellectuals and the Gulf War* (1992)). However, this book is consistent with much that others regard as positive in Baudrillard's work inasmuch that it questions the truth of appearances. Baudrillard did not deny that the US had sent a ground assault force into Kuwait and Iraq, but he did question whether the use of overwhelming force against a much weaker opponent could be called a war. *See also* CONSUMER SOCIETY; SIMULATION; SYMBOLIC EXCHANGE.

Further Reading: R. Butler *Jean Baudrillard* (1999).
M. Gane *Baudrillard's Bestiary* (1991).
G. Genosko *Baudrillard and Signs* (1998).
P. Hegarty *Jean Baudrillard: Live Theory* (2004).
D. Kellner *Jean Baudrillard* (1989).

SEE WEB LINKS

- Links to online resources relating to Jean Baudrillard's biography and his work.

Bauman, Zygmunt (1925–) A UK based, Polish-born sociologist. Bauman grew up in Poznan, Poland, but moved to Russia as a youth with his family to escape the German invasion. He fought with the Polish army, rising to the rank of major, but was sacked in 1953 because of his Jewishness. He then turned to academia, but was persecuted by anti-Semites within the academy, so he decided to leave Poland. He moved to the UK via brief stints in Tel Aviv and Canberra. A prolific writer, he is the author of over 50 books, dealing with a wide variety of topics, but principally focused around the issues of *modernity, *postmodernity, and the Holocaust. His major works include: *Modernity and the Holocaust* (1991); *Wasted Lives: Modernity and its Outcasts* (2003); *Postmodernity and its Discontents* (1997) and *Globalization: The Human Consequences* (1998).

As this brief list of titles indicates, Bauman's work is primarily focused on three questions: what constitutes *modernity? What are its effects? And what follows modernity? He charts the movement from what he characterizes as 'solid' modernity to the present situation of *liquid modernity in which the strong social bonds of family, religion, and country have been dissolved by the *deterritorializing effects of capital. Like Jean *Baudrillard, Bauman argues that consumption and consumerism have overtaken the place of work as the main organizing principle of both the economy and social life. As a consequence, he argues, social cohesion has been reduced to what he calls 'cloakroom' groups, i.e. groups which come together over a specific issue such as an anti-war rally only to disperse again when the event is over. This loss of cohesion is further exacerbated in his eyes by the premium *late capitalism places on the individual. Somewhat damningly, but on good evidence, he argues that modernity has not delivered its promise of emancipation. Polemically, Bauman equates the Holocaust with modernity, thus squaring the circle.

Further Reading: P. Beilharz *Zygmunt Bauman: Dialectic of Modernity* (2000).
T. Blackshaw *Zygmunt Bauman* (2005).
D. Smith, *Zygmunt Bauman: Prophet of Postmoderntity* (2000).
K. Tester *The Social Though of Zygmunt Bauman* (2004).

Bazin, André (1918–58) French film critic, co-founder and editor of the highly influential journal *Cahiers du cinéma*, the key organ of **auteur* theory. His essays, published posthumously in a four-volume set entitled *Qu'est-ce que le cinema?* (1958–62), translated as *What is Cinema?* (1967–71) were a major influence on the young **nouvelle vague* directors. Bazin was one of the first critics to write about cinema as a specific kind of artform and though some of his ideas have dated, he nonetheless deserves credit as one of the founders of the field of film studies. Bazin constantly sought to determine what is possible in cinema. He was one of the first to appreciate the possibilities of montage. He was also a great classifier of films and was always ready to invent a new genre to accommodate a new kind of film. Cinema, Bazin famously said, is an art of the real. Not because of its subject matter, however, but rather because the aesthetic space it creates is one that commands our credulity. We believe in what we see on the screen, even if we don't believe what we see is factual or truthful, because we believe in the objectivity of the mechanical recording device used to create it.

Further Reading: D. Andrew *The Major Film Theories* (1976).

Beauvoir, Simone de (1908–86) French feminist philosopher and author. Her landmark text *Le Deuxième Sexe* (1949), translated as *The Second Sex* (1952) is one of the foundational texts of 20th-century feminist theory. Its central thesis that women are made rather than born, which rejects *biological determinism *tout court*, continues to inform feminist theory today, even though Beauvoir herself tends to be neglected because her *existentialist approach adapted from *Sartre is out of fashion.

Born in Paris to middle-class but downwardly mobile parents, Beauvoir's childhood was marked by the anxiety of having to keep up appearances and the longing to be free from any such pretension. She went to an excellent Catholic girls' school, which

b

enabled her to gain entry to the prestigious École Normale Supérieure (ENS), where she met Jean-Paul *Sartre, with whom she would maintain a life-long relationship, and Maurice *Merleau-Ponty, who would also become a close friend. She graduated in 1923 (only the ninth woman in France to do so in the field of philosophy) and took a series of jobs in rural France teaching philosophy in secondary schools.

Beauvoir did not see herself primarily as a philosopher, even though she had trained in and excelled at philosophy. Rather what she wanted to write was fiction, but her first efforts weren't very successful. It wasn't until she adopted a more autobiographical approach that she hit on a winning formula and she became one of the most important chroniclers of her generation with works such as *Mémoires d'une jeune fille rangée* (1958), translated as *Memoirs of a Dutiful Daughter* (1987), which captured well the difficult situation of women in the middle of the tumultuous 20th century.

Throughout her life, Beauvoir was an active and 'engaged' (to use the phrase Sartre would make famous) intellectual. She was on the editorial board of *Les Temps modernes*, which since its founding has been one of the most important intellectual organs in France, providing a strong counter-hegemonic perspective. Although widely acknowledged as a key intellectual of her time, feminist theorists have always been ambivalent in their reception of her work either because she herself did not identify with feminism or because of the suspicion that her work merely replicated Sartre's. Toril Moi's important *Simone de Beauvoir: The Making of an Intellectual Woman* (1994) has, however, gone a long way towards overturning this assessment.

Further Reading: D. Bair *Simone de Beauvoir: A Biography* (1990). H. Rowley *Tête-à-Tête: Simone de Beauvoir and Jean-Paul Sartre* (2005).

Beck, Ulrich (1944–) German sociologist best known for developing the concept of *risk society (*Risikogesellschaft*). Beck was born in Stolp, which is now known as Slupsk and is in Poland, but was then under German control. He studied for his undergraduate and postgraduate degrees at Munich University, which is where he obtained his first job as well. In 1979 he moved to Münster and from there to Bamberg in 1981, where he remained for a decade. He then returned to Munich. He also holds a concurrent position at the London School of Economics. Beck first came to international attention with the publication of *Risikogesellschaft: Auf dem Weg in eine andere Moderne* (1986), translated as *Risk Society: Towards a New Modernity* (1992). Appearing shortly after the disaster at Chernobyl, *Risk Society* offered an attractive theory of society rendered vulnerable by its technological sophistication. Beck's argument is that more and more decisions affecting daily life are being made in what he terms the sub-political realms of business and bureaucracy, a fact that threatens the quality if not the existence of democracy: for instance, the decision to place a road in one place and not another is a bureaucratic one, requiring minimal input from the people affected by the decision. In more recent work, such as *Was ist Globalisierung?* (1997), translated as *What is Globalization?* (2000), and *Der kosmopolitische Blick oder: Krieg ist Frieden* (2004), translated as *The Cosmopolitan Vision* (2006), Beck has extended this thesis to the state of the entire planet, giving his theory both an epochal and global dimension. Describing the present situation as 'second modernity' (a deliberate refusal of the term postmodernity), which in his view sits alongside 'first modernity', Beck argues that the potential for a new *cosmopolitanism can be seen in twin drivers of the expansion of capital and the relaxing of territorial borders. But, as he is also careful to point out, cosmopolitanism in this form is not free from the effects of depoliticization he described in *Risk Society*—it too must confront the fact that business and bureaucracy can impose changes on society that society itself has no wish to see implemented.

behaviourism In psychology, the methodological conviction that only the body's measurable physical responses to stimuli can be used to determine the true nature of psychological states. The most well-known example of this approach is Pavlov's experiments with dogs, showing that the sound of the dinner bell was sufficient to stimulate a saliva response. The most prominent exponent of this form of psychology was B.H. Skinner, who tried to show that humans act according to experience, rather than intention. The problem with this account of human behaviour, apart from its obviously mechanistic modelling, is that it cannot account for human inventions that cannot have been caused by mere accident. For example, the malleability of copper wasn't discovered by accidentally dropping copper ore into a cooking fire because it doesn't melt at that temperature, but needs superheating, which requires the application of engineering principles. The same can be said for virtually all cognitive achievements, they are not explainable as reactions to stimuli.

Bell, Daniel (1919–) American sociologist, highly influential in the 1950s and 1960s. He is best known for his claims that western society has entered a period that is at once *post-industrial and post-ideological.

b

Bell grew up in a poor family in New York. His father died when he was an infant and his mother worked in the garment industry. He studied ancient history at City College of New York, graduating in 1939. For the next two decades, he worked as a journalist, reporting on labour and industrial issues, picking up some part-time teaching at the University of Chicago and Columbia University along the way. In 1958 he made a definitive move into academia, taking a full-time position at Columbia in the Department of Sociology. Already prominent as a journalist, he was part of the group known as the 'New York Intellectuals' (who were generally left wing, but vehemently anti-communist), Bell's star rose even higher with the publication of *The End of Ideology* (1960). Seemingly capturing the spirit of the times, Bell argued that technological and indeed technocratic solutions had replaced ideological solutions to the problem of how best to organize society. On the strength of this book, he was invited to join the President's Commission on Technology in 1964. It was in this capacity, as a policy advisor, that he was able to exert the most influence, by translating his theoretical conclusions into practical suggestions. Bell moved to Harvard in 1969, and has remained there for the rest of his career.

The 1970s saw the publication of the two works that for many people summed up the decade as a whole and foreshadowed the rise of what would subsequently be known as *postmodernism: *The Coming of Post-industrial Society* (1973) and its sequel *The Cultural Contradictions of Capitalism* (1976). Both these works argued for a sea-change in the composition of both the economy and the society of the West, particularly North America. In the first work he noted a trend in the US economy away from manufacturing towards the service industry or what today would be known as the information economy. In the second work, he argued that this change in the composition of the economy would present challenges to social cohesion because mass labour would no longer function as a ready source of integration. Both works have been subject to considerable debate, and are widely rejected by the Left, but they nonetheless remain influential testaments to the birth of the present era, which many still call post-industrial.

Further Reading: M. Waters *Daniel Bell* (1996).

Benjamin, Walter (1892–1940) German cultural critic and essayist, best known for his account of the impact of new technology on aesthetics. Born to a genteel and reasonably well-to-do Jewish merchant family in Berlin, Benjamin grew up in Charlottenburg and Grünewald, which at that time were outside the city limits of

Berlin. Although Jewish, his family were not especially observant. Benjamin took an interest in *messianism in later life, but he never developed an affinity for Judaism or Zionism, much to the distress of friends like Gershom Scholem who tried to persuade him to relocate to Israel.

His undergraduate career, like much of his life, was peripatetic. He did two years of an undergraduate degree in philology at the Albert Ludwig University in Freiburg (where his fellow students included Martin *Heidegger), but did not find the city congenial and returned to Berlin to continue his studies at the Royal Friedrich Wilhelm University (where he attended lectures by Georg *Simmel). Exempted from military service when war broke out in 1914 because of extreme short-sightedness, Benjamin moved again and completed his philosophy degree in Munich, where he studied with Heinrich Wölfflin (though he found his seminars oppressive) and met the great German poet Rainer Maria Rilke.

In 1916 he moved to Switzerland and completed his doctorate at the University of Berne, where he met Ernst *Bloch. Thereafter he returned to Germany, but his career did not progress smoothly from doctorate to habilitation, the prerequisite to a professorial appointment. Indeed, his thesis, *Ursprung des deutschen Trauerspiels* (1928), translated as *The Origin of German Tragic Drama* (1977), which sought to explain in allegorical terms the type of drama known as Trauerspiel (mourning play), popular in Germany in the early part of the Baroque period (i.e. the 16th century). Central to Benjamin's work is the claim that Trauerspiel is of a different order from tragedy, with which it is generally compared, because it is rooted in history rather than myth. Unfortunately for Benjamin, his examiners at the University of Frankfurt were not persuaded by this claim and his thesis was failed in 1925, effectively destroying his chances of an academic career.

Of necessity, he took to freelance writing as a means of supporting himself and though he never ceased to think about academic subjects, he never wrote another strictly academic book. Predominantly he wrote book and theatre reviews for *Frankfurter Zeitung* (at the invitation of Siegfried *Kracauer) and *Literarische Welt* (at the invitation of Hugo von Hofmannsthal). Living and working in Frankfurt, Benjamin maintained a peripheral but significant relation with key members of the *Frankfurt School, particularly Theodor *Adorno, with whom he sustained an important and longstanding correspondence. He travelled to Moscow in this period and wrote a highly sympathetic journal recording his experience there.

More typical of his new style was *Einbahnstrasse* (1928), translated as *One-Way Street* (1978), an enchanting collection of travel vignettes and street-level observations published in the same year as the book on Trauerspiel. In 1929 he began writing for radio as well. In the same year Asja Lacis, whom he had met on Capri a few years earlier, introduced him to Bertolt *Brecht, who was to have a significant influence on him. He would later write a series of essays on Brecht that were put together and posthumously published as *Versuche über Brecht* (1966), translated as *Understanding Brecht* (1973). Benjamin was also engaged in a long-term translation project at this time as well; he was part of a small team producing a German version of Proust's magnum opus, *Á la recherche du temps perdu*.

The next ten years were very productive for Benjamin, in spite of the enormous turmoil in his life. He began work on, but didn't complete (the posthumously published) *Das Passagen-Werk* (1982), translated as *The Arcades Project* (1999), an enormous compilation of images and quotations relating to Paris in the 19th century. He also completed a series of essays on Baudelaire that were intended to preface this project, which developed Baudelaire's idea of the *flâneur as a sociological icon of the 19th century. In 1936 he published what is probably his most famous essay, 'Das Kunstwerk im Zeitalter seiner technischen Reproduzierbarkeit' (1936), translated as 'The Work of Art in the Age of Mechanical Reproduction' (1968), proposing that art in the modern age lacks the *aura of previous eras.

As a Jew, his life was made very difficult by the rise of fascism in Germany and like many of his *Frankfurt School colleagues he was forced into exile, though sadly he ultimately acted too late. He left Germany in 1933, but didn't try to get out of Europe until 1940, by which time France had already fallen. He managed to get as far as the border town of Port Bou, where he died of a morphine overdose, whether accidentally or intentionally isn't known. His posthumous reputation, particularly in the Anglophone world, was assured by the collection entitled *Illuminations* (1968), edited and introduced by Hannah *Arendt. It was further enhanced by Terry *Eagleton's short book, *Walter Benjamin: or, Towards a Revolutionary Criticism* (1981), written, as he says, to get to Benjamin before his enemies did. Eagleton highlights Benjamin's technique of reading history 'against the grain' as a strategy for doing critical theory in the age of *postmodernity.

Further Reading: M. Brodersen *Spinne im eigen Netz. Walter Benjamin—Leben und Werk* (1990), translated as *Walter Benjamin: A Biography* (1996).

S. Buck-Morss *The Dialectics of Seeing: Walter Benjamin and the Arcades Project* (1991).

T. Eagleton *Walter Benjamin: or, Towards a Revolutionary Criticism* (1981).

F. Jameson *Marxism and Form* (1971).

M. Jay *The Dialectical Imagination* (1973).

E. Leslie *Walter Benjamin* (2007).

Benveniste, Émile (1902–76) French linguist, generally regarded as one of the main precursors to *structuralism. Born in Aleppo in Northern Syria, then a French Mandate, Benveniste's family, who were Sephardic Jews, sent him to Marseilles to attend rabbinical school, but one of the scholars there, recognizing his talent, suggested he go to the Sorbonne instead to study Indo-European linguistic forms under Antoine Meillet (a former student of Ferdinand de *Saussure). The connection proved fortuitous and Benveniste flourished. His early work was highly specialist and for that reason little known outside the closed circles of linguistics, but it was distinguished enough to see him elevated to a chair at the Collège de France at the comparatively young age of 35. Although he worked in the shadows for most of his academic career, Benveniste was propelled into the spotlight with the publication in 1966 of *Problèmes de linguistique générale*, translated as *Problems in General Linguistics* (1971). The two doyens of Parisian structuralism, Claude *Lévi-Strauss and Jacques *Lacan recognized him as an important ally in the development of their projects, thus encouraging Benveniste to broaden his range of interests and cease to write exclusively for linguists (who ignored him in any case). Benveniste's work set him apart from other linguists of his generation for his willingness to embrace ideas drawn from analytic philosophy at a time when French thought was dominated by the work of *Nietzsche and *Heidegger, and for his interest in the *problematic of the subject. Benveniste broke once and for all with the idea that language is a signal system by arguing that bees do not have language because while a bee can report back to the hive what it has seen, it cannot use an intermediary to do the reporting on its behalf; language, for Benveniste, arises only with the possibility of reported speech (a notion that is central to Gilles *Deleuze's theory of literature). By the same token, if language is not purely a signal system, then there must be a dimension to it that exceeds the basic requirements of signalling—a dimension often referred to as the poetic. In order to grasp this, Benveniste distinguished between the *énoncé* (*statement) and the *énonciation* (utterance), or to put it more simply the thing said and the way it is said. This in turn created a logical paradox that would prove central to Lacan's reformulation of psychoanalysis, namely that the 'I' of the statement is not the same as the 'I' of the utterance, that in effect the 'I' is always an 'other'.

Bergson, Henri (1859–1941) French philosopher of science interested principally in the operations of consciousness, particularly with regard to time. One of the most famous and influential writers of his age, he received the Nobel Prize for literature in 1928. He is acknowledged as an important influence by writers as diverse as Marcel Proust, Paul Valéry and Charles Péguy, as well as psychologists like William James (who claimed that like Kant, Bergson had induced yet another Copernican turn in philosophy), Pierre Janet and Jean Piaget. The rise of *existentialism in France saw his work fall into disfavour only to be revived again by Gilles *Deleuze who, in his books on cinema particularly, manages to make what others have perceived as Bergson's weaknesses appear as strengths.

Born in Paris, to Jewish parents, he studied at the École Normale Supérieure, where his classmates were Jean Jaurès (anti-war activist and socialist leader assassinated in 1914) and Émile *Durkheim. He received his doctorate in 1889 for a thesis entitled: *Essai sur les données immédiates de la conscience*, translated as *Time and Free Will: An Essay on the Immediate Data of Consciousness* (1919), a work that continues to be studied to this day. For the next decade he taught in various lycées, including the prestigious Henri IV. In 1900 he was offered the Chair in Philosophy at the Collège de France, where he remained until his retirement in 1921. Suffering from acute arthritis, he had to give up teaching in 1914. This did not prevent him from joining a diplomatic mission to the US in 1917 in a bid to persuade America to join the war. After the war he chaired a section of the League of Nations devoted to international intellectual cooperation.

Bergson's most influential and best known conceptual invention is the notion of *élan vital* (vital impulse). Ironically, it is used as much by his detractors to deride his work as it is by his supporters to explain what is significant about his work. Bergson's so-called vitalism is in this respect a double-edged sword. The most straightforward way of thinking about *élan vital* is that it encompasses the gap in mechanistic explanations of evolution and names those aspects of evolutionary change scientific theory cannot explain. It could thus be seen as a virtual power of differentiation, or adaptation to use the Darwinian term, namely a creative force able to respond to obstacles and develop creative but 'unthought' solutions. Species development can be thought then in terms of an arresting or stabilizing of this flow of creative energy and thus as much a matter of involution as evolution. This idea has lately caught the attention of *complexity theorists.

Further Reading: G. Deleuze *Bergsonisme* (1965), translated as *Bergsonism* (1988).
S. Guerlac *Thinking in Time: An Introduction to Henri Bergson* (2006).
J. Mullarkey *Bergson and Philosophy* (1999).

Bettelheim, Bruno (1903–90) Viennese-born, American-based *psychoanalyst best known for his (not uncontroversial) work on autism. Born in Vienna, Bettelheim studied philosophy and art history (which included a compulsory psychology component) at the University of Vienna. His studies were twice interrupted, first because of his father's death and the necessity of taking over the family business, and second because of Austria's *Anschluss* with Nazi Germany in 1938. Although raised in a secular family, Bettelheim's Jewish ancestry meant that he was incarcerated by the Nazis in concentration camps at Dachau and Buchenwald. Fortunately, he was amnestied after eleven months in April 1939, and was able to make his way to the US as a refugee. He wrote a moving, bestselling memoir of this experience, *The Informed Heart* (1960), which used psychoanalysis to try to understand the behaviour of both guards and inmates. He eventually settled in Chicago where he was appointed professor of psychology at the University of Chicago and made the director of the Sonia Shankman Orthogenic School. It was as director of the Orthogenic School that Bettelheim made his mark. Established as a treatment facility for psychologically disturbed children, it enabled him to develop his theories in a practical setting. In 1967 he published a series of case studies of autistic children, all of them residents in his facility, *The Empty Fortress: Infantile Autism and the Birth of the Self*, which sold very well and became a highly influential text. Unfortunately, its central thesis that bad parenting is to blame for autism (since disproved) had a terrible effect on parents struggling to raise autistic children. The same work has also been praised by Gilles *Deleuze and Félix *Guattari for not reducing children's psychological problems to a failure to adequately deal with their *Oedipal complex. Probably his most lastingly important book is *The Uses of Enchantment* (1976), which is a psychoanalytic reading of fairy tales. Interestingly, Bettelheim is highly critical of Disney's rendering of fairy tales like Snow White and Cinderella for the way they edit out the violence of the originals. Without exposure to that violence, Bettelheim argues, children do not learn about the realities of life and aren't given the opportunity to psychologically prepare themselves for the traumas of loss they inevitably must face as they grow older. Bettelheim's legacy is uneven because while some of his theories, particularly those relating to the genesis of autism, have now been discredited, many of his other insights remain as cogent as ever.

Further Reading: D. Fisher *Bettelheim: Living and Dying* (2008).

Bhabha, Homi (1949–) An Indian-born, but American-based literary critic and theorist, Bhabha is one of the three most prominent

b

*postcolonial theorists of recent times, along with Edward *Said and Gayatri *Spivak. Of Parsee descent (an Indian minority group that originally migrated from Persia in the 8th century), Bhabha was born and raised in Mumbai. He took his undergraduate degree from the University of Mumbai, then went to Oxford to complete his DPhil on V.S. Naipaul. Thereafter he taught at the University of Sussex for a decade before relocating to the US where he has held a series of prestigious appointments culminating in his decision to join Harvard in 2001. Bhabha is very far from being a prolific author: to date, he has only published one monograph (though several more are said to be in the pipeline), *The Location of Culture* (1994), which collects several previously published essays. Despite his comparatively meagre output, Bhabha's work has had an astonishingly broad impact. Difficult though his writing famously is, his combination of *poststructuralist theory, *postmodern sensibility, and *postcolonial themes resonates strongly with the critical concerns of the present moment. Bhabha's basic argument, tested via the interrogation of a rich variety of literary and artistic texts, is that culture cannot any longer (if it ever could) be conceived in monolithic terms, but has to be thought rather in terms of *hybridity. Culturally, thanks to movement of peoples, ideas, capital, and commodities made possible by the forces and processes of *globalization, 'we' are never wholly of or in one place. Our sense of self and location is a product of a combination of factors that are never entirely local or 'native' in origin. To take only one example, more than two thirds of all toys and clothing retailed in the US today are manufactured in China, yet those toys and clothes are not recognizably Chinese in form or design. For Bhabha, this hybridity is ambivalent: it means that power is always limited in its ability to determine identities and control representations. Bhabha thus criticizes Said's *orientalism thesis for portraying the effects of power as singular and inexorable and not taking into account the postmodern subject's ability to *mimic and therefore transmute what is expected of them.

Further Reading: E. Byrne *Homi K. Bhabha* (2009).
D. Huddart *Homi K. Bhabha* (2006).

Bildungsroman **(development novel)** A sub-genre of novel focusing on the personal development of the protagonist, usually from childhood through to adulthood. The prototype is J.W. Goethe's *Wilhelm Meisters Lehrjarhre* (Willhelm Meister's Apprenticeship, 1795–6), but the form was widely adopted in Europe throughout the 19th century. Other famous examples include: Charlotte Brontë's *Jane Eyre* (1847), Charles Dickens's *David*

Copperfield (1850) and Thomas Hardy's *Jude the Obscure* (1895). As these examples suggest, the development is not merely personal, inasmuch as it generally takes the form of both a move away from rural origins towards the modern city and an upward movement from one social class to another. In this regard, the personal history can be read as an allegory of a particular trajectory within a national history.

Further Reading: M. Bakhtin *Speech Genres and Other Late Essays* (1986).
F. Moretti *The Way of the World: The Bildungsroman in European Culture* (new edn, 2000).

binary opposition A pair of terms that although opposed to one another are necessarily bound together as each other's condition of possibility. Common examples of binary oppositions include: male/female, nature/culture, hot/cold, gay/straight, signifier/signified and so on. *Structuralism is predicated on binary oppositions to the extent that its basic account of meaning is that something means what it does by virtue of what it does not mean. *Post-structuralism, and more especially, *deconstruction, arose as a challenge to the absolute nature of these oppositions.

biological determinism The now largely discredited notion that it is biology, specifically the instincts, that shape the relations between sexes and, more particularly, defines their respective social roles. Typically, this viewpoint would hold that because women are the childbearing sex they are naturally more 'caring' and more inclined to want to stay at home and nurture children than men. The extension of this idea is that biology is itself a destiny, for example that women are destined to have children and that shapes their lives. Understandably, feminists have rejected this viewpoint, arguing instead that men and women are culturally conditioned to accept the traditional gender roles as normal. The first sustained attack on this position came from Mary Wollstonecraft's *A Vindication of the Rights of Women* (1792).

biopolitics *See* BIOPOWER.

biopower A form of political power that revolves around populations (humans as a species or as productive capacity) rather than individuals (humans as subjects or citizens). The focus of much of his late work, biopower was conceived by Michel *Foucault as a distinctively new form of political rationality. Traditionally, according to Foucault's own schematization, western political thought was primarily concerned with the twofold problem of what constitutes the just and good life and how can men

b

(in the period in question, from the time of Aristotle until the early Renaissance, women were excluded from politics) be persuaded to adhere to it. As an art, politics was supposed to serve a higher goal, namely God's purpose. Then, from the early 1500s, a less spiritually virtuous and more politically calculating way of thinking emerged, for which the name Machiavelli is a universally recognized shorthand. Now, political thought focused on the practicalities of obtaining, maintaining and extending the power of the prince, ignoring the freedom and virtue of the citizens. Beginning at the same time as Machiavelli, but only rising to prominence much later, still another form of thinking about power began to be formulated by the nameless bureaucrats and policy-makers who actually run governments, which had no other concern than the power of the state. It viewed the population of the state as a resource and developed knowledge about its people accordingly: on the one hand, it wanted to learn about humans as a species and come to know their biological secrets, and on the other hand, it wanted to develop the capacity of humans as machines by disciplining their bodies. Foucault termed this new kind of political rationality biopower because it concerned itself with every aspect of life, right down to its most minute parts, though only in the abstract. It was interested in the health of the people in statistical terms, not existential terms—it cared about how people live and die, but not who lives and dies. For the first time in history, Foucault argues, biological existence was reflected in political existence, and in consequence the very existence of the species itself was wagered on political questions. Giorgio Agamben's theory of *bare life originates in this thesis as does *Hardt and *Negri's concepts of *Empire and *multitude.

Further Reading: H. Dreyfus and P. Rabinow *Michel Foucault: Beyond Structuralism and Hermeneutics* (1983).

M. Foucault *La Volonté de savoir* (1976), translated as *The History of Sexuality: An Introduction* (1978).

M. Hardt and A. Negri, *Empire* (2000).

Blanchot, Maurice (1907–2003) French philosopher and author, Blanchot is a major figure in 20th-century French intellectual history, but one whose presence is often and perhaps deliberately hard to detect. Consistent with his view that literary and philosophical works are not reducible to either a psychological or sociological explanation, Blanchot was in his last years famously reclusive in his habits. His prose style is similarly enigmatic—in his fiction he habitually erases the markers of place and person readers rely on to coordinate their understanding of the text; and his philosophy, concerned as it is with the unsayable (death, silence, and solitude are among his key preoccupations, the others being friendship, work, and space), constantly strives to say that which, it acknowledges, can only be gestured towards.

Blanchot was born in Quain in the Saône-et-Loire district of Burgundy. He did his undergraduate degree at the University of Strasbourg, studying German and philosophy. There he met Emmamuel *Levinas, who would become a lifelong friend. As an undergraduate Blanchot was actively involved with the extreme right-wing group Action Française. He wrote articles for such right-wing publications as *Journal de Débats, Réaction, Le Rempart, Combat,* and *L'Insurgé,* perhaps explaining his later reticence with respect to biography. However, following the defeat of France in 1940 he refused to collaborate with the Vichy regime and retreated almost completely from public life, not surfacing again until the *May '68. He is widely believed to have authored the famous 'Manifeste de 121', a declaration signed by 121 intellectuals (mostly from the left) proclaiming the right of insubordination in protest to the Algerian war.

Gilles *Deleuze, Paul De Man, Jacques *Derrida and Michel *Foucault, among many others, have all paid homage to Blanchot, praising him for articulating the gap—which Blanchot designated as the Outside—between the sayable and the non-sayable and more particularly for attempting to say what it is that belongs only to art. Like his friend Georges *Bataille, Blanchot pursued this project via the dual pathways of literature and philosophy. Blanchot's novels, such as *Thomas l'Obscur* (1941), translated as *Thomas the Obscure* (1973) and *L'Arrêt de mort* (1948), translated as *The Death Sentence* (1978), are every bit as experimental as Bataille's, and only slightly less confronting. His best known philosophical works are: *L'Espace littéraire* (1955), translated as *The Space of Literature* (1982), and *L'Entretien infini* (1969), translated as *The Infinite Conversation* (1993).

Further Reading: G. Bruns *Maurice Blanchot: The Refusal of Philosophy* (2005).
U. Haase *Maurice Blanchot* (2001).
K. Hart *The Dark Gaze: Maurice Blanchot and the Sacred* (2004).
L. Hill *Blanchot: Extreme Contemporary* (1997).

blaxploitation (neologism constructed from black exploitation) A sub-genre of Hollywood films produced in the USA in the 1970s with the deliberate aim of attracting an African-American audience. Capitalizing on the success of *Sweet Sweetback's Baadassss Song* (director Van Peebles, 1971), *Shaft* (director Parks Snr 1971) and

Superfly (director Parks Jnr 1972), blaxploitation's aesthetic emulated their gritty storylines and streetwise heroes and created a new type of film which challenged Hollywood's stereotypes of black people. Blaxploitation storylines generally revolved around black men and women winning one over the white system. In doing so it brought black actors into the foreground of the narrative action in a way not previously seen in Hollywood, which tended to consign them to the role of victim or servant. Some 40 movies were produced in this mould, including pastiches of horror films and westerns, before the market was saturated and the genre burnt out in the late 1970s. Quentin Tarantino's (1998) *Jackie Brown* is a homage to the genre and features one of its greatest stars, Pam Grier.

Bloch, Ernst (1885–1977) German Marxist philosopher, social critic and utopianist. Bloch was born in the industrial town of Ludwigshafen. His father was an assimilated Jew of modest means who worked as an official on the railways. Bloch studied philosophy in Munich and Würzburg, before making a definitive move to Berlin where he was mentored by Georg *Simmel (their friendship ended when Simmel spoke in favour of Germany's entry to World War I). In Berlin, Bloch also met and became a firm friend of Marxist literary critic György *Lukács with whom he would later have very public disagreements concerning *Expressionism, which he favoured and Lukács did not.

At the outbreak of World War 1, Bloch (declared unfit for military service) moved out of Berlin, first to Grünewald, and then to Switzerland, where he struck up a friendship with cultural critic Walter *Benjamin. After the war, he returned to Berlin and was part of the large circle of intellectuals who were resident there in the heady Weimar Republic days—Theodor *Adorno, Bertolt *Brecht, Hanns Eisler and Otto Klemperer. He moved back to Switzerland in 1933 (to escape persecution under the new race laws implemented by the Nazis) and subsequently to the US where he waited out the war. Interestingly, for reasons which aren't clear, and unlike many other German exiles from the same circle, Bloch was not given employment by Horkheimer's Institute for Social Research, and was forced to live a hand-to-mouth existence supported by his wife's job as a waitress. After the war he returned to the now divided Germany and initially lived in the socialist East Germany, but after falling out with the authorities there he moved to the West, and spent his remaining years at Tübingen. It was during his period in the US that he began but did not complete his magnum opus, for which he is best known, the three volume colossus *Das Prinzip Hoffnung* (1959), translated as *The Principle of Hope* (1986). A sprawling work that takes in virtually every cultural form of its time, *The Principle of Hope* argues that every historical age contains its own horizon, its Front over which what he calls the Not-Yet-Conscious spirit of utopia (or wish for change) flows. Thus even the darkest moments in history are said to contain elements of 'Vor-Schein' (pre-appearance or shining ahead), signs which point towards imminent transformation. Translations of Bloch's work into English have been inexplicably slow in coming, which has hampered appreciation of his thought in the Anglophone world. However it is now generally agreed that Bloch is one of the 20th-century's most important theorists of utopia. He transformed the concept from a weak idea associated with unfulfillable dreams into a strong concept connected to the material reality of everyday life.

Further Reading: F. Jameson *Marxism and Form* (1971).

Bloom, Allan (1930–92) American cultural critic and philosopher, Bloom was born in Indianapolis but his family moved to Chicago when he was a teenager. He gained a scholarship to study politics and philosophy at the University of Chicago, where he met his mentor and key influence Leo *Strauss. He completed his PhD in 1955 and after three years in Europe, to study first with Alexander *Kojève in Paris, and then in Germany, he returned to the University of Chicago to teach adult education classes. Subsequently he worked at Cornell, Yale, Tel Aviv University and the University of Toronto. While he was at Cornell, Bloom served as a faculty member of the Telluride House, whose student residents included Paul Wolfowitz (future Deputy Secretary of Defence under Donald Rumsfeld and disgraced President of the World Bank), and Francis *Fukuyama. Bloom was rocketed to international celebrity status with the publication of the huge-selling *The Closing of the American Mind* (1987), a jeremiad for the decline of 'proper' teaching in the US. Drawing heavily on *Nietzsche, its central thesis is that social movements that sprang up in the 1960s—such as the civil rights movement—are a sign of moral decay. Its success was not without controversy and the book sparked stern ripostes from Martha Nussbaum, David Rieff, Alexander Nehamas, and Benjamin Barber. Nevertheless the book was, and continues to be, championed by the Right and remains an icon of the so-called 'culture wars'. Bloom wrote several other books, but none so widely received as this. His novelist friend Saul Bellow immortalized and 'outed' Bloom in the roman à clef *Ravelstein* (2000).

Bloom, Harold (1930–) Jewish American literary theorist and critic best known for his notion of the *anxiety of influence. Born in New York, Bloom grew up in the South Bronx. In 1947 he was admitted to Cornell University. There he was mentored by M.H. Abrams, a specialist in the study of romanticism, a subject that Bloom would make his own too. He graduated from Cornell in 1952, then spent a year at Pembroke College, Cambridge, before going to Yale to complete his doctoral studies. He finished his PhD in 1955 and was employed more or less immediately by Yale and has worked there ever since. Bloom is an incredibly prolific writer and editor and his range is enormous—he seems to have read everything of literary significance in seemingly every language. At the core of his work is the idea that all writers are engaged in a kind of creative *Oedipal struggle with their literary predecessors. This thesis is spelled out in a short but highly influential book entitled *The Anxiety of Influence* (1973). The history of poetry, Bloom argues, is the history of poetic influence. Strong poets creatively misread their precursors so as to open a poetic space for their imaginative voice; weak poets, meanwhile, idealize and imitate, lacking both the courage and the talent to do better. Oscar Wilde, he says, is just such a failure, because his poetry owes everything to Coleridge. The strong poet, as Bloom calls them, digests, or better yet *sublimates, their precursor (the exception to this rule is Shakespeare who had neither a precursor or successor who was his equal). Bloom has been criticized by *feminist scholars like Elaine Showalter for his almost entirely masculine view of literary history; but has equally been an inspiration for feminist critics like Sandra Gilbert, Susan Gubar, and Camille Paglia. His theory of inspiration and influence is at the heart of virtually everything Bloom has written. A champion of an elitist or Olympian view of literature, Bloom never hesitates to state what he thinks is good or bad in literature. He was even bold enough to propose a definitive reading list in his bestseller *The Western Canon: The Books and the School of the Ages* (1994).

Further Reading: G. Allen *Harold Bloom: Poetics of Conflict* (1994).
P. De Bolla *Harold Bloom: Toward Historical Rhetorics* (1988).
R. Sellars and G. Allen (eds.) *The Salt Companion to Harold Bloom* (2007).

body Critical theory's interest in the body (usually, though not exclusively, taken to mean the human body) is quite diverse and dates back to French philosopher René Descartes's famous splitting of the mind from the body. With the exception of Baruch de Spinoza, who vigorously decried philosophy's ignorance of what the body can do, philosophy has tended to treat the body with mistrust as the site of uncontrollable impulses and instincts. This only began to change in the early 20th century with the advent of *phenomenology, especially the work of Maurice *Merleau-Ponty, who was probably the first philosopher to attempt a genuine philosophy of the body. In the latter half of the 20th century, however, it is *feminism in all its forms that has given the greatest attention to the body. On a philosophical level, French feminist philosophers, starting with Simone de *Beauvoir, have shown that philosophy's neglect of the body is at one with its neglect of the issue of sexual difference. The body, in this regard, is the site of an almost essential form of sexual difference, which has in turn led to the formation of a sex/gender binary. But as Judith *Butler has pointed out, it is fallacious to think that there is a natural body that is distinct from a cultural body, so to correlate sex with biology and gender with culture is similarly mistaken. Along the same lines, Donna *Haraway has challenged the formal boundaries of the body in two ways: on the one hand, she has shown that the distinction between animal and human is difficult to sustain in any absolute sense (not only are we genetically alike, we also depend on animals in a range of different ways), while on the other hand, she has argued that the human body itself has become a cyborg because of its integration with machines. On a political level, using the slogan 'body politics', feminism has confronted issues such as prostitution, pornography, rape, contraception, abortion, and other concerns which directly involve the body both physically and symbolically such as anorexia, bulimia, and self-harm. As a lateral extension of this kind of work *cultural studies has examined the way the body has become an object of cultural concern, even panic, by exploring its representation in the media and the corresponding attempts by people to imitate these images. Here the work of Michel *Foucault, particularly his concepts of *biopower and *discipline, has been crucial.

body without organs A core concept in Gilles *Deleuze and Félix *Guattari's account of the genesis of the schizophrenic subject. The concept underwent a number of transformations from its first usage in Deleuze's *Logique du sens* (1969), translated as *Logic of Sense* (1990) to its more well-known deployment in *Mille plateaux* (1980) translated as *A Thousand Plateaus* (1987). Interestingly, it fades almost completely from view in Deleuze's work after his book on Francis Bacon, which was published immediately after *A Thousand Plateaus*. Guattari tends not to use the term much in his later works either, but one should certainly consult his recently published journals in *The Anti-Oedipus Papers* (2006) for an instructive account of how he used the term in relation to himself. The phrase 'body without organs' was borrowed from schizophrenic French playwright and poet Antonin *Artaud, but Artaud's work taken in isolation cannot be used to explain the concept. Deleuze reads Artaud in counterpoint to Melanie *Klein (and to a lesser extent, Gisela Pankow) and it is only in this context that the term becomes meaningful. As Deleuze explains in *Logic of Sense*, Klein proposed that in addition to the anal *object in *psychoanalysis there is a urethral or liquid object, and whereas the former attracts our desire the latter absorbs it, effectively negating it. Deleuze regards it as a missed opportunity that Klein did not pursue this idea very far and adopts it for his own purposes to describe the schizophrenic subject who feels so persecuted by his or her desire that they decide to renounce desire altogether and become a body without objects (object and organ are the same thing in this context). In subsequent work, Deleuze adds a second function to this concept: when the subject has become a body without organs, the desire seems to issue from this body as a 'miraculate'.

Bourdieu, Pierre (1930–2002) French cultural anthropologist, sociologist and public intellectual. The son of a minor civil servant, Bourdieu was born in Béarn in south-western France. He completed his *agrégé de philosophie* at the prestigious École Normale Supérieure, where his classmates included such future luminaries as Jacques *Derrida and Gérard *Genette. He then taught for a year in a provincial lycée before being called up for military service in 1956, which saw him spend two years in Algeria. He worked on a Doctorat d'État under the direction of Georges *Canguilhem, but like France's other great social anthropologist Claude *Lévi-Strauss, he never completed it. Algeria proved a transformative experience for Bourdieu and rather than return to France after his tour of duty was over, he stayed on for another two years, teaching at the University of Algiers. He returned to France in 1960, first as a research assistant for Raymond Aron at the Sorbonne, then as a junior lecturer at the University of Lille. In 1964 he finally obtained a job in Paris at L'École Pratique des Hautes Études, where he remained for two decades until his elevation to the Collège de France.

Although professionally speaking Bourdieu turned his back on his philosophical training in order to pursue a career in anthropology and sociology, his work betrays a keen sense of the importance of well-founded concepts and it is precisely his conceptual inventions that brought international attention to his work. At the core of his work there are three concepts that taken together comprise the basic methodological apparatus Bourdieu conceived for himself very early on in his career and applied with increasing sophistication throughout the rest of his life: *practice, *habitus, and *field. His first attempt to sketch out his theoretical model in detail can be found in *Esquisse d'une théorie de la pratique* (1972), translated as *Outline of a Theory of Practice* (1977), which uses his fieldwork in Kabylia in Algeria as a springboard. An inveterate reviser (the English translations of his works are often dramatically different from their putative French originals), Bourdieu produced a second, more rigorous version of his method a decade later in *Le Sens pratique* (1980), translated as *The Logic of Practice* (1990). As is indicated in the French title of this work (and mysteriously lost in the translation), Bourdieu's work focuses on identifying and articulating what he calls 'practical sense', or what he also calls the subjective understanding and manipulation of objective structures.

Practical sense amounts to knowing how to 'play the game' (an analogy Bourdieu himself frequently uses). For instance, his analyses of both the art world and the academic world, *Les Règles de l'art* (1992), translated as *The Rules of Art* (1996), and *Homo Academicus* (1984), translated as *Homo Academicus* (1988), illustrate the importance of patronage, which as Bourdieu argues is in many cases more important than actual talent because it is perfectly possible for mediocre talents to rise to prominence in their respective fields by being adept at making use of its possibilities. By field, then, Bourdieu means the relatively closed system of a specific commercial, professional or social milieu and its internal set of rules, as for instance the paradox in both art and academia that the most valuable works are those which were produced without the intent to create value. Value, as Bourdieu demonstrated in what is undoubtedly his best known work *La Distinction: critique sociale du jugement* (1979), translated as *Distinction: A Social Critique of the Judgement of Taste* (1984), is never only ever a simple matter of assigning a price, but must always be considered in its cultural and social dimension.

A prolific author of more than 30 monographs, Bourdieu wrote right up until his untimely death. In his last years, he found time to assume a more public role as an intellectual and write on more directly social matters. Typical in this respect, is the massive collective project *La misère du monde* (1993), translated as *The Weight of the World* (1999), in which Bourdieu and a large team of collaborators set out to record the voices of the socially repressed and to speak against the economic system that places them in such terrible conditions.

Further Reading: P. Bourdieu *Esquisse pour une auto-analyse* (2004), translated as *Sketch for a Self-Analysis* (2007).
B. Fowler *Pierre Bourdieu and Cultural Theory* (1997).
M. Grenfell *Pierre Bourdieu: Key Concepts* (2008).
J. Lane *Pierre Bourdieu: A Critical Introduction* (2000).
R. Jenkins *Pierre Bourdieu* (1992).
L. Wacquant, *Pierre Bourdieu and Democratic Politics* (2004).

Braudel, Fernand (1902–85) French historian, best known as a leading light of the **Annales* School, and from his elevation to the Collège de France in 1949 until his death one of the most influential historians in France.

Born in rural France, Braudel wanted to become a doctor but in accordance with his father's wishes studied history instead. On graduation he taught high school history in Algeria for nearly a decade from 1923 to 1932. He then returned to France to teach in a lycée, where he met Lucien Febvre, future co-founder of the journal *Annales*. In 1934, along with anthropologist Claude *Lévi-Strauss, he was invited to Brazil to help establish the University of São Paulo. He remained there until the outbreak of the Second World War in 1939, when he returned to France to enlist in the army. He was captured by the Germans in 1940 and spent the remainder of the war in a prison camp.

It was in prison, working from memory, that he wrote the first draft of his PhD, *La Méditerranée et le Monde Méditerranée à l'époque de Philippe II* (1949), translated as *The Mediterranean and the Mediterranean World in the Age of Philip II* (1996), which established his reputation. Commencing as a study of Spain's Philip II, this massive book of over 600,000 words soon grew into a dense, but marvellous account of virtually every aspect of life and culture relating to the Mediterranean in the second half of the 16th century. Importantly, it sketches Braudel's three-level model of history, which would become the signature of the **Annales* School: the first level, which he termed the **longue durée*, or 'geo-history', is the practically imperceptible level of humans' interaction with the physical environment; the second level refers to the formation of social groups, from the tribe to the state, incorporating the problem of the operation of political structures and economies; while the third level refers to the lives of individuals.

Braudel thus redefined historical time as simultaneously geographical, social, and individual (he was in this sense, as recent work by Manuel DeLanda has recognized, a precursor to the development of complexity models of history). This model was clarified further in Braudel's next great undertaking, the three-volume *Civilisation matérielle et capitalisme* (1967–79), translated as *Civilization and Capitalism* (1981–83). This work was a major influence on Immanuel *Wallerstein, particularly his concept of *world-system theory. Braudel's approach to history entailed a paradox: he took great pains to situate individuals, such as Philip II, in their historical context, only to demonstrate their relative unimportance when compared to the deeper historical patterns of society and geography. Despite its aspiration to a 'total history' of the region, Braudel has been criticized for his comparative neglect of social values, attitudes and beliefs. His insistence on the material details of life, right down to soil quality and climate, has however had a lasting impact on the fields of history and *cultural studies.

Further Reading: P. Burke *The French Historical Revolution: The Annales School* 1929–89 (1990).

Brecht, Bertolt (1898–1956) German Marxist playwright, novelist, poet and theorist. One of the most influential writers of the 20th century and arguably the most important dramatist of his time. His writing displays what Wolfgang Haug usefully calls 'unity-in-dispersal', which is to say it ranges across an impressive variety of genres and styles, but at its core there is a consistent political conviction.

Brecht was born in Augsburg in Southern Germany. His father was the managing director of a paper mill and solidly middle class. Brecht enrolled at Munich University in 1917 to study drama, but took on medical courses as well in the hope of avoiding being drafted into the army. He was partially successful in this gambit in that while he was eventually drafted, he was posted to a VD clinic in Augsburg as an orderly. After the war Brecht launched himself into his theatre career and was rewarded with early success. His first play, *Baal* (1918), won the prestigious Kleist Prize. In 1927 he joined the company of Erwin Piscator, widely regarded as the most important experimental theatre group in Germany. He borrowed a great deal from Piscator in his own later experiments in staging.

Considerable wealth and genuine fame soon came his way with his adaptation of John Gay's *The Beggar's Opera* (1728), *Die Dreigroschenoper* (1928), translated as *The Threepenny Opera* (1933), which he worked on with composer Kurt Weill. One of the most popular pieces of musical theatre of the 20th century, it has been performed more than 10,000 times and many of its songs, such as 'Mack the Knife', have become jazz and cabaret standards sung by the likes of Ella Fitzgerald and Nina Simone. Two years later Brecht and Weill collaborated on *Aufstieg und Fall der Stadt Mahagonny* (1930), translated as *Rise and Fall of the City of Mahagonny*, a powerful critique of the rising tide of fascism in Germany.

His anti-Nazi stance would necessitate him leaving Germany when they came to power in 1933. He fled first to Denmark, where he was joined by Walter *Benjamin, then to Sweden and thereafter, like so many of his compatriots, particularly the *Frankfurt School, to the US. He ended up in Los Angeles, which he famously described as God's way of economizing by having heaven and hell in the one place. He got work in Hollywood, despite not being able to speak English, and continued to write highly political plays, such as *Mutter Courage und ihre Kinder* (1939), translated as *Mother Courage and her Children* (1941), *Leben des Galilei* (1943), translated as *Life of Galileo*(1947), and *Der gute Mensch von Sezuan* (1943), translated as *The Good Person of Szechuan* (1948). Politics for Brecht—at least in his theatre—means two things: on the one hand, there is the pleasure (but also the pain) of the acquisition of knowledge, while on the other hand, there is the torment of the impossible situation in which no 'right' decision can be made.

Brecht remained in the US until 1947, the year he was called before the House Un-American Activities Committee to account for his communist links. He was quickly blacklisted in Hollywood as a result, effectively making it impossible for him to continue working in the US. He returned to Europe, first to Switzerland, then to East Germany, where the Communist Government gave him his own theatre company, the soon-to-be world-renowned Berliner Ensemble, which continues to perform his works today, and his own theatre, The Theatre am Schiffbauerdamm, where *The Threepenny Opera* premiered. In his last years, Brecht wrote comparatively little, concentrating instead on directing his plays, which he toured to several European capitals, including Paris, where the young Roland *Barthes was captivated.

Brecht is important to critical theory because he sought to make the theatre into a vehicle for political debate and in this regard he responded forcefully (perhaps more so than any other artist of the 20th century) to the challenge of creating an aesthetics that is neither simply art for art's sake nor pure agitprop. His name is synonymous with *Epic Theatre, a method of staging he devised over a number of years with the goal of making performances more intellectual. He famously said that theatre ought to be viewed with the same detachment and disinterested judgement as that with which boxing enthusiasts view fights. To achieve this *estrangement-effect, as he called it, Brecht staged things so as to thwart the feeling of empathy audiences 'naturally' feel for what they see on stage. Technically this was achieved in a number of ways: actors were instructed to break out of their roles and comment on their characters, or else intertitles might be dropped from the ceiling narrating the action ahead of time so as to diminish suspense.

Further Reading: F. Jameson *Brecht and Method* (1998).
P. Thompson and G. Sacks *The Cambridge Companion to Brecht* (2006).
J. Willett *Brecht in Context: Comparative Approaches* (1998).

Breton, André (1896–1966) French writer and poet best known as one of the founders of *Surrealism. He was the author of the *Surrealist Manifesto* (1924) and one of the movement's principal theorists. Because of his outspoken attitude and doctrinal approach—he frequently 'excommunicated' people from the movement for not agreeing with his vision of how things should be—Breton was known as the 'Pope of Surrealism'.

Breton was born in Normandy. His family were not wealthy. He studied medicine and psychiatry in Paris, but World War I interrupted his studies and he did not complete his training. During the war he worked in a neurological ward for soldiers with 'shell-shock' (i.e. post-traumatic stress syndrome) in a hospital in Nantes. There he began exploring the potential of *psychoanalysis to unlock the creative side of the *psyche. One of his patients was an eccentric young writer, Jacques Vaché, whom Breton later credited as a major influence, describing him as the spiritual son of Alfred *Jarry.

After the war, Breton returned to Paris and became involved with several *Dada artists and writers. In 1919 he co-founded the journal *Littérature* with Louis Aragon and Philippe Soupault. Breton and Soupault were particularly interested in a procedure they called automatic writing which, inspired by Sigmund Freud's notion of *free association, they thought would provide a window into the operations of the *unconscious. Together they published a novel utilising this method, *Les Champs magnétiques* (1920), translated as *The Magnetic Fields* (1985)—almost incomprehensible by traditional standards of writing, this novel signalled a departure from Dada because it was active rather than reactive. It proved highly influential and soon a great number of artists began experimenting with this technique, including visual artists like André Masson and musicians like Edgard Varèse.

In 1924 Breton published the first of three manifestos for Surrealism, which served to define the movement as a revolution in the arts. Breton joined the Communist Party in 1927, but was expelled in 1933. His sympathies never deviated from *Marxism, however, and his work continued to explore the *dialectic. He travelled to Mexico in 1938, ostensibly for a conference on Surrealism at the National Autonomous University of Mexico. There he got to meet the great socialist artists Diego Rivera and Frida Kahlo as well as the exiled Leon Trotsky, with whom he wrote yet another manifesto, this time for revolutionary art.

He returned to France at the outbreak of World War II and once more volunteered his services in the medical corps. After France's surrender, however, the Vichy government banned his writings and declared him an enemy of the state. He escaped from France to Martinique, where he met Aimé *Césaire. He returned to France in 1946. He was an outspoken critic of France's involvement in Algeria and was one of the signatories of the *Manifesto of the 121* written to protest against the Algerian War. Surrealism continued after the war, but its influence declined. It was succeeded by *Situationism in France and *Abstractionism in the US.

Further Reading: M. Gale *Dada and Surrealism* (1997).
D. Hopkins *Dada and Surrealism: A Very Short Introduction* (2004).
H. Richter, *Dada: Art and Anti-Art* (1964).

bricolage The French word for 'tinkering', 'making do', or even 'DIY'. Someone who engages in *bricolage* is known as a *bricoleur,* which is the equivalent of 'handyman' or 'jack of all trades'. It has passed into the *critical theory lexicon because of French anthropologist Claude *Lévi-Strauss's comparison of western science and 'primitive' mythic thought in *La Pensée sauvage* (1962), translated as *The Savage Mind* (1966), arguing that the latter is a kind of *bricolage* because it is constrained to work with existing material and is therefore only ever the contingent result of the combination of things that were ready to hand. In contrast to an engineer, the profession that personifies western science for Lévi-Strauss, the *bricoleur* cannot plan or make projects since to do so implies both that the necessary tools and materials can be obtained as required and do not have to be ready to hand. Gilles *Deleuze and Félix *Guattari describe schizophrenic productions as *bricolage* in *L'Anti-Oedipe* (1972), translated as *Anti-Oedipus* (1977).

Butler, Judith (1956–) American feminist philosopher and gender theorist, Butler was born in Cleveland, Ohio. She completed her PhD in the Department of Philosophy at Yale University in 1984, where she attended seminars by Paul de Man and Jacques *Derrida, whose work would influence her in interesting ways. After holding visiting positions at Princeton, Cornell, and Johns Hopkins, Butler obtained a permanent position at the University of California, Berkeley. She is probably the most widely read and influential gender theorist in the world.

A highly sophisticated work, Butler's PhD, which was published as *Subjects of Desire: Hegelian Reflections in Twentieth-Century France* (1987), maps out a clear project that subsequent works would set out to complete, namely the attempt to understand how social constructs like *gender come into being and more especially how they come to be seen as naturally occurring rather than historical. As Butler points out, while it is possible to choose a gender one wishes to identify with, it is presently impossible to choose not to have any gender at all. Society constrains us to have a gender, whether we want to or not. Her subsequent books, *Gender Trouble: Feminism and the Subversion of Identity* (1990) and *Bodies that Matter: On the Discursive Limits of 'Sex'* (1993), try to theorize this situation in terms of the concept of performativity (which she adapts from J.L. *Austin's concept of the *performative).

In *Gender Trouble*, Butler argues that contrary to popular wisdom both sex (generally assumed to be a biological 'fact') and gender are culturally constructed terms and the binary relation between the two is mutually reinforcing. By refusing this binary relation and showing that sex is fully as much a cultural construct as gender, Butler opens the way for a genuine critique of both terms. Both, she subsequently claims, can be understood in terms of performativity: sex and gender are, she argues, using Drag Queens as her case in point, the coded constructs that result from countless performances of gender and sex roles. Drag Queens turned out to be an unfortunate choice of example for Butler as many of her readers misunderstood her as saying that ultimately gender is simply a matter of choice. *Bodies that Matter* corrects this viewpoint with an extremely rigorous account of the various discursive ways in which gender is regulated.

Outside of her work on gender theory, Butler identifies herself as an anti-Zionist Jew and is a stern critic of Israeli politics. Her later works, especially *Excitable Speech: A Politics of the Performative* (1997), *Precarious Life: The Powers of Mourning and Violence* (2004), and *Frames of War: When is Life Grievable?* (2009) extend the notion of performativity to contemporary politics, while *Giving an Account of Oneself* (2005), basing itself in a critique of Emmanuel *Levinas, offers an ethics for the contemporary world.

Further Reading: S. Chambers and T. Carver *Judith Butler and Political Theory* (2007).

G. Jagger *Judith Butler: Sexual Politics, Social Change and the Power of the Performative* (2008).

V. Kirby *Judith Butler: Live Theory* (2006).

S. Salih, *Judith Butler* (2002).

BWO *See* BODY WITHOUT ORGANS.

Calvino, Italo (1923–85) Italian journalist and writer. Calvino was born in Cuba, where his parents both worked as scientists—his father researched in agriculture, while his mother was a botanist. When he was 2 his family returned to Italy, settling in San Remo on a small rural property. Calvino dutifully took courses in agriculture at the Universities of Turin and Florence, but war interrupted his studies. He refused compulsory military service and instead went into hiding and joined the Italian Resistance, an act for which his parents (who supported his decision) were imprisoned for the duration of the war. After the war he returned to university, but abandoned agriculture and studied arts instead. After graduation, he worked in publishing and journalism. He was an active and committed member of the Communist Party, but like many European intellectuals he resigned his membership following the Soviet invasion of Hungary in 1956. He moved to Paris in 1967, where he met Raymond Queneau (who encouraged him to join *OULIPO), Roland *Barthes, and Claude *Lévi-Strauss. Calvino wrote a wide variety of fiction and non-fiction, and though some of his early work is realist in style, it is his later more experimental work, variously labelled *postmodern, *magical realist, and *metafictional, that earned him his huge international following. His most widely read work is *Se una notte d'inverno un viaggatore* (1979), translated as *If on Winter's Night a Traveller* (1981).

Canguilhem, Georges (1904–95) French philosopher and historian of science. Born in Castelnaudary in the Languedoc region, Canguilhem studied at the École Normale Supérieure in the same year as Raymond Aron, Paul Nizan, and Jean-Paul *Sartre. Graduating in 1927, he held a series of jobs in lycées in regional France, the last of which was in Toulouse. From 1940–1944 he was active in the Resistance, though in a humanitarian rather than combat capacity (he provided clandestine medical treatment, an offence punishable by death nevertheless), for which he was awarded the Croix de Guerre. He began his study of medicine in Toulouse and finished it in Strasbourg, submitting a thesis entitled: *Essai sur quelques problèmes concernant le normal et le pathological* (1943), translated as *The*

Normal and the Pathological (1978). He argued that the normal and pathological differ quantitatively, not qualitatively, that the difference between the two is not to be found in their essence, but rather the distribution of their elements (putting it crudely, a single pimple is normal, but hundreds of pimples is pathological). As a historian of science, Canguilhem was centrally concerned with what Gaston *Bachelard called the *epistemological break, that is, the radical shift from one conception of science to another. Canguilhem is also notable in critical theory for his early recognition of the importance of scholars such as Jacques *Lacan and Michel *Foucault and the assistance he gave to their careers. In 1956 he gave a lecture at the Collège Philosophique criticizing his school friend Daniel Lagache, a pre-eminent psychologist, famously saying psychology was equivalent to philosophy minus its rigour, ethics minus its demands, and medicine without verification. He objected to the way the latter's project of unifying psychology and psychoanalysis seemed to lend itself to a kind of instrumentalism that would enable governmental interference in the very psychic lives of individuals. This attack on behavioural psychology created an opening for Lacan's more individualistic psychoanalysis. Similarly, he directed Foucault's thesis and then later advocated his candidature to the Collège de France.

Further Reading: E. Roudinesco, *Philosophy in Turbulent Times* (2008).
D. Lecourt *Marxism and Epistemology: Bachelard, Canguilhem and Foucault* (1975).

carnivalesque Mikhail *Bakhtin, a Russian linguist and literary critic writing in the first half of the 20th century, used this term to characterize writing that depicts the de-stabilization or reversal of power structures, albeit temporarily, as happens in traditional forms of carnival. Although this may take the form of writing about, or otherwise representing (in film, painting, sculpture, etc.), actual or imagined carnivals, for Bakhtin it was important that the work itself should come to embody the spirit of carnival too. It can do this, as Bakhtin shows in *Rabelais and his World* (1968), by mobilizing humour, satire, and grotesquery in all its forms, but especially if it has to do with the body and bodily functions. François Rabelais, a French author from the early 1500s, is regarded by Bakhtin as an almost perfect exponent of carnivalesque writing. His most famous work *Gargantua and Pantagruel* is a vivid illustration of Bakhtin's thesis. It shows a world in which transgressive social behaviour thrives beneath the veneer of social order, constantly threatening to upend things. Conceived in the dark days of the great purges and the Second World War, Bakhtin's concept is often read as a utopian antidote to repressive forms of power everywhere and a celebration of the possibility for affirmative change, however transitory in nature. *The Politics and Poetics of Transgression* (1986) by Peter Stallybrass and Allon White makes a very strong case along these lines, as does Robert Stam in *Subversive Pleasures: Bakhtin, Cultural Criticism and Film* (1989). In contrast, however, Terry *Eagleton argues in his book on Walter *Benjamin that carnival is a licensed or approved form of transgression and therefore offers nothing more than the mirage of change. *See also* DIALOGISM; HETEROGLOSSIA; POLYPHONY.

Further Reading: K. Clark and M. Holquist *Mikhail Bakhtin* (1984).
M. Holquist *Dialogism* (2002).
D. Lodge, *After Bakhtin* (1990).

Castoriadis, Cornelius (1922–97) Paris-based Greek political philosopher and psychoanalyst. Born in Constantinople (present-day Istanbul) and educated in Greece, Castoriadis lived in France from the end of the Second World War until his death. At 15 he joined the Kommounistike Neolaia (Communist Youth) in Athens and in 1941 he joined the Communist Party, but left after only a year to become a Trotskyist. His association with communist groups caused him considerable trouble during the Nazi occupation of Greece. When he moved to Paris he joined the Trotskyist Parti Communiste Internationaliste, but cancelled his membership after three years in response to Tito's break with Stalin in 1948 and helped to establish the breakaway group (which included Guy *Debord, Claude Lefort, and Jean-François *Lyotard) who have come to be known by the name of the journal they founded, *Socialisme ou Barbarie* (Socialism or Barbarism).

The *Socialism or Barbarism group was always very small, but its journal provided an important outlet for Castoriadis. He did not obtain an academic job until very late in life and for most of his professional career he was employed as an economist by the Organization for Economic Cooperation and Development (OECD). Neither did he have French citizenship until 1970, which meant he could have been deported back to Greece at virtually any time. Consequently most of his early writings were written under a variety of pseudonyms (Paul Chardan and Pierre Chalieu were the most commonly used).

His work as an economist influenced his view of Marxism. Although a committed Marxist, Castoriadis was an anti-Soviet. He saw the USSR as a bureaucratic state rather than a communist country and was highly critical of its centralized power structure. He came to reject Marxist economic theories and focused more on the idea of revolution, stressing that it was the spirit not the doctrine of Marx that was important. Although an activist throughout the 1960s, he also started to move in this period towards a more psychoanalytic view of the world as he tried to understand the relationship between individuals and social formations.

He trained as a psychoanalyst (though not with Jacques *Lacan or his *Ecole Freudienne) and obtained a licence to practise in 1974. His most well-known publications date from this period, such as *L'institution imaginaire de la société* (1975), translated as *The Imaginary Institution of Society* (1987), in which Castoriadis set out to articulate his theory of the autonomous subject. For Castoriadis the subject is not completely self-producing; he or she must constitute themselves using the pre-existing resources of society. So revolutionary change can come only insofar as it is possible to increase one's autonomy in relation to these resources of the psyche. This was consistent with his earlier political writings that insisted neither capital nor the state could be entrusted with the control of society and that the only hope for socialism lay in the autonomy of the workers.

Castoriadis was a prolific writer until his untimely death. His writings have largely been translated into English. For an excellent cross section of his work see the three-volume work *Political and Social Writings* (1988–93).

catachresis The improper use of a word, or its misapplication. The financial pages of any newspaper abound with examples, e.g., 'grow your business', which misapplies an agricultural term. It can also mean the application of a word to a thing or action for which no proper word exists. For example, we 'board' trains and aeroplanes, but since these are both relatively recent inventions there was no pre-existing term to describe how one enters these machines so one was borrowed from seafaring. Similarly, catachresis can be a means of creating thought-provoking metaphors such as Nietzsche's famous pronouncement that 'truth is a woman'.

cataphora A means of linking two or more phrases, sentences, or ideas, by depriving the reader of information in the first instance, thereby compelling the reader to continue forward. In the example, 'It was beautiful, that rainbow', 'It' functions cataphorically, pointing us towards the rainbow. Contrast this with: 'The rainbow was beautiful'. *See also* ANAPHORA.

catharsis A Greek word from a verb meaning 'to purify', 'to cleanse', or even 'to purge', used in drama studies to describe a peak moment in a play when a sequence is brought to a close in such a way as to prompt laughter, tears, or some other form of affective and emotional release. The term was first used by Aristotle in his *Poetics*, which is generally thought to have been written in reply to Plato's hostile view of poetry and drama as something that induces hysteria in men. Borrowing the term from medicine, where it was used to describe menstruation, Aristotle argued that, contrary to Plato, poetry and drama enable men to expel their hysterical emotions, effectively making them stronger not weaker.

cathexis The standard translation used in English (although it is in fact a Greek word) of Sigmund *Freud's concept of '*Besetzung*', which in German ranges in meaning from military occupation of a town to filling a bus. Freud's translator James Strachey took the term from Greek, contrary to Freud's own practice of using ordinary words. In Freud's work cathexis refers to the process of libidinal energy—i.e. affective, emotional, as well as sexual energy drawn from within the *psyche—being attached to a specific *object. A shoe *fetishist, then, to take an extreme example, is somebody whose cathexis is directed at shoes. The French translation of '*Besetzung*' as '*investissement*' (investment) is in many ways a happier choice as it captures Freud's sense that cathexis is an investment of psychical energy in a specific object. It should in this sense be contrasted with mere excitation, which is spontaneous and instinctual and not in receipt of input from the unconscious.

Certeau, Michel de (1925–86) French religious historian and cultural critic. He is especially well known for his critique of *historiography and his analyses of the *practices of *everyday life (particularly its spatial dimension) which he undertook in the middle part of his career. The work he did in the early and later parts of his career are less well known, especially in Anglophone countries, though no less significant or important.

After studying philosophy and the classics at the universities of Lyon and Grenoble, Certeau entered the Society of Jesus at the age of 25. Ordained into the Catholic priesthood in 1956, he went on to complete a doctorate in religious history at the Sorbonne in 1960. Certeau's principal theoretical interest in the early years of his career was the question of why we need history in the first place. Rather than inquire into the ideological meanings of histories, Certeau asked: What specific cultural need does history fulfil? Using as his model *Freud's concept of *dreamwork, Certeau argued that history should be seen as a kind of machine for easing the anxiety most westerners seem to feel in the face of death. By speaking of the past in the way it does, history raises the spectre of our inevitable demise within a memorial framework that makes it appear we will live forever after all. History is not, in other words, an innocent or straightforward documenting of the past, but an integral component of the structuring of the present. The main essays from this period were later collected in *L'écriture de l'histoire* (1975) translated as *The Writing of History* (1988).

Then in *May '68 the streets of Paris erupted in a paroxysm of student and blue-collar protest. Certeau later described his personal experience of the 'events of May' (as they are often euphemistically called) as 'shattering'. In trying to theorize what happened during the long weeks of strikes and street protests, Certeau drew a distinction between law and *authority, arguing that although law prevailed during the course of the events of May authority was diminished. When authority is lost, he argued, law has only the naked exercise of violence at its disposal. Certeau's work on May 1968, was written as an immediate response to what was happening on the streets of Paris. It was initially published in the monthly magazine *Études*, published by the Society of Jesus, and later printed in pamphlet form as *La prise de parole* (1968), translated as *The Capture of Speech and Other Political Writings* (1997). It inaugurated a change of direction in Certeau's career which saw him move away from questions of history to more contemporary issues.

This new direction led to the work for which Certeau is best known, particularly in *Cultural Studies, namely his writings on everyday life: *L'Invention du quotidien 1. arts de faire* (1980), translated as *The Practice of Everyday Life* (1984) and *L'Invention du quotidien 2. habiter, cuisiner* (1980), translated as *The Practice of Everyday Life Volume 2: Living and Cooking* (1998). The second volume was written in collaboration with his research associates Pierre Mayol and Luce Giard. A third volume on *futurology was planned, but never completed. Certeau proposed that everyday life could be seen as a balance between two types of practices which he termed *strategy and tactics: the one referring to the set of practices Foucault theorized as *discipline and the other being a kind of anti-discipline or *resistance.

The final period of Certeau's career was something of a return to origins, or a closing of a circle. Returning to France after nearly a decade abroad, teaching at the University of California, San Diego, Certeau revisited the topic with which his career began, namely 17th-century French Mysticism. Completed shortly before his death, this two volume work, *La Fable Mystique* (1982, 1986), of which volume 1 is translated as *Mystic Fable Volume One: The Sixteenth and Seventeenth Centuries* (1992), used *semiotics to argue that the discourse of mysticism exhausted itself because its project of trying to resurrect the word of God in an era that no longer knew its God simply could not be sustained. Through its bold linguistic experiments Mysticism could occasionally evoke the essential mystery of God, but it could not convert that into an enduring presence.

Overlapping the second and third periods was Certeau's unfinished project on the anthropology of belief, or what he also termed *heterology. This project would in all likelihood have constituted a fourth period, but was cut short by his untimely death. Three essays from this unfinished project exist. They deal with three forerunners to modern anthropology (Montaigne, Léry and Lafitau) and their encounter with the New World. *See also* PRACTICES; EVERYDAY LIFE; FLÂNEUR; MAY '68; SOCIETY OF THE SPECTACLE; SPACE.

Further Reading: J. Ahearne *Michel de Certeau: Interpretation and its Other* (1995). I. Buchanan *Michel de Certeau: Cultural Theorist* (2000). B. Highmore *Michel de Certeau* (2006).

Césaire, Aimé (1913–2008) Francophone poet and activist, Césaire was one of the key thinkers behind the *négritude movement. Born in Martinique, he went to Paris in 1931 on a scholarship, where with Léopold Sédar Senghor and Léon Damas he founded *L'Étudiant Noir* (The Black Student). He returned to Martinique to teach in 1939—one of his students was Frantz *Fanon, who would go on to write a series of powerful anti-colonial books. He also became close to the self-appointed pope of *Surrealism André *Breton, who spent part of World War II in Martinique. In 1945, as a member of the Communist Party, Césaire was elected mayor of Fort-de-France. In the following year he helped draft the departmentalizing laws France put in place for its various colonies, for which he was later criticized by pro-independence thinkers and activists. Similarly, he was heavily criticized by the *Creoleness writers for the fact that he always wrote in French, and never Creole, which is the first language for most Martinicans. Following Stalin's death in 1953, Césaire became disenchanted with communism, particularly its Stalinist variant, writing a stirring denunciation of it in a text that has also become a cornerstone of *Postcolonial Studies—*Discours sur le colonialisme* (1955), translated as *Discourse on Colonialism* (2001). After the Soviet invasion of Hungary in 1956, Césaire resigned from the Communist Party, but he remained active in politics until 2001. He wrote powerful biographies of black revolutionary leaders Toussaint Louverture (who led a slave uprising in Haiti in 1791) and Patrice Lumumba (who became the first Prime Minister of the newly decolonized Congo 1960), the latter in the form of a play. He also wrote an adaptation of Shakespeare's *Tempest*, highlighting the role of Caliban. But he will probably always be best remembered for his magnificent surrealist poem *Cahier d'un retour au pays natal* (1939), translated as *Notebook of a Return to My Native Land* (2001), which functioned as négritude's poetic manifesto. In honour of his memory, and as a measure of his contribution to his country as both politician and poet, Martinique named its principal airport after him.

chiasmus A figure of speech in *rhetoric composed of two parallel clauses, the second of which reverses the first, e.g. 'when the going gets weird, the weird turn pro' (Hunter S. Thompson). The term derives from the Greek meaning to shape like a cross and its form was considered significant to early Christian authors who used it to signify the crucifixion of Christ.

Chomsky, Noam (1928–) American linguist, cognitive psychologist, philosopher and political activist. It's almost as if Chomsky has had two separate careers (both of them luminous) because his linguistics work is so complex it is difficult to imagine him being able to write for a popular audience and yet from the time of the Vietnam War, which he vehemently opposed, that is precisely what he has managed to do. Consequently he is one of he most widely cited and widely known scholars alive today. That said, in the academic world his name remains very closely associated with generative grammar, which was his invention.

Born in Philadelphia in the US to immigrant parents—his father was from the Ukraine and his mother from Belarus—he was raised in a family that consciously immersed itself in Hebrew culture and literature, in spite of the blatant anti-Semitism they encountered in their largely Catholic neighbourhood. His father was a renowned Hebrew scholar with a strong interest in politics—he was a member of the Industrial Workers of the World (or 'Wobblies' as they were affectionately known)—and an obvious influence. Chomsky went to high school in Philadelphia and completed his BA and PhD at the University of Pennsylvania. While writing his PhD he was supported by a fellowship at Harvard. On graduation in 1955 he took a job with MIT (Massachusetts Institute of Technology) and has worked there ever since.

His first book, a reworked version of his dissertation, *Syntactic Structures* (1957), was a watershed in linguistics. Chomsky sought to shift the emphasis in linguistics from the study of existing examples of language use with a view to describing the regular patterns contained therein to the more speculative matter of how language users know how to use language in the first place. This ability to use languages, which he labels *competence in contrast to performance which refers to the actual use of language, is, he claims, innate, meaning all humans have it even if they don't know it. Otherwise, he argues, we could not explain how it is possible for children to learn language so quickly. Thus, in a famous review of *behavioural psychologist B.F. Skinner's *Verbal Behaviour* (1957) published in 1959, Chomsky rejected the stimuli-response model of language acquisition and use. Human language, in contrast to the language of animals (e.g. the dance bees perform to inform the rest of the hive where the honey is), is 'open', and characterized by creativity and transformation (hence Chomsky's theory is sometimes referred to as 'transformational grammar').

In 1967, Chomsky contributed an essay to the *New York Review of Books* entitled 'The Responsibility of Intellectuals' which attracted international attention. Inspired by Dwight MacDonald's essays about World War II which asked whether and to what extent the people of the belligerent countries are responsible for the actions their governments take, Chomsky argues that it is only those people who actively resist allowing their government to act in a way they find morally reprehensible who can say they are without responsibility for what is committed in their name. It is a standard that Chomsky holds himself to: his means of taking action has been to work tirelessly to expose government (particularly, but not limited to, the US government) cover-ups, deceptions, and falsehoods in both domestic and foreign policy. Apparently blessed with an indefatigable capacity for work, Chomsky has written an average of one book a year for the past 30 years dealing with this subject. The best known of these are: *American Power and the New Mandarins* (1969), *Year 501: The Conquest Continues* (1993), *Hegemony or Survival: America's Quest for Global Dominance* (2003), and *Failed States: The Abuse of Power and the Assault on Democracy* (2006).

A controversial figure, Chomsky's views are not universally shared, or without their particular problems, but by his persistence in exposing political malfeasance he has surely helped in some measure to make the world a better place.

Further Reading: R. Barsky *Noam Chomsky: A Life of Dissent* (1997).
A. Edgley *The Social and Political Thought of Noam Chomsky* (2002).
N. Smith *Chomsky: Ideas and Ideals* (1999).
W. Sperlich *Noam Chomsky* (2006).

chora *See* KHŌRA.

chronotope Literally 'time-place', it denotes the intrinsic interconnection of these two dimensions, but also connotes an author's specific attitude to the passing of time and the location of events in a narrative. The chronotope, according to its inventor Russian linguist and literary critic Mikhail *Bakhtin, is a formally constitutive category of literature, which means that it is a feature of every piece of literature. In other words, literature cannot *not* have a chronotopic dimension, but this dimension may vary quite considerably from example to example. Variations in the formation of chronotopes can be used to specify genre, Bakhtin suggests. His extensive historical account of the development of different types of chronotope in *The Dialogic Imagination* (1981) offers a vivid illustration of the importance of this concept. As he shows, in classical Greek narratives the hero often spends years away from home, having adventure after adventure, all without ever aging and when he returns home his youthful bride is still as youthful as she ever was. The departure from the constrictions of biological time is necessary for the type of tale being told and its peculiar effects clearly depend on this departure too. Chronotope should not be confused with duration or setting, which are surface features. *See also* CARNIVALESQUE; HETEROGLOSSIA; POLYPHONY.

Further Reading: K. Clark and M. Holquist *Mikhail Bakhtin* (1984).
M. Holquist *Dialogism* (2002).
D. Lodge, *After Bakhtin* (1990).

***cinema-vérité* (film-truth)** A documentary style of film-making in which, according to Russian director Dziga Vertov (who originally coined the term in 1940), there are no actors, no sets, no scripts, and no acting. The objective of *cinema-vérité* is to capture *everyday reality on film. The camera supposedly acts as an innocent recording device, allowing subjects to speak for themselves. So *cinema-vérité* treats editing and staging as distortions—albeit inevitable—of reality, and these typical aspects of film-making are deliberately kept to a minimum. It might seem that so-called 'reality TV' is simply a glitzy version of *cinema-vérité*, but the truth is that these are highly staged and carefully edited programmes with very little interest in objectivity. A better example is Michael Apted's remarkable *Up* series of documentary films, which began in 1963 with a series of short interviews with 14 seven-year-old children and has been followed up every 7 years since, thus creating an astonishing 42-year record of the changing lives of a cross section of Britain.

citizen A human *subject or agent with legally prescribed rights and responsibilities. Citizenship status is granted by states and nations, it is a political privilege rather than a right. Citizenship is conferred in different ways—most often, it is by virtue of birthright, i.e. if you are born in a particular country, then you have the right to citizenship in that country. But in an era of increased immigration, this right is steadily being withdrawn, particularly in Europe. Citizenship carries with it the obligation to behave in certain ways, to respect the laws of the land, and to perform such duties as are asked; failure to do so can result in citizenship being withdrawn. This obligation is usually thought of as mutual in that by virtue of your being a citizen the state is required to treat you in a certain way, but as the work of Giorgio *Agamben, among others, has shown, the state retains the right to make exceptions, and thereby negate the very rights it is supposed to guarantee.

Further Reading: R. Bellamy *Citizenship: A Very Short Introduction* (2008).

civil society The private or non-governmental dimension of the organization or administration of the state. It is generally contrasted with political society, which is the coercive, governmental dimension of the state. But the separation of civil and political society is artificial. As *Marxist political theorist Antonio *Gramsci argues, the reality is that the state is a dual system comprising both a coercive and consensual apparatus. Standard elements of civil society include trade unions, workers cooperatives, and mutual aid societies. The concept has a long and varied history and there is an immense literature on the subject which is divided on two key issues: what exactly comprises civil society (i.e. where to draw the line between those institutions that do and do not form part of it), and what is it capable of (i.e. is it really a forum for progressive, non-violent change?).

Further Reading: M. Edwards *Civil Society* (2004).

Cixous, Hélène (1937–) French feminist philosopher, playwright and novelist. She is best known for her notion of **écriture féminine*. Cixous was born in Oran, Algeria. Her father was a Sephardic Jew. She studied in Algeria to university entry level but left Algeria in 1955 during the Algerian War, and completed her undergraduate degree in English at the University of Bordeaux. She taught English in Bordeaux for several years before obtaining a position in Paris, first at the Sorbonne and then at Nanterre. In 1968, she defended her Doctorat d'État (her thesis was on James Joyce), making her the youngest person in France to have received that degree. In the same year she was invited by the Minister of Education to help establish the faculty of arts at the experimental university at Vincennes (now University of Paris VIII). Michel *Foucault was offered a similar position and the two worked closely together to recruit several exceptional scholars, creating one of the most star-studded faculties imaginable. In 1974 Cixous established the first European doctoral program in women's studies and despite several high level attempts to disestablish it she managed to preserve it.

For Cixous, language is trapped in a male economy, but within it there is the possibility of a female economy, which can be reached via experimental writing—this is what she means by *écriture feminine*. It is an other form of writing, both a writing of and in the space of the other (a space Cixous defines as that of the *real and the *body). Cixous does not offer a specific theory of *écriture feminine*, indeed she says the *écriture feminine* is precisely the untheorizable, the uncodifiable, the almost but not quite unsayable. Rather, *écriture feminine*, is a practice, or an experiment.

Cixous is well known in France as a playwright and novelist—her works often contain highly sophisticated and therefore virtually untranslatable wordplay, thus limiting their international appeal. Her friend, Jacques *Derrida aptly described her as a 'poet-thinker', meaning both that she is a poet and a thinker and that her thinking and poetry are inseparable, that her thinking takes place in her poetry and her poetry takes form in her thinking. *La Jeune née* (1975), translated as *The Newly Born Woman* (1986), co-written with Catherine Clément, best exemplifies this generic ambivalence in which poetry and philosophy cease to be different from one another. Probably her most famous and widely known play is *Portrait de Dora* (1976), translated as *Portrait of Dora* (1983), which explores Sigmund *Freud's famous case study from the perspective of the patient herself. Cixous frequently collaborates with Ariane Mnouchkine's improvisational Théâtre du Soleil. Her 1969 novel *Dedans* (Inside) won the Prix Médicis.

Further Reading: V. Andermatt Conley *Hélène Cixous: Writing the Feminine* (1984).
I. Blyth and S. Sellers *Hélène Cixous: Live Theory* (2004).
J. Dobson *Hélène Cixous and the Theatre: The Scenes of Writing* (2002).
S. Sellers *Hélène Cixous: Authorship, Autobiography and Love* (1996).
M. Schiach *Hélène Cixous: A Politics of Writing* (1991).

class A social category that on the one hand acknowledges a shared state of affairs amongst a large group of people whose material conditions are very similar and on the other hand recognizes that significant and real differences do exist between groups. From the perspective of their material conditions (i.e. how much money they have at their disposal, the kinds of houses they can afford, and so on), the group of people who are either unemployed or underemployed have more in common with each other than they do with professional people, who are better paid and have greater financial security. Therefore the unemployed or underemployed constitute one class and the professionals constitute another class. This concept is central to *Marxism, although Karl *Marx himself did not invent the term, nor did he ever provide a satisfactorily complete definition. On Marx's understanding, class is an essentially antagonistic concept: it defines not merely lines of difference, but lines of struggle. The history of class, Marx famously said, is the history of *class struggle. Class is not simply a matter of the passive membership of a group. Marx assumes that classes arise out of a sense of common interest born of a common situation and a common idea of who the enemy is, or what he terms *class consciousness. When it is said, as it sometimes is (especially by the right wing), that class no longer exists and that we live in a classless society, it is in fact class consciousness that is at issue, not class itself, which as an economic category is manifestly still with us. In this respect, it is crucial to note that Marx connected class to his concept of the *mode of production, arguing that classes are defined according to the relationship to the means of production. Do they own the means of production or not? That is the essential question for Marx, who using that metric identified three basic classes: the proletariat (wage earners who have nothing but their labour to sell), bourgeoisie (the owners of the means of production, or capitalists), and land-owners (rentiers). Viewed in this strict fashion, the professional class (inasmuch as they do not own factories, but receive wages) are closer to the unemployed or underemployed than they are to bourgeoisie, even though they may share the latter's cultural tastes and habits. This is a problem Pierre *Bourdieu addresses in his concept of *habitus. As Marx conceived it, class crosses all geographical boundaries—the proletariat are the same whether they are based in America or Asia—and it was always his hope that the workers of the world would recognize their common situation and unite and together overthrow the capitalist class. A similar vision animates Michael *Hardt and Antonio *Negri's concept of *multitude.

Further Reading: A. Milner *Class* (1999).

class consciousness The collective awareness of both a common material situation and a common set of interests arising out of that situation. It also entails the perception of a common enemy and is in this regard a cornerstone of what Karl *Marx referred to as *class struggle. According to Marx, a *class only truly becomes a class when it is conscious of its situation and acknowledges the implications of a shared identity. Class in the general sense of a group of people with common material circumstances is referred to as a class-in-itself by Marx, but once it develops consciousness and ceases to be passive with respect to its interests it becomes a class-for-itself. Marx tended to think class consciousness would occur more or less spontaneously once people had been made aware of their true situation, which is to say once the veil of *false consciousness had been lifted. History does not bear this out and later theorists, such as Lenin and Mao, usually insist that class consciousness must be produced. The implication, though, is that class consciousness amounts to a willingness to take action to change the situation by revolutionary means. Again, history does not bear this out, so theorists like Michael *Hardt and Antonio *Negri have suggested that a shift in class consciousness is already a revolution and that there is no need for armed insurrection if people think differently about how they want the world to be organized.

class struggle The inherent antagonism of *class, according to Karl *Marx, who famously said that the history of class is the history of class struggle. If, as Marx argues, class is both a condition of existence and an awareness of a common situation amongst a *multitude (which Marx referred to as *class consciousness), then he reasoned it was to be expected that that awareness would provoke the desire for change, by revolutionary means if necessary. His reasoning is that awareness of class is implicitly awareness of the fact that different classes have different, even contradictory interests, and that cannot but result in conflict. The owners of the means of production (the bourgeoisie) have an interest in driving down wages as low as they can so as to maximize profit, a fact that conflicts with the interest of wage labourers (the proletariat), who would obviously prefer to see wages increase as much as possible. The interest of one thus contradicts the interest of the other, the result of which is conflict. Marx saw this conflict taking a number of different forms: cultural, economic, political, and finally revolutionary overthrow. But this struggle could only succeed if it became general, if all the workers united together in a common cause.

COBRA Artistic movement founded in 1948 by a group of artists from Denmark, Belgium and the Netherlands (the name itself is an acronym constructed from the names of the principal cities of the respective countries: *Co*penhagen, *Br*ussels and *A*msterdam) who had become disenchanted with *Surrealism. Unwilling to obey André

*Breton's anti-communist dictates, these artists, many of whom had participated in the Resistance during World War II, decided to branch out on their own. The key figures were Asger Jorn, Christian Dotrement, and Constant Nieuwenhuys. The group's aim was to integrate Surrealist practices and revolutionary politics in order to make art that was experimental, festive, and vital. More broadly, they wanted to displace Paris as the art capital, get away from the orthodoxy of Breton's Surrealism, and move on from abstract and non-figurative art. They did not manage to displace Paris as the capital of the art world, but COBRA did have a lasting influence on 20th-century art. The group was, however, very short-lived: it was dissolved in 1951 after the core members fell out over the role and place of politics in art. Jorn would later team up with Guy *Debord to help establish *Situationism. COBRA's signature style was a kind of creative disfigurement that was close to Surrealism and Art Brut, but rejected the unconscious as overly individualistic or subjectivistic. It sought a collective basis for art and society and to this end emphasized totemic and mythic subjects.

Further Reading: W. Stokvis *COBRA: The Last Avant-Garde Movement of the Twentieth Century* (2004).
P. Wollen *Raiding the Icebox: Reflections on Twentieth-Century Culture* (1993).

SEE WEB LINKS

• Translations of COBRA manifestos.

code **1.** In a famous and highly influential essay 'The Television Discourse—Encoding and Decoding' (1974) Stuart *Hall used the notion of coding to map the different and potentially oppositional ways in which TV producers and consumers make and receive texts. Television producers may encode a text one way only to find that the audience decodes it in a completely different way (decoding in this sense is equivalent to Harold *Bloom's notion of creative misreading). Studies of fan culture, particularly the so-called slash versions of texts created by fans—that is, texts which appropriate characters from a popular show like *Star Trek* and write new stories in which they are made gay or bisexual—bear this out. Hall was particularly interested in trying to discern the ways in which the *hegemonic viewpoint is embedded in texts in a natural-seeming fashion.

2. In his late work *S/Z* (1970), translated as *S/Z* (1974), Roland *Barthes attempted to classify all the different types of signifieds (*see* SIGN) to be found in a literary text according to five codes: the *hermeneutic* code (the posing of an enigma or riddle—the standard forms are: What has happened? What is going to happen?); the *semic* code (the multiple meanings or *connotations specific words, phrases, and scenes may contain); the *symbolic* code (reversibility and transformation, the logic of dreams, fantasies, and the body); the *proairetic* code (code of action sequences, genres and tropes); and lastly the *cultural* code (the sum of tacit knowledge required to interpret a particular text, e.g., the stereotypes, proverbs and such like by which a culture gives itself particularity). The five codes are not mutually exclusive and it is possible (indeed almost impossible for it to be otherwise) for two or more codes to be present in the one place at the one time.

3. Gilles *Deleuze and Félix *Guattari deploy the notion of coding in *L'Anti-Oedipe* (1972), translated as *Anti-Oedipus* (1977), to analyse the way *desire is captured and channelled by social institutions. Coding subordinates the individual to the collective. It takes both an actual and virtual form—tribal tattoos, scarification, and so forth which renders group identity visible, but also collective belief in higher powers such as totems, and gods. They specify three separate processes: coding (the installation and policing of belief), decoding (separation from specific codes, either by means desacralization or secularization—it does not mean interpretation, as in Hall's use of the term), and overcoding (the super-inscription of new codes over old—for example, the celebration of Easter incorporates both Christian and Pagan elements).

cognitive estrangement A concept derived by Darko Suvin from *Russian Formalism's notion of **ostranenie* and Bertolt *Brecht's closely related (but *Marx inflected) notion of the *estrangement-effect in his *Metamorphoses of Science Fiction* (1979), a *structuralist attempt to distinguish the genre of science fiction writing from other forms of fiction. As Fredric *Jameson points out in *Archaeologies of the Future* (2005), this is a rather exclusive definition, which emphasizes the rational scientific dimension of science fiction and rigorously excludes the kinds of flights of fancy associated with fantasy fiction. For Suvin, the key to cognitive estrangement is the presence in a story or novel of what he calls a 'novum', that is a device or machine that is absolutely new and whose presence compels us to imagine a different way of conceiving our world.

cognitive map **1.** A concept conceived by the American urbanist Kevin Lynch in his book *The Image of the City* (1960) to account for the way city residents use landmarks rather than maps to spatially orient themselves. Lynch researched this by stopping people in the street in three different cities—Boston, Jersey City, and Los Angeles—and asking them to draw impromptu maps of the city. What he found was that residents in dense cities like Boston, which has a great number of well-known and clearly defined landmarks (e.g., the Charles River, Faneuil Hall, and Boston Common), were more readily able to complete this task than residents in dispersed cities like Los Angeles, which at the time had relatively few such landmarks. Landmarks make the city 'imageable' he argued, meaning they enable residents and visitors alike to form images in their mind of the city as a whole. He concluded from this that cities require landmarks, real or artificial, in order to make them habitable.

2. In his essay 'Postmodernism, or, the Cultural Logic of Late Capitalism' (1984), Fredric *Jameson adapts this concept to characterize the contribution cultural texts—particularly film and literature—make to our orientation in the world as a whole. Jameson combines Lynch with *Lacan and *Althusser to suggest that contemporary texts, in mapping our place in the world, provide a representation of our imaginary relation to the real conditions of our existence. His principal argument is that since the advent of *globalization (which he equates with the enormous expansion of capitalism following the end of World War II), the world has become too complicated to represent by means of standard mimetic forms. This orientation in the world is, for Jameson, a synonym for *class consciousness. *See also* GEOPOLITICAL AESTHETIC; NATIONAL ALLEGORY; POSTMODERNISM.

Further Reading: I. Buchanan *Fredric Jameson: Live Theory* (2006).
D. Gregory *Geographical Imaginations* (1994).

collective unconscious The inherited dimension of the *psyche according to the analytical psychology of Carl *Jung. Consisting of the entirety of human history and manifesting itself in the form of a system of *archetypes, the collective unconscious is what every human being has in common according to Jung. So although it is a very general idea, it also has quite specific manifestations, which can be seen instantiated in myths, symbols, and rituals. Within the psyche itself, the collective unconscious can be thought of as the most primitive dimension. The collective unconscious is mediated by the personal unconscious in the formation of the unified self.

Further Reading: A. Stevens *Jung* (1994).

College of Sociology (*Collège de Sociologie*) An informal group of intellectuals which, like the *Vienna Circle, was founded with the purpose of sharing ideas and with the aim of changing research in the humanities. It was founded in Paris in 1937 by three exiles from *surrealism Georges *Bataille, Michel Leiris and Roger Caillois—other participants include Pierre *Klossowski, Alexandre *Kojève, Jean

Paulhan and Jean Wahl. The group met fortnightly to discuss a wide range of subjects, but with a common purpose of trying to discern the fundamental nature of human society. They paid particular attention to indigenous cultures, which they regarded as windows into the prehistory of western society. They were fascinated by and wanted to explain the existence and experience of the sacred and its complement, the festival. The College was disbanded in 1939 at the outbreak of World War II.

Further Reading: D. Hollier *The College of Sociology* (1988).

collocation Words that are regularly used together in vernacular speech, such as 'clean and tidy', or 'neat as a pin'. Interrupting the regular pairing of words is an important, albeit easy way of achieving poetic *estrangement—for example, instead of saying 'I'm afraid I cannot do that', one might also write, 'I'm scared that I cannot do that'. The collocation in the second case is completely wrong and is typical of the kind of error a non-native speaker might make. The point is that there is no logical reason why one should say 'afraid' rather than 'scared' in this context, but the habit of national speech dictates that the former is right and the latter is wrong.

commodity An object or process produced for the purpose of exchange or sale rather than personal consumption or use by the producer. A key concept in Karl *Marx's work, the commodity is defined by him as having a dual character consisting of two very different types of value: use-value (the satisfaction of a particular human need) and exchange-value (what it can be exchanged for). Value is measured in terms of how much labour goes into producing a particular item. In this sense, the commodity can be seen as so much stored or as Marx put it 'dead' labour. From a *Marxist perspective, the most important commodity of all is labour itself, that which the worker sells to the owners of the means of production, because of its ability to create value. What is sometimes referred to as *modernity is in reality the historic shift in western countries towards an economy organized around the manufacture of commodities.

commodity fetishism The mistaken view that the value of a commodity is intrinsic and the corresponding failure to appreciate the investment of labour that went into its production. Karl *Marx created this term, borrowing the notion of the fetish from anthropology, where it refers to a sacred or symbolic object that according to its worshippers has supernatural power. For example, in certain indigenous cultures in Australia it is believed that a 'witch doctor' can point a bone at a person and thereby bring about their death—such a bone is a fetish. Commodities are fetishes in this same sense because by power of our belief in them we create an obscure hierarchy of value that rates a diamond over fresh water (to use Adam Smith's famous example from *The Wealth of Nations* (1776)), in spite of the fact that the diamond serves little or no purpose. By the same token, as with the witch doctor's bone, it isn't clear to the people who believe in commodities why they should believe in them, nor how they came to occupy the position they presently enjoy. Diamonds might be valuable because they are rare, but that does not by itself explain why society should choose to prize them so highly. Not only are there similarly rare items that might have been seized upon, there is no intrinsic reason why rarity itself should matter as much as it does. Commodity fetishism can also be understood in terms of social relations: neither the producer nor the consumer of a commodity has a necessary or full relation with the other. The fetishization of the commodity shields us from *alienation. Sigmund Freud's use of the term *fetish, which occurs later than Marx's, also borrows from anthropology. Freudo-Marxian theorists like Slavoj *Žižek have combined the psychoanalytic definition of fetish with Marx's own to create a theory of the commodity that uses the notion of *fantasy to explain its peculiar power to deceive. Commodity fetishism is an important concept in *Marxist and so-called post-Marxist theory: It is central to the work of György *Lukács, particularly his concept of *reification; it is also central to the work of Guy *Debord, who famously argued the final form of the commodity would be the image; and it is central to Jean *Baudrillard's theory of *consumer society.

communicative action The primary human activity, according to Jürgen *Habermas, who argues that philosophy should be focused on language and its capacities rather than consciousness (the focus of much of continental philosophy prior to Habermas, e.g. *Hegel and *Kant). Habermas's assumption is that language was at its origin communicative, that its purpose was to relay information and convey instructions. That is to say, at its origin language was transactional, its purpose was to achieve socially necessary goals. Communicative action is an extension of *pragmatics beyond the realm of one-on-one interaction to the level of the social.

community *See* IMAGINED COMMUNITY; INOPERATIVE COMMUNITY.

competence and performance A binary distinction between the ability to speak a language (competence) and the actual instances of that ability (performance) proposed by American linguist Noam *Chomsky. This distinction can be applied to virtually any kind of skilled behaviour. The interest in using this distinction arises from the fact that performance can vary considerably even when competence is uniformly distributed.

complex A crucial concept in Carl *Jung's analytic psychology. A complex is an assemblage of images, ideas, associations with a consistent emotional tone, gravitating around one or more *archetypes. Complexes are the personifications of the archetypes, they are what the psyche knows and sees of the archetypes. This notion has passed into popular discourse and the connection to Jung is very often unknown. The best known and mostly wide recognized examples of complexes, after the 'Oedipal complex' (*Freud borrowed the term from Jung) are the 'father complex' and the 'mother complex'—what these point to is the fact that our relationship to certain people can, for a variety of radically differing reasons, resemble and share many of the same characteristics as our relation with our parents. Perhaps the most important implication, though, of the notion of the complex is that it presupposes that the self is neither unified nor singular but always multiple and in a state of flux.

Further Reading: A. Stevens *Jung* (1994).

complexity theory A general term for a wide range of scientific research in two key problematics: (i) the interconnectedness of the apparently unconnected (e.g., what effect does a butterfly flapping its wings in Beijing have on weather in London?); (ii) the emergence of change. Complexity in this context does not mean complicated because complex systems can in fact be relatively simple; rather it means that a particular phenomenon, such as air quality, cannot be considered in isolation from a diverse range of other factors, which in this case might include prevailing winds, the location of heavy industry, and so on. Research in this field aims to identify the critical causal agents in a particular system and separate out that which is accidental, or just background noise. In *critical theory, complexity theory is utilized to engage cultural and social questions. For instance, it has been used by Manuel DeLanda to analyse the formation of cities. *See also* NON-LINEAR SYSTEM.

compulsion to repeat (*Wiederholungszwang*) A highly complex concept in *psychoanalysis with at least two orders of meaning: firstly, in the weakest sense, it refers to the myriad rituals and routines many people seem to adhere to in their *everyday lives which, if interrupted, would cause mild to severe discomfort; secondly, in the strongest sense, it refers to the persistence of unconscious thoughts and their ability to evade even the most determined forms of *repression. Aptly,

Slavoj *Žižek often uses the image of the zombie in cinema to characterize the compulsion to repeat—the image is apt because as a compulsion it lies outside of the control of conscious thought and because in Freud's view the compulsion to repeat belongs to the order of the *death drive. Freud treats the compulsion to repeat as a symptom of a disturbed *unconscious—most likely that disturbance is caused by a trauma the unconscious has not yet been able to process, so it relives it over and over again until it can. The much talked about 'pop psychological' notion of 'closure' is directed precisely at this phenomenon: we desire closure so as to bring the compulsion to repeat a traumatic memory to an end.

conceptual art A non-representational form of art which sees its purpose as the creation of ideas. The artistic object, as such, is not then the finished work, but the idea it provokes in its audience. It does not concern itself, therefore, with the need for physical permanency; indeed, very often a photograph of the event is the only record of its existence. Noted conceptual artists include: Joseph Beuys, Claus Oldenburg, and Joseph Kosuth.

condensation (*Verdichtung*) One of four key mechanisms of Sigmund *Freud's concept of *dreamwork. It is also to be found at work in the symptom-formation of both *hysterics and *neurotics and, as Freud showed in *Der Witz une seine Beziehung zum Unbewussten* (1905), translated as *Jokes and their Relation to the Unconscious* (1960), it is essential to the functioning of jokes. First introduced in *Die Traumdeutung* (1900), translated as *The Interpretation of Dreams* (1953), condensation takes three basic forms: (i) a series of elements of a dream-thought or multiple repetitions of the same dream-thought can be condensed into one; (ii) a variety of otherwise disparate and different dream-thoughts may be combined into a single composite image; (iii) the differences between dream-thoughts may be blurred so as to enhance the appearance of their connectedness. As with *displacement, another of the key dreamwork mechanisms, condensation presupposes that the *affect (*Affekt*) associated with the representations (*Vorstellung*) we make to ourselves of the *instincts is independent of that representation: in this way it is possible for the *libidinal charge of several such images to be compressed and not lose any of their power. All dreams are works of condensation inasmuch that they may only last a moment, yet contain within them substantial amounts of psychical information as becomes obvious when all the associations that can be made with a dream are teased out in detail.

connotation *See* DENOTATION AND CONNOTATION.

constative English language philosopher J.L. Austin's term for a type of speech that merely conveys information and does not perform an act. It is in this sense the logical opposite of a *performative. Unlike a performative, a constative phrase may be true or false.

constellation Walter *Benjamin famously proposed in the 'Epistemo-Critical Prologue' to *Ursprung des deutschen Trauerspiels* (1928), translated as *The Origin of German Tragic Drama* (1977), that ideas are to objects as constellations are to stars. That is to say, ideas are no more present in the world than constellations actually exist in the heavens, but like constellations they enable us to perceive relations between objects. It also means ideas are not the same as concepts, nor can they be construed as the laws of concepts. Ideas do not give rise to knowledge about phenomena and phenomena cannot be used to measure their validity. This is not to say the constellation is purely subjective or all in our heads. The stars in the night sky are where they are regardless of how we look at them and there is something in how they are positioned above us that suggests the image we construct of them. But having said that, the names we use for constellations are embedded in history, tradition and myth. So the constellation is simultaneously subjective and objective in nature. It is not, however, a system, and this is its true significance for Benjamin, who rejects the notion that philosophy can be thought of as systemic, as though it were mathematical or scientific instead of discursive. Benjamin developed this notion further in his account of the arcades in 19th-century Paris. Theodor *Adorno adopts and adapts constellation in his account of *negative dialectics, transforming it into a model. The notion of constellation allows for a depiction of the relation between ideas that gives individual ideas their autonomy but does not thereby plunge them into a state of isolated *anomie.

Further Reading: F. Jameson *Late Marxism: Adorno, or, The Persistence of the Dialectic* (1990).

constructivism 1. Artistic movement originating in post-revolutionary Russia, at the start of the 1920s. Active until the mid 1930s, when it was replaced by *socialist realism, constructivism was typified by its rejection of the romantic idea of art for art's sake, and instead insisted that art should serve a social and political purpose. Confined largely to the visual arts, (composer Dmitri Shostakouich was briefly a constructionist, though this is not how he is generally regarded) constructivism's best remembered works tend to be posters produced in support of the revolution. Its influence was felt most keenly in Weimar Germany, where similar revolutionary sentiments were prevalent until the Nazis took power. The principal constructivist artists were El Lissitzky, Vladimir Mayakovsky, Vladimir Tatlin, and film-maker Dziga Vertov.

2. In philosophy, the position that reality is independent of human perception and any knowledge that we have of it is necessarily a construction. This is not the same thing as *relativism, however, because it does not question the existence of reality or our ability to know that reality actually exists.

consumer society (*la société de consummation*) A term adopted by French cultural critic Jean *Baudrillard to characterize a trend in society to treat consumption (i.e. the purchasing of material goods) as a socially valuable activity in its own right. His point is that in the post World War II boom economy consumption became decoupled from production; whereas previous economic models focused on production as the only source of growth, in the 1950s and 1960s economic modelling began to focus more on consumption. Perhaps the most important sign of this was the new availability of relatively easy to obtain cheap credit, enabling people to buy now what they could only afford later. Consumer society also constitutes a change of mindset, a shift away from the 'save then buy' mode of thinking to a 'buy now pay later' attitude. The result of this change of mindset was, according to Baudrillard, a massive proliferation of objects whose purpose was no longer justified by need, but instead catered solely to want. *See also* POSTMODERNISM.

contact zone Mary Louise Pratt's term in *Imperial Eyes: Travel Writing and Transculturation* (1992) for social places (understood geographically) and spaces (understood ethnographically) where disparate cultures meet and try to come to terms with each other. It is used quite widely in literary studies and *Cultural Studies as well as *Postcolonial Studies as a general term for places where white western travellers have encountered their cultural, ethnic, or racial other and been transformed by the experience. Contact zones are most often trading posts or border cities, cities where the movement of peoples and commodities brings about contact. *See also* CREOLENESS; HYBRIDITY.

contradiction The combination of two logically incompatible propositions. A contradiction arises when one statement negates the other as in Beckett's wonderful phrase (quoted by Michel *Foucault in his inaugural lecture at the Collège de France), 'I can't go on. I'll go on.' If one literally cannot go on, then obviously one cannot go on, so to put these two phrases together is a contradiction. This is also what gives it its poetic power. In Karl *Marx's view contradiction is the motor of history—in his theory, the relationship between the owners of the means of production (i.e. the bourgeoisie) and the proletariat is contradictory because their interests do not coincide: it is not in the interest of the bourgeoisie to pay high wages because it reduces profits and it is not in the interest of the workers to accept low wages. This is the basic form of what Marx called *class struggle. Marx always thought that this contradiction would become so acute in real terms that it would lead to an upsurge of revolutionary unrest such that the workers would topple the bourgeoisie and bring an end to capitalism. History, to date, suggests he was wrong about this. Consequently, there has arisen a branch of Marxist thinking known as post-Marxism which tries to rethink history minus contradiction.

contrapuntal reading Borrowed from music, where it refers to the relationship between themes (e.g. the relation between the famous 'da-da-da-dum' in Beethoven's *Fifth Symphony* and its subsequent exploration), this term is used by Edward *Said in *Culture and Imperialism* (1993) to describe the relationship (in what he calls the cultural *archive) between narratives set in metropolitan centres, or at least in the countryside, of the dominant colonial nations such as England and France, and the colonies upon which the great powers depended for their wealth. His key example is Jane Austen's *Mansfield Park* (1814), which is about an estate owned by the Bertram family whose wealth derives from sugar plantations in Antigua. But as Said notes, there is almost no mention of Antigua in the novel, despite the fact that in a structural sense the story depends on it because without their holdings in the colonies the Bertrams would neither be so rich as they are, nor obliged to spend so much time away from the estate, thus opening up the narrative possibilities the novel explores. Said's strategy, then, is to read the novel in the light of this structural dependency and read the forgotten other back into the text.

Cooper, David (1931–86) South African-born psychiatrist and a leading figure of the *anti-psychiatry movement. After graduating with a medical degree from the University of Cape Town, Cooper moved to London. He worked in several hospitals here, including the unit for young schizophrenics called Villa 21. In 1965, he and R.D. *Laing, along with several other colleagues, founded the Philadelphia Association, which established the experimental, community psychiatry project at Kingsley Hall with a view towards putting into practice the ideas on psychiatry they had developed in their theoretical works. Influenced by *Freud, *Marx, and *Sartre, Cooper, like Laing, held that it was society that made people mad, particularly its key institution the family. By the same token, he also held that madness was not necessarily an illness so much as an *existential journey beyond the confining strictures of society-imposed rules. He coined the term anti-psychiatry in 1967 to describe his position. His most important works include *The Death of the Family* (1971), *Grammar of Living* (1974), and *The Language of Madness* (1978). Like Laing's, Cooper's work was very much in the spirit of its times and his work was widely read by students. It also influenced anti-psychoanalysis theorists like Félix *Guattari, although he ultimately rejected anti-psychiatry as a failed experiment. But by the end of the 1970s, both traditional psychiatry and critical theory had set aside Cooper's work as impractical. Consequently his work has now fallen into neglect.

Further Reading: Z. Kotowicz *R.D. Laing and the Paths of Anti-psychiatry* (1997).

cosmopolitanism A mode or 'way' of being in the world commensurate with the condition of *globalization, characterized by a high level of mutual respect for the rights of others and a generalized tolerance of ethnic, cultural, political and national differences. It is in this sense a paradoxical concept because it implies identification with one's difference or singularity and an empathetic acknowledgement of one's sameness. It can in this sense be compared to pluralism and internationalism. The word derives from a combination of the Greek for world or universe (*Kosmos*) and the city or polity (*polis*) and is said to originate with the founding father of the Cynics, Diogenes of Sinope who famously declared himself to be a 'citizen of the world' (*kosmopolitēs*), implying that he answered to a 'higher' power than that of the city-state to whom his allegiance was in fact owed. Cosmopolitanism is a *utopian concept inasmuch that it cannot be legislated into being and nowhere exists in its pure state, though it is often claimed that so-called 'world cities' like London, New York, Paris, and Istanbul embody many of its ideals. It has attracted commentary from some of the finest commentators in western philosophy from Immanuel *Kant to Jacques *Derrida, but it is not without its ambiguities.

Further Reading: K. Appiah *Cosmopolitanism: Ethics in a World of Strangers* (2006).
U. Beck *Cosmopolitan Vision* (2006).
T. Brennan *At Home in the World: Cosmopolitanism Now* (1997).
P. Cheah and B. Robbins (eds.) *Cosmopolitics: Thinking and Feeling Beyond the Nation* (1998).
J. Derrida *On Cosmopolitanism and Forgiveness* (2001).
J. Kristeva *Strangers to Ourselves* (1991).
S. Toulmin *Cosmopolis: The Hidden Agenda of Modernity* (1990).

Creoleness (Créolité) Literary and cultural theory elaborated in the 1980s by a small group of Francophone authors from the Caribbean, particularly Martinique and Guadeloupe, the most prominent of whom are Patrick Chamoiseau, Jean Bernabé, and Raphaël Confiant. Its main theorist is Edouard *Glissant, who joined the group later, and acknowledges the influence of Gilles *Deleuze and Félix *Guattari. Creoleness was established in opposition to *négritude, a literary movement established in the 1930s by the (also Francophone) Caribbean and African writers Aimé *Césaire, Léopold Sédar *Senghor, and Léon Damas. These authors sought to define themselves in terms of their links to the African continent, seeing their shared heritage as part of the black *diaspora as a source of empowerment for colonial peoples. In contrast, the Creoleness writers reject this stance as backward looking, but also unfeasible inasmuch that Caribbean peoples and Africans are too unlike to ever be fully integrated, preferring instead to look forward to a post-essentialist future. Ultimately Creoleness is a celebration of diversity and a negation of what it sees as false universality.

critical theory **1.** The term coined by Max *Horkheimer in 1937 to describe the work of the *Frankfurt School. Defined against the traditional conception of theory governing the sciences (including the social or human sciences such as sociology), which holds that it is a system of abstract (i.e. ahistorical, asubjective, and asocial) propositions which can be verified empirically, critical theory holds the opposite view, namely that theory is historical, subjective, and a part of society. Critical theory is in this regard a highly reflexive enterprise—it is never satisfied with asking what something means or how it works, it also has to ask what is at stake in asking such questions in the first place.

Indeed, critical theory takes self-reflexivity a step further and asks whether or not its objects of research are not artefacts of the theory. Recent work by critical theorists like Donna *Harraway, who writes about the relationship between humans and animals, has shown the degree to which this concern is justified. For critical theorists, the idea that it is possible to derive 'mind-independent' concepts, that is, concepts that do not involve the subjectivity of the theorist in some way in either their conception or application, is both illusory and *ideological. The attempt to separate concepts from their producers, gives rise to what Horkheimer scathingly referred to as *instrumental reason. Thus critical theory is ultimately concerned with what it is possible to know, given that the ontological status of neither the subject nor the object of theory can be taken for granted.

The word 'critical' should thus be understood to mean, as it does in Immanuel *Kant's work, the opposite of 'analytical': it refers to the set of concepts whose reach is always and of necessity greater than their grasp. For example, we can neither see, hold, nor properly think something as vast as the universe, in its totality, yet without the concept of the universe we would be unable to situate ourselves in time and space. The same can be said of concepts like nation, *society, *community, politics, and so on, all of which are necessary for thinking about the state of the world, even though none are verifiable in a strictly scientific sense.

In general, critical theory explores the connections, overlaps, intersections, and interferences between the three spheres of economic development, psychic life, and *culture. Its starting premise, derived in part from Karl *Marx, but also inspired by Émile *Durkheim and Max Weber, is that midway through the 19th century the world as a whole underwent a major transformation and entered a new period of history known as *modernity. This entails three consequences: tradition cannot be used as a guide for thinking about either the present or the future; society has splintered into semi-autonomous sub-systems (e.g. the market, the various professions, industry), making it difficult but necessary to find ways of speaking of 'the whole'; the good, the true, and the beautiful have been disaggregated, presenting new challenges to ethics, philosophy and aesthetics.

Under such conditions, critical theory is interested in why human society has (in its eyes) failed to live up to the promise of enlightenment and become what it is today, unequal, unjust, and largely uncaring. Witnesses to the barbarity of both the First and Second World Wars, the first generation of critical theorists can perhaps be forgiven for the bleakness of their outlook.

2. Today the term is also used to refer—very loosely, it has to be said—to any form of theorizing in the humanities and social sciences, even when this isn't politically consistent with the outlook of the original Frankfurt School. This has tended to empty the term of any meaning and rendered both its political and methodological concerns invisible.

Further Reading: S. Bronner *Of Critical Theory and its Theorists* (1994).

D. Couzens Hoy and T. McCarthy *Critical Theory* (1994).

P. Dews *Logics of Disintegration* (1987).

D. Frisby *Fragments of Modernity* (1985).

D. Held *Introduction to Critical Theory* (1980).

F. Rush (ed.) *The Cambridge Companion to Critical Theory* (2004).
P. Stirk *Critical Theory, Politics and Society* (2000).

SEE WEB LINKS

- A collection of resources, based in the Frankfurt School of thought, from many contemporary writers of and about critical theory, as well as links to other websites.

Cultural Materialism Welsh Marxist literary critic Raymond *Williams used this term in the 1960s to describe how his own work combined criticism of specific cultural texts with the material facts of history. In the 1980s, it was widely taken up as the name for any kind of literary or cultural research concerned with the relation between history and text. The main names we associate with this particular trend are Catherine Belsey, Jonathon Dollimore, and Alan Sinfield. Often, especially in relation to *Cultural Studies, the name Cultural Materialism was invoked polemically to distinguish those forms of criticism which pertain to the 'real' world as opposed to those which deal only with the 'inside' of texts, never connecting them to the 'outside' world (such as *New Criticism, *Practical Criticism, and according to some lights Cultural Studies). It is often compared with *New Historicism, in large part because the latter's key figure Stephen *Greenblatt studied with Williams, but their approaches to the relationship between history and text are quite different. Cultural Materialism treats *culture as a 'whole way of life' (to use Williams's famous phrase), and not just as a series of high points along the lines of Matthew Arnold, who regarded culture as the 'best' that has been thought and written. If culture is a whole way of life, then virtually anything can and must be treated as cultural: in this way, Williams helped to create Cultural Studies, as the field of research dedicated to interrogating all forms of cultural production. In classical *Marxism, culture is merely the expression of the economic base, but Williams argued against this by problematizing the assumption that the relation between the two is direct, allowing that a work may simultaneously reflect and contest the established order determining it. Downplaying economic and technological determinism, Williams shifted the emphasis to social relations, arguing that texts can only be fully understood in relation to Antonio *Gramsci's concept of *hegemony. In other words, the essential question for cultural material with respect to any text is: does it challenge, alter, reject, or endorse the prevailing ideology?

Further Reading: J. Brannigan *New Historicism and Cultural Materialism* (1998).
C. Colebrook *New Literary Histories* (1997).
A. Milner *Cultural Materialism* (1989).
S. Wilson *Cultural Materialism: Theory and Practice* (1995).

Cultural Studies An interdisciplinary approach to the study and analysis of *culture understood very broadly to include not only specific texts, but also *practices, and indeed ways of life. The most influential works in the field have tended to be large edited collections like Lawrence Grossberg, Cary Nelson, and Paula Treichler's mammoth *Cultural Studies* (1991) and introductory textbooks like John Fiske's *Reading the Popular* (1989), which reflects not only the heterogeneous nature of work calling itself Cultural Studies, but the fact that in a very real sense Cultural Studies is theoretically provisional and avant-garde (its practitioners tend to be avid consumers of new concepts drawn from a wide variety of fields).

Cultural Studies began in Britain in the late 1950s. Richard *Hoggart's *The Uses of Literacy* (1957) is often held up as the inaugural text, with Raymond *Williams's *Culture and Society: 1780–1950* (1958) running a close second. Both these authors rejected the Leavisite model of *practical criticism, which was largely concerned with identifying works suitable for inclusion in a highly select canon of 'great works', in favour of a more expansive view of *culture. As *Marxists they were both concerned to point up the importance of traditional and working class culture and to show how changes in society threatened their very existence. In contrast to practical criticism, Cultural Studies employed history and sociology as well as 'close reading' in its analysis of cultural texts. Cultural Studies achieved institutional status in 1964 when Hoggart founded the Birmingham Centre for Contemporary Cultural Studies (CCCS).

For the next decade or so the CCCS provided much of the focus for the developing field and many of the most famous names in the field were based in Birmingham at this time. Stuart *Hall succeeded Hoggart as director and (arguably) gave Cultural Studies the shape it has today by importing the then quite new and radical thinking coming out of France known as *theory, e.g. *structuralism *semiotics, and (later) *poststructuralism and theories of power as well. Britain fell into steep economic decline during the 1970s, falling so far as to require an IMF loan to staunch its currency, which of course had widespread social repercussions. Cultural Studies was at its peak documenting this, but when Thatcher came to power in 1979 it found it impossible to account for the profound swing to the right that followed. Stuart Hall's magnificent *Hard Road to Renewal: Thatcherism and the Crisis of the Left* (1988) is the last will and testament of this species of left-sympathetic (when not avowedly Marxist) Cultural Studies.

In the 1980s Cultural Studies spread its wings and its focal point shifted to Australia, not least because many of its pioneering practitioners like Tony Bennett, John Fiske, and John Hartley migrated there. Cultural Studies flourished in Australia, becoming in two decades the dominant discipline in the humanities, at least in part because of its facility for adaptation to the demands of the so-called 'reform' of the higher education sector in the 1980s and 1990s. This came at the price of its radical roots, the previously crucial notions of dissidence and resistance all but vanished from the vocabulary, but gave rise to a discipline ready, willing, and able to work in partnership with government. Cultural Studies moved from being a discipline largely concerned with the critique of government policy (as the most explicit manifestation of power) to one that wants to help write that policy. The field's principal organ, the journal *Cultural Studies*, began life in Australia as the *Australian Journal of Cultural Studies*.

Cultural Studies also took root in the US thanks to the efforts of several American CCCS students (particularly Hazel Carby, Michael Denning, and Lawrence Grossberg) who brought it back home with them like an intellectual contagion. But in contrast to the situation in Australia it did not achieve hegemony. Rather it tended to be swallowed up or placed alongside the much bigger fields of area studies, race studies, African-American studies, and American studies. The fate of Cultural Studies elsewhere has been uneven—it is still resisted in most parts of Europe, particularly France and Germany, but even there it has gained a foothold. Reflecting its global spread, an international Cultural Studies association was formed in Finland in the 1990s.

After more than 50 years of existence, Cultural Studies still does not have a specific methodology or a discrete area of interest: its approach tends to be needs-based, meaning that it applies theory according to the case at hand; and there is literally nothing that falls outside of the scope of Cultural Studies. And that for its detractors and supporters alike is both its strength and its weakness.

Further Reading: P. Bowman *Interrogating Cultural Studies: Theory, Politics and Practice* (2003).

C. Barker *Cultural Studies: Theory and Practice* (2007).

J. Hartley *A Short History of Cultural Studies* (2002).

J. Lewis *Cultural Studies: The Basics* (2002).

G. Turner *British Cultural Studies* (1996).

SEE WEB LINKS

- Articles and extensive links to academic resources.

culture A set of beliefs, *practices, rituals, and traditions shared by a group of people with at least one point of common *identity (such as their ethnicity, *race, or *nationality). At its core is the sense that it is different from nature in that it is a product of conscious choice and not the *instincts. But as authors like Donna *Haraway have shown, the nature/culture divide is difficult to sustain. A wide range of disciplines—predominantly anthropology, archaeology, *Cultural Studies, history and sociology—make use of the concept of culture, each one adding its own qualification, making it problematic to say that what is meant by this word is exactly the same in any two disciplines. Obviously there are common themes and the differences tend to be related to scope, and turn on the question of whether or not a limit can be placed on what counts as cultural. In the social sciences, particularly history and sociology, culture has usually been opposed to *society, and given a lower status, as it was thought to refer to pastimes rather than the serious business of holding the collectivity together. However, the general trend with this term, even in the social sciences, has been expansive, so that even within the confines of specific disciplines it has been enlarged to encompass virtually every facet of human behaviour. And in recent times it has overtaken *society as the dominant term as doubts have grown as to the existence or even the possibility of society. Culture has thus come to stand for 'weak' rather than 'strong' ties between people within a given collectivity. The types of cultures that are now said to exist are innumerable—there is banking culture, work culture, music culture, sports culture, and so on. In the humanities, from the time of Matthew Arnold in the late 19th century up until very late in the 20th century, culture referred to artistic production of all types, and was further classified into categories of 'high' and 'low' reflecting the perceived relative aesthetic merit of a particular work. The advent of Cultural Studies in 1950s Britain began to change that, as it combined ways of thinking about culture from history and sociology and conceived of culture as the glue holding society together. Culture came to refer to any form of creative production, from the self-consciously artistic work of professional artists to the relatively banal *habits and practices of *everyday life. It is this sense of the word that has lately become dominant. The principal theoretical problem culture raises is one of reproduction: why do people adhere to a given culture and to what extent are their actions determined by this?

culture industry Max *Horkheimer and Theodor *Adorno's term for the commercialization of art in all its forms—music, literature, the visual arts—and its subsequent permeation of every aspect of daily life that occurred in the first part of the 20th century. Written in exile in Los Angeles in the 1940s, Horkheimer and Adorno's essay 'The Culture Industry: Enlightenment as Mass Deception' is a central plank in their account of the transformation of life in *modernity offered in *Dialektik der Aufklärung* (1944), translated as *Dialectic of Enlightenment* (1972).

The choice of terms—culture industry rather than 'mass culture' (their original choice) or 'popular culture'—provides a significant clue as to how this concept should be understood: the emphasis should be placed on the second word not the first. For what Horkheimer and Adorno were struck by in their analyses of Hollywood was the fact that the application of industrial processes of production, distribution, and consumption to culture resulted in the complete deterioration of culture as they knew it. In effect, their implication is: where there is industry there cannot be culture. This is because, as Herbert *Marcuse would later explain, under such conditions culture is performed rather than lived.

The culture industry's singular aim is to produce a form of culture compatible with the aims of capitalism. In order to make culture into the means of reliably turning a profit it has to be standardized and its disruptive power neutralized. Standardization primarily occurs at the level of form, a fact that is masked by the apparent variety of what Horkheimer and Adorno scathingly refer to as psuedo-individualization of content. For example, as several formalist studies of genre fiction (particularly crime, romance, and westerns) have shown, difference tends to be confined to the incidentals of setting and character and even then there are restrictions. Because of its commitment to market principles, the culture industry tends to try to repeat success via duplication and avoid failure by minimizing innovation. This doesn't mean it cannot make entertaining, complex, and interesting products, but it does mean at the end of the day all it makes is products.

Consequently, as Jameson explains in *Late Marxism* (1990), *critical theory regards the offerings of the culture industry as inauthentic (meaning false or deceitful in both an ontological and ideological sense) because like all commodities they proclaim that happiness and pleasure already exists and is readily available for consumption. Authentic art, by contrast, offers no such consolation and instead affirms the sheer negativity of existence. The culture industry reverses Immanuel *Kant's famous dictum that art is 'purposiveness without purpose' and gives rise to 'purposelessness for purpose', or what Marcuse referred to as *desublimation.

Lastly, it is perhaps worth mentioning that the culture industry is not the same thing as the creative industry, although from a certain perspective one could rightly say their referent is the same. Creative industry is a techno-bureaucratic term whose precise ideological purpose is to erase the negativity implicit in Horkheimer and Adorno's coinage, and as such is a clear-cut example of what they themselves would have called *instrumental reason. The culture industry thesis has been criticized by Anglo-American *Cultural Studies for failing to perceive the power of consumers to consume cultural products in their own highly individualized manner.

Further Reading: T. Adorno *The Culture Industry* (1991).
D. Held *Introduction to Critical Theory* (1980).
F. Jameson *Late Marxism: Adorno, or, The Persistence of the Dialectic* (1990).

cynical reason (zynische Vernunft) German philosopher Peter *Sloterdijk's term for what he calls enlightened *false consciousness. In his unexpectedly bestselling book, *Kritik der zynischen Vernunft* (1983), translated as *The Critique of Cynical Reason* (1987), Sloterdijk describes cynical reason as the end of the ideal, central to both the *Enlightenment and *Marxism, that an increase in our understanding of the true nature of the world will necessarily bring about social change. Slavoj *Žižek defines cynical reason as the feeling that we know very well that our present situation is invidious, but all the same we act as though it isn't. Global inaction, relatively speaking, in the face of knowledge about climate change is a perfect case in point. Even though we tell ourselves we know we are heading for a planet-wide disaster, we act as though nothing is wrong. *See also* INSTRUMENTAL REASON.

Dada Artistic movement (encompassing literature, the performing and visuals arts) formed in response to World War I and the imperialist bourgeois culture that fomented and prosecuted the war. Volatile and short-lived, it flourished in Europe and America from about 1916 until roughly 1924. It paved the way to *Surrealism and is often lumped together with Surrealism, but in fact its aesthetic was distinctive, as the *Situationists would insist in the 1950s and 1960s.

If André *Breton is Surrealism's pope, then the pope of Dadaism would have to be Hugo Ball. His Cabaret Voltaire, which opened in 1916 in the Spiegelgasse in Zurich, is generally thought of as the birthplace of the movement. Its denizens included Tristan Tzara, Hans Arp, Richard Huelsenbeck, and Hans Richter. Ball coined the name Dada, the title of the movement's magazine. As Ball explained it, Dada is 'yes yes' in Romanian, 'rocking horse' in French, a sign of naivety in German, and the first words out of a baby's mouth. It simultaneously stands for everything and nothing, which was Dada's aesthetic in a nutshell.

Dada aimed to produce a form of art that functioned as anti-art, as art that put to the sword the decadent pretensions of pre-war art. Its anti-art was also intended to make a social statement. Its signature look is that of the 'ready-made', an ordinary object such as a urinal, re-contextualized and transformed into art, and the 'collage' or 'cut up', ordinary items juxtaposed in forceful and creative ways so as to produce art.

The movement was as peripatetic as its members. Just as the very word Dada has several meanings, so there are several Dadas. In New York, at almost the same time as the events in the Cabaret Voltaire, expatriate French artists Marcel Duchamp and Francis Picabia were making a sensation at the famous 'Armory Show' with what Duchamp called anti-retinal art, i.e. art designed to stimulate rather than please the eye. In his account of *postmodern art as that which brings forth the unpresentable, Jean-François *Lyotard singles out Duchamp as one of the key artistic precursors to the postmodern aesthetic.

Besides New York and Zurich Dada, there are at least two other forms of Dada usually recognized: Berlin Dada and Paris Dada. Unlike New York and Zurich, Paris and Berlin were not neutral cities; the war was being fought literally on their doorsteps. Consequently Berlin and

Paris Dada were bleaker than their predecessors. George Grosz's blood-soaked *Homage to Oskar Panizza* (1917–18) perhaps best typifies this changed outlook. Berlin Dada also invented the technique known as photomontage (the best known exponent is undoubtedly Man Ray), which influences *avant-garde arts still. Paris Dada was the product of Duchamp and Picabia, who returned from New York in 1919 and connected with Tzara and a vibrant group of young intellectuals and artists like Paul Éluard who were determined to defy convention and produce something radically new.

Dada didn't really end so much as implode. The group couldn't sustain so many fractious personalities and fell apart. But the ideas and techniques it pioneered continue to exert an effect today.

Further Reading: M. Gale *Dada and Surrealism* (1997).
D. Hopkins *Dada and Surrealism: A Very Short Introduction* (2004).
H. Richter *Dada: Art and Anti-Art* (1964).

SEE WEB LINKS

- A site providing definitions and biographical overviews of notable Dada artists together with examples of artwork.

Daly, Mary (1928–2010) American *radical feminist philosopher and theologian. Daly was born in Schenectady in New York State. She obtained two doctorates—one in philosophy and one in theology—and taught for more than 30 years at the Jesuit-run Boston College (she was eventually forced into retirement because of her refusal to teach male students, which ran foul of College policy). A provocative figure in the feminist movement, Daly is best known for *Gyn/Ecology: The Metaethics of Radical Feminism* (1978), which argues that western culture reduces women to object status and that this, in turn, destroys women both mentally and physically. She argues that western society is not merely patriarchal in its organization, but that reality itself (by which she means, language, experience, and consciousness) is patriarchal and that feminism cannot succeed unless it addresses this basic fact. A highly influential figure, Daly has been criticized from within the feminist movement, particularly by Audre Lorde, for her failure to appreciate the unequal way oppression is distributed according to differences in race and class.

Dasein German philosopher Martin *Heidegger's word for the individual *subject. Produced from two words in German 'Da' and 'sein' which separately mean 'there' and 'being' but together are usually translated as 'existence', *Dasein* is usually left untranslated and the most literal reading of it is the one that is recommended. In other words, *Dasein* is not the same as the subject, but replaces it in Heidegger's philosophy with the precise aim of eliminating from his thinking all the baggage and presuppositions associated with the notion of the subject. Only by making this break in our thinking are we able to understand the subject in its being as a subject, which is first of all a matter of *Dasein*.

death-drive (*Todestriebe*) The tendency inherent in all organic things to return to an inorganic state. The concept is part of a dualism developed late in Sigmund *Freud's career consisting of two forces the life-drive (*Lebenstriebe*) and the death-drive, also known as Eros and Thanatos after the Greek Gods for love and death respectively, which exist in a state of equilibrium (for this reason Freud sometimes referred to it as the 'Nirvana principle'). According to Freud, the death-drive manifests in the *psyche as a tendency toward self-destruction, or more precisely the elimination of tension, which can also be turned outwards, whereby it becomes aggression. The idea of the death-drive originates, to some degree, with the concept of the *compulsion to repeat, which refers to behaviour which cannot be explained by the concept of the *pleasure principle. For example, it does not give us pleasure to dwell on a humiliating incident and yet very often we cannot seem to get it out of our head, we keep going over and over it. This being so, Freud reasoned there must be another drive at work besides Eros. Similarly, Freud could not conceive that *ambivalence, or aggression, or melancholia could be derived from the pleasure principle either. The death-drive is a highly contested concept in *psychoanalysis and there is no agreement as to its coherence or cogency. Jacques *Lacan maintains the concept of the death-drive within his own schematization of the drives, but renders it part of every drive, thus undoing Freud's dualistic conception of it. Gilles *Deleuze rejects it out of hand as ridiculous, while Slavoj *Žižek shows in countless works that it is a very useful concept for thinking through many of the inanities of *consumer society. The death-drive, which Žižek visualizes as a kind of zombie-drive, is used to explain the empty satisfaction of consumerism, the fact that no matter how much we buy it never extinguishes the urge to buy more.

death of the author Taken from the title of an essay by Roland *Barthes, 'La mort de l'auteur' (1968), translated as 'The Death of the Author' (1977), this phrase is widely regarded in academia and the media as emblematic of both *post-structuralism and *postmodernism in that its purpose is to signal the absolute relativity of the text and the correspondingly enhanced status of the critic. Put simply, Barthes's basic point is that the author's life (the intricate details of their biography, in other words) is not part of the literary object. Although Barthes makes no mention of it, his argument echoes and extends the work of W. K. Wimsatt and Monroe Beardsley who, in two famous essays

'The Intentional Fallacy' (1946) and 'The Affective Fallacy' (1946) (both appear in revised form in Wimsatt's *Verbal Icon* (1954)), argued that neither our knowledge about an author nor the particular affect a piece has on its readers are valid grounds for judging the quality of the text. Barthes's point differs in that, in contrast to these two forerunners of *New Criticism, he is not interested in judging the relative merits of certain literary objects, but is rather trying to unravel the specific ontology of the literary object. His argument has three strands to it, each one reflecting the influence of ideas that were in circulation at the time of writing, though not yet synthesized as they are here: first, when an author creates a character and gives that character a voice the author ceases to be the one who is speaking (this point echoes Mikhail *Bakhtin's notion of *dialogism); second, all writing is simply words on a page, so it is language itself that speaks not an author (this is a fundamental premise of *structuralism); third, all writing is quotation (this point echoes Julia *Kristeva's notion of *intertextuality). *See also* READERLY AND WRITERLY; WORK AND TEXT.

Debord, Guy (1931–94) French Marxist, activist, film-maker, social commentator and philosopher. Born in Paris, he was raised by his mother and grandmother in the southern resort towns of Nice, Pau, and Cannes. In Pau, situated in the foothills of the Pyrenees, Debord studied at the same lycée as his future hero the Comte de Lautréamont (Isidore Ducasse), author of *Chants de Maldoror* (1868) and *Poésies* (1870) from which *Situationism's watchword that plagiarism is necessary was lifted. Shortly after the war, he moved back to Paris, ostensibly to study law at the University of Paris, though he never took study seriously, preferring instead a Bohemian life.

In 1951, at a film festival in Cannes he met Isidore Isou, Romanian eccentric and founder of the Lettrist International movement. Debord joined the movement and quickly asserted himself as one of its most inspired proponents. At first, the movement found sustenance in *Surrealism's channelling of the unconscious, but in a pattern that was to be replayed again and again in Debord's life this was soon rejected in favour of *Dada's polemical lampooning of established values. The movement founded its own journal *Potlatch*, named after the Native Americans' feast discussed by Marcel Mauss in his influential work *Essai sur le don* (1925), translated as *The Gift* (1954). Debord's first film produced in 1952, *Hurlements en faveur de Sade* (Howlings in Favour of Sade), was a Lettrist exercise in anti-cinema.

Lettrism ended without a bang and barely a whimper in 1957 at a meeting with the remnants of the Movement for an Imaginist Bauhaus (led by Asger Jorn, who had also been involved in *COBRA) at a remote Italian village. There, 'in a state of semi-drunkenness', as Debord would later famously put it, *Situationism was formed with a show of hands by five votes to one. The idea of the situation, which was to be the focus of the group's artistic and political activities, was the product of a commingling of two antithetical sources: Jean-Paul *Sartre's concept of the situation and his rival Henri *Lefebvre's demand for the transfiguration of the everyday. Lefebvre, with whom Debord formed a short-lived but intense friendship, was probably the most important living influence on Debord. Not only in terms of ideas, but also in terms of contacts: it was through Lefebvre that Debord met the two other key figures of Situationism, Raoul *Vaneigem and Constant Nieuwenhuys.

Debord's name will forever be associated with Situationism, in spite of the fact that the group dissolved in 1972 amidst bitter, factionalist infighting, much of it provoked by Debord himself, who had a talent for the caustic put-down. Not the least reason for this is the fact that the concepts or practices of **détournement* (turnaround/reversal) and **dérive* (drift), which they invented as a means of protesting against what they saw as the encroachments of capitalism upon the authenticity of life, continue to be mobilized by cultural activists today. Culturejamming and adbusting are perfect examples of *détournement*. Similarly, Situationism's notion of *psychogeography, an experimental procedure for mapping the city from the perspective of desire rather than habit and obedience to design, still has its enthusiasts among cultural geographers some 50 years after it was first mooted.

Debord's most influential work was *La Société du spectacle* (1967), translated as *Society of the Spectacle* (1970), which made the famous prophecy that postmodernity seems to have realized in full, namely that the final form of the commodity would be the image. By no means prolific in his output, preferring a dense aphoristic style to the sprawling ramble of his older friend Lefebvre, Debord's total output is comparatively meagre in volume but exceptional in its impact. Debord's films are available on DVD and, appropriately enough, on the internet in bootleg form. A small band of diligent fans have performed Herculean labours to collect, edit and in most cases translate into English the bulk of his writings, including his correspondence (four volumes) and make most of them freely available on the Internet as he undoubtedly would have wished.

Suffering the painful effects of a lifelong abuse of alcohol, Debord took his own life with a bullet to the heart in his cottage in Champot.

Further Reading: J-M. Apostolidès *Les Tombeaux de Guy Debord* (1999).
C. Bourseiller *Vie et mort de Guy Debord: 1931–94* (1999).
A. Hussey *The Game of War: The Life and Death of Guy Debord* (2001).

A. Jappe *Guy Debord* (1999).
V. Kaufman *Guy Debord: Revolution in the Service of Poetry* (2006).
A. Merrifield *Guy Debord* (2005).

Debray, Régis (1940–) French left-wing intellectual, journalist, academic, and policy advisor who became internationally renowned (if not infamous) for his links to Fidel Castro and Che Guevara as well as for his advocacy of guerrilla warfare. Born in Paris, he studied at two of that city's most prestigious schools, the Lycée Louis-le-Grand and the École Normale Supérieure, where he worked with *Marxist philosopher Louis *Althusser. Debray visited Cuba in 1961 to report on its highly successful literacy campaign and became interested in Latin American politics. He returned there in 1963 and 1964 to study guerrilla tactics and subsequently took a position at the University of Havana in 1966. Based on his experiences, he wrote *Révolution dans la révolution* (1967), translated as *Revolution in the Revolution* (1967), which became a kind of revolutionaries' handbook, a status that was surely helped to a very great extent by the fact its Cuban publishers printed 200,000 copies on its first print run. In 1967 he accompanied Guevara on his last fateful trip to Bolivia, as a correspondent for a Mexican newspaper, and was himself captured and imprisoned on the charge of aiding insurrection. After an international campaign for clemency, led by such prominent figures as Jean-Paul *Sartre, André Malraux, and President de Gaulle, he was released in 1970. He then moved to Chile, taking the opportunity to conduct interviews with its Marxist President Salvador Allende, which he published as *The Chilean Revolution* (1971). Following the coup by Pinochet in 1973, Debray returned to Paris. From 1981 to 1995 he worked as a policy advisor to President Mitterrand on Foreign Affairs, later reporting that the President ignored his ideas. Over the last two decades he has also developed himself as a media theorist, completing doctorates at the University of Paris and the Sorbonne. He has also written a three-volume autobiography, *Le temps d'apprendre à vivre* (1992–2000).

decadence A general word for a decline in cultural standards that was adopted to name an aesthetic style that emerged in the latter part of the 19th century in Europe. In the first instance decadence was, in spite of its subject matter which tends to recall ancient myths and supernatural tales, a kind of *Avant-garde, or *modernism inasmuch as it marked a break with the established aesthetic of its own time. Indeed, in his book on postmodernism, Fredric *Jameson describes decadence as a kind of premonition. The first use of the word 'decadence' in this aesthetic sense occurred in Théophile Gautier's 1868 preface to Charles Baudelaire's collection of poems *Les Fleurs du*

Mal (1857). However the work that has come to be regarded as the quintessential example of decadence is Joris-Karl Huysman's *À rebours* (1884), translated as *Against Nature* (1926), which interestingly enough is also regarded as one of the more important examples of naturalism. Decadence was also a crucial concern for Friedrich *Nietzsche, although in his case it was something that philosophy had to figure out how to overcome.

Further Reading: M. Calinescu *Five Faces of Modernity* (1987).

decentred structure French *Marxist Louis *Althusser's term for *Marx's conception of the social totality as opposed to *Hegel's. In Althusser's view, Hegel's structure of the whole is expressive, meaning that each part of the whole is capable of expressing or representing the whole—so, for example, the economy can be used to describe the state of society as a whole. Althusser rejected the idea that one part can stand for the whole and instead argued that every part is mutually dependent on every other part (a relationship he described as semi-autonomous).

decoding *See* CODE.

decolonization The historical process whereby countries under colonial rule by foreign (usually European) powers transitioned to self rule. The term is very broad in its sweep and encompasses both a vast geographical territory (the majority of the global South or former *Third World) and a complicated timeline (it didn't take place all at once), but also significant differences in how it was achieved (violent or peaceful) as well as divergent outcomes (relative prosperity and crushing poverty). Decolonization began in the immediate aftermath of World War II, in part because European powers like Britain and France were no longer capable of holding on to their empires, but also because (in the case of India at least) independence had been promised in return for assistance during the war. But as the Vietnam War demonstrates, the colonial empires were not always given up without a fight. And as often as not it led to bloody wars, sometimes with the colonial power, but just as frequently internal civil wars erupted in the wake of the departing colonial power as factions fought to control the newly decolonized nation's future. Not all decolonizing nations decolonized to the same extent, indeed in many cases the nations endeavoured to preserve the basic civic structure the colonial powers had created but with all the key positions of government placed into indigenous hands. The Ghanaian independence leader Kwame Nkrumah designated this kind of change in government without change in the way government is conceived *neo-colonialism. Decolonization is a foundational moment for *Postcolonial Studies. It brings together a variety of questions, too, about nationalism, national identity, *nativism, and the *transcultural.

Further Reading: R. Betts, *Decolonization* (2004).
D. Brydon and H. Tiffin *Decolonising Fictions.*
I. Szeman, *Zones of Instability: Literature, Postcolonialism, and the Nation* (2003).

deconstruction A reading strategy developed by French philosopher Jacques *Derrida whose essential gesture is to demonstrate that every philosophical position, irrespective of how coherent it seems on the surface, contains within it the means of its own self-undermining. Adapting the word from Martin *Heidegger's terms 'Destruktion' (destruction) and 'Abbau' (unbuilding), Derrida himself describes it as a double gesture—the first move consists in reversing the hierarchy of a particular philosophical opposition, while the second move amounts to a displacement of the very system in which the hierarchy operates. Derrida's work is often described as a critique of the philosophy of presence because he destabilizes the opposition between presence and absence, particularly with regard to the *sign, which as Derrida explains in his account of **différance* is always the present mark of an absence. Thus, as Jonathon Culler explains in his seminal account of Derrida's thought and its influence, *On Deconstruction* (1982), it undermines both the philosophy it asserts and the hierarchical oppositions upon which it relies. As a reading strategy, deconstruction is particularly interested in identifying those aspects of a concept or text whose peculiar state of being is to be undecided, neither this thing nor that thing and not nothing either. His main example of this is the sign: the sign *as* sign is a sign of something else, thus it is most fully itself when it is perceived as something else, but to remain a sign it must also continue to be perceived as different from the thing it represents.

Further Reading: S. Critchley *The Ethics of Deconstruction* (1992).
J. Culler *On Deconstruction: Theory and Criticism after Structuralism* (1982).
C. Norris *Deconstruction: Theory and Practice* (1982).

defamiliarization *See* OSTRANENIE.

deictic Any of an important class of words whose meaning can only be fully determined by context. Also known as a *shifter (Roman *Jakobson's preferred choice), a deictic is a word like the pronouns 'I' or 'you' whose meaning varies according to context because their principal function is indicative rather than semantic. Their role is of particular interest in literary and critical studies because of the complexities of their use in reported speech.

Deleuze, Gilles (1925–95) See overleaf.

DELEUZE, GILLES (1925–95)

Undoubtedly one of the most influential philosophers of the 20th century, the century his friend Michel *Foucault mischievously suggested would be named after him. Deleuze's work became the height of fashion in the early part of the 21st century spawning literally hundreds of books about his work. Although notoriously difficult to read and often frustratingly elusive, Deleuze has broad appeal as a thinker because his work invites creative application not slavish adherence.

Born in Paris, Deleuze studied for his *baccalauréat* at the Lycée Carnot and then his *khâgne* at the Lycée Henri-IV. From there he went to the Sorbonne to study philosophy, graduating in 1948. His classmates included François Châtelet, Jean-François *Lyotard, Michel Butor, Pierre *Klossowski, Claude Lanzmann, maker of the epic film *Shoah* (1985), and the novelist Michel Tournier, who remembers Deleuze in his memoir, *Le Vent Paraclet* (1977), translated as *The Wind Spirit* (1988). His first book, *Empirisme et subjectivité. Essai sur la nature humaine selon Hume* (1953), translated as *Empiricism and Subjectivity: An Essay on Hume's Theory of Human Nature* (1991), was written while he was still a student. What is interesting about this, besides the obvious fact Deleuze was a prodigy, is that in later life Deleuze repudiated everything else he wrote in this period. In his own eyes then, his work on Hume marks the true starting point of his career.

As is customary in the French academic system, Deleuze then did his time in the Lycée system, first in Amiens, then Orléans, and finally back in Paris, for nearly a decade before obtaining a post as a junior lecturer at the Sorbonne in 1957. He remained there until 1964, when he moved to the Centre National de la Recherche Scientifique. In 1962, after an eight-year publishing furlough, Deleuze published his second book, *Nietzsche et la philosophie*, translated as *Nietzsche and Philosophy* (1983), which many regard as his most important. It is credited with sparking a profound 'return to *Nietzsche' after more than half a century of neglect because it overturned the gloomy image of Nietzsche as the ultimate nihilist and dismissed the suspicions of those who bought the distorted picture of him as a Nazi philosopher created by his sister Elisabeth. Instead it presented Nietzsche as a philosopher of joy, calling on us to overcome our **ressentiment* and embrace life fully, that is to say in an *active rather than reactive manner.

This theme would remain constant throughout Deleuze's work, although the terms themselves would disappear by the end of the

1960s, evolving into what many see as a *vitalist philosophy. His next books explore this problematic, somewhat obliquely it has to be said, through an examination of literature. Inspired by Nietzsche's idea that the philosopher is a kind of physician, Deleuze looked to the work of Proust and Sacher-Masoch to see whether this idea applied to literature as well. *Proust et les signes* (1964), translated as *Proust and Signs* (1972), and *Presentation de Sacher-Masoch* (1967), translated as *Coldness and Cruelty* (1971), inaugurate a trajectory in Deleuze's work he named the 'clinical' that culminated in the publication of *Critique et clinique* (1993), translated as *Essays Critical and Clinical* (1997). In between the books on Proust and Sacher-Masoch, Deleuze wrote on commission textbooks on Bergson and Kant. The former is generally taken as evidence that Deleuze was indeed a vitalist, while the latter is read as a sign that Deleuze's philosophical project consisted in completing Kant's critique—this is made explicit in Deleuze's later collaborative works.

From 1964 until 1969 Deleuze taught philosophy at the University of Lyon, during which time he prepared the requisite two theses for his Doctorat d'État, both of which appeared in the watershed year of 1968: *Différence et répétition*, translated as *Difference and Repetition* (1994), and *Spinoza et le problème de l'expression*, translated as *Expressionism in Philosophy: Spinoza* (1990). By his own account, *Difference and Repetition* was the first book in which he did *his own* philosophy, the first book in which he broke away from writing the history of philosophy and began to create new philosophy for himself. Written in the same period, though not published until a year later, *Logique du sens* (1969), translated as *The Logic of Sense* (1990), ostensibly a study of Lewis Carroll's work, but really a profound meditation the philosophy of language, completes this phase of Deleuze's career.

Deleuze did not participate in the events of *May '68 and was generally ambivalent about its results. On the one hand, he was impressed by the fact that such a large number of people, some 10 million students and blue collar workers, had coordinated their action to show their dissent, but on the other hand he detected fascist elements in the operations of some of the groups. In the summer of 1969, a young psychoanalyst and political activist by the name of Félix *Guattari sought Deleuze out because he admired his work and it proved to be a meeting of true minds. Now Deleuze knew how to respond philosophically to May '68. He and Guattari agreed to work together and over the next several months they met and shared ideas and developed a work that was simultaneously a critique and a rethinking of both *Marx and *Freud (particularly the *Lacanian interpretation of the latter) and a synthesis of a new methodology they proposed to call *schizoanalysis, the core concept of which is the *desiring-machine. Guattari's notebooks, *Écrits pour l'Anti-Oedipe* (2005), translated as *The Anti-Oedipus Papers* (2006), provide a partial but nonetheless illuminating picture of how they worked. On its publication in 1972, *L'Anti-Oedipe*, translated as *Anti-Oedipus* (1977), was an immediate sensation, but it divided opinion quite sharply between those like Fredric *Jameson who heralded it as a radical intervention and those like Perry *Anderson who dismissed it as irrationalist nonsense.

Deleuze spent the remainder of the decade developing his collaborative project with Guattari. The next instalment was an attempt to apply schizoanalysis to literature focusing on one of their mutually favourite authors, the great Czech writer Franz Kafka. As the title suggests, *Kafka: Pour une literature mineure* (1975), translated as *Kafka: Towards a Minor Literature* (1986), introduced a new category of literature and a new way of thinking about minority. Minor literature has become an important concept in *Postcolonial Studies. Perhaps recognizing the difficulty of his work, Deleuze next published a collection of conversations or exchanges (he refused to use the word interview) with his friend Claire Parnet, *Dialogues* (1977), translated as *Dialogues* (1987), which like the previous book served as an appetizer for the sequel to *Anti-Oedipus*, which finally appeared in 1980. An even more prodigious synthesis of new concepts and new ideas, *Mille Plateaux* (1980), translated as *A Thousand Plateaus* (1987), is arguably one of the most important philosophical works of the 20th century. The outpouring of ideas it initiated continues to fascinate scholars today and has given rise to a veritable industry of exegetical works seeking to explain the meaning of such suggestive concepts as *abstract machine, assemblage, becoming, *body without organs, *nomadology, *rhizome, and *war machine.

After *A Thousand Plateaus* Deleuze said he needed to find himself again and his next works were in some ways quite personal. First he wrote a short book on the art of Francis Bacon, *Francis Bacon, logique de la sensation* (1981), translated as *Francis Bacon: The Logic of Sensation* (2003), this book makes use of some of the concepts developed in *A Thousand Plateaus*, but places more emphasis on new terms like *affect and sensation, which would be important to his fourth collaborative work with Guattari, *Qu'est-ce que la philosohie?* (1991), translated as *What is Philosophy?* (1994). He followed this with two volumes on film, *Cinéma 1. L'Image-mouvement* (1983), translated as *Cinema 1: The Movement-Image* (1986) and *Cinéma 2. L'Image-temps* (1985), translated as *Cinema 2: The Time-Image* (1989). The books proposed not a philosophy of film, but rather to articulate the specifically philosophical dimension of film. Anglo-American film studies was very slow to appreciate these books, but has in the last couple of years become deeply fascinated by the way they reorient the discussion of film.

His next two books were monographs on authors that were close to him personally and intellectually. The most personal of all these books in this period was the one he wrote about his friend Foucault, published two years after the latter's death: *Foucault* (1986), translated as *Foucault* (1988). His next book was on Leibniz, an author not often mentioned in the rest of his work yet clearly important to him. *Le Pli: Leibniz et le baroque* (1988), translated as *The Fold: Leibniz and the Baroque* (1993) has been well received by creative artists and geographers who see in it a radically new way of thinking about space and spatial relations. By the end of the 1980s, Deleuze's health had deteriorated dramatically and he found it difficult to work, yet he continued to produce new works, the already mentioned collaboration with Guattari as well as the essays on the clinical approach to literature. But perhaps his most important work in these years was the magnificent eight-hour video of him in conversation with Claire Parnet, *L'Abécédaire de Gilles Deleuze.*

He took his own life in November 1995. It is difficult to classify Deleuze's achievement. He saw himself as overturning Plato and creating a form of transcendental empiricist philosophy that took philosophy past the various impasses it had got itself into. How successful he was in this venture is still being decided. But it is widely agreed that he was one of the most important thinkers of the 20th century.

Further Reading: R. Bogue *Deleuze and Guattari* (1989).
I. Buchanan *Deleuze and Guattari's Anti-Oedipus* (2008).
C. Colebrook *Gilles Deleuze* (2002).
F. Dosse *Gilles Deleuze et Félix Guattari: Biographie Croisée* (2007).
M. Hardt *Gilles Deleuze* (1993).

SEE WEB LINKS

- An excellent resource, which contains transcriptions in English of Gilles Deleuze's lectures and interviews as well as links to ongoing research in the field.
- An excellent resource, but in French. It contains original recordings and video of Gilles Deleuze's lectures.

denotation and connotation Two interrelated orders of meaning operating simultaneously in a single cultural object: the first order, denotation, functions to state 'what is'; the second order, connotation, functions conceptually and ideologically. French literary critic Roland *Barthes, who transformed these concepts into a full-blown semiotic system by adapting the work of Danish linguist Louis *Hjelmslev, offers an extended example of how this dual system works in his afterword to *Mythologies* (1957), translated as *Mythologies* (1970) in the form of a meditation on the cover page of a random issue of *Paris Match*. The image in question is of a uniformed black soldier saluting the French flag—at the level of denotation, the image signifies or can be read as simply that, a black soldier saluting a flag; but the same image also offers another order of meaning, or connotation, which Barthes muses might be that it is an answer to the critique of colonialism (what could be more patriotic and thus less inclined to insurrection than a soldier in uniform saluting a flag?). Within that analysis, the same dual function is clearly at work: the French flag denotes the national flag of France, but connotes patriotism, belonging, identification, and so forth. This *dialectical way of reading cultural texts was especially influential in film and media studies in the 1970s and 1980s.

dependency theory An attempt to explain the persistent poverty of the *Third World as a symptom of the global system of capital, which in its very structure seems to require an impoverished global South as a source of cheap labour and raw materials. Developed by Paul Baran (among others) in the 1960s and 1970s from a *Marxist perspective, dependency theory challenges the neo-liberal notion that Third World poverty is simply a matter of underdevelopment, which is to say in time and with the right entrepreneurial spirit it will catch up with the First World. It argues instead that the impoverished state of the Third World is the result of deliberate policies on the part of First World nations, dating back to colonial times. Britain's deliberate destruction of India's nascent textiles industry and forced transformation of that country into an exporter of raw cotton and importer of cloth at the start of the Industrial Revolution is often held up as a textbook example of the way the Third World is in fact the creation of the First World. As Mike Davis points out in *Late Victorian Holocausts* (2002), at the time this was occurring,

Indian peasants actually had a better standard of living than did British peasants, but Britain used its disproportionately greater military and economic power to its advantage and in the process created conditions that many of its former colonies still struggle to overcome to this day. Dependency theory scholars like André Gunder Frank and Immanuel *Wallerstein reject the concept of *globalization because in their view capitalism has always been global in scale and scope.

See also WORLD-SYSTEM THEORY.

Further Reading: M. Blomstrom and B. Hettne *Development Theory in Transition: The Dependency Debate and Beyond: Third World Responses* (1984).
A. G. Frank *Capitalism and Underdevelopment in Latin America* (1979).

dérive **(drift)** An experimental technique of walking or moving through the urban space in a manner contrary to its design yet consistent with one's own desire, devised by the *Situationists. Its purpose is twofold: on the one hand, it is meant to expose a particular city's *psychogeography; on the other hand, it is a deliberate attempt to break away from what the Situationists deplored as ordinary life. Owing an obvious debt to the *Surrealist practice of aimlessly strolling through the city so as to experience it unconsciously, but highly critical of its dependence on automatism *dérive* does not involve surrendering one's will in this way, nor is it interested in chance or the happenstance. Instead its purpose is to notice and become aware of the way different parts of the city resonate with different states of mind, passions and desires. Interestingly, the Situationists thought that this attitude to space could only be sustained for a day or two without risking mental collapse; they also thought it could only be applied to the city. Rebecca Solnit's *Wanderlust: a History of Walking* (2000), suggests they were wrong on the second count. While Deleuze and Guattari's caution against *deterritorializing (a term with obvious if unacknowledged debts to Situationism) too far and too fast in *Mille Plateaux* (1980), translated as *A Thousand Plateaus* (1987), would seem to confirm that they were right on the first count. *See also* COGNITIVE MAPPING; *DÉTOURNEMENT*; DETERRITORIALIZATION; *FLÂNEUR*.

Further Reading: K. Knabb (ed.) *Situationist International Anthology* (2007).
S. Plant *The Most Radical Gesture: The Situationist International and After* (1992).

Derrida, Jacques (1930–2004) See overleaf.

DERRIDA, JACQUES (1930–2004)

French philosopher and one of the most influential intellectuals of the 20th century, Derrida is best known as the originator of *deconstruction. A prodigious talent and prolific author, Derrida is generally regarded (not uncontroversially, it has to be said) as one of the most important philosophers of all time. Certainly if notoriety can be used as a measure, there can be no doubting his importance. Yet unlike his peers Gilles *Deleuze and Michel *Foucault, his influence is largely confined (with notable exceptions, of course) to literature departments and the handful of philosophy departments admitting the possibility of a 'continental philosophy'.

Born in Algeria, Derrida began his preparation for university at a lycée there but his education was interrupted because of the restrictions on Jews imposed by the Vichy government. He moved to Paris in 1949, where he attended the prestigious Lycée Louis-le-Grand before entering the École Normale Supérieure (where his tutors included Louis *Althusser and Michel *Foucault). On his second attempt, he passed his agrégation in 1956. Between 1957 and 1959, in lieu of military service, Derrida taught English and French at a lycée in Le Mans. He returned to Paris in 1960 to a position as an assistant lecturer at the Sorbonne. In 1964 he was given a full lectureship at his alma mater, the École Normale Supérieure, and remained there until 1983, when he was made Directeur d'études at the École des Hautes Études en Sciences Sociales. From 1966 onwards, Derrida held regular visiting appointments at Johns Hopkins University, Yale, SUNY Buffalo, and the University of California at Irvine.

Derrida rose to international fame on the strength of a talk he gave in 1966 at a conference in Baltimore criticizing Claude *Lévi-Strauss, 'La structure, le signe et le jeu dans le discourse sciences humaines', translated as 'Structure, Sign and Play in the Discourse of Human Sciences' (1978), which is generally credited as the founding moment of *post-structuralism. The following year, a watershed year for Derrida, saw the publication of three books, each one destined to become a landmark in the field, *La Voix et la Phénomène* (1967), translated as *Speech and Phenomena* (1973), *L'Écriture et la difference* (1967), translated as *Writing and Difference* (1978), and *De la Grammatologie* (1967) translated as *Of Grammatology* (1976), the last of them containing the instantly infamous phrase by which Derrida's thought would become known: 'il n'y a pas de hors-texte' (there is nothing outside the text). Read by his detractors as evidence of his nihilism, it is generally thought to mean that there is no higher authority that can be appealed to in order to decide the meaning of a text.

As Derrida helpfully explains in the useful collection of interviews, *Positions* (1972), translated as *Positions* (1981), these three works—*Voix et la Phénomène, L'Écriture et la difference,* and *De la Grammatologie* (1967)—announced at once a project (the critique of *logocentrism) and a method (deconstruction). By logocentrism he means the idealism of language philosophy which always assumes that both speech and writing can only be thought by presupposing an exterior and abstract form of language he designates as logos. Although the word deconstruction has passed into popular parlance, its meaning is both more complex and subtle than its various appropriations have tended to present. Simplifying a great deal, it can usefully be understood as a practice of reading interested in articulating the operative elements of a text, concept, or idea in their full complexity, paying particular attention to the peculiar paradoxes of mutual interdependencies. For example, in his late work on the notion of 'forgiveness' Derrida argues that it is only the unforgivable that can truly be forgiven because it is only the unforgivable that meets the demand of that which can be forgiven, his point being that if something can be forgiven that forgiveness is in a sense given in advance and therefore not really in need of forgiveness, which by rights should only be given after the fact.

At the core of deconstruction is Derrida's notion—he explicitly says it isn't a concept—of **différance*, which is at once the means of doing deconstruction and an example of it. In a widely read essay, entitled simply '*Différance*' (1968), Derrida explains that the term is spelled the way it is to bring together two senses of the verb to differ, which as Derrida reads it means both to defer and to identify the different. This he explains is the basic condition of the *sign—the sign stands for a thing that is absent, so in a sense it defers contact with that thing; by the same token, the sign is by definition different from that which it signifies. *Différance* is the origin of difference itself, but inasmuch as the very notion renders problematic the very idea of an origin (as Derrida points out) it is better thought of as a condition or state of affairs that manifests itself as 'play', a word Derrida uses in its full range of senses from the ludic to the performative to the architectural. *Différance* has been enormously influential in literary studies, where it has been used to license a microscopic or 'playful' form of close reading that to the uninitiated can seem quite laboured. The best known exponents of this are the members of the so-called *Yale School of Deconstruction.

But it also has to be said that Derrida made his name with a combative 'take-no-prisoners' style of argumentation from which not even his friends were spared, as Michel *Foucault (the first of Derrida's many scalps) discovered in 1963 when his former student presented an excoriating critique of his *Folie et déraison* in a public lecture Foucault himself attended. Other notable scalps include John *Searle, who got into a spirited debate with Derrida over *speech act theory. Sometimes, as was the case with his book-length eulogy for his friend Paul de Man, *Mémoires, pour Paul de Man* (1988), his combative style could be turned to defensive purposes as well. Probably his most consequential work in this latter respect is *Spectres de Marx* (1993), translated as *Spectres of Marx* (1994), which, as Fredric *Jameson argued in his review of it, functioned both to renew and more importantly re-legitimate critical interest in Marx in France and elsewhere. It also offered a stirring riposte to Francis *Fukuyama's celebration of neo-liberalism. In the last decade of his life, Derrida turned increasingly to political questions, endeavouring to map out an ethics of hospitality he called *cosmopolitanism.

Further Reading: R. Gasché *The Tain of the Mirror* (1986).
C. Norris *Deconstruction: Theory and Practice* (1982).
N. Royle *Jacques Derrida* (2003).
J. Smith *Jacques Derrida: Live Theory* (2005).

desire One of the fundamental powers of reason according to Immanuel *Kant, which is able to exercise its judgement without the mediation of *pleasure. In *critical theory desire and pleasure are usually opposed to one another—desire is treated as a continuous flow, while pleasure is treated as an arrest of that flow, or an irruption that somehow brings desire to an end. For this reason desire is often categorized as sacred, while pleasure is consigned to the profane. There are two different debates concerning desire. The first is whether desire is cognitive or *instinctual, or to put it another way, voluntary or involuntary. The second is whether desire is self-motivating or not. The general consensus, with regard to the first question, is that desire belongs to the instincts, it is a force that flows through us which we have to learn to channel and contain in order to become 'civilized'. There are two vehemently opposed camps with regard to the second question: on the one side there is Jacques *Lacan, who argues that desire is motivated by *lack (that it constantly flows toward an *object it cannot obtain), while in the other camp is Gilles *Deleuze, who, rather like Kant, treats desire as one of the basic forces of nature itself.

desiring-machine The actual mechanism of *desire according to Gilles *Deleuze and Félix *Guattari. Deleuze and Guattari give as their example the machine formed by the child and the maternal breast. The idea seems to derive in part from a reaction to Melanie *Klein's overly *Oedipal theory of *object relations (particularly her case study of Richard), but more directly from Bruno *Bettelheim's case study of a schizophrenic boy, little Joey, in *The Empty Fortress* (1967). Looking at these case studies of how children play, Deleuze and Guattari argue that the objects that the children play with are not *symbolic (e.g. they aren't representatives of the *phallus), but machinic, meaning they give desire the means to not merely express itself, but form something constructive. It is in light of this they would later describe their work as *constructivist. The concept first appears in *L'Anti-Oedipe* (1972) translated as *Anti-Oedipus* (1977), but interestingly is dropped thereafter. In the sequel to *Anti-Oedipus, Mille Plateaux* (1980), translated as *A Thousand Plateaus* (1987), they instead speak of abstract machines and assemblages, but they retain the core idea that desire's basic function is to assemble and render machinic.

Further Reading: I. Buchanan *Deleuze and Guattari's Anti-Oedipus* (2008).

desiring-production The term used by Gilles *Deleuze and Félix *Guattari in *L'Anti-Oedipe* (1972), translated as *Anti-Oedipus* (1977), for the process of *desire. In spite of the title of their book, Deleuze and Guattari are not anti-*psychoanalysis—as they put it, their goal is to renovate psychoanalysis by re-engineering its principal conceptual mechanisms. From this perspective then, desiring-production may be seen to replace the *Freudian concept of the *id and thereby render the *instincts productive. Similarly, it also replaces the *Lacanian conception of *lack as the principal motor of desire with the notion that desire is a productive, assembling force. But they also use the notion of desiring-production to infuse some *Marxism into psychoanalysis and argue that *society could not function as it does if desire was not the synthesizing force it is. Borrowing from Kant,

Deleuze and Guattari develop a kind of ethics of desire by distinguishing between legitimate and illegitimate syntheses of desire.

Further Reading: I. Buchanan *Deleuze and Guattari's Anti-Oedipus* (2008).

desublimation Herbert *Marcuse's term for the process whereby art (in the strictest sense) is rendered banal and powerless. In *One-Dimensional Man* (1964), his million-selling account of the changes to society wrought by *late capitalism, Marcuse argues that the real problem posed by the *culture industry for *critical theory and hence *society itself is not its blurring of the distinction between high culture and low culture, but rather its blurring of the distinction between art and reality. Consistent with fellow *Frankfurt School theorists Max *Horkheimer and Theodor *Adorno (the authors of the culture industry thesis) and more particularly Walter *Benjamin's account of art in the age of mechanical reproduction, Marcuse argues that the mass production and distribution of art and its concomitant permeation of almost every aspect of daily life has destroyed what was most potent in art to begin with, namely its antagonism toward the ordinary (Benjamin's word for this is *aura). This antagonism is achieved via the process Freud called *sublimation, which according to *psychoanalysis is what happens when the *libido is brought under the control of the *reality principle: gratification of sexual desire is delayed and transformed into an aesthetic achievement or what Marcuse refers to as Eros. Under such conditions, Marcuse argues, the artistic realm is an 'other' dimension, radically distinct from and intrinsically antagonistic to *everyday life, and society can therefore be said to be two-dimensional at least. It is the loss of this dimension through the process of desublimation whereby Eros is reduced to sexuality that results in society becoming one-dimensional and therefore unable to resist the transformations imposed upon it by the changes in the *mode of production. Where before in art and literature representations of artists, prostitutes, adulterers, and so forth testified to an other, perhaps *utopian, life, now they are simply an affirmation of the existing order and carry no power of negation. Desublimation is in this sense repressive. So-called sexual liberation, Marcuse argues, comes at the price of the destruction of Eros, which leaves us with an intensified sexual existence but no resistance to the present, no space that can be considered 'other'.

deterritorialization Gilles *Deleuze and Félix *Guattari's concept for *desire that operates in an unorganized (not to say disorganized) way, by which they mean a mode of desiring that does not require an *object to motivate it and give it direction. In *L'Anti-Oedipe* (1972) translated as *Anti-Oedipus* (1977), Deleuze and Guattari redefine Jacques *Lacan's concept of the *drive as a territory, so to deterritorialize means to sever desire from its connection to the drive. But they also argue that desire is constantly looking to reterritorialize, to restore its connection to the drive in other words. Deterritorialization is an optimal process for Deleuze and Guattari, necessary to the release of creative energies. However, at its extreme deterritorialization is synonymous with schizophrenic psychoses, and in their later work Deleuze and Guattari are careful to state that one must exercise caution in deterritorializing. But, they nevertheless hold to the idea that at least a little bit of deterritorialization is needed to stop things from stagnating. *See also* DÉRIVE.

Further Reading: I. Buchanan *Deleuze and Guattari's Anti-Oedipus* (2008).

***détournement* (turnaround/reversal)** An artistic practice conceived by the *Situationists for transforming artworks by creatively disfiguring them. In 'A User's Guide to Détournement' (1956), Guy *Debord, a key Situationist theorist, and Gil Wolman, argue that *détournement* has a double purpose: on the one hand, it must negate the ideological conditions of artistic production, the fact that all artworks are ultimately commodities; but on the other hand, it must negate this negation and produce something that is politically educative. It achieves negation in two main ways: either it adds details to existing works, thus revealing a previously obscured ambiguity, or it cuts up a range of works and recombines them in new and surprising ways. The enemy of this practice is, however, sheer novelty, and it is this that must be guarded against in producing the negation of the negation. The Situationists take the position that the literary and artistic heritage of humanity should be used for what they term partisan propaganda purposes, by which they mean the promotion of radical politics. The advantage of *détournement*, Debord and Wolman argue, is that it is cheap but powerful and that makes it a weapon anyone can use to break through what they famously call the Chinese walls of understanding. Marcel Duchamp's moustache on the *Mona Lisa* is regarded as consistent with this aim, but too tame; similarly, Bertolt *Brecht's re-staging of classical plays by Shakespeare is regarded as a crucial prototype, but again it is seen as being too conservative. The *poète maudit* Lautréamont (pen-name of Paris-based Uruguayan writer Isidore Ducasse) is generally regarded as the main precursor; his *Les Chants de Maldoror* (1868) is cited by Debord and others as the perfect example of an extended *détournement*. The main exponent of the practice of *détournement* was Danish painter Asger Jorn who, along with Guy Debord, was one of the founders of the Situationist movement. *See also* COGNITIVE MAPPING; *DÉRIVE*; DETERRITORIALIZATION; *FLÂNEUR*.

Further Reading: K. Knabb (ed.) *Situationist International Anthology* (2007). S. Plant *The Most Radical Gesture: The Situationist International and After* (1992).

diachronic *See* SYNCHRONIC AND DIACHRONIC.

dialectic A method of argument based on the idea of two people in dialogue each putting forward a proposition that the other counters and by this means arriving at an ultimate truth. The word originates in Classical Greek philosophy—its invention is sometimes attributed to Zeno, but it was Socrates and Plato who popularized it as a means of obtaining truth by a process of asking questions. German *Enlightenment philosopher, Immanuel *Kant rejected this method as sterile, as producing nothing but illusions. In contemporary critical theory, however, it is the names G.W.F. *Hegel and Karl *Marx which are most often associated with the dialectic, each one credited with having reinvented the concept. Central to Hegel's notion of the dialectic is the constant presence of contradiction: as Hegel points out, identity contains its opposite, namely difference, inasmuch that to be one thing something must also not be another thing. His best known demonstration of this argument is his essay on the relation between the master and the slave in *Phänomenologie des Geistes* (1807), translated as *Phenomenology of Spirit* (1977), in which he famously argues that because the master is conscious of the need to dominate the slave he is enslaved and therefore not fully himself. For Hegel, history can be understood in the same terms as a constant progression from the abstract to the concrete, mediated by a process he referred to as negation. To become a true master, the master must negate that part of himself which is enslaved, but in doing so he does not thereby become whole; on the contrary, he merely becomes deficient in a different way, so the negation itself must be negated. Hegel called this process *Aufhebung* which in German means the superseding, surpassing, and cancelling out of what was. It is generally translated into English as sublation, but this isn't wholly satisfactory. Marx felt that Hegel got things around the wrong way and described his own version of dialectics, also known as *dialectical materialism, as a standing of Hegel back on his feet. His complaint was that Hegel treated the real world as merely the phenomenal form of the idea, whereas for him it is the real world that gives rise to ideas. However, like Hegel, Marx gives a central role to contradiction, which in its empirical form of *class struggle is the motor of history. Marx wanted to show that capitalism is simultaneously the best and the worst thing that has happened in human history and that it is only by grasping its dual nature that it can truly be understood. In Marx's view, capitalism created tremendous productive capacity, enabling necessity to finally be conquered, but did so at the price of the monstrous exploitation of the many by the few. Marx saw his dialectical method as a 'scandal to the bourgeoisie' because implicit in it is the view that its recognition of the present state of affairs is also a foretelling of its inevitable destruction. In his development of *dialectical criticism, Jameson insists that this sense of scandal must be preserved.

Further Reading: F. Jameson *Valences of the Dialectic* (2009).

dialectical criticism Fredric *Jameson's term for his approach to literary and cultural analysis. The essential tenets of the approach—he insists that it is not a method as such, which would imply a 'one size fits all' attitude which Jameson rejects—were worked out in detail in *Marxism and Form* (1971) and then further elaborated in *The Political Unconscious: Narrative as a Socially Symbolic Act* (1981). As in Karl *Marx's conception of the *dialectic, Jameson insists that dialectical criticism must strive for the scandal of the unexpected revelation that comes from the demonstration that the *Other is not as different from the same as we initially thought. Dialectical criticism should proceed from the abstract to the concrete, from the imperfectly understood to the concretely understood, where that would mean comprehending the true historical nature of existence. In this regard, dialectical criticism can also be compared to Bertolt *Brecht's notion of the *estrangement-effect, which was doubtless an inspiration in any case. Ultimately, dialectical criticism should strive to reveal obscure effects of *class struggle in any given text by reconstructing the historical conditions—particularly the *ideological conditions—that yielded it. Jameson's life-work can be seen as an astonishingly long and diverse series of demonstrations of both the versatility and utility of this approach. *See also* METACOMMENTARY; TRANSCODING.

dialectical materialism The official name given to *Marxist philosophy, although it is not a phrase that Karl *Marx himself used. Current from the time of the Second International onwards, it was the official *ideology of the USSR, where (under Stalin's direction) the vast body of work by Marx and his followers was codified and transformed into a set of laws that went by the appropriately imposing name of *Diamat*. Stalin himself contributed to this task with a book of his own,

Dialectical and Historical Materialism (1938), although it has to be said that there are serious doubts as to whether he actually authored the work himself. Dialectical materialism combines the dialectical approach of G.W.F. *Hegel with the philosophical materialism of Ludwig Feuerbach (one of the so-called 'Young Hegelians'). Following Feuerbach, who attempted to create a secular version of Hegel's dialectic of spirit, Marx repudiated Hegel's idealism, claiming in a famous phrase that in doing so he had stood Hegel back on his feet, and prioritized matter over spirit. At its core, dialectical materialism is of the view that the world exists independently of our perception of it and that as it is the sole reality it has primacy over the ideal, the imagined, and the spiritual. Moreover, as Friedrich *Engels insisted, the world is characterized by constant revolutionary changes driven by its own internal contradictions. Engels codified his view as three laws, drawn from classical philosophical sources as well as Hegel: first, the world consists of opposites that are simultaneously in state of conflict and unity (e.g. night and day); second, quantitative changes give rise to qualitative 'leaps' (e.g. the boiling of water, when the temperature passes 100°C—which is a quantity—it turns into steam—a change in its quality); third, change is a process of negation (e.g. a seed germinates into a plant, and in doing so negates its previous existence as a seed, and in turn negates that state of negation by becoming a plant, and so on). Dialectical materialism has been criticized, both from within Marxism and without, for being overly dogmatic and rather too programmatic in its approach. Jürgen *Habermas critiques it for being a scientism, for mistaking a philosophy for a science in other words; meanwhile, Louis *Althusser lauds it precisely because in his view it transforms philosophy into science.

Dialectic of Enlightenment Theodor *Adorno and Max *Horkheimer's modification of Immanuel *Kant's thesis that *Enlightenment means the end of the intellectual immaturity of humans and the advent of the Age of Reason. Adorno and Horkheimer accept that the Enlightenment did bring about the Age of Reason, but argue that reason is a double-edge sword, or in their words a *dialectic, because as humankind exercises its reason and transforms its environment according to its own needs it also allows an 'instrumental' way of thinking to dominate every aspect of thought with the paradoxical result that rational ways of thinking give rise to irrational acts. Written during World War II, *Dialektik der Aufklärung* (1944), translated as *The Dialectic of Enlightenment* (1972), is primarily concerned to understand how a country like Germany, so rich in its intellectual tradition, could have succumbed to the atavistic appeal of Nazism. Their answer, in part, was that thought had been allowed to become a mere commodity, something to be exchanged, rather than something that influences life.

dialogism A principle or condition of interconnecting performative differences underpinning all forms of communication according to Mikhail *Bakhtin. We cannot understand how meaning is produced, Bakhtin argues, unless we grasp that the meaning of individual words is the result of a negotiation, not only between actual speakers in dialogue with one another, but also with language itself. All language users shift and reshape the meaning of words according to the demands of their situation. Dialogism is, in this sense, an extra-linguistic function inasmuch as it is not intrinsic to words or any of the other parts of speech, yet it is also the sphere where language *lives* (as Bakhtin puts it) so it cannot be separated out and treated as surplus to linguistics. It is always possible, however, for language to sink back into a monologic state, such as one finds in official discourse. So it is the task of literature, Bakhtin says, to strive to produce dialogism at every level by orienting it towards another's discourse with the aim of creating what he calls double-voiced discourse. Hence his interest in the *carnivalesque, which by its very nature is doubly-determined: it juxtaposes the official order of things with its subversive transgression. For Bakhtin, the pinnacle of this type of writing is arrived at when the author's own voice disappears and the characters appear to be autonomous, as though speaking for themselves. Bakhtin first conceived of the concept of dialogism in his book on Dostoevesky, whom he considered a master of this form of writing. *See also* CARNIVALESQUE; HETEROGLOSSIA; POLYPHONY.

Further Reading: K. Clark and M. Holquist *Mikhail Bakhtin* (1984).
M. Holquist *Dialogism* (2002).
D. Lodge *After Bakhtin* (1990).

diaspora Derived from the Greek for 'scattering of seeds', it is used to describe population migration and dispersal (voluntary and involuntary). Originally used to refer to the Jewish peoples' forced exile from Israel (as it is now known) in the pre-Christian era and their subsequent removals from Spain, Portugal, and Russia, where they had resided for well over a thousand years, diaspora is now used to refer to virtually any mass migration. Slavery in Europe and the Americas resulted in an African diaspora, whereby millions of Africans were forcibly relocated to distant lands. Similarly, European colonialism resulted in millions of Europeans relocating to far-off continents. This in turn led to Indian and Chinese diasporas as cheap labour was imported to South Africa, Australia, Fiji and elsewhere to solve various production problems. Diaspora is generally thought in terms of 'homelessness', a sense of trauma and exile, but lately it has come to be viewed more positively as a kind of post-national *cosmopolitanism or *Creoleness in which the diasporic subject represents a new, more advanced stage of politically and culturally heterogeneous citizenry. *See also* GLOBALIZATION; MULTITUDE.

d

Further Reading: E. Said *Reflections on Exile* (2000).

diegesis The opposite of *mimesis, according to Plato. In diegesis the author speaks in their own voice, whereas in mimesis they do not (instead they try to create the illusion that it is someone else who speaks). In the 1960s, French *structuralist scholars like Christian *Metz and Gerard *Genette adapted it to refer to the actual succession of events in a story—i.e. what happens—which they opposed to the narration or telling of the story (effectively the new form of mimesis). This distinction found two particular uses in literary and film studies. First it allowed the separation of narrators who participate in the story which they are telling and those who do not—think of Conrad's *Heart of Darkness* (1900): Marlow participated in the action of the story he tells, so he is a diegetic narrator; but the person he tells the story to, who is in fact the one who reports to us as readers does not, therefore he is extra-diegetic, that is, outside of the story. Similarly, music in film can be either diegetic or extra-diegetic, part of the story being told, or an aural backdrop.

différance French philosopher Jacques *Derrida's term—he explicitly rules out calling it a concept—for the condition of possibility for meaning. As he explains in the extremely helpful collection of interviews, *Positions* (1972), translated as *Positions* (1981), Derrida conceived this neologism in order to make apparent the way in which the French verb *différer* has both a temporal and a spatial dimension: on the one hand, it signals delay or reprieve (a deferred payment such as a pension, or a pre-recorded broadcast of a TV programme may both be referred to in this way); and on the other hand, it is the movement which separates like from unlike. To which Derrida adds a third observation to the effect that *différance* is the process which gives rise to the very differences it announces. As such, *différance* is an origin one never arrives at (its presence is permanently delayed), a difference one never fully succeeds in making, and the perpetual and necessary attempt to do both these things. The term is difficult to translate because the first of the three senses is not available in the English cognate 'to differ', making it hard for Anglophones to 'hear' its inner complexity. But if one bears in mind that it refers to a condition of possibility rather than a particular form of causality or even effect then its purpose can be understood relatively easily. In the interview already mentioned, Derrida goes on to discuss the notion of transgression in a way that illuminates quite helpfully what he is endeavouring to articulate with this notion of *différance*: transgression, he says, can never be achieved once and for all, because insofar as a law is transgressed it proves itself transgressible and by that measure the act itself ceases to be a transgression; so transgression must move ceaselessly to restore the integrity of the law it wishes to transgress. For this reason, as Jacques *Lacan and other *psychoanalysts have pointed out, the supposedly arch-transgressor, namely the Marquis de Sade, is also of necessity an enthusiast of the law. Derrida's reading strategy, which he calls *deconstruction, assumes that *différance* underpins every aspect of meaning-making.

Further Reading: S. Critchley *The Ethics of Deconstruction* (1992).
J. Culler *On Deconstruction: Theory and Criticism After Structuralism* (1982).
C. Norris *Deconstruction: Theory and Practice* (1982).

differend (différend) A wrong or injustice that arises because the *discourse in which the wrong might be expressed does not exist. To put it another way, it is a wrong or injustice that arises because the prevailing or *hegemonic discourse actively precludes the possibility of this wrong being expressed. To put it still another way, it is a wrong or injustice which cannot be proved to have been a wrong or injustice because the means of doing so has (also) been denied the victim. Jean-François *Lyotard, who coined this term in his book *Le Différend* (1983), translated as *The Differend: Phrases in Dispute* (1988), took as his key exhibit Holocaust denier Robert Faurisson, whose position is that the only person who can legitimately testify to the existence of gas chambers is somebody who actually died in one. One might also point to the situation of the detainees at Camp X-Ray in Guantanamo Bay who as suspects or persons of interest in the so-called 'War on Terror' are denied the right to a trial on the grounds that they are neither enemy combatants (which would be covered by the Geneva convention) nor on US soil (which would place them under jurisdiction of the US judiciary). The language, the opportunity, and the means to articulate any wrong that may have befallen them is also denied them. *See also* BARE LIFE; BIOPOWER.

Dilthey, Wilhelm (1833–1911) German philosopher who worked on *hermeneutics and *Lebensphilosophie* (life philosophy) and influenced Martin *Heidegger, Hans-Georg *Gadamer and Jürgen

*Habermas. He was a colleague and important supporter of Georg *Simmel at the University of Berlin. His work on 'lived experience' was an important precursor to *phenomenology.

Further Reading: R. Makkreel *Dilthey: Philosopher of the Human Studies* (1993).

discipline Michel *Foucault's concept to describe a broad scale movement he detected in European history away from spectacular and grotesque forms of punishment towards more subtle modes of coercion that take the individual body as their target. Commencing in the mid to late 18th century, at the start of the era that Foucault would later characterize as the age of *biopower, techniques were developed in a number of quarters—particularly the armed services—to harness more fully the potentiality of the human body. These new training techniques were distinguished by the fact that they no longer looked upon the body as an indissociable whole, but instead treated it as an interconnected series of parts that could be thought of as so many components of a machine. By means of a meticulous training of the body, its productive capacity could be enhanced and at the same time its will to resist reduced, the attraction of this outcome to the holders of power is obvious. What Foucault shows is that this new logic of discipline, which first took shape in the preparation of soldiers, found application in virtually every aspect of modern life.

Further Reading: M. Foucault *Surveiller et punir: naissance de la prison* (1975), translated as *Discipline and Punish: The Birth of the Prison* (1977).

discourse A specific form of language use shaped and determined by situational rules and context. Discourse can be thought of as the performance of language, but even this is too limiting because the concept is used in place of language precisely as a way of encompassing the extra-linguistic dimension of all forms of communication. In *critical theory, it is Michel *Foucault who has done the most to develop this concept. In his work, discourse is expanded to include the operation of power: Foucault asks who has the right to use a particular discourse, what benefits accrue to them for using it, how is its usage policed, and where does it derive its *authority from? His examples include medical discourse (including psychiatry), penal discourse, and sexual discourse.

Further Reading: S. Mills *Discourse* (2004).

discursive formation French historian Michel *Foucault's term for a system of *statements produced by force of a single *discursive practice (the underpinning system of rules of a particular society at a certain moment in its history). Foucault created this concept as a means of rethinking causality in a nonlinear or dispersed fashion. For instance he wanted to be able to show that transformations which took place in such diverse and geographically dispersed entities as factories, hospitals, prisons, and schools in Europe throughout the 17th and 18th centuries were consistent with one another, because there is a discursive link connecting them all. The changes are not the product of a single consciousness, or a specific intention. The changes accrue over time as a specific discursive practice—in this case *discipline—moves more and more into the foreground. Discursive formations emerge, then, in a slow and uncertain way; they aren't born or created by fiat; and they are anonymous and objective.

Further Reading: J. Bernauer *Michel Foucault's Force of Flight* (1990).
M. Foucault *L'Archéologie du savoir* (1969), translated as *The Archaeology of Knowledge* (1972).
C. O'Farrell *Michel Foucault* (2005).

discursive practice French historian Michel *Foucault's term for the system of rules governing the production of *statements in a particular society at a certain moment in history. These rules are anonymous, unintended and objective; they are not simply the laws or social regulations either. They are rather the rules for the production of statements, determining not merely what can and cannot be said at one moment, but also—and more importantly—what it is possible to say. To be able to say someone is 'mad' for instance requires that madness exist as a concept and that the rules for its use are established. It is the production of these rules that interested Foucault as a historian.

Further Reading: M. Foucault *L'Archéologie du savoir* (1969), translated as *The Archaeology of Knowledge* (1972).

displacement (*Verschiebung*) One of four key mechanisms of Sigmund *Freud's concept of *dreamwork. It is also to be found at work in the symptom-formation of both *neurosis and *hysteria. The concept of displacement depends on the prior thesis, developed by Freud, that a representation (*Vorstellung*) of an *instinct one makes to oneself and its *affect (*Affekt*) or *libidinal charge are effectively semi-autonomous. The *fetish is a classic instance of this: to someone with a foot fetish, for example, the image of a naked foot has the same affect as does the image of a naked body as a whole (indeed, if they were a true fetishist in the clinical sense, the foot alone would give pleasure). Similarly, advertising constantly uses this strategy, aiming to shift the libidinal charge of sexual imagery onto products in the hope that the idea of that product will have a libidinal affect too. In dreams, the displacements tend to be found in the apparently irrelevant details of the dream which seem to occupy a place of undue prominence—they become apparent in therapy when in discussing them patients have a disproportionate reaction to them (i.e. the affect of their response is greater than the apparent affect of the idea). In *Die Traumdeutung* (1900), translated as *The Interpretation of Dreams* (1953) Freud gives the example of a dream in which someone sees themselves climbing up a staircase, an activity that at first glance seems relatively insignificant; but on closer examination, he argues that its true significance is that the person concerned was worried about the dangers of sexual relations with someone of lower social class. The Russian linguist Roman *Jakobson has argued that displacement is in fact a form of *metonymy and as such one of the fundamental poles of language. Jacques *Lacan adopts this thesis in his work, arguing that *desire is in its nature metonymic.

dispositif An organization of *statements. The term is used by Michel *Foucault to describe the systemic connection of statements. It is for this reason often translated as 'apparatus', although this doesn't really work as it is a virtual process rather than an actual entity. Its nearest cognate is probably Gilles *Deleuze and Félix *Guattari's concept of the assemblage (certainly their writing suggests that they appropriated the concept and made it their own).

Further Reading: C. O'Farrell *Michel Foucault* (2005).

distributive justice Socially just allocation of goods and resources. Research in this field tries to determine what would be a 'fair' way of distributing limited resources. For instance, it is manifestly unfair that rich countries like the US use vastly more of the earth's resources than very poor countries like Guatemala, but it would be equally unfair to scale back the US's allocation in line with Guatemala's usage since this would result in a cataclysmic drop in standard of living. Given these uneven conditions, what is the best path forward so that a socially just allocation of resources can be achieved? This is the central question asked by distributive justice. *See also* RAWLS.

Further Reading: S. Fleischacker *A Short History of Distributive Justice* (2005).

double-consciousness A concept conceived by W.E.B. *Du Bois in his landmark work *Souls of Black Folk* (1903) to describe the mental situation of African-American people in early 20th-century America. Du Bois argued that the exclusion of black Americans from mainstream American life meant that black people not only had consciousness of themselves as black, they also had consciousness of themselves as not-white as well.

dreamwork (*Traumarbeit*) The process which, according to Sigmund *Freud, transforms dream-thoughts (*latent content) into actual dreams (*manifest content) by distorting them in such a way that the implicit desires the dream-thoughts contain do not become apparent to the conscious. There are two separate functions in a dream—the first is to produce dream-thoughts, which are created from bodily stimuli, *instincts, and what Freud called the day's residues (i.e. the many threads of psychic activity that are left unresolved at the end of the day); the second is the transformation of those dream-thoughts (many of which are unacceptable to the conscious), into dream images. This process, the dreamwork proper, consists of four different mechanisms: *condensation (*Verdichtung*), *displacement (*Verschiebung*), consideration of representability (*Rücksicht auf Darstellbarkeit*), and secondary revision (*sekundäre Bearbeitung*). Dreams are not creative, Freud maintains, they are transformative, and it is the transformations inherent in them that are crucial from the perspective of analysis. In other words, in analysing a dream Freud doesn't ask what a particular image stands for; rather, he wants to know why the thing it does stand for had to be represented in that way.

drive (*Trieb*) A compulsion to act originating in the *psyche which does not have a specific *object. In contrast to the *instinct, it cannot be satisfied. Although there is considerable dispute about it in *psychoanalysis, it is clear that in his work Freud maintained a clear distinction between instincts and the drive. Unfortunately, this distinction was obliterated in English at least by James Strachey's unhappy decision to translate both *Instinkt* and *Trieb* as drive. The drive differs markedly from instinct in that it is variable in both formation and action, but more particularly because its aim is its object. Take for example, the nutrition instinct (one of the seven basic instincts according to *ethology), its aim is to provide sustenance for the body and its object is food. When we eat we satisfy that instinct. So why do some of us have such difficulties with eating—either we eat too much, or don't eat enough? The answer is that eating is not purely a matter of instinct; there is another dimension to it which needs to be thought in terms of *desire, which is the drive. Understood as a drive, the nutrition instinct becomes a kind of oral drive for which eating is something that is enjoyable in itself, the object is no longer food it is the mouth itself, but it is not a proper object in that it does not extinguish the drive or provide satisfaction. Now there is no aim except the joy of eating. The paradox of the drive, as its keenest theorist Jacques *Lacan tirelessly argued, is that it is driven by what it cannot have; it is, in other words, motivated by lack. What it lacks is precisely an object that could give it satisfaction. Freud argued that there were two basic types of drive, which he called the life-drive (Eros) and the *death-drive (Thanatos), that exist side by side in a state of equilibrium. Pathological symptoms emerge, according to Freud, when these drives fall into a state of disequilibrium.

Du Bois, W.E.B. (1868–1963) Founding figure of black *Cultural studies, writer, sociologist, economist and activist, of whom it has been said he attempted virtually everything possible to overcome western racism short of armed insurrection. Born in Massachusetts, a descendant of Haitian slaves, he was raised by his mother after his father deserted the family. Although very poor, Du Bois nonetheless had access to excellent education and excelled in school. He studied at Harvard and the University of Berlin. He wrote over 4,000 articles in his lifetime, but most of these pieces (many of which are minor editorial essays written while he was editor of *Crisis*, the organ of the NAACP (National Association for the Advancement of Colored People), of which he was a co-founder) are hard to find and astonishingly there is no collection of his works. Undoubtedly his most famous work, though, is *Souls of Black Folk* (1903), which a century on is still widely studied and taught. An advocate of assimilation and integration (but on a level playing field) Du Bois disagreed profoundly with Marcus Garvey's separatist strategies. Black people have to endure a *double-consciousness, Du Bois argued, in that they have to know when and how to act 'white' as well as 'black'. Thus, they live conscious of the fact that to some 'they' are a problem. Paul Gilroy, in his *The Black Atlantic: Modernity and Double Consciousness* (1993), argues that this thesis can be extended to the black *diaspora as a whole.

Durkheim, Émile (1858–1917) French sociologist, widely considered one of the founders of the field of sociology. He was born in the Lorraine region of France into a family of devout Jews (his father, grandfather and great-grandfather were all rabbis). Although expected to follow the family tradition and go to rabbinical school, Durkheim instead studied at the prestigious college, the École Normale Supérieure (his classmates included Henri *Bergson and Jean Jaurès). He determined to take a scientific approach to the study of society, which put him at odds with the humanist establishment and made his career progression difficult as a consequence. He obtained a post at the University of Bordeaux in 1887 and for the next 15 years this was his base from which to launch his assault on the French academic system and begin the work of establishing sociology as a discipline. His PhD dissertation, *The Division of Labour in Society* was published in 1893 and was shortly followed by *Rules of Sociological Method* (1895), which became a manifesto for the fledgling field. In 1898 he founded the journal, *L'Année Sociologique*, which, with interruptions for war, continues to be published today. The first of the two books for which Durkheim is best known, *Suicide*, was published in 1897. Comparing the suicide rates of Protestants and Catholics, he tried to explain why it was lower for Catholics than for Protestants in terms of social control mechanisms. His data gathering methods have since been challenged, but the work remains an important early example of a sociological case analysis because of the way it classifies suicide types into categories. Having served his time in the provinces, as virtually all French academics are expected to do, in 1902 he was offered a position as chair of education at the Sorbonne. The second of his two famous books, which also happened to be his last, *The Elementary Forms of Religious Life* was published in 1912, the same year in which he finally obtained a tenured chair at the Sorbonne. In contrast to his contemporaries, Max Weber and Ferdinand *Tönnies, Durkheim's focus was not the individual, but rather the large scale institutions whose existence cannot be thought of in terms of the actions of individuals such as government, religion, and education. He was concerned to explain how society holds together in the face of *modernity, which for him meant a social situation not defined by the assumption of a common background.

Further Reading: J. Alexander and P. Smith (eds.) *The Cambridge Companion to Durkheim* (2005).

A. Giddens *Durkheim* (1978).

S. Lukes *Émile Durkheim: His Life and Work* (1975).

K. Thompson *Émile Durkheim* (1982).

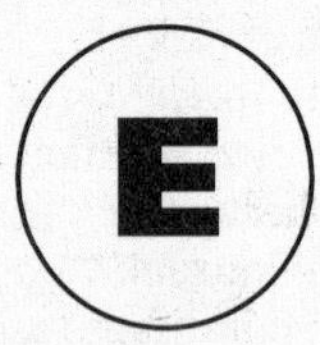

Eagleton, Terry (1943–) Marxist cultural critic. The son of a working-class family of Irish descent, Eagleton was born in Salford in the north-west of England. He was educated at De La Salle College and Cambridge University, where he came under the influence of Raymond *Williams. He is best known for his witty, combative and indeed sniping reviewing style. His *Literary Theory: An Introduction* (1983) introduced an entire generation of Anglophone literature students to theory. He achieved proper notoriety when the Prince of Wales decried him to a group of Oxford students as 'that dreadful Terry Eagleton'.

When Eagleton gained admission to Trinity College, Cambridge to read English in 1961, it coincided with the high point of the influence of the doyen of *practical criticism, F. R. *Leavis, and though he would later write scathingly of both, practical criticism's combative tone and its emphasis on close reading left its mark. However, the greater personal and intellectual influences were the Dominican theologians Laurence Bright and Herbert McCabe and cultural critic Raymond *Williams, whom he encountered at Jesus College, where he moved to undertake his postgraduate research. Eagleton's PhD, written under the direction of Williams, examined the work of the minor Victorian poet and writer Edward Carpenter.

In his student years, Eagleton was heavily involved with the Catholic Left. He was one of the founding editors of *Slant*, a radical Catholic journal which sought to challenge the structures of the Catholic Church in the wake of Vatican II and bring a distinctly Christian perspective to debates central to the concerns of the New Left. He also wrote two book-length treatments of this subject in this period, *The New Left Church* (1967) and *The Body as Language* (1970). Through his publications in *Slant* as well as in *New Blackfriars* (the Catholic theological journal), Eagleton sought to demonstrate common ground between Christian thought and socialism and between religion and politics more generally. Christ, he proposed, offered a way out of the existential angst caused by the alienating forces of modern life.

Eagleton left Cambridge in 1969 to take up a position at Oxford, where he remained for three decades. He then moved to Manchester University which caused a scandal by imposing mandatory retirement on him when he reached 65. The publication in 1976 of *Criticism and Ideology* brought international attention to Eagleton, and established him as one of Britain's leading Marxist critics. This was followed in quick succession by *Marxism and Literary Criticism* (1976), a study of Walter *Benjamin and an introductory textbook on literary theory. He also wrote regularly for *New Left Review*. During this period, Eagleton's work was distinguished by two main preoccupations: Irish literature and history and postmodernism. Equally outspoken about both, in *Heathcliff and the Great Hunger* (1995) he showed himself to be one of the staunchest champions of Irish literature and in *The Illusions of Postmodernism* (1996) one of the sternest critics of postmodernism.

Since leaving Oxford Eagleton has also settled accounts with theory in *After Theory* (2001) and made a pronounced turn toward spiritual matters, going so far as to write a book entitled *The Meaning of Life* (2007). But he hasn't deserted politics altogether. In 2002 he published perhaps his most controversial book of all, *Holy Terror*, which in the aftermath of 9/11 infuriated right-wing critics by (bravely, it has to be said) highlighting the connection between terrorism and state terror. He made international news in 2006 when the Australian Archbishop was accused of plagiarizing his review of Richard Dawkins's polemical book *The God Delusion* (2006). Showing that advancing age has not dulled his spirit or wit, Eagleton caused a highly public stir in 2007 by deriding Kingsley Amis and Martin Amis for their conservatism.

Further Reading: D. Alderson *Terry Eagleton* (2004).
J. Smith *Terry Eagleton: A Critical Introduction* (2008).

Eco, Umberto (1932–) Italian medievalist, semiotician, cultural commentator, and novelist. He is world renowned as the author of the huge bestseller, *Il nome della rosa* (1980), translated as *The Name of the Rose* (1983), which was made into a film starring Sean Connery and Christian Slater (director, Annaud, 1987). However, before that he was already highly regarded as scholar, initially for his work on medieval aesthetics, but then more generally for his contributions to *semiotics.

Eco was born in the northern city of Alessandria in the Piedmont region of Italy. His father was an accountant, but his grandfather was a foundling (hence the name Eco, which is an acronym derived from *ex caelis oblatus*, which roughly translates as 'gift from heaven'). His father wanted him to be a lawyer, but he chose to study medieval literature and philosophy instead at the University of Turin. He graduated with a PhD in 1954 and took a job with the state broadcasting station, Radiotelevisione Italiana (RAI), working as a cultural editor. From 1956, following the publication of his first book *Il problema estetico in San Tommaso* (Aesthetic Problems in St Thomas Aquinas) he also lectured part-time at the University of Turin. He did compulsory military service in 1958–9, but did not return to his old job at RAI. Instead took a job as a non-fiction acquisitions editor at Casa Editrice Bompiani in Milan.

It was the publication in 1959 of 'L'opera in movimento e la coscienza dell'epoca', translated as 'The poetics of the open work', which in presenting a new dialectic of the *open and closed work first drew international attention to Eco's work. Anticipating by more than a decade fellow semiotician Roland *Barthes's distinction between the *readerly and writerly text, Eco argues that works of art are fields of possibilities which to a greater or lesser degree invite and require the audience to contribute to the production of meaning. Works which try to constrict the range of meanings the audience can produce are naturally enough called 'closed' works (examples would include religious doctrines, political manifestoes, textbooks and user's manuals), while those works which compel the audience to produce multiple meanings are called open works. Eco does not thereby agree with the rather empty claim that the reader is free to produce whatever meaning they like in response to a text. He sees it, rather, as a creative collaboration.

Throughout the 1960s and early 1970s, Eco was preoccupied with the problem of how in fact readers do produce meanings and what part the text plays in that production of meaning. Although not formally a part of the *reader-response school, his work was nevertheless congruent with it on a number of levels. This work is best exemplified by the collection of essays spanning the period from 1959 to 1977 published in English as *The Role of the Reader: Explorations in the Semiotics of Texts* (1981). The collection contains his essays on James Bond and Superman, which have virtual canonical status in genre studies as examples of the advantages of the *structuralist approach to narrative analysis. His two key theoretical works, both written in English, *A Theory of Semiotics* (1976) and *Semiotics and the Philosophy of Language* (1984), stem from this period as well. Drawing extensively on the work of the American semiotician C. S. *Peirce, Eco sought to develop a theory of unlimited semiosis.

Following a series of trips to America in the early 1960s and 1970s, taking in the sights in California and Las Vegas, Eco wrote a series of essays for Italian newspapers and magazines that in 1986 were translated and edited as a single collection titled *Faith in Fakes* for the US edition and *Travels in Hyperreality* for the UK edition. Both titles apply equally well and can be regarded as corollaries—to travel in *hyperreality is in effect to have faith in fakes. What Eco found intriguing, but also confounding, about the hyperreal world he encountered in places like Disneyland is the fact that not only do these places replicate the *real, somehow they seem to replace it as well. It's as though the unreal is more real than the real. Although Eco doesn't use the word *postmodern, the phenomenon he describes is a staple concern of postmodern theorists like Jean *Baudrillard.

Since the publication of *The Name of the Rose*, Eco has more or less abandoned his technical semiotic work and returned to his roots as a medievalist. He has written big books on ugliness, beauty, and the Knights Templar as well several more novels and collections of journalisms.

Further Reading: M. Caesar *Umberto Eco: Philosophy, Semiotics and the Work of Fiction* (1999).

ecocriticism The first person to use the term appears to have been William Rueckert in 1978, whose purpose in doing so was to suggest that ecological terms and concepts can usefully be applied to the study of literature. This, however, is not the dominant meaning of the term. It tends to be interpreted more loosely as a general term for the study of the relationship between literature and the natural environment. Although a number of critics have considered the importance of the environment in literature (e.g. Leo Marx and Raymond *Williams), it was not until the late 1980s and early 1990s that it became a recognizable sub-branch of literary and cultural studies. One explanation for this may be that it was not until then that the environment itself became of broad and perhaps even urgent concern for many people. Ecocriticism defines itself as a practice of reading literature from an earth-centred (rather than human-centred) perspective. There is also an activist dimension to ecocriticism: at least part of the reason ecocritics want to discuss the centrality of nature in literature is to raise awareness more generally about the need for concern and indeed action with regard to the environment. Unsurprisingly, many ecocritics are also active in the environmental justice movement, whose concern is the uneven and generally inequitable distribution of the burden of environmental degradation (e.g. poorer countries tend to be more polluted than richer countries). *See also* ECOLOGICAL IMPERIALISM.

Further Reading: L. Buell *The Environmental Imagination* (1995).

G. Garrard *Ecocriticism* (2004).

C. Glotfelty and H. Fromm (eds.) *The Ecocriticism Reader: Landmarks in Ecology* (1995).

L. Marx *The Machine in the Garden: Technology and the Pastoral Ideal in America* (1964).
D. Phillips *The Truth of Ecology: Nature, Culture, and Literature in America* (2003).
R. Williams *The Country and the City* (1973).

ecofeminism A philosophical and political position which posits that there is a connection between the social mentality underpinning the domination of women in patriarchal society and the domination and degradation of nature by industrial capitalism. The term was coined by French feminist and science fiction writer, Françoise d'Eubonne in *Le Féminisme ou la mort* (1974) (Feminism or Death), a work that envisioned a future in which feminist attitudes prevailed, thus saving the planet from its seemingly inexorable course towards eco-death. Ecofeminism challenges the meaning of 'productivity', arguing that industrial, value-adding productivity is very far from the only form of productivity there is and that the hegemonic form is environmentally unsustainable. There is no single form of ecofeminism, but all forms have at their core the belief that addressing the causes of the imbalance of power between the sexes is essential to averting environmental disaster, that in other words it is only by changing deep-seated social and cultural attitudes that effective steps to save the planet can be made. Disagreement between the various branches of ecofeminism tends to hinge on whether the connection between women and nature is a source of power or oppression. A substantial body of work has developed under this rubric in most of the major languages.

Further Reading: G. Gaard and P Murphy *Ecofeminist Literary Criticism: Theory, Interpretation, Pedagogy* (1998).
M. Mies and V. Shiva *Ecofeminism* (1993).
K. Warren and N. Erkal *Ecofeminism: Women, Culture, Nature* (1997).

***École Freudienne de Paris* (Freudian School of Paris)** Founded by Jacques *Lacan in 1964 after he was expelled from the International Psychoanalytical Association, to train analysts to practise as psychoanalysts. The founding members of the School included Michel de *Certeau, Cornélius *Castoriadis, Félix *Guattari, and Luce *Irigaray. At the invitation of Louis *Althusser, the school was based at École Normale Supérieure. Its membership fluctuated between 150 and 600 according to the changes in political tides. Lacan dissolved the School abruptly in January 1980.

ecological imperialism A theory conceived by Alfred Crosby in his 1986 book *Ecological Imperialism: The Biological Expansion of Europe, 900–1900,* which proposes that colonization was not only a form of cultural and political tyranny, it was also a form of environmental terrorism. Indeed, Crosby goes so far as to argue that the ecological dimension was in fact primary. His reason for suggesting this is the evident fact that wherever colonists settled they brought with them diseases that devastated the local populations (of both people and plants and animals) as well as invasive pests and weeds that encroached on the existing flora and fauna, and eventually starved them out of existence. European-style agricultural practice utilized in dry regions like Australia and South Africa has had a catastrophic environmental impact. Crosby's work has sparked an enhanced interest in the role and significance of the environment in understanding colonial history in *Postcolonial Studies.

***écriture feminine* (feminine writing)** Hélène *Cixous coined this term in the widely read essay 'Le Rire de la Méduse' (The Laugh of Medusa) to describe a kind of writing that is outside of the masculine economy of patriarchal discourse. Cixous envisages *écriture feminine* as a form of writing that would, in psychoanalyst Jacques *Lacan's terms, reside or take place in the realm of the *real, rather than the *symbolic. In *psychoanalytic terms it therefore takes the form of the expression of the inexpressible and can only be arrived at via experimentation and play. Interestingly, Cixous's canonical examples of writers capable of attaining this effect are Shakespeare, Kleist, and Genet.

Further Reading: V. Andermatt Conley *Hélène Cixous: Writing the Feminine* (1984). I. Blyth and S. Sellers *Hélène Cixous: Live Theory* (2004).

ego (*Ich*) A central concept in *psychoanalysis which is present in Sigmund *Freud's earliest writings, but gains in prominence with the elaboration of the second *topography in 1920. The ego is that part of the psychical apparatus which acts as an agent of the self. However, it is only one part of the psychical apparatus and cannot be fully understood in isolation from the other components, namely the *id and the *superego. It is the product of a gradual process of differentiation in early childhood between the internal impulses of *desire rising up from the id and the equally powerful pressures of external reality (whose avatar is the superego). In contrast, Jacques *Lacan treats the ego as a kind of mirage, an illusory product of what he calls the *mirror phase. The ego is organized, whereas the id is not; it is a focal point for ideas, and more importantly for *cathexis. It is the ego which calibrates *pleasure and decides what is and what is not pleasurable. Freud described the ego as being like a rider sitting on a horse, the horse being the id; like a rider, the ego draws on the energy of the forces it sits astride (namely the *instincts), but it must also take care to defend itself against those very same forces, which have the power to unseat it. Symptoms like *anxiety and *hysteria are the ego's pathological response to the pressures of the id.

ego-ideal (*Ichideal*) The ideal form of 'I' the *ego *projects after it has overcome the *narcissism of childhood (or what *Freud calls the *ideal ego). In his early work, Freud makes little distinction between the ego-ideal and the *superego, but he gradually distinguishes it as that in the psychical apparatus which makes human collectivity possible. As he explains in his 1921 book on group psychology, in his view large groups are formed out of a collective fascination for powerful leaders: in submitting to their will, the subject effectively substitutes their ideal-ego for his or her own. The leader becomes the image of the ego the subject wishes he or she actually had.

Eisenstein, Sergei (1898–1948) Russian pioneer film-maker and film-theorist. He was born in Riga (then part of Imperial Russia, but now the capital of Latvia) to a middle-class family. His parents separated in 1905 and he moved with his mother to St Petersburg. He studied architecture and engineering at the Petrograd Institute of Civil Engineering. He participated in the 1917 revolutions and in 1918 he joined the Red Army. He was stationed in Minsk for three years, which brought him into contact with Japanese culture (Kabuki theatre, with its aesthetic of the unexpected, in particular, impressed him). In 1920 he moved to Moscow and joined the artistic fray there between *realism and *constructivism, siding with the latter. He worked initially in the theatre as a designer and progressed from there to film, which is where he made his mark, creating several enduring masterpieces such as *Battleship Potemkin* (1925), *October* (1927), and *Ivan the Terrible* (1944). As both film-maker and film-theorist, Eisenstein took a *dialectical view of cinema: it was, for him, at once a powerful rhetorical device and a higher means of knowing the universe. This is the principle behind the concept for which Eisenstein is best known, namely montage. Inspired by Japanese haiku poetry, but clearly owing a debt to both *Hegel and *Marx, montage achieves its effect through the collision of different kinds of *signs forcing the mind to reach for a higher unified meaning. Montage works in two directions at once: by pushing the audience towards a synthesis of meaning not present in the film itself, it also compels the audience to pay more attention to what is before them. In contrast to his Hollywood contemporaries, Eisenstein was not interested in obtaining a completely realistic look in his films; in his view, reality did not speak for itself. Eisenstein's *Film Form* (1949) and

Film Sense (1942) are standard starting points for virtually any study of the history of film.

Further Reading: D. Andrew *The Major Film Theories* (1976).

Empire A prophetic and utopian concept which attempts to theorize in philosophical terms the nature of the new paradigm of power and right that emerged alongside *globalization in the latter half of the 20th century. Conceived by Italian Marxist Antonio *Negri and American Marxist Michael *Hardt in their bestselling book *Empire* (2000), Empire is in effect a new form of *sovereignty, which is at once a brutal new power-regime bathed in blood and a new set of possibilities for liberation. Hardt and Negri claim that the sovereign authority of nation-states has declined absolutely in the post World War II era. Taking its place is a new logic of rule or *governmentality, Empire, which yokes together multinational corporations and supranational organizations (e.g. the International Monetary Fund) to produce not only a new form of subjectivity, but also a new form of value as well. Proof of its existence, they say, is to be found in the fact that no nation, not even the USA, is capable by itself of controlling the whole world in all its facets. Similarly, the fact that all nations are at the mercy of global trends in finance capital (as the sub-prime loan meltdown in 2007 made apparent) is symptomatic of their relative lack of *authority in the postmodern world. In contrast to the nation-state model of sovereignty, Empire is a decentred and *deterritorialized apparatus of rule, which has no history, no fixed centre and no boundary lines demarcating its territory. Contra *Lyotard, it endlessly espouses a master narrative in which it presents itself as universal and all-inclusive, as having always been there and encompassing the entire world right down to its ganglia. The acknowledged inspirations for the concept of Empire are *Foucault's notion of *biopower and *Deleuze and *Guattari's concept of desiring-production, but Hardt and Negri tax Foucault with failing to grasp biopower's true dynamism and Deleuze and Guattari with spoiling their concept by rendering power too chaotic. Although it appears bleak in that it is a form of power that, as Foucault argued with respect to biopower, is interested in populations rather than people, Empire has its affirmative dimensions too. Its modification of sovereignty has created a new political constituency, which Hardt and Negri refer to as the *multitude, which in their view is destined to invent new forms of democracy that will take us beyond Empire's uninviting landscape toward a more hopeful and egalitarian space. Empire has provoked fierce debate. The Right dismiss it out of hand as fanciful, while the Left demand more rigour in its empirical analyses.

Further Reading: G. Balakrishnan (ed.) *Debating Empire* (2003).
A. Boron *Empire and Imperialism: A Critical Reading of Michael Hardt and Antonio Negri* (2005).
M. Hardt and A. Negri *Empire* (2000).
M. Hardt and A. Negri *Multitude: War and Democracy in the Age of Empire* (2004).
A. Negri *Empire and Beyond* (2008).
P. Passavant and J. Dean *The Empire's New Clothes: Reading Hardt and Negri* (2003).

e

empiricism A mode of philosophical reasoning which holds that the only reliable source of knowledge is experience (i.e. that which can be observed). It denies that there is any knowledge outside of the realm of the observable. The main empiricist philosophers are: David Hume, John Locke, and John Stuart Mill. It therefore rejects concepts like Immanuel *Kant's notion of the categories, which cannot be sensed directly, but whose existence must be inferred (we cannot observe the universe in its entirety, but its existence may be inferred). Kant's entire philosophical career was directed against the empiricist philosophy and towards building an alternative, which he termed critical philosophy (the philosophical basis of *critical theory). In the wake of Kant, philosophy has split into two: continental and empiricist. The former, which is Kantian or critical in outlook, is so named by the latter because it is primarily European in origin, whereas empiricism is almost exclusively British and North American (also known as *analytic philosophy).

Empson, William (1906–84) British literary critic, often regarded as one of the greatest of his generation, and poet. A keen and intuitive exponent of 'close reading', Empson is often associated with *New Criticism and *Practical Criticism, but despite certain family resemblances his work differs from those schools in important ways. Perhaps most importantly, Empson always emphasized the importance of both the author's biography and historical context in understanding literature, two things the New Critics and Practical Critics assiduously avoided.

He was born in Yorkshire into a family of well-off intellectuals. At the age of 7 he won a scholarship to Winchester College, where he excelled in spite of the school's famous emphasis on sports and rugged discipline. From there he succeeded in obtaining a scholarship to Magdalene College at Cambridge, where he took a double first in Mathematics and English, graduating in 1929. His director of studies in English was I.A. *Richards, who recognized his genius and encouraged him to pursue his studies in that field. Legend has it that Empson wrote his first book, *Seven Types of Ambiguity* (1930) as undergraduate essays for Richards. It was an immediate and substantial success; it not only sold well, it was received warmly by the doyens of literary criticism is the UK and US, T.S. Eliot and John Crowe Ransom respectively, and quickly became required reading for university students.

In spite of his success, Empson's career faltered at this point. Condoms were found in his rooms by a servant and worse still so was a young woman. The University's reaction was swift and harsh. Empson was not only excluded from the university, he was forbidden to live in Cambridge. This prevented him from obtaining either an MA or PhD there. He moved to London, briefly, making a living with freelance writing and editing, then took a three-year post teaching English in Tokyo. There he acquired an interest in Noh theatre, becoming expert enough to write a book on it, which sadly was lost on his return to London in 1934. He remained in London for three years, in which time he completed his second major book, *Some Versions of Pastoral* (1935) as well as a major collection of poetry.

In 1937 he accepted a job at the National Peking University, but by the time he arrived in China the Japanese had invaded and there was in fact no job for him. He remained in China for two years, eking out a living teaching at various universities in exile there, constantly on the run from the Japanese forces. Relying on a prodigious memory and precious few books he was able to continue working, and started on his magnum opus *The Structure of Complex Words* (1951). He returned to China after the war, for another brief stint. In the early 1950s he accepted a Professorship at the University of Sheffield and worked there until his retirement. Empson wrote vehemently against *theory, and saw in *structuralism, *post-structuralism and *deconstruction a profound betrayal of good writing. Empson was a singular writer and though his work is widely admired it is difficult to emulate so it has not given rise to a school, or a large following.

Further Reading: J. Haffenden *William Empson* (2 volumes, 2005–6). C. Norris and N. Mapp *William Empson: The Critical Achievement* (1993).

encoding/decoding *See* CODE.

Engels, Friedrich (1820–95) German social scientist, philosopher and co-author with Karl *Marx of *The Communist Manifesto* (1848), one of the most influential texts of the 19th century. Engels's work is greatly overshadowed by his more famous collaborator, but it is often said with some justification that it was Engels who created *Marxism. Not only did he provide Marx with crucial financial assistance enabling him to carry out his work, he did a great deal to promote his work as well.

Engels was born in Barmen in what is now Wuppertal, a northern Rhineland city in Germany. The eldest son of a textile manufacturer, he was compelled to join the family business at a young age, though his inclinations actually tended in the opposite direction towards radical philosophy and politics, a passion he kept alive by writing. In 1842, his father sent him to work in his company's Manchester factory in an effort to distract him from his leanings. On the way to Manchester, as fate would have it, he stopped in Cologne to visit the offices of the *Rheinische Zeitung*, a radical periodical for which he had contributed several articles, and there he met Karl Marx. The two famously did not hit it off immediately, but the seeds of a powerful working friendship were nonetheless sown in this encounter.

Manchester, then the global centre for textile manufacturing, and one of the most ghastly examples of how cruel laissez-faire capitalism can be, brought Engels face to face with the effects of the transformation in the *mode of production brought about by the Industrial Revolution. His observations were brought together in *Die Lage der arbeitenden Klasse in England* (1845), translated as *The Condition of the English Working Class in 1844* (1887) as a cautionary tale to his countrymen about the dangers of industrialization. He showed that the workers and their families in Manchester suffered considerably higher rates of illness and premature death than their counterparts in less industrialized cities.

Engels returned to the continent in 1844, stopping first in Paris to once again visit Marx. This time their meeting went well and they began a collaborative partnership that was to last for the rest of their lives. Engels helped Marx finish his attack on the so-called 'Young Hegelians', *Dieheilige Familie* (1845), translated as *The Holy Family*. The following year they were both forced to move to Brussels for political reasons. There they were contacted by the German Communist League and asked to prepare a programme statement outlining their goals. The result, which was published in February 1848, one of the most tumultuous years in European history, was *Manifest der Kommunistischen Partei*, translated as *The Manifesto of the Communist Party* (1850). Engels would later say, rather modestly, that although both their names were on the book's cover, the reality was that it was all Marx's work.

Both Marx and Engels returned to Germany in 1848 and together started and edited a new daily newspaper *Neue Rheinische Zeitung* (New Rhinelander Times) in Cologne. But the newspaper was soon suppressed for its anti-government stance. Engels took part in the revolution of 1848–49 as an aide-de-camp to August Willich, but the uprising was soon crushed and he was forced to flee. He escaped to Switzerland and from there he made his way back to England, where he remained for the rest of his life. Although he hated it, he took a position with his father's firm in Manchester, using his income to support both himself and Marx. He retired from business in 1870 and moved to London, where Marx was living.

From 1870 until his death, Engels occupied himself with editing Marx's great, but unfinished work *Das Kapital*. He also found time to write a number of works himself, the best known of which are translated as: *Anti-Dühring: Herr Eugen Dühring's Revolution in Science* (1878), *Socialism: Utopian and Scientific* (1880); and *The Origin of Family, Private Property and the State* (1884).

Further Reading: T. Carver *Friedrich Engels: His Life and Thought* (1989).
J. Green *Engels: A Revolutionary Life* (2008).

Enlightenment (*Aufklärung*) A broad intellectual movement in Europe characterized by a foregrounding of the power of reason and a setting aside of superstition. There is no consensus as to when exactly the Enlightenment began, but it is not generally thought to have started much before the publication in 1637 of René Descartes's *Discours de la méthode pour bien conduire sa raison, et chercher la verité dans les sciences* (Discourse on the Method of Rightly Conducting One's Reason and of Seeking Truth in the Sciences), in which the famous slogan celebrating the centrality of reason '*Je pense, donc je suis*' (I think, therefore I am) appears. Other highpoints include: The Encylopédistes, the group of authors led by Denis Diderot and Jean le Rond d'Alembert who wrote the massive *Encyclopédie, ou dictionnaire raisonné des sciences, des arts et des metiers* (Encyclopedia, or a systematic dictionary of the sciences, arts, and crafts), between 1751 and 1772, with the express purpose of changing the way people think by foregrounding scientifically acquired knowledge and banishing superstition; the Scottish Enlightenment, contemporaneous with the Encylopédistes, whose leading figures were David Hume, Adam Smith, and Robert Burns; in the US the group of statesmen who wrote the bill of rights were also considered part of the Enlightenment movement. In *critical theory, however, Enlightenment is usually dated by the publication in 1784 of Immanuel *Kant's essay 'Beantwortung der Frage: Was ist Aufklärung?' (Answering the Question: What is Enlightenment?), which famously defines Enlightenment as the coming to an end of humanity's period of intellectual immaturity. *See also* DIALECTIC OF ENLIGHTENMENT.

Further Reading: M. Foucault 'What is Enlightenment?' in P. Rabinow (ed.) *The Foucault Reader* (1984).
J. Israel *Enlightenment Contested: Philosophy, Modernity, and the Emancipation of Man 1670–1752* (2008).
R. Porter *The Enlightenment* (2001).

epic A long, narrative poem praising the deeds and person of a hero, often for their efforts in either founding or saving a particular community. The epic is an extremely old form in literature. Indeed, the oldest known written text is *The Epic of Gilgamesh*, whose origin is put at more than 3000 years BC. Other well-known epics include: Homer's Trojan War poems, *The Iliad* and *The Odyssey*, thought to date from around 800 BC, the slightly later Indian work, *Mahābhārata*, and the Anglo-Saxon *Beowulf* from 800 AD. The principal defining feature of the epic is the grandness of scale and the sense that the destiny of the individual is the destiny of the whole world. In contemporary literature it is primarily the fantasy genre, typified by J.R.R. Tolkien's work, which adheres to the epic form, in prose, though, rather than verse.

Epic Theatre A highly politicized, *Marxist-oriented form of theatre developed in Germany in the early part of the 20th century by Erwin Piscator. It is, however, Piscator's one-time collaborator Bertolt *Brecht who is the better known exponent of Epic Theatre. Indeed Brecht's name is virtually synonymous with Epic Theatre, despite the fact that it had a number of other quite prominent adherents including both Mayakovsky and Meyerhold. Doubtless this is due to Brecht's fame as well as his extensive writings on the subject. Epic Theatre is typified by its deliberately anti-realist and anti-naturalist approach. It aims to shatter the sometimes stupefying 'spell' theatre can cast over its audience by constantly reminding the audience that what they are seeing is both artificial and contrived and something that should be evaluated and judged. Brecht rejected theatre that was spectacular or melodramatic; he wanted theatre that made people think. For example, actors move in and out of character and comment on what their character is doing, perhaps expressing distaste; the dialogue and the narrative play havoc with continuity and temporality, so characters say things like 'I'm just off to the thirty years war'; and intertitles, like they use in silent cinema, are used to create a counterview to what is occurring on stage. Brecht often said theatre should be like a car crash with the audience called on to bear witness to what happened and determine for themselves how the event should be assessed. *See also* THEATRE OF CRUELTY; THEATRE OF THE ABSURD.

episteme French historian Michel *Foucault uses this term, which literally means knowledge in Greek, to name the set of conditions which enable something to be known. The episteme, for Foucault, is the condition of possibility of knowledge, and in his view there can only ever be one episteme at any one moment in history. It is not, however, the body of knowledge itself. In this regard, it is similar in many respects to Gilles *Deleuze and Félix *Guattari's later concept of the *rhizome inasmuch that what it actually names is the dispersed and discontinuous *relations* between the multitude of elements that combine to produce so-called knowledge.

epistemological break The moment of rupture separating science from its non-scientific past. After the rupture the non-scientific past comes to be seen as so much superstition. In this way, the history of science is understood not so much a process of discovery as the overcoming of the obstacles to thought posed by knowledge itself. It thus entails not simply the addition of new knowledge, but the reorganization of the very possibility of knowledge. It changes the conditions of what is and can be known. The concept was conceived by Gaston *Bachelard and further developed by Georges *Canguilhem, but it is perhaps the work of Michel *Foucault which has done the most to demonstrate the importance of this concept by taking it outside of the strictly scientific domain Bachelard and Canguilhem remained in. Foucault described epistemological breaks not only in the history of medicine, but also in the history of prisons, sexuality, and psychiatry.

epistemology The study or inquiry into the origin, possibility, and constitution of knowledge. Its central questions are: what does it mean to know something and by what means are we able to have knowledge? In asking these questions it also brings into play issues to do with doubt, scepticism, and truth, because implicit in the question of what it means to know something is the issue of whether one's knowledge can ever be complete.

epochē In Classical Greek philosophy it refers to the suspension of judgement or scepticism so that an argument may be heard in full before a decision concerning its merit is taken. German *phenomenologist Edmund *Husserl uses this term (although it is usually rendered in English as 'bracketing') to describe a methodological procedure of setting aside one's personal knowledge about the world so as to see more clearly its conceptual core. The aim is to achieve a pure perception of phenomena, cleansed of presuppositions and prejudices.

essence The singular property or attribute that makes a particular thing what it is. To put it another way, the singular property or attribute that must be there for a particular thing to be that thing. The contemporary form of this is DNA sequencing, which identifies exactly what genetic material must be present for a certain type of organism to be that organism. DNA markers are in this sense the scientific equivalents of essences. *See also* ESSENTIALISM.

essentialism A mode of philosophy which determines *ontology, that is the nature of being, by distinguishing between two types of properties a particular thing may have: those which are essential to it, and those which are merely accidental. The former are sometimes referred to as *essences. In contemporary critical theory the most common form of this way of thinking is to be found in gender studies, where sexual difference is held by certain thinkers to be an essential difference between men and women and by extension a common cause for action (in both a positive and negative sense—*sexism is the bias of one *gender against another, while *feminism is similarly an action of one gender against another). The work of Judith *Butler, however, challenges the essentialist position by offering a conception of gender that focuses more on the 'accidents' of *performativity. Similarly, Donna *Haraway challenges the essentialist view of gender by challenging the underlying assumption that it is possible to distinguish between male and female in an absolute sense to begin with. *See also* STRATEGIC ESSENTIALISM.

estrangement-effect (*Verfremdung, seffekt*) Bertolt *Brecht's term (also sometimes translated as alienation-effect) for the moment in a work of art when that which used to appear natural suddenly appears historical, when that which was thought of as timeless and eternal is seen as deliberately caused and altered across time. Its purpose is political because it aims to overturn the paralysing sense that things have always been 'this way' and therefore that there is nothing that can be done to change them. Brecht's principal means of doing this was to stage theatre in such a way that the viewer is denied the habitual comfort of forgetting that they are watching a play and becoming (what *psychoanalytic film critics call) *sutured into the events on stage. Thus he would discourage actors from 'becoming' their characters and using that to elicit the empathy of the audience, preferring that they create a sense of 'distance' between themselves and their character that would put the audience in two minds about what they were watching (Brecht's ideal manner of viewing, he famously said, was that of the sports fan evaluating a boxing match). French cultural critic Roland *Barthes deployed this principal in *Mythologies* (1957), translated as *Mythologies* (1972), which is a spirited attack on everything that appears 'natural' in modern life in the era of *late capitalism. *See also* COGNITIVE ESTRANGEMENT; *OSTRANENIE*.

Further Reading: F. Jameson *Brecht and Method* (1998).

devote to Facebook while they are at work. For Certeau, the everyday is that which escapes any and all attempts to either control it or document it. As such, it doesn't even leave a trace and Certeau is scathing of attempts by sociologists to quantify it statistically or otherwise. Inspiring though this work has been from the point of view of trying to think about the possibility of resistance, it is also self-defeating inasmuch as its research object is by its own definition impossible to grasp.

Between these two poles of interest in and indifference to the material, defined by Lefebvre and Certeau, there are a number of important authors whose work has touched on the question of the everyday. Most prominently, these include, Maurice *Blanchot for whom the everyday is the ineffable; Fernand *Braudel whose exhaustive trilogy *The Structures of Everyday Life* (1975–9) plumbs the depths of the everyday in all its minutiae going back to the Middle Ages; Erving *Goffman for whom the everyday is a performance; Raoul *Vaneigem, the Belgian *Situationist, and Agnes Heller for whom (following *Lukács) the everyday is the site of possible redemptive politics. To this list must be added the name Roland *Barthes, whose great *Brecht-inspired *Mythologies* (1957), translated as *Mythologies* (1972) continues to set the standard for perceiving the extraordinary in the ordinary.

Further Reading: M. Gardiner *Critiques of Everyday Life* (2000).
B. Highmore *Everyday Life and Cultural Theory* (2002).
A. Kaplan and K. Ross, (eds.) 'Everyday Life', special issue of Yale French Studies vol 73 (1987).
J. Roberts *Philosophizing Everyday Life* (2006).

existentialism A mode of philosophy which emerged in the latter part of the 19th century and came into prominence in the middle part of the 20th century. It foregrounds the perplexing condition of the modern *subject who, in the absence of God, is forced to contend with the meaninglessness of life. This does not necessarily mean that existentialism is a secular philosophy, though largely speaking it is, because the absence of God can be understood to mean that humans have forsaken God or that God has forsaken humans (i.e. God still exists, He just doesn't involve Himself in human affairs). Both of the so-called 'fathers' of existentialism, Søren Kierkegaard and Friedrich *Nietzsche, start from this position and argue for a *metaphysics of truth and freedom in response—*authenticity thus replaces piety as the new condition for the righteous to aspire to. Instead of being true to God, one must rather be true to oneself, but this is difficult for two reasons: first, there is the apparent logical impossibility of the self knowing the self; second, there is the problem of knowing how one should act. In the early 20th century, *phenomenology confronted the question of how the subject makes sense of their world, and although it did not concern itself overly much with the metaphysical question of how one should act it had a significant influence on existentialism all the same because of its account of *apperception (derived from *Kant), which solves the first problem. The second problem, namely the question of how one should act preoccupied existentialism's most important theorist Jean-Paul *Sartre and answering it effectively became his life's work. Sartre popularized the term existentialism (which he borrowed from Gabriel Marcel, who first used it in the mid 1920s), in his short book *L'existentialisme est un humanisme* (1946), translated as *Existentialism and Humanism* (1948), which summarized and simplified his previous book, *L'Être et le Néant* (1943), translated as *Being and Nothingness* (1958), which is for many the definitive work on the subject. Sartre's novels, particularly *La Nausée* (1938), translated as *Nausea* (1959), are also taken to be important contributions to existentialism because they dramatize the situation of the subject confronted by the brute fact of existence. The label existentialism has also been applied to the work of both Martin *Heidegger and Karl *Jaspers, though neither of them accepted the term themselves.

Further Reading: S. Earnshaw *Existentialism: A Guide for the Perplexed* (2006). T. Flynn *Existentialism: A Very Short Introduction* (2006).

SEE WEB LINKS

- A basic introduction to existentialism.

Expressionism A pan-European movement in the arts—especially painting—that developed in the first third of the 20th century. Rejecting impressionism and naturalism, expressionism is anti-realist in both approach and subject matter. It aims to 'render visible' (to use one of its leading artists Paul Klee's famous phrase) that which escapes representational painting, such as the raw affects of emotion, sexuality and spirituality. Inspired by the writings of the founder of *psychoanalysis, Sigmund *Freud, which explore the hidden world of the *unconscious, expressionism wants to shed light on the complex impulses underpinning daily life. The leading figures of this movement were the Viennese painters Gustav Klimt and Egon Schiele and the Norwegian Edvard Munch whose 'Scream' paintings are perhaps the sine qua non of the Expressionist style. *See also* GERMAN EXPRESSIONISM.

***fabula* and *sjužet* (story and plot)** A distinction drawn by *Russian Formalism between the story told (*fabula*) and the imaginative way in which that story is actually narrated (*sjužet*). As Victor Erlich observes in his definitive account of the movement, *Russian Formalism* (1955), the basic story of Tolstoy's *Anna Karenina* (1869) is fairly meagre—reduced to its barebones it is a melodramatic account of a young woman who falls in love with an unworthy man and is driven to suicide—but that gives no indication of the richness of the telling of the story, which in the view of many (not least the author himself) places the novel high up in the pantheon of all time greats. The distinction is especially useful for thinking about crime fiction, which relies for its effect on the disjunction between the events as they must have happened (*fabula*) and the order in which they are discovered or narrated (*sjužet*). The Russian Formalists tended to regard such disjunctions as a measure of a particular work's literariness (**literaturnost*). *See also* DEFAMILIARIZATION.

face (*visage*) Emmanuel *Levinas's term for the presence of the *Other. It is an ambiguous concept because it simultaneously does and does not refer to actual human faces. It does refer to human faces inasmuch as the face is the most expressive part of the human body, but does not refer to actual human expressions. The face is not an object of experience or perception for Levinas, it is rather an epiphany or revelation—it transforms us, but does not yield knowledge. Levinas uses the notion of the face to think through the problematic of the self's relation with the infinitely Other. The face is what separates the self from the Other, thus stopping the Other from annihilating it. By the same token, the face appears in 'my' world, but I cannot harm it. It is not *of* this world.

Further Reading: C. Davis *Levinas: An Introduction* (1996).

false consciousness A *Marxist concept describing the masking effect of *ideology, which cloaks the true conditions of things, thus inhibiting the mobilization of political activism. Thomas Frank's bestselling *What's the Matter of Kansas* (2004) offered a convincing portrait of what false consciousness looks like in contemporary society by documenting the fact that voters in Kansas in the first part of the

21st century seemed unaware that voting Republican meant they were effectively voting against their own interests. By prioritizing cultural issues, and neglecting labour and industrial issues, voters demonstrated that they were not conscious of what is politically significant. Obviously, from a Marxist perspective, the economic considerations are always given primacy. But one might just as well argue that the cultural issues are primary. Marxist tradition, dating back to *Marx himself, holds the rather *utopian view that false consciousness can be shattered by knowledge, but later critics like Slavoj *Žižek, who aligns false consciousness with *fantasy, argue that people resist taking on board the implications of knowledge. This position, of knowing the truth of one's situation, but not acting as though it were true, is known as *cynical reason.

Fanon, Frantz (1925–61) Psychiatrist, activist, and revolutionary theorist. Fanon was born on the Caribbean island of Martinique. His father was the descendent of slaves and his mother of mixed race. His family were comfortably middle class and he attended an excellent school. One of his teachers was poet and activist Aimé *Césaire, who would be an influence for the rest of his life, although he rejected the latter's theory of *négritude. During World War II, he fought with the Free French Forces in Europe. He was wounded in 1944 and received the Croix de Guerre. After the war he returned to Martinique in order to complete his Baccalaureate. While he was there he assisted in Césaire's mayoral campaign. He then returned to France to study medicine and psychiatry in Lyon, where he was also able to attend lectures by Maurice *Merleau-Ponty. Qualifying in 1951, he practised in France for a couple of years and then went to Algeria in 1953 to take up the position of *chef de service* at the Blida-Joinville Psychiatric Hospital. He stayed there until 1957, when he was deported.

His first book, *Peau noire, masques blancs* (1952), translated as *Black Skin, White Masks* (1986), was written while still in France, but drew on his experiences in Martinique and Algeria, where he had been stationed during the war. It is a study of the psychological damage done by colonialism and racism combined. Theoretically it draws on Jean-Paul *Sartre (who would later write an infamous preface for his last book), particularly his analysis of anti-Semitism, and the *psychoanalysis of Jacques *Lacan, in a bid to analyse what he saw as a debilitating inferiority complex amongst his black peers. He also recognized that there was a superiority complex at work in white people that also needed to be addressed if progressive change was to be made.

Over the next few years, he concentrated on the practical matters of psychiatry, developing therapeutic strategies that Gilles *Deleuze and Félix *Guattari would later acknowledge as a precursor to what they called *schizoanalysis. Fanon ceased to focus exclusively on the psychosexual history of the individual and began to factor in socio-cultural concerns. His extensive writings on this subject have not been fully studied nor anthologized, though there is a useful selection published in a special issue of the journal *Information psychiatrique* (1975) dedicated to Fanon. When the Algerian Revolution erupted in 1954, Fanon got to see at first hand the effects of colonial violence. He joined the Front de Libération Nationale (FLN) almost immediately, and used his position to assist the revolution. It was for this reason that he was expelled from Algeria in 1957.

Following his expulsion, Fanon made his way in secret to Tunis. There he joined the editorial collective of the journal *El Moudjahid* for which he wrote to the end of his life. He attended conferences on decolonization throughout Africa and reported on these for the journal. Some of these pieces are collected in *Pour la révolution Africaine* (1964), translated as *Toward the African Revolution* (1994). It was in this period, too, that Fanon wrote the work which made him internationally famous, albeit posthumously: *Les Damnés de la terre* (1961), translated as *The Wretched of the Earth* (1965), the title of which is drawn from Karl *Marx. This work became infamous for its discussion of the necessity of violence, not just to win power, but also to imprint the minds of the revolutionaries with the significance of their undertaking. Its message reverberated throughout the *Third World, which was then in the throes of a radical process of *decolonization.

He was diagnosed with leukaemia in his early 30s. At first he sought treatment in the USSR. When this didn't work, he tried his hand in the US. But it was all to no avail. He died at Bethesda hospital, Maryland at the age of 36. Little known in his own lifetime, particularly in France where his books sold hardly at all (not helped by the fact they were frequently banned for discussing the war in Algeria, which the French government did not want to admit to or discuss), Fanon has become a symbol of postcolonial struggle. His name is placed in the same pantheon of legendary figures of the 20th century as Che Guevera, Malcolm X, and Steve Biko, all of whom were themselves inspired by his writings.

His life has inspired at least one novel, John Edgar Wideman's *Fanon* (2008), and at least one film, Isaac Julien's 1996 documentary *Frantz Fanon: Black Skin White Mask*. The great Italian director Gillo Pontecorvo drew on *Les Damnés de la terre* in filming *The Battle of Algiers* (1966). Rage Against the Machine cite him in their 1996 release *Evil Empire*. Virtually all the major *postcolonial theorists from Homi *Bhabha to Henry Louis *Gates pay homage to his work.

Further Reading: N. Gibson *Fanon: The Postcolonial Imagination* (2003).

L. Gordon, *Fanon and the Crisis of European Man* (1995).
D. Macey *Frantz Fanon: A Life* (2000).
A. Sekyi-Otu *Fanon's Dialectic of Experience* (1996).

fantasy In *psychoanalysis, fantasy is the *imaginary staging of an *unconscious *desire. Sigmund *Freud's rejection of his own *seduction theory hinged on his realization of the importance fantasy plays in the psychic life of the subject. What he realized is that it is enough for a particular act to be fantasized about for it to be significant to a particular subject, and that it doesn't have to have actually taken place. Jacques *Lacan makes fantasy the central concept in his account of psychoanalysis, but gives it another role to play. Whereas Freud saw fantasy as being in some sense in conflict with reality, for Lacan, fantasy is at once a defence against reality and a necessary support for reality. This latter proposition is fundamental to the work of Lacanian psychoanalyst Slavoj *Žižek.

femininity The culturally relative ideal *gender *identity for women. Varying substantially from one historical period to the next and from one geographic region to another, femininity is considered by *feminism to be an imposed system of rules governing how women should act, look, feel, and even think within a particular society. Femininity is generally portrayed as the weaker, lesser *Other of *masculinity; a fact that clearly underpins the *psychoanalytic concept of penis envy, which supposes that all young girls actually want to be boys on some level. So internalized are these rules and cultural assumptions supposed to be, they define not merely how a woman should comport herself, but what it actually means to be a woman. This can readily be seen by doing a book search using 'femininity' as a keyword—the plethora of titles this throws up, from works in philosophy and critical theory to self-help manuals (both of the psychological and beauty tips variety) and autobiographies, is astonishing. A similar search for masculinity yields only a fraction of the results and nothing like the variety. That femininity is a constrictive demand placed on women by society has been recognized by female writers throughout the ages, but it was Simone de *Beauvoir who first theorized it. Her argument was that by consenting to play the roles femininity demands, women effectively consent to their own oppression. Recent work on femininity has been powerfully influenced by Judith *Butler, particularly her concept of performativity (which she derives from J.L. *Austin's linguistic concept of the *performative), by means of which she argues that gender roles are paradoxical inasmuch that they aren't fixed and can be varied—women can dress and act like men if they want to and vice versa—but one cannot choose not to have a gendered identity.

Further Reading: J. Butler *Gender Trouble: Feminism and the Subversion of Identity* (1990).

feminism See overleaf.

feminist theory The extension of *feminism (understood as a practical social movement concerned to address the inequality of the sexes) into theoretical discourse. Undoubtedly one of the most important and influential intellectual currents of the 20th century (every bit the equal of *Marxism and *psychoanalysis), Feminist theory encompasses most disciplines from art and architecture through to science and technology, but it is predominantly concentrated in the social sciences and the humanities. As diverse as it is, and the varieties of feminist theory are almost without limit, at its core it has four principal concerns, which are to: (i) elucidate the origins and causes of *gender inequality; (ii) explain the operation and persistence of this state of affairs; (iii) delineate effective strategies to either bring about full equality between the sexes or at least ameliorate the effects of ongoing inequality; and (iv) imagine a world in which sexual inequality no longer exists. Of the four, feminist theory has tended to prioritize the first two, leaving the strategic questions to women working in the field, so to speak, in the various advocacy groups like the National Organization for Women founded in the US in 1966; while the task of imagining the future has been parcelled out to creative writers, particularly those working in SF like Ursula LeGuin and Marge Piercy. The decision to prioritize one or other of these four problematics is what gives shape to the specific feminisms.

The causes of sexual inequality are almost impossible to trace since for all of recorded history it was already an established fact. Therefore it is ultimately a matter for pure speculation. The most widely accepted hypothesis is that in prehistoric times biology placed women in a subordinate position to men because pregnancy and childrearing render them vulnerable and in need of assistance both to obtain food and fend off predators. While there is probably some truth to this strand of the *biological determinism hypothesis from an anthropological point of view, the practical need to protect women does not explain the widespread denigration of women and their socialization as lesser beings. By the same token, as societies became more prosperous and their technology more sophisticated women's vulnerability diminished, but if anything the positioning of them as

FEMINISM

One of the most important social movements of the past two centuries and certainly the social movement which has brought about the most enduring and progressive transformation of human society on a global scale. It is customary to divide the history of feminism into a *First, *Second, and *Third Wave, with each period signalling a different era in the struggle to attain equality between the sexes. Today feminism means many different things to different people, but at its core, if one goes back to its origins in the late 18th century, it is primarily a social movement for the emancipation of women. That movement was slow to start, and it wasn't until the late 1880s that the term 'feminism' actually appeared. Before then, the more usual term was 'women's rights'. The first advocates for women's rights were for the most part lonely voices pleading against obvious and manifest iniquities in society's treatment of women.

This was certainly the case in one of the earliest self-consciously feminist works, namely Mary Wollstonecraft's *A Vindication of the Rights of Woman* (1792), which was written at the height of the French Revolution. Establishing what would become a common theme throughout much feminist writing, Wollstonecraft conducts her critique on two fronts: on the one hand, she criticizes *patriarchal society (as it would later be called) for the unjust way it limits women's rights, as well as their opportunity for education, self-expression, and economic independence; while on the other hand, she criticizes women for buying into *femininity which, in her view, turns women into mere 'spaniels' and 'toys'. Wollstonecraft's solution was better education for young women, not the granting of equal rights. So in this sense, one might say feminism begins not with Wollstonecraft but rather with the various Women's Suffrage movements that sprang up in the early 1800s.

Achieving full voting rights for all women regardless of age, *race, or marital status took more than a century of struggle, easily justifying Juliet Mitchell's claim that feminism is 'the longest revolution'. The focus on voting rights, as important as these are, tends to obscure the fact that it was not only the right to vote that women were fighting for, though this was of course emblematic inasmuch that once they could vote they would be able to use the democratic process to bring about other forms of change. In point of fact, however, even after women obtained the right to vote in most parts of the world at the turn of the 20th century, it was still several decades before full equality was obtained. And many would say that it has not yet been obtained.

It is worth mentioning that throughout the long First Wave of feminism women fought against several other injustices as well, of which three are key. (i) Women were restricted in terms of the ownership of property, requiring them to marry so as to inherit, thus preventing them from attaining true independence (it is this issue which exercises proto-feminist writers like Jane Austen and Charlotte Brontë). (ii) Women did not have full rights over their own body, which meant they had no legal protection against sexual violence (e.g. the idea that a husband could rape his wife was not admitted as law until late in the 20th century). (iii) Women were discriminated against in the workplace, which not only meant women were paid less than men for the same work, it also restricted them from applying for certain jobs, denied them promotion, and made no allowance for maternity leave. Many of these problems persist today.

Once suffrage was granted, the women's rights movement fell into decline, and remained quiescent until the late 1950s and early 1960s when it was reignited by a new generation of activists who called themselves the Second Wave of feminism. Betty *Friedan's *The Feminine Mystique* (1963) is generally credited as the tipping point for this second round of political struggle. Echoing Wollstonecraft, she argued that women were victims of a false belief in the promise of femininity and urged them to look beyond their domestic situation for fulfilment. The National Organization for Women (NOW) was formed in 1966 and became the central focus, in the US, for feminist activism. Its goal was the ratification of an Equal Rights Amendment to the Constitution, which it did not manage to achieve in full, but it nonetheless made giant strides towards it. Second Wave feminism also took the view that equality between the sexes would only come about if there was a sea change in cultural attitudes on the part of both women and men. Authors like Germaine *Greer and Kate *Millett called for a sexual liberation as well, arguing that women could alter their status as the second sex (to borrow the title of Simone de *Beauvoir's important book) by overturning the double standards applied to their sexuality and behaviour.

The Second Wave of feminism came to an end in the early 1980s partly as a result of its successes—many women felt that all the relevant battles had been fought and won—but primarily because of the change in political climate. The Reagan-Thatcher era was very unfriendly to equal rights and it rolled back many of the gains that had been made. This is the period of the so-called 'culture wars' when feminism was caricatured as mere political correctness and its political agenda scorned in the press. Third Wave feminist scholar

Susan Faludi documents this in her *Backlash: The Undeclared War Against Women* (1991). But there were also problems within feminism. Feminist scholars of colour, particularly those from the *Third World, argued very forcefully that feminism neglected *race and *class. These issues are central to the Third Wave, which many cite as beginning with the outraged response of feminist critics to the treatment of Anita Hill during the Senate-confirmation hearings for US Supreme Court nominee Clarence Thomas in 1991. Hill testified that Thomas sexually harrassed her when she was working in the Department of Education, and later at the Equal Employment Opportunity Commission. Thomas flatly denied this, and was subsequently confirmed by the Senate.

Further Reading: C. Colebrook *Gender* (2004).
M. Walters *Feminism: A Very Short Introduction* (2006).
C. Weedon *Feminist Practice and Poststructuralist Theory* (1996).

subordinate seemed to harden. For obvious reasons, then, the issue that has exercised feminist theorists the most is the one of persistence: why does *sexism continue after the principal justification for it has long since ceased to obtain?

There are three basic answers to this question: first, biology continues to be a determining factor; second, that it is in men's interest to maintain the subordination of women; and third, women have been complicit with their own oppression. Surprisingly, perhaps, *radical feminists like Shulamith *Firestone support the first answer, although she then uses it as a stage to call for the use of biotechnology to put an end to women's reproductive role. Not surprisingly, the second answer has very widespread support, and shows the influence of Marxism. In effect, it equates feminist struggle with *class struggle. The third answer, which is perhaps the most painful inasmuch as it is a form of self-criticism, has given rise to the most debate, and perhaps for that reason has contributed the most in the way of ideas for achieving the strategic goal of equality between the sexes. Both *First Wave and *Second Wave feminists agree that *femininity—understood as a male-imposed ideal of how women should look and act—is a major limiting factor for feminist politics. So from Mary Wollstonecraft to Germaine *Greer and Kate *Millett feminist writers have advocated to a greater or lesser degree the abandoning of the practice of self-denial most versions of femininity demand. Interestingly, some *Third Wave feminists have argued against this, calling instead for a celebration of femininity.

Setting aside an imposed *identity is of course liberating, but it also creates an identity crisis. Simone de *Beauvoir, one of the most important feminist writers of the 20th century, famously declared that woman is made not born, thereby making identity a key agenda item for feminist research, particularly amongst the so-called French feminists—Hélène *Cixous, Catherine Clément, Luce *Irigaray, Julia *Kristeva, and Michèle *Le Douffe—who draw on a wide variety of philosophical sources, but focus particularly on *psychoanalysis, to try to elucidate what 'woman' means in our time. The answers to this question are not unproblematic and within the field there has been considerable debate as to how to handle the material differences between women (e.g. differences of *class, *race, ethnicity, religion, and sexuality). This debate has progressively refined a feminist standpoint from which to view and evaluate the world, which has in turn enabled the development of *ecofeminism and feminist ethics as well as feminist film criticism and literary criticism. In this way feminist theory does not so much imagine an alternative future as carve out a new way of thinking and acting in the present.

Further Reading: C. Colebrook *Gender* (2004).
M. Walters *Feminism: A Very Short Introduction* (2006).
C. Weedon *Feminist Practice and Poststructuralist Theory* (1996).

fetishism A psychological process in which an apparently non-sexual thing (animate or inanimate) is given the value of a sexual *object. For example, the proverbial shoe fetishist finds the sight of shoes arousing. On Freud's reading, the fetishist starts by desiring to look at the sexual parts of the body (e.g. face, breasts, and genitals), but out of fear and shame does not, and looks away; however, by looking away consistently, the thing they look away at, such as another person's feet, rather than their face, is able to remind them of the thing they actually wanted to see. The process is complete when the alternate object becomes the actual object of desire.

See also COMMODITY FETISHISM.

Feyerabend, Paul (1924–94) Austrian philosopher of science. Born in Vienna, Feyerabend was drafted into the *Arbeitsdienst* (Works Service) upon graduation from High School in 1942. He then volunteered for the army, hoping the war would be over before he finished his training. But that was not to be and he was sent to the Eastern Front where he was wounded. After the war he tried his hand at several things, even working for a time in theatre. He then went back to school initially studying sociology and history, but soon switching to physics, before settling finally on philosophy. He then studied with Karl *Popper at the London School of Economics. Feyerabend was employed for most of his life at the

University of California, Berkeley, but he also held a variety of visiting appointments outside the US Feyerabend's work was notable for his argument against the accepted position that there is only one form of science and that the key to scientific progress is the application of rigorous scientific methods. He shows rather that there are multiple forms of science, none with a particular claim to privilege and that progress occurs in an anarchistic fashion, i.e. when rules are broken rather than adhered to. Feyerabend's principal works include: *Against Method: An Outline of an Anarchistic Theory of Knowledge* (1975); *Farewell to Reason* (1987); and *Conquest of Abundance* (1999).

Further Reading: J. Preston *Feyerabend: Philosophy, Science and Society* (1997).

field The network of social relations, regulations and adaptive possibilities specific to a social group, which may be defined in terms of location (such as a town or village), profession (artists, academics, and so forth), or class (blue collar, white collar, etc.). Developed by French sociologist Pierre *Bourdieu, the field is an objectifiable structured space, which means its rules for inclusion and exclusion, as well as the nature of the strategies one may employ while operating within its boundaries, can be identified and articulated. As Bourdieu demonstrates in *Homo Academicus* (1984), translated as *Homo Academicus* (1988) and *Les Règles de l'art* (1992), translated as *The Rules of Art* (1996), it is possible to identify the structure of both academia and the art world and indeed any other sphere of life. With respect to art, Bourdieu dismisses the idea of the creative genius labouring in isolation as an impossibility—the artist, he shows, must be aware of a field (not just the 'art world' as it is sometimes said, but the very possibility of art itself looked at from a social perspective) in order to know what counts as art and to know where its ontological boundaries are so they can be pushed. It is in the encounter with this field that the artist is formed. Bourdieu developed this term in conjunction with *habitus and *practice.

Further Reading: M. Grenfell *Pierre Bourdieu: Key Concepts* (2008).

film noir A film movement—or, better yet, film style—that began in the US in the early 1940s and persisted until the late 1950s. The term was created by French film critics by analogy with *roman noir*, the French term for hard-boiled crime novels. Following the end of World War II large quantities of American films were imported into France, forcing French critics to take notice of Hollywood productions whereas previously they had written them off almost as a matter of course. John Huston's 1941 film of Dashiell Hammett's *Maltese Falcon* (1930) is widely considered the first *film noir*, but Marcel Carné's prior *Le Jour se lève* (1939) also has a claim on this title. In both cases, there is also an obvious influence of 1920s German Expression, not the least because many of the most important *film noir* directors were in fact German émigrés (e.g. Fritz Lang, Josef von Sternberg, Billy Wilder, Otto Preminger, Douglas Sirk, and Max Ophuls). Although it is predominantly associated with detective thrillers, there are also *film noir* westerns and melodramas, so it cannot be considered a *genre in the true sense of the word. Stylistically, it is typified by three distinctive characteristics: first, and most prominently, its visual style is characterized by stark contrasts between light and dark used to symbolize 'good' and 'evil'; second, its narratives are morally ambiguous, frequently ending on a bathetic 'winner loses' note; third, its characters are of a limited variety of stereotypes—the grotesque villain, the beautiful but flawed *femme fatale*, and the emotionally damaged hero who seeks for justice in an unjust world, even if he has to break the law to do it. The best-known example, in this regard, is undoubtedly Howard Hawks's 1946 adaptation of Raymond Chandler's *The Big Sleep* (1939), starring Humphrey Bogart and Lauren Bacall. *Film noir* has been of particular interest to film critics interested in *psychoanalysis because its stories seem to be more about the complexities of human sexuality than their ultimately mundane crime and punishment plots. Because of the way the *femme fatale* uses her sexuality and breaks with the Hollywood convention of depicting women as passive (mother, whore, wife, or mistress), she has been subject to considerable theoretical attention. *Film noir* has also drawn the attention of film critics interested in the relationship between film and architecture because of its intensely urban character and the way it represents buildings.

Further Reading: J. Copjec (ed.) *Shades of Film Noir* (1993).
J. Naremore *More than Night: Film Noir in its Contexts* (1998).
S. Žižek *Enjoy Your Symptom! Jacques Lacan in Hollywood and Out* (2001).

Firestone, Shulamith (1945–) Canadian born *feminist scholar, activist, and writer. A central figure in the establishment of *radical feminism, her best known work *The Dialectic of Sex: The Case for Feminist Revolution* (1970) remains a crucial milestone in the field of *gender studies. Firestone's thesis is that the political inequality of women originates with their reproductive capacity, which forces them into a state of dependency on men (which in turn strengthens the power of the *patriarchy by making a political choice appear a political necessity). Her political programme is built around the need for women to alter their circumstances by seizing control of the means of reproduction. At the extreme, she advocates non-human means of reproduction through the use of sophisticated biotechnology. Her work is cited as an influence by Riot Grrrl Kathleen Hanna and SF novelist Marge Piercy. It has been criticized for its *biological determinism and failure to take into account other social factors such as *class and *race. Firestone was a vanguard author in the *Second Wave of feminism.

First Wave feminism The work of the first *feminist activists in the early 1800s up to and including the Suffragists (as retrospectively designated by the *Second Wave feminists). These feminists laid the groundwork for future feminists by fighting for the conditions that enabled them to go to university, vote, and have economic independence. The First Wave feminists campaigned for both equal rights in terms of laws and regulations, but also equal cultural rights, so as to give women the opportunity to pursue whatever career or life choice they decided on.

Fish, Stanley (1938–) American literary theorist and cultural critic. Born in Providence, Rhode Island, Fish studied at the University of Pennsylvania and Yale. He has taught at the University of California, Berkeley, Johns Hopkins and Duke Universities, the University of Illinois, and Florida International University. Fish began his career as a Milton scholar and has written a number of highly regarded books on that subject. In critical theory he is best known for the concept of the *interpretive community, which displaces the problem of how meaning is produced onto society itself and makes meaning the practical production of readers rather than texts. Fish is a high-profile cultural commentator who writes columns for *The New York Times* and *The Wall Street Journal*, generally taking a counter-intuitive view of things. For instance, he has famously argued that the humanities have no use and that is a good thing, and that political correctness is a waste of time.

flâneur A psycho-social type emblematic of *modernity. The essentially untranslatable term was introduced into the critical theory vocabulary by German cultural critic Walter *Benjamin in his uncompleted posthumously published *Das Passagen-Werk* (1982), translated as *The Arcades Project* (1999). Adapting the term 'flâneur' from the work of French poet and critic Charles Baudelaire, especially his essay 'Peintre de la vie moderne' (1863), translated as 'The Painter of Modern Life' (1964), Benjamin uses it to theorize the emergence of what would later be called *consumer society, i.e. a society in which practices of consumption rather than production are predominant. Belonging neither to the poorest class nor the wealthiest class, the 'flâneur' existed on the margin of both the city and the bourgeoisie, consuming images of both as a spectacle or *phantasmagoria. *Cultural Studies uses the concept of the 'flâneur' to theorize the experience of consuming the built environment for itself, particularly the space of shopping malls. The most influential work on the 'flâneur' is still Benjamin's posthumously published *Charles Baudelaire, Ein Lyriker im Zeitalter des Hochkapitalismus* (1969), translated as *Charles Baudelaire: A Lyric Poet in the Era of High Capitalism* (1973). But important and more contemporary adaptations are also to be found in John Fiske's *Popular Culture and Everyday Life* (1988) and Anne Friedberg's *Window Shopping* (1985). *See also* EVERYDAY LIFE; PRACTICES; SOCIETY OF THE SPECTACLE; SPACE.

f

Further Reading: S. Buck-Morss *The Dialectics of Seeing: Walter Benjamin and the Arcades Project* (1989).
K. Tester *The Flâneur* (1994).

floating signifier A signifier without a specific signified (*see* SIGN). Also known as an 'empty signifier', it is a signifier that absorbs rather than emits meaning. For example, Fredric *Jameson suggests that the shark in the *Jaws* series of films is an empty signifier because it is susceptible to multiple and even contradictory interpretations, suggesting that it does not have a specific meaning itself, but functions primarily as a vehicle for absorbing meanings that viewers want to impose upon it.

flow Welsh cultural critic Raymond *Williams's concept of how television operates. In a short book entitled *Television: Technology and Cultural Form* (1974), Williams observes that television cannot be thought of in terms of single programmes because the actual experience of watching television is like dining from a smorgasbord—there is a vast amount of choice. Just as importantly, television doesn't begin or end with a single programme; there is always another programme to follow, so its content does not have a defined shape. Rather it flows like a river. Although he'd been a television critic for a number of years, writing for the BBC's publication, *The Listener*, Williams didn't develop his theory until he spent a sabbatical in California. Perhaps it was only when he'd moved away from the highly structured and regulated television environment of the BBC to the looser and highly commercialized television environment of California that he was able to see television for what it really is. Williams's concept had enormous influence in British *Cultural Studies for a number of years, but it also had its critics. American critic John Ellis argued against it in *Visible Fictions* (1982), proposing as an alternative a theory of television as a segmented commodity.

Further Reading: R. Dienst *Still Life in Real Time: Theory After Television* (1994).

Fordism Named after Henry Ford, it refers to both a model of production (namely the assembly line) and a social phenomenon characterized by rising wages and falling commodity prices. Henry Ford not only developed a means of massively increasing industrial productivity through the assembly line idea (adapted from slaughterhouses), he used that increase in productivity to reduce the cost of his cars and make them more widely affordable. Ford thus matched mass consumption with mass production. He also recognized the value to his company a skilled workforce represents and he put in place a number of innovative ideas to retain his workers, including regular pay increases and a credit plan to enable them to buy his cars. Italian critic Antonio *Gramsci was attracted to the Fordist model and it became for him a kind of *utopian vision of how development should be managed.

foreclosure (*Verwerfung/forclusion*) The psychoanalytic term for the repudiation of a specific *desire. It differs from *repression in that the incompatible desire is not merely prevented from entering the consciousness, all trace of its existence is denied, as if the thought had never arisen. In his reading of Freud, Jacques *Lacan treats foreclosure as the specific mechanism of psychosis (in contrast to *neurosis); he argues that the psychotic *subject forecloses on the Name-of-the-Father (that which organizes the subject's symbolic field and gives them their identity and meaning to their reality). In effect, then, foreclosure is the repudiation of the organizational structure of reality, hence Lacan's treatment of it as a flight into psychosis.

fort/da Sigmund *Freud's name for a game played by his 18-month-old grandson involving a cotton reel which the boy would repeatedly throw out of his cot, exclaiming 'Oo' as he did so, forcing his mother to retrieve it for him, at which he would utter an appreciative 'Ah'. Freud interpreted these noises as babyish approximations of '*fort*', meaning 'gone', and '*da*', meaning 'there'. The significance of the game, which Freud discusses in 'Beyond the Pleasure Principle' (1920), is that it shows the child transforming an unhappy situation, one in which they have no control over the presence of their parents, into a happy one in which the parents are at the beck and call of the child. Freud also interpreted it as a kind of revenge on the parents, a way of saying to them that they aren't so important. *See also* COMPULSION TO REPEAT.

Foucault, Michel (1926–84) See opposite.

FOUCAULT, MICHEL (1926–84)

French philosopher, social historian, political activist and in later life *Queer Theory icon. Associated with both the *structuralist and *poststructuralist movements, he never really identified with either, preferring to describe himself as either an *archaeologist or a *genealogist. At his death he was one of the most influential intellectuals in the world, his work studied in practically every branch of the humanities and social sciences. He died of AIDS at the age 57, cutting short an immensely productive career.

The son of wealthy, upper middle-class parents, Foucault was born in Poitiers, a small provincial city of approximately 40,000 people in west-central France. His father was a surgeon, and his mother was the daughter of a surgeon, and it was expected in due course that he too would take up medicine. An excellent student, in 1946 he gained entry into the prestigious Parisian institution, the École Normale Supérieure (ENS) on the rue d'Ulm, where he studied philosophy. His contemporaries at ENS included such future luminaries as Louis *Althusser (who was briefly his tutor) and Jean Laplanche. Like most of his generation, Foucault's intellectual horizon was dominated by what Vincent Descombes terms the 'three Hs', namely *Hegel, *Husserl, and *Heidegger. Indicatively, he wrote his undergraduate dissertation on Hegel. He joined the Communist Party in 1950, but had little involvement with their activities and resigned his membership in 1952 in the wake of the 'doctors' plot'.

Foucault graduated from the ENS in 1951. Thanks to the intervention of his father he was able to evade military service and continue his studies. He was granted a three-year scholarship by the Fondation Thiers to complete a doctorate, but he relinquished it after only one year in favour of a teaching assistant position in the northern university of Lille. His first book, *Maladie mentale et personalité* (1954), which he would later disavow for being too psychological, displayed what would prove to be a lifelong interest in the distinction between the normal and the abnormal. A revised version was published in 1962 under the new title *Maladie mentale et psychologie*, translated as *Mental Illness and Psychology* (1976), but Foucault disowned this as well. Foucault considered studying medicine at this point in order to pursue his interest in psychiatry further, but chance played a part and in 1955 at the behest of the great mythologist Georges Dumézil Foucault took a position teaching French at the University of Uppsala in Sweden.

It was here in Uppsala's vast Bibliotheca Walleriana that he began the monumental work that would eventually become his PhD, *Folie et Déraison: Histoire de la Folie à l'âge classique* (1961), translated in abridged form as *Madness and Civilization* (1965) and in complete form as *History of Madness* (2006). Presented as an archaeology of the silence of madness, the final manuscript ran to more than 943 pages, with a further 40 pages of notes on top, and brought to bear an incredible range of material, scientific, medical, artistic, and the sheerly arcane, the accuracy and interpretation of which has not gone unchallenged. Indeed Foucault has been accused of gross exaggeration and outright error, particularly with respect to his reading of the *Narrenschiff* or 'ship of fools'. The most telling attack, though, came from his own former pupil Jacques *Derrida, who gave a devastating critique of *Folie et Déraison* in a lecture Foucault himself attended in 1963 (it has since been republished in his *L'Ecriture et la différence* (1967), translated as *Writing and Difference* (1978)).

Foucault moved twice more before his thesis was finished—firstly to Poland for a brief stint heading up the Centre Français at the University of Warsaw, occasionally doubling as cultural attaché as well; then to Hamburg, and the Institut Français, where he completed the compulsory complementary thesis, an introduction to and translation of Immanuel Kant's comparatively minor work, *Anthropologie in pragmatischer Hinsicht* (1798) (Anthropology from a Pragmatic Point of View). In 1960 Foucault returned to France to take up a position teaching psychology at Clermont-Ferrand, six hours by train from Paris where he continued to live throughout the six years of his appointment there. Foucault's next two books appeared simultaneously in 1963: *Naissance de la clinique*, translated as *The Birth of the Clinic* (1973) and *Raymond Roussel*, translated as *Death and the Labyrinth* (1986). The former brought the archaeologist's eye to the work of the medical gaze itself, inquiring into the way in which it developed, while the latter extended his interest in the work of *déraison* or 'unreason'.

Foucault's career was until 1966 solid, respectable and respected but confined exclusively to the halls of academia. This changed, much to his own surprise, with the publication of *Les Mots et les choses* (1966), translated as *The Order of Things* (1970). Despite being every bit as recondite and dense as his previous books, it was the breakout bestseller of 1966, its original print run of 3,000 selling out in a week. His audience now greatly enlarged, Foucault was henceforth able to assume a role similar to that of Jean-Paul *Sartre as a public intellectual. It is notoriously difficult to pin down why a particular book should succeed, but it is generally thought that it was its apocalyptic ending, effectively pronouncing the death of man, that somehow caught the mood of the times. Academically, though, it was the book's dramatic opening which drew stark attention to the peculiarity of thought and asked how and why it is possible to think certain things in one historical period and not another. In doing so, it introduced several new terms which would become Foucault's stock-in-trade and influence the human and social sciences for decades, especially *archive, *discourse, and *episteme. These rather mysterious terms were rendered rather more concrete with the publication of *L'Archéologie du savoir* (1969), translated as *The Archaeology of Knowledge* (1972), which in many ways reads as kind of user's guide to *Les Mots et les choses*.

In spite of, or perhaps because of, his newfound fame, Foucault chose to move to Tunis in 1966. However, he was obliged to leave Tunisia after only two years because of his involvement with pro-Palestinian students. He was in Tunis when the events of *May '68 erupted in Paris, and visited the city soon after. But because of what he had seen in Tunisia he always felt the students in Paris had it much easier than their colleagues on the other side of the Mediterranean. It was in Tunis that Foucault wrote *L'Archéologie du savoir*, his only purely methodological work. In part it is written as a defence against criticisms his previous work had received, but it was also an attempt to systematize his thought and set his conceptual house in order. It didn't have the sales success of its predecessor, but it soon became—in spite of its author's intentions—something of a structuralist's handbook.

On his return from Tunis in October 1968, Foucault was offered the foundation chair of philosophy at the newly created 'experimental' university of Vincennes. He used his position to create a stellar department. His appointments included Alain *Badiou, Etienne *Balibar, François Châtelet, Gilles *Deleuze, Jacques-Alain Miller (Jacques *Lacan's son-in-law and anointed successor), and Michel *Serres, to name only some. His tenure at Vincennes again proved to be brief. In 1970 at the age of only 42, Foucault was appointed to the Collège de France, the most prestigious research institution in the country, where he remained until his death 14 years later. Interestingly, Foucault didn't publish a single-authored book again until 1975. His first years at the Collège were spent on collaborative projects—in conjunction with his students he published a dossier with notes on the infamous case of Pierre Rivière who murdered his mother, sister, and brother in 1835; outside academia he formed the Groupe d'Information sur les Prisons (Group for Information on Prisons) which sought to expose conditions in French prisons by interviewing prisoners, ex-prisoners, social workers, and guards and compiling the information.

These two strands were woven together with Foucault's next book, *Surveiller et punir: Naissance de la Prison* (1975), translated as *Discipline and Punish: The Birth of the Prison* (1977). As with his previous books on the asylum and the clinic, *Surveiller et punir* pursues two lines of historical inquiry: on the one hand it tries to identify the historical conditions necessary for this particular type of institution to come into being, while on the other hand it inquires after the changes in thought itself that were required to have conceived of such an institution in the first place. Many readers have found this book to be incredibly gloomy because of the way Foucault charts the spread of the idea of incarceration and its mechanisms of surveillance—the *panopticon—into the reality of everyday life, arguing that schools, factories, offices, and shops are all organized along the same lines. With Foucault's characteristic flair for the astonishing example, *Surveiller et punir* combined case material with theoretical speculation to argue that power and knowledge are synonymous. This work was championed by the *nouveaux philosophes* (*New Philosophers), a tribute about which Foucault remained ambivalent.

Foucault now turned his eye towards the self. In 1976 he published the first of what was projected to be a six-volume history of sexuality, *La Volonté de savoir*, translated as *The History of Sexuality: An Introduction* (1978). Following the publication of this book it is thought by some (especially Dreyfus and Rabinow) that Foucault underwent some kind of personal or at least intellectual crisis and that the work that follows is radically different. This thesis is hotly disputed (by Deleuze, among others), but supported by the fact that the next two volumes in the series didn't appear until 1984. In the intervening years Foucault seemed to undergo a kind of 'conversion' experience and whereas before he had spoken insistently about the dialectic of power and resistance, now he began to speak about the possibility of self-fashioning (a term he adopted from Stephen *Greenblatt). His political activity in these years took on a more geopolitical hue—he travelled to Iran in 1979 to report on the revolution there, and in 1981 and 1982 he publicly supported the Solidarity movement in Poland.

Foucault's next book, *L'Usage des plaisirs* (1984), translated as *The Use of Pleasure* (1985), the last to appear in his lifetime, examines the ways in which the self is regulated via its *pleasures. He corrected the proofs of the third volume of the history of sexuality, *Le Souci de soi* (1984), translated as *The Care of the Self* (1986), on his deathbed. A fourth volume on the confessions of the flesh was all but completed, and it is rumoured that a fifth on pornography had been drafted, but Foucault's dying decree was that there be no posthumous publications and so far that has been honoured, with the exception of his lectures at the Collège de France, six volumes of which (at last count) have been transcribed and published. Foucault isn't the fashionable name he once was, but it can safely be said his legacy is far from exhausted. A considerable corpus of his unpublished works may be consulted at the Bibliothèque du Saulchoir in Paris.

Further Reading: G. Deleuze *Foucault* (1986).

H. Dreyfus and P. Rabinow *Michel Foucault: Beyond Structuralism and Hermeneutics* (1983).

G. Gutting *Foucault: A Very Short Introduction* (2005).

D. Halperin *Saint Foucault: Towards a Gay Hagiography* (1995).

D. Macey *The Lives of Michel Foucault* (1993).

foundationalism The position in philosophy that all knowledge must be grounded on certain unassailable facts or truths, usually secured via a combination of experience and reason. The two most famous examples of this are René Descartes's assertion 'I think, therefore I am' and Immanuel *Kant's designation of reason as the ground of philosophy.

See also ANTI-FOUNDATIONALISM.

fragmented body (*corps morcelé*) Jacques *Lacan's conceptualization of the disconnected and unorganized state of the psyche prior to the *mirror stage. As Lacan theorizes it, the child under the age of 18 months is unaware that their body is distinct from their mother's body, and similarly unaware that their body is a unitary whole. The memory of this feeling of disassociation remains with the subject throughout their life, buried in the *unconscious, but constantly threatening to return to the surface and shatter the illusion of wholeness the subject lives by.

Frank, Manfred (1945–) German philosopher and cultural critic. A prolific author of books on the German Romantic tradition in philosophy (especially the work of Friedrich Schleiermacher and Johann Gottlieb Fichte), very few of which have been translated into English, Frank is probably best known though for his sympathetic critiques of *deconstruction and *post-structuralism, or what he himself labels *neostructuralism. Operating in the hermeneutic tradition of Hans Georg *Gadamer and Paul *Ricoeur, but radicalizing their positions significantly, Frank charges Roland *Barthes, Gilles *Deleuze, Jacques *Derrida, Michel *Foucault, and Jean-François *Lyotard with underplaying the importance of the *subject and overplaying the arbitrariness of the *sign. Frank upholds the *structuralist position that the sign is constituted in a systematic network of interconnections between other signs, but resists the implication that the meaning of specific signs is completely arbitrary. He insists rather that meaning is multi-layered and that the network of signs is influenced by history. But rather than argue, as structuralism does, that it is the system of signs that confers meaning, Frank takes the contrary view and suggests that it is the historically sedimented meaning of signs that produce structures.

Frankfurt School The collective name for the group of scholars and the body of work associated directly and indirectly with the Institut für Sozialforschung (Institute for Social Research), an independent research centre affiliated with Frankfurt University. In 1937, Max *Horkheimer defined the Institute's approach to social and culturalanalysis as *critical theory, a label that has become virtually synonymous with the Frankfurt School. Today, for many people, particularly in Anglo-American *Cultural Studies, the Frankfurt School means a dour, elitist outlook and a hostile attitude to popular culture. Such gross underestimations of the real achievements of the school suggest not only ignorance of the work, but also ideological prejudice. The Frankfurt School regarded capitalist society with suspicion and was not taken in by its glossier blandishments as some versions of Cultural Studies have been.

Established in 1923 with the financial backing of Felix Weil, the son of wealthy grain-merchant Herman Weil, the Institute for Social Research was intended to be a place for the development of and experimentation with *Marxist ideas broadly construed. Private funding gave the Institute the luxury of real autonomy. It was not obliged to take on students or do any research except that which coincided with its goals. The first director was Carl Grünberg, an Austrian, Marxist professor of law and politics, but the younger members of the Institute found him lacking in imagination, and it wasn't until the appointment of his replacement Max *Horkheimer that the Institute took on the quality we are familiar with today.

Under Grünberg's direction, the Institute maintained close links with the Marx-Engels Institute in Moscow and imported samizdat copies of unpublished manuscripts by Marx and Engels, which in the political climate of the times was courageous and provocative. Indicative of this pro-communist stance, which would be toned down dramatically in later years, among the Institute's early appointees was Richard Sorge, the spy who famously told a disbelieving Stalin that Germany was going to invade the USSR. Other early appointees included Karl Wittfogel, a specialist in the now mostly discredited notion of the 'Asiatic mode of production' and a playwright whose works were staged by Piscator and others. The better known names associated with the Frankfurt School—e.g. Theodor *Adorno, Leo *Löwenthal, Erich *Fromm, and Herbert *Marcuse—joined the Institute a few years later. Grünberg suffered a stroke in 1927 from which he never fully recovered, and stepped down from the role as director in 1929. His successor was Max Horkheimer and it was under his direction that the Institute's reputation was made.

Horkheimer brought new fellows to the Institute and with them new ideas and in this way transformed it into one of the most influential intellectual movements of the 20th century. In contrast to his predecessor, Horkheimer encouraged the questioning of the basic premises of Marxism and encouraged a philosophical approach to issues of Marxist doctrine. He also encouraged the use of *psychoanalysis, then still a relatively new and radical methodology, for the purposes of social analysis. He also established, under the editorship of Leo *Löwenthal, a sociologist of literature interested in mass market fiction, the Institute's journal, *Zeitschrift für Sozialforschung* (Journal for Social Research). Contributors to the journal included figures like Walter *Benjamin who was never part of the school's inner core, but is nevertheless crucial to its reputation. In the 1930s, Horkheimer mapped out an ambitious programme of social research inquiring into the nature of political character that took over a decade to complete.

Watchful of the rise of Nazism in Germany, Horkheimer had the presence of mind to transfer the Institute to Geneva in 1931 to protect its largely Jewish membership from the newly implemented race laws. In 1934 the Institute relocated to New York, where it was attached to Columbia University, and not (as might have been expected given its Marxist leanings) to the USSR. Using his new position as a base, Horkheimer was able to employ the Institute's influence and resources to assist a number of intellectuals in their bid to get visas so as to escape the Nazis. However, in 1939, following some bad investments, the Institute found itself in financial difficulty, and was no longer able to fund as many researchers or projects as it had been accustomed to doing. Some of its key members, like psychoanalyst Erich Fromm, were obliged to leave and take work elsewhere, and this caused a great deal of internal friction and disruption. But the Institute survived and relocated again in 1941, this time to Los Angeles, were it remained in much looser form for the duration of the war.

After the war, at the invitation of the West German government (in recognition of, and as partial compensation for, the injustices of the Nazi period) the Institute and several of its key members returned to Frankfurt. It is really only in this period that the label 'Frankfurt School' actually begins to be used. Horkheimer stepped down as director of the Institute in favour of Adorno in 1958. Adorno's tenure though brilliant was marred by his poorly judged decision to call in the police to restore order following student protests in 1969. He nonetheless drew some important students to the centre, including future luminaries like Jürgen *Habermas. The Institute continues to do research today, continuing the tradition of its creators. It is impossible to measure the influence the Frankfurt School has had on the development of research in the humanities and social sciences in the past century. But probably its most important contribution has been its promotion and legitimating of interdisciplinary research. Recognizing that the split between disciplines is an artefact of modernity and that in any case no one discipline is equipped to deal with the complexity of the modern world, the Frankfurt School happily combined philosophy, psychoanalysis, Marxist theory, sociology, and economics.

Further Reading: S. Bronner *Of Critical Theory and its Theorists* (1994).
D. Held *Introduction to Critical Theory* (1980).
M. Jay *The Dialectical Imagination* (1973).
R. Wiggershaus *The Frankfurt School* (1994).

SEE WEB LINKS

- A history of the Frankfurt School, biographical detail of major figures, and links to other websites.

free association (*freie Assoziation*) A therapeutic technique in *psychoanalysis developed by Sigmund *Freud as a means of gaining access to the *unconscious thoughts underpinning dreams, fantasies, and symptoms. The technique consists in asking the *analysand to say whatever comes to mind during the course of analysis without regard for relevance or fear of embarrassment. Thus, it is free in the sense of being free from censorship and constraint; its specific purpose is to eliminate voluntary responses to questions, which by their very nature, aim to control the flow of information. Freud initially used hypnosis with his patients in order to try to access unconscious thoughts, but soon replaced it with free association, which he found much more effective.

free indirect style (*le style indirect libre*) A form of writing that enables a narrative told in the third person to give voice to a first person perspective. In doing so, it blurs the distinction between narrator and character, thus allowing the writer to present the character's innermost thoughts and concerns in an immediate fashion. The most celebrated example of the use of this mode of writing is Gustave Flaubert's *Madame Bovary* (1857).

Frege, Gottlob (1848–1925) German philosopher, mathematician, and logician whose work had a strong influence on 20th-century linguistics and language philosophy. Born in Wismar in Pomerania, Frege studied at Jena and Göttingen. He worked for most of his life in the mathematics department at Jena. He never published a monograph on philosophy in his own lifetime and it was only thanks to influential admirers like Bertrand Russell, Rudolf Carnap, and Ludwig *Wittgenstein that his philosophical work became widely known. His first major work was *Begriffsschrift* (1879), translated as *Conceptual Notation and other Writings* (1972), which set out to create a formal notational system for logic. In spite of a very poor initial reception (it was dismissed by the leading figures of the time), it has nonetheless had a tremendous influence on the development of the field of mathematical logic ever since. His real masterpiece, though, came a few years later: *Die Grundlagen der Arithmetik: eine logische mathematische Untersuchung über der Begriff der Zahl* (1884), translated as *The Foundations of Arithmetic: A Logico-Mathematical Enquiry into the Concept of Number* (1968). This was met with a similarly hostile response. Frege then turned to problems in the philosophy of language and it was this work which led to him becoming known in *critical theory. In particular, it is the distinction between *Sinn* (sense) and *Bedeutung* (reference) outlined in the paper 'Uber Sinn und Bedeutung' (1892), translated as 'On Sense and Reference' (1969), that has proved the most consequential for the development of *analytic philosophy. Frege noted that two expressions might have the same point of reference (*Bedeutung*); his famous example is that of the morning star and the evening star, inasmuch that the morning star and the evening star are in fact one and the same thing, namely the planet Venus, but have a very different sense (*Sinn*) according to the different expressions. Frege was directly influential on Edmund *Husserl, who as a young scholar wrote a critique of Frege only to be roundly chastised by him in return. In so doing, however, Frege directed him away from the psychologism of Brentano and put him on the road to creating his concept of *phenomenology.

Further Reading: M. Dummett *Frege: Philosophy of Language* (1973).
A. Kenny *Frege: An Introduction to the Founder of Modern Analytic Philosophy* (1995).
H. Noonan *Frege: A Critical Introduction* (2001).

French New Wave *See* NOUVELLE VAGUE.

Freud, Anna (1895–1982) Austrian psychoanalyst and youngest daughter of the founder of *psychoanalysis Sigmund *Freud. Close to her father, she recounted her dreams to him from a young age (many of which are analysed in his book *The Interpretation of Dreams*, which was published when she was 5 years old), and began reading his work as a teenager. She underwent analysis with her father as part of the training to become a psychoanalyst herself in 1918, was admitted to the Vienna Psychoanalytic Society in 1922, and began taking patients of her own shortly thereafter. Her research and practice was primarily focused on children, which made her a rival of Melanie *Klein, with whom she did not see eye to eye. Indeed, their rivalry briefly threatened to split the British Psychoanalytic Association, but was in the end resolved amicably. From 1925 until 1934 she was secretary of the International Psychoanalytic Association. In 1938, fleeing the Nazis, she moved with her father, by then very ill with jaw cancer, to London, where she oversaw the building of his house in Hampstead (in which she lived for the rest of her life). Posterity, rather unkindly, tends to regard Anna Freud as having little that was original to say, a perception her immense labour of editing and translating her father's work did little to change. And though it is true her own thought is very much an extension of her father's she nevertheless developed her own take on things, emphasizing the role of the *ego (rather than the *id, which was her father's interest). Her key publication was the *Ego and the Mechanisms of Defence* (1936).

Further Reading: E. Young-Bruehl *Anna Freud: A Biography* (1988).

Freud, Sigmund (1856–1939) See opposite.

Friedan, Betty (1921–2006) American feminist, political activist, and co-founder of the National Organization for Women (NOW). Her book, *The Feminine Mystique* (1963), a huge bestseller, is generally

FREUD, SIGMUND (1856–1939)

Founder of *psychoanalysis and one of the most influential intellectuals of the 19th and 20th centuries. Michel *Foucault described him as a 'founder of discourse', meaning that Freud's work enabled a new way of thinking and speaking. The basic tenets of psychoanalysis as a *talking cure are widely known (even if they aren't widely understood), underpinning as they do virtually every 'talk show', whether it be Rikki Lake, Jerry Springer, Dr Phil, or Oprah.

Freud was born in Příbor (Freiberg) in Moravia, which was then part of the Greater Austrian Empire, but is now part of the Czech Republic. His father was a wool merchant, but his business failed in 1857 and the family relocated to Vienna, where Freud spent the remainder of his life bar his final year. Although he was not raised an orthodox Jew, he nevertheless retained an attachment to Judaism. His family, like many Jewish families at that time were assimilated, but perhaps because of the prevailing anti-Semitism they resided in Leopoldstadt, the Jewish quarter of Vienna.

Freud commenced medical school at the University of Vienna in 1873 and graduated in 1881. He combined the study of medicine with comparative anatomy. His first published research paper was on the sexual anatomy of eels. He spent considerable time in his student years working in Ernst Brücke's laboratories and it was there that he met Josef Breuer, the man who effectively started him on the path that would lead to the invention of psychoanalysis. In 1883 he began a three-year internship in the psychiatric department of Vienna's General Hospital. It was during these years that Freud undertook his now infamous research on the medicinal properties of cocaine (he published a paper on it in 1884, extolling its benefits as a mental stimulant, aphrodisiac, and withdrawal cure for morphine addicts).

In 1885 Freud was awarded a travelling grant that enabled him to go to Paris to study with Jean-Martin Charcot, known as the father of neurology. He was impressed by Charcot's use of hypnosis to treat *hysteria and though he would later reject hypnosis as a useful means of dealing with psychological problems, it was an important clinical stepping stone for him. On his return to Vienna in 1886 he set up private practice as a neurologist. He continued to do scientific research for the next decade, publishing papers on cerebral palsy and *aphasia. But it was his collaboration with Breuer, published in 1895 as *Studien über Hysterie,* translated as

Studies on Hysteria (1955), which was decisive in terms of his future career path. Freud and Breuer worked on the assumption that under hypnosis patients recalled forgotten or repressed psychical traumas. Therapy consisted in enabling patients to remember the trauma and by talking about it, make sense of it and resolve it. For this reason, one of the first patients, known as Fräulein Anna O (later identified as Bertha van Pappenheim), referred to their technique as the talking cure, a label that stuck and became a standard code phrase for psychoanalysis.

Freud noticed that many of the traumas his patients recalled involved sexual relations between the patient as a child and their parents. At first, he assumed these recollections were true and he developed his theory of hysteria around it, which became known as *seduction theory. But he gradually came to realize that the recollections had to be false, the product of fantasy rather than actual memory, because it was simply impossible that so many childhood rapes could go unreported. At first he thought his project of trying to understand hysteria had failed, but then after extensive self-analysis he saw that it is precisely the fact that the memories are false that is crucial. He modified his thesis accordingly: now he worked from the premise that imagined events can and do have real effects, and in this sense psychoanalysis as we know it now was born.

What he still had to work out was the psychical mechanism by which these imagined events were produced. The answer came to him in a dream—now known as the 'dream of Irma's injection'—which he analysed himself and felt afterwards that he had finally cracked the mystery of how dreams work. Freud himself helped to create the legend: a few years after this epiphany, he wrote in a letter to his close friend Wilhelm Fliess that he wondered, not a little vainly, if one day a plaque would be affixed to Bellevue (a summer resort near Vienna) stating: 'In this house, on July 24th, 1895, the secret of dreams was revealed to Dr Sigmund Freud'. This dream and its analysis is a centrepiece in *Die Traumdeutung* (1900), translated as *The Interpretation of Dreams* (1953), the book which effectively launched Freud's career and spawned psychoanalysis. Although it is arguably one of the most influential books written in the past century, it was not, however, an immediate sensation, and it was anything but a bestseller—it sold only 351 copies in its first six years of being in print!

After extensive self-analysis—Freud deliberately slept on a hard bed for several months to deny himself proper, deep sleep and recorded his dreams immediately upon waking—Freud concluded four things that became the cornerstones of his method: first, the biological function of dreams is to protect sleep, to stop us from waking up in other words (this is true even of nightmares according to Freud); second, all dreams are an *unconscious 'working through' of the previous day's thoughts and activities (that is the source of their imagery); third, all dreams contain a *wish-fulfilment (usually in the form of a symbolic satisfaction of something the conscious mind finds unacceptable); to protect sleep, dreams must overcode our anxieties in such a way that we can simultaneously acknowledge their existence and not have to think about them. The latter process Freud termed *dreamwork.

Consisting of two processes—*condensation and *displacement —the mechanism of the dreamwork (which is convincingly explained and exemplified in *The Interpretation of Dreams*), is arguably Freud's most important conceptual legacy. To understand its significance, one has to place it within the context of the *topography of the mind Freud constructed: the dreamwork stands between the conscious and the unconscious, functioning like an active filter. It presupposes two things: first, that the unconscious is a lively space where the *instincts are represented; second, that the conscious is both largely unaware of what happens in the unconscious and generally disapproving of the little it knows. This in turn supposes the *psyche is constructed of three 'characters': the *id, the *ego, and the *superego. The id is the realm of pure instinct; the ego rests like a membrane over the id, but is not driven by the instincts; and the superego is a governing force watching over the ego making sure it doesn't succumb to the temptations of the id.

However, it is undoubtedly the concept of the *Oedipus complex, which makes its appearance about a third of the way through *The Interpretation of Dreams*, that is the best known (and most controversial!) aspect of this book. Musing on his experience as an analyst, Freud states that being in love with one parent and hating the other is an essential part of the neurotic's stock of psychical impulses. He then makes an incredible leap and suggests that this perhaps explains the universal appeal of Sophocles' play *Oedipus Rex* (429 BC) some 2,500 years after it was written: it appeals to everyone because it describes the basic dynamic of the development of human sexuality.

The next few years after the publication of *The Interpretation of Dreams* were highly creative and productive ones for Freud. He was promoted to the coveted position of Professor Extraordinarius and he published a string of books which gave shape to psychoanalysis, taking it beyond dream analysis. In short order he published the following three books, which made more concrete his understanding of the unconscious and the importance of sexuality: *Zur Psychopathologie des Alltagslebens* (1901) translated as *The Psychopathology of Everyday Life* (1914), *Der Witz une seine Beziehung zum Unbewussten* (1905), translated as *Jokes and the Relation to the Unconscious* (1960), and *Drei Abhandlungen zur Sexualtheorie* (1905), translated as *Three Essays on the Theory of Sexuality* (1949). His fame grew and the remainder of his career is in many ways coextensive with the career of psychoanalysis itself.

In the years that followed, Freud's writing became both more speculative and more adventurous—he offered psychoanalytic profiles of people he hadn't met, such as the American President Woodrow Wilson. He published a selection of his case histories (though sadly he burned all his notes), and he wrote a kind of psychohistory of humanity tracing the rise of so-called civilized man. Freud's legacy is beyond calculation. His work is known virtually everywhere. It is taught in most universities, though pointedly not in psychology departments. And it has inspired a great number of intellectuals, some of whom like Jacques *Lacan and Slavoj *Žižek explicitly continue his work, and many others like Jean-Paul *Sartre and Fredric *Jameson who use the basic architecture of his concepts to do their own work. Then there are others like Carl *Jung and Gilles *Deleuze and Félix *Guattari who developed their work in explicit opposition to Freud.

Further Literature: H. Ellenberger *The Discovery of the Unconscious: The History and Evolution of Dynamic Psychiatry* (1970).

C. Surprenant *Freud: A Guide for the Perplexed* (2008).

T. Thwaites *Reading Freud: Psychoanalysis as Cultural Theory* (2007).

SEE WEB LINKS

- Biographical information, as well as information on Sigmund Freud's ideas, theories, and his psychoanalytical approach. The site also contains an extensive bibliography and other resources regarding Freud.

credited with initiating the so-called *Second Wave of feminism. Friedan's book spoke of that claustrophobic existence of the suburban 'housewife' and as later feminist critics would point out she seems to have been oblivious of *class, *ethnicity, *race, and the other cultural and legal barriers to equality that women face. Nevertheless, her book was a rallying cry for women to demand the right to define their own social role. The feminine mystique she spoke of was the social role constructed for women by men that women have been persuaded or coerced into accepting, namely that women are caregivers, that they are nurturers and so on, by reason of biology, and therefore better suited to jobs in fields like nursing and teaching. She wrote a number of other works, but none that had the effect of her first book.

Fromm, Erich (1900–80) German *psychoanalyst and critical theorist. He was associated with the *Frankfurt School for many years, but in later life forged his own path. Fromm completed his undergraduate and postgraduate training at the University of Heidelberg, where philosopher-psychiatrist Karl *Jaspers taught. He graduated with a PhD in 1922 and then began his training as a clinical psychoanalyst, starting his own practice in 1927. In 1930 he joined the Institute for Social Research in Frankfurt and when the Nazis came to power he moved with the Institute to Geneva and then to Columbia University in New York. He obtained a teaching position at Bennington College in 1941 and remained there for the duration of World War II all the while continuing his private practice as a psychotherapist. In 1950 he moved to Mexico City taking a job at the national university there, where he worked until his retirement in 1965. Fromm's work pioneered the social psychological application of psychoanalysis and his writing reached a mass audience with its key message that the psyche constantly adapts to meet the challenges of its environment. The key psychological challenge, as he saw it, was the need to resist the urge to subordinate oneself to authority and thus deny oneself the burden of freedom. A prolific author, Fromm's best known books are: *Escape from Freedom* (1941), *Man for Himself* (1947), *The Art of Loving* (1956), and *To Have or To Be?* (1976).

Further Reading: R. Funk *Erich Fromm: His Life and Ideas* (2004).

Frye, Northrop (1912–91) Canadian literary critic and theorist renowned for his innovative use of Carl *Jung's theory of *archetype and *myth. Born in Sherbrooke, Quebec, Frye studied English at Victoria College in Toronto. He then studied theology and completed his orders to become a minister in the Uniting Church of Canada in 1936. He did pastoral work for a short period, and then took a scholarship to go to

Merton College, Oxford. After completing his studies at Oxford he returned to a position at Victoria College, where he remained for the rest of his career, eventually rising to the rank of Chancellor. He was very much a public intellectual determined to raise the profile of literary criticism and demonstrate its importance to non-academic readers. The lectures in *The Educated Imagination* (1963) were originally broadcast on Canadian radio and from 1968 to 1977 he served as a board member for the Canadian Radio-Television and Telecommunication Commission, which regulates the media in Canada.

Frye's first book, a study of the English poet William Blake, *Fearful Symmetry* (1947), brought him immediate international attention because it offered a powerful counterpoint to the dominant *New Criticism, overturning its textual isolationist policy, but retaining its close reading technique in modified form. Frye describes the New Critics as being like visitors to an art gallery who stand so close to the picture all they can see is the texture of the paint, whereas his preference is to stand so far back that the content blurs and reveals itself as a pure archetypal outline. In contrast to the New Critics, Frye read literary texts in relation to both other literary texts (indeed, for Frye this literally meant all literary texts—his viewpoint was astoundingly synoptic) and the social context which yielded them in the first place. Literature has to mean something to its readers Frye thought, by which he meant it has to serve a social purpose. Hence his interest in *myths, which for Frye are complex allegories concerning the relation between humans and their gods. Frye systematized his thinking on myth in what is by far his best known work, and indeed for many one of the most important works of criticism of the 20th century, *Anatomy of Criticism* (1957).

Myth, for Frye, centres on the mobilization of archetypes (which he conceives slightly differently from Carl *Jung, though with an obvious awareness and admiration for him), arguing that it is the production of archetypes that saves literature from creating mere stereotypes. Frye uses the notion of displacement (comparable, though not the same as Sigmund *Freud's notion of *displacement) to account for the way mythic structures can permeate realist or naturalist texts, even though the magical elements have been stripped away—James Joyce's *Ulysses* (1922) is the best-known example of this. Between the extreme of pure myth and so-called realist texts (a word Frye objected to) lies romance. Thus, Frye proposes that there are three orders of myth. He balances his analysis of myth with a study of modes, symbols, and genres, thus creating one of the greatest literary typologies ever produced. Some critics have found his ceaseless classification of types oppressive, while others have seen it as a precursor to *structuralism, and for both these reasons Frye's work has fallen into a state of relative neglect. Yet as Fredric *Jameson shows in *The Political Unconscious* (1981), Frye's typologies can be used to great effect for contemporary criticism, even if one does not agree fully with his ontology.

Frye was a prolific author right up until his death. He wrote books on Canadian literature, T.S. Eliot, Shakespeare, Milton, and the Bible.

Further Reading: J. Ayer *Northrop Frye: A Biography* (1989).
I. Balfour *Northrop Frye* (1988).
C. Cotrupi *Northrop Frye and the Poetics of Process* (2000).
J. Hart *Northrop Frye: The Theoretical Imagination* (1994).

Fukuyama, Francis (1952–) American political philosopher. He was born in Chicago, to a well-educated middle-class family. Fukuyama's father was a second generation Japanese-American with a doctorate in sociology (as well as religious training) and his mother a Japanese-born daughter of the founder of the economics department at Kyoto University. He obtained his BA at Cornell University, where he studied classics and political philosophy. There he met one of his key influences, the conservative cultural critic Allan *Bloom, author of the bestselling polemical account of the decline of American culture *The Closing of the American Mind* (1987). He then went on to complete a doctorate at Harvard with Samuel P. Huntington, author of the highly influential *neo-racist tract *The Clash of Civilizations and the Remaking of the World Order* (1998). His career has been divided between positions at the RAND Corporation and the US State Department, where he specialized in policy and planning relating to the former Soviet Union and the Middle East, and prestigious American universities such as George Mason and Johns Hopkins. Fukuyama shot to prominence with a short essay published in the right-wing journal, *The National Interest* entitled 'The End of History?' (1989). Written on the eve of the collapse of so-called 'actually existing socialism' with the fall of the Berlin Wall in November 1989, Fukuyama's essay seemed to capture the spirit of what took place: it was not merely the triumph of the capitalist West, it was also final confirmation of the universal legitimacy of liberal-democratic order. History had come to an end, Fukuyama claimed, because (following a highly *Hegelian line of thinking) the pinnacle of possible social formations had been attained. Fukuyama converted this essay into a bestselling book entitled *The End of History and the Last Man* (1992), sparking an intense debate that included sophisticated repudiations from several critical theory luminaries, such as Jacques *Derrida in *Spectres de Marx* (1993) translated as *Spectres of Marx* (1994), Fredric *Jameson in *The Cultural Turn* (1998), and Perry *Anderson, in *A Zone of Engagement* (1992). His work since, which has focused on such issues as trust, the inhuman, and governance, has not attracted the same level of critical interest (although it continues to sell well), perhaps because it has not entertained the same philosophically grandiose pretensions as his debut work.

Further Reading: G. Elliott *Ends in Sight: Marx, Fukuyama, Hobsbawm, Anderson* (2008).

f

functionalism A term used in architecture, linguistics, philosophy, psychology, and sociology. It has a slightly different meaning in each context, but in every case it implies a conscious emphasis on delineating how things function within a specific field of inquiry. In architecture, which is in many ways emblematic of the term's meaning across all disciplines, functionalism refers to a style of building in which design reflects purpose. The so-called *international style architects were adherents of this principle. In sociology, linguistics and philosophy, functionalism refers to the starting premise that all aspects of society, from language through social rituals such as marriage to thought itself exist only to serve a particular purpose.

fundamentalism A strict adherence to a religious or political doctrine often coupled with an extremely dogmatic interpretation of the founding text of that religion or political position (e.g. Bible, manifesto, etc.). Fundamentalism can also refer to the practice of treating religious works such as the Bible or Koran as the literal word of God.

Futurism Artistic movement originating in Italy in the early 1900s. An *Avant-garde movement led by the poet F.T. *Marinetti, Futurism rejected artistic and cultural tradition in favour of a technologically oriented future. It celebrated war as a liberating force, freeing the present of the weight of the past, and admired speed, machines, youth, and violence. There also existed a Russian form of Futurism, which shared the same values, but was rapidly subsumed by *constructivism.

futurology The study of the possible (and assumed to be likely) nature of the world in the near future based on what is known about present trends in demography, technology, and economic geography. Undoubtedly the best-known example of futurology is Alvin Toffler's 1970 bestseller, *Future Shock*, which predicted (with some degree of accuracy) the digital revolution that occurred in the early 1990s. But it also worried that people were not ready for the changes to come. Government and business are the two stakeholder groups with the most interest in futurology. Interestingly, Michel de *Certeau's work on *everyday life was funded by the French government on the understanding that it would deal with futurology, but Certeau's research team did not get around to writing that particular volume (in part because Certeau left France for a job in California, but also because neither he nor his fellow researchers were sure they knew what the concept actually meant)—but there are traces of it in the first volume of his work on *everyday life.

Gadamer, Hans-Georg (1900–2002) German philosopher best known for his work on *hermeneutics. Born in Marburg, his father was a professor of pharmacy. Despite parental pressure to study the natural sciences, Gadamer instead studied humanities as an undergraduate, first in Breslau (now Wrocław in Poland), then in Marburg, where he completed his doctorate on the essence of pleasure in Plato in 1922. A polio epidemic was sweeping through Marburg at the time and Gadamer was unlucky enough to fall victim. Polio was untreatable then, and Gadamer had to endure a long, painful convalescence, during which he was confined to bed. To help him pass the time, his mentor Paul Nastorp sent him an unpublished manuscript on the *phenomenological interpretation of Aristotle by a then unknown young scholar called Martin *Heidegger. Solely on the strength of this essay, Gadamer moved to Freiburg when he regained his health to work on his habilitation under the direction of Heidegger, joining a highly select group of young philosophers, many of whom, like Leo *Strauss, Karl Löwith, and Hannah *Arendt, went on to become major figures in their own right. Gadamer completed his studies in 1928 and was given a non-tenured teaching post at Marburg, where Heidegger had also moved. His doctoral thesis on Plato's dialectical method was published in 1931—it was to be his only book of substance for nearly 30 years! In part this was because in contrast to his former teacher, Gadamer was not a Nazi and he never joined the Nazi Party, and felt silenced by the regime. This stance served him well in the post-war years, despite the fact that he never actively opposed the Nazi regime. He was made rector of Leipzig University in 1945. He used his position to host several conferences around the need for a spiritual reconstruction of Germany and in defence of the autonomy of philosophical thought. But he did not find life in East Germany congenial so in 1947 he moved to the West, initially to Frankfurt, where his colleagues included Theodor *Adorno and Max *Horkheimer, and then definitively to Heidelberg, where he remained from 1949 until his death half a century later. There Gadamer wrote the work for which he is best known, *Wahrheit und Methode: Grundzüge einer philosophischen Hermeneutik* (1960), translated as *Truth and Method* (1975), in which he set out to produce a philosophical hermeneutics. He rejected the psychologism of Schleiermacher and his emphasis on authorial intention, and instead sought to ground the truth of the text in an understanding of the collective consciousness produced by history (*wirkungsgeschichtliches Bewußtsein*). His aim in doing so was to delineate the fore-structures (as he called them) that come into play in interpreting and understanding texts.

Further Reading: J. Grondin, *Hans-Georg Gadamer: A Biography* (2003). C. Lawn *Gadamer: A Guide for the Perplexed* (2006).

Gates, Henry Louis Jr (1950–) American literary critic and historian specializing in African-American studies. Born in Virginia, Gates completed his undergraduate degree at Yale, during which time he spent a year volunteering at a mission hospital in Tanzania. He was then awarded a Mellon Foundation scholarship (the first African-American ever to be awarded it) to study for his PhD at Cambridge University. There he met Nigerian writer and scholar Wole Soyinka (the first African to win the Nobel Prize for literature), who would become his mentor. He also worked with Raymond *Williams and George Steiner. He returned to the US before completing his dissertation and has since held appointments at Yale, Cornell, Duke, and Harvard, where he is the director of the W.E.B. Du Bois Institute for African-American Research. Gates's career can be viewed as having a singular purpose pursued by dual means: his purpose is to modify the western canon so as to accommodate African and African-American voices; his means of doing this are theoretical and historical. On the one hand, through works like *The Signifying Monkey* (1989), he has endeavoured to offer an aesthetic of black writing that articulates its distinctiveness without at the same time universalizing black experience (as *negritude is criticized for doing); on the other hand, he has undertaken a vast rehabilitation programme (for the want of a better term), whereby he has unearthed rare published and unpublished works by African-American writers, such as our *Our Nig* by Harriet E. Wilson, which was the first novel written by a black person in the US, and brought these into the public sphere. This has been accompanied by the compilation of encyclopaedias of black lives and writings. Gates is a high-profile intellectual who has done a lot of work on television and written for the mainstream press. He is routinely identified as one of the most influential African-Americans.

gay Originally an adjective to describe a light-hearted, frivolous, or joyful attitude, it was used in the early part of the 20th century to refer to someone with an open-minded or unconventional approach to sexual propriety. And until the 1950s, this was its most widely recognized meaning; but in the middle part of the century it also began to be used as a synonym for homosexuality in general. This latter meaning emerged as the dominant meaning of the word in the 1970s. The annual Gay Pride parades held around the world in memory of the 1969 Stonewall riots have helped transform the word gay into a generally positive and affirmative term. In the early part of the 21st century, gay has acquired a new meaning, apparently unrelated to its other meanings, as a pejorative with the approximate meaning of 'uncool, outdated, pathetic, and generally undesirable'.

gaze (*le regard*) A concept used by both Jean-Paul *Sartre and Jacques *Lacan, though with slightly different meanings, to formulate the *existential problem of being looked at by another (for this reason, it is also sometimes translated as 'the look'). Simply put, the problematic is this: If 'I' as an observing subject have consciousness and the object 'I' gaze at does not, then what does that mean to 'me' when another gazes upon me, thus transforming 'me' into an object of their consciousness? The gaze of the other inevitably degrades 'my' being-for-oneself and transforms it into a being-for-others. In other words, it is the gaze that enables the subject to recognize that the *Other is also a subject. Commenting on Sartre's work, in a very early seminar, Lacan twists this problem further and argues that in fact it is the object that gazes at 'us' and not the other way round. The gaze is not 'me' looking at the other, but rather the other looking at me. Film theorists, particularly Christian *Metz and Laura Mulvey have used this concept to great effect in their analysis of the function of cinema.

Further Reading: J. Rose *Sexuality in the Field of Vision* (1986).

Geertz, Clifford (1926–2006) American cultural anthropologist. Born in San Francisco, Geertz served in the Navy during World War II, and then studied for a BA at Antioch College on the 'GI Bill'. This was followed by a PhD at Harvard, for which he did extensive fieldwork in Java (in Indonesia). Most of Geertz's fieldwork was done in Indonesia, but he also spent a considerable period of time in Morocco. He held appointments at the University of Chicago and at Princeton. It was Geertz's fifth book, *The Interpretation of Cultures* (1973), that brought him international attention, and more importantly won him a large readership outside of professional anthropological circles. He proposed a new method of thinking about anthropological research, which he called 'thick description', borrowing the term from British analytic philosopher Gilbert Ryle. Describing culture as an 'acted document', Geertz argues that the object of anthropology, i.e. what it is anthropologists actually study, is a 'thick description' in itself, because it is a multi-coded 'text' that is simultaneously constructed and interpreted by the anthropologist. All human behaviour is, he argues, symbolic action, so anthropological fieldwork consists in learning the various ways in which symbols are manipulated in culture, without at the same time falling into the trap of thinking these symbols are fixed or immutable. Anthropological interpretations are thus fictions, he argues, not in the sense of being false, but rather (as in the original meaning of the term) made up or constructed, and therefore cannot be schematized. He developed this thesis further in the subsequent work *Local Knowledge* (1983). Geertz's method chimed well with the shift toward *relativism and *pragmatism which *postmodernism heralded and his work was enormously influential in a wide variety of fields, notably literary studies and *Cultural Studies. *New Historicism's leading scholar Stephen *Greenblatt has openly acknowledged a theoretical debt to Geertz. In the latter part of his career, Geertz's work took a more biographical and ultimately autobiographical turn: first, he wrote a short book on the lives of four key anthropologists, *Works and Lives: The Anthropologist as Author* (1988), then a book about his own life in the field, *After the Fact: Two Countries, Four Decades, One Anthropologist* (1995).

Further Reading: F. Inglis *Clifford Geertz: Culture, Custom and Ethics* (2000).

Gellner, Ernest (1925–95) Czech historian and social anthropologist. Born in Paris to a family of Bohemian Jews, Gellner grew up in Prague. In 1939 his family moved to Britain to escape persecution by the Nazis. Gellner won a scholarship to Balliol College, Oxford, where he studied philosophy, politics, and economics. But after only a year of study, he left university to join the Czech army. He returned to Prague after the war, but disgusted by the communist takeover he left after only a few months and resumed study at Balliol. His first job in 1947 was at the University of Edinburgh in the Department of Moral Philosophy. Two years later he took a position in the Sociology Department at the London School of Economics, where he was to remain for two decades. In 1974, he moved to Cambridge as the head of the Department of Anthropology, remaining there for nearly 20 years before fulfilling a lifelong dream of returning to Prague as the head of a George Soros funded institute to study the rise of nationalism in Eastern Europe. Gellner shot to prominence in 1959 with the publication of *Words and Things*, which attacked the so-called ordinary language philosophers, particularly Ludwig *Wittgenstein, for the way they privilege convention and community-established norms of meaning. Probably his most-read work, though, is *Nations and Nationalism* (1983), which, alongside the work of Benedict *Anderson, continues to set the agenda for debate about the subject of what constitutes nationalism.

Further Reading: J. Hall *The State of the Nation: Ernest Gellner and the Theory of Nationalism* (1998).

S. Malešević and M. Haugaard (eds.) *Ernest Gellner and Contemporary Social Thought* (2007).

gender The set of behavioural, cultural, psychological, and social characteristics and practices associated with *masculinity and *femininity. The notion of gender was used in *Second Wave feminism to separate individual attitudes and actions from physiology in order to undermine the *biological determinist thesis which holds that cultural attitudes are simply a reflection of the specific nature of the *body. By contrast, feminism claimed that attitudes are fluid with respect to biological sex and that it is *culture rather than nature which shapes these. As Simone de *Beauvoir famously put it, one is not born a woman. Gender is rather an *identity one adopts or creates. American *ethnomethodologist Harold Garfinkel and American sociologist Erving *Goffman argue that gender identity is something that has to be learned and constantly managed. Their work chimed well with American psychologist Robert Stoller who showed that in the case of sex reassignment surgery it was a relatively simple procedure to correct the body, but much more problematic to undo the learned social behaviour. It was further argued by feminism that the very notion of gender is itself influenced and shaped by other equally powerful cultural forces such as *race and *class, there being a significant difference in terms of relative opportunities between being a white middle-class woman living in a western city and a poor non-white woman. In recent times, work on gender has been dominated by Judith *Butler, who argues that the sex/gender distinction should be regarded as regulatory apparatus that positions sex as 'natural' so as to make gender roles appear 'normal'. Society, she argues, calls upon us to perform masculinity and femininity and though it appears that we may choose between the two, the crucial point is that we cannot choose not to have any gender at all. Thus gender is a highly *ambivalent category in Butler's view. As Donna *Haraway points out in an extended essay on the question of gender in *Simians, Cyborgs and Women* (1991), the sex/gender distinction is also an artefact of the English language—German, for instance, uses only one word, *Geschlecht*, to encompass both meanings, while not coinciding exactly with either—and other cultures confront this issue in different ways, according to different social and cultural pressures.

Further Reading: C. Colebrook *Gender* (2004).

genealogy French historian Michel *Foucault's term, borrowed in this sense from Friedrich *Nietzsche, for his research methodology, which was in turn superseded by the notion of *archaeology. First outlined in a 1971 essay entitled, 'Nietzsche, Genealogy, History' (reprinted in the collection, *Language, Counter-Memory, Practice,* edited by Donald Bouchard), genealogy aims to uncover the implicit systems or unwritten rules (what Foucault himself later referred to as *discursive practices) which taken together comprise lived society. As is true of so many of Foucault's concepts, genealogy was intended to break with the conventions of the history of ideas. In particular, Foucault wanted to challenge three postulates he saw as fallacious, namely the assumptions that history is an attempt to uncover the essence of things, or some primordial truth; that the most important moment is the moment of birth; and that the origin of a thing is also its truth. Instead he proposed that history should concern itself with descent and emergence. History, Foucault argues, is not the result of the deliberate acts of individuals; it is rather the product of the unintended and unexpected coalescence of millions of individual acts. So the only way to chart it is to try to see how certain accidents and departures give rise to new solidities over time. Foucault's career was devoted to devising the conceptual means of articulating such silent events.

Further Reading: P. Barker *Michel Foucault: An Introduction* (1998).

Genette, Gérard (1930–) French, *structuralist literary theorist. Born in Paris, Genette studied at the École Normale Supérieure, where his classmates included Jacques *Derrida and Pierre *Bourdieu. After an obligatory period of teaching in lycées, Genette obtained a position at the Sorbonne in 1963 and then a more permanent post at the École des Hautes Études en Sciences Sociales in 1967. Together with Tzvetan *Todorov and Hélène *Cixous, he founded the journal *Poétique* in 1970, which became a key organ of the structuralist and *post-structuralist movements in Paris and a significant rival to *Tel Quel.* Genette's work focuses on the question of how literary writing works, that is, what sets it apart from other forms of non-literary writing, but also how does it achieve certain of its effects. His approach, consistent with *Lévi-Strauss's original geological inspiration for structuralism, tends to be stratified: he investigates the ways different parts of the literary text interact and devotes considerable attention to identifying and analysing these parts. He enlarges the *Russian Formalist binary of **fabula* and *sjužet* to a trinity by adding what he calls the narrative instance, namely the act of telling the story itself, thus taking into account its *performative dimension. Genette's star has waned in recent years with the movement away from such purely formal questions towards more politically motivated problems in literary theory. His key works are collected in a series of volumes entitled *Figures I* (1966), *Figures II* (1969), and *Figures III* (1972), a selection of which has been compiled and translated into English as *Figures of Literary Discourse* (1984).

Geneva School **1.** A small group of linguists based in Geneva at the turn of the 20th century. The most prominent figure was Ferdinand de *Saussure, whose work on the linguistic *sign was a vital precursor to the founding of both *structuralism and *semiotics. Saussure's contribution to scholarship might never have been known were it not for the efforts of his former students, and fellow members of the Geneva School, Charles Bally and Albert Sechehaye. It was they who transformed incomplete lecture notes into the posthumously published *Cours de linguistique générale* (1916), translated as *Course in General Linguistics* (1959), upon which Saussure's lasting fame rests.

2. A small group of literary scholars using a combination of *phenomenology (inspired by the work Edmund *Husserl) and *Russian Formalism to analyse the *ontology of literature as a specific art form and affective experience. The text was treated as the realization of the author's consciousness and the critics sought its deep structure by looking for and interpreting recurrent images and symbolic patterns. All material facts, such as the biography of the author, or the historical context, were set aside as extraneous. Its core membership consisted of Georges Poulet, Jean-Pierre Richard, Marcel Raymond, and Jean Starobinski. American literary critic J. Hillis *Miller was influenced by their approach.

Further Reading: T. Eagleton *Literary Theory: An Introduction* (1983).

genre Derived ultimately from the Latin word 'genus' (used in biology to classify sub-groups of a particular species), it is used in literary and film studies to distinguish different types of works bearing a 'family resemblance' in terms of composition, structure, or subject matter. In literary studies it is used in two ways: first, on a meta-level, it is used to distinguish between prose, poetry, and drama; second, it used to distinguish between different types of compositions within those groups (e.g., lyric poems, epic poems, haiku, and so on). In film studies it tends to be used only to separate conventional narrative types (e.g. romance, thriller, action-adventure, and so on).

Further Reading: J. Frow *Genre* (2005).

geopolitical aesthetic A type of narrative whose essential subject is the inter-relations between nation states. Fredric *Jameson coined the concept for a series of lectures he gave at the British Film Institute in London in 1990 dealing with the differences between First World, Second World, and *Third World cinemas. Subsequently published as a book entitled *The Geopolitical Aesthetic* (1992), these lectures highlight the difficulty film-makers face in representing the relationship between nations. In later work Jameson has suggested that films like *Dirty Pretty Things* (director Frears, 2001), *In This World* (director Winterbottom, 2003), and the British TV miniseries *Traffik* (director Reid, 1989), which revolve around international criminal conspiracies—illegal human organ trading, people smuggling, and drug smuggling respectively—call to attention the way the lives of people in different parts of the world are inextricably linked.
See also COGNITIVE MAPPING; NATIONAL ALLEGORY.

German Expressionism A *modernist film movement that developed in Germany in the first part of the 20th century, lasting roughly from 1919 until 1924. The best-known examples of German Expressionist film are: *The Cabinet of Dr Caligari* (director Wiene, 1919), *Metropolis* (director Lang, 1926), and *Nosferatu* (director Murnau, 1921). Contemporaneous with the tumultuous Weimar period and the rise of German fascism, its dark, anti-realist aesthetic was inspired by the pan-European movement of *Expressionism in the arts, typified by such diverse figures as Gustav Klimt, Edvard Munch, and Vincent Van Gogh; more locally, it took inspiration from the Munich-based der Blaue Reiter (the blue rider) group of artists and the Dresden-based die Brücke (the bridge) group, whose members included Franz Marc, Wassily Kandinsky, Ernst Kirchner, and Fritz Beyl. Like Expressionist art, which was similarly influenced by *psychoanalysis, its subject matter tends to be focused on ambivalent questions to do with sexuality and emotion, which it explores via supernatural and science fictional tales. German Expressionism was very influential on Hollywood, particularly **film noir* (many of the directors, including Lang, Lubitsch, and Murnau, migrated to the USA when the Nazis came to power in 1933).

Further Reading: T. Elsaesser *New German Cinema: A History* (1989).

Gestalt The German word for 'configuration', 'pattern', and 'whole' which has passed into English because English lacks a precise equivalent. Its use in *critical theory originates with Gestalt psychology developed by Max Wertheimer, Kurt Koffka, and Wolfgang Köhler, which explored the psychology of perception and argued that the operational principle of perception is holistic (i.e. we see the outline of the whole first and fill in the details in stages). Gestalt theory passed easily into art theory, where it was used by the influential art historian Ernst Gombrich to create a dialectic between figure and ground.

GIP *See* GROUPE D'INFORMATION SUR LES PRISONS.

Glissant, Édouard (1928–) Caribbean writer and critical theorist. He is best known as one of the principal architects behind *Creoleness, the movement to celebrate the cultural, ethnic, and political heterogeneity of the Caribbean. Shortlisted for the Nobel Prize in 1992, the year fellow Caribbean Derek Walcott won it, Glissant is the author of several novels as well as collections of poetry and essays. Perhaps because he is Francophone, his work has not received the attention it deserves in *Postcolonial Studies. In his theoretical writings he acknowledges the influence of Gilles *Deleuze and Félix *Guattari, especially their concept of the *rhizome.

globalization A complex process involving the worldwide diffusion of cultural products, the streamlining of international manufacturing and trade, the standardization of global financial markets, and the prevalence of new media technology capable of simultaneous real-time transmission of content everywhere in the world. Often described in terms of a 'shrinking' of the planet, the reality is in fact the opposite: globalization is the result of the massive expansion of processes and enterprises that were once national or at most regional in scale and scope.

Globalization is a highly contested term. First of all, there is no agreement that it actually exists; second, where there is agreement that it exists, there is considerable argument about when it began; third, where there is agreement about both its existence and its origin, there is disagreement about whether this constitutes anything new. Complicating matters is the fact that globalization is not 'owned' by any single discipline and could even be said to have been simultaneously invented by several disciplines at once. So, when an economist, a historian, and a sociologist speak about globalization, it cannot be taken for granted that what they have in mind is exactly the same thing. Not surprisingly, perhaps, there is also very little agreement about whether globalization is a good or bad thing—there is no consensus view on either the Left or the Right.

Does globalization exist? The evidence would seem to be overwhelming. The existence of institutions like the World Bank, the International Monetary Fund, the World Trade Organization, the International Criminal Court, and the United Nations, not to mention multinational corporations like Ford®, Coca-Cola®, and Microsoft® whose businesses reach to almost every corner of the globe, is a compelling argument for the affirmative case. But there are those, like American anthropologist James Clifford, who make the counter-claim that there are still hundreds of millions of people in the poorer parts of the world completely unaware of globalization. This view holds true if globalization is viewed strictly as a phenomenon that one has to be conscious of or directly participate in for it to exist. Ulrich *Beck and other *risk society theorists have shown, however, that this is not the case. For example, it is widely accepted that climate change is a global phenomenon brought about by human actions that affects every person on the planet whether they are aware of it or not.

Assuming that globalization does exist, that there are enough processes and enterprises of a global scale and scope to agree that it is a reality, then when did it start? This is a *periodization hypothesis and as such the answer turns on whether one can point to what amounts to *paradigm shift, a moment when things became different in kind. *Dependency theory and *world-system theory scholars like André Gunder Frank and Immanuel *Wallerstein, among others, argue that what we know of as globalization today is simply international trade by another name and that has been going on since ancient times. On this view, globalization is simply the latest and most extensive phase of process that has been ongoing for more than 2,000 years, and therefore nothing particularly new.

The counter argument is that the latter half of the 20th century has seen such seismic changes in international trade regulation, business practice, technological advancement, geopolitical alignment, and *culture in general, that one is compelled to take the view that there is something radically different happening today compared to even the recent past (i.e. pre World War II). The two most obvious indicators of this change are the financial markets and the media—the fact that the latter has taken to almost obsessive reporting of the former is doubtless the reason for its visibility, but its genuine global potency was made abundantly apparent in the so-called credit crunch of 2007–9. Anyone watching a major news service like CNN or BBC cannot help but have the impression that globalization is a fact: almost everything is reported in terms of its global impact (or alternatively in terms of the way the global impacts on the local).

In cultural terms, globalization manifests itself in two ways: (i) the global diffusion of products originally associated with a single culture or nation (e.g., sushi, hamburgers, French fries, coffee, chocolate, and so on are available practically everywhere in the world); (ii) a global breaking down of local tastes, or to put it another way, a global cosmopolitanism of taste (e.g., sushi is available everywhere because tastes have changed to accommodate it). American sociologist George *Ritzer has tried to characterize globalization as *McDonaldization, but this is a simplification—it assumes that globalization spread like a virus from a single site, namely the USA, whereas in fact it is the product of concurrent changes of the kind that only something like *complexity theory would be capable of theorizing properly.

g

Further Reading: F. Jameson and M. Miyoshi *The Cultures of Globalization* (1998).
A. MacGillivray *A Brief History of Globalisation: The Untold Story of Our Incredible Shrinking Planet* (2006).
M. Steger *Globalization: A Very Short Introduction* (2003).

glocalization A neologism conflating the terms 'global' and 'local' to express the paradoxical manner in which processes of *globalization, which seem to erode the very possibility of the local, in fact demand an intensified attention to it. Glocalization highlights the inextricability of the two views of the world: global and local. Global processes, such as the movement of international finance flows, have a local effect, and vice versa, as the 'credit crunch' of 2007–9 demonstrated—failing mortgages in America almost brought down the entire global financial sector.

Glocalization was first used by Manfred Lange to describe the goal of the 1989 Global Change exhibition he curated in Bonn, which was to show the interconnection between the different levels of perception—local, regional, and global. In academic circles it was popularized by British sociologists Roland Robertson and Zygmunt *Bauman. The relation between the global and the local has also been of great concern to *Postcolonial Studies, particularly the critics Arjun *Appadurai, Homi *Bhabha, Arif Dirlik, and Gayatri *Spivak.

Independently of academia, global businesses (particularly in Japan) have discovered that a one-size-fits-all approach to marketing does not work and that what is required is rather an embedding of their products in a local context. Thus at the start of the new millennium CNN abandoned its model of one centralized newsdesk broadcasting to the world and created instead several localized newsdesks, each one tailored to the specific cultural, ethnic, and political concerns of its region. There is also an activist dimension to this term, as is exemplified in the slogan 'Think globally, act locally'.

Further Reading: Z. Bauman *Globalization: The Human Consequences* (1998).
M. Featherstone et al. (eds.) *Global Modernities* (1995).
F. Jameson and M. Miyoshi (eds.) *The Cultures of Globalization* (1998).

glossematics (Glossematik) Louis *Hjelmslev's name for his theory of language. Like Ferdinand de *Saussure, one of his key inspirations, Hjelmslev took the position that language is arbitrary in relation to the real world, which is to say there is nothing about a tree, for example, that necessitates it being called a tree, a fact that is amply proven by the great variety of different words different languages use for ostensibly the same object. By the same token, not all languages name things in the same way—his two demonstrations of this have become quite famous: the first compares Welsh and English words for colours, showing that the Welsh word 'glas' covers a spectrum of colours that in English would be shared between green, blue, and gray; the second compares Danish, German, and French words for trees individually and collectively and again shows that there is a disparity in the way they name the world. His conclusion, which has much in common with Saussure, was that words are *signs and as such do not refer to the real world, but rather express our sense of it.

His comparison between languages served another, deeper purpose. Hjelmslev's ultimate goal with glossematics was to abstract what is common to all languages. Thus he compares the phrases 'jeg véd det ikke', 'je ne sais pas', and 'I don't know' in Danish, French, and English respectively and suggests that although constructed differently they can all be said to share a single thought or 'purport'. The rather odd word 'purport' translates the Danish word 'mening', which might also have been rendered as meaning, although this too would have been problematic because it would have obscured the originality of Hjelmslev's theory. The French translation (the one Barthes, Deleuze, Greimas, and others relied on), which renders purport as 'sens', is perhaps a better choice, inasmuch that in English it implies both the words 'meaning' and 'direction' without implying direct intent as purport does. Julia *Kristeva, among others, has criticized the notion of purport for preserving a transcendental element in what is otherwise meant to be an immanent theory of language.

For Hjelmslev, as a process purport is equivalent to substance, as though the intent of a particular statement is like clay that can be moulded into a variety of different forms. But, having said that, looked at from a system point of view, it does not have an independent existence—it can only be a substance insofar as it has form. Thus, in addition to content as substance, there is always a content-form as well that is independent of the content and forms it into a content substance. The shape of a building is, for all intents and purposes independent of the materials used to build it; but it is also constrained by those materials, in that there are only certain things concrete and steel can be made to do. Hjelmslev recognizes this and accounts for it in his system by adding a dimension of expression to his grid, again distinguishing system and process within it. As process, expression refers to the acquired limits in the range of references of particular words (as he points out, the Welsh 'glas' has a greater range of reference than its putative cognate in English 'blue'); as system, he notes that the same sound can have different meanings in different languages ('got' in English sounds the same as 'Gott' (god) in German, but doesn't mean the same thing). Thus expression-purport and content-purport must be seen as independent of each other.

Not unjustifiably, the Italian linguist and bestselling novelist Umberto *Eco describes Hjelmslev's theory as having 'Byzantine complexity'. This becomes apparent as soon as one tries to unravel the way Hjelmslev weaves together four new terms to explain purport and its relation to language: form of content, form of expression, content of form, and content of expression. These may be considered rewrites of Saussure's basic binary pair, *signifier and signified, although the truth is they go way beyond Saussure's thinking.

Goffman, Erving (1922–82) Canadian-born sociologist; born in Mannville in Alberta, but raised near Winnipeg. His parents were lower middle-class Ukrainian Jews. Goffman originally enrolled to study chemistry in Manitoba, but after a spell working for the National Film Board became interested in sociology and switched his major, moving to Toronto where he was taught by eminent social scientists C.W.M. Hart and Ray Birdwhistle. He did his PhD, a study of rural life in the Shetland Islands (Scotland), at the University of Chicago, graduating in 1953. From 1955 to 1958 Goffman worked on a National Institute of Mental Health-funded ethnographic project at St Elizabeth's Hospital in Washington DC. He used this as an opportunity to gather material for his book, *Asylums* (1961), one of the most influential pieces of sociology in the 20th century as well as a moving and affecting account of the dehumanizing processes mental patients are subjected to. Goffman was particularly interested in the social and political mechanisms whereby certain behaviours come to be coded as clinically insane and not merely eccentric. This built on his previous work on the performance of social roles in the similarly influential *The Presentation of Self in Everyday Life* (1959). He attempted to synthesize his observations on everyday interactions in *Frame Analysis* (1974), a work he himself thought of as his magnum opus. Although Goffman continues to be read today, his work has been criticized, somewhat paradoxically, for being on the one hand overly impressionistic and on the other hand overly systemic.

Further Reading: T. Burns *Erving Goffman* (1992).
P. Manning *Erving Goffman and Modern Sociology* (1992).

Goldmann, Lucien (1913–70) Romanian-born, Paris-based *Marxist sociologist of literature whose theory of structural parallels or homologies was very influential in the 1950s and 1960s. Born in Bucharest, he began his studies there, but soon moved to Vienna to study German philology. It was there that he first came into contact with the work of György *Lukács, which proved to be a lifelong interest. During World War II he was initially incarcerated in Paris, where he was studying at the time, but he was able to get away to Switzerland where he got a job as an assistant to the great child psychologist Jean Piaget. He completed a doctorate there on Kant. After the war he returned to Paris. He held positions at the Centre Nationale de Recherche Scientifique and the École Pratique des Hautes Études. His work foregrounded the problems of *class consciousness and *reification. In *Le dieu caché: étude sur la vision tragique dans les Pensées de Pascal et le théâtre de Racine* (1955), translated as *The Hidden God: A Study of Tragic Vision in the Pensées of Pascal and the Tragedies of Racine* (1964), Goldmann posited a homology between class situation, world view, and artistic form, the implication being that each of these three things can be treated as synonymous with the other two, so that a study of an artistic object can yield knowledge of both class and world view. Because of this facility, enabling the study of one thing to function as the study of another thing, the theory of homology was initially quite attractive, but would subsequently come under fire for oversimplying things. Goldmann enlarged upon the idea in his posthumously published *Pour une sociologie du roman* (1973), translated as *Towards a Sociology of the Novel* (1974), making what he called a 'rigorous homology' between the novel form and *everyday life in capitalist society.

Further Reading: M. Cohen *The Wager of Lucien Goldmann: Tragedy, Dialectics, and a Hidden God* (1994).

governmentality (*gouvernementalité*) Michel *Foucault's word for the set of assumptions underpinning a particular mode of government. Studying it amounts to a deciphering of its logic. Foucault coined this term in the course of his lectures on security, territory, and population and suggested that where before he had spoken of *biopower this was what he had in fact meant. Although the words are obviously related and share a common point of origin, they are nonetheless distinct: governmentality defines a general problematic, while biopower refers to a specific historical example. In a separately published lecture from the aforementioned series from 1977/78 entitled 'Governmentality' Foucault explains that he means three things by this term: (i) the ensemble of institutions and procedures that enable the exercise of a very specific type of power; (ii) the tendency that has over time led to the predominance of a specific model of power (i.e. *biopower); (iii) the processes by which previous models of power came to be governmentalized. In Foucault's view, what he terms 'government' (by which he means something approximating bureaucracy, though he has in mind something rather more active than that) has basically supplanted the state and the sovereign. Governmentality also implies something like the old sociological notion of 'mentality', meaning a way of thinking as much as a set of practices. Mitchell Dean's *Governmentality: Power and Rule in Modern Society* (1999) provides both an excellent account of the concept and its uses in the field of social research as well as a very comprehensive bibliography of the secondary research that has sprung up around this concept.

Further Reading: G. Burchell (ed.), *The Foucault Effect* (1991).

M. Foucault 'Governmentality' in P. Rabinow (ed.), Essential Works of Foucault 1954–84, Volume 3 (2000).

M. Foucault *Security, Territory, Population: Lectures at the Collège de France 1977–78* (2007).

Gramsci, Antonio (1891–1937) Italian *Marxist philosopher and political activist and theorist. Gramsci was born in the small town of Ales, near Cagliari, in Sardinia. His family were of Albanian origin. When he was only 7 years old, his father was imprisoned for embezzlement, placing considerable financial strain on the family. Gramsci himself was forced to take on part-time work to help support the family until his father's release in 1904. He was nevertheless able to complete high school and win a scholarship to the University of Turin, where he studied linguistics and literature, but due to ill-health and poverty he was unable to complete his studies.

From 1914 he started writing for socialist newspapers to support himself. For the next ten years or so he combined journalism with political activism. Fiat and Lancia were then setting up factories in

Turin, moving it towards the giant industrial city it would become, and Gramsci helped the new factory workers to organize trade unions. He joined the Partito Socialista Italiano (PSI, Italian Socialist Party) in 1913. In 1919 he helped found the weekly newspaper *L'Ordine Nuovo* (The New Order), which was recognized by Lenin as ideologically closest to his own Bolshevik programme. The editors of this periodical formed the core of the splinter group Partito Communista d'Italia (PCI, Italian Communist Party) which Gramsci helped form in 1921. Gramsci became leader of the PCI in 1924.

In 1924 Gramsci was elected to the Italian parliament as a representative of the Veneto region. Gramsci was vocally anti-Mussolini, which was a highly dangerous stance to take. In spite of his parliamentary immunity he was arrested in 1926 by the Fascist government under its 'emergency powers' act. At his trial, the prosecutor famously declared that it was imperative to stop Gramsci's brain from functioning! This manifestly did not happen: that Gramsci is known at all today is because of the 3,000 pages of notes he compiled while in prison, which were later smuggled out and published. However, the miserable conditions in prison aggravated his already poor health and he died in a prison hospital half way through his 20 year sentence at the age of 46.

Gramsci's 'Prison Notebooks' as they came to be known cover an astonishing range of topics, including close readings of Marx's work which had to be written entirely from memory because communist books were not allowed in prison. His writing was also subject to the scrutiny of the prison guards and for this reason he had to create an elaborate new vocabulary. Many of his new concepts, then, are not entirely new; they are rather new words for already existing concepts—the best known instance of this is *hegemony, which is in many ways simply a recasting of the traditional Marxist concept of *ideology. There is considerable debate in Marxist discourse about the merits of these changes, some arguing that they are not simply new words but genuinely new concepts, with others taking the view that the changes are had at the price of a loss of a sense of intellectual heritage. In the UK, Gramsci's deviations from textbook Marxism won him a wide readership in *Cultural Studies and the New Left.

The reason for this is fairly simple. Gramsci theorized the role *culture plays in politics in a new and compelling way. He defines the state as a kind of dual system comprising the coercive forces of political society and the private realm of business and work or what Gramsci called *civil society. With his concept of hegemony he showed that the reason the much anticipated revolution of the proletariat had not yet occurred was because within the realm of civil society the working class had come to identify their own best interests as being one and the same as the best interests of the bourgeoisie. The banking crisis or 'credit crunch' of 2007–9 provided a clear example of what this looks like in practice: taxpayers' money was used by governments in the UK, US, and elsewhere to prop up failing banks on the basis that we would all be worse off if they were allowed to fail. This rationale was largely effective because—as Gramsci argued several decades earlier—the ruling class control the cultural means of production, not only the media, but 'common sense' itself.

To defend against this, Gramsci argued, the proletariat needs its own intelligentsia, in other words a standing army of what he called *organic intellectuals. These are intellectuals raised up from the working classes, who in direct contrast to the ivory-tower intellectuals do not see themselves as separate from society. The organic intellectual shares the experiences and understands the situation of the working classes, but unlike them no longer feels *subaltern, and for that reason is in a position to facilitate progressive change. Gramsci advocated 'popular' education, that is, education for everyone at every stage of their life. His notebooks contain wonderful essays on the political significance of popular literature and film, seeing in them both the source of the reactionary nature of the oppressed and a promise of change.

Further Reading: P. Anderson 'The Antinomies of Perry Anderson' in *New Left Review* (1976).

C. Bambery *A Rebel's Guide to Gramsci* (2006).

C. Buci-Glucksmann *Gramsci and the State* (1975).

S. Jones *Antonio Gramsci* (2006).

grand narrative (*grand récit*) Jean-François *Lyotard's term for ideas, concepts, notions, or beliefs which can function to legitimate certain social actions and practices. For instance, the notion of revolution, since the French Revolution, has served to legitimate large-scale programmes of social change. Similarly, the notion of *Enlightenment has served to legitimate a movement toward secular reason. Such grand narratives no longer function, according to Lyotard who defines the *postmodern age as being characterized by incredulity towards all grand narratives. Several critics have argued that it is too early to say that all grand narratives have become defunct. *Marxism (it is thought by many) still retains its power to give social life coherence and meaning. In Anglo-American *Cultural Studies, grand narrative has been interpreted to mean any form of overarching *ideology, which it then codes as oppressive.

Greenblatt, Stephen (1943–) American literary critic, specialist in Shakespeare and Renaissance studies, and one of the founders of *New Historicism. Born in Boston and educated at Yale and Cambridge, where he worked with Raymond *Williams. Greenblatt taught for nearly 30 years at the University of California, Berkeley and is now based at Harvard. He first used the term New Historicism (which would in due course be taken up as the name of a movement) in his 1982 book *The Power of Forms in the English Renaissance* to describe his way of connecting the literary text to its historical context with a view to using that as a means of interpreting it and understanding it. For Greenblatt, the text must always be seen as arising out of the material of its time: ideas, stories, concepts, do not just fall from the sky, he insists, but have a definite (albeit not necessarily knowable) origin. His reputation had already been established with his previous book *Renaissance Self-Fashioning*, which introduced an idea that Michel *Foucault admitted to finding useful in his theorization of the care for the self. Self-fashioning, the conscious construction of one's self, both interior and exterior, is in many respects the key to Greenblatt's entire oeuvre: his most famous work, the *New York Times* bestseller *Will in the World: How Shakespeare became Shakespeare* (2004), takes this idea to its logical limits. Greenblatt's work has been highly influential, particularly in *postcolonial literary studies, which has an obvious sympathy with his historical approach to interpretation. However, his work is also viewed by many as anti-theoretical and not all that congenial to *critical theory.

Further Reading: C. Gallagher and S. Greenblatt *Practicing New Historicism* (2000). M. Robson *Stephen Greenblatt* (2007).

Greer, Germaine (1939–) Australian *feminist scholar, political activist, and journalist. She became a household name with the international bestseller *The Female Eunuch* (1970), a vanguard text in *Second Wave feminism. Greer argued that culture has separated women from their *libido, their *desire, and their sexuality, thus rendering them virtual eunuchs. Her larger quarrel is that this separation of women from their libido is in effect a separation of them from their capacity to act, and as such it is politically stifling. If *feminism is to achieve its goals, she argues, and actually liberate women from the confining strictures of *patriarchy then it needs to put women back in touch with their sexuality. To do this, Greer argued, women should give up celibacy, monogamy, even the nuclear family. Not surprisingly, Greer's theses were regarded as provocative and her work drew considerable criticism as well as lavish praise. Following the success of this book, Greer has maintained a high-profile existence championing the cause of feminism, not always in a way that is greeted with widespread agreement, but rarely if ever in a way that doesn't provoke thought and comment. She has published several books since, but none as successful as her first.

Greimas, Algirdas Julien (1917–92) *Structuralist, semiologist, whose work influenced figures as diverse as Roland *Barthes and Fredric *Jameson (an avid exponent of Greimas's semiotic squares). He was part of a great generation of (mainly) French scholars who, in the aftermath of World War II, thought it both possible and desirable to take a more scientific approach to the study of culture in all its forms.

Born in Lithuania, Greimas moved to France in 1936 to study law at the University of Grenoble. He went back to Lithuania in 1940 and, after enduring successive military occupations by the Germans then the Soviets, returned to France in 1944 to complete a doctorate on the vocabulary of clothing. In 1949 he took a job in Alexandria in Egypt, where he met and became friends with Barthes, who had similarly been posted there by the French Department of Cultural Affairs. Drawing on three principal sources—namely, the Swiss linguist Ferdinand de *Saussure, the Danish linguist Louis *Hjemslev, and Russian morphologist Vladimir *Propp—Greimas pioneered a method of analysis he called structural semantics. This was the subject of his magnum opus *Sémantique structurale* (1966), translated as *Structural Semantics* (1983).

Greimas's aim was not to determine the meaning of specific words or texts, but rather to understand how meaning is produced. Effectively a generational model akin to Noam *Chomsky's model of generational grammar, structural semantics is an extreme form of formalism. Also known as semiotic reduction, structural semantics treats the content of the text as a superficial expression (or enunciation-spectacle) of a deeper drama played out between two interrelated structures he called *actants and functions. In this way, virtually all forms of textual production from the writing of scientific treatises through to folktales and cookbooks (to list only some of the types of text Greimas analysed) can be treated as narratives. Moreover, it holds that the content is independent of the narrative, or what amounts to the same thing it shows that a particular narrative function or actant can be fulfilled by a near infinite variety of content.

Further Reading: F. Dosse *History of Structuralism* (1997).
F. Jameson *The Prison-House of Language* (1972).
R. Schleifer *A.J. Greimas: Linguistics, Semiotics and Discourse Theory* (1987).

SEE WEB LINKS

- An overview of a number of semioticians including Algirdas Greimas.

Groupe d'Information sur les Prisons (GIP, Group for Information on Prisons) Established in 1970 by Michel *Foucault in collaboration with Jean-Marie Domenach and Pierre Vidal-Naquet for the purpose of distributing information about conditions in French prisons. It was not primarily a prison-reform advocacy group, though of course its purpose in making known the terrible conditions in which prisoners were forced to live was to foster the call for change. Operating in the age before email and the Internet, the various members of the group gathered information by interviewing prisoners, their wives, and guards, and distributing the results of their research via samizdat pamphlets. The group attracted as members such luminaries as Gilles *Deleuze, Jean Genet, and Jean-Paul *Sartre.

Further Reading: D. Macey *The Lives of Michel Foucault* (1993).

group-in-fusion (group-en-fuson) French philosopher Jean-Paul *Sartre's term for a group of people united by a common purpose. A crucial component of *Critique de la Raison Dialectique* (1960), translated as *Critique of Dialectical Reason* (1976), Sartre's theory is that the majority of people are *alienated from one another for the majority of time, a state he refers to as *seriality. What they lack, he argues, is *praxis, namely the will to get involved in the political process. The group-in-fusion is not an 'innocent' or 'ideal' form in that it can refer to both progressive and fascistic types of *social movement.

Guattari, Félix (1930–92) French psychoanalyst, political activist, and philosopher. He is best known for the books he co-wrote with French philosopher Gilles *Deleuze: *L'Anti-Oedipe: Capitalisme et Schizophrénie* (1972), translated as *Anti-Oedipus* (1977); *Kafka: Pour une Littérature Mineure* (1975), translated as *Kafka: Towards a Minor Literature* (1986); *Mille Plateaux: Capitalisme et Schizophrénie 2* (1980), translated as *A Thousand Plateaus: Capitalism and Schizophrenia* (1987); and *Qu'est-ce que la Philosophie?* (1991), translated as *What is Philosophy?* (1994). He was also the author of several important works in his own right: *Psychanalyse et Transversalité* (1972) (Psychoanalysis and Tranversality); *La Révolution Moléculaire* (1980), translated as *Molecular Revolution* (1984); and *Cartographies Schizoanalytiques* (1989) (Schizoanalytic Cartographies).

Before he met Deleuze, Guattari had already gained notoriety in France as a political activist. He was known in the French press as

'Mr Anti-' for his public campaigning for a range of causes from the decolonization of Algeria, the improved treatment of prisoners in French prisons (he was a member of Michel *Foucault's *Groupe d'Information sur les Prisons), the improved treatment of the mentally ill in French insane asylums, and the establishment of free radio, to gay rights and green politics. In 1973 he outraged national sensibilities by publishing a special issue of the journal *Recherches* edited by Guy Hocquenghem and René Scherer provocatively entitled 'Trois milliards de pervers: Grande Encyclopédie des Homosexualités' (Three Billion Perverts: An Encyclopedia of Homosexualities). French courts banned it and ordered all copies destroyed. Guattari was also fined 600 francs, but he proudly never paid. More controversially, he collaborated with the Italian Marxist theorist, Antonio *Negri, who was arrested in 1977 on charges of terrorism for his association with the Red Brigades. Guattari also spoke against the extradition from Germany to France of Klaus Croissant, a German lawyer sympathetic to the Baader-Meinhof Group; and in the late 1950s and early 1960s he carried cash for the Front de Liberation Nationale Algérien (Algerian National Liberation Front), the guerrilla army fighting for independence from French rule in Algeria.

Guattari's activism was informed by his clinical practice as a psychotherapist in the private psychiatric clinic La Borde founded in 1953 by Jean Oury, with the aim of providing a radically new form of care which 'de-institutionalized the institution'. At La Borde all staff, including cooks and cleaners, participated in providing therapy for the patients, many of whom were psychotic, and all staff, including doctors and nurses, participated in the maintenance of the hospital. Guattari was enlisted by Oury because of his ability to organize collective action and thus help break down the barriers between staff and patients. Guattari received formal training in psychoanalysis from France's most important interpreter of Freud, Jacques *Lacan, achieving the status of 'analyste membre' (member analyst) in 1969. Although he remained a member of Lacan's school, the *Ecole Freudienne de Paris, until its dissolution in 1980 shortly before the master's death, Guattari's relationship to Lacan and Lacanian psychoanalysis was at best ambivalent. The publication of Guattari's notebooks, *The Anti-Oedipus Papers* (2006), has made it clear just how strained relations were between them, especially after the publication of *Anti-Oedipus* (even though that work was, in the words of its authors, designed to save Lacan from the Lacanians).

Like the anti-psychiatrists R.D. *Laing and David *Cooper, although he did not agree with their strategies, Guattari was much inspired by Jean-Paul *Sartre's *existentialist philosophy. Deploying the rubric *schizoanalysis to describe his approach to psychotherapy, Guattari's presiding goal was to re-invent psychoanalysis, particularly its Freudian and Lacanian forms, from the inside. His principal argument against psychoanalysis was that it is too normative: its basic therapeutic move is to try to restore the patient to something it supposes is a prior state of normalcy. Whereas in Guattari's view there is no going back after a psychotic episode, one must go forward. Towards the end of his life, Guattari developed a theory of World Integrated Capitalism, a forerunner to theories of globalization, and a major influence on Michael *Hardt and Antonio Negri's concept of *Empire.

See also ANTI-PSYCHIATRY; LACAN; MARXISM; SCHIZOANALYSIS.

Further Reading: F. Berardi *Félix Guattari: Thought, Friendship, and Visionary Cartography* (2008).
F. Dosse *Gilles Deleuze et Félix Guattari: Biographie Croisée* (2007).
G. Genosko *Félix Guattari: A Critical Introduction* (2009).
J. Watson *Guattari's Diagrammatic Thought: Writing between Lacan and Deleuze* (2009).

gynocriticism A term introduced by American *feminist literary critic Elaine Showalter to classify critical work such as her own which focuses exclusively on literature written by female authors. Its twofold aim is to recover 'lost' or 'neglected' women writers and to understand in its specificity women's construction of textual meaning. The term is not widely used today, but the two key examples of gynocriticism, namely Sandra Gilbert and Susan Gubar's *The Madwoman in the Attic* (1979) and Elaine Showalter's *A Literature of their Own* (1977), are still read today, so the practice of gynocriticism, if not the word, is very much alive.

Habermas, Jürgen (1929–) German philosopher, best known for concepts of *communicative action and the *public sphere. An immensely influential figure, particularly in his native country, Habermas's shadow looms large over almost every aspect of research in the human and social sciences. The only comparable figures in terms of impact in this field are Michel *Foucault and Niklas Luhmann.

Habermas was born in Düsseldorf in Northern Germany, but he spent his early life in Gummersbach, where his grandfather was the director of a Protestant seminary. His father was the director of the Chamber of Industry and Commerce in the neighbouring city of Cologne. In interviews he has described his father as a Nazi sympathizer and admitted that like Günter Grass he was a member of the Hitler Youth. This experience, particularly Germany's defeat and the aftermath, including the Nuremberg 'War Crimes' trials, could not but be formative for Habermas, and they left him a stern critic of politics. He completed his undergraduate studies in philosophy at Göttingen and Zürich, then completed a doctorate in 1954 at the University of Bonn entitled, *Das Absolute und die Geschichte. Von der Zwiespältigkeit in Schellings Denken* (The absolute and history: on the contradiction in Schelling's thought). In 1956 he moved to Frankfurt to complete his habilitation at the home of *critical theory, the Institute for Social Research, under the direction of Theodor *Adorno and Max *Horkheimer.

Interestingly, although Habermas would remain connected in some way or another to the Institute for Social Research for the rest of his career, he did not finish his habilitation there. He fell out with Horkheimer over the direction his thesis should take, so he transferred to the University of Marburg. In 1962, at the instigation of Hans-Georg *Gadamer, Habermas was offered a position at Heidelberg University, which he accepted, but two years later he was lured back to Frankfurt by Adorno to take over Horkheimer's recently vacated chair. He remained there until 1970, when he moved to the Max Planck Institute in Starnberg. A decade later he returned to Frankfurt and took over as director of the Institute for Social Research. Beginning in the early 1980s, Habermas also accepted a number of visiting professorships in the US.

Unusually for a dissertation, Habermas's first work, *Strukturwandel der Öffentlichkeit; Untersuchungen zu einer Kategorie der Bürgerlichen Gesellschaft* (1962), translated as *The Structural Transformation of the Public Sphere: an Inquiry into a Category of Bourgeois Society* (1989), proved an enduring success. It introduces the important concept of the public sphere, which is a realm in society where citizens can freely express opinions relating to general or public interest topics. Habermas treats the public sphere as a historical category and his research focuses on how specific types of public sphere emerge and correspondingly what causes their demise.

Post-structuralist critics like Jean-François *Lyotard are sharply critical of the concept's inherent idealism, but it has nevertheless proven highly useful for thinking through the transformations that have shaped what is generally known today as *postmodernism. One of Habermas's most influential pieces of work was a short essay he wrote entitled 'Modernity—An Incomplete Project' (1983), which was a polemic shot across the bow of postmodernism at the moment of its birth. Rather than recognize the advent of a new era as many critics (e.g. Fredric *Jameson) did at the start of the 1980s, Habermas took the counter-intuitive position that *modernity, i.e. the logical precursor to postmodernity, had not yet reached its zenith, and, moreover, that its emancipatory project was worth continuing with and shouldn't be abandoned so lightly.

Habermas's interest in the public sphere developed over the next two decades into a general theory of society, culminating in his magnum opus *Theorie des Kommunikativen Handelns* (1981), translated as *The Theory of Communicative Action* (1984). Habermas's theory is that all social life can be explained in terms of the ability of humans to communicate with one another. Most important for Habermas is the ability to use language to do things, not merely to command other people to perform a particular act, but to change the very symbolic status of a person, place, or object. In this last respect, he draws on and extends the theory of *performative language developed by J.L. *Austin and J. *Searle and Ludwig *Wittgenstein's theory of *language games. Since the publication of *The Theory of Communicative Action* Habermas has tried to use the central theses of that work to analyse and critique ethical and political issues relating to contemporary world events. The culmination of this work is the magisterial *Faktizität und Geltung. Beiträge zur Diskurstheorie des Rechts und des demokratischen Rechtsstaats* (1992), translated as *Between Facts and Norms: Contributions to a Discourse Theory of Law and Democracy* (1998).

Further Reading: A. Bowie *Introduction to German Philosophy: From Kant to Habermas* (2003).
A. Edgar *The Philosophy of Habermas* (2005).
R. Holub *Jürgen Habermas* (1991).
T. McCarthy *The Critical Theory of Jürgen Habermas* (1984).
D. Rasmussen *Reading Habermas* (1990).

habitus An acquired but structuring disposition towards the world constituted in practice (i.e. as a consequence of actual, practical experience) and always oriented towards practical situations and problems. French sociologist Pierre *Bourdieu, developed the concept to theorize cultural behaviour as simultaneously subjective and objective. Habitus refers to those aspects of cultural behaviour such as taste in food or definitions of beauty which appear 'natural' but are in fact 'learned'. It manifests as 'savoir faire' ('know-how') or more precisely as an understanding of how to 'play the game'—as Bourdieu points out, in sport, the rules of the game only create the conditions of possibility, but they do not determine how the game will actually be played, nor in fact how one will best succeed at the game. Knowing this—how to succeed in the game—is the practical knowledge Bourdieu has in mind when he refers to habitus. Crucially, the habitus is the locus of those actions—which Bourdieu defines as *practices—which are performed unthinkingly, without intention or specific goal, save that of conforming to the demands of the *field, which the subject has internalized. Bourdieu says habitus is embodied history, it is the lessons of the past transmuted into a 'second nature' and, though forgotten as history, constant as a presence in everything we do.

Further Reading: P. Bourdieu *Le sens pratique* (1980), translated as *The Logic of Practice* (1990).

Hall, Stuart (1932–) Left-wing British sociologist and cultural critic instrumental in the foundation of *Cultural Studies as an academic discipline in the UK. Born in Jamaica and educated there, Hall moved to Bristol in the UK in 1951. He went to Merton College, Oxford as a Rhodes Scholar, gaining an MA. He then took a position at Birmingham University. Together with Raymond *Williams, and E.P. *Thompson, he helped found the Marxist journal *New Left Review* in 1960 and edited it for two years before relinquishing the role to Perry *Anderson. In 1964 he was invited by Richard *Hoggart to join the Centre for Contemporary Cultural Studies. He remained with the centre for 15 years, becoming its director in 1968. Over the years, Hall worked on a variety of collaborative projects at Birmingham (a pattern that obtained for much of his career), each analysing a different aspect of British life, such as those published as *Policing the Crisis: Mugging, the State and Law and Order* (1978) and *Resistance through Rituals* (1976), that were to form the basis of the discipline today known as Cultural Studies. In contrast, to many of his sociology colleagues around Britain, Hall was an early adopter of what came to be known simply as 'theory', particularly the work of Italian Marxist, Antonio *Gramsci and the French *structuralists Louis *Althusser and Michel *Foucault. In 1979 he moved to the Open University, where he remained until retirement in 1997. With the election of Margaret Thatcher in 1979, Hall seemed to find his vocation—documenting both the defeat of the Left and the seemingly irrepressible rise of the Right—and wrote what is arguably his most important book, the magisterial, if grim, *The Hard Road to Renewal: Thatcherism and the Crisis of the Left* (1988). As with all his work, this book sought to identify the representational means by which *hegemony is captured, paying particular attention to the ideological manipulation of *identity.

Further Reading: K-H. Chen and D. Morley (eds.) *Stuart Hall: Critical Dialogues in Cultural Studies* (1996).

H. Davis *Understanding Stuart Hall* (2004).

P. Gilroy et al. (eds.) *Without Guarantees: In Honour of Stuart Hall* (2000).

J. Procter *Stuart Hall* (2004).

C. Rojek *Stuart Hall* (2002).

Haraway, Donna (1944–) American cultural critic renowned for her works on the intersections between humans and machines and humans and animals. Born in Denver, Colorado, Haraway studied zoology and philosophy at Colorado College and then completed a PhD at Yale on the role of metaphor in shaping research in developmental biology, later published as *Crystals, Fabrics and Fields: Metaphors of Organicism in Twemtieth-Century Development Biology* (1976). She taught women's studies and general science at the University of Hawaii and Johns Hopkins University before her appointment to the History of Consciousness programme at the University of California, Santa Cruz, where she has worked for more than two decades. Haraway's work has gone through three distinct phases. In her earliest works, such as *Primate Visions: Gender, Race, and Nature in the World of Modern Science* (1989), she showed that human assumptions about themselves are reflected in their analyses of animals, which in theories of animal aggression, for example, mirror our own view of ourselves as creatures driven by instincts. In the second phase, which produced the essay for which she best known, 'A Cyborg Manifesto: Science, Technology, and Socialist-Feminism in the Late Twentieth Century', which is included in the collection

Simians, Cyborgs and Women: The Reinvention of Nature (1991), Haraway argued that we are not as human as we think we are—our dependence on machines is so great, she argues, we have effectively become cyborgs. The third phase takes this argument in a different direction—again she wants to argue that we are less human than we think we are, but this time she does so by highlighting our dependence on animals. This latter work, particularly *The Companion Species Manifesto* (2003), also contains a strong ethical demand for more equitable treatment of animals.

Further Reading: J. Schneider *Donna Haraway: Live Theory* (2005).

Hardt, Michael (1960–) American *Marxist philosopher, social theorist, and cultural critic best known for his collaborative work with Italian Marxist philosopher Antonio *Negri with whom he has co-authored four books.

Hardt was born in Rockville, Maryland in the USA, and raised in the suburbs of Washington DC where his father worked as a Sovietologist (specializing in economics) at the Library of Congress. He studied engineering at Swarthmore College in Pennsylvania during the prolonged 'energy crisis' of the 1970s. His choice of major was motivated by a political desire to help develop alternative energy technology for the poor. He spent his summers in Italy working in a factory making solar panels. In 1983 he moved to Seattle to do a PhD in Comparative Literature, again because it seemed to offer the best way forward for him to advance his political thinking. At this time, too, he was volunteering for the Christian 'Sanctuary Movement' in Guatemala and El Salvador, which provided shelter for refugees trying to escape the CIA-funded wars ravaging those countries. With characteristic modesty, Hardt would later say his time in South America helped him more than he was able to help others.

In the summer of 1987, Hardt travelled to Paris to meet with Antonio Negri to go through some questions he had regarding the English translation of *L'anomalia selvaggia. Saggio su potere e potenza in Baruch Spinoza* (1981), translated as *The Savage Anomaly: The Power of Spinoza's Metaphysics and Politics* (1991). The meeting proved fortuitous. Negri suggested to Hardt that he move to Paris, which he did, and invited him to join the editorial board of the journal he was founding, *Futur Antérieur.* Then when an editor at the University of Minnesota Press asked Negri to put together a collection of his early writings for publication, Negri countered by suggesting a collaborative book written with Michael Hardt dealing with contemporary issues. The resulting work, combining essays from Negri's previous books *Operati e Stato* (1972) (Work and State) and *La*

Forma Stato (1977) (The Form of the State) with new essays by both him and Hardt, was the first step towards the work which would bring them both such international renown.

Hardt's first solo work, *Gilles Deleuze: An Apprenticeship in Philosophy*, a reworked version of his PhD, was published in 1993. One of the first full-length monographs published on *Deleuze and still one of the most important, Hardt's book offered an astute reading of Deleuze as a political philosopher. In 1994, after spending two years at UCLA (University of California, Los Angeles), Hardt was appointed to the Literature Programme at Duke University. Over the next several years he worked on another collaborative project with Negri, which would be published in 2000 as *Empire*. Resonating strongly with the optimistic fervour for change ignited by the anti-WTO (World Trade Organization) movement that took to the streets in such numbers in Seattle, Genoa, and elsewhere as the 20th century drew to a close, the concept of *Empire captured the millennial spirit of the moment perfectly and the book became an instant worldwide bestseller.

Empire is only the first instalment of a vast and vastly ambitious project to rethink the political composition of our time (the second instalment, *Multitude: War and Democracy in the Age of Empire* appeared in 2005, and the third, *Commonwealth*, in 2009). It argues that the worldwide processes of economic, political, and social transformation generally referred to as *globalization have created the necessary conditions for the emergence of a new form of global sovereignty which will rein in the interests of specific nation-states and give more space to the needs of specific subjects, regardless of their place in the world. The new people rising up to assume this new form of sovereignty are referred to as the *multitude by Hardt and Negri. By the same token they argue that the old forms of imperial thinking no longer work as well as they used to. The Empire project is a controversial one and just as it has many enthusiastic supporters, it also has a number of stern critics on both the Left and the Right.

Further Reading: G. Balakrishnan (ed.), *Debating Empire* (2003).

A. Boron *Empire and Imperialism: A Critical Reading of Michael Hardt and Antonio Negri* (2005).

A. Negri *Empire and Beyond* (2008).

P. Passavant and J. Dean *The Empire's New Clothes: Reading Hardt and Negri* (2003).

Harvey, David (1935–) British *Marxist geographer. Born in Kent, Harvey completed both his BA and PhD at St Johns College, Cambridge. His first appointment was at the University of Bristol, where he remained for a decade. He then moved to Johns Hopkins University, where he worked for two decades, with a six-year interregnum at Oxford in the middle. In 2001 he took a position at CUNY (City University of New York). Harvey's work is characterized by its trenchant critique of the effects of capitalism. In *Social Justice and the City* (1973) he argued that geography could not and should not remain objective in the face of urban poverty and its causes and he showed that in many cases it is the result of a deliberate strategy on the part of capital. In *The Limits of Capital* (1982), his most theoretically sophisticated work, Harvey argues that real estate speculation is essential to capitalism's dynamic and its Achilles heel (the 'credit crunch' of 2007–9 clearly bears this out). His most widely known work, however, was his bestselling 1989 book, *The Condition of Postmodernity*, which offered a rich account of the social, cultural, and economic conditions of the era then widely known as *postmodernism. In contrast to the accounts of postmodernity given by Jean-François *Lyotard and Fredric *Jameson, which are in many ways better known, Harvey's account of postmodernity is able to propose a cause for the changes it describes: he points the finger at what he calls 'flexible accumulation', by which he means the system-wide movement away from capital investment in fixed assets like factories towards more fluid investments like shares. Effectively what Harvey provides is a much more sophisticated version of the *post-industrial society thesis of Daniel *Bell and Alain *Touraine. His most recent works, particularly *The New Imperialism* (2003) and *A Brief History of Neoliberalism* (2005) are powerful polemics against the geopolitics of the George W. Bush administration and its origins in Reaganism and Thatcherism.

Further Reading: N. Castree and D. Gregory *David Harvey: A Critical Reader* (2006).

Hegel, Georg Wilhelm Friedrich (1770–1831) German philosopher, one of the most influential thinkers of all time. His work casts an extremely long shadow and virtually every thinker in *critical theory acknowledges his influence, even when—as in the case of someone like Gilles *Deleuze—they go to great lengths to avoid being or sounding like Hegel. Karl *Marx was an enthusiastic, albeit highly critical, reader of Hegel, and as a consequence in Marxism there is a very important stream of work known as Marxist-Hegelianism, of which the best-known exponents are undoubtedly Fredric *Jameson and Slavoj *Žižek. In France, led by Louis *Althusser, there was an equally powerful movement in Marxism aimed at severing the connection between Marx and Hegel and it largely succeeded, with the effect that *post-structuralists tend to neglect Hegel, or worse, caricature him as a figure of evil (Jameson even suggests that in French philosophy Hegel is a codeword for Stalin). Hegel was a similarly potent influence on *deconstruction, *existentialism, *hermeneutics, and *pragmatism.

Hegel was born in Stuttgart, in south western Germany. His father was a secretary in the Duke of Württemberg's revenue office. His mother died when he was 13. A precocious talent, Hegel read extensively as a child and excelled at school. At the age of 18, he entered a Protestant seminary attached to the University of Tübingen, where his fellow students included the future poet Friedrich Hölderlin and the future philosopher Friedrich Schelling. The three became firm, lifelong friends. After graduation, from 1793 until 1801, Hegel worked as a private tutor for wealthy families in Berne and Frankfurt. Then, with the assistance of Schelling, he moved to Jena, where he was given an unsalaried position in the philosophy department. It was in Jena that Hegel encountered Napoleon, whose armies devastated the city, whom he famously described as a 'world-soul'.

His finances made precarious by the war, Hegel moved to Bamberg and accepted the job of editor of the local newspaper there in 1807. His first major book, *Phänomenologie des Geistes* (1807), translated as *Phenomenology of Mind* (1910), appeared in the same year. Written against tough deadlines, Hegel sent individual chapters to the publisher and never had time to revise the whole text. The result is a text whose very structure has been the subject of considerable debate. One of the most influential philosophical works ever written, the *Phenomenology of Mind* (also translated as *Phenomenology of Spirit*) serves as the point of introduction for Hegel's entire philosophical edifice. Hegel takes the radical step of arguing—contrary to *empiricism—that there is nothing prior to the process of producing concepts that can serve as the foundation for philosophy. There is in this sense no immediate given, according to Hegel; all sense data are subject to the prior existence of a conceptual apparatus that enables the mind to make sense of its perceptions. This process of making sense is described by Hegel as *dialectical.

The dialectic is undoubtedly the concept most closely associated with Hegel's name (it is the concept that drew Marx's interest), but it is also relatively poorly understood. The key to the dialectic is the moment of transformation Hegel referred to as the negation of the negation. Understanding is produced when the 'negative' sense data are combined with the equally 'negative' concepts, each one supplying the latter with what it lacks: sense data are negative because they are insufficient to ground truth, while concepts are negative because they are in and of themselves empty abstractions, but in combination they each negate the other's negativity. According to Hegel, all knowledge is produced in this fashion: we start with what is known and as more information becomes available we negate that knowledge and obtain newer, more sophisticated knowledge. This process is known as *Aufhebung*, sometimes translated into English as 'sublation', though more often than not left untranslated: it has the complex triple meaning of raising up, preserving, and negating. Ultimately, what interests Hegel is the process by which the self becomes conscious of itself.

A year after the publication of the *Phenomenology of Mind* he moved again, to Nuremberg, this time to take on the job of headmaster of a *Gymnasium* (high school), where he remained until 1816. During these years he conceived of then composed his enormous three-volume *Enzyklopädie der philosophischen Wissenschaften* (1817), translated as *Encyclopedia of the Philosophical Sciences* (1970). In 1816 he was given an appointment at Heidelberg University, then in 1818 he accepted the chair in philosophy at the University of Berlin, at that time the most prestigious position in the field in Germany. He continued to write prolifically on art, history, and philosophy, contributing several works to the philosophical canon that continue to be studied in detail today. His magnum opus, according to most of his commentators, *Wissenschaft der Logik* (1812–16; 2nd edn, 1832), *The Science of Logic* (1989), lays out in intricate detail Hegel's *metaphysical system.

Hegel is often described as either an idealist or a historicist or both because his work is embedded in a model of history that is constantly thrusting forward towards some—perhaps unrealizable—image of the perfection which Hegel calls absolute being. It is this aspect of his work that *post-structuralism rejects. The progress of human history, for Hegel, is the march towards self-determination, which is only achieved when full self-consciousness is attained. In his view, self-consciousness is synonymous with freedom and this is the basic story his later work tells. The best known instance of this in Hegel's work is his account of the master/slave relationship in the *Phenomenology of Mind*, an essay which is for many readers emblematic of Hegel's work as a whole. Hegel famously argues that the self-consciousness of both master and slave is in fact the opposite of what they initially think it is: the slave thinks they have no freedom but discovers that because of their servitude they have been relieved of the burden of having to think about their *situation, thus they really do have freedom of consciousness; while the master realizes that having to think about the need to enslave the other is in itself a burden that reduces his freedom.

Further Reading: S. Houlgate *An Introduction to Hegel* (2005).
R. Pippin *Hegel's Idealism: The Satisfactions of Self-Consciousness* (1989).

SEE WEB LINKS

- An extensive set of resources regarding G.W.F. Hegel's biography, work, and articles.

hegemony Italian *Marxist scholar Antonio *Gramsci adopted this term (possibly as a codeword for *ideology) in his prison notebooks to theorize what is known today as 'soft' power, that is to say power that maintains its *authority without the need for violent coercion. Hegemony is not something governments can achieve on their own; they require the active complicity of the population they administer. As is obvious, revolution is impossible, or at least highly unlikely under such conditions, and that is what concerned Gramsci. He realized, too, that *culture is in this respect a more potent political tool than mere force of arms. For Gramsci the clearest sign of this is the willingness of a population to not only tolerate dreadful living and working conditions, but to die to preserve them too. Benedict *Anderson's work on the *imagined community demonstrates how the concept of nation functions in a hegemonic manner to create a sense of bonded coherence amongst a large group of people who could not possibly know each other.

Further Reading: E. Laclau and C. Mouffe *Hegemony and Socialist Strategy* (1985).

Heidegger, Martin (1889–1976) German philosopher, generally regarded as one of the most important of the 20th century, not least because he is one of the most divisive. He is a controversial figure too because of his active involvement with the Nazis. His work is a major focal point for post-World War II continental philosophy, particularly in France where the backlash against *psychoanalysis, *Marxism, and Jean-Paul *Sartre manifested as a return to Heidegger. With the conspicuous exception of Gilles *Deleuze, most of the leading figures of *post-structuralism have engaged extensively with Heidegger's thought (e.g. Pierre *Bourdieu, Jacques *Derrida, Jean-Luc *Nancy, Philippe *Lacoue-Labarthe, Jean-François *Lyotard, and Bernard *Stiegler).

Heidegger was in born in the town of Messkirch, in the Baden region of Germany. His father was a sexton in the local parish and a cooper of modest means. The local priest in Messkirch recognized his talent and undertook to teach him Latin, thus enabling him to gain entrance into a prestigious grammar school in Konstanz and from there into academia. He completed his undergraduate and postgraduate degrees at Freiburg University, where his teachers included Edmund *Husserl, the founding father of *phenomenology. Initially Heidegger studied theology, but when ill-health showed him to be unsuited to a life of the cloth he switched to philosophy. He completed his studies in 1916, and then undertook war service, but not active duty. After the war he worked as Husserl's assistant until 1923, when he obtained a post at Marburg University.

Marburg dithered for years over making Heidegger's post permanent and in the end managed to do so just in time for Heidegger to be lured back to Freiburg to succeed his stalwart mentor Husserl. In the five years he was at Marburg, however, Heidegger managed to complete the book that many regard as the most significant work of philosophy of the 20th century, *Sein und Zeit* (1927), translated as *Being and Time* (1962). Heidegger set out to tackle the one great philosophical problem philosophy had in his view assiduously ignored, namely the problem of being itself; his aim was to uncover the process whereby being-ness is possible. His argument is that it is only possible because there is an entity to whom being matters, this entity he termed **Dasein*. Owing to the difficulty of translating this neologism, which literally means there-being, it is usually left untranslated (in some translations *Dasein* is rendered as 'man', but in spite of the fact that *Dasein* does imply humans, 'man' is too humanistic to be satisfactory).

In 1933, four months after Hitler was made Chancellor of Germany, Heidegger was appointed Rector of Freiburg University. On the 1st of May that year he joined the Nazi Party, and ostentatiously wore a swastika lapel pin for years afterwards, even in the company of Jewish friends; then on the 27th of May he gave his (now infamous) inaugural address as rector in which he exhorted students to align themselves with the Führer and embrace Germany's national destiny. As rector he implemented the Nazi race laws, which meant extinguishing the university privileges of his mentor and staunchest supporter Husserl. In spite of his obvious support for National Socialism, the Nazis did not support Heidegger in return and within a year he felt compelled to resign his post. He thereafter described his period as rector as a failure.

At the end of the war, when the Allies occupied Germany, Heidegger was called to account for his association with the Nazis. The Denazification commission labelled him *Mitläufer* (fellow traveller) and in view of his influence as an intellectual he was prohibited from teaching. He was rehabilitated in 1951 and continued to teach until 1976. Today, no one seriously disputes that Heidegger expressed sympathy for Nazism, the question that remains is whether this sympathy was personal, or born of philosophical conviction. His defenders argue that it was an unfortunate quirk of character that had nothing to do with his philosophical thinking, while others—notably Karl *Jaspers and Theodor *Adorno—claim his philosophy was fascist at its core. His stunning failure to publicly condemn the Holocaust is often cited as evidence of the latter case, as is his seemingly callous equation of *modernity with gas chambers.

Further Reading: R. Bernasconi *Heidegger in Question: The Art of Existing* (1993).
M. de Beistegui *Heidegger and the Political: Dystopias* (1998).
C. Fynsk *Heidegger: Thought and Historicity* (1986).
M. Inwood *Heidegger: A Very Short Introduction* (2000).
H. Ott *Martin Heidegger: A Political Life* (1994).
M. Wrathall *How to Read Heidegger* (2005).

hermeneutics The study of the theory and the practice of interpreting texts. It dates back to ancient times, when it was closely associated with the study of *rhetoric. Since the beginning of the Christian era, however, it has mostly been connected to religious study, both Christian and Muslim. At issue in both cases is determining the correct way of reading scriptural texts. In the case of the Bible, it is far from self-evident how it should be read. The problems that have to be considered are manifold: first, there is perpetual question of translation (it was not all written in the same language); second, there is the question of the change in the meaning of words over time (the Bible was not written all at once); third, there is question of whether each of the contributing authors meant the same thing by the same words; fourth, should the stories be treated as allegories?; fifth, should the scripture be treated as fact? The list of problems to be considered could easily be extended. It was not until the 18th century that a secular form of hermeneutics was developed by Friedrich Schleiermacher, who demonstrated that the interpretation of all texts, not just sacred texts, is problematic for essentially the same reasons, namely language's capacity for multiple meaning. His solution was to anchor meaning in the psychology of the author. Thus, Schleiermacher was the first to raise the question of authorial intention, which would remain central to textual studies until the middle of the 20th century, arguing that it has to be understood in context (a perspective that *New Historicism maintains today). In the latter half of the 20th century, it is the work of Hans Georg *Gadamer and Paul *Ricoeur that has been most closely associated with hermeneutics.

Further Reading: R. Palmer *Hermeneutics: Interpretation Theory in Schleiermacher, Dilthey, Heidegger and Gadamer* (1969).

heteroglossia An extension of the concept of *dialogism conceived by Russian linguist and literary critic Mikhail *Bakhtin. Literally it means a mixture of tongues. For Bakhtin literature should strive to be what he called double-voiced, by which he meant it should incorporate the voice of others. The best examples of this type of literature should, he thought, submerge the voice of the author altogether. But Bakhtin also realized that the presence of different voices by themselves was not sufficient to produce the utopian effect he prized, particularly not if those different voices were all of the same type or class of people. Tolstoy's work, according to Bakhtin, suffers especially acutely from this problem in that it is almost entirely populated by the aristocratic class and their various retainers, such that even the peasants whom Tolstoy is said to have held in such high esteem are only seen from the point of view of their masters. The better writers, from this perspective, are those like Dickens and Dosteoevsky whose works give voice to every class of people. For Bakhtin this can never be achieved simply by representing or depicting other classes (this is Tolstoy's fault); one must incorporate their voice into the very style of the text itself. By means of parody and comedy (the larger effects of which Bakhtin called *carnivalesque) the socially subordinate can be not merely depicted or quoted but brought to life, for in this way their subversive attitude to the social system that imprisons them in their class position can also be felt and understood. It is Dickens's combination of social realism and satire that stands him above the other authors of his era (the other English writer he approves of is Thackeray, who obviously shares this trait with Dickens, albeit articulated differently). *See also* CARNIVALESQUE; DIALOGISM; POLYPHONY.

Further Reading: K. Clark and M. Holquist *Mikhail Bakhtin* (1984).
M. Holquist *Dialogism* (2002).
D. Lodge *After Bakhtin* (1990).

heterology Traditionally the branch of philosophy concerned with the problem of the existence of the *Other or 'unknowable being', which has been variously interpreted as referring to God (*Levinas) and the Indigenous Subject (*Certeau).

In medical pathology heterology refers to morbid, abnormal tissue composed differently from surrounding healthy tissue. Inspired by this, Georges *Bataille developed a notion of heterology as an anthropology of the unassimilable, or the excessive.

Further Reading: G. Bataille *Visions of Excess* (1985).
M. de Certeau *Heterologies* (1986).
E. Levinas *Time and the Other* (1987).

heterotopia In his 1967 lecture '*Des espaces autres*' (Of other spaces) Michel *Foucault proposed the concept to describe spaces such as that of the cinema and the cemetery which have the 'curious property' of being connected to other places via a complex network of relations, but in such a way that they either suspend, cancel out, or reverse those relations designated, reflected, or represented by them. Heterotopias are explicitly defined in contradistinction to Gaston *Bachelard's 'inner spaces', yet one senses that it is precisely the way these spaces seem to externalize the inner realms of our imagination that captivates Foucault's interest.

Foucault speculates that there are two kinds of spaces that have this property of being at once in a network of relations and outside it as well: *utopias and heterotopias. He dismisses utopias as essentially unreal and concentrates on heterotopias which he insists are real places built into the very institution of society, adding that they are in some way realized utopias. There are, he thinks, two main types of heterotopia: what he calls (doubtless for the want of better words) 'crisis heterotopias' and 'deviation heterotopias', the former corresponding to what anthropologist Victor Turner would more productively call 'liminal spaces' and the latter what Foucault himself would more productively call 'disciplinary spaces'. His examples of 'crisis heterotopias', primarily taken from primitive society, include sacred or taboo places reserved for adolescents, menstruating women, women in labour, and so on. His impression is that such spaces have all but disappeared from western society, although he hazards that there are some remnants still around (the honeymoon hotel being his prime example). Anticipating *Deleuze's notion of the 'any-space-whatever', Foucault calls these places 'anywhere places', that is places that are precisely not 'just anywhere' but nowhere. His 'deviation heterotopias' read like a catalogue of his past and future works—he lists psychiatric hospitals, prisons, and old peoples' homes. He qualifies this preliminary attempt at a typology by stating that society can, more or less at will, change the nature and function of heterotopias and indeed bring into existence new types of heterotopias.

In total Foucault offers six principles for a description of heterotopia: the two already given—(i) heterotopias are of a specific type; (ii) heterotopias can be transformed, reinvented, or made afresh—and the following four: (iii) heterotopias have the ability to juxtapose in a single real place several emplacements that are incompatible in themselves (cinema is his prime example of this); (iv) heterotopias are connected to what he calls heterochronias, ruptures or breaks in time; (v) heterotopias always presuppose a system of opening and closing that isolates them and makes them penetrable at the same time; (vi) heterotopias transform our relations with other real spaces either to make us see them as less real or to compensate us for their relative shoddiness (Jean *Baudrillard and Umberto *Eco are exponents of the first proposition, while Edward *Said is an exponent of the latter).

historical materialism A branch of *Marxism that—following Karl *Marx's own prescription—takes the position that the development of history is not determined by the *desires or actions of specific human subjects, but is instead shaped by the objective facts of material existence. History unfolds as the attempt by humans to alter their natural environment to suit their particular needs—this explains, in part, why technology developed at a faster pace in colder climates, the need to defend against the environment was much greater there than in, say, the tropics, where the climate is more congenial. In order to meet their needs humans must work together and produce not only the specific goods they need but *society itself. In doing so, however, divisions between different groups of people whose interests differ arise, the result of which is social antagonism. These groups, which might have been artisans, farmers or merchants to begin with, evolve into *classes, of which there are three basic types: landowners, bourgeoisie (i.e. manufacturers and merchants), and workers. The relationship between the classes is *dialectical according to Marx inasmuch as their respective interests do not coincide. The working through of this dialectic is referred to as *class struggle.

Further Reading: P. Anderson *In the Tracks of Historical Materialism* (1983).

historicism The view that past events must be understood and judged within the context of their own times. This is because, as G.W.F. *Hegel argued, all societies are the product of their history. So, for example, *New Historicism argues that to read Shakespeare properly one has to read it from the perspective of his peers, and see it as his original audiences did. Historicism also refers to the view that history unfolds according to certain inexorable laws, such as the economic laws of supply and demand. For this reason *Marxism is often regarded as a form of historicism, though not all Marxist scholars accept this label (Louis *Althusser, for one, rejects it completely). Karl Popper wrote derisive critiques of historicism, which was a codeword for Marxism for him in any case, arguing (quite mistakenly) that it is totalitarian in that it tries to describe everything that happens and in that it imposes a single narrative on the unfolding of events.

historiography The study of the writing of history, the way style, narrative, metaphors, and so on affect how the historical record is received and understood. It can also refer to debates within a particular field of academic history (e.g. the history of Australia). The key point is that it does not refer to actual events, or history as such, it only refers to the interpretation and articulation of those events. It thus asks what counts as history and more particularly which methods reliably produce history. Key figures in this field include: Michel de *Certeau, Michel *Foucault, and Hayden *White.

Hjelmslev, Louis (1899–1966) Danish linguist. Born in Copenhagen, Hjelmslev studied comparative linguistics in Copenhagen, Prague, and Paris. In 1931 he helped found the Linguistic Circle of Copenhagen, which modelled itself on (and in some respects against) the *Prague Linguistic Circle founded six years earlier by a small group of like-minded linguists that included such luminaries as Roman *Jakobson, Jan Mayakovsky, and Nikolai Trubetzkoy.

Although his own work concentrated specifically on understanding language, aiming to develop a general theory of language, it has been expanded upon by others—particularly Roland *Barthes, Michel de *Certeau, Gilles *Deleuze, Umberto *Eco, Michel *Foucault, and Algirdas *Greimas—to analyse a broad range of cultural phenomena. He called this general theory *glossematics and intended it to be a kind of algebra of language which cut across what he saw as false distinctions between phonetics, morphology, syntax, lexicography, and semantics. The reality of language usage, Hjelmslev argued, necessitates a more complex system than traditional linguistics provides and in his best-known book, *Omkring sprogteoriens grundlæggelse* (1943), translated as *Prolegomena to a Theory of Language* (1969), he set out to provide exactly that.

Hobsbawm, Eric (1917–) British Marxist historian. Born in Alexandria, Egypt, Hobsbawm went to school in Vienna and Berlin before moving to London in 1933. He gained his BA and PhD from King's College, Cambridge, where he took an active role in the Communist Party and met fellow Marxist Raymond *Williams. During World War II Hobsbawm served in the Royal Engineers and the Royal Army Education Corps. He was appointed lecturer in history at Birkbeck College, London, in 1947, and apart from visiting positions in the US at Stanford and the New School, effectively remained there for the rest of his career. A prolific author, with an engaging style, and a capacious knowledge of the arts and sciences, Hobsbawm is equally at home writing short pieces for popular magazines and newspapers or in lengthy treatments. He even did a ten-year stint between 1955 and 1965 as the *New Statesman*'s jazz critic, writing under the pseudonym Francis Newton (these pieces were later collected and published under Hobsbawm's own name as *The Jazz Scene* (1989)). He is best known for the tetralogy on the 'ages of world history', commencing with the *Age of Revolution 1789–1848* (1962) and progressing from there to *The Age of Capital 1848–75* (1975), and *The Age of Empire 1875–1914* (1987), concluding with the controversial *Age of Extremes 1914–91* (1994), which offered an incisive account of what Hobsbawm called the 'short 20th century'. Together with Terence Ranger he edited *The Invention of Tradition* (1983), a collection of essays which by demonstrating that many of the so-called traditional elements of contemporary life (such as Scottish tartan) are in fact of recent origin has had an enormous influence on *Cultural Studies.

Further Reading: G. Elliott *Ends in Sight: Marx, Fukuyama, Hobsbawm, Anderson* (2008).
E. Hobsbawm *Interesting Times: A Twentieth-Century Life* (2002).

Hoggart, Richard (1918–) Left-wing British literary historian and sociologist who was instrumental in establishing *Cultural Studies. Born and educated in Leeds, Hoggart was with the Royal Artillery during World War II, reaching the rank of captain. Hoggart's first academic job (like Raymond *Williams's) was as a tutor in adult education at the University of Hull, a position he held from 1946 until 1959. It was during these years that he wrote the semi-autobiographical work for which he is still best known today: *The Uses of Literacy* (1957). A bestseller at the time, it was influential for two main reasons: firstly, it broke with the *Leavisite tradition's emphasis on high culture and demonstrated that there was an authentic working-class culture worthy of consideration; second, it argued that this tradition of working-class culture (which was his own) was under threat of destruction from imported American popular culture. From Hull he moved briefly to the University of Leicester and from there to Birmingham University in 1962. There, together with Stuart *Hall, he founded the Centre for Contemporary Cultural Studies, which is regarded by many as the birthplace of Cultural Studies as an academic discipline. He directed the centre for a decade, then took a three-year position with UNESCO, and finished his academic career as warden of Goldsmith's College in London. Hoggart retired in 1984, but has maintained an active publishing schedule since then, producing several further works reflecting on the state of British cultural traditions.

homo sacer Translated literally as 'sacred man', this classical concept has attracted significant attention in contemporary critical theory because Italian philosopher Giorgio *Agamben has devoted several books to exploring the intricacies of its multi-layered meaning. *Homo sacer* is a paradoxical figure: it is the one who may not be sacrificed, yet may be murdered with impunity. In this sense, the *homo sacer* is outside or beyond both divine and human law. Agamben's provocative thesis is that the *homo sacer* is evidence not merely of an original ambivalence in the notion of the sacred, as anthropology has long contended, but that the realm of the political itself is constituted by making an exception of the very people in whose name it is created. The *homo sacer* thus emblematizes the sovereign's power over life and death, the power to designate a life that is worth neither saving nor killing. For Agamben, the most complete realization of *homo sacer* is the concentration-camp inmate, particularly the hapless figures known in the colloquial language of the camps as '*die Muselmänner*' (i.e. the 'Muslims') because of their apparent surrender to God or Fate. But rather than argue that *homo sacer* is a product of Nazism, or totalitarian politics more generally, Agamben contends that on the contrary it is the sheer possibility of so regarding human life that enabled Nazism's exterminationist politics. The very same possibility, he argues, is at the origin of democracy too, a fact that is displayed in the way politics has been constituted as a *biopower focused on the population not the individual. *See also* BARE LIFE.

Further Reading: G. Agamben *Homo Sacer: Sovereign Power and Bare Life* (1998). G. Agamben *Remnants of Auschwitz: The Witness and the Archive* (1999).

hooks, bell (1952–) The pen-name of African-American feminist and social activist Gloria Watkins. The pen-name combines the names of her mother and grandmother and is written in lower case to signify that it is the content of her books rather than the name on the spine that is important. Since the publication in 1981 of *Ain't I a Woman?: Black Women and Feminism*, hooks has been highly critical of both *Second Wave feminism for its neglect of *race, and race studies for its neglect of *gender. Thus she writes against sexism within feminism and against racism within black liberation movements. She has also written extensively on the mutually reinforcing ways in which race and gender are used to subordinate women in the *public sphere, particularly media and politics. Like Henry Louis *Gates, she also has an abiding concern for the preservation and popularization of African-American culture. She is a vanguard author in *Third Wave feminism.

Horkheimer, Max (1895–1973) German philosopher and one of the founders of the *Frankfurt School. Horkheimer was a superb organizer, who did an enormous amount behind the scenes to facilitate the research of the Frankfurt School scholars both in Germany and the US. From an early age, and in spite of—or perhaps because of—his privileged upbringing, Horkheimer had a powerful sense of the social injustices of the capitalist system.

He was born in Stuttgart, into a family of wealthy Jewish textile manufacturers. Initially he followed his father's footsteps into the family business, but his heart was never in it. He was conscripted in 1917, but was rejected as unfit for service on medical grounds. In 1919 he finally enrolled at university to study psychology, philosophy, and economics in Munich. While living in Munich, he was mistaken for the revolutionary playwright Ernst Toller and arrested and imprisoned. On his release, he transferred his studies to Frankfurt. He spent a year at Freiburg studying with Edmund *Husserl and met his research assistant Martin *Heidegger. He completed a doctorate and habilitation under the direction of Hans Cornelius (the same professor who would later fail Horkheimer's friends Theodor *Adorno and Walter *Benjamin).

In 1930 Horkheimer became director of the Institut für Sozialforschung (Institute for Social Research in Frankfurt). His inaugural address, given in 1931, 'The Present Situation of Social Philosophy and the Tasks of an Institute for Social Research' outlined three key tasks: the development of an inter-disciplinary approach to the study of society (by which he meant combining philosophy and sociology, hitherto unheard of in the German academic system); the reconstruction of the Marxian project, so as to emphasize social and cultural issues rather than exclusively economic problems; the explication of the interconnections between society, economy, culture, and consciousness.

Under his direction the Institute funded and carried out research on the German working class's 'psychic structure', which given the political conditions of the time—the fact that the Nazi party was everywhere in ascendance—was incredibly brave and provocative. Aware, albeit not fully aware, of the danger this shift in the political situation betokened, the Institute transferred its affairs to Geneva in 1931. It relocated again in 1934, this time to Columbia University in New York. Horkheimer moved to the US first and then arranged for his other similarly exiled colleagues to follow, and in due course most of them did with the signal and sad exception of Benjamin. There the Institute began on an extensive qualitative and quantitative project on *authority and the family. However, in 1939, due to some bad investments, the Institute found itself in financial difficulty and the amazing team of researchers it had assembled began to break up and of necessity take jobs elsewhere.

'Traditionelle und Kritische Theorie' ('Traditional and Critical Theory'), Horkheimer's most famous essay, and a kind of signature piece for the Frankfurt School as a whole, was published in 1937 in the Institute's house journal, *Zeitschrift für Sozialforschung* (Journal for Social Research). This established *critical theory as a codeword for a materialist form of social analysis which nonetheless eschewed any connection with science, or what it referred to as *instrumental reason. It could maintain its connection with *psychoanalysis precisely because it was not recognized as a science. This article foreshadowed in many ways what is undoubtedly Horkheimer's best-known work, namely his collaboration with Adorno, *Dialektik der Aufklärung* (1944), translated as *Dialectic of Enlightenment* (1972), completed in the Institute's new residence in exile, Los Angeles. In part this project set out to explain the conditions under which Nazism could take hold of a society, but it also wanted to show that it was very far from a uniquely German phenomenon, which it did by demonstrating that mass media diminished resistance to ideological messaging. This view would hold sway until the early 1980s when *Cultural Studies decided it was elitist and overturned it in favour of more reception-oriented theory.

Horkheimer returned to Frankfurt in 1949 and the Institute reopened there in 1950. Between 1951 and 1953 he was rector of the university. In 1954 he returned to America to lecture at the University of Chicago. He retired in 1955. Horkheimer wrote little in his last years, but he remained an influential figure.

Further Reading: S. Benhabib, W. Bonss and J. McCole (eds.) *On Max Horkheimer* (1985).

D. Held *Introduction to Critical Theory* (1980).

M. Jay *The Dialectical Imagination* (1973).

R. Wiggershaus *The Frankfurt School* (1994).

humanism Any philosophy, or political stance which emphasizes or privileges the welfare of humans and assumes that only humans are capable of reason. In doing so, humanism treats the human as an abstract universal; it is premised on the paradoxical idea that all people should be treated the same, regardless of who they are and what they have done as individuals, solely on account of their humanity. In the 1950s, humanism was endorsed by radical critics like Jean-Paul *Sartre, who used it as a slogan to counter nationalist and racist discourse. In the 1960s and 1970s, particularly with the rise of *structuralism, authors like Michel *Foucault rejected the term humanism for its assumption that human means only one thing and more especially for failing to register the degree to which the human is a construction of history. Consistent with this view, there has in fact arisen a *posthumanism movement which tries to describe a vision of the world which does not start from a position that prioritizes the human.

Husserl, Edmund (1859–1938) German philosopher, founder of *phenomenology and one of the most influential thinkers of the 20th century. His work was a significant influence on Martin *Heidegger, Maurice *Merleau-Ponty, Emmanuel *Levinas, Alfred Schütz, Rudolf Carnap, Roman *Ingarden, and Jacques *Derrida. Husserl was a prolific author, although he published relatively little in his own lifetime—he left work amounting to some 40,000 pages, which is steadily being published (at last count there were more than 27 volumes in the growing edition of his complete works). There is a major archive dedicated to his work in Leuven, Belgium.

Born in Prostějov in the Austro-Hungarian Empire (now in the Czech Republic), into a Jewish family. He initially studied mathematics as an undergraduate at the Universities of Leipzig and Berlin, then completed a doctorate on calculus at the University of Vienna in 1883. Franz Brentano was lecturing on psychology and philosophy at the University of Vienna at that time and Husserl found himself drawn more and more in that direction. Brentano was forced to resign his position because of religious differences, so he advised Husserl to complete his habilitation with Carl Stumpf at the University of Halle.

His habilitation, published in 1891 as *Philosophie der Arithmetik* (Philosophy of Arithmetic), was still on mathematics, but with a decided bent in the direction of psychology. Although he set out to provide a logical foundation for the existence of numbers, his project was severely criticized for psychologism by the logician Gottlob *Frege. Husserl subsequently amended his ideas and developed his own critique of psychologism in his next book, *Logische Untersuchungen* (1901), translated as *Logical Investigations* (1913), which attempted to show that concepts are not psychological. On the strength of this he was appointed to a position at the University of Göttingen in 1901 and he remained there until 1916, publishing two further volumes under the same title. In doing so he created phenomenology as a science. Phenomenology as Husserl conceived it is interested in discovering the specific processes of the mental synthesis and the concepts by which they are apprehended.

Phenomenology differs from psychology in that it is not *empiricist in its approach and deals with the *essence of acts of consciousness. It isn't empiricist because it questions the nature of the given, i.e. it does not assume that what appears does so without being shaped in some way by the determining influence of consciousness. There is a difference between sense data being registered by our mind and actually knowing what those sense data mean to us—even raw *affect, such as the feeling of heat, needs to be processed so as to be read by the mind as meaning 'danger'. How this processing takes place is more or less the sole concern of Husserl's research for the remainder of his career. Phenomenology assumes that the world is as it appears to consciousness and that the mind is capable of intuiting the reality of the world. Phenomenology is not a form of *relativism, but to avoid the consequences of its own starting position it has to show that the mind's processes are capable of doing this independently of what is going on in the world. Husserl invented a method he called **epochē* (usually translated as 'bracketing'), or phenomenological reduction, which enabled him to separate the act of consciousness—apperception— from the intentional objects of consciousness.

In 1916, Husserl was appointed to a professorship in philosophy at the University of Freiburg. He taught there for the remainder of his career. It was there that he encountered his most famous students, such as Martin Heidegger and Emmanuel Levinas, but also future *Vienna Circle philosophers Rudolf Carnap and Moritz Schlick.

In his final years, he was treated extremely poorly by the Nazi regime, which came to power in 1933. He was made to suffer considerable ignominy by his illustrious but politically misguided protégé Martin Heidegger, who (in his capacity as rector of Freiburg University) revoked his emeritus status and even deleted the dedication to him from his book (it was later restored). His books were added to the bonfires the Nazis held to cleanse their libraries of the writings of Jewish authors. His unpublished papers might have met the same fate were it not for the actions of Belgian priest Hermann van Breda. It is for this reason that the Husserl archive is today located in Leuven.

Further Reading: A. Bowie *Introduction to German Philosophy: From Kant to Habermas* (2003).

M. Russell *Husserl: A Guide for the Perplexed* (2006).

D. Woodruff Smith *Husserl* (2006).

D. Zahavi *Husserl's Phenomenology* (2003).

hybridity A term used in contemporary *Postcolonial Studies to theorize and to a certain degree celebrate a global state of mixedness —a mixedness of cultures, races, ethnicities, nations, and so on. The term is drawn from biology, where it is used to describe the intermingling of different strains or species of plants and animals to produce 'new' species (the mule, which is the offspring of a donkey and horse, is a perfect example of a hybrid). Interestingly, in colonial and imperial discourse of the 19th century, the term hybridity carried negative connotations and was used primarily to signal what the 'white' races had to fear if miscegenation was left unchecked. Its meaning has effectively been reversed. In part, this is because an alternative affirmative use of the term is available in the work of Russian literary critic and theorist Mikhail *Bakhtin, who uses it in the development of his key concepts of the *carnivalesque and *dialogism. Today, the term is probably most closely associated with Homi *Bhabha, who uses the term to stress the interdependence of colonizer and colonized, and to therefore argue that one cannot claim a 'purity' of racial or national identity. All identity, he maintains, is produced in a kind of *third space, which is 'in between' the subject and their idealized other. The term is not without its critics, however, even from within *Postcolonial Studies: Aijaz Ahmad, Chandra Talpade Mohanty, and Benita Parry have all offered critiques of the term on the grounds that it is idealist and doesn't accurately reflect the reality on the ground (in other words it doesn't pass what Toni Morrison has wittily described as the 'taxi test', i.e. a hybrid identity might be fine in theory but will a taxi still stop for you?). These critics rightly point out that hybridity is too often used simply to uncritically describe a state of being, rather than analyse it. However, Nestor Garcia Canclini also offers a *utopian account of this term, which suggests a far greater depth than Ahmad, Parry, and Mohanty are prepared to credit.

Further Reading: A. Ahmad *In Theory: Classes, Nations, Literatures* (1992).
H. Bhabha *The Location of Culture* (1994).
R. Young *Colonial Desire* (1995).
N. Garcia Canclini *Hybrid Cultures* (1995).

hyperreality An aesthetic mode of reproduction or replication that strives to produce an effect that is more real than the real thing being copied. Italian author, semiotician, and cultural critic, Umberto *Eco, coined the term in an essay entitled 'Travels in Hyperreality' (1975) which tries to account for the particular attraction to Americans of waxwork museums, Ripley's 'Believe it or Not!', and the seemingly relentless replication of icons of European culture, such as Las Vegas's mini Eiffel Tower. Somewhat snobbishly, Eco regards the logic behind such exhibitions as compensatory. For the lack of an authentic culture of its own, he argues, America creates *pastiches of European culture.

But because their inauthenticity cannot really be disguised, they strive to be more real than the original by trying to recall the affect of the presence of the original object. More generously, Jean *Baudrillard, in his account of *simulation, sees the hyperreal as part of global shift in the way culture communicates itself.

hypertext Most often seen on Internet pages, it is a kind of text which although not actually present is nonetheless immediately available, usually by clicking on a hyperlink. Its purpose is generally to embellish or add information to the text preceding it. A footnote may also be considered a kind of hypertext. The hypertext is in this sense on a separate spatial plane to the regular text, but somehow on the same temporal plane. The design idea behind hypertext is that it can be read simultaneously with the main body of the text. Jacques *Derrida's more creative works, like *Glas* (1974), play on precisely this problematic.

hysteria (*Hysterie*) A widely used term to designate pathological symptoms of either a physical or psychical nature for which no physiological cause is apparent. Hysteria in this sense is often used as a pejorative for an imagined illness. The word is derived from '*hystera*', the Greek word for 'uterus' or 'womb', and has its origin in the idea current in ancient Egypt as well as classical Greece and Rome that the female reproductive organ is able to move throughout the body and that this movement is triggered by an unsatisfied longing for a child. For this reason, at least until the middle part of the 19th century hysteria was thought to be an exclusively 'female malady' (as it was commonly referred to in the Victorian era). Inspired by the great French neurologist, Jean Charcot, Sigmund *Freud became interested in hysteria and in the course of the development of *psychoanalysis he proposed an aetiology which starts from the premise that hysteria is the product of psychical conflict between thoughts generated in the *unconscious and the censor protecting the conscious. He identified two types of hysteria: (i) conversion hysteria—in which this conflict is expressed in bodily symptoms; (ii) *anxiety hysteria—in which the conflict is deflected onto an object, manifesting as a phobia (e.g. fear of spiders).

hysterical sublime Fredric *Jameson's suggested term for a reformulated vision of the *sublime (in *Kant's sense) focused on technology rather than nature. Kant defined nature as sublime because it consistently exceeds the capacity of human concepts to grasp either its particularity or its generality. More practically, the caprices of nature (e.g. variable soil quality, water supply, and so on) are, as Marx recognized, what must be overcome in order for human society to be able to satisfy its elementary needs. Until the middle of the 20th century, then, nature has been feared and admired in equal measure because of humanity's seeming inability to control its forces. But with the rapid advances technology made in the second half of the 20th century nature's pre-eminent position in western metaphysics began to slide and technology took its place. At first, machines like steam trains and motor cars made humans seem equal to or greater than nature, but with the advent of digital technology a new type of machine emerged that proved difficult to respond to cognitively: the awesome capabilities of computers are beyond question, but as physical objects they are rather unimpressive. We get no sense of what a computer is capable of simply by looking at it, so from a representational point of view what is always the most significant about computers is the vast network of other computers they are able to tap into. The image of a global matrix of interlocked machines from humble handheld mobile phones to orbiting satellites is, Jameson suggests, a new form of the sublime because technology is presented as exceeding human capacities and categories. Jameson's key exhibits are drawn from cinema—e.g. *The Parallax View* (director, Pakula, 1974)—but he also acknowledges the importance of literature, particularly cyberpunk, in developing this notion. The hysterical or technological sublime is a constituent component of Jameson's account of *postmodernism and a vital precursor to his later notion of a *geopolitical aesthetic.

Further Reading: I. Buchanan *Fredric Jameson: Live Theory* (2006).
F. Jameson *The Geopolitical Aesthetic* (1992).
F. Jameson *Postmodernism, or, the Cultural Logic of Late Capitalism* (1991).

icon Derived from the Greek 'eikon', *meaning 'resemblance' or 'image', it is generally used to refer to sacred images of Christian saints and other religiously significant figures. American* *semiotician Charles Sanders *Peirce adopted this term as one of three classifications of types of *sign (the other two being the *index and the *symbol). For Peirce, the icon is an example of what he called firstness because it is able to signify by virtue of its own qualities (i.e. without reference to an object or convention). A pure icon in Peirce's sense is an image of a thing so closely resembling the thing it represents that we forget we are looking at an image. It is, in this sense, a theoretical possibility, not an actuality.

iconography The field of art history interested in the analysis of the specific image components of pictures. The term itself is a neologism constructed from the Greek words for image and writing, a fact that gives a clue to its main concern. Art historians like Aby Warburg and Erwin Panofsky show that Medieval, Baroque, and Renaissance Christian art use a limited number of images, which also have a fairly stable set of meanings. In the Romantic period, forests, mountains, and rivers were used in a similarly iconic manner to the standard Christian symbols of the previous era. Identifying these images and their specific, coded meanings, enables these works to be read. The practice of iconography was popularized by Dan Brown's bestselling novel *The Da Vinci Code* (2003) in which a historian deciphers the meaning of several different artworks in order to solve a mystery.

Further Reading: R. van Straten, tr. P. de Man *An Introduction to Iconography* (1994).

id (*das Es*) The part of psychical apparatus where the *instincts are located in Sigmund Freud's *topography. Freud himself did not use the term 'id', it was introduced by his English translator James Strachey, who also used Latin terms for the other two key constituents of the psychical apparatus, namely the *ego and *superego. Freud borrowed the concept of the id from German psychiatrist Georg Groddek who, in turn, most likely adapted the idea from Friedrich

*Nietzsche's opposition between the 'I' and the 'it' in *Beyond Good and Evil* (1886). The id is a reservoir of energy that the other parts of the psychical apparatus draw on, but must also contain if they are not to be overwhelmed by it. The id does not understand 'no'; it is the *pleasure principle unconstrained by the *reality principle.

ideal ego (*Idealich*) The *ego's *narcissistic and idealized image of itself as omnipotent. Although *Freud did use this concept in his work on narcissism, it does not figure very largely in his work. *Lacanian *psychoanalysts, particularly *Žižek, have found it useful to contrast with the *ego-ideal, and create a binary between an image others have of the 'I' and the 'I' as it wants to see itself.

identity The image of who one is. This may be either a self-composed image, i.e. the image one has of oneself, or, it may be imposed from the outside, i.e. the image others have of one. These two images are not always in harmony with one another. Identity is at stake in questions and problematics to do with sexuality, *gender, *race, and ethnicity.

identity politics A form of politics premised on the idea that all people are different and that difference not only has to be respected, it also makes it impossible for one person to completely understand or empathize with another. At this level, identity politics would just be another word for *anomie, but it is rarely played out at the level of the individual subject. *Identity in this context is generally thought of in terms of belonging to collectives determined by one or more of several basic social categories such as *class, *race, *gender, religion, ethnicity, and so on. The effect can be paradoxical, as the women's movement discovered in the 1970s, when lesbians, women of colour, women from the *Third World, and others, began to argue that gender by itself was not a universal category capable of uniting all women under one banner. By the same token, as a politics it is fraught with the difficulty of separating it from a special interest view of the world which might just as well serve the interests of merchant bankers as any other minority group. Since the late 1990s, however, the politics of *social movements, which is issue-driven and inclusive, has largely replaced identity politics. *See also* STRATEGIC ESSENTIALISM.

Ideological State Apparatus (ISA) French *Marxist philosopher Louis *Althusser's concept for what is known in contemporary political discourse as 'soft power', i.e. the form of power that operates by means of ideological persuasion rather than violent, physical coercion. The latter 'hard power' form is referred to as the *Repressive State Apparatus (RSA). Ideology, for Althusser, is an essential part of the smooth running of any form of government, even the most violent and repressive governments, because without the active support of at least a portion of the general population it cannot hope to succeed. Power, Althusser argues, does not only come out of the barrel of a gun (as Mao famously said), but must also be crystallized in the minds of individual subjects. In so saying, Althusser separates the state from the apparatuses the state requires in order to maintain itself, his implication being that revolutionaries not only need to take power, they also need to control the apparatuses of power. The Ideological State Apparatus is not unified like the RSA, but consists rather in a loose coalition of largely private or nongovernmental entities such as churches, schools, universities, trade unions, the media, and even the family. Each of these entities is semi-autonomous, which is to say they have their own area of efficacy and are not necessarily subordinated in any direct way to a higher authority. In order to explain this collective but independent acting together Althusser constructed the notion of *structural causality. Despite their diversity, all ISAs contribute to a single result, namely the reproduction of the relations of production. *See also* HEGEMONY.

Further Reading: L. Althusser *Lenin and Philosophy* (1971).

ideology A set of beliefs, convictions or ideas which both binds a particular group of people together and determines the actions they take. For this reason, ideology is often used—particularly in the media—as a pejorative, as though to say only certain types of people have (indeed 'suffer from') ideology, and it renders them incapable of thinking for themselves. But, as commentators like Fredric *Jameson and Slavoj *Žižek argue, this position is itself ideological because it is built on the tacit, but obviously deeply held belief that its own position, i.e. the allegedly non-ideological position, is the 'normal' or 'commonsense' view of things, while the so-called ideological position is aberrant. The notion of a non-ideological position is thus a *myth or better yet a *projection. This in turn points to two other characteristics of ideology: it is frequently invisible to its adherents and it serves to create rules or regimes of inclusion and exclusion. Because of its invisibility, ideology is often equated with *false consciousness. To escape his censors, the imprisoned Italian *Marxist, Antonio *Gramsci used the term *hegemony in place of ideology and in doing so explained the invisibility of ideology—it is, he argued, the role of ideology to define and police that which counts as commonsense, that which everybody knows to be so, and insofar as it does that it is invisible. The task of any politics, then, according to Gramsci is to overturn this state of affairs, but not so as to get rid of ideology altogether—impossible, in any case—but rather to make way for a new ideology, one which is clear about interests. Marxists generally refer to this formation of ideology as *class consciousness. Perhaps the most widely used definition of ideology is the one given by French Marxist, Louis *Althusser who conceived it as an *imaginary relation to real conditions.

imaginary (*imaginaire*) A concept used by Gaston *Bachelard, Jacques *Lacan, and Jean-Paul *Sartre to indicate (in their own differing ways) a process of the mind or the psychical apparatus susceptible to the seductions of the image. For Lacan, the imaginary is the state or order of mind of the child before it is inducted into the *symbolic order via the process he referred to as the *mirror stage. The child sees itself in the mirror and *misrecognizes the image it sees reflected there as its true self. The 'I' in this sense is an image, which is to say a product of the imaginary. The imaginary is not a 'childish' state of mind, it is rather a state of mind ignorant of the limits of the *real and therefore highly creative. But it can also be disturbing—the experience of *psychosis is akin to being trapped in the imaginary.

imagined community Benedict *Anderson's definition of nation. In *Imagined Communities* (1983) Anderson argues that the nation is an imagined political community that is inherently limited in scope and sovereign in nature. It is imagined because the actuality of even the smallest nation exceeds what it is possible for a single person to know—one cannot know every person in a nation, just as one cannot know every aspect of its economy, geography, history, and so forth. But as Anderson is careful to point out (contra Ernest *Gellner) imagined is not the same thing as false or fictionalized, it is rather the unselfconscious exercise of abstract thought.

The imagined community is limited because regardless of size it is never taken to be co-extensive with humanity itself—not even extreme ideologies such as Nazism, with its pretensions to world dominance, imagine this; in fact, as Giorgio *Agamben has argued such ideologies tend to be premised on a generalization of an exception. Its borders are finite but elastic and permeable. The imagined community is sovereign because its legitimacy is not derived from divinity as kingship is—the nation is its own authority, it is founded in its own name, and it invents its own people which it deems citizens. The nation can be considered a community because it implies a deep horizontal comradeship which knits together all citizens irrespective of their class, colour, or race. According to

Anderson, the crucial defining feature of this type of comradeship is the willingness on the part of its adherents to die for this community.

The nation as imagined community came into being after the dawning of the age of *Enlightenment as both a response to and a consequence of secularization. It is the product of a profound change in the apprehension of the world, which Anderson specifies as a shift from sacred time to 'homogeneous empty time', a notion he borrows from Walter *Benjamin. In sacred time, present and future are simultaneous. Because everything that occurs is ordained by God, the event is simultaneously something that has always been and something that was meant to be. In such a conception of time there is no possibility of a 'meanwhile', or uneventful event, that is a mode of time that is empty of meaning rather than full of portent. Secularization, however, gave prominence to empty time, the time of calendars, clocks, and markets, which is concerned with temporal coincidence rather than destiny and fulfilment. This mode of time is perfectly embodied by the newspaper which places in contiguity news of events that share only their temporality.

It was the establishment of print culture, firstly through the mechanical production of Bibles and then even more strongly through the distribution of newspapers, that was the most important causal factor in creating the cultural conditions needed for the idea of nation to become the political norm. Print had three effects according to Anderson: first, it cut across regional idiolects and dialects, creating a unified medium of exchange below the sacred language (Latin in Europe) and above the local vernacular; second, it gave language a fixity it didn't previously have, and slowed down the rate of change so that there was far greater continuity between past and present; and thirdly it created languages of power by privileging those idiolects which were closest to the written form. Anderson's emphasis on the print culture in all its forms, but particularly the newspaper and the novel, has been extremely stimulating for a number of scholars working in a wide variety of different disciplines.

See also POSTCOLONIALISM.

imago Swiss *psychoanalyst Carl *Jung's term for the unconscious prototypes of its parents the child constructs in order to mediate between itself and the social environment. It is an unconscious representation, which may or may not be reflected in reality. The child may hold the imago of a fierce father, yet in reality its father may be rather mild. Sigmund *Freud did not use this concept. References to it appear in the early work of Jacques *Lacan, but he dropped it in the 1950s.

immanence A mode of philosophy grounded in itself. It rejects the idea of an external or transcendent ground, but is not thereby *anti-foundational. Spinoza is probably the most important philosopher of immanence—in his work, God is treated as immanent rather than transcendent, meaning that God does not sit on high judging humans, rather we are at one with His substance. In the 20th century the principal philosopher of immanence is Gilles *Deleuze—although he substitutes being for God, his *ontology is derived from Spinoza.

immaterial labour A *Marxist concept designating a type of labour that produces a nonmaterial good such as a cultural product, communication, information, or knowledge. The kinds of productions associated with the so-called creative industry, or the 'knowledge economy' are the result of immaterial labour. Michael *Hardt and Antonio *Negri specify two kinds of immaterial labour: (i) problem-solving or analytic labour of the type we associate with professional service and management; (ii) affective labour of the type we associate with the service sector, so-called because it is the *affect the staff display in themselves and evince in others that is the primary form of their labour (the waiter's smile is part of their job, in other words).

implied reader Wolfgang *Iser's concept for the reader a literary work appears to be written for, or seems to invite (as opposed to the actual reader of the work). The implied reader is assumed to be both sympathetic and receptive to the text's strategies. By the same token, the implied reader—in contrast to the actual reader—has no ideological 'baggage' that might interfere with the text's schemes. The concept clearly owes a debt to Wayne Booth's prior concept of the implied author and can be usefully compared to Stanley *Fish's later notion of the *interpretive community.

Further Reading: R. Holub *Reception Theory: A Critical Introduction* (1984).

index In Charles Sanders *Peirce's *semiotics, the second part of his tripartite model of the *sign's relation to its *object (the other two elements are the *icon and the *symbol). The index sign is characterized by the fact that it shows the object—examples for Peirce include weathervanes, thermometers, yardsticks, and photographs.

Ingarden, Roman (1893–1970) Polish literary theorist who worked on *phenomenology and had a significant influence on the establishment of both *Reception Theory and *Reception Aesthetics. Born in Kraków, then a part of the Austro-Hungarian empire, Ingarden studied mathematics in Lviv (in the Ukraine), and philosophy in Göttingen under Edmund *Husserl. He moved to Freiburg with Husserl and completed his doctorate on Henri *Bergson under his supervision in 1918. He then returned to Poland, teaching first at Lviv University, until it was closed because of war in 1941, then at the Nicolaus Copernicus University after the war. Ingarden's career suffered under communist rule—he was frequently banned from teaching, accused of being either an idealist or an enemy of materialism. In the early part of his career, up until the outbreak of World War II, Ingarden wrote in German as was common, but he switched to Polish out of solidarity with his invaded homeland. Consequently, it is really only his early works that are known outside of Poland. Of these early works, the best known is undoubtedly *Das literarische Kunstwerk. Eine Untersuchung aus dem Grenzgebiet der Ontologie, Logik und Literaturwissenschaft* (1931), translated as *The Literary Work of Art* (1973). This work, which attempts to theorize the ontology of literature as it is being read, had a significant influence on René *Wellek and Wolfgang *Iser, particularly the latter, as well as on the development of *reader-response criticism. Ingarden argues that neither of the key metaphysical categories of the real and the ideal is adequate to describe the ontology of the literary work, and proposes instead that it be understood as a stratified intentional object.

Further Reading: A. Chrudzimski (ed.) *Existence, Culture, Persons: The Ontology of Roman Ingarden* (2005).

in-itself/for-itself (*an sich/für sich, en-soi/pour-soi*) In *phenomenology, a dichotomy distinguishing between the two basic modes of existence, the difference being the latter form has consciousness and the former does not. The distinction is central to the work of *existential philosopher Jean-Paul *Sartre, who uses it to demonstrate that the being of an object such as a stone is not of the same variety as the being of a human being. However, for Sartre, not all human beings have being that is for-itself; this status must be arrived at via the conscious pursuit of a state of freedom.

inoperative community (communauté désoeuvrée) A theory of community put forward by French philosopher Jean-Luc *Nancy which rejects the idea that community can be produced through work. By inoperative ('désoeuvrée') Nancy does not mean dysfunctional or failing, but rather a spontaneous or 'unworked' inclination to come together that has no object or purpose other than itself. Community does not confer a higher purpose upon its constituents, Nancy claims. It does not, as religious, quasi-religious, and metaphysical philosophers argue (he has in mind Martin *Heidegger, but one could also name Alain *Badiou), transform humans from animals into men and women. The coming together is not motivated by individual desire or collective insecurity, but inheres in the human situation as a passion for sharing. This model of community is resolutely set in the present and Nancy explicitly rejects those models of community (particularly Marx-inspired models) that situate community as either a lost idyll or future ideal that can never be realized.

Further Reading: J-L. Nancy *La communauté désoeuvrée* (1986) translated as *The Inoperative Community* (1991).
B.C. Hutchens *Jean-Luc Nancy and the Future of Philosophy* (2005).
I. James *The Fragmentary Demand* (2006).

instinct An inner compulsion to act in a certain way 'hard-wired' into the body. According to *psychoanalysis, instincts operate on a level different to that of the system of the conscious and *unconscious, one that might be thought of as purely biological or physiological. Instincts have four features: a biological source (opinion varies as to what this source is, but usually it is assumed to be genetic); a supply of energy from that source (e.g. the *libido); a specific aim which, when achieved, gives rise to satisfaction, or discharge of energy (e.g. *cathexis); and an *object, namely the means of attaining a specific aim. *Ethology, which is in part the study of instincts, postulates that there are six basic instincts: sex, fighting, parenting, sleeping, territoriality, and grooming. The key implication of this is that instincts are thought to be unstoppable because they originate in a part of the body that is outside of the realm of thought; they are urges to action we cannot easily ignore. By the same token, some instincts—like parenting and grooming—might be learned behaviour and not instinctual at all; similarly, even the apparently obvious instincts like sex, necessary to the reproduction of certain species, are anything but straightforward. For *Freud, instincts are something which both the conscious and *unconscious must come to terms with either by channelling them into socially acceptable practices, or dealing with them in some other way. He suggested there are four possibilities with regard to the latter course: reversal into its opposite (i.e. an active demand converted into passive acceptance); turning against the self (i.e. making the self into an object); *repression; and *sublimation. Freud always distinguished between the *Instinkt* and the *Trieb*, but rather unhelpfully this distinction is obliterated in the English translation because James Strachey translates both as *drive. The difference between the two is, however, crucial, and one could say that Jacques *Lacan's career is built on emphasizing the latter over the former. Indeed he all but rejects the existence of the instincts as a kind of myth.

instrumental reason Max *Horkheimer and Theodor *Adorno's term for the social and political shift in priority from ends to means, from worrying about the larger meaning and purpose behind goals to caring only for the efficiency with which those goals are achieved. Comparable to Max *Weber's concept of *rationality (economic rationality being the best known example of this), instrumental reason refers not only to a rise in what Weber called bureaucratic thinking, it also refers to a larger trend in philosophy to privilege the objective at the expense of the subjective. Now, as Horkheimer and Adorno argue in *Dialektik der Aufklärung* (1944), translated as *Dialectic of Enlightenment* (1972), the subjective is treated as though it is sheer representation without any cognitive content, while the objective is treated as though it is pure cognitive content. A contemporary example of this line of thinking would be the work of Manuel DeLanda, particularly *Intensive Science and Virtual Philosophy* (2002). This way of thinking, Horkheimer and Adorno argue, obscures the fact that what we think of as reason is always the product of a negotiation between the rational and the irrational, the subjective and the objective, between that which can be proved empirically and that which cannot. Even more problematically, by rigorously trying to purge itself of all its subjective elements, thought winds up producing a mythology in which it remains trapped. The objective is made to seem equivalent to that which is unchanging, eternal, universal, effectively placing it on the same plane as a deity. In his later work on aesthetics, Adorno argues that this process of expelling the subjective altogether is not yet complete and suggests that art has continued importance in our society precisely because it creates a place for the irrational, thus tempering the relentless pursuit of the rational in every other dimension of contemporary life.

Further Reading: S. Jarvis *Adorno: A Critical Introduction* (1998).

intensity Gilles *Deleuze's term, derived from language philosophy, for the specific criteria that determine that something is one kind of thing and not another. Because Deleuze uses it to theorize the ontology of literally everything, including *affect, it is often mistakenly thought that intensity refers to a species of experience that is particularly intense. But this is false. The true origin of the term is the logical relation between intension and extension. If we take the colour blue as our example, the extension of blue is all the objects in the world that are blue, while intension is the specific set of characteristics that make a thing recognizable as blue. In this sense, intensity may also be understood, paradoxically enough, as the extension of difference. *See also* SINGULARITY.

intentionality In philosophy, the relation between thought and the object in the world being thought about. So if one is thinking of a car, then it is the relation between one's thought about that car and the actual car itself. Intentionality does not only have to be directed towards a solid object; it can also point towards an idea, or an emotion. Thus, it can also be thought of as the directedness of consciousness. It does not, however, refer to the idea of intention as motive for action (e.g. whether someone's intentions are honourable or not).

intentional fallacy A core idea of *New Criticism. In a famous paper, entitled 'The Intentional Fallacy' (1954), W.K. Wimsatt and Monroe Beardsley argue that the author's intentions—that is, the vision the author has of what they are trying to achieve in a particular work—is not a valid source of critical judgement about a text's relative worth as literature. Crudely put, the fact that an author thought they were writing the great realist of novel of their time is not sufficient to make it so. By the same token, just because they failed to realise their intention to write a great realist novel, that is no reason to disregard the work's other potential merits. Rather one must concentrate on its formal properties because these and these alone are sufficient to distinguish good literature from bad. *See also* AFFECTIVE FALLACY.

international style An austere, anti-ornamental, ultra *modernist style of architecture associated with the work of the great European architects Walter Gropius, Le Corbusier, and Ludwig Mies van der Rohe, among others. The term derives from the title of an exhibition (and accompanying book written by Henry Russell Hitchcock and Philip Johnson) staged in 1932 to showcase this new style of architecture which emerged after the end of World War I and was then at its peak. Characterized by its smooth, balanced rather than symmetrical lines, its lack of decorative flourishes, and its emphasis on volume, and preference for cheap modern materials like steel, glass, and concrete the international style is highly distinctive. Mies van der Rohe's most famous quote 'less is more' could serve as a motto for the style aimed at by the entire movement, while Le Corbusier's description of buildings as 'machines for living' perhaps sums up its functionalist attitude—architecture was supposed to change how people act, think, live, and work. In this sense it was *utopian.

interpellation Proposed by the French Marxist philosopher Louis *Althusser, the term is central to his account of *ideology as the imaginary relationship of individuals to their real conditions of existence. It names the non-coercive process whereby a *subject is called upon by a particular social formation to *misrecognize themselves as a subject and thereby forget that they are constituted by society rather than constitutive of society as they henceforth imagine themselves to be. Ideology recruits individuals and transforms them into subjects (which for Althusser implies that they are simultaneously the subjects of society, meaning the products of society, and subjected to society, meaning subordinate to society) by persuading them to occupy a subject position it has prepared for them and see themselves in that otherwise vacant position. The most straightforward example of this process is probably that of nationality, which government is constantly exhorting its citizens to adopt as the basis of both individual and collective identity. But this process should not be thought of as a kind of becoming; for Althusser ideology is eternal, so one is always already interpellated, or to put it another way ideology has no outside—one is always already inside ideology. The pivotal notion of misrecognition is drawn from French psychoanalyst Jacques *Lacan's account of the *mirror stage in the developmental psychology of very young children. Althusser hypothesizes that just as babies look in the mirror and misrecognize their virtual image as their actual self, so under conditions of ideology individuals misrecognize socially produced virtual representations as their actual self. This concept (directly and indirectly) has been used to great effect by a variety of radical minority groups to argue the social and cultural importance of affirmative representations of politically marginalized groups. *See also* HEGEMONY; IDEOLOGICAL STATE APPARATUS; IMAGINED COMMUNITY.

Further Reading: L. Althusser *Lenin and Philosophy* (1971).

interpretive community Stanley *Fish developed this concept to explain how diverse readers consistently produce similar readings of certain types of texts. His argument, which borrows Noam *Chomsky's distinction between *competence and performance, is that readers in a particular country at a particular time internalize a set of expectations about how texts work and what counts as a text, amounting to a kind of literary competence, such that whenever they encounter a new text they already know how to respond to it. Pierre

*Bourdieu makes a very similar argument using his concept of the *habitus.

Further Reading: S. Fish *Is There a Text in this Class? The Authority of Interpretive Communities* (1980).

intertextuality Julia *Kristeva is generally credited with the invention of the term, but the concept can also be found in the work of Roland *Barthes and Roman *Jakobson. Derived from a synthesis of Mikhail *Bakhtin's concept of *dialogism and Sigmund *Freud's notion of *dreamwork, intertextuality is a theory of meaning and meaning-production. It holds that all texts (in the expanded sense of the term *post-structuralist theory maintains) are composed of other (pre-existing) texts (in the ordinary sense of the word) held together in a state of constant interaction. It means that there are no original texts, no complete texts and no singular texts: all texts exist in a state of partiality and inter-dependency with other texts. This is not simply a fact of language, according to Kristeva, but its necessary pre-condition. Every writer is first of all a reader, Kristeva argues, so their works are created from textual resources they've digested in a lifetime of reading; by the same token, readers are like writers, they build up a picture of what they read by associating it with everything they've read before. Meaning is therefore always 'in between'.

introjection The transposition in fantasy of an *object or any other source of *pleasure that is usually outside the subject to a position inside the subject. For example, the child may perceive the strength of its father or kindness of its mother as agreeable attributes and unconsciously incorporate these into its *ego and *superego. Consequently, if one or other parent dies, the work of mourning the subject enters into is in part a kind of mourning for the loss of a part of the self too. The concept was conceived as the opposite of the notion of *projection, by Sigmund *Freud's friend and fellow *psychoanalyst Sandor Ferenczi in 1909; it was adopted by Freud himself in 1915. The concept is central to the work of Melanie *Klein, though she restricts its use to the discussion of objects.

invented tradition It has every appearance of being an actual tradition, in that it repeats images and symbols drawn from the past (real or imagined), but is in fact both of a relatively recent origin and artificially created. British historian Eric *Hobsbawm identified this phenomenon in a collection of essays he edited with Terence Ranger, *The Invention of Tradition* (1983). One of the most striking examples of an invented tradition adduced in this collection is Scottish tartan—the colourful clan tartans tourists purchase along the Royal Mile in Edinburgh are in fact an early 19th-century invention, not an ancient tradition as is claimed. Hobsbawm's point, however, is not to mock such fictions, but to highlight the *ideological importance of at least the perception of continuity with the past.

Irigaray, Luce (1932–) Psychoanalyst, philosopher and French feminist theorist. One of the handful of scholars known by the generic term 'French feminists' in spite of the fact that many of them are not French by birth (the others being Hélène *Cixous, Michèle Le *Doeuff, and Julia *Kristeva), Irigaray has had an enormous influence on feminist theory since the early 1970s.

Born in Belgium, Irigaray took her Master's degree in philosophy at the University of Leuven in 1955. She then taught at a high school in Brussels until the end of the decade before moving to Paris, where she initially studied psychology. She gained her Master's degree in psychology from the University of Paris in 1961 and a Diploma in psychopathology the following year. During this time she also attended Jacques *Lacan's seminars and trained as a psychoanalyst. However her first doctorate was in linguistics and it was this that she first taught at Vincennes from 1970–74. Her second doctorate, *Speculum de l'autre femme* (1974), translated as *Speculum of the Other Woman* (1985), which inaugurated a radical break with Lacan, led to her dismissal from Vincennes. Since 1980 Irigaray has been ensconced at the Centre Nationale de Recherche Scientifique in Paris.

In interviews, which rarely dwell on the personal, Irigaray describes her work as having gone through three distinct phases: first, she set out to critique the way the western subject was formed in the image of the white male and viewed the entire world through that lens; then she began to think about the ways and means by which a specifically female subjectivity might be articulated; and, finally, but still ongoing, she started to think about new models for relations between the sexes not built on the idea of domination and submission.

In the first phase, Irigaray mobilized *deconstructive reading strategies to expose the narrow way in which the subject is conceived. Mindful of the fact that it is impossible—at least from a deconstructive perspective—to create a position that is completely pure, which is to say uncontaminated by the phallogocentrism she wants to escape, Irigaray advocates a *strategic essentialism of the feminine.

In the second phase, Irigaray used body morphology as a rhetorical weapon against anatomy, aiming to reconceive the body (particularly the female body) as a positivity rather than a lack. It was in this phase that she famously proposed the image of the lips (by which she means both the mouth and the labia) as a sex which is neither singular nor plural (see *Ce Sexe qui n'en est pas un* (1977), translated as *This Sex Which is Not One* (1985)). She has been accused of biological essentialism for this move, but such a criticism misses the point that what is at stake is the elaboration of a female *imaginary (in Lacan's sense) that does not reduce the female sex to either a weaker version of the phallus (the clitoris) or that which completes the phallus (the vagina).

The third, ongoing phase, has been marked by an attempt to mobilize the polymorphically perverse body of the pre-oedipal subject (to use Sigmund *Freud's famous description) in order to think about the inherently destabilizing *Other to the white male standard around which western subjectivity is conceived. Irigaray does not conceive the pre-oedipal in a nostalgic fashion, but sees it rather as the constant potential of all subjects. Involved, too, is the rethinking of the relation between mother and daughter (which is also central to *Kristeva's work).

Beyond this, drawing on the work of Emmanuel *Levinas, Irigaray has attempted to construct an ethics of sexual difference. Not forgetting her training in linguistics, in *J'aime à toi* (1992), translated as *I love to you* (1996), Irigaray locates the root of the problem posed by ethics in language itself and shows the way various languages subordinate women in their very structure.

In her more recent work, such as *Democracy Begins between Two* (2000), Irigaray has (in collaboration with the Commission for Equal Opportunities for the Italian region of Emilia-Romagna) tried to give her ethical thinking a practical twist. Irigaray is a prolific writer, with a sometimes difficult or elusive style, who engages the western philosophical canon in a debate about the place for and of women in thought, politics, and indeed love.

Further Reading: C. Burke et al. (eds) *Engaging with Irigaray* (1994).
T. Chanter *Ethics of Eros: Irigaray's Rewriting of the Philosophers* (1995).
E. Grosz *Sexual Subversions* (1989).
T. Lorraine *Irigaray and Deleuze* (1999).
M. Whitford *Luce Irigaray: Philosophy in the Feminine* (1991).

irony A type of *rhetoric in which there is a deliberate and obvious disparity or incongruity between the statement made and its intent, as when we say one thing, but mean the opposite of what we say. When somebody says, 'lovely weather we're having', and it is raining, they are being ironic. Irony in this sense is a very close relative of sarcasm. But it can take more complex forms and its intent does not always have to be humour. For instance, when Romeo kills himself because he thinks Juliet is dead, that is also ironic. Literary theory distinguishes at least five types (or *tropes) of irony: (i) verbal irony—the simplest form involving a discrepancy between statement and intent (e.g. sarcasm); (ii) structural irony—a more complex or extended form in which a character's world-view is at odds with the world they find themselves in (e.g. Sade's *Justine, or Good Conduct Well Chastised* (1791), which is doubly ironic in that the author is clearly unsympathetic towards his naive heroine who is constantly surprised by the cruelties and injustices meted out to her); (iii) dramatic irony—routinely found in TV sitcoms, it involves a situation in which the audience possesses more information than the characters on stage (all pantomimes play on this, with the audience deriving great amusement from knowing the monster is behind the hero, who for some reason is unable to see the monster for himself); (iv) tragic irony—a version of dramatic irony in which the audience can see that a character's course of action is destined not to have the outcome the character thinks it will (e.g. Arthur Miller's *Death of a Salesman* (1949)); (v) cosmic irony—a version of dramatic irony in which it seems that despite the best intentions of characters, fate is always going to crush their dreams (e.g. Thomas Hardy's *Jude the Obscure* (1895)).

Further Reading: C. Colebrook *Irony* (2003).

ISA *See* IDEOLOGICAL STATE APPARATUS.

Iser, Wolfgang (1926–2007) German literary scholar, best known for establishing *Reception Theory. Together with his colleague Hans Robert *Jauss, he is the founder of the Konstanz School of reception aesthetics which has had a significant influence on Anglo-American *reader-response criticism. Born in Marienberg, Germany, he studied literature in Leipzig and Tübingen as an undergraduate. He then completed a PhD in English at Heidelberg, writing a dissertation on the work of the 18th-century English novelist Henry Fielding. His most significant books are *Der implizite Leser: Kommunikationsformen des Romans von Bunyan bis Beckett* (1972), translated as *The Implied Reader: Patterns of Prose Communication in Prose Fiction from Bunyan to Beckett* (1974) and *Der Akt des Lesens: Theorie ästhetischer Wirkung* (1976), translated as *The Act of Reading* (1978). The concept of the *implied reader. has been widely used in literary studies. In a marvellous cameo written about himself in the middle of a textbook published near to the end of his life entitled *How to do Theory* (2006), Iser explains that his theoretical explorations arose not from philosophy (although they owe an obvious and acknowledged debt to *phenomenology), but out of a recognition that the study of literature was in a state of crisis in the 1950s. Cultural heritage, he argues, could no longer serve as the unquestioned justification for studying literature and readers could no longer be expected to mine canonical texts for a standard set of 'improving' meanings. Having set aside the idea that all texts contain a specified set of meanings readers should find, Iser then set about trying to understand how meanings are in fact formed. His key publications pertain to this problem.

Jakobson, Roman (1896–1982) Russian linguist, formative member of both the *Russian Formalists (the *Moscow Linguistic Circle as well as **Opoyaz*) and the *Prague Linguistic Circle, and one of the founding fathers of *structuralism. An incredibly prolific author—he wrote over 600 articles—Jakobson is widely regarded as the pre-eminent linguist of the 20th century.

Born in Moscow, he studied historical philology at Moscow University. He was, by then, already friends with the greatest poets and painters of his time, including the futurist poets Velimir Khlebnikov and Vladimir Mayakovsky as well as the great revolutionary artist Cazimir Malevich. In 1915, Jakobson helped establish the Moscow Linguistic Circle (the first meeting took place in his parent's dining room), with the purpose of promoting a linguistic approach to poetics. Its membership included such key figures as Victor Shklovsky and Yuri Tynyanov. Around the same time he met Nicolai Troubetzkoy, who shared his interest in *Husserl's *phenomenology and with whom he would form a fast friendship that proved highly influential on his thinking. Although Russia was in a real state of tumult at the time, in 1917 Jakobson took part in the creation of *Opoyaz*, a St Petersburg based society for the study of poetic language and the group mostly responsible for what we think of as Russian Formalism today.

Jakobson chose to leave Russia in 1920, which proved a wise decision as many of his former colleagues who remained behind were eliminated by the new Bolshevik regime. Initially he went to Prague, where he worked as a translator for the Soviet Red Cross mission, then as a cultural attaché. Legend has it that structuralist linguistics was born in Prague because Jakobson realized, while listening to Russian poetry translated into Czech, that while their words were similar on paper they were quite different sounding and therefore had a dissimilar musicality. Jakobson thus began to concentrate on sound, an approach that led him to focus his research on the notion of the phoneme (a unit of sound meaning). It was in Prague too that Jakobson first read the work of *Saussure, realizing straightaway the importance of the distinction between *langue and parole. After nearly a decade in the city, Jakobson established the Prague Linguistic Circle, again with the intention of focusing on poetic language. Its early membership included René Wellek and Jan Mukařovský.

The threat of war interrupted the Circle's work in 1938 when in defiance of world opinion Germany absorbed large sections of Czechoslovakia into the Third Reich. Jakobson fled, first to Denmark, where he collaborated with the other great linguist of his generation Louis *Hjelmslev, and then like so many other European exiles to New York, where he met Claude *Lévi-Strauss. He remained in the US for the rest of his life, holding posts at the New School for Social Research, Harvard, and MIT (Massachusetts Institute of Technology). Aside from the countless incidental analyses Jakobson produced, his major mark on critical theory was his problematic but nonetheless striking assertion that poetic language is autonomous, meaning that while it may be constructed from ordinary language there is something distinctive about it that makes it stand apart. Jakobson called this difference **literaturnost* (literariness), a code phrase that together with **ostranenie* (defamiliarization or estrangement) would become synonymous with Russian Formalism itself.

Jakobson's concept of poetic language is, however, only one part of his larger model of communication. According to Jakobson, verbal communication has six constitutive functions: the *phatic (it conveys no meaning, but serves to keep the communication channels open); referential (that which refers to the speech context); emotive (the speaker's attitude to their own speech); poetic (the autotelic dimension, i.e. it has no purpose except itself); conative (the orientation of the speech toward its addressee); and metalingual (the reflective dimension which focuses on the properties of language itself, as for instance when we ask 'what do you mean?'). Jakobson argues that all six functions are present in all speech, but different functions may have greater or less prominence according to the occasion.

Further Reading: T. Bennett *Formalism and Marxism* (1979).
V. Erlich *Russian Formalism: History—Doctrine* (1955).

Jameson, Fredric (1934–) Marxist cultural critic. Born in Cleveland Ohio, Jameson was educated at Haverford College and Yale University. He is renowned for his landmark essay, 'Postmodernism, or, the Cultural Logic of Late Capitalism' (1984), which for admirers and detractors alike continues to serve as a focal point for attempts to define the nature of the contemporary *situation. Few authors display Jameson's intellectual range, which encompasses a command of several languages and an encyclopedic knowledge of works in architecture, art, film, history, politics, and literature.

Reticent about allowing his work to be turned into something he disparagingly calls a 'brand', Jameson has held back from developing a singular method that could be easily emulated. His method, which he has variously called *metacommentary, *transcoding, and *dialectical criticism, is, he insists, in a permanent state of incompletion. There is no one form of the dialectic, he argues, and neither can there be a final form, it must constantly adapt to meet the new challenges of a rapidly changing historical situation. Jameson has brought together his thoughts on his dialectical method in *The Valences of the Dialectic* (2009).

Jameson completed his doctorate at Yale in 1959. It was published in 1961 as *Sartre: The Origins of a Style*. Focused on *Sartre's novels and plays rather than his philosophical writing, it established a template for future work by exploring the degree to which an author's style can be read dialectically as a symptom of their engagement with their political situation. In essence, as he articulates more directly in the work that follows, for Jameson all cultural works can be treated as *allegories for which the master text is history itself.

In the succeeding decade, Jameson wrote a series of long essays on key thinkers of the Left, including *Adorno, *Bloch, *Benjamin, *Lukács, and *Marcuse, which sought both to make these authors (whose works were not translated into English at the time) more widely known in the Anglophone academy and to examine their usefulness for contemporary cultural politics. These essays were brought together in *Marxism and Form* (1971), undoubtedly the most important book on Marxist aesthetics of the latter half of the 20th century. In a companion volume, *The Prison-House of Language* (1972), Jameson provided a critical account of *Russian Formalism and *structuralism.

In *The Political Unconscious: Narrative as a Socially Symbolic Act* (1981), Jameson continued his investigation of the link between style and politics. Highly influential in literary studies and *Cultural studies, the concept of the *political unconscious adapts the psychoanalytic concept of *wish-fulfilment to explain the unconscious social and political presuppositions of cultural works. Jameson's thesis is that cultural texts are symbolic solutions to real historical problems. They bring into existence in textual form a vision of society that society itself is incapable of realizing. Textual analysis, following this logic, tries to reconstruct (or reverse engineer) the historical sub-text or problematic driving a particular text by asking how it works. His key exhibit in this regard is the 19th-century's obsession with the notion of **ressentiment* (particularly in the work of Friedrich *Nietzsche and Joseph Conrad), which, as he shows, served the ideological purpose of discrediting all forms of political action.

In 1982, Jameson gave a talk at the Whitney Museum of Contemporary Art entitled 'Postmodernism and Consumer Society'. In the words of one commentator, namely Perry *Anderson, it redrew the map of the whole field of humanities at a single stroke. A revised version of this talk was published in 1984 in *New Left Review* with the new title of 'Postmodernism, or, the Cultural Logic of Late Capitalism'. It quickly became one of the most discussed and cited articles of the decade because of the way it sought not only to elucidate the specific features of *postmodernism, but to explain their underlying causes as well. Jameson rejects the idea that we have entered a *post-industrial age in which the internal contradictions of capitalism have at last been resolved and argues instead (adapting Ernest Mandel's argument in *Der Spätkapitalismus* (1972), translated as *Late Capitalism* (1975) in the process) that the present should be understood as the age in which capitalism has finally permeated every aspect of life, including consciousness itself. Culture, for Jameson, is thus both a response to and registration of the underlying economic and political forces of the *mode of production itself.

An extended working out of the implications of his thesis is presented in book form in *Postmodernism, or, the Cultural Logic of Late Capitalism* (1991). The postmodern situation, Jameson argues, is conditioned by two historical drivers: (i) the so-called 'Green Revolution', or the industrialization of Third World agriculture, which had two powerful effects—on the one hand, it massively increased food production, thus enhancing food security, but it is also put millions of peasants out of work, forcing them to move to cities in search of employment; (ii) the refocusing of the First World economy around tertiary enterprises (i.e. knowledge and information) rather than primary and secondary enterprises (i.e. agriculture, mining, and manufacturing). These changes took effect in the 1950s, but in Jameson's view it wasn't until the 1970s that they began to be recorded in what he terms the political unconscious of global culture. Examining a wide range of texts across all the arts, Jameson identifies five symptoms of the cultural shift toward full-blown postmodernism—the *waning of affect; *pastiche; *hysterical sublime; *geopolitical aesthetic; and a mutation in built space interfering with our ability to produce a *cognitive map of our situation.

Jameson's subsequent books, *The Geopolitical Aesthetic* (1992), *The Seeds of Time* (1994), and *A Singular Modernity* (2002) have extended this discussion further by examining in more detail the problem of what came before postmodernism and inquiring into its continued significance. In contrast to many Marxist critics, Jameson does not engage in either doctrinal battles relating to the correct interpretation of Marx's thought or factionalist battles relating to the political uptakes of Marx's thought (e.g. Leninism, Maoism, Stalinism, Trotskyism, etc.). For Jameson, the crucial measure of any form of thought and indeed work of art is whether or not it enables us to imagine a future different from our present, even if it is brought about by cataclysm. For this reason, Jameson has nurtured a lifelong interest in *modernism and science fiction, which in his view offer the most important examples of this type of utopian thinking. Two recent books, both of which collect essays written over a 30-year period, are devoted to precisely these topics: *The Modernist Papers* (2007) and *Archaeologies of the Future* (2005).

Jameson was awarded the prestigious Holberg Prize in 2008.

Further Reading: P. Anderson *The Origins of Postmodernity* (1998).
I. Buchanan *Fredric Jameson: Live Theory* (2006).
S. Homer *Fredric Jameson* (1998).
C. Irr and I. Buchanan *On Jameson* (2006).
F. Jameson *Jameson on Jameson: Conversations on Cultural Marxism* (2007).

Jarry, Alfred (1873–1907) French novelist and playwright who influenced *Surrealism and *Dada, but also the *Situationists and the *OULIPO authors who were attracted to his concept of *'pataphysics, or the science of imaginary solutions. A conspicuously eccentric figure, Jarry is best remembered for his play *Ubu Roi* (King Ubu, 1896) which caused such a scandal on its opening night, largely because of the swearing it contained. It wasn't staged again for more than a decade. It has since become a cornerstone of the *absurdist theatre canon. His late novel, *Le Surmâle* (1902), translated as *The Supermale* (1964), is an inspiration for Gilles *Deleuze and Félix Guattari's concept of the *desiring-machine.

Further Reading: K. Beaumont *Alfred Jarry: A Critical and Biographical Study* (1984).

Jaspers, Karl (1883–1969) German psychiatrist and philosopher, considered one of the fathers (along with Martin *Heidegger) of German *existentialism. Born in the northern German town of Oldenburg, Jaspers initially followed his father's footsteps into law, but soon switched to medicine. He obtained a doctorate in medicine in 1908 and then took his habilitation in psychology. He worked briefly as a psychiatrist, but spent the bulk of his professional life as an academic. However, his earliest publications were clinical in orientation. His two-volume work, *Allgemeine Psychopathologie*

(General Psychopathlogy, 1913) remains an important reference point today as one of the pioneering works of the so-called 'biographical method' of diagnosis. In the early 1920s, Jaspers shifted into philosophy and it is as a philosopher that he is best known. Because his wife was Jewish, Jaspers was removed from his university post in 1937 by the Nazis. This made for difficult times for Jaspers during the war years, but in the aftermath of the war because he was untainted by any direct association with the Nazis (in contrast to his rival Heidegger) he was able to take on a leadership role in rebuilding the German university system. Jaspers wrote widely, and for a broadly popular audience, on the question of Germany's future, including the difficult issue of how it should deal with its guilt. In the years following the war, Jaspers became a high-profile spokesperson for the humanist viewpoint. Perhaps because of this, inasmuch as the humanist perspective became very outmoded in the *structuralist period, Jaspers's work is quite neglected today.

Jauss, Hans Robert (1921–97) German literary theorist, best known for establishing *Reception Aesthetics. Together with his colleague Wolfgang *Iser, he is the founder of the Konstanz School, which has had a significant influence on Anglo-American *reader-response criticism. Born in Göppingen, Germany, Jauss studied in Esslingen and Geislingen. In 1939 he joined the army and saw service on the Russian Front. He was briefly imprisoned at the end of the war as an enemy combatant, thus delaying his university studies until 1948. He completed his undergraduate and postgraduate degrees at the University of Heidelberg, graduating in 1957 with a dissertation on Marcel Proust. Between 1959 and 1966, Jauss held jobs in Münster and Giessen. In 1966, he was invited to join the newly established University of Konstanz to set up the subject area of literary studies. He did this in collaboration with several colleagues and the end result became known as the Konstanz School. Jauss's own inaugural lecture in 1967, entitled 'Literary History as a Challenge to Literary Theory', was seminal in launching what he describes as Reception Aesthetics, which is a mode of literary history interested in the interaction between readers and writers. His most important works include: *Toward an Aesthetic of Reception* (1982) and *Aesthetic Experience and Literary Hermeneutics* (1982).

***jetztzeit* (now-time)** Walter *Benjamin uses this term in his 'Theses on the Philosophy of History' to describe a notion of time that is ripe with revolutionary possibility, time that has been detached from the continuum of history. It is time at a standstill, poised, filled with energy, and ready to take what Benjamin called the 'tiger's leap' into the future. It isn't naturally occurring, however, and takes the intervention of the artist or revolutionary to produce it by 'blasting' it free from the ceaseless flow in which it would otherwise be trapped. Benjamin contrasts *jetztzeit* with the 'homogeneous empty time' of the ruling class, which is history written from the perspective of the victors (as Benedict *Anderson shows in his account of nation as *imagined community).

jouissance The French word for enjoyment. It has become part of the vocabulary of Anglophone *critical theory and more particularly *psychoanalysis because of the translations of the work of Roland *Barthes, Georges *Battaile, Julia *Kristeva, and Jacques *Lacan, among others. In contrast to the English word 'enjoyment', jouissance can also mean orgasm. Early attempts at translating it as 'bliss', as for instance in Richard Miller's translation of Barthes's *The Pleasure of the Text* (1975), lack this dimension, and though it captures something of the spiritual dimension of the word it still lacks its intensity. Central to its usage in critical theory is its opposition to 'plaisir' (*pleasure)—pleasure is usually seen as the opposite of jouissance in that it is seen as a coming to an end, whereas jouissance is regarded as limitless. The connection to orgasm is quite ambiguous in this respect because the implication is that jouissance occurs on a higher plane to that of the merely physical; it is an orgasm of the mind or spirit not just the body. The opposition between pleasure and jouissance is modelled on G.W.F. *Hegel's opposition between 'Lust' (pleasure) and 'Genuss' (enjoyment), as discussed by Alexandre *Kojève. In psychoanalysis this opposition is interpreted as a prohibition on jouissance—the *pleasure principle regards jouissance as excessive and destabilizing. On this view, pleasure can only be pleasurable so long as it is not too pleasurable. In contrast, jouissance can only be jouissance if it goes beyond mere pleasure and risks death and courts disaster.

Jung, Carl (1875–1961) Swiss psychiatrist and founder of analytical psychology whose work on *archetypes and *myth had a significant influence on Anglo-American literary criticism in the 1950s and 1960s, particularly via the work of Northrop *Frye. Jung's work was less influential on continental literary criticism, but it did have at least one significant advocate in France, namely Gaston *Bachelard. Gilles *Deleuze may also be cited in this context, but despite Christian Kerslake's heroic effort in *Deleuze and the Unconscious* (2007), his connection to Jung is relatively little perceived.

Jung was born in Kesswil in Switzerland. His father was a relatively poor clergyman in a rural parish, while his mother belonged to the wealthy Preiswerk family. His paternal grandfather, after whom he was named, was a prominent physician and rector of Basel University (he was also rumoured to be the illegitimate son of the great German author Wolfgang Goethe). Jung studied for a medical degree at universities in Basel and Zurich, writing his doctorate on the psychopathology of the occult. Reading Richard von Krafft-Ebing's work decided him on a career in psychiatry, then the least respected branch of medicine. He took a resident's position at Burghölzli Asylum (attached to the University of Zurich) under the direction of Eugen Bleuler, who coined the term schizophrenia. He was dismissed from his post by Bleuler who found out he'd been having an affair with his patient, Sabina Spielrein, a Russian Jew who became a psychoanalyst in her own right; she died in 1942 at the hands of the Nazis.

During his time at Burghölzli, Jung read and admired the works of Sigmund *Freud, particularly *Die Traumdeutung* (1900), translated as *The Interpretation of Dreams* (1953), and in a gesture of homage he sent a copy of his book on word associations to Freud, believing it provided empirical support to the latter's theory. Freud reciprocated the gesture several months later, spawning an intense friendship which lasted six years. For a time, Freud thought of Jung as his natural successor, making him the first president of the International Psychoanalytic Association, but they broke from each other in 1912 for a variety of personal and professional reasons (they continued to snipe at one another for the rest of their lives in their published work). Their main theoretical differences concerned the *libido and the *unconscious—in contrast to Freud, Jung conceived the libido as a kind of life-force, thinking Freud's version overly reductive; while his concept of the unconscious allowed for an inherited dimension he called the *collective unconscious. Like Freud, however, most of Jung's most important theories were developed out of self analysis, particularly of his own childhood recollections of dreams and events.

Jung's theory of developmental psychology revolves around a fundamental confrontation between the self, which yearns to be realized (a process Jung referred to as individuation), and the unconscious, the domain of the *archetypes, which constantly seek actualization. In contrast to Freud's theory, which focuses almost exclusively on childhood, and treats the unconscious as an unknowable other, Jung's theory holds that the unconscious is a constant presence and the developmental confrontation between self and unconscious is lifelong. The process of individuation is highly complicated and by no means linear—the confrontation with the archetypes, particularly, gives rise to several different types of response in the psyche. These varying responses are what differentiate people from one another. Jung argued that people can be classified according to psychological type, of which there are eight basic varieties; this concept has been very influential in the development of management theory.

Further Reading: D. Bair *Jung: A Biography* (2003).
A. Stevens *On Jung* (1990).
A. Stevens *Jung* (1994).
A. Storr *C.G. Jung* (1991).

Kant, Immanuel (1724–1804) German philosopher, one of the most influential thinkers of all time. His influence is so great, European philosophy is generally divided into pre-Kantian and post-Kantian schools of thought. Outside of philosophy, Kant's essays on the *sublime and the meaning of *Enlightenment have been hugely influential in setting the agenda for research in aesthetics.

Kant was born in Königsberg, then the capital of Prussia, but now a Russian exclave—it was renamed Kaliningrad at the end of World War II when the city was occupied by Soviet forces. Even by the standards of his own time, Kant was extremely unworldly, he never travelled more than 100 miles from his hometown, and almost his entire professional life was spent as a university academic. His father was a harness-maker and a strict disciplinarian who maintained an austere and pious household. Kant studied literature, philosophy and natural science at the University of Königsberg. He did not complete his degree, however, and there is speculation that he was forced out of the university because of his sympathy with Leibniz's thought. After three years working as a private tutor he was able to return to the university and complete his degree and commence work as a lecturer.

Kant's career progressed slowly. He wrote prolifically, initially in Latin, then in his native German, but his work did not receive wide distribution (not least because in one case his publisher went bankrupt). He also found his progress was slowed by the demands of teaching and the necessity of earning a living. He was finally given a salaried position in 1770 and he was able to devote himself more fully to philosophy. It still took him another decade, however, to complete and finally publish *Kritik der reinen Vernunft* (1781), translated as *Critique of Pure Reason* (1929), the work which established him as one of the greatest philosophers of all time. Kant himself described the work as producing the philosophical equivalent of the so-called Copernican Revolution because it reversed the usual assumption that the apprehension of empirical sense-data necessarily precedes the production of the concepts we assign to them.

Critique of Pure Reason, or First Critique, as it is usually known because it was followed by two further critiques, sought to overcome what Kant saw as the problem of the *empiricist David Hume's scepticism concerning causation. He agreed with Hume that it is impossible to prove that every event has a cause by power of experience, but disagreed with him that one should thereby abandon the general principle that every event has a cause. Kant's solution is to divide the psychical apparatus in two: on the one side there are 'intuitions', the perceptions of given sense data, and on the other side there are categories and concepts (such as space and time), the universal laws of the mind. His rationale is that we could not describe the world in a variety of different ways if we did not have concepts that enable us to see it differently too. But even more importantly, Kant argued that even when a specific cause is not perceptible we nonetheless know that it must exist and that necessity is sufficient to found knowledge.

Kant describes the process of attaining knowledge as judgement and identifies three stages in its composition: first there is the apprehension of something that affects the mind, then the imagination reproduces it in the mind, and thirdly it is recognized by the mind which assigns it a concept. Judgement is the application of the rules of understanding to intuitions. These rules are said to be 'transcendental' by Kant because they function as conditions of possibility for knowledge. In the subsequent Second and Third Critiques, *Kritik der praktischen Vernunft* (1788), translated as *Critique of Practical Reason* (1909), and *Kritik der Urteilskraft* (1790), translated as *The Critique of Judgement* (1952), Kant turned his attention to aesthetic, moral, and political questions. Such is the force of these later works Kant is regarded by many readers as fundamentally a moral philosopher.

As a moral philosopher, Kant is austere and uncompromising: the only act that is unconditionally good in his view is one that is done selflessly out of a sense of duty and for the sake of duty. Acting out of duty deprives the will (or what after *Freud we would call the *ego) of an *object of *desire, meaning that the act is carried out in accordance with universal law rather than for personal gain. His ethics are developed on the principle that they must not presuppose a specific object or will, but must always reflect universal laws, or what Kant called the 'categorical imperative', which is a law that any rational being would recognize as valid without exception in all imaginable situations.

Further Reading: H.E. Allison *Kant's Transcendental Idealism* (1983).
P. Guyer *Kant* (2006).
R. Scruton *Kant: A Very Short Introduction* (2001).

SEE WEB LINKS

- A website claiming to be the most comprehensive list of resources on Immanuel Kant available on the web.

Kautsky, Karl (1854–1938) Marxist intellectual and political activist. He was born in Prague, but his family moved to Vienna when he was 7 years old. He studied history, economics and philosophy at the University of Vienna. It was there that his active involvement with politics began. He joined the Austrian Social Democratic Party. In 1881 he visited Friedrich *Engels in London and the two became firm friends. In Stuttgart in 1883 he founded the journal *Die Neue Zeit* (The New Time), and edited it until 1917, which provided him with a basic means of living, even while living abroad, as he frequently did. Kautsky was an outspoken critic of the First World War. After the November Revolution in Germany (the chaotic period from the end of the First World War in November 1918 until the establishment of the Weimar Republic in August 1919), he was given a senior position in the Foreign Office of the briefly reigning revolutionary government, which he used to try to prove Germany's war guilt. A prolific author, he wrote a biography of Engels as well as a detailed account of *Marx's economic theory. His writings were held in high enough regard in his own lifetime to attract strong (negative) responses from both Lenin and Trotsky.

Further Reading: M. Salvadori and J. Rothschild *Karl Kautsky and the Socialist Revolution* (1990).

khōra **(chora)** The pre-linguistic or inchoate point of origin of the subject, for which the womb may stand as a figure, though the pre-biotic soup out of which all life is supposed to have emerged according to evolutionary theory might stand just as well. Paris-based, Bulgarian linguist and psychoanalyst Julia *Kristeva adapted the term from Plato's *Timaeus*, where it means quite simply a receptacle for meaning, to theorize a semiotic network or nonexpressive totality out of which individual words and meanings are produced. It is for her the potentiality for meaning that must pre-exist meaning-making, but it has no meaning itself. It is in this respect neither sensible nor intelligible, although Kristeva insists it is nonetheless regulated and not anarchic as Jacques *Derrida charges in his account of the concept. As the potential for meaning, the *khōra* is also the limit or disruption of meaning. It makes its appearance then wherever meaning-production is pushed to its limits, as in modern and postmodern art and literature. In *psychoanalytic terms, the *khōra* is the realm of the *drives, which are pre-symbolic, unrepresentable, yet motivating: they give the subject the energy they need to act.

Further Reading: J. Derrida *On the Name* (1995).
J. Kristeva *Revolution in Poetic Language* (1984).

kitsch Bad, tasteless, gaudy, flashy art or pseudo-art. The *Frankfurt School, particularly Theodor *Adorno, used the term kitsch in conjunction with *Avant-garde to define the polar extremes of contemporary art, condemning kitsch on the one hand for merely reproducing the values of *late capitalism and praising the Avant-garde on the other hand for challenging or refusing those values. The great American art critic Clement Greenberg adopted a similar binary in his writings on modern art, again condemning kitsch for its failure to yield anything new or interesting. Although kitsch is generally used in a derogatory fashion, it can also be used in an affirmative sense when it refers to items of nostalgia—propaganda items from former communist countries like China and Russia might be considered 'good' kitsch because to people on the Left they recollect a 'lost' world of socialist dreams and to people on the Right they confirm capitalism's victory. Similarly, artists like Andy Warhol and Jeff Koons exploit nostalgic kitsch in their work.

Kittler, Friedrich (1943–) German media theorist born in Rochlitz. His family moved to Lahr in 1958 to escape from East Germany. He went to University in Freiburg, studying Romance philology, German studies, and philosophy. He completed his doctorate on Swiss author and poet Conrad Ferdinand Meyer in 1976 and his habilitation on modern German literary history in 1984. He worked at Kassel University and the Ruhr University between 1986 and 1993. In 1993 he was appointed to the chair of media aesthetics and history at the Humboldt University of Berlin. Influenced by the work of Jacques *Derrida, Michel *Foucault, and Jacques *Lacan, and writing against the *hermeneutic conventions embodied in the work of Hans-Georg *Gadamer, Kittler develops a discourse analysis of media history that focuses on the fact of media technology, rather than its specific content. In contrast to Marshall *McLuhan, Kittler does not treat media as a prosthetic extension of 'man', but rather argues that media—or, the inscription system (*Aufschreibesysteme*) as he calls it—creates the necessary conditions in which 'man' can come into being. Kittler's most well known works in English are *Discourse Networks 1800/1900* (1990) and *Gramophone Film Typewriter* (1999).

Klein, Melanie (1882–1960) Austrian-born child *psychoanalyst and leading exponent of *object relations theory. She was born in Vienna into a family of middle-class, non-practising Jews. She married young, which prevented her from completing her studies at the

University of Vienna. In 1910 she moved with her husband and family to Budapest, which is where she encountered psychoanalysis for the first time. She even got to meet Sigmund *Freud in 1917. She trained as an analyst with Freud's friend Sándor Ferenczi, and began her own practice in 1919. After meeting Karl Abraham she moved (with his encouragement) to Berlin in 1921, where she practised for five years. Due to her rivalry with Anna *Freud, Berlin proved an unhappy city to practise in, so when Freud's biographer Ernest Jones suggested she move to London she leapt at the chance. She lived the rest of her life there and became a central figure in British psychoanalytic circles. She trained a number of quite eminent psychoanalysts, including Hanna Segel, Wilfred Bion, and Herbert Rosenfeld. Klein pioneered a form of 'play therapy' as a way of psychoanalysing children too young to verbalize their thoughts in feelings the way adults do in the process Freud called 'free association'. A detailed account of her technique is given in *Narrative of Child Analysis* (1961), which is an extensive case history of one patient, known as little Richard or little Dick. Both Jacques *Lacan and Gilles *Deleuze are highly critical of Klein's interpretation of her patient's play, pointing out that she is a little too willing to see children's toys as symbols. Yet, it also has to be said, both theorists draw on her work for their own conceptual inventions. Her principal contribution to psychoanalytic theory is the concept of the *part-object, which is central to the development of object relations theory. Klein argued that the child initially perceives its mother as a disconnected series of part-objects, centring on the breast as its primary source of nutrition. But the child is *ambivalent about the breast because sometimes it gets food from it and sometimes it is denied food, so it splits the breast into a 'good' object and a 'bad' object. As the child grows up it has to learn to integrate these two objects and recognize the mother as a whole person. The former ambivalence induces feelings of guilt which the child then tries to make reparations for. This is a constant cycle for Klein.

Further Reading: P. Grosskurth *Melanie Klein: Her World and Her Work* (1986).
J. Kristeva *Melanie Klein* (2004).
H. Segal *Melanie Klein* (1992).

Klossowski, Pierre (1905–2001) French philosopher, novelist, and artist, born in Paris. Klossowski's parents—both of whom were artists, as was his younger brother Balthus Klossowski, who rose to considerable fame as a painter (Bono sang at his funeral)—were originally from Poland and probably of Jewish descent. He travelled a lot with his family in his youth. From the start of World War I in 1914 until 1923 he lived in Switzerland, Germany, and Italy. When he returned to Paris in 1923, his mother's lover the German poet Rainer Maria Rilke arranged a job for him as private secretary to the French author André Gide who was then working on his masterpiece *Les Faux-monnayeurs* (1925), translated as *The Counterfeiters* (1931). At the same time he commenced his university studies at the École Pratique des Hautes Études. However, he did not pursue a conventional academic career. Instead he made a precarious living as a freelance critic and translator. This brought him into contact with a number of the leading thinkers of the 1920s and 1930s—George *Bataille and Walter *Benjamin (whose works he translated into French) numbered among his close friends. During World War II, Klossowski spent his time in a seminary training to be a Catholic priest, but he did not complete his training and lost his vocation, which inspired his first novel *La Vocation suspendue* (Suspended Vocation, 1950). It is for his work on Sade, *Sade, mon prochain* (1947), translated as *Sade My Neighbour* (1991), and Nietzsche, *Nietzsche et le cercle vicieux* (1969), translated as *Nietzsche and the Vicious Circle* (1998), that Klossowski is best known. The former influenced Roland *Barthes, Simone de *Beauvoir, Maurice *Blanchot, and Michel *Foucault, each of whom would add their own contributions to the growing catalogue of works devoted to Sade (a measure of his lasting influence may be seen in Pier Paolo Pasolini's acknowledgement of him in the credits to his 1975 film *Salo*), while the latter would prove especially significant to Gilles *Deleuze, with whom Klossowski would also become friends, and Jean-François *Lyotard. After 1970 Klossowski stopped writing and concentrated on drawing.

Further Reading: A. Arnaud *Pierre Klossowski* (1990).
I. James *Pierre Klossowski: The Persistence of a Name* (2000).

Kojève, Alexandre (1902–68) Russian-born French philosopher and political theorist. The nephew of the great Russian painter Wassily Kandinsky, Kojève had a privileged upbringing in pre-revolutionary Russia. In 1918 he was imprisoned by the Bolsheviks for small-time black market activities. He was duly released and because he was unable to further his studies under the new regime he fled to Poland. From there he moved to Heidelberg in Germany where he studied with Edmund *Husserl, and Karl *Jaspers. He started reading *Hegel then, but would later claim that he was unable at that point to make head or tail of it. He soon moved on again, this time to Paris, where he was to spend the rest of his life. There he met his countryman Alexandre Koyré, whose lectures he attended along with Georges

*Bataille. In 1933, at Koyré's invitation, Kojève commenced lecturing on Hegel's religious philosophy at École Pratique des Hautes Études. Among the regular attendees was *psychoanalyst Jacques *Lacan, *Surrealists Raymond Queneau (who would later edit the lectures and publish them) and André *Breton, and the philosophers Maurice *Merleau-Ponty and Eric Weil. Accordingly it is generally said that Kojève taught the French how to read Hegel. Influenced by his friend and mentor Koyré, Kojève emphasized the importance of Napoleon's victory at Jena to Hegel, claiming this episode was the embodiment of Hegel's thesis concerning the 'end of history' in which the *dialectic of master and slave is finally transcended. He later corrected this claim by saying Hegel was premature in his pronouncement by a century and that it was in fact Stalin who most perfectly realized this thesis, only to renounce it a few years later and revert to his original position. For Kojève the end of history arrives with the advent of the universal and the homogenous. Initially he thought this was realized in communism, but he subsequently changed his mind and saw that it is actualized fully in the abundance of American-style capitalism. Kojève's most famous work was *Introduction à la 'Phenoménologie de l'esprit'* (1947), translated as *Introduction to the Reading of Hegel* (1980). After the war, at the invitation of one of his former students Robert Marjolin he joined the Ministry of Finance and worked as an adviser in the international trade section, though he continued to write as well and engaged in a famous debate with the American conservative philosopher Leo *Strauss. *See also* FUKUYAMA.

Further Reading: P. Anderson *A Zone of Engagement* (1992).
D. Auffret *Alexandre Kojéve* (1990).
J. Butler *Subjects of Desire* (1987).
M. Roth *Knowing and History* (1988).

Korsch, Karl (1886–1961) German *Marxist philosopher, Korsch was born in Tostedt, near Hamburg. Korsch's family were from peasant stock, although his father held a white-collar job in a bank. He attended universities in Munich, Berlin, Geneva, and Jena, where he obtained his doctorate in 1910 for a thesis on law. For two years prior to the First World War he lived and worked in Britain, but returned to Germany at the outbreak of war in 1914. He opposed the war and never carried a weapon, but was nonetheless forced to serve on the western front and was wounded and twice decorated with the Iron Cross. After the war Korsch was an active participant in the anarcho-syndicalist movements that flourished in the first couple of years of the Weimar Republic. His writings in this period concentrated on elaborating a hypothetical economic system appropriate for a national economy organized around the existence of workers' councils. In the 1920s his writing would be forced to try to take stock of and account for the failure of the workers' movements, which he did in socio-psychological terms (arguing that the people lacked the necessary belief in the possibility of a socialist economy to realize it). His work in this period has been compared to the Italian Marxist Antonio *Gramsci, who was similarly interested in the spontaneous rise and fall of workers' power. Probably his best-known book *Marxismus und Philosophie* (1923), translated as *Marxism and Philosophy* (1970) was published in this period by Carl Grünberg, the inaugural director of the Institute for Social Research in Frankfurt. Korsch became friendly with Felix Weil, who provided the funds for the Institute, and was instrumental in bringing together several of the *Frankfurt School's founding members. In spite of that, however, he never became part of the inner core of the Frankfurt School, although he did work for the Institute again in New York from 1945 until 1950. He tried to diagnose why theory had become detached from revolutionary practice by applying a materialist method to theory itself. His analyses were resonant with (though not identical to) those of the contemporaneously published *History and Class Consciousness* (1923) by fellow Marxist Georg *Lukács and were met with a similarly hostile reception. He was denounced by Zinoviev and Kautsky for ultra-leftism. A member of the Communist Party, Korsch held a seat in the Weimar Reichstag, but was expelled from the Party in 1926 over differences with party leadership. After stepping down from parliament he returned to writing and lecturing and began a close friendship with the dramatist Bertolt *Brecht, who attended his lectures on Marxism. He had to flee Germany and go into exile following the Reichstag fire in February 1933, which Hitler blamed on the Communists. From 1933 until 1936 Korsch lived in Denmark, as did Brecht. He then emigrated to the US, as did Brecht a few years later. Brecht acknowledged his friend's importance by giving him a cameo role as the characters Ko and Ka-osh in posthumously published *Me Ti: Buch der Wendungen* (Book of Changes, 1965). Korsch remained in the US until his death. Among a variety of posts, he taught sociology at Tulane University in New Orleans. It has been said that Korsch grew disillusioned in his final years, cut off from his roots and seemingly trapped in McCarthyist USA, though at his death he was working on a biography of Bakunin.

Further Reading: S. Bronner *Of Critical Theory and its Theorists* (1994).
M. Buckmiller, *Karl Korsch und das Problem der materialistischen Dialektik* (1976).
M. Jay *Marxism and Totality* (1984).
D. Kellner (ed.) *Karl Korsch: Revolutionary Theory* (1977).

Koyré, Alexandre (1892–1964) Russian-born French philosopher and science historian. The son of middle-class importers, Koyré was born in Taganrog in Southern Russia. As a teenager, he took part in the political activities of the failed 1905 revolution, for which he was briefly imprisoned. At 17, he went to Göttingen in Germany to study with Edmund *Husserl and from there to Paris to work with Léon Brunschvicg. He also attended the lectures of Henri *Bergson, then one of the most famous philosophers in France—Koyré would later be the first philosopher to introduce Bergson's work in Germany. He was also instrumental in smuggling Husserl's thought into France. When war broke out in 1914, he returned to Russia and joined the infantry. He took part in the unsuccessful February Revolution in 1917, but opposed the successful October Revolution in the same year. He left Russia permanently in 1919, settling in France where he resumed his studies in philosophy. He taught religion and philosophy at the Fifth Section of the École Pratique des Hautes Études from 1931 onwards. In the academic year of 1932–3, Koyré wrote a series of articles and lectures to mark the centenary of *Hegel's death. He then took a job teaching in Cairo, which gave his friend and fellow Russian Alexandre *Kojève an opportunity to teach in his place. In his work, Koyré emphasized the significance of the Napoleonic wars to Hegel in the so-called Jena period during which he wrote *Phänomenologie des Geistes* (1807). Koyré argued that if a Hegelian mode of history is possible, then it is conditioned on the possibility of history being able to come to an end. Napoleon's victory at Jena was one such moment because in Hegel's view it precipitated the end of the old order of the world and ushered in a new order for which a new philosophy was required. It was a provocative thesis and one that profoundly influenced a number of scholars, particularly Kojève. During the Second World War he took refuge in New York, introducing fellow exiles and future collaborators Roman *Jakobson and Claude *Lévi-Strauss to one another.

Kracauer, Siegfried (1889–1966) German cultural critic, journalist and film theorist. Jewish, Kracauer was part of the talented intellectual diaspora that fled to the United States to escape the Nazis. Although never part of the inner circle of the *Frankfurt School, he was close friends with two of its core members, Theodor *Adorno and Leo *Löwenthal.

Born in Frankfurt am Main, Kracauer originally trained as an architect, writing a doctorate on ornamental metalwork in Berlin and Potsdam. He worked as an architect until 1917 when he was drafted into the army. He tried to return to his profession after the war, but it proved impossible and he drifted into writing, eventually joining the editorial staff of *Frankfurter Zeitung* in 1921 as an arts journalist writing primarily about film and literature.

Die Angestellten. Aus dem neuesten Deutschland (1930), translated as *The Salaried Masses* (1998), his first academic book, is an ethnological study (indebted to Max Weber and Georg *Simmel, under whom he studied) of white-collar workers in Berlin, written as though they were representatives of 'primitive tribes' whose habits were foreign and strange. An early and important but underrated attempt to think and write about *everyday life, *The Salaried Masses* anticipates the critical sociological work of the Frankfurt School's Institute for Social Research under Max *Horkheimer.

Between 1921 and 1933 (when he was forced into exile), he wrote over 700 film reviews, as well as hundreds of articles on a wide range of other cultural topics. He also found time to write a semi-autobiographical novel, *Ginster* (1928). A sample of these essays is available in *Das Ornament der Masse* (1963), translated as *The Mass Ornament* (1995), the title of which is taken from his essay on chorus-line dancers. The collection also contains a fragment of the book *Der Detektiv Roman: Ein philosophischer Traktat* (The Detective Novel: A Philosophical Treatise), completed in 1925 but never published in full in his lifetime. Like Ernst *Bloch, also a fellow-traveller of the Frankfurt School, Kracauer saw in the detective novel a microcosm of *modernity.

Like his friend Walter *Benjamin, Kracauer left it somewhat late to escape Europe but happily, whereas the former did not make it, he did, though his family were not so fortunate. With the assistance of the Institute for Social Research he managed to get to the US in 1941 and at the age of 51 had to start all over again. He made ends meet writing for *The Nation*, *Harper's Magazine*, and *The New York Times Book Review*, as well as reports for government agencies like UNESCO. He was given a job as film curator at New York's Museum of Modern Art, which gave his life some measure of stability and enabled him to complete his most ambitious and best-known work, *Theory of Film: The Redemption of Physical Reality* (1960), which was written in English.

Theory of Film ranks with *What is Cinema?* (1958) by André *Bazin, as one of the pioneering works of cinema studies. Kracauer theorized that film was at once part of modernity, which for him meant socially-fragmenting change, and a possible source of redemption: the cinematic image was capable of providing a *utopian image of totality which society itself was unable to do. But this image was to be grasped only by a close analysis of the micrological details of the film.

As Miriam Hansen puts it in her excellent introduction to the Princeton edition of *Theory of Film*, Kracauer's work has fallen into relative neglect in recent years because his emphasis on the connection between film and reality does not accord with cinema studies' interest in virtuality. That said, the journals *New German Critique* (1991) and *New Formations* (2007) have devoted special issues to Kracauer's work suggesting a renaissance may be in the wind.

Further Reading: M. Brodersen *Siegfried Kracauer* (2001).
T. Forrest *The Politics of the Imagination* (2008).
D. Frisby *Fragments of Modernity* (1985).
G. Koch *Siegfried Kracauer: An Introduction* (2000).
I. Mülder-Bach *Siegfried Kracauer—Grenzgänger zwischen Theorie und Literatur* (1985).

Kristeva, Julia (1941–) Bulgarian-born, Paris-based linguist, philosopher, and psychoanalyst. One of the most significant feminist authors in the latter half of the 20th century, Kristeva's career seems to fall into three distinct periods, each distinguished by a different primary interest: *poststructuralist linguistics, *psychoanalysis, and critical biography. These shifts of interest are not so much departures as stepping stones toward an ever more sophisticated theorization of language, desire, and the unconscious. She was awarded the prestigious Holberg Prize in 2004.

Kristeva came to Paris to study in 1965 and enrolled in Roland *Barthes's seminars. Already very well versed in Eastern European linguistics and philosophy, particularly the work of the *Russian Formalists and Mikhail *Bakhtin, she gave seminar presentations that helped introduce this work in France. Perceiving the limits of *structuralism as a methodology, Kristeva used Bakhtin's work to endow it with a sense of dynamism and history that it so critically lacked. In 1966, in a famous essay for the French journal *Communication* (later incorporated into *Séméiotiké* (1969), partially translated as *Desire in Language* (1980)), she proposed the concept of *intertextuality to explain the interconnectedness of all aspects of communication. Consistent with Bakhtin's notion of *dialogism, intertextuality holds that there are no intrinsic meanings, that rather all meaning is produced in a negotiation between previously established meanings. She found inspiration for her theory in modernist authors, particularly Louis-Ferdinand Céline, James Joyce, and Marcel Proust. Her teacher, Roland Barthes, adopted the concept of intertextuality in his *S/Z* (1970), as did her contemporary Jacques *Derrida.

In 1965 she joined the *Tel Quel group, a small band of philosophers and thinkers (among them Barthes, Derrida and *Klossowski) who wrote for and identified with the journal of that name founded and edited by her then husband Philippe *Sollers. Kristeva participated in the 1974 *Tel Quel* study trip of China, then in the grip of the 'Cultural Revolution', following the group's conversion to Maoism in the late 1960s, and afterwards wrote a highly idealized account of Chinese life *About Chinese Women* (1986). Throughout this period, Kristeva undertook psychoanalytic training, eventually attaining the status of analyst in 1979. She attempted to blend her interests in politics, semiotics, and psychoanalysis by synthesizing a new methodology she christened *semanalysis. Out of this work arose the influential concept of the **khōra*, which is a pre-linguistic, pre-subjective realm of psychosexual development.

As the 1970s unfolded, Kristeva drifted away from the *Tel Quel* group and began to focus more on psychoanalysis. She wrote a trilogy of studies on *abjection, love, and depression: *Powers of Horror* (1982), *Tales of Love* (1983), and *Black Sun* (1987). The focus of her work is consistently the situation of the subject and its relation to itself and others.

Beginning in the late 1980s Kristeva worked on a trilogy on the theme of 'female genius', writing comprehensive critical biographies of Hannah *Arendt, Collette, and Melanie *Klein. As much feminist acts of historical recovery as demonstrations of psychoanalytic prowess, these works seem to portend a move beyond strictly academic work into a more 'pop' philosophical realm aimed at a broad readership. She has also written a number of semi-autobiographical works, starting with *Les Samouraïs* (1990), which are for the post-structuralist generation what Simone de *Beauvoir's works were for the *existentialists. *See also* CIXOUS; IRIGARAY.

Further Reading: M. Becker-Leckrone *Julia Kristeva and Literary Theory* (2005).
A. Benjamin and J. Fletcher (eds.) *Abjection, Melancholia and Love: The Work of Julia Kristeva* (1990).
E. Grosz *Sexual Subversions* (1989).
J. Lechte *Julia Kristeva* (1990).
K. Oliver *Reading Kristeva: Unravelling the Double-Bind* (1993).

Kuhn, Thomas Samuel (1922–96) American historian and philosopher of science. Born in Cincinnati, Kuhn obtained his Bachelor of Science, Master of Science, and PhD in physics from Harvard University. He taught the history of science at Harvard from 1948 until 1956. He then moved to California for a few years before returning (via Princeton) to take up a position at MIT

(Massachusetts Institute of Technology). His most famous work, *The Structure of Scientific Revolutions*, was published in 1962. Kuhn argued against Karl *Popper's thesis that scientific knowledge progresses in a linear fashion via the progressive repudiation of thoughts, models, and ideas. Popper believed that science's true concern is not with 'what is', but rather with what can be proven false or impossible. In contrast, Kuhn argued that science proceeds via 'paradigm shifts' (comparable to *Bachelard's concept of the *epistemological break, though much narrower in scope) amounting to wholesale revolutions in thought. His rationale is that some scientific discoveries do not merely refute previous theories, they redraw the map of knowledge itself—for example, when Christopher Columbus sailed across the Atlantic he not only proved once and for all that to do so did not risk falling off the edge of the earth, he also created a vast new colonial enterprise. Kuhn proposed a three-phase model of scientific progress: first there is prescience, which follows certain discoveries, but lacks an overall hypothesis; then there is 'normal science' in which the initial discoveries are converted into a paradigm or platform of thought upon which future work can be built; the third phase is crisis, which is what happens when the second phase ultimately fails. The crisis is resolved with the irruption of a new paradigm in the place of the old. Kuhn maintained that each new paradigm was incommensurable with what went before, but this has since been rejected as unnecessarily relativistic.

Further Reading: S. Fuller *Thomas Kuhn: A Philosophical History of Our Times* (2000).

J. Preston *Kuhn's 'The Structure of Scientific Revolutions': A Reader's Guide* (2008).

Lacan, Jacques (1901–81) See overleaf.

lack (*manque*) The motive cause of *desire in Jacques *Lacan's theory of *psychoanalysis. What the subject lacks is being, or rather the sense of being fully themselves—the concept is indebted to Jean-Paul *Sartre's *existentialist philosophy. Lack is in this sense synonymous with castration, which in Lacan's work manifests as a rupture in the signifying chain preventing access to the *signified.

Laclau, Ernesto (1935–) UK-based, Argentine sociologist and political theorist known for his extensive work on the concepts of popular struggle and *hegemony. Born in Buenos Aires, he was educated at the University of Buenos Aires and at Oxford. Since 1973, he has taught in the department of government at the University of Essex. He is best known for the work he co-authored with Chantal Mouffe, *Hegemony and Socialist Strategy: Towards a Radical Democratic Politics* (1985). Adopting a *post-structuralist stance, the authors reject *Marxism for being both essentialist and determinist and argue instead that political thinking needs to grapple with the real uncertainty and undecidability of contemporary existence. In this, and subsequent works, Laclau rejects the notion that *class by itself brings about the necessary level of group cohesion to effect political change; similarly, he rejects the notion that group cohesion can only take place along prescribed lines of identification. This is simultaneously both more hopeful than traditional Marxism inasmuch as it is open to the possibility of multiple constituted solidarities and much more pessimistic in that it does not accept that awareness of a common plight will be sufficient to galvanize people into action. In 2000 Laclau contributed to a book co-written with Judith *Butler and Slavoj *Žižek called *Contingency, Hegemony and Universality*, ostensibly with a view to demonstrating their different approaches to a common problematic. Despite the friendly spirit with which that project appears to have been undertaken, it seems to have had the opposite effect, at least insofar as relations between Laclau and Žižek were concerned. For the next few years, in the pages of *Critical Inquiry*, and in their own books, the two carried out a running

LACAN, JACQUES (1901–81)

French psychoanalyst and founder of *École Freudienne de Paris. Undoubtedly the most influential psychoanalyst after Freud, Lacan combined *psychoanalysis with *semiotics to produce a powerful theoretical synthesis that had an enormous influence over almost the whole field of the human and social sciences, though nowhere more so than in *film studies where it became a virtual doctrine. Today, Lacan's work continues to exert a strong influence thanks to the tireless efforts of followers, particularly Slavoj *Žižek.

The son of a wealthy merchant family, Lacan was raised a Catholic and educated at the same school as future French President Charles de Gaulle. He studied medicine and psychiatry at university but took an active interest in the arts as well. As a student, he met the *Surrealists André *Breton and Philippe Soupault and he heard James Joyce give readings of *Ulysses* (1922) at the famous Paris bookshop Shakespeare and Co. He read *Nietzsche in the original German and in 1923, at the tender age of 22, he encountered Freud's theories.

It took several years, however, for Freud to become the focal point of Lacan's interests. It was his reading of the Spanish Surrealist Salvador Dalí's provocative essay 'L'Âne pourri' (The Rotten Donkey) that paved the way by suggesting a new way of thinking about the connection between the mind and language and shifting his focus of attention from *hysteria to *psychosis. Dalí argued that paranoid delusions are not errors of perception, but creative interpretations of reality that have their own distinctive logic. While Dalí developed this thesis into a method he termed *critical paranoia, Lacan set about rethinking what paranoia meant in clinical terms. The first fruit of this labour was his PhD thesis, *De la psychose paranoïaque dans ses rapports avec la personnalité* (Paranoid psychosis and its relation to personality), defended in 1932. Although Lacan scrupulously avoided any mention of his Surrealist inspiration in his thesis so as not to put off the medical establishment, it was the Surrealists rather than the psychiatric community who first recognized its brilliance.

For the next four years, as part of his training as a psychoanalyst Lacan underwent analysis with the Jewish-Polish exile Rudolph Loewenstein, during which time he wrote very little. In 1936 he began attending the seminars of the Russian émigré philosopher Alexandre *Kojève who together with his countryman Alexandre *Koyré introduced *Hegel's thought to an entire generation of French scholars. Following Kojève Lacan recognized the distinction between an 'I' that thinks and an 'I' that wants, and this became the basis of his renovation of psychoanalysis as a philosophy of *desire. Lacan's first major statement to this effect, which after a stumbling start was to be his entrée to the world stage as a major psychoanalyst, occurred in 1936 at the International Psychoanalytical Association (IPA) congress in Marienbad. Lacan presented the first version of his paper on the *mirror stage, arguing that the child's sense of self is based upon a *misrecognition ('méconnaissance'). The child sees the image of itself in a mirror and says 'that's me!' even though in actuality it is merely a reflection. By this means the child attains an imaginary mastery over self. This insight would later be taken up by the French Marxist Louis *Althusser in his rethinking of the concept of *ideology.

During World War II, Lacan worked as a military psychiatrist, writing nothing for the duration of hostilities. He maintained his hand in the field by corresponding with Melanie *Klein, Michael *Balint, D.W. *Winnicott, and others, but increasingly found himself at odds with them. After the war, Lacan's profound disagreements with his peers in France and abroad over theoretical issues as well as his refusal to desist from his controversial practice of shortening analytic sessions to as little as 10 minutes instead of the IPA prescribed 60 minutes resulted in his being ostracized by a large proportion of the professional psychoanalytic community. In 1964, he founded his own group, École Freudienne de Paris (The Freudian School of Paris), and broke definitively with both the national and international psychoanalytic statutory bodies. The membership list of this new school reads as a virtual who's who of French theory—it includes such as figures as Michel de *Certeau, Félix *Guattari, and Luce *Irigaray. Shortly before his death Lacan unilaterally dissolved the École Freudienne de Paris.

Lacan's published output in his own lifetime was comparatively small. He never wrote a straightforward or complete account of his theory. He developed it in a peripatetic fashion through interventions at conferences and his weekly seminars. In 1966 a large collection of his conference papers running to some 900 pages was published under the bland title of *Écrits* (the English translation is published under the same title). In spite of its unwieldy size it sold 5,000 copies in two weeks, which is unheard of for such an abstruse work. In the main, however, Lacan's thought has been disseminated via the haphazard publication of his seminars edited by his son-in-law Jacques-Alain Miller. The product of transcriptions of Lacan's actual seminars and subject to variable editorial control, these books are both stimulating and frustrating, as rich in ideas as they are elusive in their explanations of those ideas. Sadly, less than half of the seminars are available in this form, but bootleg versions abound. Lacan's writing is notoriously difficult and it is probably best to approach his work via an expert guidebook.

Lacan's version of psychoanalysis is distinctive for its emphasis on the concept of *lack ('manque'). According to Lacan, having is never sufficient by itself to extinguish wanting, therefore desire must be thought of as the gap between the two. Even when we have what we want, it doesn't stop us from wanting more, so in theory we never really have what we want. Desire is in this sense impossible to fulfil.

Lacan was a prodigious inventor of concepts, many of which have passed into the standard idiom of critical theory, e.g. *floating signifier, *imaginary, *phallus, *objet (petit) *a*, *symbolic, and *real. Perhaps his most famous statement was his rallying cry that we must return to Freud. He meant two things by this—firstly, and obviously, that we should read Freud's texts (and not those of his followers), preferably in the original German; secondly, and much more importantly, he meant that we should focus on the analytic situation, namely the relation between analyst and analysand, which is where psychoanalysis first took form. *See also* PSYCHOANALYSIS; SEMIOTICS; STRUCTURALISM.

Further Reading: E. Grosz *Jacques Lacan: A Feminist Introduction* (1990).
S. Homer *Jacques Lacan* (2005).
J. Rose *Sexuality in the Field of Vision* (1986).
E. Roudinesco *Jacques Lacan* (1997).
S. Turkle *Psychoanalytic Politics: Jacques Lacan and Freud's French Revolution* (1992).
S. Žižek *Looking Awry* (1991).

battle, each accusing the other of misunderstanding Marx, politics, and pretty much everything.

Lacoue-Labarthe, Philippe (1940–2007) French post-structuralist philosopher. Often working in collaboration with his Strasbourg colleague, Jean-Luc *Nancy, Lacoue-Labarthe's writing is chiefly concerned with the metaphysics of the *subject in the wake of *post-structuralism. He explores this problematic by investigating the relationship between literature and philosophy, or more rigorously put between aesthetics and politics. In this regard, his work is sometimes seen as a form of *deconstruction, but although he was close to Jacques *Derrida he was neither his student nor his acolyte. He is perhaps best known for his engagement with the issue of *Heidegger's Nazism and its implication for philosophy, *La Fiction du politique* (1987), translated as *Heidegger, Art and Politics* (1990). His previous work can be seen as the clearing of a path to this particular summit. In a book co-written with Nancy, he traced the trajectory of German Romanticism and connected it to Nazism in *L'Absolu littéraire* (1978), translated as *The Literary Absolute* (1988), and then worked directly on one of the poets Heidegger was interested in, namely Paul Celan, in *La poésie comme experience* (1986), translated as *Poetry as Experience* (1999). He did not simply condemn Heidegger's philosophy out of hand, as many have, but argued instead that his philosophy contained pathways to a philosophical confrontation with Nazism that he failed to take. He did, however, condemn Heidegger for his silence on the Holocaust.

Further Reading: J. Martis *Philippe Lacoue-Labarthe: Representation and the Loss of the Subject* (2005).

Laing, Ronald David (1927–89) Controversial British psychiatrist and leading member of the *anti-psychiatry movement. Born in Glasgow, Laing studied medicine at the University of Glasgow. He was then drafted into the army, in spite of poor health, serving as a psychiatrist in the medical corps. He left the army in 1953 and after a brief stint at a Glasgow hospital moved to London to undertake training in *psychoanalysis at the Tavistock Clinic, where he worked with W.D. *Winnicott. In 1965, along with several colleagues, among them David *Cooper, Laing founded the Philadelphia Association and began an experimental community psychiatry project at Kingsley Hall with a view to putting into practice the reconceptualization of schizophrenia worked out in his books, *The Divided Self* (1960), *Self and Others* (1961), and *Sanity, Madness and the Family* (1964). The idea was to create a shared living space for schizophrenics and psychiatrists and approach the disease as a shamanistic journey rather than an illness that can be cured with drugs or electro-shock therapy. A famous, but in many ways discrediting account of life at Kingsley Hall, written by one of the patients there, Mary Barnes, and her psychiatrist, Joseph Berke, *Mary Barnes: Two Accounts of A Journey Through Madness*, was published in 1971. Probably his most influential book, *The Politics of Experience and the Bird of Paradise* (1967), was written during this period. Very much a work of its time, it draws on *Marx, *Nietzsche, *Freud, *Heidegger, and *Sartre, to argue that society as we know it in the west is mentally straitjacketing and that is the reason so many people are unhappy. In this regard his work anticipated the student protests of *May '68 and was similarly quite influential on Félix *Guattari, though he ultimately rejected anti-psychiatry. Because the anti-psychiatry movement is generally seen to have failed, both by professional psychiatrists and by critical theorists, as its therapeutic techniques don't provide any relief from the distressing experiences schizophrenia can induce, Laing's work has fallen into neglect.

Further Reading: Z. Kotowicz *R.D. Laing and the Paths of Anti-psychiatry* (1997).

Lakatos, Imre (1922–74) Hungarian philosopher of science and mathematics best known for his fallibility thesis. Born in Debrecen, Hungary's second largest city, to a Jewish family, Imre Lipschitz (as he was originally named) studied philosophy, mathematics, and physics. When the Nazis invaded, he changed his name to Molnár to disguise his Jewish descent. After the war, he changed his name to Lakatos to honour General Géza Lakatos who overthrew the Nazi puppet government in Hungary in 1944 and halted the deportation of Jews to death camps. He worked as a public servant in the Education Department while he worked on his PhD, which he completed in 1948. He then went to Moscow University to continue his studies, but on his return to Hungary in 1950 he was imprisoned for three years on charges of revisionism. He left Hungary for good when the Soviet Union invaded in 1956 and moved to the UK. He completed a PhD at Cambridge, which was published posthumously as *Proofs and Refutations* (1976), and then took a post at the London School of Economics in the newly formed philosophy department headed by Karl *Popper. *Proofs and Refutations* attempts to reconcile what Lakatos saw as a rift between Popper's falsification model of scientific progress and T.S. *Kuhn's paradigm change model; for Popper, change in scientific thought should occur as soon as it is discovered that a theory is in part or in whole false, whereas Kuhn argued that scientists frequently cling to theories even when their imperfections are known. His solution, later heavily criticized by his colleague and friend Paul *Feyerabend, was to describe scientific theories as 'research programmes' and treat them as provisional (not to say *ad hoc*) attempts to search for truth. Research programmes can then be evaluated in terms of whether they are progressive or not.

language games A use of language which has its own internal rule system or sense regime. Most often language games take the form of a conscious mutation of an already existing language, such as the children's language Pig Latin, but it may also consist of entirely new words, such as one finds in certain highly technical jargons. Viennese philosopher Ludwig *Wittgenstein conceived the notion of language games to explain the origin of language as an arbitrary and game-like association between certain sounds and particular objects and actions. French philosopher Jean-François *Lyotard uses the notion of language games to describe the conditions under which a *differend may arise: if the notion of a wrong in one language game, that of the victim, cannot be translated into the language game of another, say that of the courts, then it is impossible for that wrong to be heard. The proliferation of language games and the corresponding impossibility of an authentic politics is for Lyotard one of the characteristics of *postmodernism.

langue* and *parole A binary pair introduced by Ferdinand de *Saussure distinguishing between, on the one hand, the set of possible ways of making meaning contained by any one language and, on the other hand, its various specific, concrete instantiations. In learning another language, our primary goal must be to gain an appreciation of its *langue* because only then will we be able to make sense of it, which for Saussure would mean being able to manipulate it and create new meanings. If we simply build up a vocabulary of foreign words we will never understand a language in the way a native speaker of that particular language does because we lack an appreciation of the rules of combination of those words that comprise that language's *langue.* The terms are generally left in the original French because of the difficulty of their translation; where they are translated they are rendered as 'language' and 'speech' which is misleading to the extent that it obscures the fact that for Saussure *langue* refers to the internal structure of a language, not language itself, for which he used the term *langage.* For Saussure, *langue* is the system or machine of language developed in the collective unconscious of a specific community of language users. In contrast, *parole* is the event of language. This distinction is one of the cornerstones of *structuralism.

Further Reading: F. Jameson *The Prison-house of Language: A Critical Account of Structuralism and Russian Formalism* (1972).
J. Sturrock *Structuralism* (1986).

late capitalism (*Spätkapitalismus*) A term used in *Marxism since the 1930s, but brought into prominence in *critical theory by the work of economic historian Ernest Mandel with the publication of *Der Spätkapitalismus* (1972), translated as *Late Capitalism* (1975). By late capitalism Mandel meant simply the latest or most current stage of capitalism's development, namely the transformations that had taken place in the capitalist *mode of production since the end of World War II, particularly the explosive growth experienced in the USA, Germany, and Japan. Fredric *Jameson adopts this term and Mandel's analysis in his account of *postmodernism as the most appropriate description of the present epoch.

latent content *See* MANIFEST AND LATENT CONTENT.

Leavis, Frank Raymond (1895–1978) English literary critic, leading exponent of *Practical Criticism. It is impossible to overestimate Leavis's influence as a literary critic. In 'The Rise of English' (chapter one of *Literary Theory: An Introduction*, 1983), Terry *Eagleton goes so far as to say we are all Leavisites, in the same way we are all Copernicans, because we all operate in the wake of the revolution in how literature is viewed that he inaugurated.

Leavis was born and educated in Cambridge, where his father ran a music shop, selling pianos and other instruments. World War I broke out when Leavis was 19, but unlike millions of his countryman he objected to the war. So rather than enlist in the infantry to fight he joined the Friends Ambulance Unit, which was anything but a 'soft' option. Indeed, he was gassed during the war and suffered permanent effects. He commenced his university studies in 1919, initially in history, but switching to English Literature in his second year. He completed a doctorate on 'The Relationship of Journalism to Literature' in 1924 and was given his first full-time teaching appointment in 1927. In 1929 he married his former student Queenie Dorothy Roth, thus forming one of the most formidable partnerships in literary criticism.

It is as the uncompromisingly stern editor of the journal *Scrutiny* which he and his wife founded in 1932 that Leavis is best known. He remained at the helm for over 20 years, using the journal as a vehicle both to defend the new method of analysing literature he advocated, namely Practical Criticism, and to attack the lack of rigour he perceived in other approaches to literary criticism, particularly in that of the so-called Bloomsbury Group, whose middle-class elitism irritated him. Practical Criticism, or 'close reading' as it is also known, which Leavis adopted (with due modification) from his former teacher I.A. *Richards, became his means of assessing (assaying might be a better word) the relative 'greatness' of a piece of work. Leavis insisted that the work had to stand on its own, which meant setting aside such ponderous notions as authorial intention, but also ignoring weightier issues like historical context. For Leavis a 'great' work was one which contained 'life', which he never defined, but seemingly meant immediacy of experience and a grasp of the unconscious forces underpinning quotidian existence. By this measure, it is easy to see why he was a great champion of D.H. Lawrence.

Concerned with greatness as he was, it is perhaps not surprising that Leavis spent so much time on questions of canonicity. His best-known collection of essays, *The Great Tradition* (1948), is a powerful exercise in canon formation, tracing a line from Austen, through Eliot and James to Conrad and of course Lawrence (but famously overlooking Hardy, whom he detested). Leavis is generally viewed now as a reactionary, anti-theoretical critic, and though there is a certain truth in this, Eagleton's insight that his real achievement was the creation of a discipline means that no history of literary studies (including histories of literary theory) can ignore him. Moreover, it is very far from the case that his legacy has been completely negated, there are still a great many Leavisite critics writing today. Leavis created an assessable pedagogy for literary studies that was readily comprehensible to high school students and as a consequence it became the standard methodology throughout the Anglophone world in the 1950s.

Further Reading: M. Bell *F. R. Leavis* (1988).
I. MacKillop *F. R. Leavis: A Life in Criticism* (1995).
F. Mulhern *The Moment of Scrutiny* (1979).

Le Doeuff, Michèle (1948–) French feminist philosopher and playwright. A less well-known member of the small group of thinkers collectively known as French Feminists, Le Doeuff's work is more exclusively philosophical than her better-known peers Luce *Irigaray and Julia *Kristeva. She is best known for the collection of essays *Recherches sur l'imaginaire philosophique* (1980), translated as *The Philosophical Imaginary* (1990), which according to her most important commentator Elizabeth Grosz comprises her key project. The concept of the imaginary Le Doeuff proposes should not be confused with Jacques *Lacan's concept of the same name. Grosz identifies three separate components to Le Doeuff's concept: it refers in a loose sense to imagery (texts), to the image (the opposite of the rigorous concept), and *psychoanalysis (*Freudian rather than Lacanian), specifically the repressed. A specialist in early modern English thought, she has written on Francis Bacon, Thomas More, and William Shakespeare.

Further Reading: M. Deutscher (ed.) *Michèle Le Doeuff: Operative Philosophy and Imaginary Practice* (2001).
E. Grosz *Sexual Subversions* (1989).

Lefebvre, Henri (1901–91) French *Marxist philosopher and sociologist. Lefebvre published 70 books in his lifetime on an incredibly wide array of topics, and is generally regarded as one of the great theoreticians of the 20th century. Because of his interests in *space and *everyday life (indeed his name is virtually synonymous with these concepts), he tends to be read more in geography departments than philosophy departments. Unfortunately for Anglophone readers, the English translations of his work reflect this bias.

Lefebvre was born in the rural town of Hegetmau just outside the Pyrenees, France. And though he moved to Paris at an early age to study at the Sorbonne, he retained a strong link with the countryside throughout his life. In the 1920s Lefebvre taught philosophy in Paris and was part of the small group of anti-*Bergson, Marxist thinkers known as the *Philosophies* group. He joined the Communist Party (PCF) in 1928. In this period he took a keen interest in the work of the *Surrealists, and was a familiar of Tristan Tzara and André *Breton, but it was a short-lived passion. He soon came to think of Surrealism as an inauthentic mode of critique and broke with it quite acrimoniously.

His career stalled in the late 1920s and early 1930s and he found work as a cab driver and factory hand, a fact he would later claim gave him greater right to speak about existence than *existentialists like *Sartre who had never done any physical labour. After a bad car accident, he was able to find work as a teacher. Around this time he started reading *Hegel and through Hegel discovered *Marx. During the German occupation of France, Lefebvre was removed from his teaching post because of his association with the PCF and his book on Nietzsche was seized and burnt. He then went on to join the Resistance, writing anti-Vichy pamphlets and (it is alleged) helping to blow up German trains. Following the war he worked as an artistic director for a radio station in Toulouse.

The first instalment of what would become a trilogy of works on *everyday life, *Critique de la vie quotidienne* was published in 1947, the second and third instalments appearing in 1962 and 1981 respectively. Translation into English (as *Critique of Everyday Life*) followed a decade later. Lefebvre takes the view in these works that a radical politics interested in change must commence with a thoroughgoing knowledge of the day-to-day routines and rituals of everyday people. This for Lefebvre is the true meaning of critique, which he designated as 'revolutionary' in opposition to what he saw as the useless 'poetic' critiques of the Surrealists. The critique of everyday life initiated by Lefebvre had two strategic goals: on the one hand he wanted to convince fellow Marxists of the utility of the concept of *alienation for the analysis of *superstructure; on the other hand he wanted to convince philosophers of the importance of the mundane.

These strategic aims would also underpin what is undoubtedly Lefebvre's most influential work: *La Production de l'espace* (1974), translated as *The Production of Space* (1991). Importantly, Lefebvre's work on space is, as was his work on everyday life, concerned with 'moments', that is to say, he doesn't forsake time in favour of space, but rather tries to see how one can think these two dimensions together to produce a critical account of contemporary life. His final book, *Éléments de rythmanalyse: Introduction à la connaissance de rythmes* (1992), translated as *Rhythmanalysis: Space, Time and Everyday Life* (2004), would make this connection more concrete and offer an explicit methodology for its analysis. But having said that, Lefebvre also showed that space and time, in their abstract form, were not by themselves sufficient to articulate space fully. So he developed a range of supplementary dimensions to enable history, movement, and change to be incorporated into our understanding of space.

Lefebvre's work has cast a long shadow, particularly in contemporary *Cultural studies (broadly understood). The three theorists most influenced by Lefebvre are Fredric *Jameson, David *Harvey, and Edward *Soja—in all three cases, it is Lefebvre's insistence on the significance of urbanization that is key to the respective conceptualizations of *postmodernism as a historical period. It should be noted that although Michel de *Certeau cites his work as an influence in writing about the *practices of everyday life, the differences between their respective approaches are significant—Certeau jettisons Lefebvre's commitment to Marx. Lefebvre's former research assistant, Jean *Baudrillard also acknowledges an influence, as is obvious in his work on objects, but similarly rejects his commitment to Marx.

Further Reading: B. Burkhard *French Marxism Between the Wars: Henri Lefebvre and the 'Philosophies'* (2000).

S. Elden *Understanding Henri Lefebvre: Theory and the Possible* (2004).

R. Hess *Henri Lefebvre et l'aventure du siècle* (1988).

R. Shields *Lefebvre, Love and Struggle: Spatial Dialectics* (1998).

Levinas, Emmanuel (1906–95) Paris-based philosopher and commentator on the Talmud. Born in Kovno, Russia (now Lithuania) to Jewish parents, Levinas began his studies in philosophy in Strasbourg in 1923 where he met Charles Blondel, Maurice Pradines, Henri Carterton, and Maurice *Blanchot. In 1928 he moved to Freiburg University to study *phenomenology with Edmund *Husserl. There he met Martin *Heidegger, who was also studying with Husserl.

Heidegger's *Sein und Zeit* (1926), translated as *Being and Time* was to have a profound influence on him.

In 1930 Levinas returned to France and became a naturalized French citizen. When Germany declared war on France, he was required to report for military duty. He was duly mobilized and quickly captured and spent most of the war, from 1940, as a prisoner in a camp near Hanover in Germany. As a Jew, he was assigned to a barracks for Jewish prisoners. It was during this period that he wrote *De l'existence à l'existant* (1947), translated as *Existence and Existents* (1978), and the series of lectures *le Temps et l'Autre* (1948), translated as *Time and Other* (1987). Blanchot assisted Levinas's wife and daughter to find refuge in a monastery. His mother in-law, as well as his father and brothers were not so fortunate. They all perished at the hands of the Nazis.

After the war, Levinas worked as the Director of the Alliance Israélite Universelle and he studied the Talmud with Monsieur Chouchani. He published five volumes of Talmudic commentaries, the last of which was published shortly after his death. Levinas's thinking was coloured by his experiences in the war. Not surprisingly, he found it difficult to forgive Heidegger, but at the same time felt he could not simply be dismissed. Heidegger mapped out a boundary philosophy that had to move beyond, and much of Levinas's later works can be viewed as an attempt to do precisely this. During the 1950s and 1960s Levinas became increasingly critical of Heidegger, phenomenology, and ontology. In contrast to Heidegger who continued to emphasize being in his work in this period, Levinas wondered what there was other than being. His work in this period shifted focus to ethics, which he argued can only be thought in terms of our relationship with the *Other, which for Levinas was not simply God, but Mystery itself, that which can never be reduced to or incorporated by the Same.

The concept of the Other, which Levinas contrasts to the other (by which he meant other people), is central to much of Levinas's thought. In effect, his entire philosophy revolves around this problematic and many of the concepts he subsequently invents owe their origin to it as well. If the Other cannot be reduced to the Same, then our relationship to it has to be a 'relation without relation' as Levinas puts it. It is the presence of the Other, which we can only sense as a kind of *face (visage), which is Levinas's codephrase for the sense of epiphany the Other provokes in us, that makes us realize that we share the world, that it is not ours by right. His notion of ethics flows from this. Ethics for Levinas does not simply mean determining how one should act, for him it entails a way of both seeing and questioning the world: ethics is optics, he famously pronounced.

Levinas's work in the late 1950s and early 1960s began to take on a more distinctive character, becoming more his own thinking and less and less a commentary on existing philosophies. It developed into what might be termed an ethics of *alterity, or perhaps even a *heterology. In 1961, Levinas published his Doctorat d'Etat, the monumental *Totalité et Infini*, translated as *Totality and Infinity* (1969) and in the same year was appointed Professor of Philosophy at Poitiers, where he remained until 1967 when he took up an appointment at Paris-Nanterre. In 1972 he published *Humanisme de l'autre homme*, translated as *Humanism of the Other* (2003). He moved to the Sorbonne in 1973. In 1974 he published *Autrement qu'être ou Au-delà de l'essence*, translated as *Otherwise than Being or Beyond Essence* (1978). He retired in 1976, but continued to publish prolifically as well as teach. *De Dieu qui vient à l'idée* (1982), translated as *Of God Who Comes to Mind* (1998), and *Entre Nous* (1991), translated as *Entre Nous* (2000), among several other books were completed in the last two decades of his life.

Levinas's work was a major influence on French *existentialism. His attempts to develop an ethics of alterity influenced Maurice *Merleau-Ponty, Jean-Paul *Sartre, and Jacques *Derrida. He died in Paris on Christmas Day in 1995.

Further Reading: H. Caygill *Levinas and the Political* (2002).
S. Critchley *The Ethics of Deconstruction* (1992).
C. Davis *Levinas: An Introduction* (1996).
J. Derrida *Adieu to Emmanuel Levinas* (1999).
R. Eaglestone *Ethical Criticism: Reading after Levinas* (1997).

SEE WEB LINKS

- The Emmanuel Levinas webpage.
- The Institute for Levinassian Studies website.

Lévi-Strauss, Claude (1908–2009) French anthropologist and key proponent of *structuralism. He was born in Brussels, but his family moved to France when he was 6. He went to the Lycée Condorcet in Paris, but elected not to take the entrance exam to the prestigious École Normale Supérieure and instead studied law and philosophy at the University of Paris, graduating in 1932. In 1929 he began teacher training at the Lycée Janson-de-Sailly, along with Simone de *Beauvoir and Maurice *Merleau-Ponty. On graduation, he taught philosophy without enthusiasm until 1935 when, at the suggestion of Céléstin Bouglé, he relocated to Brazil to take up a position as visiting Professor of Sociology as part of a French cultural mission. Based at the University of São Paulo, Lévi-Strauss used his time in Brazil to do ethnographic fieldwork among the indigenous peoples of the Amazon basin and the Mato Grosso. He lived briefly among the Caduveo, Nambikwara, Tupi-Kawahib, and Bororo peoples, collecting information about their kinship structures, belief systems, and religious symbols. A first-hand account of his experiences in Brazil (including his post-war return visit), which by his own estimation transformed him into an anthropologist, can be found in *Tristes Tropiques* (1955), translated as *Tristes Tropiques* (1974), which was an international bestseller.

When Germany invaded Poland in 1939, Lévi-Strauss felt duty-bound to return to France, which he duly did. He was assigned to a liaison position on the Maginot line. When France surrendered he resumed teaching at a Lycée in Montpellier, but because of his Jewish ancestry he was forced to resign because of the race laws imposed by the Nazis. In 1941, he was fortunate enough to be offered a post at the New School for Social Research in New York and gain both an admission to the US and exit from France (others in the same situation, such as Walter *Benjamin, were not so lucky). Lévi-Strauss made several important connections while in New York, which were to prove highly influential on his research. Perhaps most important of all, he met the similarly exiled Russian linguist Roman *Jakobson, considered by many to be (along with Lévi-Strauss himself) one of the founding figures of structuralism. He also met the great American anthropologist Franz Boas who, in a strange twist of fate, died in Lévi-Strauss's arms after suffering a heart attack during a dinner at the Faculty House at Columbia University.

From 1946–7 Lévi-Strauss worked as a cultural attaché at the French Embassy in Washington DC. He at last returned to Paris in 1948, initially to a job as associate director of the Musée de l'Homme. In the same year, he submitted his minor and major theses, respectively: 'La Vie familiale et sociale des Indiens Nambikwara' ('The Family and Social Life of the Nambikwara Indians') and 'Les Structures élémentaires de la parenté' ('The Elementary Structures of Kinship'). The latter was published in 1949, it was translated into English in 1967, but the translation was so controversial it was retranslated in 1990. Simone de Beauvoir famously read a draft copy of it and pronounced it a 'brilliant awakening' of sociology in a long review in Jean-Paul *Sartre's journal *Les Temps modernes*. She even claimed to perceive in it a profound compatibility with the *existentialist project, a claim Lévi-Strauss himself laid to rest in *La Pensée sauvage* (1962), translated as *The Savage Mind* (1966). In 1950 Lévi-Strauss was appointed to a professorship at the École Pratique des Hautes Études, a position he retained until his elevation to the Collège de France in 1959.

It was, however, the publication in 1955 of the short essay 'The Structural Study of Myth' which transformed Lévi-Strauss from obscure anthropologist to paradigm-changing intellectual. Republished in the first volume of *Anthropologie Structurale* (1958), translated as *Structural Anthropology* (1963), this essay was one of the inaugural works of the analytic method that would come to be known as structuralism. Utilizing the insights of his friend Jakobson, as well as the work of Nikolai Troubetzkoy, Lévi-Strauss reasoned that *myth could be treated 'like a language', i.e. as a complex system of relations between a variety of different types of elements. Languages may vary widely in terms of grammar and vocabulary, but they have in common the fact of grammar and vocabulary. Understanding this is the basic point of structuralism.

From this point of view, which departs radically from the accepted anthropological practice of only going with what can be empirically shown, it isn't the specific content of a myth that is important, but the set of relations it contains between myth elements, which for Lévi-Strauss are recurrent across time and space. Using this method, Lévi-Strauss is able to show that versions of the Oedipal myth can be found in practically every culture. His question, then, is why do cultures need myths? His answer, simplified a great deal, is that myths provide symbolic solutions to real problems; myths are a culture's way of resolving the contradictions inherent in its own rules. This thesis has been adopted by Fredric *Jameson in *Signatures of the Visible* (1992) to analyse contemporary culture.

At the peak of his fame in 1966, Lévi-Strauss was invited to a conference at Johns Hopkins University, to which was also invited the relatively unknown young philosopher Jacques *Derrida, who offered a devastating critique of Lévi-Strauss and it is now legend that on that day *post-structuralism was born. Devastating though the critique was, Lévi-Strauss's career did not come to an end, though his influence did decline. He nevertheless continued to publish prolifically for the next three decades, putting out several more books enlarging upon the ideas laid down in *Structural Anthropology.*

Further Reading: E. Leach *Claude Lévi-Strauss* (rev. ed. 1989).
J. Sturrock *Structuralism* (1986).

libido The Latin word for desire or wish appropriated by *psychoanalysis to name the psychical energy of the *id. Sigmund *Freud was the first to use this term in this way, but it is now widely used, even outside of psychoanalytic literature where it has become a 'polite' code phrase for an individual's sexual appetite. Freud initially thought the libido was exclusively sexual in nature, and confined to the *instincts, so he opposed it to the *ego, which is the product of a compromise with the instincts; but he later came to think that the ego also has libidinal energy and revised his theory accordingly. In his more mature works, libido is the psychical dimension of sexual excitation—its effects may be felt somatically, but it is not a somatic concept. Libido is perhaps better understood as belonging more to the order of the *drive than the instincts, which chimes well with Freud's later positioning of it as the opposite of the *death-drive. Some scholars, Carl *Jung and Gilles *Deleuze in particular, reject Freud's idea that libido is necessarily a sexual energy and treat it as a kind of life-force, an energy pervading all human activity.

lifeworld (*Lebenswelt*) The context in which any given consciousness is inevitably immersed, even if it is incapable of registering it directly. Although it is intended to describe a kind of background to consciousness, it should not be thought of as inert; it is rather a constantly shifting and changing horizon in which consciousness is enveloped. In this regard, the lifeworld is both subjective and intersubjective. Edmund *Husserl introduced this concept in his late work, *Die Krisis der europäischen Wissenschaften und die transzendentale Phänomenologie: Eine Einleitung in die phänomenologische Philosophie* (1936), translated as *The Crisis of European Sciences and Transcendental Phenomenology: An Introduction to Phenomenological Philosophy* (1970). The concept was further developed by Maurice *Merleau-Ponty and Alfred Schütz, among others in the field of *phenomenology. In *critical theory, lifeworld is central to the work of Jürgen *Habermas, who incorporates it into his theory of *communicative action as a kind of minimum level of linguistic consciousness. Used in a less technical way, the concept of lifeworld has also featured in studies of *everyday life as a codeword for the human environment.

liminality A ritual space or phase of transition in which a person is no longer what they were, but is not yet what they will be. The liminal is the in-between, the neither one thing nor the other. The term was coined by anthropologist Arnold van Gennep in his classic work *The Rites of Passage* (1908), which describes the variety of rituals performed by so-called primitive tribes which facilitate the passage of children to adulthood. Victor Turner develops this concept further in his work *The Ritual Process: Structure and Anti-Structure* (1969). Radical theatre theorist and director Richard Schechner explored the possibilities of this concept with the Performance Group in New York.

linguistic criticism A mode of literary criticism that focuses on the linguistic structure of a text pioneered by English linguist Roger Fowler. It is particularly noted for its interest in the way power is conveyed in language.

Further Reading: R. Fowler *Linguistic Criticism* (1986).

linguistic turn The recognition in western philosophy that language poses an insurmountable limit to philosophical thinking because there is no absolute way of reducing all expressions to their propositional form. Many of the philosophers who adhere to this position began their careers as *analytic philosophers, determined to prove the opposite. The most famous example is Ludwig *Wittgenstein. The extreme form of this position, usually attributed to Jacques *Derrida, though it is a caricature of his thought, is that language is all that there is, meaning that language is our only means of knowing and engaging the world. The influence of this line of thinking was felt outside of philosophy as well. For example, American historian Hayden *White foregrounds the role language plays both in the formation of the historical record and the subsequent construction of historical narrative; Clifford *Geertz makes a similar case for anthropology.

liquid modernity Zygmunt *Bauman's term for the present historical condition of globalized capitalism. It is defined by a chronic weakening of the relationship between labour and capital and the unleashing of capital's power to dissolve social and communal bonds. It is characterized by the pervasiveness in contemporary society of what Bauman refers to as the 'unholy trinity' of uncertainty, insecurity and unsafety, or as he more bluntly puts it the failure of government to act as the principal guarantor of existence. *See also* MODERNITY; POSTMODERNISM; SECOND MODERNITY.

Further Reading: Z. Bauman *Liquid Modernity* (2000).
Z. Bauman *Liquid Love* (2003).

***literaturnost* (literariness)** The principal object of interest for *Russian Formalism, the elusive quality of language use that distinguishes the poetic from the ordinary. This quality is best seen in—indeed, is produced by—what the Russian Formalists referred to as **ostranenie*, the process of making the already familiar seem unfamiliar or strange, thereby awakening in us a heightened state of perception. Just as people who live by the sea no longer hear the waves, Victor Shklovsky wrote, we no longer hear the words we utter, and as a consequence perception has withered into mere recognition. It is this habit-dulled state of affairs that literature, by power of its ability to defamiliarize the familiar, is supposed to address, according to Russian Formalism. A simple example of how this might work, which film directors like Jean-Luc Godard and Quentin Tarantino have both exploited to good effect, is to tell a story out of order (as Godard famously said, 'a story has to have a beginning, a middle, and an end, just not necessarily in that order'), thus challenging the viewer to reconstruct the correct order for themselves.

logical positivism A school of philosophy originating in fin-de-siècle Vienna with the work of the so-called *Vienna Circle founded by Moritz Schlick and Hans Hahn. Its principal theoreticians were A.J. Ayer, Rudolf Carnap, Ernst Mach, and Ludwig *Wittgenstein. Its aim was to create a new kind of philosophy informed by the principles of science and logic. By doing so it hoped to demonstrate the irrelevance (and indeed the wrong-headedness) of *metaphysics, and the synthetic thinking of post-Kantian thought. It applied a verification principle to all statements about the world and rejected all those that could not be verified as true. For example, the statement 'the universe is infinite' cannot be verified because neither universe as such nor the idea of infinity can be verified. Logical positivism has had very little influence on *critical theory. *See also* ANALYTIC PHILOSOPHY; EMPIRICISM.

logocentrism French philosopher Jacques *Derrida's term, now widely used, for what he sees as a pervasive form of idealism in language philosophy which assumes that neither speech nor writing can be thought without first of all presupposing an abstract and idealized notion of language which actual speech and writing imperfectly represent. Derived from the Greek word 'logos' meaning 'word' in the sense of the word of God or some other authority, logocentrism names a tendency in philosophy to suppose that there must be some kind of ultimate authority guaranteeing the meaning of language. When Roland *Barthes writes of the *death of the author, it is precisely the death of *this* logocentric notion of language that he is referring to. In the little collection of interviews, *Positions* (1972), translated as *Positions* (1981), Derrida states that logocentrism is the principal focus of the reading strategy he developed, namely *deconstruction, for which he is best known. For Derrida, particularly in his earlier work, the most pernicious symptom of logocentrism is the widespread privileging of speech over writing in philosophy, usually taking the form of the assumption that writing is secondary or parasitical to speech.

longue durée A term that literally means 'long duration' introduced by the French historian Fernand *Braudel. It is a standard term of reference in the work of the **Annales* School, which Braudel helped to establish. It is used to indicate a perspective on history that extends further into the past than both human memory and the archaeological record so as to incorporate climatology, demography, geology, and oceanology, and chart the effects of events that occur so slowly as to be imperceptible to those who experience them, such as the changing nature of the planet or the steady increase in population in a particular area.

Löwenthal, Leo (1900–93) German sociologist of literature and original member of the *Frankfurt School. Born in Frankfurt am Main to a middle-class Jewish family, he met future Frankfurt School colleagues Theodor *Adorno and Siegfried *Kracauer while still in high school. He studied literature at universities in Frankfurt, Heidelberg, and Giessen and received a doctorate in philosophy in 1923. He became an assistant at the Institute for Social Research under the leadership of Max *Horkheimer and was given responsibility for editing the Institute's journal, *Zeitschrift für Sozialforschung* (Journal for Social Research), a task he continued even as the journal's base was switched to Paris and then New York. Along with virtually all the other members of the Frankfurt School, Löwenthal relocated to the US to escape persecution by the Nazis. But he did not move with them to California. He instead took up an administrative job in Washington DC for the duration of the war. Neither did he return to Germany as Adorno and Horkheimer did, but like Herbert *Marcuse he stayed on in the US, taking jobs at Stanford and Berkeley. Although an integral member of the inner core of the Frankfurt School he is not remembered as one of its key innovators. His significance as a scholar stems rather from his extensive analyses of popular literature, which might be read as practical examples of the kind of analyses his colleagues Adorno and others were attempting to theorize in their own more abstract way.

Further Reading: M. Jay *The Dialectical Imagination* (1973).
R. Wiggershaus *The Frankfurt School* (1994).

Luhmann, Niklas (1927–1998) German sociologist and systems theorist. Luhmann is renowned for his attempt to develop a sociological model capable of accounting for every aspect of contemporary society. His work is enormously influential, particularly in Germany, where it rivals Jürgen *Habermas' dominance of the social sciences.

Luhmann was born in Lüneberg in northern Germany. His family were relatively well off brewers. In 1943, when he was only 16, he was conscripted to serve in the Luftwaffenhelfer, also known as Flakhelfer since the principal task of those who served in the Luftwaffenhelfer was to assist the anti-aircraft gunners. Günter Grass, Pope Benedict XVI, and Habermas also served in the Luftwaffenhelfer. He was captured by the Americans in 1945. After the war he moved to Freiburg to study study law. He took a job in the civil service following graduation. In 1961, he was granted a sabbatical leave, which he used to go to Harvard, where he met and studied with the great American sociologist Talcott Parsons. He then completed postgraduate qualifications in the School for Administration in Speyer, after which he moved to the University of Münster to complete his habilitation. In 1970 he was appointed professor of sociology at the University of Bielefeld, where he spent the remainder of his career, retiring in 1993.

As the title of his best known work, the monumental *Soziale Systeme: Grundriß einer allgemeinen Theorie* (1984), translated as *Social Systems* (1995), makes apparent, Luhmann was primarily interested in the way society functions. Very far from being a rigid *structuralist, as the notion of systems theory might seem to imply, Luhmann was particularly concerned to understand the way society adapts, the way it deals with risk and cataclysm. Luhmann was, in part, inspired by the work of Humberto Maturana and Francisco Varela, particularly their groundbreaking book, *Autopoiesis and Cognition: The Realization of the Living* (1972), which introduces the idea of *autopoiesis, or the self-creating system.

Further Reading: C. Borch *Niklas Luhmann* (2010).

Lukács, György (1885–1971) Hungarian *Marxist philosopher and literary critic, widely considered the founding figure of western Marxism. Born to a wealthy Jewish family in Budapest—his father was an investment banker—he studied in Budapest, Berlin, and Heidelberg. In Germany he became friends with Max Weber, Ernst *Bloch, and the poet Stefan George. At this stage of his career, Lukács was still strongly influenced by the work of *Kant, *Hegel, and *Dilthey, a fact reflected in his still rather idealist early books: *Soul and Form* (1910) and *The Theory of the Novel* (1916).

The First World War and more particularly the Russian Revolution had a profound effect on Lukács. In 1918 he joined the Hungarian Communist Party, serving as a People's Commissar for Education and Culture in the short-lived Hungarian Soviet Republic. When the Soviet collapsed he was forced into exile in Vienna and was only saved from extradition and probable execution (he was condemned to death in absentia) by the intervention of writer friends like Thomas Mann (who reputedly based the character Naphta in *Der Zauberberg* (1924), translated as *The Magic Mountain* (1927) on Lukács). Vienna brought Lukács into contact with a number of other similarly exiled Marxist intellectuals and fellow revolutionaries like Antonio *Gramsci, Adolf Joffe, and Victor Serge and proved a rich environment in which to rethink many of his previously held positions. The result was *History and Class Consciousness* (1923), probably his most important book.

Although it was condemned at the time for being 'ultra leftist' by the Comintern, and later subjected to excoriating self-criticism by Lukács himself, *History and Class Consciousness* has been immensely influential in a number of disciplines. Lukács's goal in writing it was to stimulate debate about the *dialectic and place it at the centre of Marxist philosophy. As Fredric *Jameson explains in *Marxism and Form* (1971), *History and Class Consciousness* criticizes philosophy before Marx for its inability and/or unwillingness to come to grips with the *totality* of social life. In particular, he denounces as a false problem *Kant's concern for the impossibility of grasping the *Ding an sich* (thing in itself), which according to Lukács is the result of middle-class *alienation and a corresponding tendency to view the objects of the world contemplatively rather than with an understanding of their materiality.

Lukács thus argues that the middle class can understand specific objects but not the larger historical problem of how such things are possible in the first place. In contrast, the *class conscious proletariat is able to penetrate the truth of their situation and dissolve the glacial state of *reification into which the middle class are held fast by their *commodity fetishism. Works that demonstrate this awareness are designated *realist by Lukács (he singles out Balzac, Scott, and Tolstoy as his key exemplars), thus setting the stage for one of the great literary critical debates of the 20th century between himself and Bertolt *Brecht, whom he mistook for an avatar of a *modernism understood as mere formal experimentation. For Lukács realism means works that are expressive of social forces. That is to say, the work must expose not merely the living conditions of the poor as Dickens does, but also the degree to which society at large is responsible for those conditions. For this reason, he also rejected naturalism, particularly its chief exponent Émile Zola, whose work he regarded as superficial.

In 1929 Lukács moved to Berlin, staying there until 1933 when the Nazis came to power. He then fled to Moscow, where he remained until after World War II, surviving both the German invasion of Russia and perhaps more astonishingly Stalin's purges. His writings from

Moscow, perhaps out of political necessity, took on a dogmatically Stalinist tone. He defended Soviet-dictated *socialist realism and denounced modernism. His key works from this period were *The Historical Novel* (1937), *The Young Hegel* (1938), and *Studies in European Realism* (1948). He returned to Budapest after the war and took an active, if ambivalent role, in the political reconstruction of Hungary. In the late 1950s he joined Imre Nagy's revolutionary government, which opposed the USSR. After the 1956 uprising, he was deported to Romania, once again narrowly escaping execution. Fortunately, he was able to return to his home country the following year and he engaged in an extended period of self-criticism, which lasted more or less until his death, in which he repudiated his former 'Stalinist' positions.

Further Reading: A. Kadarkay *Georg Lukács* (1991).
M. Löwy *Georg Lukács: From Romanticism to Bolshevism* (1979).

Lyotard, Jean-François (1924–98) French philosopher, author of more than 25 books on diverse topics, including aesthetics (especially the *Avant-garde), ethics, justice, and political theory, but undoubtedly best known for his work on *postmodernism, *La Condition postmoderne: rapport sur le savoir* (1979), translated as *The Postmodern Condition: A Report on Knowledge* (1984).

In the early part of his career, from 1954–64, Lyotard was actively involved with the group 'Socialism ou Barbarie' (socialism or barbarism), whose members included such luminaries as Jean Laplanche, Claude Lefort, and Gerard *Genette, among others. Led by its founder Cornelius *Castoriadis, Socialism ou Barbarie sought to critique *Marxism from within, arguing that it was more important to hold to the revolutionary spirit of Marx's ideas than the exact letter of his writings. In this period, Lyotard also actively campaigned against France's involvement in Algeria. Although he parted with the group in 1964, Lyotard remained in solidarity with the Left until the failure (as he saw it) of the events of *May '68 led him to break with Marxism altogether. He would come to see Marxism as a discourse of terror, as the vituperative account of the 'desire called Marx' in *Economie libidinale* (1974), translated as *Libidinal Economy* (1993) makes clear.

Written for the provincial government of Quebec's Conseil des Universités, *La Condition postmoderne: rapport sur le savoir* (1979) lifted the term *postmodernism out of its relative obscurity as the name for a new stylistic trend in architecture, literature, and the arts, and transformed it into an indictment of the present age. Lyotard's principal thesis, summed up in the famous phrase that the present age is defined by 'incredulity towards *grand narratives', is that scientific discourse (knowledge in general) has entered a new phase characterized by the unavailability of its traditional legitimating narratives, namely Revolution (the idea that detecting faults in a particular society will spontaneously give rise to a social movement to correct them) and *Enlightenment (the idea that through the sophistication of arts and sciences human society necessarily becomes more humane than it was). In the absence of grand narratives, knowledge today is forced to fall back on highly localized values, or 'little narratives', particularly the idea of efficiency.

Perhaps Lyotard's most provocative idea is that these little narratives should be thought of as highly specific and completely incommensurable *language games (a term he borrows from *Wittgenstein). Although Lyotard took care to state that this did not mean that society is in a state of chaotic Brownian motion, nor that language games are the only form of social relation there is, he nonetheless conveyed the strong impression that the absolute relativism (or *anti-foundationalism) such a thesis implies should be regarded as a virtue because it means no single language game is capable of either dominating or integrating all the other language games. Indeed, Lyotard goes so far as to say that political struggle should consist in 'waging war on totality', by which he means any form of *hegemonic discourse. As meagre a notion of freedom as this is, many readers of Lyotard have seen it as hopeful because it seems to betoken the idea that *resistance is possible. It is, however, a highly problematic notion of resistance because by definition it lacks any possibility of coordinating individual language games so as to create a genuine *social movement.

Lyotard never pursued the social implications of his thesis at any great length, although in subsequent works, he would argue that it is the incommensurability between language games—the inability of one language game to communicate fully with another—that is the source of what can properly be called injustice. This problematic is a central preoccupation for Lyotard in the latter part of his career and gave rise to what is for many his most important philosophical work, namely *Le Différend* (1983), translated as *The Differend: Phrases in Dispute* (1988). A *differend (which might be loosely translated as a 'wrong' or 'injustice') arises when a conflict occurs in such a way that the wronged party is unable to find the means of representing their position. Lyotard uses as his case example the extreme relativist position adopted by Holocaust-denier Robert Faurisson in which the only person who can testify to the existence of gas chambers is somebody who actually died in one.

Lyotard's last works concentrated on this question of representability. In works such as *L'inhumain* (1988), translated as *The Inhuman: Reflections on Time* (1991), Lyotard develops an aesthetic around the idea that only what is unrepresentable is the proper subject for art. Accepting that this is a logical impossibility, but arguing that it is nonetheless an aesthetic and indeed epistemological necessity, Lyotard praises postmodernist art for 'bringing forth' the unrepresentable, at least in the minds of the beholder, seeing in this a source of hope for future politics.

Further Reading: G. Bennington *Lyotard: Writing the Event* (1988).
B. Readings *Introducing Lyotard* (1991).
S. Malpas *Jean-François Lyotard* (1996).
J. Williams *Lyotard: Towards a Postmodern Philosophy* (1998).

Macherey, Pierre (1938–) French literary theorist. He was born in Belfort, in the Franche-Comté region. Macherey attended the École Normale Supérieure from 1958 to 1963, where he met Louis *Althusser with whom he would work very closely for a number of years. He completed an MA in 1961 on Spinoza (a lifelong interest) under the direction of Georges *Canguilhem. In 1962–3, Macherey, along with fellow students Étienne *Balibar, Michel *Pêcheux, and Jacques *Rancière, undertook a year-long study of the then still relatively new critical methodology *structuralism under the direction of Althusser. Next the group tackled Karl *Marx's *Das Kapital*, eventually publishing a long multi-authored volume entitled *Lire le capital* (1968), partially translated as *Reading Capital* (1970). In the ensuing years, as the group disintegrated over personal, political, and theoretical differences, the contributions by Macherey and Rancière were deleted. In 1966, Macherey published *Pour une théorie de la production littéraire*, translated as *A Theory of Literary Production* (1978), which for many readers is not only his most important work, but also the most enduring example—at least in literary studies—of an Althusserian approach to textual analysis. In subsequent work, Macherey focused on Spinoza, completing a five-volume interpretation of his *Ethics* in 1998.

Further Reading: C. Belsey *Critical Practice* (1980).

magical realism A style of literature which integrates a *realist mode of writing with fantastical or marvellous events treated as perfectly ordinary occurrences. The term derives from a mistranslation of Cuban writer Alejo Carpentier's notion 'lo real maravilloso' (marvellous reality), which occurs in the prologue to *El Reino de este Mundo* (1949), translated as *The Kingdom of This World* (1957), where it is used to characterize the life of the people Carpentier encountered on a visit to Haiti. The key here is that the aim is to describe a reality in which the magical is part of *everyday life and not an extraordinary dimension. Thus, it should not be confused with either the fantastic (as Tzvetan *Todorov defines it) or fantasy fiction, because its purpose is not simply to go beyond the bounds of realism. As is evident in the best-known examples of magical realism, namely Gabriel García Márquez's novel, *Cien años de soledad* (1967), translated as *One Hundred Years of Solitude* (1970), and Salman Rushdie's *Midnight's Children* (1981), there is a distinct political purpose behind introducing the marvellous, which sets it apart from the merely fantastic. At its best, as in Márquez and Rushdie, but one can also cite the work of Mikhail Bulgakov, Angela Carter, and Günter Grass, the device of magical realism (as the *Russian Formalists would undoubtedly call it) enables the writer to critique belief, memory, and the imagination as historical forces.

Further Reading: M. Bowers *Magic(al) Realism* (2004).
L. Parkinson Zamora *Magical Realism: Theory, History, Community* (1995).

manifest and latent content In *Die Traumdeutung* (1900), translated as *The Interpretation of Dreams* (1953), Sigmund *Freud calls the dream that the *analysand or patient recalls the manifest content because this is how the dream appears to them; but, he argues, that appearance conceals a deeper truth, which he calls the latent content, and designates as the dream's thought. It is latent in the sense that it is implicit in the manifest content, but because of the transformations and distortions enacted by the *dreamwork it is for all intents and purposes invisible. It is the latent content that his analysis seeks to reveal.

Marcuse, Herbert (1898–1979) German cultural critic and one of the most influential members of the *Frankfurt School. Late in life, he became an intellectual superstar and a celebrity figure, particularly among dissident students, with the publication of *One Dimensional Man* (1964), which spoke to the baby-boomer generation of their velvet-lined repression under capitalism and sold over a million copies.

Marcuse was born in Berlin into a family of assimilated, upper middle-class Jews. He was in the army during the First World War, but did not see active service. Following the war, he got involved with the Soldier's Council but soon left it. Disillusioned with politics, he decided to focus on his studies. He completed a doctorate on the *Künstlerroman* (novels about artists) in German literature at Freiburg University. He worked in bookselling and publishing for the next six years. Then, after reading *Sein und Zeit* (1927), translated as *Being and Time* (1962), he decided to complete his habilitation under the supervision of its author Martin *Heidegger. Owing to their political differences, however, this didn't work out quite as planned. Marcuse completed the thesis, which was published as *Hegels Ontologie und* *die Grundlegung einer Theorie der Geschichtlichkeit* (Hegel's Ontology and the Foundations of a Theory of Historicity, 1932), but it didn't result in him being confirmed as a professor.

Jobless and uncertain of his academic future, Marcuse was recommended to Max *Horkheimer, director of the Institut für Sozialforschung (Institute for Social Research), by Edmund *Husserl, via a number of intermediaries, and duly given a job, initially as a librarian. It was at this time that Marcuse first read *Marx, finding there (especially in the so-called 'early Marx' of the *Economic and Philosophical Manuscripts* (1844)) a materialist ontology that in his view surpassed not only Heidegger, but also *Hegel and *Dilthey. Marcuse rejected Heidegger's view and developed a philosophy of the present as an inhuman form of existence that could only be rectified by means of a revolution. The rise to power of the Nazis in 1933 necessitated leaving the country. Marcuse followed the Institute first to Switzerland and then to the USA, where he took up permanent residence.

During the war, Marcuse was forced to find employment outside of the Institute because of its financial difficulties, so he was unable to publish a great deal between 1942 and 1950. He did, however, manage to publish *Reason and Revolution* (1941), which attempted to reclaim Hegel's philosophy for the left. His next book, published a decade after the war, *Eros and Civilization* (1955), is probably his most important book. It brought about the fusion of Marx and Freud that critical theory had been attempting to produce since the 1930s and in doing so launched the analytic approach known as Freudo-Marxism, which even today, continues to influence research in the humanities and social sciences. Contrary to his Frankfurt School colleague, the psychoanalyst Erich *Fromm, *Eros and Civilization* argues that civilization does not depend upon the renunciation of instinct and indeed could be said to be fuelled by the instincts. Marcuse positions Eros as a unifying power that can be pitted against the fragmenting power of *modernity.

His next books, *Soviet Marxism* (1958) and *One Dimensional Man* (1964) focused more closely on the question of repression. This research can be read as an extension of *Adorno and Horkheimer's critique of the *culture industry. In 1965, in a high-profile essay published as part of book co-written with Robert Wolff and Barrington Moore, *Critique of Pure Tolerance*, Marcuse coined the famous concept of *repressive tolerance, by which he meant that the fact that a particular state allows certain practices should not deceive us into thinking genuine freedom prevails and by the same token nor should we tolerate the repressive elements of the state. He dedicated the essay to his students at Brandeis University in a gesture of solidarity. Throughout the 1960s and 1970s, Marcuse was very active in speaking for and to the student protest movement both in the US and in Europe.

Marcuse died of a stroke, during a visit to Berlin to speak at the Max Planck Institute at the invitation of Jürgen *Habermas.

Further Reading: D. Held *Introduction to Critical Theory* (1980).
M. Jay *The Dialectical Imagination* (1973).
R. Wiggershaus *The Frankfurt School* (1994).

Marinetti, Filippo Tommaso (1876–1944) Italian author best known as the founder of *Futurism. He shot to international prominence when his short and provocative text 'The Founding and Manifesto of Futurism' was published on the front page of the French daily newspaper *Le Figaro* in 1909. It celebrated art as violence, cruelty, and injustice; it called for the destruction of museums and libraries; and it glorified war as a kind of cultural hygiene. His reputation is, however, more than a little tarnished by his enthusiastic, albeit idealistic, support for Mussolini's fascist regime. He even tried, unsuccessfully, to make Futurism the official art of Italian fascism. Today Marinetti is generally remembered, particularly by Paul Virilio, as a prophet of speed.

m

Further Reading: C. Poggi *Inventing Futurism: The Art and Politics of Artificial Optimism* (2009).

Marx, Karl (1818–83) See opposite.

Marxism The political *discourse and a revolutionary *social movement inspired by the work of Karl *Marx. At its most elementary, Marxism is a science of history premised on the view that the economy, or more precisely the *mode of production, determines and decides the conditions of existence for all people. There is a *utopian dimension to it as well inasmuch as its basic conviction is that the needs of all people should be met by *society. In the capitalist mode of production, however, this is impossible because there is a divide between the owners of the means of production and the workers who must sell their labour to survive—the relationship between the two, which Marx refers to as a *class struggle, is fundamentally iniquitous in Marx's view. Marx theorized that once workers became aware of this inequality and the fact that it could not be overcome without making changes to the very mode of production that they would rise up in protest and overturn capitalism and replace it with socialism. History proved him wrong on this last count. The history of Marxism as a revolutionary social movement begins with the founding of the

MARX, KARL (1818–83)

German Jewish economist and social theorist and one of the most influential thinkers of all time. Born in the Rhineland town of Trier, shortly after it passed from French rule to Prussian rule. As the Prussian state was much less tolerant of Jews than the French, Marx's father converted to Christianity in order to continue to be able to work as a lawyer. His father he wished that his son would follow him into the law, but it was not to be. Although he studied law at the Universities of Bonn and Berlin, Marx never became a lawyer. His father transferred him to Berlin in the hope of improving his attitude to study, but if in Bonn he was distracted by duelling and gambling, in Berlin he was distracted by ideas, particularly the work of *Hegel, and of the two distractions it was the latter that proved the most enduring in its effects.

An academic job was Marx's initial career goal, and he obtained a PhD from the University of Jena, but the political situation in Prussia at that time made it impossible so he instead turned to journalism and took a job with the Cologne-based liberal newspaper *Rheinische Zeitung*, becoming its editor at age 24. It was in the offices of *Rheinische Zeitung* that he met his future collaborator Friedrich *Engels in 1842. Marx used his position to publicly critique the monarchical state, which retaliated by censoring his editorials and effectively forcing the paper to close. Marx's so-called 'early writings', *On the Jewish Question* (1843), *A Contribution to the Critique of Hegel's 'Philosophy of Right'* (1843–4), and *Economic and Philosophical Manuscripts* (1844), among other works, date from this period. Following the closure of *Rheinische Zeitung*, Marx moved to Paris in 1843, hoping to find there greater freedom to write and think.

Abandoning the idea of a professional career, Marx dedicated himself to developing a 'science' of the capitalist economy, living off loans, gifts from benefactors, inheritances, and his meagre royalties. It was a hand-to-mouth existence about which he would later say that he only regretted that his wife and family had to endure it. Marx and Engels published their first collaborative work, *The Holy Family*, in 1845. Although it was written almost in its entirety by Marx, it was published under a joint name, most likely because at that time Engels was better known. A response to the criticism this book received was written, but never published in Marx's lifetime. The manuscript was preserved however and published as *The German Ideology*. Expelled from France, Marx moved to Brussels, and began to think in more international terms. His writing no longer focused exclusively on German authors, as it had done in his previous work which contains attacks on Feuerbach, *Hegel, and Stirner among others. He now attacked internationally renowned writers such as Proudhon, a radical thinker and rival.

In Brussels Marx was involved with the international movement, the Communist League. The League held two conferences in London in 1847, following which Marx and Engels were assigned the task of preparing a manifesto to guide the nascent movement. Engels wrote the initial drafts, and Marx wrote up the final manuscript, which was published in German in London in 1848. A French translation soon followed, as did an English translation in 1850. Yet despite the fact that 1848 was a turbulent year in Europe (the insurrection in Paris, which affected both Baudelaire and Flaubert so deeply, being the most prominent), *Manifest der Kommunistischen Partei*, translated as *The Manifesto of the Communist Party* (1850) had little immediate impact on revolutionary thought or practice. Provocatively Marx urged the working class to fight alongside the bourgeoisie, insofar as the latter fought against the static conservatism of the feudalist property holders and the monarchy; but he also predicted that the working class would eventually have to overthrow the bourgeoisie as well. Interestingly, the revolutionary programme *The Communist Manifesto* espoused was primarily democratic in character.

Owing to the failure of the liberal revolutions in Europe in 1848 and 1849, both Marx and Engels were forced to flee to England, where they remained until their deaths. Engels found employment in the family firm, overseeing its interests in textile manufacturing and marketing in Manchester. Supported by Engels, Marx settled in London, near to the vast resources of the library in the British Museum, which opened in 1857 and contained over 40 kilometres of shelving (the library itself has since been moved to St Pancras, but Marx's favourite desk is preserved in the now mummified 'reading room'). Marx also wrote hundreds of short articles for various English and German newspapers on diverse topics of contemporary and historical interest, including Britain's imperial occupation of India. His notebooks from the winter of 1857–8, largely compiled whilst seated in the British Museum, were published posthumously as the *Grundrisse der Kritik der politischen Ökonomie (Rohentwurf)* (1939), translated as *Grundrisse: Foundations of the Critique of Political Economy (Rough Draft)* (1973). Here one sees Marx throw off the influence of Hegel once and for all and begin the process that would lead to the writing of his master work *Das Kapital: Kritik der Politischen Ökonomie* (Capital: Critique of Political Economy).

Throughout the 1860s Marx worked on, but never completed, and only sporadically published what would come to be known simply as *Das Kapital*. The first volume appeared in 1867, and was the only volume to appear in Marx's lifetime; the other two volumes were published posthumously under Engels's editorship (a fourth volume was written, but it was published by Karl *Kautsky under the separate title of *Theories of Surplus Value*) in 1884 and 1894 respectively.

From the *Grundrisse* onwards Marx's work became increasingly minutely focused on the precise economic mechanisms of the capitalist system. He admired the productive capacity of capitalism and the way it unleashed tremendous productive forces, but also saw that the system was innately unequal in its distribution of prosperity and ultimately exploitative. More importantly, perhaps, Marx also saw that the logic of capitalist production was such that it was bound to swing from one crisis to another because its very premise, namely the endless pursuit of profit, was destabilizing.

Marx's health deteriorated throughout the 1870s, slowing down his rate of work, which had always been prodigious and painstaking, preventing him from finishing his project. Fortunately Engels was able to oversee his legacy. Marx's influence on *critical theory is immense, albeit uneven. Indeed, his legacy can be seen in the very constitution of critical theory, particularly in its earliest formulation by the *Frankfurt School, in the attention it gives to the real world considerations of economics and politics. His work has also had a significant influence on literary criticism, via the work of artists like Bertolt *Brecht and scholars such as Georg *Lukács, Pierre *Macherey, Terry *Eagleton, Fredric *Jameson, and others, and history, through the work of Perry *Anderson and Eric *Hobsbawm, among many others. Philosophers like Jean-Paul *Sartre, Jacques *Derrida, and Gilles *Deleuze, all claim as an essential resource Marx's contribution to political thought. Like any great thinker, Marx has given rise to rival schools of thought, some of which—like *Althusser's followers—became highly influential in their own right, as well as powerful opponents. Outside academia, Marx's work has proven to be a powerful intellectual and ideological weapon in the hands of the oppressed everywhere.

Further Reading: E. Balibar *The Philosophy of Marx* (2007).
P. Osborne *How to Read Marx* (2005).
P. Singer *Marx: A Very Short Introduction* (2000).
F. Wheen *Karl Marx* (2000).

First International in 1864 and to a certain degree ends with the fall of the Berlin Wall in 1989. In between, of course, there were three more Internationals as well as highly successful revolutions in Russia, China, Korea, and Cuba. As a form of political discourse, Marxism has had a varied history—it experienced a major rupture following the Russian Revolution in 1917. Marxist scholars in the western parts of Europe felt cut off from the events in Russia, but also felt defeated by the failure of revolution to occur in their own country. A new form of Marxism, generally known as *Western Marxism, emerged at this point and to a certain degree developed independently of the more pragmatic version of Marxism that obtained in the USSR.
See also CRITICAL THEORY.

Further Reading: D. McLellan *Marxism After Marx* (2007).

SEE WEB LINKS

- An exhaustive range of resources and information about Marxism which can be searched by subject, author or history.
- A Socialist Party website that provides an overview of Marxism.

Marxist Criticism A form of cultural criticism that applies *Marxist *theory to the interpretation of cultural texts. Since neither Karl *Marx nor his collaborator Friedrich *Engels ever developed a specific form of cultural criticism themselves, Marxist Criticism has been extrapolated from their writings. As there is no one form of *Marxism, so there is no one form of Marxist Criticism. This is not to say that the different variants of Marxist Criticism do not have certain features in common, but it is nevertheless also true that there is considerable debate within the field concerning those differences. In common, then, all forms of Marxist Criticism assume the following: (i) that no artistic object can be understood in isolation from the social, cultural, and historical conditions in which it was produced; (ii) that all categories by which artistic objects might be measured are themselves constructions that need to be evaluated from the perspective of the social, cultural, and historical conditions that gave rise to them; (iii) that all artistic productions are commodities that can and must be understood in terms of the production of surplus value; (iv) that art is a site for the playing out of a *symbolic form of *class struggle. The principle area of difference in Marxist Criticism is the issue of whether or not it should be prescriptive or not: in other words, is it the job of Marxist Criticism to determine what art should be like? There have been powerful movements in favour of this position—the most noted is of course *socialist realism. This position has also been championed very strongly by such critics as György *Lukács. But there is a similarly powerful movement against it and in recent years it has generally been agreed that it is neither possible nor desirable to prescribe what art should be like. But if that isn't the task of Marxist Criticism, then what is? As is the case with *psychoanalysis, the response to this question is twofold: there is an attempt to understand the nature of the object (i.e. what makes it art and why) and alongside it there is the attempt to understand the subject's response to particular art objects. In both cases, the primary conceptual tool is the notion of *ideology. Some of the major Marxist critics are: Terry *Eagleton, his *Marxism and Literary Criticism* (1976) was immensely influential; Fredric *Jameson, his *Marxism and Form* (1971), and more particularly *The Political Unconscious* (1981), are perhaps the most sophisticated attempts to synthesize the critical methodologies from a broad spectrum of approaches; Lukács, although a troubled figure, his *History and Class Consciousness* (1923) continues to be studied today and it is in many ways a foundational text for the field; Pierre *Macherey, whose *Pour une théorie de la production littéraire*, translated as *A Theory of Literary Production* (1978), is generally regarded as the definitive application of *Althusser's work to literature; and Raymond *Williams, a hugely influential figure, particularly in the nascent field of *Cultural Studies.

masculinity The culturally relative ideal *gender *identity for men. Studies of masculinity, a now quite considerable body of work, show that the specific nature of masculinity varies across time and geography—men in 19th-century Britain were expected to act and behave quite differently from the way they are expected to act and behave today; similarly in the 21st-century men in Britain are expected to act and behave quite differently from men in Iraq. Thus, it is more usual in critical discourse to speak of masculinity in the plural rather than the singular. The study of masculinity is an offshoot of the study of *gender pioneered in *feminism and *Cultural Studies, and as such its research has at its core the problem of identity formation. In particular it has overturned the idea of *biological determinism which holds that gendered behaviour is a function of physiology—e.g. men are stronger and more aggressive than women and are therefore naturally supposed to be hunter-warriors—and shown very clearly that masculinity is culturally defined. Research in the field has been greatly influenced by Judith *Butler's concept of performativity (which she derives from J.L. *Austin's linguistic concept of the *performative), which claims that all gender roles are performances requiring constant self-management. Along the same lines, some researchers have wanted to argue that men are under just as much stress to conform to cultural expectations of the ideal body as women, though many in *feminism see this as overstating things since in most parts of the world the *patriarchy is still firmly in place.

Further Reading: R.W. Connell *Masculinities* (2005).
S. Whitehead *Men and Masculinities: Key Themes and New Directions* (2002).

masquerade Used in *psychoanalysis to designate a psychological phenomenon of adopting an expected social role or *persona and maintaining appearances. It was first used by British psychoanalyst Joan Rivière in a paper entitled 'Womanliness as Masquerade' (1929). Although the term is frequently used by feminist cultural critics like Germaine *Greer, it has not really been developed into a fully fledged concept. It can, in this sense, be seen as a precursor to the much more sophisticated concept of *performativity developed by Judith *Butler.

matheme French *psychoanalyst Jacques *Lacan's term for his equations, graphs, schemata, and symbols which function like *axioms in his thinking and teaching. One finds similar notations in the work of Alain *Badiou, who similarly treats mathematical equations as an *ontology. In both cases, the matheme is used in preference to language, which is by implication deemed too imprecise to express a particular problem or concept.

May '68 A series of street protests that began in a number of universities in Paris but rapidly spread to incorporate a wide cross section of French society. Some historians estimate that as many as 10 million people participated in the mass strikes over the course of several weeks. Known by a variety of different epithets such as 'the events of May', and the 'long summer', May '68 was not a single event, but rather a series of events interlinked by a common theme or purpose, which is difficult to define but essentially boils down to a nationwide transformation of what Raymond *Williams called, in a different context, the *structure of feeling. For the first time in French history, workers and students (effectively the future managerial class, and therefore the class enemies of the workers) united together to stage their dissatisfaction with the state of French society and more especially the way it was governed. Whole sections of the workforce went out on strike, perhaps most notably the garbage collectors, with the result that Paris was soon inundated by trash piled high on street corners. The police did not know how to respond, and many peaceful marches became violent, the cobblestones in the older parts of Paris being turned into handy missiles. The reason these events, rather than the numerous other protest events that occurred that year around the world (e.g. 1968 was also the year of the so-called

'Prague Spring'), have such significance for critical theory is not clear, though in all likelihood it is simply a matter of it happening at a time when French theory was hegemonic. Consequently, the reflections of French critical and cultural theorists (e.g. Alain *Badiou, Michel de *Certeau, Gilles *Deleuze, Raymond Aron) on their national situation were transformed by an international readership into thoughts of more universal significance. In particular they raised the question of whether *resistance is possible and if change can be achieved by non-violent means. Interestingly, in French politics May '68 is often derided as 'nothing', but in such a way as to confirm that it really was 'something', although no one is ever quite sure what.

Further Reading: K. Ross *May '68 and its Afterlives* (2002).

McDonaldization A process whereby all businesses and indeed institutions conform to the model of practice established by the fast-food chain giant McDonald's. American sociologist George *Ritzer first proposed this thesis in his bestselling book *The McDonaldization of Society* (1993). Ritzer identifies four key features of McDonaldization which, adapting Max Weber for the *postmodern era, he refers to as a rational system: its efficiency (the food fills you up quickly); calculability (transformation of quantity into quality); predictability (the product is the same everywhere from Boston to Beijing); and control through non-human technology (supply gives shape to demand). His complaint is that despite the productive advantages of rational systems, they give rise to numerous unintended disadvantages—e.g. the large scale potato and beef farms necessitated by the McDonald's menu and the unhealthy cost-cutting farming practices the low budget demands. Somewhat nostalgically and not all that persuasively, Ritzer suggests that what he calls 'premodern' businesses like 'mom and pop' grocery stores and privately run B&Bs can be considered to have escaped McDonalization. But this is naive: at the very least it overlooks the highly McDonaldized supply chains and service regulations such enterprises must adhere to. As persuasive as the anecdotal evidence is, Ritzer supplies very little detail on the degree to which society, rather than businesses and bureaucracies, is becoming McDonaldized. Ultimately, it is therefore a rather gloomy and impressionistic jeremiad against change.

McLuhan, Herbert Marshall (1911–80) Canadian media theorist, one of the most influential intellectuals of his time. Born in Edmonton, McLuhan grew up in Winnipeg. He completed a BA and MA in English at the University of Manitoba, then he went to

Cambridge to complete a PhD in English Literature. When he arrived in the UK he found that Cambridge did not recognize his Canadian degrees, so he was forced to start all over again. At Cambridge he studied under I.A. *Richards and F.R. *Leavis. He returned to North America in 1937 to take a position at St Louis University and continue working towards his PhD, which he finally completed in 1943. Published in 1951 as *The Mechanical Bride: Folklore of Industrial Man* McLuhan's thesis explores the changing nature of *rhetoric in contemporary culture. In 1944 he returned to his native Canada, where he spent almost all of the remainder of his professional career. In the early 1950s McLuhan turned his attention increasingly towards communication and media, tracking the rise of what would later be known as the *consumer society. McLuhan's career took off in the early 1960s with the publication of a number of books that would transform him into an academic superstar: *The Gutenberg Galaxy: The Making of Typographic Man* (1962); *Understanding Media: The Extensions of Man* (1964); *The Medium is the Message: An Inventory of Effects* (1967), and *War and Peace in the Global Village* (1968). McLuhan's work saw past the content to the form—he grasped before almost anybody else that new media technology did not just mean new ways of distributing old or familiar content; it meant a whole new way of thinking and being in the world. His concept of the 'global village' has been widely adopted as a description of the world as it is in consequence of the processes of *globalization. Consequently, although he died decades before the Internet became part of *everyday life, he is generally seen as one of its key prophets. His work was enormously influential too on *Cultural Studies, particularly in its formative stages.

Further Reading: T. Gordon *Marshall McLuhan: Escape into Understanding: A Biography* (1997).
P. Marchand *Marshall McLuhan: The Medium and the Messenger* (1989).

mentality (*mentalité*) A historical form of collective *unconscious (extrapolated from *Durkheim's idea of collective consciousness rather than *Jung's own concept of collective unconscious) conceived by the **Annales* group of historians in France to explain how a large population of individual subjects can act and think in a similar fashion without direct coercion. The concept is particularly useful for characterizing the apparently spontaneous shift in national character that precedes revolutions. It is also used to discuss such **longue durée* processes as secularization.

Merleau-Ponty, Maurice (1908–61) French philosopher. A key proponent of *phenomenology, Merleau-Ponty is one of the most important commentators on the work of Edmund *Husserl. He was also one of the first to recognize the significance of the work of Swiss linguist Ferdinand de *Saussure and is considered by many to have provided the link from phenomenology to *structuralism. Undoubtedly, though, Merleau-Ponty is most widely known as a philosopher of the *body.

Born in Rochefort-sur-Mer, he grew up in the Charente-Maritime region, but studied in Paris, first at the Lycée Janson-de-Sailly and then, following a familiar pathway, the Lycée Louis-le-Grand and the École Normale Supérieure (ENS), where his classmates included Simone de *Beauvoir and Jean-Paul *Sartre. He completed his studies at the ENS in 1930 and then along with Beauvoir and Claude *Lévi-Strauss began his teacher training at his alma mater the Lycée Janson-de-Sailly. He was invited back to the ENS in 1935 to take up a position as tutor and remained there until the outbreak of World War II in 1939. During these years he developed his ideas on perception in preparation for his Doctorat ès Lettres. He also attended the lectures of Alexandre *Kojève. During the war, Merleau-Ponty served briefly in the infantry and then following France's surrender he took an active role in the Resistance.

After the war, Merleau-Ponty's career really took off. Having already submitted his minor thesis, *La structure du comportement* (the structure of behaviour), in 1938 (it was published in 1942), he was finally able to submit his major thesis, *Phénoménologie de la perception* (1945), translated as *Phenomenology of Perception* (1962). On the strength of this he was offered a Chair in Child Psychology and Pedagogy at the Sorbonne. Part of his research for this project was done at the Husserl archive in Belgium—he was the first French scholar to visit, he was also instrumental in establishing a Paris-based Husserl archive as well. In 1946, together with Sartre and Beauvoir, Merleau-Ponty founded the journal, *Les Temps Modernes*, serving as its political affairs editor until 1952, when he resigned over disagreements with the editorial board concerning their support for North Korea's invasion of South Korea. In the same year he was elevated to a Chair in Philosophy at the Collège de France, the youngest ever appointment.

Merleau-Ponty's lifelong project was to explain the lived world. He rejected purely scientific explanations as overly simplified, pointing out that in their attempt to present realist explanations they rely on idealist models. Merleau-Ponty rejected virtually all dualisms, particularly those which separated the mind into parts such as Sigmund *Freud's distinction between conscious and *unconscious and those which separated subjects from objects. Merleau-Ponty thought rather in terms of continuums of existence, hence his concepts of flesh (*chair*) and chiasm, which try to explain the interlocking of the differentiated but not isolated components of existence. In this latter respect he was clearly influenced by Henri *Bergson. Merleau-Ponty died suddenly and unexpectedly and left behind a large corpus of unfinished material. Thanks to the efforts of diligent editors, two unfinished books, *Le Visible et l'invisible* (1964), translated as *The Visible and the Invisible* (1968) and *La Prose du Monde* (1969), translated as *The Prose of the World* (1973), have since been published, as have a selection of his lectures from the Collège de France.

Further Reading: T. Baldwin *Reading Merleau-Ponty* (2007).
T. Carman *Merleau-Ponty* (2008).
T. Carman and M. Hansen (eds.) *The Cambridge Companion to Merleau-Ponty* (2004).
L. Hass *Merleau-Ponty's Philosophy* (2008).

messianism The belief that a divine saviour will return to earth and 'save' the true believers. This concept was brought into prominence in *critical theory by the work of German philosopher Walter *Benjamin. In his late essay, 'Theses on the Philosophy of History' (included in the collection of his essays selected by Hannah *Arendt, *Illuminations* (1968)), Benjamin compares the moment of revolutionary rupture to that of the arrival of the messiah. Messianism has since become a codeword in political philosophy for the belief that history is not a continuum that progresses inexorably from one moment to the next, but is instead a series of punctuations. Jacques *Derrida's work on Benjamin focuses almost exclusively on this aspect of his work.

metacommentary American cultural critic Fredric *Jameson's term for his comparative analysis of competing interpretive methods. Jameson says that the metacommentary implies a model not unlike Sigmund *Freud's conception of the relationship between the symptom and its underpinning, but repressed idea (minus his theory of the *libido, of course). The content of a text is the distorted product of lived experience subject to censorship—there are always certain ideas, thoughts, phrases, and so forth that are not appropriate in a particular historical context so they have to be distorted to escape that censorship. This is Freud's basic idea for dream analysis: dreams are distorted images of our unconscious thoughts created in such a way as to escape censorship. So understanding a text means coming to grips with this process of censorship, which Jameson suggests can be accomplished by means of a reconstruction of its original context. What must be explained, then, is why a particular text had to be distorted in that way. A simple, literal example of this is the much discussed effects of the Hays Code on Hollywood: for instance, since the act of sex could not be depicted explicitly, visual metaphors for it had to be found, hence the famous smoking in bed scene following the first kiss which became a universal symbol of sex. In his later works, Jameson tends to use the term *dialectical criticism rather than metacommentary to describe his analytic approach. *See also* TRANSCODING.

Further Reading: F. Jameson *Marxism and Form* (1971).

metafiction Fiction that draws attention to and directly comments upon its status as fiction. Most often this takes the form of an intrusion of the 'author' into the work. One of the earliest and most celebrated cases of metafiction is Laurence Sterne's *Tristram Shandy* (1760–7), which has the author commenting frequently on his failure to get on with telling the story. But it can also take the form of a work of fiction about either the reading or writing of fiction, as one finds (again quite famously) in Italo *Calvino's *Se una notte d'inverno un viaggatore* (1979), translated as *If on a Winter's Night a Traveller* (1981). The device is more common in late 20th-century fiction writing than it is in earlier periods and for this reason is often associated with *postmodernism, although there is no direct correlation between the two. The device can also be witnessed in film and television.

Further Reading: P. Waugh *Metafiction: The Theory and Practice of Self-Conscious Fiction* (1988).

metahistory The consideration of what history is in a philosophical sense. The Canadian literary critic Northrop *Frye was the first person to use this term, but it is American historian Hayden *White who has given the term its most complete meaning. For Frye it meant simply the speculative philosophy of history, while for White it is the examination both of what history is and how that has changed over time. White is particularly interested in the problematic posed by the fact that history is a form of narrative, a feature it shares with fiction, and as he shows in *Metahistory: The Historical Imagination in 19th-Century Europe* (1973), this has a significant influence on the range of meanings that can be given to a set of basic facts. Was the French Revolution inevitable? If so, why didn't similar revolutions occur elsewhere? Was it a tragedy? If so, from whose perspective? Fredric *Jameson's concept of *metacommentary takes a similar approach to the analysis of *critical theories.

metalanguage Language about language. In this sense, virtually all of linguistics and all of literary criticism falls into the category of metalanguage inasmuch as both disciplines are essentially concerned with using language to write about and understand language use. Understood in this rather straightforward fashion the concept poses no real difficulties, but if one takes it literally, then as critics like Jacques *Derrida show, you have a real problem because how can language be outside of itself? It is in effect a logical fallacy to suggest it.

metalepsis A second-order device in *rhetoric in which one *metonym refers to another metonym as for example in the famous description of Helen of Troy as the 'face that launched a thousand ships'. In *narratology, metalepsis refers to the collapsing of an embedded tale and the frame narrative, such as one often finds in *postmodern *metafiction (e.g. Italo *Calvino).

metanarrative *See* GRAND NARRATIVE.

metaphor A figure in *rhetoric in which the meaning of one word is transferred onto and in a certain sense combined with that of another. It is constructed in the same manner as a simile, but the comparative terms 'like' and 'as' are removed. So instead of saying 'that man behaves like a pig' one says 'that man is a pig' and in so doing the attributes of the pig (generally the disagreeable ones) are transposed onto the man. Metaphors can also take extended forms, from a few a paragraphs to entire books—Joseph Conrad's *Heart of Darkness* (1902), for instance, is often read as an extended metaphor for imperialism and its effects.

metaphysics The study of that which lies outside of or beyond the physical realm; (i.e. outside of the realm of the measurable and indeed the knowable). It aims to know and describe the world in its totality, including everything that is not immediately available to the naked eye. It is in this sense inevitably speculative since it deals with such unknowns and perhaps unknowables as causality, existence, and possibility. As such, both empirical philosophers like David Hume and critical philosophers like Immanuel *Kant have been severe on metaphysics. The term derives from Aristotle and refers to works he wrote after his essays on physics. Aristotle himself did not use the word metaphysics—the subject matter he considered, which has since been labelled metaphysics, he referred to as 'first philosophy'. Jacques *Derrida defines *deconstruction as a critique of western metaphysics, which seems to mean the whole of western philosophy. In contrast, Gilles *Deleuze's work might be thought of as a lifelong attempt to discern the physical underpinnings of metaphysics.

metonym A type of figure in *rhetoric in which a part of a thing, or something closely related to it, is used to represent that thing. For example 'the Oval Office' and 'the White House' are often used to represent the US Presidency. Similarly, 'Washington' is frequently used to represent the US government as a whole.

Metz, Christian (1931–93) French film theorist. Metz introduced film studies to both *structuralism and *psychoanalysis and in the process helped initiate the establishment of film theory. Instead of asking what films mean, Metz set out to discover how they make meaning, and in doing so revolutionized the way film was written and thought about in the academy. Born in Béziers in southern France, Metz studied classical languages and ancient history at the École Normale Supérieure and then completed a doctorate in general linguistics at the Sorbonne. Always a cinephile, Metz began to think of ways of applying Ferdinand de *Saussure's theories of language (then much in fashion in Paris thanks to the work of Claude *Lévi-Strauss and Roland *Barthes, among others) to cinema in order to deduce the universal syntax of narrative film. How, in other words, does a film tell a story in pictures? In the 1970s, realizing that the structuralist approach to film analysis he had adopted privileged the cinematic text over the audience, Metz began to incorporate the insights of psychoanalysis, particularly its *Lacanian variant (itself already influenced by structuralism), so as to think through how viewers receive films. Metz hypothesized that films are the equivalent of dreams or hallucinations so Sigmund *Freud's theory of the dreamwork can be applied directly to them. This has proved a highly influential suggestion. Metz's most important publications are *Essai sur la signification au cinéma* (1968), translated as *Film Language: A Semiotics of the Cinema* (1980) and *Le Signifiant imaginaire. Psychanalyse et cinema* (1977), translated as *The Imaginary Signifier: Psychoanalysis and the Cinema* (1982).

Miller, J. Hillis (1928–) American literary critic (primarily a Victorianist) who was part of the group of scholars who were known as the *Yale School of deconstruction. Born in Virginia, Miller attended Oberlin College and Harvard University, graduating from the latter in 1952 with a PhD entitled *Symbolic Imagery in Six Novels of Charles Dickens*. His first appointment was to Johns Hopkins University, where he remained for 20 years, coming under the influence of *Geneva School critic Georges Poulet, who advocated a *phenomenologically inflected critique of consciousness. He then moved to Yale in 1972, where he stayed for 14 years, working with Paul de Man, Harold *Bloom, and Geoffrey Hartman, moving away from his strictly phenomenological interests towards deconstruction (as Derrida's various essays on *Husserl show, these two approaches are not completely incompatible). He became a key popularizer of *deconstruction, mediating its move out of French and Comparative Literature departments into more mainstream English departments. He then moved to the University of California Irvine, where the originator of deconstruction Jacques *Derrida was based. In 1976, in a presentation at the annual MLA (Modern Languages Association) conference entitled 'The Critic as Host', Miller effectively summed up his view of deconstruction as a kind of parasitical practice which dwells within and feeds off, but also poisons, the text it is working on. The presentation became famous for the elegant, yet utterly comprehensive way it repudiated M.H. Abrams attempt to refute deconstruction and in the process showed that when it comes to the close reading of texts deconstruction is more than a match for its predecessor *New Criticism. Miller's work tends to highlight the points of undecidability or tension in texts, showing that they never quite mean what they say, and somehow always mean more than they say.

Millett, Kate (1934–) American feminist scholar and activist best known for her book *Sexual Politics* (1970). Originally her PhD in English Literature at Columbia University, *Sexual Politics* offered a powerful critique of sexual inequality in western art and literature. She demonstrated the deeply embedded *patriarchal values in the works of writers like D.H. Lawrence, Henry Miller, and Norman Mailer (who retaliated with a waspish essay denouncing *political correctness in writing). By contrast, she argued, writers like Jean Genet offer a more nuanced account of the politics of sexuality. The book was an instant *cause célèbre*. Millett was featured on the cover of *Time* magazine and touted as the new face of *feminism and though she soon ceased to be a 'media darling' because she was outed as bisexual her work was nevertheless a vanguard text in *Second Wave feminism. However, despite being a committee member of the National Organization for Women, Millett did not pursue a position as spokeswoman for feminism, unlike Germaine *Greer, whose own breakthrough bestseller *The Female Eunuch* (1970) was published in the same year as *Sexual Politics*. She continued to write, and contribute to feminist debate, but focused more on developing an artists' colony in upstate New York.

mimesis The imitation of nature. Both Plato and Aristotle wrote extensively about mimesis, both were worried about its capacity to present the truth in contrast to the more reliable form of philosophy. In classical literature, mimesis is the opposite of *diegesis in that it refers to the attempt by an author to speak in a voice other than their own, specifically a character's. In more recent critical discourse mimesis has become a code phrase for *realism, or more precisely works of art that attempt to present reality in its most *everyday and mundane sense. The famous debate in the 1930s between Bertolt *Brecht and György *Lukács, two of the 20th-century's most important *Marxist critics, centred on the relative artistic value of mimesis, with Lukács arguing in favour of it, saying it was necessary to get away from the tales of aristocracy if the truth of society was to be told, and Brecht arguing against it by saying that the imitation of reality dulled the audience's mind and instead what they needed was to be shocked (the so-called *estrangement-effect). In the immediate aftermath of World War II, and perhaps in response to the shock of the war itself, mimesis was foregrounded as the pinnacle of artistic achievement, especially in literature, by Eric Auerbach's magisterial book *Mimesis* (1953), which showed that the goal of art since the earliest times had been to represent nature just as it is. In critical theory, mimesis has been important to a range of scholars, but most notably French *psychoanalyst Jacques *Lacan, and after him (adapting his ideas), the *postcolonial critics Homi *Bhabha and Michael *Taussig, who see in it the origins for a theory of *resistance. Bhabha, in particular, plays on the idea that the *subaltern, by imitating the *hegemonic other, i.e. the colonial master, escapes scrutiny and thereby creates the conditions necessary for political subversion. By the same token, inasmuch as the subaltern looks like their master in manner and dress, they compel the master to recognize that the *Other looks like them.

Further Reading: M. Potolsky *Mimesis* (2006).

mimicry A term used in *Postcolonial Studies to describe the paradoxical (or doubly articulated) state of affairs in colonial countries whereby the colonial power desires its subjugated others, namely the indigenous population of the occupied country, to look or at least act the same as the occupiers and yet fear that very outcome because it would dilute their own sense of difference and superiority. Mimicry is thus, as Homi *Bhabha theorizes, an ambivalent strategy whereby *subaltern peoples simultaneously express their subservience to the more powerful and subvert that power by making mimicry seem like mockery. A contemporary form of this can be seen today in the way in which call centre jobs from Australia, the UK, US, and elsewhere are exported to India precisely because as a direct result of colonization there are operators there who can mimic English speakers from those countries.

Further Reading: H. Bhabha *The Location of Culture* (1994).

mirror stage (*stade du miroir*) The stage of childhood development in which the *ego is formed according to Jacques *Lacan's *psychoanalysis. His theory is based on the so-called 'mirror test' conducted by his friend, the psychologist Henri Wallon, who compared the reactions to a mirror of 6-month-old human babies with similar aged chimpanzees. What was noteworthy about the experiment to Wallon, and hence Lacan, was the fact that the chimpanzees showed only limited interest in their reflection, whereas the human babies were utterly fascinated. Lacan concluded from this that the human babies had *misrecognized the image in the mirror as their actual selves. For the first time in their lives, the babies obtained an image of themselves as a whole (thus creating in them the *narcissistic sense that before that moment their body was *fragmented); by the same token, the babies see that their body is distinct from both their environment and the body of others. In this way, too, the subject is *alienated from itself. It introduces the subject into the *imaginary order.

misrecognition (*méconnaissance*) A process of self-identification in which a *subject assumes an identity they mistake for their own. The concept derives from Jacques *Lacan's account of the *mirror stage of childhood development in which the young child (under 18 months) sees itself in the mirror and mistakes that image for itself. While the image in the mirror is obviously an image *of* them, it isn't *actually* them, but the child fails to make this distinction. Thus the child's 'I' is the product of its *imaginary and the result of an illusion. Marxist critic Louis *Althusser adapts this idea in the development of his concept of *interpellation, which holds that *society constantly calls on its subjects to adopt a particular *identity (citizen, consumer, voter, etc.). But in doing so the subject is *alienated from their 'true' self.

mode of production Karl *Marx created this concept to distinguish between different periods in history according to the varying ways in which the forces and relations of production were organized. Forces of production are the tools, machinery, and energy sources a society is able to put at its disposal, while the relations of production are the network of social rules regarding the ownership and the use of the forces of production (this distinction effectively corresponds to that between *base and superstructure, which Marx also uses). Marx's thesis is that the composition of the economy—meaning, the relative forces available in a society and the distribution of access to those forces—conditions all other aspects of social life. As the great Marxist archaeologist V. Gordon Childe has pointed out, for a society to have artists and shamans it must first of all produce sufficient surplus food to support non-producing members. The greater the amount of surplus it produces the greater its potential to focus on addressing wants rather than needs. Thus, for Marx the essential point of distinction between modes of production is the amount of surplus it generates and who benefits from that surplus. He identifies four modes of production, Asiatic, ancient, feudal, and bourgeoisie, and prophesies a fifth, namely communism. He also speaks of three prehistorical modes of production corresponding to the Stone, Bronze, and Iron Ages. In contemporary critical theory, this concept is used by Louis *Althusser, and updated by Ernest Mandel, but probably its most widely debated incarnation is to be found in Fredric *Jameson's account of *postmodernism.

modernism An international artistic movement, encompassing all the arts from architecture to arts and crafts, film, and literature, that began in the latter part of the 19th century and finished in the middle of the 20th century. It falls between *realism, which it repudiated, and *postmodernism, which was faced with the task of trying to find something new and interesting to do after apparently every possible experiment had already been performed by its predecessor. And it encompasses, albeit uncertainly, a range of artistic movements, including: *Abstractionism, *Avant-gardism, *constructivism, cubism, *Dadaism, *Futurism, *Surrealism, and even *Situationism (to list only a few of the many creative factions that flourished during this period).

Its defining characteristic is captured by two famous phrases: Arthur Rimbaud's 'Il faut être absolument moderne!' (One must be absolutely modern!) and Ezra Pound's 'make it new', both of which enjoin artists to jettison tradition and experiment with the possibilities inherent in every medium, regardless of the apparent senselessness or indeed ugliness of the outcome. Pound's fellow American modernist Gertrude Stein thought that it was the duty of the work of art to strive for ugliness because only in that way could it be assured of being truly new (beauty being a lingering trace of past traditions).

The stem word 'modern', which derives from the Latin 'modo' (meaning current or of the moment), has been in use for nearly two thousand years. Its usage until the middle of the 19th century was generally unmarked, signalling no particular privilege or significance save that of currency. In *A Singular Modernity* (2002), Fredric *Jameson lists 14 different uses of the term modern from the Classical period up until the 1960s. The real question, then, he argues, is when and how did modern become the demand for the new? There is no straightforward answer to this question, but it is generally thought (although the details are hotly disputed) that modernism is the aesthetic complement of *modernity (change in the social sphere) and that its drive for change is rooted in the disruptions to social life brought about by *modernization (change in technology). That is to say, it was the changes in the conditions of daily life that enabled modernism to blossom.

This argument, which was presented powerfully and persuasively by Marshall Berman in *All that is Solid Melts into Air* (1982), reflects certain historical facts: modernism was an urban aesthetic—it celebrated and agonized over the new forms of life (and the various problems they entail) that the crowded cities of industrializing Europe afforded. The key change was the *alienation of individuals from their families, their villages, and their connection to the land: factory workers moved to the city to become wage-earners, but in doing so became separated from everything that they knew and took for granted.

Industrialization was thus a powerful force of change: it changed the structure of cities, it created a new class of people (the proletariat) and new things to spend money on (commodities). Ultimately, though, it was the First World War which brought about the most sweeping changes: it literally killed off the hidebound traditionalism of the Victorian era and introduced a new sense of urgency about the need to live life for all that it had to offer. Sigmund *Freud's theory of sexual repression struck a powerful chord with the post-war generation for precisely this reason: it sensed personal, social, and cultural constraints it was no longer prepared to accept or tolerate. It was in this flux that the first artists began to think of themselves as modernists and their art as modernism emerged.

Modernism was not a singular enterprise: it varied according to history and geography, or to put it another way it did not occur in the same way or at the same time in all countries. It was inspired and repulsed by the political experiments of the period: communism, fascism, Nazism, and socialism. Paris led the way, through the work of its poets Charles Baudelaire and Arthur Rimbaud, and its painters Edouard Manet and Paul Cézanne, and because of them expatriates like James Joyce, Pablo Picasso, and Igor Stravinsky flocked there, further enhancing its reputation. But modernism was a properly global phenomenon, if predominantly a white Anglo-Saxon male phenomenon, and variants of it occurred on virtually every continent. The highpoints of modernism are for the most part still revered and avidly studied today.

Further Reading: M. Calinescu *Five Faces of Modernity* (1987).
A. Compagnon *The Five Paradoxes of Modernity* (1994).
P. Childs *Modernism* (2000).
F. Jameson *The Modernist Papers* (2008).
T.J. Clark *Farewell to an Idea* (1999).

modernity The cultural and social world produced by and in reaction to the processes of *modernization, namely the advent of new ways of thinking (e.g. secularization) and the emergence of new technology (e.g. the steam engine). Modernity is used in two main ways in history and sociology: first, it can refer to any period of radical change, and in this sense there have been several periods of so-called modernity dating back to ancient times; second, it can refer to a very specific moment in history—but there is no general rule or agreement as to when this moment should be (other than that it should be one of the moments referred to in the first sense of the word). As Fredric *Jameson records in *A Singular Modernity* (2002), the word 'modern' has been in use since the 5th century AD and by his reckoning has been used to refer to at least 14 periods in history since then. Modernity in this first sense might be thought of as qualitative in that it refers only to a change in attitude; in contrast, then, we might thus specify that modernity in the second sense is quantitative in that it refers to a change in the very composition of society, not just in its attitudes. But there would still be the problem of which period counts as genuinely modern in this expanded sense and historians are divided in this regard between two principal moments in European history; the end of the 'dark ages' and the start of the industrial revolution. The choice itself depends on whether attitudes or technology is foregrounded (arguably, too, the change in attitudes was a necessary precursor to the invention of new technology). Generally, though, most uses of the term modernity tend to refer to the period also known as the Victorian era, particularly the latter half, i.e. from the 1870s onwards. As Jameson also points out, modernity is also the back-projection of *postmodernism—it is the mythical moment when 'now' began. *See also* ALTERNATE MODERNITY.

m

Further Reading: A. Appadurai *Modernity at Large: Cultural Dimensions in Globalization* (1996).
M. Berman *All That is Solid Melts into Air: Experience of Modernity* (1982).
A. Giddens *The Consequences of Modernity* (1991).

modernization The transformation of culture and society brought about by embracing a combination of new ways of thinking and new technology. A highly problematic concept in sociology and development studies, modernization theory assumes that all societies are on an evolutionary trajectory taking them from 'primitive' to 'modern' and that if they are not yet modern it is because they are reactionary and/or underdeveloped. This is problematic because it assumes that the western standard of living and lifestyle is the norm to which all societies should aspire; it also assumes that the western standard of living and lifestyle is implicitly the best available (in spite of the contrary evidence from environmental science). *Modernism is often thought of as a reaction to modernization, a means by which a particular society can absorb the shocks that rapid and radical change can cause. Modernization is also of interest to the **Annales* School of historians—their research asks why modernization occurred in one place and not another.

Further Reading: J. Timmons Roberts and A. Bellone Hite *From Modernization to Globalization: Social Perspectives on International Development* (1999).

moral criticism A tendency—rather than a recognized school—within literary criticism to judge literary works according to moral rather than formal principles. Moral criticism is not necessarily censorious or 'moralizing' in its approach, although it can be; nor does it necessarily imply a Christian perspective, although it often does. Moral critics include D.H. Lawrence, whose position was pagan, and extolled the virtue of 'life' as a force to be nourished through literature; T.S Eliot, who was Christian, and judged works in terms of their ability to clarify life, and give it meaning; F.R. *Leavis, who thought literature should be 'improving', that by reading it one should become a better person. Moral criticism is also concerned with the 'seriousness' of a work and whether its purpose is worthy of its means—it is from this perspective than one speaks of such things as 'gratuitous' sex in a novel, or nudity in a film, when it isn't seen to serve the moral purpose of the narrative.

Moscow Linguistic Circle Discussion group founded by Roman *Jakobson for the purpose of investigating the poetic function of language which, together with the St Petersburg-based **Opoyaz*, formed the core of *Russian Formalism. Its membership included such key figures as Victor *Shklovsky and Yuri Tynyanov, who would both also play a major part in advancing the theoretical development of Russian Formalism. The group sought to connect poetics and linguistics to show you could not properly understand one in the absence of the other.

Further Reading: T. Bennett *Formalism and Marxism* (1979).
V. Erlich *Russian Formalism: History—Doctrine* (1955).

multitude In *Empire* (2000) and (more explicitly) in *Multitude* (2004), Michael *Hardt and Antonio *Negri adapt the Spinozian term to conceive of a new form of political subjectivity. Consisting of *singularities rather than individuals, that is to say social subjects who cannot be reduced to their *bare life, the multitude is, according to Hardt and Negri, the only form of political subjectivity capable of realizing democracy for what it truly is, namely the rule of everyone by everyone. It is an immanent rather than transcendent concept, so it should not be confused with the idea of a people—it is not unified, but multiple and plural; by the same token, it is not anarchic or incoherent, but joined up by power of what its constituents have in common. Hardt and Negri emphasize the changing composition of labour, particularly the increase in what they refer to as *immaterial labour, in support of this point. In the era of the multitude, they argue, race and gender (among many other possible identity differences) will still be important, but they will no longer determine hierarchies of power, or, what amounts to the same thing, regimes of inclusion and exclusion. Hardt and Negri claim, somewhat problematically (as many commentators have remarked), that the multitude is constantly being brought into being by the changes to the composition of capital and society that capitalism itself is unwittingly bringing about.

Further Reading: G. Balakrishnan (ed.) *Debating Empire* (2003).
M. Hardt and A. Negri *Multitude: War and Democracy in the Age of Empire* (2004).
P. Virno, *A Grammar of the Multitude* (2004).

myth **1.** The Swiss psychoanalyst Carl *Jung proposed that the comparative study of myths could be used to understand and interpret the dreams and hallucinations of psychotic patients. For Jung myths are metaphors or dramatizations of the inner workings of the dimension of the *psyche he calls the *archetype, which in Jungian theory is the inherited part of the mind, namely our link to the *collective unconscious. In a manner that Jung thought potentially therapeutic, myths illustrate to us the dangers of an archetype being given free rein. Myths can thus be treated as revelations of the structure of the pre-conscious psyche, that is, the psyche of pure archetypes as yet undomesticated by consciousness. The crucial implication here is that Jung assumes that the behaviour of the unconscious resembles the structure of myths, so when mythic elements appear in the course of treatment they are accorded a high level of significance. Canadian literary critic Northrop *Frye adapts Jung's theory in *Anatomy of Criticism* (1957) to develop his own powerful form of analysis of literature as essentially mythic.

2. The great French anthropologist Claude *Lévi-Strauss transformed the study of myth in a famous essay, 'The Structural Study of Myth' (1955), which asked the apparently innocent question: if the content of myths is contingent, if anything can be incorporated into a myth as seems apparent from the incredible richness of the world's vast collection of myths created throughout the centuries, then how do we account for their apparent similarity of form? Lévi-Strauss answers this question, which encapsulates the *structuralist approach in a nutshell, by drawing on the insights of Swiss linguist Ferdinand de *Saussure who observed that similar sounds recur in different languages, but have different meanings and argued that in the case of spoken language it is the combination of sounds (i.e. the form) that is significant, not the specific sounds themselves (i.e. the content). Applied to myth, as Lévi-Strauss explains, this logic results in the almost completely opposite view to Jung—now the elements of a myth (the challenges the hero must face, the special powers brought to bear, and so on) can be considered significant only in terms of the combination of their relations with other elements and not for themselves. The specific combination of elements will vary from myth to myth, but the way of producing this combination is unique to myth and universal according to Lévi-Strauss. Myths have the following constitutive characteristics: they are timeless or simultaneously historical and ahistorical (e.g. as Benedict *Anderson argues in his account of *imagined communities, although nations are only a comparatively recent invention in history, they always present themselves as eternal, as having always been there); they are the opposite of poetry inasmuch as they can be translated from language to language, from one type of media to another, without loss of coherence or consequence (and thus, there is no such thing as the 'true' or 'original' form of a myth—the myth consists of all its variations taken together); and they are effective or *performative (their telling is itself a kind of message). This last idea has been taken up by Fredric *Jameson in *Signatures of the Visible* (1992) to suggest that contemporary Hollywood films can be read as symbolic solutions to real problems, and that is why cinema has such an important place in society today.

3. Inspired by Bertolt *Brecht's concept of *estrangement, French literary critic Roland *Barthes developed a concept of myth as a critique of 'naturalness' (i.e. that which appears to simply occur without any historical determination, just as the sun does every morning). In a series of short essays initially published in the cultural journal, *Les Lettres nouvelles*, and subsequently republished in book form as *Mythologies* (1957), translated as *Mythologies* (1972), Barthes used myth as a codephrase for that which 'goes without saying' because it is so widely accepted as a 'truth', and by this means he tried to demonstrate that what passes for 'truth' is in fact the result of careful *ideological stage-managing. As Barthes puts it in the afterword to *Mythologies*, the widely read essay 'Myth Today', myth's key principle is to transform history into nature. In the same essay, Barthes attempted to synthesize his theory of myth as follows: myth is a special type of speech (by which he means coded form of language use or communication); myth is not an object, idea, or concept, but rather a form of signification (it is a process rather than a thing); anything can be turned into a myth, though not everything is a myth (they are subject to history); myths are constructed from material that has already been worked on (they are a second-order or meta system that uses pre-existing symbols and icons); myths are not universal, they have to be dealt with in the specificity. Myths can thus take a variety of different forms—at the end of his essay, Barthes lists seven common varieties, all of which can be found in abundance in virtually any newspaper.

myth criticism The study of both myths as literature and literature as myths—in the former case, myths are read for their own specific literary merit and as historical precursors to later literary texts (Sophocles' trilogy of plays surrounding the myth of Oedipus would be one example); in the latter case, which has been the more influential of the two approaches, literary texts are read as creative reworkings of myths. A number of prominent scholars have operated in this field: the most notable are Mircea Eliade, Leslie Fiedler, Northrop *Frye, René Girard, Carl *Jung, G. Wilson Knight, and Paul *Ricoeur.

mythopoeic A form of literature that has the structure, look and feel of a myth, but is in fact a contemporary creation rather than a story passed down by tradition. The word was created by one of the genre's great practitioners, J.R.R. Tolkien, author of *The Lord of the Rings* (1954–5). Although the bulk of mythopoeic texts tend to be works like Tolkien's, namely fantasy, this is not exclusively the case. As Richard Slotkin demonstrates in a powerful work, *Regeneration* *through Violence* (1974), works of so-called serious literature to do with the history of a nation can also be classified as mythopoeic. For example, the cycle of *Rambo* films taken together offer a potent counter-narrative to standard accounts of American history—in Rambo's universe the Vietnam War was won by its soldiers, but lost by the politicians.

Nancy, Jean-Luc (1940–) French post-structuralist philosopher. A prolific author of books on the German Romantic tradition in philosophy, including its 20th century adherents such as Martin *Heidegger.

Born in Caudéran, near Bordeaux, Nancy studied at lycées in Baden-Baden and Bergerac, before pursuing university studies in Toulouse, then the Sorbonne. At the Sorbonne, he studied with Georges *Canguilhem and Paul *Ricoeur, the latter directing his thesis on *Hegel's philosophy of religion. After graduating from the Sorbonne he was given a position at the University of Strasbourg, where he intended to complete a doctorate in theology, though in the end he wrote on *Kant. For his Doctorat d'État, which he completed at Toulouse in 1987, he wrote on the problem of the experience of freedom in Kant, Schelling, and Hegel (Jacques *Derrida and Jean-François *Lyotard were both on the examining committee).

Often seen as fellow traveller of Jacques Derrida, the latter in fact saw Nancy as 'postdeconstructionist', which is a backhanded way of acknowledging the originality of his work while stipulating that deconstruction nevertheless conditions it. Nancy's work is primarily concerned to develop philosophical critiques of political concepts such as community, freedom, and indeed humanity. The principal purpose of these critiques—which is consistent with Derrida's *deconstructionist project—is the identification of an ontologically 'pure' form of political concepts, freed from their contamination by the philosophically suspect interests of party and *ideology. Purity is, however, impossible in Nancy's view because unity is impossible; for Nancy *ontology is only ever a matter of fragments whose relation to one another is at best uncertain. In the years since his heart transplant, Nancy's focus has shifted away from commentaries on other thinkers towards the development of a philosophy of his own, albeit one guided by the conviction that philosophical systems are impossible. It is in this phase that he has produced what are widely regarded as his most important works: *La Communauté désoeuvrée* (1986), translated as *The Inoperative Community* (1991), *Être singulier pluriel* (1996), translated as *Being Singular Plural* (2000), and *La*

Création du monde; ou, La Mondialisation (2002), translated as *The Creation of the World or Globalization* (2007). Nancy is also widely known outside of academia for his bestselling account of his heart transplant operation, *L'intrus* (2000) which was made into a film of the same name by Claire Denis. He has also written several books in collaboration with his University of Strasbourg colleague Philippe *Lacoue-Labarthe.

Further Reading: J. Derrida *Le Toucher, Jean-Luc Nancy* (2000), translated as *On Touching, Jean-Luc Nancy* (2005).
B. Hutchens *Jean-Luc Nancy and the Future of Philosophy* (2005).
I. James *The Fragmentary Demand* (2006).
D. Sheppard et al. (eds.) *On Jean-Luc Nancy: The Sense of Philosophy* (1997).

narcissism An intense form of self-regard, or attraction to one's image. The term is derived from Ancient Greek mythology, which tells of a young man called Narcissus so fascinated by his own reflection that he drowns trying to embrace it. *Psychoanalyst Sigmund *Freud adopted the term from British sexologist Havelock Ellis to theorize male homosexuality as sexual attraction to an image of oneself. Freud later rejected this as an explanation of homosexuality, but he retained the concept of narcissism to describe the situation in which *libido is withdrawn from external *objects and redirected towards the *ego. According to Freud, this is how children begin life (a stage he refers to as primary narcissism), and only gradually move away from this towards a situation in which *cathexis is sought in the outside world.

narratology The study of the structure, function, and effect of narrative initiated by *Russian Formalism and developed into a highly specialist sub-discipline by *structuralism. In particular, narratology draws on the crucial distinction between **fabula* and *sjužet* developed by Russian Formalism which distinguishes between the actual events in a story and the imaginative way these events are described. In this respect, Vladimir *Propp's analyses of the formal structure or morphology of Russian folktales, which compared hundreds of traditional stories and broke them down into 31 basic narrative functions and 7 character types, was foundational. By emphasizing form over content, narratology is able to show similarity between stories that might otherwise appear to contain quite different subject matter. Popular fiction studies provides a good example of this by demonstrating the structural similarity of Mills & Boon romances and Jane Austen's novels. The major narratological theorists after Propp are Claude *Lévi-Strauss, Roland *Barthes, Algirdas *Greimas, and Gerard *Genette.

Further Reading: M. Bal *Narratology: Introduction to the Theory of Narrative* (1997).

national allegory A type of narrative whose essential subject is the nation state. Because the life of a nation, large or small, exceeds the capacity of what any novel can actually accommodate, narrative fiction of this type uses *allegory as a means of expressing a dimension of existence greater than that of the lives of its individual characters. National allegory tends to be focused on the lives of ordinary people, however, rather than heads of state or aristocracy, using their mundane daily struggles as a means of illustrating the state of the nation. First conceived by Fredric *Jameson in his monograph on Wyndham Lewis, *Fables of Aggression* (1979), and developed further in an article entitled 'Third-World Literature in the Era of Multinational Capitalism' (1986), national allegory is a highly controversial concept and has been the subject of considerable debate, particularly in *Postcolonial Studies. Jameson suggests that Sembène Ousmane's novel *Xala* (1974) is a perfect illustration of a national allegory because the predicament of its central characters can only be fully understood from the perspective of the nation. *See also* GEOPOLITICAL AESTHETIC.

Further Reading: A. Ahmad *In Theory* (1992).
J. Beverley *Subalternity and Repression: Arguments in Cultural Theory* (1999).
C. Irr and I. Buchanan (eds.) *On Jameson* (2006).
I. Szeman *Zones of Instability: Literature, Postcolonialism, and the Nation* (2003).

nativism The desire to return to, or restore, indigenous practices, beliefs, and cultural forms inhibited, destroyed, or outlawed by a colonizing power. It generally holds the view that indigenous practices are more authentic and therefore more culturally nourishing than the adopted or imposed western practices. The discourse of nativism became especially prominent in the 1950s, when the *decolonization process was at its peak. It can be compared with **négritude*, but its focus is more narrow—rather than celebrate the shared fate of a *race, it tends to foreground absolute difference. Nativism is problematized in *Postcolonial Studies in two ways: first, there is the question of to what extent it is even possible to restore indigenous practices under conditions of modernity (Cambodia's destruction of its western-style hospitals under Pol Pot in the 1970s is an extreme version of this dilemma); second, there is the question of the desirability of doing so, especially when these practices would lead to the reduction of gains in rights on the part of minority groups, women, and so on (as for example in Rwanda in the 1990s when the assertion of one ethnic group's nativist ideas led to the near genocide of the other). Chinua Achebe's novel *Things Fall Apart* (1958) is a vivid working through of these troubling paradoxes.

Further Reading: J. Beverley *Subalternity and Repression: Arguments in Cultural Theory* (1999).
I. Szeman *Zones of Instability: Literature, Postcolonialism, and the Nation* (2003).

negative dialectics A new form of *dialectical thinking developed by Theodor *Adorno in *Negative Dialektik* (1966), translated as *Negative Dialectics* (1973), which many regard as his magnum opus. Written with the explicit aim of radicalizing western philosophy as a whole by generating a mode of what he termed non-identity thinking, *Negative Dialectics* offers a bold programme for an immanent and self-reflexive critique of philosophy rather than a specific concept. This programme can be understood as the attempt to resolve, though not once and for all, two different problems: first, if concepts are not identical with their objects then in a certain sense they are inadequate to the task of defining objects; second, if we are aware of this, but accept that philosophy has no other resource for understanding and defining objects except the concept, then we have to figure out how to create an adequate form of philosophy using means we know to be inadequate. Concepts cannot be identical with objects by definition. So this isn't simply a problem of a poorly conceived concept that could be remedied by creating a better concept. The problem is exacerbated by the fact that both concepts and objects change over time. Thus, every concept has a history and is embedded within history. Adorno's solution to this twofold problem is to build a critique of concepts into his critique of philosophy. Since this is a working with (rather than a resolving of) the fundamental problem of the inadequacy of concepts it is described as *negative* dialectics. That is to say, it is a restless form of thinking which does not proceed from, or expect to arrive at a transcendental or transcendent ground or principle. Negative dialectics directs philosophy to confront the interfaces between concepts, objects, ideas, and the material world.

Further Reading: D. Held *Introduction to Critical Theory* (1980).
S. Jarvis *Adorno: A Critical Introduction* (1998).

Negri, Antonio (1933–) Italian *Marxist political philosopher best known for his collaborative writings with Michael *Hardt. A measure of his significance may be gauged from Michel *Foucault's remark in 1980 that Negri had been imprisoned for his ideas—very few theorists can claim that status.

Negri was born in Padua, in Italy. He became politically active at a young age, via the Roman Catholic youth organization, 'Gioventú

Italiana di Azione Cattolica', which he joined in the early 1950s. He joined the Italian Socialist Party in 1956. He studied political theory at the University of Padua and obtained a position there as a professor upon graduation, teaching state and constitutional theory. In 1969 Negri co-founded 'Potere Operaio' (Workers' Power), a 'workerist' (*operaismo*) political group that organized protests in factories on behalf of labour. The group disbanded in 1973 and Negri joined the Autonomia Operai Organizzata (Autonomous Workers' Organization), contributing numerous theoretical articles.

In April 1979 Negri was arrested along with several other members of the Autonomia movement and charged with several offences alleging a connection with the 'Brigate Rosse' (Red Brigades). Negri was also charged with masterminding the Red Brigades' 1978 kidnapping and murder of Aldo Moro, the leader of the Christian Democratic Party. He was exonerated of the latter charge, but was nevertheless convicted on the association charge and in 1984 sentenced (in absentia) to 30 years in prison. He was given an additional four years on the charge of being 'morally responsible' for the violence of political activists in the 1960s and 1970s. He spent four years in jail waiting for his trial, in which time he was elected to the Italian legislature on the Radical Party's ticket. He was freed from prison on parliamentary privilege grounds, but this was revoked by the Italian Chamber of Deputies. Rather than return to prison he fled to France with the aid of Amnesty International and Félix *Guattari.

In France, he obtained a position at the University of Paris VIII in Saint Denis, where his colleagues included Alain *Badiou and Gilles *Deleuze. It was while he was teaching in Paris that he met a young student by the name of Michael Hardt, with whom he would produce a number of collaborative works in the decades to follow. In 1997 he returned to Italy to voluntarily serve out his sentence, hoping the gesture would raise awareness concerning the situation of the hundreds of other political exiles involved in radical activities in the 1960s and 1970s. His sentence was commuted and in 2003 he was released. The time in prison was productive for Negri: the first of his collaborations with Michael Hardt were completed there, *The Labor of Dionysus* (1994), which combined translations of older pieces by Negri with some new pieces written by Hardt, and the international bestseller *Empire* (2000).

It was the publication of *Empire* that catapulted both Negri and Hardt to the front ranks of *critical theory. The book appeared shortly after the so-called 'Battle in Seattle' (November 1999) in which the worldwide anti-globalization *social movement shot to prominence and it seemed to offer a powerful new message of hope. Hardt and Negri propose that a new form of *sovereignty has emerged since

World War II, which they term *Empire, and argue that it is global in nature and already more potent than any nation state. They also argue that the new global processes of manufacturing, managing labour, and finance, known as *globalization, are changing the very composition of capital, and in doing so creating a new class, which they term the *multitude, and thereby opening up a new chapter in the history of *class struggle. In an era when most other writers on the Left are making gloomy pronouncements about the rise of neo-conservativism, Hardt and Negri's work is a breath of fresh air. Not surprisingly, then, *Empire* was a runaway bestseller.

The events of September 11, 2001, changed the international political climate quite dramatically and Hardt and Negri's sequel to *Empire*, *Multitude: War and Democracy in the Age of Empire* (2005) was, comparatively speaking, cold-shouldered. The critics who greeted *Empire* enthusiastically now sharpened their knives. In part this was because *Multitude* does not really answer the questions raised by the previous book—it still doesn't explain how the multitude will bring about social change. Hardt and Negri tend to take the view that the sheer fact that the multitude exists means that social change has already occurred, and regardless of how technically accurate this might be it doesn't satisfy most readers. Time will tell if the third volume of the trilogy, *Commonwealth* (2009), will answer this demand.

The decade since the publication of *Empire* has been incredibly productive for Negri. In addition to the Empire trilogy he has produced several volumes of essays and interviews adding to and explaining the basic theses entailed in that trilogy.

Further Reading: T. Murphy and A-K. Mustapha (eds.) *The Philosophy of Antonio Negri*, 2 vols (2005, 2007).

***négritude* (blackness)** A neologism coined by Martinican poet and politician Aimé *Césaire that appropriates the derogatory 'nègre' (whose cognates in English would include 'negro' and 'nigger') and turns it into a positive. The most famous instance of this is in Césaire's powerful prose poem *Cahier d'un retour au pays natal* (1939), translated as *Notebook of a Return to My Native Land* (2001), which contains the line 'Haiti, where négritude stood up for the first time and said it believed in its humanity'. The reference to Haiti is in fact a reference to the leader of the slave revolt of 1791, Toussaint Louverture. As a movement, *négritude* was established by a small group of African-Caribbean scholars in Paris in the 1930s—including the future leader of Senegal Léopold Sédar Senghor and the poet Léon Damas—who, under the influence of the Harlem Renaissance in the US (particularly the poet Langston Hughes, who spent time in Paris in the early 1920s, but also W.E.B. *Du Bois and Jamaican-born Marcus Garvey) as well as *Surrealism in Paris, undertook a kind of mental decolonization through poetry and writing. It was primarily aimed at celebrating African heritage (in a deliberately essentialist manner), specifically an African personality or affectivity, as a means of affirming existence in a racist, white-dominated world. It took as its purview the entire black *diaspora as well as Africa itself. This bold standpoint was praised by Jean-Paul *Sartre in his famous preface to Senghor's 1948 collection of poetry, *Anthologie de la nouvelle poésie nègre et malgache de langue française* (Anthology of New Black and Malagasy Poetry). *Négritude* was not without its critics, however, even from within the black community. It was attacked by the *Creoleness writers for its monolithic outlook; it was also attacked by Nigerian Nobel laureate Wole Soyinka for accepting the inferior term handed out by the European powers instead of constructing its own positive term. Soyinka saw in *négritude* what he thought of as an unhealthy fetishism of the 'native' state. Although it was an important movement for several decades, its force is all but spent now.

Further Reading: B. Moore-Gilbert *Postcolonial Theory: Contexts, Practices, Politics* (1997).
V. Mudimbe *The Idea of Africa* (1994).
E. Said *Culture and Imperialism* (1993).

neo-colonialism The perseverance or renewal of colonial institutions (particularly models and style of governance), practices and thinking after *decolonization. The term was proposed by the Ghanaian independence leader Kwame Nkrumah in *Neo-Colonialism: The Last Stage of Imperialism* (1965). His thesis is that although countries such as his own Ghana achieved independence from their previous colonial overlords, their economies and hence their political situations continued to be defined and shaped by external powers under the structural conditions now known as *globalization. This is particularly true of resource-rich nations like Nigeria, which has abundant oil, but little in the way of manufacturing, and is therefore dependent on global markets for its wealth. Theorists of *Empire, such as Michael *Hardt and Antonio *Negri, see this condition of neo-colonialism as central to the new world order in which power exerts itself temporally (through the flows of finance or people) rather than spatially or territorially.

neo-racism Étienne *Balibar's term for the prevalent new modality of racism he calls 'racism without race', which emerged in the 1970s. Whereas racism used to be premised on the idea of *race as biological heredity, now in the postcolonial era it tends to be focused on 'cultural differences'. It surfaces in debates about immigration, assimilation, and multiculturalism and although its tone tends to be respectful its intent is always to preserve the pillars of racial segregation both ideologically and practically. Indeed, the very question of whether or not immigration might cause 'cultural' difficulties (whatever form these might take—e.g. the loss of cultural distinctness, or dilution of tradition) is neo-racist in form according to Balibar. Samuel P. Huntington's highly influential *The Clash of Civilizations and the Remaking of the World Order* (1998) is a highly sophisticated example of neo-racism inasmuch as it insists on the universality and immutability of ethnic characteristics.

Further Reading: Ê. Balibar and I. Wallerstein *Race, nation, classe: les identités ambiguës* (1988), translated as *Race, Nation, Class: Ambiguous Identities* (1991).

neo-realism An Italian cinematic movement that lasted from 1942 to 1952. Luchino Visconti's *Ossessione* (Obsession, 1942) is generally credited as being the first neo-realist film, but Roberto Rossellini's *Roma città aperta* (Rome Open City, 1945) is usually regarded as the archetype of the genre. Conceived in response to the regulation of film content imposed by Mussolini's fascist regime which prohibited the depiction of crime or immorality (indeed, anything that did not show Italy in the best possible light), neo-realism sought to counter the unreality of the propaganda films with an aesthetic described by Rossellini as moral because its central purpose was to confront audiences with their own reality. Neo-realism's aesthetic had four basic principles: (i) it should project a moment of *everyday life rather than construct a fictional tale; (ii) it should focus on social reality, i.e. the lives of the majority of people, the poor peasants and urban dwellers eking out an existence under difficult conditions, not the privileged few; (iii) it should use non-professional actors and improvised script so as to preserve the natural speech rhythms of the people it represents; (iv) and for the same reason it should film on location using hand-held cameras, rather than in a studio. Only one film, namely Vittorio De Sica's *Ladri di bicicletti* (The Bicycle Thieves, 1948), actually adhered to all four of these precepts. Neo-realism was a significant influence on the *French New Wave as well as a host of other directors such as the great Indian novelist and film-maker Satyajit Ray. Gilles *Deleuze, in his two-volume 'natural history' of cinema, cites neo-realism as the moment when cinema finally breaks free of an action-reaction mode of narrative and develops a true cinema of ideas.

neostructuralism Manfred *Frank's term for what is more usually referred to as *poststructuralism. Frank argues that post-structuralism is inappropriately named because the body of work it refers to cannot be thought of or understood independently of *structuralism. In his view, it is better thought of as neostructuralism because it can be seen as a continuation of the structuralist project, with new means. As Frank sees it, neostructuralism is an essentially French movement, albeit one with adherents all over the world, that owes its impetus to the events of *May '68. Astutely, Frank identifies a common distaste for the metaphysical concepts of domination and system linking the otherwise quite disparate work of Jacques *Derrida, Gilles *Deleuze, Michel *Foucault, Julia *Kristeva, and Jean-François *Lyotard. But he is troubled by what he sees as an amoral celebration of the death of the subject that goes together with this position.

Further Reading: M. Frank *Was ist Neostrukturalismus?* (1984), translated as *What is Neostructuralism?* (1989).

neurosis A general term for a 'nervous' disease, i.e. a psychological disease without an organic cause. The term was first used in 1777 by Scottish doctor William Cullen. By the 19th century the term was in widespread use for a large variety of disorders ranging from stomach complaints to heart palpitations. Present-day usage, however, tends to conform to Sigmund *Freud's conceptualization of it in his account of *hysteria. Freud adopted the term in the 1890s and it soon became central to the development of *psychoanalysis as the prime example of a type of psychological disturbance that, in contrast to *psychosis, is susceptible to the *talking cure. On Freud's understanding of it, neurosis is the outward, symbolic expression of a psychical conflict in the subject's *unconscious—it manifests itself in a variety of symptoms, such as *compulsion to repeat, *fetishism, and so on. We become neurotic, according to Freud, as a defence against, or compromise with, an unconscious conflict. Freud also found that in conscious life the subject seems to derive satisfaction from their neurosis (which Freud referred to as the secondary gain of illness), and often exhibit considerable reluctance to 'cure' themselves in therapy.

New Criticism A mode of literary analysis that developed in the southern US in the 1930s and 1940s and became the dominant way of reading and thinking about literature in the American academy until the advent of *structuralism in the 1960s.

New Criticism treats the literary work of art as a stand-alone, self-sufficient object that can only be properly appreciated in isolation. Careful attention to the specificity of language use, a process usually referred to as 'close reading', should tell the reader everything they need to know about a text. The New Critics regarded every text (providing it was of a sufficiently high standard to be deemed literary in the first place) as singular and ineffable, its meaning unique and incapable of being expressed by any other means. For this reason New Critics prized and all but insisted on 'difficulty' with regard to language use (a preference which would later earn them the charge of elitism), making it an essential cornerstone in their attempt to define the 'good' literary object. By 'difficulty' the New Critics essentially meant polysemy (as the *structuralists would subsequently call it) or multiple meanings. Like the *Russian Formalists before them, and with a similar zeal for the technical side of writing, the New Critics wanted to distinguish literature from non-literature in purely formal terms, which is to say purely on the basis of the language use.

The New Critics were inspired by I.A. *Richards' famous experiment with Cambridge students in which he gave them poems to analyse but told them neither the title nor the author of the pieces selected and interrogated their responses, finding them wanting in both sensitivity and skill. The results of this experiment, written up in *Practical Criticism: A Study of Literary Judgement* (1929), struck a chord with the New Critics who also thought that literary studies needed to be taught differently, with more rigour than it had been in the past. New Criticism's immense influence in North America, which lasted well into the 1980s, stems from the fact that it paid serious attention to the problem of how to teach literature. In contrast to *Practical Criticism, which was very much centred around F.R. Leavis in Cambridge, New Criticism had several focal points—the key names in the field were: John Crowe Ransom, Allen Tate, Cleanth Brooks, R.P. Blackmur, W.K. Wimsatt, and Monroe Beardsley.

Further Reading: T. Eagleton *Literary Theory: An Introduction* (1983).

New Historicism A movement in literary and cultural criticism that began in the US in the late 1970s and early 1980s, largely in Renaissance and Shakespeare studies, but eventually branching out to connect with a variety of other topic areas such as *Postcolonial Studies. Stephen *Greenblatt's *Renaissance Self-Fashioning* (1980) is usually credited with being the inaugurating text of the movement, although the term itself wasn't minted until *The Power of Forms in the English Renaissance* (1982). Greenblatt's name is undoubtedly the one most closely associated with New Historicism, though of course there are several others involved as well such as Catherine Gallagher, Jeffrey Knapp, Louis Montrose, Stephen Orgel, and Walter Benn Michaels. New Historicism does not have a specific methodology, at least not one as rigorously worked out as, say, *psychoanalysis and is in many respects anti-theoretical in its outlook. Its actual practice of reading texts is not dissimilar to the model of 'close reading' espoused by both *New Criticism and *Practical Criticism. Where it differs from its precursors, however, is in its conviction that literary texts can in fact tell us something about the world outside of the text, something that both New Criticism and Practical Criticism explicitly proscribe. But unlike *historical materialism, with which it is frequently compared (not the least because Greenblatt studied with Raymond *Williams at Cambridge), it takes the view that the interpretation of cultural texts better enables us to understand history, rather than the other way round as historical materialism would insist. Opponents of New Historicism, like Fredric *Jameson, argue that cultural texts are symptoms of history, whereas for New Historicism cultural texts are agents of history; they are the means by which history is made. This view rests on the idea that history itself comprises performances, representations, and symbolic exchanges. New Historicism draws on the work of Michel *Foucault, particularly his late work on power and *subjectivity, as well as Clifford *Geertz, especially his concept of 'thick description'.

Further Reading: J. Brannigan *New Historicism and Cultural Materialism* (1998).
C. Colebrook *New Literary Histories* (1997).
A. Veeser (ed.) *The New Historicism* (1989).

New Philosophers (*nouveaux philosophes*) A group of young French philosophers who, despite their previous attachments to Maoism, publicly broke with *Marxism in the early 1970s, following the publication of Russian dissident writer Alexander Solzhenitsyn's account of the gulags in the Soviet Union. The very loosely knit group included André Glucksmann, Alain Finkielkraut, Bernard-Henri Lévy, and Guy Lardreau, argued that western philosophy, but especially the Marxist-Hegelian tradition, had led to and legitimated the gulags and was therefore to be rejected in favour of a new philosophy not devoted to the totalizing goals of the older styles of philosophical system. The highpoint of this line of thought, however, came from outside the group in the form of Jean-François *Lyotard's proclamation (in his book on the *differend) that our ethical duty is to wage war on totality. Michel *Foucault was claimed by the New Philosophers as one of their own and though he gave several sympathetic interviews to its members, it is clear that he was not comfortable with their wholesale rejection of the Left. Foucault's friend, Gilles *Deleuze, had no such sympathy and was utterly scathing in his rejection of the New Philosophers as being neither new nor philosophers, but just a bunch of grandstanding hacks playing to an anti-intellectual media.

Nietzsche, Friedrich (1844–1900) See overleaf.

NIETZSCHE, FRIEDRICH (1844–1900)

German philosopher, generally ranked with Immanuel *Kant and G.W.F. *Hegel in terms of his influence. Indeed, French philosopher Michel *Foucault ranks him as equal to Karl *Marx and Sigmund *Freud in terms of his influence on 20th century thought. While this claim undoubtedly has merit, it is perhaps difficult to see the justification for it at first glance. It is true that Nietzscheanism isn't as widely known as either *Marxism or *psychoanalysis is, yet in many ways it is Nietzsche's scepticism that opened the way for these other two *discursive regimes (to use Foucault's own terms). Adding to the mystery is the fact that Nietzsche was scarcely known in his own lifetime; indeed his books sold so badly he had to pay for them to be privately published. Yet in the 20th century there is no continental philosopher of note that does not acknowledge Nietzsche's importance.

Nietzsche was born in Röcken, a small town near Leipzig in Germany. His father, a former teacher, was the pastor of the local Lutheran church. Nietzsche had a younger sister and brother as well. His sister is a controversial figure in Nietzsche studies because of the hand she played in distorting Nietzsche's work by selectively editing his final unfinished manuscript, *Der Wille zur Macht* (The Will to Power) so as to make it appear utterly anti-Semitic, which would later make it appear amenable to the core ideological values of Nazism. Archival research in the 1960s by two Italian philologists, Giorgio Colli and Mazzino Montinari (who were preparing materials for a translation of the complete works of Nietzsche), showed conclusively that *Der Wille zur Macht* was a fabrication and in a very real sense 'did not exist'. Nietzsche's sister cut more than 1500 pages from his text and reordered the paragraphs to substantially alter their meaning. Indeed, the very title was a fiction—Nietzsche himself saw the project as an attempt to revalue all values.

Nietzsche's father died in 1849 necessitating a move to Naumberg, where the family resided with his father's unmarried sisters. Nietzsche went to seminary school in Naumberg, where he showed aptitude in a range of subjects, including music. In 1864 he commenced theological studies at the University of Bonn, but left after only one semester. He then moved to the University of Leipzig to study philosophy. Before he had completed his studies there he was, quite remarkably, offered a professorship in philosophy at the University of Basel in 1869. At the age of 24 he was and remains one of the youngest scholars to be offered such a post. In 1870 he served for a year as a medical orderly in the Prussian army then returned to his post in Basel, from which he observed the formation of the German State under Bismarck with some distaste. In his early years at Basel he was intimate with the musician Richard Wagner, frequently visiting him and his family at their house on Lake Lucerne.

Nietzsche's first book appeared in 1872, *Die Geburt der Tragödie aus dem Geiste der Musik*, translated as *The Birth of Tragedy* (1993), but in a pattern that was to be typical of all his books it was treated with suspicion and ultimately disdain. The main problem was its style: Nietzsche eschewed the classical model for the presentation and development of a philosophical argumentation in favour of a more speculative style that offended the sensibilities of his peers. Written in part as defence of Wagner, *The Birth of Tragedy* was later disavowed by Nietzsche, who felt the binary it constructed between Apollonine and Dionysiac tendencies in art was overly simplistic. His next book, *Unzeitgemässe Betrachtungen* (1876), translated as *Untimely Meditations* (1997), consisted of four essays on German culture, history, Wagner, and Schopenhauer. In his marvellous little portrait, *Nietzsche* (1994), Michael Tanner recommends that this largely neglected book be read alongside Matthew Arnold's near contemporary work *Culture and Anarchy* (1869) as a kind of antidote. His future work would jettison the narrative structure of these essays and aim for something less readily digestible, not aphorisms exactly but something close to that.

Nietzsche attended Wagner's music festival at Bayreuth in 1876 and was so disappointed by its populist atmosphere that he decided to break with Wagner altogether. He responded to this break, which he described as personally shattering, with a prolific outpouring of writing. He wrote almost a book a year for the next decade, including: *Menschliches, Allzumenschliches: Ein Buch für freie Geister* (1878), translated as *Human, All Too Human: A Book for Free Spirits* (1996); *Morgenröte. Gedanken über die moralischen Vorurteile* (1881), translated as *Daybreak: Thoughts on the Prejudices of Morality* (1997); and *Die fröhliche Wissenschaft* (1882), translated as *The Gay Science* (1974). This amazing productivity notwithstanding, in 1879 Nietzsche resigned his position at the University of Basel. His health, never strong to begin with, had deteriorated to such an extent that it became impractical to continue working. For the next ten years he led a peripatetic existence shuttling between Germany, Austria and Italy in search of climate conducive to good health and writing.

In Turin in January 1889, Nietzsche suffered a psychotic breakdown. Legend has it that he saw a horse being whipped in the Piazza Carlo Alberto and ran towards it to protect it by placing his arms around its neck. He then collapsed to the ground weeping. In the following couple of days he wrote a handful of postcard length letters to close friends—these are known as the *Wahnbriefe* (Madness Letters) because of their incomprehensible content—after which he never wrote again. The letters were so worrying for the recipients they arranged to bring him back to Basel and have him placed in an asylum. In 1893, his sister Elisabeth, who had been in Patagonia as part of a utopian group attempting to create a new Germany, returned home and took over the care of her brother. She also took control of his unpublished writings and remade them in her own image. It isn't known exactly what struck Nietzsche down. For a long time it was assumed that syphilis was the cause, but that has lately been brought into question.

Although he was anti-religious, his position on religion was complex: he argued that it is better to believe in God than to believe in nothing, but that the belief in God had over time become such an empty gesture it amounted to the same thing as believing in nothing. Nietzsche is sometimes described as a *nihilist, but this is a mistake because nihilism was precisely what he was most opposed to. In his philosophy he sought to trans-value or re-value the 'old' values so as to avoid the abyss of nihilism. Nietzsche argued that humanity is held back from making this leap because of its attachment to slave morality, or what he referred to as **ressentiment*, the sense that somehow the world owes the individual something and that is the reason they haven't been able to get ahead. His answer to the problem is the notion of the eternal return—if we could have life over again, it would have to repeat itself in every detail or it would not be *our* life, therefore we should live in such a way that if our life was repeated we would be able to embrace it. In other words, we shouldn't judge life, or seek to enchain it, we should live it to its maximum potential.

Further Reading: G. Deleuze *Nietzsche and Philosophy* (1983).
J. Derrida *Spurs: Nietzsche's Styles* (1979).
A. Nehamas *Nietzsche: Life as Literature* (1985).
L. Spinks *Friedrich Nietzsche* (2003).
M. Tanner *Nietzsche* (1994).

SEE WEB LINKS

- The website of the Friedrich Nietzsche Society which includes links to resources and discussion boards.

nihilism An intellectual and political position premised by the rejection of all moral and ethical values grounded in the belief that there is some kind of higher authority or being (e.g. God, humanity, justice, nature, etc.). The term itself derives from Ivan Turgenev's novel *Fathers and Sons* (1861), where it is used to describe a generation of intellectuals who had become disenchanted with bourgeois life in Russia because they saw it as hollow.

noesis and noema In *phenomenology, the act of apprehending (noesis) and the object apprehended (noema). A specific noema may give rise to multiple acts of noesis.

nomadology Gilles *Deleuze and Félix *Guattari's utopian project outlined in *Mille Plateaux* (1980), translated as *A Thousand Plateaus* (1987). The origin of the word 'nomad' is not, as many have assumed, a romanticized image of actual nomadic peoples, such as the Bedouins, but rather Immanuel *Kant's disparaging claim that the outside of philosophy is a wasteland fit only for nomads. The immediate origin of the concept would seem to be Deleuze and Guattari's discussion of the despot in *L'Anti-Oedipe* (1972), translated as *Anti-Oedipus* (1977). The despot is an intermediate figure between the primitive society without a state on the one hand and the so-called civilized imperial state on the other. What is crucial about the concept of the despot, however, is the fact that in Deleuze and Guattari's description it refers to a latent state of being, meaning it is virtual and presupposed, but never actual. Like the despot, then, the figure of the nomad stands for the power of the virtual, or what they call the *war machine. The nomad is a tendency towards *deterritorialization, Deleuze and Guattari argue, that can be found to some degree in all phenomena. Their project consists in identifying this tendency wherever it can be located and finding ways of amplifying it. Deleuze and Guattari distinguish between a royal science and a nomadic science, and though they freely admit that nomadic science creates structures that collapse, they also celebrate its ability—when juxtaposed with royal science—to open a creative line of flight.

nominalism The condition into which art, philosophy, and even thought itself descends in the absence of a unitary and overarching idea or *grand narrative (to borrow François *Lyotard's useful term). Theodor *Adorno used this term to criticize his friend Walter *Benjamin's work on the Paris arcades, condemning him for not providing a sturdy enough account of the relation between the fragments he collected in his compendium of *modernity. The notion of *constellation was in some senses meant to remedy this problem, but Benjamin didn't take it far enough in Adorno's view. In his later work on aesthetics, Adorno saw that nominalism was the problem facing all art in an era that had begun to question the very nature and existence of art as such. Nominalism is, as Fredric *Jameson points out in his book on Adorno, both a philosophical tendency and a historical event. It is the repudiation of the universal by the particular that is possible because the historical moment itself defines itself as a refusal of the universal. Jameson uses the concept of nominalism to explain certain trends in *postmoderism that he sees are born of an emphasis of the particular at the expense of the universal (by which he means history)—his specific complaints are directed at *New Historicism.

Further Reading: F. Jameson *Late Marxism: Adorno, or, The Persistence of the Dialectic* (1990).

non-linear system A mathematical concept that describes a complex situation in which inputs and outputs do not function proportionally. For example, as we have all been made aware in recent times, a small change in the temperature of the planet as a whole can cause massive changes in a great number of the earth's systems, both artificial and natural. More simply put, a non-linear system is one in which causation appears to be indirect. Climate change is the indirect, unintended result of a similarly non-linear process known as modernization. But even that does not go far enough because not all the peoples on the planet have shown an interest in *Modernity, so if we are to search for the true cause of climate change we have to ask why one group of people pursued the path of industrialization and others did not. *See also* COMPLEXITY THEORY.

non-place Marc *Augé's term for generic places such as bus depots, train stations, and airports which, however elaborate and grandiose, do not confer a feeling of place. As Gertrude Stein famously said of Oakland, there is no 'there' in a non-place. In direct contrast to places, which we tend to think of as being relational, historical, and concerned with identity, non-places are designed and intended for the frictionless passage of a nameless and faceless multitude. The paradox of non-places, according to Augé, is that anyone can feel 'at home' in them regardless of their actual background because they are equally alienating to everyone. He means that if we travel to a country that is otherwise culturally foreign to us, then the most familiar and therefore homely aspect of that country will be its generic non-places, which in this context appear universal. Non-places may usefully be thought of as machines (in the same sense in which Michel *Foucault thought of the *panopticon as a machine) whose chief utility is their ability to substitute for, and to improve upon, human interaction—the automatic turnstile is faster than the conductor, the ATM more convenient than the bank, and the credit card simpler than cash. Not as far-reaching as George Ritzer's *McDonaldization thesis, but resonant with it nonetheless, Augé's argument is that the increasing prevalence of non-places on a global scale is an index of what he terms *supermodernity, and the experience of them its defining characteristic. Non-places are not the cause of this epochal shift. The cause, though it is never actually named by Augé, is *late capitalism.

Further Reading: M. Augé *Non-Lieux, Introduction à une anthropologie de la surmodernité* (1992), translated as *Non-Places: Introduction to an Anthropology of Supermodernity* (1995).
I. Buchanan 'Non-Places: Space in the Age of Supermodernity' in R. Barcan and I. Buchanan (eds.) *Imagining Australian Space* (1999).

nostalgia for the present Fredric *Jameson's apparently paradoxical formulation naming the attraction of the spectacle of the presence in the here and now of the past that certain films seem to provide. His key exhibit is the Lawrence Kasdan film *Body Heat* (1981), starring William Hurt and Kathleen Turner. Jameson notes that although it is set in present-day Florida, it is filmed in such a way that all markers of contemporaneity are obscured, giving rise to the illusion the actual time of the film is the 1940s, the period from which its technicolour version of *film noir* mise-en-scène is borrowed. It is this desire for the present of previous films that is central to the concept. A more recent example of nostalgia for the present in cinema would be Peter Jackson's remake of *King Kong* (2005), which depicts the glamorous 'present' of 1930s New York.

Further Reading: I. Buchanan *Fredric Jameson: Live Theory* (2006).
C. Burnham *The Jamesonian Unconscious: The Aesthetics of Marxist Theory* (1995).
F. Jameson *Postmodernism, or, The Cultural Logic of Late Capitalism* (1991).

nouveau roman **(new novel)** A style of novel that emerged in France in the 1950s. A precursor to **Nouvelle Vague* (several *nouveau roman* authors either collaborated with film-makers or became film-makers themselves—Marguerite Duras is undoubtedly the best-known example), the *nouveau roman* is often referred to as 'plotless' because of its rejection of conventional narrative forms. Developed as an experiment in writing, the *nouveau roman* constantly pushed the boundaries of intelligibility by deliberately flouting the norms of realism, character, plotting, and so on. Not surprisingly, the initial critical reaction to the *nouveau roman*, at least in the popular press, was very far from favourable. And while the *nouveau roman* would be championed by critics like Roland *Barthes, it remained something that only a very small minority of readers took an interest in. The best-known proponent of the *nouveau roman* was Alain Robbe-Grillet, who effectively wrote its manifesto in 1963 with the publication of his collection of essays entitled, *Pour un Nouveau Roman*, translated as *For a New Novel* (1965). Other important *nouveau roman* authors include: Michel Butor, Nathalie Sarraute, and Claude Simon.

Further Reading: S. Heath *The Nouveau Roman: A Study in the Practice of Writing* (1972).

Nouvelle Vague A film movement, or moment, that was current in France in the late 1950s and early 1960s. Also known as the French New Wave, *Nouvelle Vague* was influenced by Italian *neo-realism and similarly rebelled against the prevailing national trend of big budget literary adaptations and costume dramas. The term *Nouvelle Vague* was coined by *L'Express* editor Françoise Giroud to describe the emergent youth culture of the period. The association with cinema grew out of the popularity of films like *Et Dieu créa la femme* (And God Created Woman, 1956), which was directed by a 28-year-old Roger Vadim. *Nouvelle Vague* was a highly intellectual cinematic form and many of its most important directors were film critics writing for *Cahiers du cinéma* who seized the opportunity the demand for a *jeune cinéma* (young or youthful cinema) presented (e.g. Claude Chabrol, Jean-Luc Godard, Jacques Rivette, Eric Rohmer, and François Truffaut). Not explicitly political, *Nouvelle Vague* was nonetheless highly critical of the consumer culture that was beginning to dominate French life at that time. Therefore it sought to make films which did not conform to the safe commercial formulas of the mainstream. So it did away with the establishing shot and introduced the jump cut instead. It did away with standard narrative trajectories and focused instead on the ambiguous complexities of human relationships, which in real life do not have neat beginnings, middles, or ends. Coinciding with the rise of **auteur* theory, *Nouvelle Vague* directors held to the idea that films could be imbued with a signature style and did not have to be anonymous commodities.

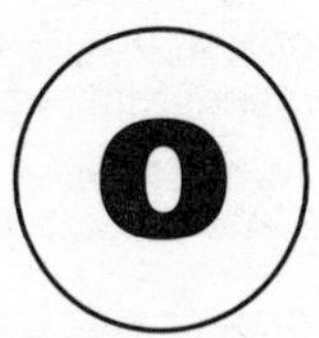

object (*Objekt*) The thing, which may be a person, body part, symbol, image, or idea, through which the *drive seeks to attain its aim, namely its satisfaction or extinction (albeit temporary). In choosing this term, Sigmund *Freud wanted to make the point that the drives (the psychological organization of the instincts) do not make a distinction between animate and inanimate, partial and whole, or even real and imagined. The notion of the object is central to *psychoanalysis, particularly its theory of sexuality. At the most basic level, object choice defines sexual orientation (whether homosexual or heterosexual); but it also defines the nature of the sexual perversions (any form of sexuality not organized around a relationship to another person). Since object choice is said to occur in childhood, the theory of the object is particularly important to child psychoanalysts like Melanie *Klein.

Objects can be both internal and external to the body—hunger, for example, feels as if it is located in the pit of the stomach, so it is internal; whereas sensation or touch, which is experienced through the skin, is external. The distinction between the internal and external object is by no means straightforward, however, because some objects appear external but only function if they are rendered internal, such as the thumb which the child sucks in order to go to sleep. Objects can thus be effective and ineffective and therefore subject to love and hate, often at the same time, a state that is known in psychoanalysis as *ambivalence.

Klein called the ineffective objects 'bad objects' and the effective ones 'good objects' and based her theory of child development around the child's need to learn to deal with the crises the bad objects apparently represent to them. The classic example of the bad object is the breast that does not provide milk. Understandably, perhaps, to the hungry child such an object can be an object of hatred. What should also be observed is that for the child the breast is not necessarily a part of the object called 'mummy', and for this reason it is known as a part object. The theory of how the child relates to a particular object (part or whole) is known as *object relations theory: it is concerned with not only the feeling of love or hate towards the object, but also its placement (*introjected or *projected, i.e. internal or external), and the way they act on or with the object.

Further Reading: J. Laplanche and J-B. Pontalis *Vocabulaire de la Psychanalyse* (1967), translated as *The Language of Psychoanalysis* (1973).

object relations theory A subsection of *psychoanalysis which prioritizes the role of the *object in childhood development. It is generally associated with the British Psycho-Analytic Society, whose most notable members included Michael *Balint, Melanie *Klein, and D.W. *Winnicott. In contrast to traditional psychoanalysis, object relations theory focuses on the relationship between the infant and the mother, not the father-child, or *Oedipal, relationship that is central to Sigmund *Freud's thought. It also conceives this relationship as subject (child) to object (mother), or even to part-object (the breast), which again contrasts with Freud who acknowledges the role of the object but still wants to see the relationship between child and parent as intersubjective.

Further Reading: G. Kohon (ed.) *The British School of Psychoanalysis: The Independent Tradition* (1986).

J. Laplanche and J-B. Pontalis *Vocabulaire de la Psychanalyse* (1967), translated as *The Language of Psychoanalysis* (1973).

objet (petit) a In Jacques *Lacan's *psychoanalysis, the *object of *desire that can never be obtained. It has a range of meanings in Lacan's work, but the most consistent and widely recognized understanding of it is that it is that which desire *lacks in perpetuity and is therefore that which causes desire. In later formulations, Lacan came to think of it as the surplus value of enjoyment (*jouissance). Lacan always insisted that the term remain untranslated so as to give it an algebraic status in English, and for the most part this is respected. Literally, it might be rendered as the 'object (little) a', but this is still not completely right since the 'a' stands for *autre* (other), so strictly speaking it should be the 'object (little) o'.

Oedipus complex The central organizing *myth of *psychoanalysis. In *Die Traumdeutung* (1900), translated as *The Interpretation of Dreams* (1913), Freud relates that in his clinical experience the child's relationship to its parents is the major determinant in the psychical lives of his more neurotic patients. This idea occurred to him a few years earlier during self-analysis. As he reports in a letter to his friend Fliess, in analysing his affection for his mother and jealousy of his father he was reminded of the Sophocles play *Oedipus Rex* (429 BC), which he thought could only continue to be so affecting some 2,500 years after it was written because its thematic concerns are universal. Freud elaborated this claim on two different levels: the individual subject, and human society.

The story of the Oedipus myth, on which Sophocles based his play, is as follows: King Laius of Thebes learns from an oracle his son will kill him. Thinking to avert this fate, he binds his son's feet (hence his name, which means swollen feet) and then orders his wife Jocasta to kill him. Unable to do so she orders a servant to carry out the evil deed, but instead he abandons the child in the fields where he is discovered by a shepherd who passes him to a fellow shepherd from Corinth who takes the infant back to his land where he is raised in the court of King Polybus. As an adult Oedipus also goes to an oracle and is told that he will marry his mother and kill his father. Hoping to avoid his fate, he leaves Corinth, and—as fate would have it—meets his biological father on the road to Thebes. The two men fall into an argument and Oedipus duly kills his father. He continues on his way to Thebes. Thebes is at that time under the spell of the Sphinx, who has cursed the city. He solves the Sphinx's riddle, thereby lifting the curse, and is rewarded with the Kingship over the city and the hand of its recently widowed Queen, namely his biological mother. The prophecy is thus fulfilled, but at this point none of the characters in the play is aware of this fact. When at last they learn the truth of what has transpired Jocasta hangs herself and Oedipus blinds himself and goes into exile.

According to Freud, this myth resonates strongly with everyone because it tells the basic story of childhood development, at least from the boy's perspective. Psychoanalysis holds that all children develop a love attachment to the parent of the opposite sex and a corresponding rivalry with the parent of the same sex: thus, the little boy loves his mother and wants to usurp his father. What the story narrates in effect is *object choice, but it also teaches compromise, or what Freud called the *reality principle. In 1910 Freud would describe this conflicted desire as the 'Oedipus complex', thus inscribing the myth at the centre of his thinking and teaching. This phrase has since passed into popular usage, which has not always been to the advantage of psychoanalysis because many people find it absurd or repugnant (Freud himself defended against such reactions by saying they just proved his point because the myth would not provoke such outbursts if it was not revealing an inner truth). At first, Freud thought this desire had to be literal, but he came to realize it could also be enacted symbolically. Freud initially confined the period of the 'Oedipus complex' to children under the age of 5, but he later modified his thinking and allowed that it didn't reach its proper resolution until puberty.

In 1972, in a work pointedly titled, *L'Anti-Oedipe*, translated as *Anti-Oedipus* (1977), Gilles *Deleuze and Félix *Guattari published a scathing attack on the centrality of the 'Oedipus complex'.

ontology In philosophy, the theory of the existence of things—at its most basic, or fundamental, it seeks to answer the question why there is something rather than nothing. It does not examine the existence of particular things; its focus is the more general level of the possibility and actuality of anything existing at all. In the 20th century, the most influential account of ontology is given by Martin *Heidegger, in his extensive writings on the subject.

open and closed work Italian semiotician and novelist Umberto *Eco proposed this binary in his 1959 essay 'L'opera in movimento e la coscienza dell'epoca', translated as 'The poetics of the open work', to describe works of art that, on the one hand, appear incomplete inasmuch as they appear to be given to the audience to make of them what they will, and on the other hand, seem finished and somehow unassailable, as though the audience's input was neither desired not needed. He refers to the former as open and the latter as closed and equates the first with freedom and the second with obedience and submission. Eco is aware that all texts, to a certain degree, can be regarded as co-productions between author and addressee, but he shows that what is at stake is in fact an issue of the world view of a text, or what Michel *Foucault would later term the *episteme. He gives examples of medieval allegories and argues that in their own time, no reader would have thought it possible not to read them for their Christian message. It is only now, in a secular age, that such a reading is possible.

Opoyaz Russian acronym created from *Obschevesto po izucheniyu poeticheskogo yazyka* (Society for the Study of Poetic Language), which along with the *Moscow Linguistic Circle was one of the precursor groups to *Russian Formalism. The group was formed in St Petersburg, Russia, in 1916, by a group of students and professors working in language studies. It was chaired by the poet Osip Brik and its membership included Victor *Shklovsky, Boris Eichenbaum, and Roman *Jakobson. The group was interested in uncovering the working mechanisms of literary technique, or more precisely identifying the specific quality of language use that separated the literary text from the non-literary text. The group, never more than a loosely knit discussion unit and occasional cooperative publishing venture, folded in 1923 and merged with the Moscow Linguistic

Circle, though by then many of its leading lights had already fled abroad.

Further Reading: T. Bennett *Formalism and Marxism* (1979).
V. Erlich *Russian Formalism: History—Doctrine* (1955).

orality The state of a language which has no written form but exists only as spoken words. This concept was created to try to gauge the effect writing technology has on a society and more especially on its language. For example, it is thought that in oral societies the meaning and pronunciation of words changes more rapidly because it isn't fixed by the standardizing power of print. By the same token, without the mnemonic power of print oral societies make greater use of myths and songs as a way of preserving knowledge. Interestingly, the father of *structuralism, Ferdinand de *Saussure, disputes both these points and argues instead for the priority of speech over writing.

Further Reading: W. Ong *Orality and Literacy: The Technologizing of the Word* (1982).

ordinary language philosophy A branch of philosophy interested in language's capacity for meaning. A product of the so-called *linguistic turn, ordinary language philosophy treats misunderstanding in philosophy as a failure to understand language. In contrast to *analytic philosophy, it does not treat with suspicion language's capacity for obfuscation, but sees this as one of language's many capabilities that philosophy ought to be able to explain. Its central claim is that meaning resides in use, that words mean what they are used to mean. The leading figures in this field are Ludwig *Wittgenstein, Gilbert Ryle, J.L. *Austin, and J.R. *Searle.

organic intellectual An intellectual or someone of professional standing (i.e. a doctor, lawyer, or priest) who rises to that level from within a social *class that does not normally produce intellectuals, and remains connected to that class. In other words, the organic intellectual is the opposite of a yuppie—they are not upwardly mobile and their concern is for the conditions of their class as a whole, not for themselves. Italian *Marxist philosopher Antonio *Gramsci develops this concept in his famous 'Prison Notebooks'.

Orientalism Traditionally, any form of scholarship or indeed fascination with the Orient, meaning the countries generally referred to today as the Middle East (but also encompassing the whole of North Africa, Turkey, Pakistan, and the northern tip of India). Edward *Said's book *Orientalism: Western Conceptions of the Orient* (1978) transformed the term from a relatively neutral, though obviously biased, name for a venerable field of study dating back several hundred years, into an indictment of bigotry and racism. Said's work emptied Orientalism of its previously positive associations and connotations and put in their place a long list of charges. Indeed, there are few critical reversals of the meaning of terms as complete as Said's demolition of Orientalism. His basic charge is that the Orient as conceived by the Orientalists (primarily, but not exclusively, English, French, and German) is a fiction of their own imagining bearing no resemblance to the actual Orient, which as Said points out is a vastly complicated region. He notes, too, that many of the most famous Orientalist scholars never even visited the Orient, relying instead on second-hand accounts of it, as though the actuality of the Orient did not really interest them. This fictional Orient conjured up by Orientalists is, Said shows (using the work of Michel *Foucault as his inspiration), a discursive production, a fantastic place that is the product of hundreds of years of mystification, exoticization, and outright deception made possible by the discrepant power relations between West and East. The problem, he argues, is that the West's ongoing fantasy of the Orient has real effects: insofar as the West understands the Orient as backward, unenlightened, irrational, sexually deviant, unhealthy, uninviting, and so on, it forms its politics accordingly (one has only to recall Donald Rumsfeld's callous disregard for the looting of Iraq's national museum following the fall of Baghdad in 2003 to see the consequences of this). In the 30 years since its publication, *Orientalism*, has become a cornerstone of *Postcolonial Studies.

Further Reading: B. Moore-Gilbert *Postcolonial Theory: Contexts, Practices, Politics* (1997).

***ostranenie* (defamiliarization or estrangement)** A central concept in *Russian Formalism's attempt to describe and define what constitutes **literaturnost* (literariness). A neologism, it implies two kinds of actions: making strange, and pushing aside. Consistent with this double meaning, the concept refers to the techniques writers use to transform ordinary language into poetic language, which for the Russian Formalists is language which induces a heightened state of perception. Habit, according to the Russian Formalists, is the enemy of art, therefore to produce art the writer has to force the reader outside of the usual patterns of perception by making the familiar appear strange or different. The principal theorist of this concept, Victor *Shklovsky, uses a famous passage in Tolstoy's *War and Peace* (1869), where an opera is described as 'painted cardboard and oddly dressed men and women who moved, spoke and sang strangely in a patch of blazing light' to exemplify this concept. Basically what Tolstoy does, according to Shklovsky in *Theory of Prose* (1990), is view things out of context, or to put it another way he fails to see the thing that makes the actions he describes either meaningful or coherent and in this way he defamiliarizes them. In *The Prison-House of Language* (1972), Fredric *Jameson enumerates three advantages of the concept of *ostranenie*: firstly, it enables literary theory itself to come into being by providing a way of distinguishing its object—namely, poetic language; secondly, it enables a hierarchy to be established within works and between works (i.e. more or less defamiliarizing); thirdly, it generates a new way of thinking literary history in terms of ruptures and breaks rather than continuities and influences. The problem with this concept, however, is that it is psychological rather than purely textual, inasmuch as it is premised on the deadened senses of the reader being awakened by clever writing rather than something specific to the writing itself. Obviously, too, this process suffers from the logic of diminishing returns—what was shocking yesterday is all too familiar today, thus demanding an ever greater level of shock to achieve a decreasingly small level of shock value (this, as many commentators have observed, is the problem contemporary non-representational art also faces). *See also* COGNITIVE ESTRANGEMENT; ESTRANGEMENT-EFFECT.

Further Reading: T. Bennett, *Formalism and Marxism* (1979).
V. Erlich *Russian Formalism: History—Doctrine* (1955).

Other Emmanuel *Levinas's concept of Ethics is centred on the problematic of the relation between being and that which is otherwise than being (the title of one of his later books), or the self and Other (which he capitalizes to distinguish it from the more ordinary form of otherness, namely the experience of unfamiliarity). Other, for Levinas, is that which the self can neither know nor assimilate. Levinas often describes it as a Mystery (in the religious sense), as that which is beyond imagining, experiencing or knowing. It is that which resists 'my' purposes absolutely. I am obligated to the Other; it commands me, but it has no authority over me. By the same token the Other is what 'I' desire to kill, but cannot kill. When 'I' kill others, i.e. actual people, it is the Other that I am really trying to kill according to Levinas, and since that is impossible, all violence is doomed to failure. 'I' encounter the Other as a *face.

OULIPO A small group of novelists and mathematicians founded in France by Raymond Queneau and François Le Lionnais for the purpose of exploring the creative interaction between the respective fields. The group's name is an acronym derived from the very *'pataphysical sounding *OUvroir de LIttérature POtentielle* (workshop on potential literature), a fact that was surely not accidental given that many of its members were also involved in the Collège de 'pataphysique, of which it is in fact an offshoot. Although the group itself has never had a particularly high profile, a number of its members have—the most prominent are undoubtedly Raymond Queneau, Georges Perec, and Italo *Calvino. The group used mathematical formulae to create what Perec referred to as writing machines. So for example the writers might adopt the constraint that they cannot use a certain letter, or they might write following the rule that each successive word in a sentence must be a letter longer than the previous word and so on.

Further Reading: W. Motte (ed.) *Oulipo: A Primer of Potential Literature* (1998).

over-determination **1.** The standard English translation of *Überdeterminierung*, the word Sigmund *Freud uses to describe the effect of the *dreamwork processes known as *condensation (*Verdichtung*) and *displacement (*Verschiebung*) whereby *either* a number of different dream-thoughts are compressed beneath a single image *or* the affect of one particularly strong dream-thought is transferred onto another comparatively innocuous image. The net result is a multi-layered image that cannot be taken at face value and whose surface is only a partial and at best unreliable indicator of what lies beneath.

O

2. French Marxist philosopher Louis *Althusser adapted this term (it is rendered in French as *surdétermination*) to articulate his thesis that all social practice is multiply determined, or has more than one cause, hence its contradictory nature and appearance. A classic example of what Althusser has in mind can be seen in the debate concerning climate change—it is the lavish western lifestyle that is allegedly the cause of the present crisis, yet that is the one thing we are apparently unwilling to give up in order to resolve the crisis. But because of our awareness of the crisis and its inherently contradictory nature we have got used to the perfectly Althusserian idea that every single aspect of our daily life, from the way we dispose of our garbage to the products we buy, is *at once* an effect of a larger process we loosely refer to as *globalization *and* a contribution to a larger process we refer to as, again very loosely, climate change. Our decision to buy Fairtrade or organic products is in this sense overdetermined because it reflects both personal desire and an awareness of the economic system as a whole. The crucial implication here is that a change at one level—our consciousness of the seriousness of the threat climate change poses to the future of the planet—does not automatically translate into action on the other level. We haven't given up our consumerist lifestyle, we've merely tried to alter its modality, as though to say we can save the planet from the effects of consumption by shopping differently.

palimpsest A manuscript written on a piece of any material (paper, parchment, stone, vellum, etc.) which has previously been written on, but whose surface has been cleaned to make way for the new text. Common in the Middle Ages before paper became widely available, today it is generally used as a *metaphor for a text with more than one layer of meaning, an allegory for example.

panopticon 18th century English philosopher Jeremy Bentham coined the term to describe a model of prison architecture (which he conceived) enabling what he thought of as a therapeutic form of total surveillance (the literal meaning of the word). Consisting of a central observation tower situated inside a circular building where the cells are located in such a way as to be fully and constantly visible to the guards who because of their location and the relative play of light are all but invisible to the prisoners. The design effectively turns the prisoner's space into a backlit stage where he or she is continuously on show. Bentham reasoned that this complete lack of privacy would have a remedial effect on prisoners who would be forced by this means to adopt socially approved standards of behaviour because they would be unable to escape the punitive eye of the guards. Owing to this ingenious structure, prisoners would internalize better standards of behaviour and thereby rehabilitate themselves for re-entry into society, or so Bentham thought. Its chief virtue, in Bentham's view, was that it reduced the need for violent forms of coercion. But for Michel *Foucault, who happened upon this work in the course of writing *Surveiller et punir: Naissance de la Prison* (1975), translated as *Discipline and Punish: The Birth of the Prison* (1977), it was this psychological dimension that was both its most fascinating and disturbing feature. For Foucault, Bentham's blueprints, which gave rise to just a handful of actual buildings (the most famous example being Stateville penitentiary in the US), are emblematic of an epistemic shift not only in the treatment of prisoners but more generally in the organizational rationality—what Foucault would himself later call *governmentality—of society as a whole. He used the term panopticism to characterize the mechanism behind this change which he charted in the transformation of the spatial disposition of factories, schools, hospitals, army barracks, and so forth throughout the 18th and 19th centuries so as to bring about what he describes as the automatic functioning of power. The panopticon is in Foucault's view the most perfect and sublime realization of the principle of *discipline, the subordination of bodies to machines and their reconfiguration as machines.

Further Reading: M. Foucault *Surveiller et punir: Naissance de la Prison* (1975), translated as *Discipline and Punish: The Birth of the Prison* (1977).
H. Dreyfus and P. Rabinow *Michel Foucault: Beyond Structuralism and Hermeneutics* (1983).

paradigm **1.** The vertical axis of communication in *Saussurian linguistics and *semiotics. The horizontal axis or *syntagm defines the deep structure of a particular piece of communication, with the vertical axis specifying the possible lexical variations that structure can meaningfully accommodate. So in the sentence 'the boy went to the shop', we can substitute girl for boy, beach for shop and so on, all without altering the 'a person went somewhere' relational structure of the sentence.

2. American historian of science Thomas *Kuhn uses this term to describe different moments in scientific development, coining the phrase 'paradigm shift' to name the ruptures that occur in thought when a new discovery is made. The best known example of so-called 'paradigm shift' is of course the Copernican revolution, namely the insight that the earth is not the centre of the solar system.

paranoid-critical method Spanish artist Salvador Dalí's proposed second phase of *Surrealism which, in contrast to the first phase, would seek to consciously exploit its explorations of the unconscious. In other words, rather than simply try to reveal the workings of the unconscious through automatic writing and so forth, it proposes to create systematic objectifications of the delirious connections made by the unconscious. The Dutch architect Rem Koolhaas provides a fine account of this method in *Delirious New York* (1978), in which he argues that Dalí's view of things can be witnessed in a range of late 20th-century building projects (his key example is the reconstruction of London Bridge in Arizona). Paranoia, Koolhaas argues, is a delirium of interpretation in which every thing perceived serves to confirm the reality of the mind. It is a perpetual feeling of the shock of recognition. In artistic terms, it is like the fabrication of facts to evidence an unprovable worldview, and the insertion of those false facts into the world in such a way as they take the place of true facts. A clear example of this is Dalí's illustrations for Lautréamont's *Chants de*

Maldoror (1868), which radically reinterpret François Millet's bucolic paintings as charged with sexual energy.

parapraxis Sigmund *Freud's actual term for what is more commonly known as a 'Freudian slip'. Able to take many forms, from the forgetting of names, to losing one's keys, to accidentally saying the wrong word, parapraxis is, according to Freud, an instance of *unconscious thoughts escaping censorship and influencing the realm of conscious action. Such slips, Freud theorized, betray what our unconscious is really thinking. If, for example, we consistently forget someone's name, that might be a symptom of our dislike for that person. As Freud shows in *Zur Psychopathologie des Alltagsleben*s (1901), translated as *The Psychopathology of Everyday Life* (1914), parapraxis is extremely common and widely occurring.

paratext French literary theorist Gérard *Genette's term for the framing devices authors and publishers use to contextualize works and generate interest (e.g. blurbs, subtitles, celebrity endorsements, and so forth). As Genette points out in *Seuils* (1987) translated as *Paratexts. Thresholds of Interpretation* (1997), although not officially part of the text, the paratext can have a significant influence over the way a text is received.

parole *See* LANGUE AND PAROLE.

part-object *See* OBJECT.

pastiche A work of art (in the broadest sense) that borrows and mixes artistic styles. In the programme essay to his magisterial account of *postmodernism, *Postmodernism, or, the Cultural Logic of Late Capitalism* (1991), Fredric *Jameson provocatively claimed that all postmodern art conforms to a logic of pastiche, which he defined as parody without purpose. That is to say, postmodernism's purpose in copying previous artistic styles is neither to exalt nor critique, but simply to use them to create interesting new works. Postmodernism is compelled to do this Jameson argues because artistic innovation was effectively exhausted by its precursor *modernism.

'pataphysics ('*pataphysique*) French author Alfred *Jarry's playful concept defined in *Gestes et opinions du Docteur Faustroll, pataphysicien* (1911), translated as *Exploits and Opinions of Dr Faustroll, Pataphysician* (1965), as the science of imaginary solutions. More than that, in contrast to so-called general science, it is meant to be a science of the particular, a science of exceptions, and a science of alternative or supplementary universes. In 1948 a group of writers, basically the core of the group that would later call themselves *OULIPO (Raymond Queneau, Jean Genet, and Eugene Ionesco, among others), founded a Collège de 'pataphysique and produced a periodical devoted to absurdist writing. The college and journal folded suddenly and without explanation in 1975. In an appropriately playful essay included in his final work, *Critique et Clinique* (1993), translated as *Essays Critical and Clinical* (1997), Gilles *Deleuze suggests that Jarry is an unrecognized precursor to *Heidegger because they are both engaged in the task of going beyond metaphysics. In no less playful fashion, though to perhaps more serious purpose, in *Fatal Strategies* (1983) Jean *Baudrillard describes nuclear arms as a 'pataphysical weapons system because it is intended not to be used, indeed it is intended to eliminate the very need for weapons. It is perhaps worth adding that Don Delillo's early novel *Great Jones Street* (1973) contains a hilarious pastiche of this concept: in a scene about a third of the way into the novel there is a character who describes himself as a Professor of Latent History whose work deals with events that almost took place. Jarry is generally credited as a vital precursor to so-called *absurdist writing, while 'pataphysics seems to become prominent anywhere politics starts to seem absurd.

Further Reading: C. Bök *'Pataphysics: The Poetics of an Imaginary Science* (2001).

patriarchy Initially this term was used in anthropology to designate a family structure in which an older male (usually a father or grandfather) is in control of family life. In *feminism this term is extended to describe an entire society in which men are in control on both a micro and macro scale, that is to say, in control of individual families as well as the principal organs of power. Patriarchal societies are inherently hierarchical, privileging one group of people, namely men, over another for no other reason than *gender. Popular expressions like 'glass ceiling' reflect this situation in which it appears that women cannot reach the highest levels in a given society because of their sex, despite being well qualified to do so.

Pêcheux, Michel (1938–83) French *Marxist philosopher and linguist. Pêcheux studied with Louis *Althusser at the École Normale Supérieure from 1959 to 1961, quickly becoming part of the select group of students subsequently known as Althusserians—these included Étienne *Balibar, Pierre *Macherey, Nicos *Poulantzas, and Jacques *Rancière. On graduation, he obtained a position in a social psychology laboratory at the Centre Nationale de Recherche Scientifique. There he attempted to apply Althusser's thinking to social science topics, focusing specifically on linguistics. He published a manifesto of sorts along these lines entitled *L'Analyse automatique du discours* (1969) (Automatic Discourse Analysis), in which he sought to understand language as a social practice that contributes both to the maintenance of certain ideological positions, but also the formation of subjectivity. Pêcheux rejects *Saussure's casting of the **langue*/*parole* distinction, arguing that such formalisms served ideological rather than analytic purposes. Pêcheux's best known work in English is *Language, Semantics and Ideology* (1982), which is a translation of *Les Vérités de la Palice* (1975).

Peirce, Charles Sanders (1839–1914) American philosopher, one of the founders of both *pragmatism and *semiotics. A true polymath with interests spanning the full spectrum from the hard sciences to the humanities, Peirce wrote voluminously on an incredibly wide range of subjects (mathematics, physics, geodesy, spectroscopy, astronomy, anthropology, psychology, and philosophy, to name but a few), but published little in his own lifetime, and even today in spite of considerable editorial efforts the vast bulk of his work remains unpublished. As it stands, his published output runs to 12,000 pages, while his unpublished output is in excess of 80,000 handwritten pages, not all of them well preserved. It is probably fair to say his true legacy is yet to be fully appreciated; certainly in his own lifetime the scale of his achievement was exceedingly little known.

Peirce was born in Cambridge, Massachusetts. His father was a prominent professor of mathematics at Harvard University. He was one of the founders of the US Coast and Geodetic Survey, where Peirce would later find employment thanks to his father's influence, and one of the founders of the Smithsonian Institute. Peirce followed in his father's footsteps and went to Harvard too, where he completed a BA, MA, and MSc in rapid succession. In his time at Harvard he was fortunate enough to gain the friendship of the great American philosopher William James, who would provide crucial assistance to him throughout his life; he was also unfortunate enough to make an enemy of Charles Eliot, who would become president of Harvard and effectively block his chances of employment there. From 1859 until 1891, Peirce was employed by the US Coast and Geodetic Survey and was by all accounts a terrible employee, using his time to pursue his own projects.

The unfortunate fact that Peirce never held a tenured university position (he was a part-time lecturer at Johns Hopkins University for years, his only academic appointment) coupled with the entirely haphazard way in which he wrote and published has meant that the dissemination of his ideas has followed a slow and uncertain path. In *critical theory, it has undoubtedly been Peirce's theory of semiotics which has been the most influential, while philosophy has tended to focus more on his theory of logic and his notion of pragmatism. But Peirce himself always held that logic and semiotics were inseparable since thought could not take place except by means of *signs. His theory of semiotics influenced scholars as diverse as Gilles *Deleuze (who makes extensive use of it in his books on cinema), Umberto *Eco, and Julia *Kristeva.

Peirce took what might be termed a pansemiotic view of things, meaning that he thought that literally everything, from chemical reactions to human communication, could be understood from a semiotic perspective. His theory of signs was constructed with this in mind. Peirce's work has at its core a system of three interrelated universal categories, which he simply named firstness, secondness, and thirdness. These terms are slippery, but taken together offer a powerful *ontology: firstness is a mode of being which does not require reference to anything else, it exists in a state of immediacy; secondness, in contrast, is precisely a category of reference, of comparison and reflection, an intermediary state of relatedness; thirdness is pure mediation, it combines first and second things with other first and second things, as in memory and synthesis. The sign, as Peirce conceives it, belongs to the category of thirdness.

Peirce's model of the sign has three components, rather than the basic two adopted by *Saussure, which he termed the *representamen, the *interpretant, and the *object. The representamen is something which creates in the mind of an observer an equivalent sign; that sign is in turn the interpretant, namely the observer's representation to themselves of what they have seen; this representation in turn becomes an object, namely the significance to the observer of the original sign. Since every sign creates an interpretant, which in turn becomes a representamen to another interpretant, and so on, semiosis (the process of sign production) must be regarded as infinite. There can be no first or last sign. To distinguish between these moments in the cycle of sign production, Peirce constructed an elaborate taxonomy of the parts of the sign.

Further Reading: J. Brent *Charles Sanders Peirce: A Life* (rev. ed. 1998).
U. Eco and T Sebeok (eds.) *The Sign of Three: Dupin, Holmes, Peirce* (1984).
C. Misak *The Cambridge Companion to Peirce* (2004).

performative British philosopher J.L. *Austin's term for a type of speech that performs an action. For example, the phrase 'I now pronounce you husband and wife' performs the action of joining two people in marriage, provided the person who utters it is so empowered. Performatives do not always have to be as direct as that. If, for example, someone says 'it is stuffy in here' and we open a window in response, then it can be said that the phrase has a performative effect.

performativity American philosopher Judith *Butler adapts J.L. *Austin's concept of the *performative in her book *Gender Trouble: Feminism and the Subversion of Identity* (1990) to redefine *gender as an action humans are compelled to perform by society rather than a state of being or bodily condition. Her case example, which as she acknowledges in subsequent books was much misunderstood, is drag or cross-dressing: drag imitates gender, she argues, and in doing so reveals the imitative structure of gender itself. Gender can be imitated because it is always already a performance to begin with. As such, gender does not have an essence, or an intrinsic nature or identity. What was misunderstood by many was the fact that this does not mean gender is something we can therefore opt out of. As Butler clarifies in *Bodies That Matter: On the Discursive Limits of 'Sex'* (1993), while it is true that we can decide which aspects of available gender identities we wish to perform, we cannot choose not to have any gender identity at all because society constantly imposes gender upon us.

periodizing hypothesis The attempt to delineate and characterize a particular period of history as an 'age', e.g. *postmodernism. It assumes two things: first, that there is difference in kind (not just degree) between one moment in history and another; second, that there is something that gives a particular segment of time a certain kind of unity. In recent memory, the 1960s stands out as the most widely talked about example of period: according to some historians, it differs significantly from the 1950s because it is dominated by the 'youth culture' of the so-called baby boomer generation; it is unified by a shift in the *structure of feeling away from believing in the idea of government towards a more dissident and rebellious position. Today, it is probably the notion of *globalization that is the most talked about example of a periodizing hypothesis, though not everyone recognizes it as such (i.e. there are those who refuse it on the grounds that international trade has always been around).

Further Reading: F. Jameson 'Periodizing the 60s' in *The Ideologies of Theory* (2008).

persona The mask, role, or character which society expects individuals to present. Swiss psychologist Carl *Jung used this term, which literally means 'mask', to describe the different social roles people are called on to play in *everyday life. The complaint made by *feminist critics that society demands that women be wives, mothers, mistresses, and so on, all at once, is in effect a statement about both the significance of personae in daily life and the difficulties they present when they come into conflict with one another. What is crucial, though, about this notion of persona is the fact the subject is always conscious of the fact that 'they' are never quite 'that', they are never quite what they appear to be. This is a potential source of both anxiety and comfort. Obeying the same logic, persona is also used in literary studies to describe the character an author adopts to tell a particular story. This concept is especially useful in the case of first person narratives to distinguish the 'I' of the text from the actual author.

phallocentrism Any theory of sexuality which gives primacy to either or both the penis and the *phallus. Sigmund *Freud's biographer Ernest Jones coined the phrase in his discussion of the sexuality of young girls, which challenged the master's view that everything can be explained by reference to the penis. In contrast to Freud, who thought that girl's sexuality is defined by their envious desire for a penis and its frustrated compensation in the form of a baby, Jones argued that young girls are in fact aware of their own sexual organs and do not require the penis as a point of comparison in order to organize their own sexuality.

phallus The imaginary and symbolic value of the penis. The phallus is not the same as the penis; it is a representation, not a part of the male anatomy. In *psychoanalysis, particularly *Lacanian psychoanalysis (indeed it is not a distinction Sigmund *Freud himself ever makes), it is at its most basic the representation of the male reproductive organ as it appears in the unconscious of both the child and the adult. The child passes successfully through the *Oedipal phase to the degree that it recognizes that the phallus is a symbol and can therefore never be possessed. The phallus is in this sense synonymous with castration and it affects boys and girls equally. As such, it is also the ultimate form of the signified (*see* SIGN), the point where the chain of signification comes to an end.

phantasmagoria A form of projection invented in France in the late 18th century. A precursor to cinema, phantasmagoria is able to make images move, thereby creating a more effective illusion. In its earliest form, the representations it projected were presented as ghosts, juxtaposing old-fashioned superstitions with new technology. This paradoxical conjunction of the old and the new caught the attention of German cultural theorist Walter *Benjamin who used the term phantasmagoria to describe the shopping arcades that emerged in

Paris in the mid 19th century. Now the term is used in *critical theory as a general term for an interest in or fascination with what later *postmodern theorists like Umberto *Eco would call *hyperreality.

Further Reading: M. Warner *Phantasmagoria: Spirit Visions, Metaphors, and Media into the Twenty-first Century* (2006).

phatic function One of the six constitutive elements of verbal communication according to Russian linguist Roman *Jakobson (the other functions are: referential, emotive, poetic, conative, and metalingual). The phatic function is the part of communication which keeps open the line of communication itself; it is the means by which two or more speakers reassure themselves that not only are they being listened to, but they are also being understood. It is in this sense a part of communication that is separate from the exchange of meaning; it is, as it were, without content of its own. Examples include such common phrases as 'are you with me?', 'do you know what I mean?' and so on.

phenomenology A philosophy of the *intentional being of consciousness, founded by German philosopher Edmund *Husserl in the latter part of the 19th century. Until the advent of *structuralism in the 1950s it was the dominant mode of philosophy in Europe: its most notable adherents include Husserl's student Martin *Heidegger (they did not see eye to eye—Husserl thought Heidegger had misunderstood phenomenology, while Heidegger thought Husserl's version of it was flawed), as well as Maurice *Merleau-Ponty and Emmanuel *Levinas. The object of phenomenology, namely intentionality, bears a superficial resemblance to what is sometimes known as 'inner experience'. This is because it is only available via reflection, i.e. after the fact. Husserl's research countered this problem with two reductions: first, he excluded all appeals to transcendent objects (i.e. objects whose meaning is intrinsic) to ground cognition; second, he separated the incidental instances of intentionality from the universal, which he termed eidetic. Consciousness, Husserl famously insisted, is always consciousness of something. This consciousness has two dimensions: (i) there is consciousness directed at an object, which Husserl refers to as *noesis and (ii) the object that consciousness is directed at, which Husserl refers to as noema. These in turn vary according to modality and temporality. Heidegger's critique of phenomenology centres on the priority Husserl gives to intentionality; in Heidegger's view, human existence itself is necessarily prior (for this reason Heidegger is sometimes referred to as an *existentialist philosopher, although he himself did not subscribe to that view). Merleau-Ponty's more sympathetic critique of Husserl also took issue with the priority of intentionality, but did so by foregrounding the pre-cognitive capacities of the body itself. It is for this reason—his emphasis on the body—that Merleau-Ponty's work continues to be read, even though phenomenology as a whole has declined considerably in importance.

Further Reading: D. Cerbone *Understanding Phenomenology* (2006). D. Moran *Introduction to Phenomenology* (1999).

philology A theory of language development which traces the 'family tree' of modern natural languages like English, French, and German back to their historical origins. The central point of interest of such research is to show the common ancestry of words dispersed across several languages. Although a highly distinguished philologist himself, Ferdinand de *Saussure inaugurated the *semiotic revolution by arguing against this account of the history of language.

phoneme A functional, i.e. meaningful, unit of sound, as in the distinction between 'bat' and 'cat'—the 'b' and 'c' sounds change or determine the meaning of the word as it would be heard in normal speech. By contrast, if one were to spell the words as follows 'batt' and 'catt', thus emphasizing the 't' sound, it would make no functional difference.

phonocentrism The privileging or prioritizing of the acoustic or phonic dimension of language over the graphic or written dimension. As Jacques *Derrida demonstrates with his concept **différance*, which in French is pronounced the same as 'différence', *phonemes are not the only meaningful unit of language; one must also take the written (or what Derrida refers to as the grammatological) into account as well.

pleasure (*plaisir*) 1. In a number of books and essays, starting with the pointedly titled *Le Plaisir du texte* (1973), translated as *The Pleasure of the Text* (1975), French literary critic Roland *Barthes used the essentially untranslatable distinction between *plaisir* and *jouissance as a crucial pivot around which his thinking on culture and literature turned. Unhappily, the English translation of *The Pleasure of the Text* blunts the significance of this distinction by rendering 'jouissance' as 'bliss', which lacks the force of the French original whose nearer cognates include 'orgasm' and 'coming'. For Barthes the distinction is political: *plaisir* is a conscious, subject-centred form of enjoyment capable of being put into words, but for that reason it is compliant and sedate; whereas jouissance is unconscious and inexpressible, and thus revolutionary and violent. Insofar as we experience *plaisir* we remain within ourselves, while jouissance threatens to dissolve or destabilize our selfhood. Extending this logic to literature, Barthes squares up this distinction with the one he later makes between *readerly and writerly texts, equating the former with *plaisir* and the latter with jouissance.

2. The second volume of Michel *Foucault's unfinished series of books on the history of sexuality, entitled *L'Usage des plaisirs* (1984), translated as *The Uses of Pleasure* (1985), problematized pleasure in a number of ways that have subsequently become influential, particularly in *Cultural Studies. At the level of language, Foucault observed that the Ancient Greeks and Romans did not have a single word, like pleasure, capable of referring to such a wide variety of acts and affects. Thus his history tries to show how and why a word like 'pleasure' became necessary. Consistent with his earlier work on medicine, Foucault shows that the term 'pleasure' performs a regulatory function, but the way that regulatory function applies varies geographically and historically. For example, Christian doctrine proscribes certain types of pleasure because they divert the believer from the true path. By contrast, the Ancient Greeks regarded pleasure as a subsidiary issue to the more important matter of the ethics of one's acts. Foucault's concept of pleasure is as open-ended as his concept of power, but interestingly he is quite adamant that pleasure is a better term than *desire (in contrast to in the work of his close friend Gilles *Deleuze).

pleasure principle (*Lustprinzip*) According to Freud, all actions—conscious and *unconscious—give rise to *pleasure or its opposite unpleasure in the psychical apparatus. In the course of daily life we try to regulate our thoughts and actions so that we have more of the first and less of the second. It is for this reason known as an 'economic model' of the psychical apparatus, where pleasure is regarded as an equivalent of money and unpleasure the equivalent of debt. It is also known as a constancy principle or nirvana principle because it is assumed that the subject's primary aim is to achieve a plateau which is just pleasurable enough. While Freud certainly has sensual pleasures in mind, pleasure does not necessarily have to take that form. The pleasure in question may also be an *ego pleasure, i.e. the pleasure the ego obtains from gaining the *superego's approval. By the same token, unpleasure takes the form of self-reproach, or more usually a kind of negative tension one experiences when a pleasure is delayed, i.e. it doesn't usually arise from having to do something one might find distasteful.

poetics The study of the formal construction of literary works of all genres, not just poetry. It is underpinned by the assumption that it is possible to delineate what it is that separates a poetic (literary) use of language from a non-poetic (ordinary) use of language. In contrast to *Russian Formalism, which is an obvious precursor, it is not primarily concerned with the problem of determining which is literary and which is not; rather, its concern is with the effectivity and unity of specific literary works. Poetics is often treated as a synonym for *structuralist literary theory.

political correctness The deliberate avoidance of language use and behaviour which may be perceived to be either derogatory or excluding of a political minority. Institutions and organizations that adopt political correctness as part of their communications policy thus expressly forbid the use of racist, sexist, and otherwise prejudicial language and require that politically neutral terms be used at all times. So, instead of 'chairman', 'chairperson' is used because it does not imply that the role is in any way gendered; similarly 'indigenous' has been substituted for 'native' and/or 'Indian' because it implies prior sovereignty of possession of the land. Right-wing commentators like to complain about and lampoon political correctness as a kind of needless or useless language tyranny, but the fact is the way language is used does matter to people so its use needs to be subject to oversight. The difficulty comes when trying to legislate against specific words such as 'nigger' which can either be an insult or an expression of solidarity depending on the context. Judith *Butler offers an important consideration of this in her discussion of 'hate speech' in *Excitable Speech: A Politics of the Performative* (1997).

political unconscious A concept created by Fredric *Jameson to articulate the implicit political dimension of creative works. First proposed in *The Political Unconscious: Narrative as a Socially Symbolic Act* (1981), the political unconscious draws on and adapts *Freud's notion of *wish-fulfilment and *Lévi-Strauss's notion of the savage mind ('pensée sauvage') to construct the hypothesis that artistic works can be seen as symbolic solutions to real but unconsciously felt social and cultural problems. The task of the cultural critic is then to find the means of reconstructing the original problem for which the text as symbolic act is a solution. This approach to textual criticism turns not so much on the question of what does a particular text mean as why it exists in the form that it does.

Further Reading: I. Buchanan *Fredric Jameson: Live Theory* (2006).
S. Homer *Fredric Jameson* (1998).
C. Irr and I. Buchanan *On Jameson* (2006).
F. Jameson *Jameson on Jameson: Conversations on Cultural Marxism* (2007).

polyphony Russian linguist and literary critic Mikhail *Bakhtin used this word, literally meaning many voiced to describe literary writing that managed to liberate the voice of its characters from under the domination of the authorial or narratorial voice. In *Problems of Dostoevsky's Poetics* (1984), Bakhtin refers to polyphony as a new kind of artistic thinking because what he has in mind goes against the grain of the traditional privileging of harmony, which means many voices heard as one. The reader of Dostoevsky, Bakhtin suggests, cannot but have the impression that he or she isn't dealing with a single author, but is in fact faced with a multiplicity of authors (Raskolnikov, Myshkin, Stavrogin, Ivan Karamazov, the Grand Inquisitor, and so on), each of whom has their own unique voice. *See also* CARNIVALESQUE; CHRONOTOPE; DIALOGISM; HETEROGLOSSIA.

Further Reading: K. Clark and M. Holquist *Mikhail Bakhtin* (1984).
M. Holquist *Dialogism* (2002).
D. Lodge *After Bakhtin* (1990).

Popper, Karl (1902–94) Austrian-born, but British-based philosopher of science and politics. He is widely regarded as one of the most influential philosophers of the latter half of the 20th century, particularly for his concept of the 'open society', which lauds western liberal democracy over the supposedly closed societies of the eastern communist countries.

Popper was born in Vienna to a middle-class family of converted Jews. His father taught law at the University of Vienna, where Popper received his education. As a student he joined the Social Democratic Party of Austria, but soon grew disillusioned with its *Marxist ideology, particularly the constraints on scientific thinking the doctrine of *historical materialism appeared to impose. He graduated with a doctorate in psychology in 1928.

In 1934 he published his first, and perhaps his most famous book, *Logik der Forschung* (which he translated himself and republished in English in 1959 as *The Logic of Scientific Discovery*), which argued that the philosophy of science needed to be rethought from the ground up. Science, Popper argued, could not be thought in terms of the discovery of universal truths, but had rather to be thought in terms of provisional, but ultimately falsifiable, propositions that are true until someone can disprove them. He rejected the empiricist model of science which holds that on the basis of the observation of data it is possible to arrive at universal truths by induction. Only that which is falsifiable is scientific he argued and on this basis he repudiated both *psychoanalysis and *Marxism's claims to that status.

Aware of the threat Austria's proposed Anschluss with Nazi Germany posed to a Jew like himself Popper emigrated to New Zealand in 1937. He remained there until after the war, and then accepted a post at the London School of Economics which he held until his retirement. His colleagues there included fellow philosophers of science Paul *Feyerabend and Imre *Lakatos and the eminent economist and free-market champion Friedrich Hayek. His most famous student, billionaire financier George Soros, named his philanthropic foundation after Popper's 1945 book *Open Society and Its Enemies.*

Popper had considerable difficulty in getting *Open Society and Its Enemies* (which was written while he was in New Zealand), published, which in light of its later fame is perhaps hard to imagine. However, it was not until the Cold War began in earnest in the early 1950s that its message began to resonate. *Open Society and its Enemies* applies Popper's critique of inductive reasoning to political philosophy, to attack 'historicism' in the political philosophy of Plato, Marx, and *Hegel, for which he blames most of what took place during World War II. But as Perry *Anderson has pointed out in *English Questions* (1992), Popper's attack is based on the rather threadbare premise that historicism means only social sciences which take historical prediction as their aim, which is hardly the case. Neither Marx nor Hegel claim to predict history.

With the end of the Cold War, Popper's stock as political philosopher has gone into steady decline, but his work as philosopher of science seems to be holding its own despite powerful critiques from his former colleagues Feyerabend and Lakatos.

Further Reading: S. Gattei *Karl Popper's Philosophy of Science* (2009).
B. Magee *Popper* (1977).
G. Stokes *Popper: Philosophy, Politics and Scientific Method* (1998).

positivism The third and highest state of human knowledge according to 19th century French philosopher Auguste Comte. According to Comte, humans evolve through three distinct states of social being: the theological, the metaphysical, and the positive. The first, primitive state of social life is the theological, in which humans progress from pagan fetishism to monotheism; the second, slightly more advanced state, is the metaphysical, so called because in it humans turn away from the supernatural, but nonetheless search for secular powers like 'nature'; the third, and final stage, is positivism, in which humans use science to ask how things work, rather than why they are there. The aim of positivism is to discover the immutable universal laws governing the known universe by virtue of scientific analysis and observation.

Postcolonial Studies A loosely-applied rubric for a large variety of work (creative and critical) across a range of disciplines—particularly anthropology, history, and literary studies—with a shared interest in the effects of colonization on the cultures of both the colonizers and the colonized. The leading theorists in the field are Homi *Bhabha, Gayatri *Spivak, and Edward *Said. The field is large enough for there to be several different sub-fields operating under its umbrella such as *feminist postcolonial studies and *Queer Theory and postcolonial studies.

The origins of Postcolonial Studies are predominantly Anglophone, but a comparative dimension has blossomed in the past two decades so that there are now substantial Francophone, Lusophone, Germanophone, and Hispanophone (as well as many other language groups) bodies of work in the area as well. The term was originally used by historians and economists in hyphenated form ('post-colonialism') to describe the political and economic situation of nations following decolonization, thus it had a specific historical point of reference. However, it is in literary studies rather than history that the term has put down its deepest roots, becoming in the process one of the most important intellectual movements in the entire discipline, easily outpacing *deconstruction and *New Historicism whose central tenets it has in any case absorbed. Postcolonial Studies offers itself as a radical alternative to the bland and ideologically naive Commonwealth Literatures project.

Literary studies has deleted the hyphen and with it the precision of reference it had in history, thus allowing the term to encompass the analysis of virtually any aspect of colonization, from the Early Modern or pre-colonial period of European exploration of the globe up to the present day. The deleting of the hyphen should be regarded as an essentially polemic gesture problematizing the very idea that colonialism is something that belongs safely in the past. Indeed, there are many who would argue that viewed globally we are very far from being postcolonial inasmuch that there are still many countries where the institutions, practices, and power relations of colonization are still very much present (from the perspective of indigenous peoples, this is true of Australia, Canada, New Zealand, and the US, to name only the most obvious). Similarly, there are those who observe that, even where the colonizers have departed, their models of governance remain so that a situation of *neo-colonialism obtains (here one might point to Israel and Palestine, whose recent history offers an even more complex case of the persistence of colonization).

It is difficult to generalize about a field of study as broad as Postcolonial Studies, but it can be observed that (i) it takes an anti-essentialist approach to *identity (though it will allow the necessity for *strategic essentialism); (ii) it privileges *difference over sameness (but acknowledges that difference is not without its *ambivalence); (iii) its political outlook is pluralist and anti-*hegemonic (it openly celebrates *Creoleness, *diaspora, and *hybridity, and at the same time problematizes all forms of *subalternity and subjugation); and (iv) it equates *representation with power (Said's *Orientalism thesis has it that the control of *representation is an index of power and the exercise of that control one of the things postcolonial critics must not tire of exposing). Theoretically, Postcolonial Studies draws on *Marxism (albeit in a non-Marxist way), *psychoanalysis (particularly on issues to do with *alterity), *Derrida, *Foucault, and to a limited extent *Deleuze and *Guattari (especially their concept of the *rhizome).

Further Reading: A. Ahmad *In Theory: Classes, Nations, Literatures* (1992).
B. Ashcroft et al. *The Empire Writes Back* (2002).
D. Gregory *The Colonial Present* (2004).
P. Hallward *Absolutely Postcolonial: Writing Between the Singular and the Specific* (2002).
R. Young *Postcolonialism: A Very Short Introduction* (2003).

SEE WEB LINKS

- The Postcolonial Studies site in the English Department at Emory University, which gives a good overview of postcolonialism, key authors, terms, and major issues.

p

post-feminism The position, variously argued, that *feminism (specifically *radical or so-called *Second Wave feminism) is no longer relevant in the present situation either because (in the affirmative case) it has achieved its goals and has therefore reached its limit of usefulness, or (in the negative case) it was wrongheaded to begin with and has been superseded by a more sophisticated version. More of a sound bite than a fully thought-out concept, it is a fundamentally conservative notion, much like Francis *Fukuyama's notion of the 'end of history', in that it wants to say both that the struggle for equality of the sexes is over and that the struggle was unnecessarily shrill and aggressive to begin with. However, as many feminist commentators have pointed out, the post-feminist position does not reflect the reality on the ground for the majority of women in the world today, who continue to face gender bias in the workplace and at home.

Further Reading: S. Faludi *Backlash: The Undeclared War against American Women* (1991).

posthumanism The critical perspective that the age of *humanism has come to an end. It is premised on the idea that humanism's twin assumptions that humans are both knowable and reasonable is false. It rejects the idea that humans can be known, largely on the grounds that the dividing line between human and non-human or animal is difficult to delineate in the first place and highly permeable too. Donna *Haraway's work on cyborgs is especially important in this regard. It also rejects the idea that because humans have reason (or at least bestow upon themselves the idea that they have reason), this is sufficient to make them the only arbiters of the fate of the planet and all its other non-human inhabitants. Posthumanism is a highly eco-conscious discourse.

Further Reading: C. Wolfe *What is Posthumanism?* (2010).

post-industrial society A society whose economy is no longer based on manufacturing. In 1973, in *The Coming of Post-Industrial Society,* influential American sociologist Daniel *Bell argued that the transition in the US economy away from manufacturing towards what he called the service sector (but would today be known as the information economy) was generalized and the economy as a whole went through a phase change. Writing at a time of real crisis in the global economy brought on by the so-called 'Oil Shock' (a massive spike in the cost of energy engineered by the OPEC member nations), which had a profoundly negative effect on manufacturing, Bell's work seemed to capture the **zeitgeist* perfectly. The term itself was coined by French sociologist Alain *Touraine in *The Post-Industrial Society. Tomorrow's Social History: Classes, Conflicts and Culture in the Programmed Society* (1969). Both Bell and Touraine argue that the transformation in the economy brings with it a transformation in society—in the preceding industrial period it was the antagonism between the proletariat and the bourgeoisie that gave society its cultural coherence. In post-industrial society, the blue-collar worker recedes in importance, and his or her place is taken by the so-called white-collar worker, but now there isn't a clear-cut class distinction to shape society because there is no real significant difference between them and the bourgeoisie. Theorists, such as Fredric *Jameson and David *Harvey, would take this same moment as the starting point for what they prefer to call *postmodernism.

postmodern *See* POSTMODERNISM.

postmodern condition *See* POSTMODERNISM.

postmodernism See next page.

postmodernity *See* POSTMODERNISM.

POSTMODERNISM

A highly contested term used to signify a critical distance from *modernism. Since it first came to prominence in the mid 1970s, it has given rise to a vast body of literature in virtually every discipline in the humanities and social sciences. Broadly speaking, though, it has been used in three main ways: (i) to name the present historical period; (ii) to name a specific style in art and architecture; (iii) to name a point of rupture or disjuncture in epistemology (for this reason it is often, mistakenly, equated with *poststructuralism and *deconstruction). Attempts have been made to standardize usage so that when the historical period is intended the term 'postmodernity' is used, whereas if it is the aesthetic dimension that is at issue the term 'postmodernism' is used, with the term 'postmodern' being reserved for epistemological references. Pedagogically useful as this standardization of terminology is, the uptake of it is very far from universal.

In *The Origins of Postmodernity* (1998), Perry *Anderson traces the first appearance of the notion of postmodernism to the work of the literary critic Frederico de Onís, who used the word 'postmodernismo' (in a foreword to a collection of contemporary Hispanophone poetry he edited in 1934) to describe what he saw as a short-lived reactionary reflux within modernism itself (i.e. precisely the opposite meaning to the one it would subsequently attain). Although it gained widespread usage in Spanish and Portuguese criticism, both in Europe and Latin America, it didn't pass into the Anglophone world until 1954, when the great English historian Arnold Toynbee used it in an essentially negative way in the eighth volume of his *A Study of History* to name the period beginning with the Franco-Prussian War (1870–1). However, Toynbee's deployment of the term didn't catch on. It was, rather, the contemporaneous usage of the term—initially only in private correspondence—by the 'Black Mountain Poets' Charles Olson and Robert Creeley, who were the first to use it in a sense consistent with how the term is understood today, that was to prove influential.

Olson and Creeley used the term 'post-modern' to describe both a shift in history and a specific poetic project they developed in relation to that shift. But neither poet produced a durable doctrine and the term fell into disuse again, only to be picked up a few years later at the dawn of the 1960s by two scions of the New York Left, C. Wright Mills and Irving Howe. If in the hands of Olson and

Creeley the term postmodern had acquired a certain affirmative meaning, Mills and Howe quickly restored its pejorative sense: they mobilized the term to describe a general slackening of commitment to the political ideals embodied in the notions of communism and socialism. At the end of the 1960s, its meaning was once more reversed by the literary critic Leslie Fiedler who used it in a CIA-sponsored conference to celebrate the emergence of a new 'youth-culture' sensibility prioritizing personal expression and civil rights over work and the needs of the state. To this point, the use of the term postmodern was sporadic and inconsistent, functioning more as a suggestive adjective than a viable concept. But that soon changed.

In 1971, Egyptian-born literary and cultural critic Ihab Hassan produced a vast survey of works (across all the arts, but focused particularly on literature and music) that in his view could no longer be described as modern because their organizing impetus was radically different from modernism, and had therefore to be labelled postmodern. Interestingly, his key exhibits of this new style were John Cage, Robert Rauschenberg, and Buckminster Fuller, all names associated with Black Mountain College. Hassan argued that these artists (together with the likes of Ashberry, Barth, Barthelme, Pynchon, and Warhol) were anarchic in spirit and inclined towards playful indeterminacy rather than the Olympian aloofness which he associated with modernism. Although willing to see the postmodern as a form of 'epistemic break' (a term he adapted from Michel *Foucault) akin to other forms of the *Avant-garde, such as *Dadaism and *Surrealism, he refused to see it as a historic break and pulled back from making any connection between the new art form and changes in society. Thus, for Hassan postmodernism was essentially a passing fad in the history of the arts and it was soon overtaken by what he called post-postmodernism.

It took the architectural historian Charles Jencks to connect the dots and link the artistic Avant-garde with social change and contrive a vision of the postmodern that would finally capture the attention of the mainstream. Somewhat gnomically, Jencks pronounced that the previous era came to an end at precisely 3.32pm on July 15, 1972, with the demolition of the Pruitt-Igoe social housing project in St Louis, designed by the architect responsible for the twin towers of the World Trade Centre in New York, Minoru Yamasaki (this coincidence has not gone unremarked and there are those who suggest that it is the destruction of the latter that actually marks the true advent of postmodernity). Jencks reasoned that the destruction of these buildings marked the end of the idea (largely associated with utopian architects like Le Corbusier) that social change could be effected through architecture and more generally the end of the idea that it is government's role to attempt to effect social change. It also signalled the acceptance of the idea that the global market is the true arbiter of the social. Jencks saw in this gesture a refreshing willingness to break with the past and it was this aspect of postmodernism that his writing emphasized. But he also hoped that the proliferation of new styles which this changed attitude to tradition enabled would give rise to a kind of *polyphonic harmony of differences.

Now widely used in architectural and artistic circles, the term postmodern was still seen as referring primarily to a new style or fashion in the aesthetic realm and was regarded by many (including those like Hassan who initially touted the term) as suspiciously modish. The next statement of the term would deepen its penetration considerably and apply it to the realm of knowledge itself thus giving the term the intellectual respectability it had hitherto lacked. Commissioned by the Conseil des Universités of the government of Quebec, Jean-François *Lyotard's *La Condition postmoderne: rapport sur le savoir* (1979), translated as *The Postmodern Condition: A Report on Knowledge* (1984) transformed postmodernism into a concept to be reckoned with, and initiated a two-decade long debate about its existence. Lyotard famously defined the postmodern as incredulity towards what he called *grand narratives. By this he meant (i) the idea that revolution was inevitable and that it would bring with it beneficial social change; and (ii) the *Enlightenment ideal that progress in social terms would be achieved through technological advancement. The credibility of these grand narratives was destroyed by World War II, which revealed the hollowness of both—revolution gave rise to Stalinism and the Enlightenment gave rise to Nazism (here Lyotard's argument extends several key tenets of Frankfurt School thinker Theodor *Adorno's work).

The destruction of the grand narratives saw the spawning of a multiplicity of 'little narratives' or what Lyotard more commonly referred to as *language games (a notion he adapted from Ludwig *Wittgenstein). Incommensurable with one another, these language games could neither be subsumed by an overarching or totalizing concept such as *contradiction nor integrated by processes like Jürgen *Habermas's notion of consensus or Niklas Luhmann's systems theory. Lyotard is careful to acknowledge that not all social relations are of this type, but he nonetheless insists that language games are the minimum form of social relation. The resulting image of society, which Lyotard terms 'realism', is that of an agonistics or even a polemics in which each language game must compete for legitimacy. Unable to appeal to pre-existing grand narratives for its legitimacy, knowledge now makes do by citing its efficiency and its practicality. It has to be said that Lyotard paints a grim portrait of the university system dominated by economic rationalism, which is only very partially offset by the faith he has in Avant-garde art to keep alive thoughts of the future by, as he puts it, 'waging war on totality'. Although Lyotard speaks of postmodernism as a historical condition and links the state of knowledge corresponding to that condition to the kinds of social changes theorized by Daniel *Bell and others as the emergence of a *post-industrial society, he doesn't name the cause of the change. A decade later British Marxist geographer David *Harvey would give a much more thorough answer to this problem in his *The Condition of Postmodernity* (1989).

The first critic to provide an economic answer to the problem Lyotard raised was however Marxist cultural critic Fredric *Jameson. Jameson's work on postmodernism was developed in instalments over a period of more than 20 years. One can read traces of it in *Marxism and Form* (1971) and *The Political Unconscious* (1981), though in these instances he used the terms *consumer society, *post-industrial society, and *society of the spectacle. He first used the term postmodernism in a talk entitled 'Postmodernism and Consumer Society' given at the Whitney Museum of Contemporary Art in the autumn of 1982. A fuller version of the essay was subsequently published in *New Left Review* in the spring of 1984 under the new title of 'Postmodernism, or, the Cultural Logic of Late Capitalism'. This essay has been enormously influential and for many it offers the definitive, but by no means infallible, definition of postmodernism. Jameson builds on Ernest Mandel's argument in *Der Spätkapitalismus* (1972), translated as *Late Capitalism* (1975), that contemporary capitalism is an intensification of trends in global economics detected by Marx, rather than proof that Marx was wrong (as Daniel Bell and others had argued).

Rejecting any suggestion that capitalism has somehow come to an end, radically changed, or worse attained its apotheosis, Jameson's thesis is that postmodern culture is the *superstructural expression of *late capitalism (meaning simply the current state of the *mode of production), which for Jameson means a global situation of economic, military, and political dominance by the US.

Jameson readily acknowledges that postmodern texts are recognizably different from modern texts, but in contrast to a lot of critics he is unwilling to accept that the symptomatic features of postmodernism are purely textual in origin. Culture, for Jameson, cannot be dissociated from the economic and political situation in which it must make its way because the traditional *Marxist distinction between them (i.e. the *base/superstructure model) has in fact collapsed. Postmodernism, Jameson argues, is the 'cultural revolution' needed to enable contemporary society to adjust and respond to these changes. His catalogue of five symptoms of postmodernism—the *waning of affect, *pastiche, *hysterical sublime, *geopolitical aesthetic, and a mutation in built space that has discombobulated our global *cognitive map—have to be read against this background.

For many, however, Jameson's account of postmodernism is too 'totalizing' (which certain careless critics have equated with 'totalitarianism', though in reality it means nothing more sinister than trying to account for the historical situation as a whole) and there remains a strong counter-current which resists his comprehensive overview in favour of a highly localized aesthetic and/or epistemological definition. Canadian literary critic, Linda Hutcheon, is probably the leading exponent of the purely aesthetic definition of postmodernism, while the late American philosopher Richard *Rorty was probably the principal authority on the epistemological version of postmodernism.

Further Reading: P. Anderson *The Origins of Postmodernity* (1998).
I. Buchanan *Fredric Jameson: Live Theory* (2006).
A. Callinicos *Against Postmodernism* (1989).
D. Harvey *The Condition of Postmodernity* (1990).
I. Hassan *The Postmodern Turn* (1987).
F. Jameson *Postmodernism, or, the Cultural Logic of Late Capitalism* (1991).
C. Jencks *The Language of Post-Modern Architecture* (1977).
J-F. Lyotard *La Condition postmoderne: rapport sur le savoir* (1979) translated as *The Postmodern Condition: A Report on Knowledge* (1984).

post-structuralism An influential movement (albeit one whose membership is ambiguous) in *critical theory that came into being as the result of an internal critique of the movement that preceded it, namely *structuralism, with which it shares a number of crucial characteristics, particularly the latter's anti-humanist de-privileging of the individual conscious and the subject. Its principal characteristic is scepticism (to the point of irrationality according to its critics) towards any form of completeness of either knowledge or understanding. It rejects all transcendental and/or idealist ontologies and epistemologies and accepts only those theories of being and knowledge that are premised on the final unknowability of these things.

Post-structuralism is generally thought to have emerged at a conference held at Johns Hopkins University in 1966 to celebrate the achievements of structuralism and showcase it to American academics. A young scholar by the name of Jacques *Derrida presented a paper criticizing the conference's keynote speaker and one of the founding fathers of structuralism, Claude *Lévi-Strauss, entitled 'La structure, le signe et le jeu dans le discours des sciences humaines', translated as 'Structure, Sign and Play in the Discourse of Human Sciences' (1978). In what would become well known as his style of thinking, Derrida shattered the illusion at the heart of structuralism, namely that language could be frozen long enough to identify its universal characteristics. But, Derrida argued, language is a continuous process, and as such, its structures (i.e. its internal rules) are subject to constant variation. What we recognize as post-structuralist thinking today is the extension of this idea to virtually every aspect of human thought, with the effect that it has become a doctrine that no idea, concept, thought, or thing is ever fully what we think it is. Derrida uses the word **différance* to name this state of affairs.

Post-structuralism is a very loosely applied term. It is often treated as a synonym for *postmodernism, but this is misleading because whereas postmodernism concerns changes at the level of the world-historical, post-structuralism refers only to an intellectual position. Similarly, it is often used as a synonym for deconstruction, but this is also imprecise because although Derrida is credited with initiating this particular intellectual position, he has his own project which does not coincide on all points with post-structuralism as it is generally understood. Along the same lines, it is often said to include authors as diverse as *Badiou, *Barthes, Derrida, *Deleuze, *Foucault, *Jameson, and Lyotard, but this is also misleading inasmuch as it makes it seem that the work of these authors has something more in common than the general agreement that structuralism was inadequate in several important respects. In the hands of its critics, like Jürgen *Habermas, and Manfred *Frank, post-structuralism is simply a codeword for irrational and irresponsible philosophy. So it is a term that should be used with considerable caution.

Further Reading: C. Belsey *Poststructuralism: A Very Short Introduction* (2002). J. Williams *Understanding Poststructuralism* (2005).

Poulantzas, Nicos (1936–79) Paris-based Greek *Marxist philosopher and sociologist. Born and educated in Greece, Poulantzas was active in the student movement in the 1950s. He was a member of the Greek Democratic Alliance, which was the euphemism used by the outlawed Greek Communist Party. After completing his law degree in the late 1950s, he moved to Paris to undertake a PhD in the philosophy of law. There he met and was influenced by Louis *Althusser. But although Poulantzas came to be considered an 'Althusserian', his work maintained its own distinctive character and edge. He came into prominence as a theorist of the state—he engaged the doyen of the British New Left, historian Ralph Miliband in a long-running debate on the theory of the state in the pages of the *New Left Review*. Poulantzas argued that the state serves the interests of capital by providing the minimum level of social order needed to enable business to flourish. It solicits the legitimation of this social order by cultural means, particularly through the imagery and rhetoric of nation, but also (and more insidiously) through tokenistic concessions to organized labour. In so doing, Poulantzas borrowed from and reinterpreted Italian Marxist Antonio *Gramsci's concept of *hegemony, giving *ideology an affirmative rather than purely manipulative role to play in the formation and reproduction of the state. He was particularly interested in examining the reasons behind the failure of dictatorships to endure in spite of their powerful repressive measures. His main works were: *Political Power and Social Classes* (1973); *Fascism and Dictatorship* (1974); *The Crisis of Dictatorships* (1976); and *State, Power, Socialism* (1978).

Further Reading: B. Jessop *Nicos Poulantzas: Theory and Political Strategy* (1985).

Practical Criticism A form of literary analysis which focuses exclusively on the text, ignoring such extraneous factors as authorial intention and historical context. The term originates with an experiment performed on Cambridge literature students by I.A. *Richards. The students were given a selection of poems to read and comment on, but they were not given the titles of the poems, nor were they told anything about who the authors of the poems were. The idea was that the students should judge the texts before them solely on the basis of what they had in front of them. Richards was amazed at how poorly (in his view) the students performed and concluded that what was needed was more practical instruction in the art of reading texts. The results of his experiments (Richards's own background was in fact in psychology) are written up in the appropriately titled *Practical Criticism: A Study of Literary Judgement* (1929), which became a kind of handbook for the discipline of literary studies and had enormous influence. It was however his former student, F.R. *Leavis, who popularized the method of 'close reading' through the journal, *Scrutiny,* which he founded. It became the default way of reading literary texts in most of the Anglophone world. Even after its influence waned in universities due to the impact of *structuralism and *poststructuralism in the 1960s, it remained very much in force in high schools and colleges well into the 1980s. The exception to this rule was the US, which was instead gripped by *New Criticism, a home-grown mutation of Practical Criticism, that was similarly concerned to focus only on the text.

The strength of Practical Criticism was that it set aside the merely impressionistic responses found in what Terry *Eagleton describes as the 'belle-lettristic waffle' of the then hegemonic Bloomsbury group of authors, and brought genuine rigour to the business of reading texts. Students were taught to better understand the effects of literary convention and technique (e.g. the role of *metaphor), and were given free rein to pronounce judgement on the relative worth of specific texts. Practical Criticism, particularly its leading avatar F.R. Leavis, was virtually obsessed with deciding what did and did not belong in the canon of 'great texts' worthy of further study. While this enabled literary studies to develop standardized texts and more importantly standardized tests in schools, thus explaining its incredible influence, it also led to standardized responses to texts and promoted the idea that only certain responses (i.e. the teacher's) could be considered valid. Because Practical Criticism ignored both the author's and the reader's background and was only interested in so-called 'universals' like 'truth', it consciously reduced the range of meanings any text might in fact yield. It was this factor more than anything that led to its eventual demise as other methods celebrating diversity of meaning came into fashion. But it was also attacked from a political perspective for ignoring the significance of *identity politics, particularly issues to do with *gender, *race, and sexuality. The plurality of possible readings that texts can give rise to is explored by *reader-response critics.

Further Reading: P. McCallum *Literature and Method: Towards a Critique of I.A. Richards, T.S. Eliot, and F.R. Leavis* (1983).

practices A code word in *Cultural Studies for what people do in the course of their *everyday life. Such activities as dating, shopping, walking, watching TV, and the like are generally regarded as examples of practices. Although the term is somewhat out of fashion nowadays, the twofold impetus behind its coinage remains current: on the one hand, the term is used to defend the position that there is no aspect of culture (no matter how banal) that is not significant and therefore worthy of critical attention; on the other hand, it is used as a tacit critique or indeed rejection of the central plank of both psychology and *psychoanalysis, namely the assumption that it is possible to know *why* people do what they do. In this regard, the uptake of the term could be said to signal an empirical turn in Cultural Studies, the basic position of which is as follows: we can know what people do because their activity can be observed and recorded, but we cannot know why they do what they do because their intentions and purposes are not visible. Behind this turn, however, there is also a stubborn repudiation of *Marxism. For Marxism, the reason why we do things can and must be explained in terms of *ideology. Practices became prominent in Cultural Studies in large part because of Pierre *Bourdieu and Michel de *Certeau, who both used the term in comparable ways. Certeau's highly influential two-volume study (produced in collaboration with Luce Giard and Pierre Mayol) *L'invention du quotidian* (1980), translated as *The Practice of Everyday Life* (1984), proposed the hypothesis that practices are the texts of everyday life and that by using the resources of *semiotics they can be made legible. He even went so far as to propose that it might be possible to develop a grammar of such activities as walking and introduced the concepts of *strategy and tactics as possible analytic terms. John Fiske popularized these ideas in several of his books, particularly *Understanding Popular Culture* (1989), while John Frow provided a comprehensive critique of them in *Cultural Studies and Cultural Value* (1995). For Bourdieu, practices are a branch of reason or 'savoir faire' ('know how') that stems from the body rather than mind.

Further Reading: B. Highmore *Everyday Life and Cultural Theory* (2002).

practico-inert Jean-Paul *Sartre's term in *Critique de la Raison Dialectique* (1960), translated as *Critique of Dialectical Reason* (1976), for the embedded or sunk (to use the economics term) results of *praxis, by which he meant deliberate, goal-oriented human action. As such, the practico-inert is the matter with which praxis must work. For example, climate change is the product of hundreds of years of human endeavour, which until very recently was (and perhaps even still is) seen as activity contributing to the welfare of humanity. Industrialization brought real rewards to at least some sections of *society, not only improving the standard of living in monetary terms, but also improving the quality of life by providing labour-saving, indeed life-saving new technology. But now it is clear that very same process has created the potential for a catastrophe on a global scale. As Sartre puts it with regard to his own highly localized example of deforestation in China, humans have done what humanity's worst enemy would have done if it had wanted to destroy humankind. The very thing that calls most urgently for praxis now is in fact the result of past praxis.

pragmatics A branch of linguistics which investigates the role context plays in the formation of meaning. It draws on the J.L. *Austin theory of the *performative, but also incorporates elements of anthropology and sociology. It is interested in the way users of a particular language draw on non-linguistic cues to disambiguate the intent of a particular piece of communication (e.g. to determine whether a comment was a jest or insult, flirtatious or harassing, etc.).

pragmatism A branch of philosophy founded by the American philosophers Charles Sanders *Peirce and William James—the latter is credited with coining the term, but he attributes the concept to Peirce. Pragmatism is distinguished by its interest in how things work and its foregrounding of belief as an effective mode of thought—we act on beliefs, even when we have no way of verifying them. It is interested in the ways by which humans and indeed all organisms mentally adapt to their environment and create a workable relationship with it via the elaboration of concepts.
See also CONSTRUCTIVISM.

Prague Linguistic Circle A discussion group founded in 1926 by a small group of Czech and expatriate Russian linguists, for the purpose of analysing the poetic function of language. The group was chaired by renowned linguist Roman *Jakobson, but also numbered amongst its membership Nicolai Troubetzkoy and Jan Mukařovský. Also known as the Prague School, the group survived World War II (though many of its members were forced into exile) but not the rise to power of the Communist Party. It was officially dissolved in 1950, but had in reality already dissipated two years earlier. As a crucial precursor to *structuralism, the group worked through a number of ideas taken from *Saussure, and created the first effective form of a structuralist linguistics (characterized by a pronounced interest in **langue* rather than *parole*). As with its predecessors, *Opoyaz and the *Moscow Linguistic Circle, from which its membership was in part drawn in any case, the group sought to bring together *poetics and linguistics.

Further Reading: T. Bennett *Formalism and Marxism* (1979).
V. Erlich *Russian Formalism: History—Doctrine* (1955).

praxis The Greek word for 'doing' which is widely used in *critical theory to signify purposive and purposeful human activity, that is to say human activity with a specific goal and a tangible outcome. The most prominent and completely theorized use of the term praxis is undoubtedly to be found in Jean-Paul *Sartre's *Critique de la Raison Dialectique* (1960), translated as *Critique of Dialectical Reason* (1976); but important discussions are also to be found in the work of the Italian *Marxist Antonio *Gramsci. In some quarters, praxis is a synonym for *resistance. It is used to designate any action that consciously interrupts the *hegemonic status quo.

primal scene (*Urszene*) In *psychoanalysis, the child's first witnessing of its parents having sexual intercourse. The child makes a threefold interpretation of the act, according to Sigmund *Freud: first, they interpret it as an act of aggression on the part of the father; second, while it excites them, it also induces fear of castration; third, the child assumes it is anal sex. Freud initially insisted that the primal scene was actual—that the child had to actually witness the event—but later came to realize that it could just as well be virtual, a figment of the imagination.

problematic French *Marxist Louis *Althusser adopted this term (from the work of Jacques Martin) to describe the source of the theoretical unity of a particular form of *discourse. His purpose in doing so was to distinguish the so-called early or Hegelian Marx from the later post-Hegelian Marx. The term is widely used in *critical theory today, usually without any reference to Althusser, as a means of indicating a theoretical starting point that is at once perplexing and productive.

problematization Probably the most influential conception of this term derives from Michel *Foucault, whose work on health, incarceration, madness, and sexuality inquires how each of these things was rendered problematic, which is to say transformed into something capable of inducing or requiring action at the level of the state. In this sense, problematization is one of *governmentality's core processes.

projection In *psychoanalysis, the process of transposing thoughts generated by the *psyche onto the outside world, thus enabling the subject to rid themselves of character traits they would prefer not to see themselves have. For example, as Sigmund *Freud argues, gothic tales and horror stories give body to nameless and essentially empty anxieties and fears as well as desires that most people have. It can take more paranoid forms, too, such as the subject who is uncertain about their ability to remain faithful who then projects infidelity onto their partner. Projection is central to the work of Melanie *Klein, who employs it in her account of childhood development to explain how children 'act out' their internal thoughts. So when a child deliberately breaks a toy they could be seen as projecting their own sense of helplessness in the family situation. *See also* INTROJECTION.

Propp, Vladimir (1895–1970) Russian literary scholar and founding father of *narratology. Born in St Petersburg, he attended St Petersburg University, studying philosophy. After graduation in 1918, he taught Russian and German at secondary schools for a number of years before attaining a position at his alma mater. In 1928 Propp published *Morfológija skázki*, which applied the principle of *Russian Formalism to the study the narrative structure of Slavic folktales. The impact of this work was quite modest to begin with; indeed, it was not until 1960 when Claude *Lévi-Strauss wrote an approving, but nonetheless searching critique of the 1958 English translation *The Morphology of the Folktale* did it become well known. Following that, however, its impact was nothing short of seismic: it reshaped the study of narrative almost completely. Roland *Barthes translated Lévi-Strauss's insights into a useable form for literary criticism in his 1966 essay, 'Introduction à l'analyse structurale des récits', translated as 'Introduction to Structural Analysis of Narratives' (1977). Probably the best known and most effective use of Propp's thought is in the study of genre fiction—Umberto *Eco's essay on the narrative structure of James Bond is perhaps the archetype. Propp set aside the content of the text, as it were, namely the actual sentences that comprise the text, and focused exclusively on the abstract form of the text, paying particular attention to the events (or functions) and character types in the tale. By sorting out those events and characters which are crucial to the tale and those which are superfluous, Propp exposed the *syntagm or that which is universal to the tale. He argued that there are 31 basic functions and 7 character types and that all folktales are created using an amalgam of these standard ingredients.

Further Reading: S. Rimmon-Kenan *Narrative Fiction* (1983).

prosopopoeia A rhetorical device whereby the perspective of another person or thing is given voice, as in the statement 'the evidence speaks for itself', or 'if X was here they would no doubt have something to say', and so on.

psyche The Greek word for breath and soul 'psukhē', and the name given to Eros's true love. Swiss analytical psychologist Carl *Jung used the term to designate the totality of mental processes, both conscious and *unconscious. Crucially, Jung's notion of the psyche allows for autonomous entities, such as *complexes, to operate within its domain. The psyche should thus be viewed as being neither homogenous nor unified. It is also capable of transformation.

psychic reality Everything that strikes a person as being real, regardless of whether it is actually real. Psychic reality feels real to the person who experiences it and they have no sense that it might not be real. Swiss analytical psychologist Carl *Jung used this term to explain the fact that two people may encounter a specific event quite differently. It also explains how one person may apprehend quite different things—poltergeists and spiders, let's say—in fundamentally the same way. In Jung's theory, psychic reality is an intermediary phase between the physical world of sense data on the one hand and the spiritual world of thought and cognition on the other hand.

psychoanalysis A means of investigating the *unconscious dimension of the human mind established by Sigmund *Freud on the basis of his self-analysis and his experience as a practising clinician dealing with *hysterical and *neurotic patients. Freud himself stated that psychoanalysis has three dimensions: it is (i) a method for investigating the unconscious meanings of the things patients say and do; (ii) a therapeutic technique; and (iii) a cluster of inter-related theories that attempt to explain systematically the functioning of the psychical apparatus.

It is described in this way, as a cluster of theories, because although Freud was responsible for initiating psychoanalysis, he was rapidly joined by a large number of other practitioners, who, in due course, contributed their own theories, sometimes building on Freud's own work and taking it further, and sometimes challenging his hypotheses and offering counter-proposals. In time, schools and factions developed and psychoanalysis as a movement fractured along a variety of faultlines, making it impossible to describe it as being just one thing. Although the different schools of thought in psychoanalysis share a number of common points, the differences between them can be quite radical, as splinter groups initiated by Carl *Jung, Melanie *Klein, and others show very well.

Jacques *Lacan, one of Freud's most important interpreters (particularly from the perspective of *critical theory), frequently insisted that Freud's theories can only be fully understood in the context of the analytic situation, that is to say, in the context of the therapeutic relation between the analyst and analysand (patient). His famous battle cry that psychoanalysis needed to 'return to Freud' meant precisely this: the core of psychoanalysis is *transference, the relationship between analyst and analysand. The history of the development of psychoanalysis tends to bear out Lacan's claim inasmuch that psychoanalysis as we know it today wasn't born until Freud abandoned both hypnosis (a technique he adopted from the great French neurologist Jean-Martin Charcot and refined further with his colleague Josef Breuer) and *seduction theory, which he did when he found them both to be therapeutically limiting.

Freud stopped using hypnosis because he realized that what people say freely, without suggestion, is *more* not less indicative of what is happening in their unconscious, provided one knows how to interpret it. As he later demonstrated at length in *Zur Psychopathologie des Alltagslebens* (1901), translated as *The Psychopathology of Everyday Life* (1914), the little repetitions, hesitations, mistakes, and so on we routinely make in everyday conversation can all betray the workings of the unconscious. He abandoned seduction theory when he realized that the stories his patients were telling him, which frequently included accounts of childhood rapes and what would later be known as *Oedipal fantasies, couldn't all be true, even if the patients insisted they were. The path of psychoanalysis was henceforward to comprehend the mechanisms of the unconscious, or what Freud called the primary processes.

Having ruled out actual seduction, Freud had to explain both the fact that fantasies can have such a strong effect and the seeming omnipresence of sex in those fantasies. He was able to do so by proposing a *topography of the psychical apparatus, separating it into three distinct but interconnected spheres: the unconscious, the preconscious, and the conscious. The unconscious, he argued, is where the *instincts (of which there are two main types—the life instinct and *death instinct, both of which are intimately related to sex) reside and these instincts exert a constant pressure on the other parts of the psychical apparatus, but they cannot pass through the preconscious into the conscious in their raw form without causing a psychic disturbance. They are held in place by a powerful counterforce he called *repression. Repression does not necessarily mean absolute negation, it can also take the form of distortion (*dreamwork), which disguises unacceptable thoughts and impulses in an acceptable form. Neuroses, he then reasoned, are caused either by the exhausting effort of maintaining this repression and/or because the effort had failed.

One of Freud's earliest patients, Fräulein Anna O (later identified as Bertha van Pappenheim), whom he wrote about in *Studien über Hysterie* (1895), translated as *Studies on Hysteria* (1955), described psychoanalysis as a *talking cure because Freud's therapeutic technique consisted in asking patients to describe their dreams, or recent activities, and then ask them to think through and talk about all the associations that came to mind as they did so. By this means his patients became gradually aware of the operations of the unconscious. Interestingly, Freud did not generally interpret people's dreams for them, but rather taught them the means of analysing them themselves. Some patients resisted this process, a fact that Freud usually interpreted as meaning they actually needed it, while others became all but addicted to it, a problem he never fully resolved.

Psychoanalysis is undoubtedly one of the most influential intellectual movements of the past century. Although he was highly critical of psychoanalysis, Michel *Foucault nevertheless described Freud as a 'founder of discourse' because his work created the possibility of a new way of thinking and speaking about the human subject. Its influence is all but incalculable—it is vital to *critical theory, the *Frankfurt School, *Dada, *Surrealism, and literary studies, just to mention a few of the more obvious fields where its impact has been substantial.

Further Reading: C. Surprenant *Freud: A Guide for the Perplexed* (2008).
T. Thwaites *Reading Freud: Psychoanalysis as Cultural Theory* (2007).

psychoanalytic criticism The application of *psychoanalysis to the understanding of cultural texts, particularly literary and filmic texts. The originator of psychoanalysis, Sigmund *Freud, was fascinated by cultural texts and made extensive references to them throughout his writings. Indeed, one might argue that the foundational concept of the *Oedipal complex is a product of Freud's interest in literature, inasmuch that he speculates that Sophocles' play still has a hold on us some 2,500 years after it is written because it dramatizes a universal experience. But Freud's most important thoughts on the subject are to be found in two short essays, one on daydreams, the other on the notion of the *uncanny. In the first essay, 'Der Dichter und das Phantasieren' (1908), translated as 'Creative Writers and Day-dreaming' (1959), Freud argued that creative writing is a form of play in which the writer creates a fantasy world that he or she takes seriously. The artistry of writing lies in disguising, or better yet *sublimating the libidinal dimensions of the fantasy world so that readers will not be put off or embarrassed by it. In the second essay, 'Das Unheimliche' (1919), translated as 'The Uncanny' (1955), Freud argued that literature's ability to unsettle us stems from the way it reminds readers of their own traumatic, but *unconscious events of childhood. In this way, Freud laid out the two main pathways that psychoanalytic criticism has followed since: on the one hand, it has tried to use the author's life to understand their work, to see their creations as the product of unconscious desires; while on the other hand, it has tried to understand the effect creative works have by discerning in them repetitions of common symptoms and neuroses that all readers can identify with. In both cases, then, the creative work is apprehended as the representation of an unconscious wish, either the author's or the reader's. The body of research in this field is immense and includes many of the leading names in *critical theory. Currently, the most prominent theorist in the field is Slavoj Žižek, but one must also mention the challenge to psychoanalysis posed by Gilles *Deleuze and Félix *Guattari—they do not reject psychoanalysis as many people think, but they do dispute the core idea of psychoanalytic criticism that all texts are so many rehearsals of unconscious fantasies. They argue that texts are better seen as machines that carry out essential psychic work.

Further Reading: E. Wright *Psychoanalytic Criticism* (1984).

psychogeography The study of the specific effects (and affects) of the built environment (intended or not) on the emotions and actions of individuals. Although generally associated with the *Situationists, it actually dates back to the days before Situationism when its originator Guy *Debord was still involved with the Lettrist International. The term first appeared in an essay by Debord, in the short-lived Lettrist organ *Potlatch*, entitled 'Introduction to a Critique of Urban Geography' (1955). Debord claims the term was suggested to him by an illiterate Kabyle as a general term for a variety of phenomena the group was investigating in 1953. Put very simply the aim of psychogeography was to see the urban space in the light of desire rather than habit. In order to do that, it experimented with different ways of getting lost, such as hiking through the Harz region in Germany using a London map as a guide. But it also implies a project to reform or re-imagine the city, to make it more desirable by making it less a product of and service agent for capitalism. Psychogeography was, and is, very far from an exact science and it is perhaps best to think of it more as a set of practices designed to escape the imperatives of the city than a precise concept or methodology. Having said that, it was not meant to be simply playful either—its purpose was always serious, even when its methods were not. Psychogeography did not come to an end with the Situationist movement, but continues to be developed today. Novelists and cultural historians such as Iain Sinclair, Peter Ackroyd, Stewart Home, and Will Self, also consider much of their writing about the secret or inner life of cities to be exercises in psychogeography. It has also been suggested that the dark and mysterious tales of the city found in the work of William Blake, Thomas de Quincy, Charles Baudelaire, and Walter *Benjamin should be considered as providing templates for what would become psychogeography. *See also* COGNITIVE MAPPING; *DÉRIVE*; *DÉTOURNEMENT*; DETERRITORIALIZATION; *FLÂNEUR*.

Further Reading: M. Coverley *Psychogeography* (2006).
K. Knabb (ed.) *Situationist International Anthology* (2007).
R. Solnit *Wanderlust: A History of Walking* (2001).

psychosis A 19th century psychiatric term for madness that was taken up by *psychoanalysis to designate severe mental disorders (e.g. schizophrenia), which it contrasted with the less severe disorders of *neurosis. In general, psychoanalysis regards psychosis as untreatable because it has as its main symptom the complete breakdown of communication, thereby making the *talking cure impossible. Yet, as the work of Jacques *Lacan makes plain, psychoanalysis also regards psychosis as an incredibly important phenomenon from the point of view of studying how the psychical apparatus functions. Lacan's theory of the genesis of psychosis hinges on the failure of the *Oedipal process and the *foreclosure of Name-of-the-Father, with the result that *symbolic order is not properly formed and the *subject is locked into a nightmarish world dominated by the *imaginary. Unable to distinguish between the real and the unreal, the psychotic subject suffers delusional episodes that can make life extremely difficult for them. Gilles *Deleuze and Félix *Guattari reject the psychoanalytic explanation of the genesis of psychosis—in their view, its genesis can only be organic, i.e. the result of physiological changes in the brain itself. As a result, their work offers no theory for the treatment of psychosis; rather, it concentrates on adapting the world (and not the 'patient') to its symptoms.

public sphere (*Öffentlichkeit*) Jürgen *Habermas's term for any realm of social life in which public opinion can be formed. It comes into existence whenever a forum is created in which citizens can express their opinions concerning topics of general—i.e. public—interest, and those opinions can be subjected to critical debate. The public sphere should be open to all citizens and everyone within it should be treated equally. Examples of possible public spheres include newspapers, magazines, radio news, TV news, and of course the Internet, but it should be noted not all of these entities necessarily satisfy the democratic rule concerning access and freedom to express opinion. Similarly, not everything that is expressed in these outlets is of public interest. In other words, public sphere is not simply another word for media. Habermas's thesis is that the public sphere that arose in the early 18th century was eroded by the rise of what Michel *Foucault called *biopower, the intervention of the state. Public spheres are historical concepts and in Habermas's view they can be thought of as being typical of their age.

qualia In philosophy, the specific phenomenal or affective qualities of a particular conscious experience. For example, the taste of wine, the colour of the night sky, and the sound of crickets chirping on a summer's day, are all qualia.

qualisign A quality (or *qualia) that is a *sign in Charles Sanders *Peirce's semiotic system. Thus colour of a rose is at once a quality of that particular rose and a sign.

quasi-cause Gilles *Deleuze's concept, derived from Stoic philosophy, for the relation between two or more (incorporeal) effects. In Stoic philosophy only bodies, that is material things, can be causes in relation to one another; effects are not causes, or even qualities, they are attributes, or events. Effects do not exist, rather they inhere or subsist.

Queer Studies The study of sexual identity and its related cultural history. It emerged as the academic response to the Stonewall Riots in 1969, initially as a challenge to the academy, but very rapidly became a standard inclusion (albeit in a very tokenistic way) in most humanities and social sciences faculties. It would be an exaggeration to claim that Queer Studies has become mainstream but its exceptional status is certainly a thing of the past. As a field it has become substantial enough to generate several subfields including Asian Queer Studies, Black Queer Studies, Queer Cinema, Queer Nation, and *Queer Theory. Although the obvious point of focus for Queer Studies is *gay and lesbian people, the deeper purpose of Queer Studies is to challenge the efficacy of such labels to begin with. It questions why *society should allocate resources and grant privileges according to sexual orientation. In this respects, its approach, which tends to be highly interdisciplinary, mirrors that of *Postcolonial Studies, *feminism, and *race studies.

Further Reading: R. Corber and S. Valocchi *Queer Studies: An Interdisciplinary Reader* (2003).

Queer Theory A *post-structuralist approach to the analysis, documenting, history, and understanding of human sexuality. It is particularly (but not exclusively) interested in forms of sexuality that fall outside of (or are defined in opposition to) the so-called heterosexual norm. It grew out of and exists alongside *Queer Studies, effectively functioning as the latter's forum for raising definitional and ontological questions concerning what it means to be bisexual, gay, lesbian, or straight. The work of Michel *Foucault, particularly his work on power and the history of sexuality, is generally credited as the principal theoretical impetus. Foucault's work sought to find out both how and why human sexuality came to be treated as an item of knowledge and the cultural and political implications of the attempt to make it knowable. In general, Foucault's work shows that power exerts itself by creating regimes of inclusion and exclusion. The point that is often missed by Foucault's readers is that it is the form of the binary itself that primarily interests Foucault, not the content. In other words, it is not the fact that straight is included and queer is excluded by a given society that concerns Foucault, but rather the fact that the elastic continuum of sexuality can be segmented so neatly despite the obvious permeability of the key categories. In the wake of Foucault's studies, there has proliferated an incredible array of works that affirm the existence of regimes of inclusion and exclusion and show the myriad ways its categories leak. The most prominent in this regard is Eve Kosofsky Sedgwick's *Epistemology of the Closet* (1990), and Judith *Butler's *Gender Trouble* (1990).

Further Reading: I. Morland and A. Willox (eds.) *Queer Theory: Readers in Cultural Criticism* (2004).

N. Sullivan *A Critical Introduction to Queer Theory* (2003).

SEE WEB LINKS

- Online resources integrated with visual and textual resources in Queer Culture, Queer Theory, Queer Studies, Gender Studies, and related fields.

quiddity Derived from the Latin '*quidditas*', meaning 'whatness', it is used in philosophy to designate the specific features of a thing that determine it as that thing. It is a form of universal knowledge and may be compared to *essence.

quilting point (*point de capiton*) A term introduced by Jacques *Lacan to define the points along a signifying chain where the signifier is attached to the signified, at least momentarily. The term is taken from upholstery and refers to the attachment of buttons. A certain number of these quilting points are necessary to the 'normal' *subject—their absence is in fact a symptom of *psychosis. Without such quilting points the subject would be incapable of navigating their *everyday life because they would be constantly questioning the meaning of every *sign they encountered, from the most mundane to the very elaborate.

race The biological, physiological, or genetic classification of humans according to distinctive features of physical appearance such as skin colour, shape of face, hair colour, body morphology. It is generally used in a *binary fashion to identify both a superior race and an inferior race. Throughout history, but especially since the rise of the African slave trade, the concept of race has been of concern to western political thinkers, who use it to justify and legitimate the invasive, exploitative, and predatory actions of their governments. In critical theory, race is thus treated as a problematic term whose history is instructive because it shows how power and *ideology combine to facilitate the unjust and unequal treatment of others by *hegemonic powers. Recent scholarship in postcolonial studies has demonstrated that race is an important issue for non-western political philosophy as well. Because of its associations with colonialism, eugenics, and slavery, race has not been used in an affirmative sense in critical theory since the 1970s, when affirmative terms such as **négritude* began to lose their currency. It has been replaced by *ethnicity in this regard.

radical feminism A loosely formed, but highly visible movement within *feminism calling for a substantial change to the structure of contemporary society (hence the designation 'radical'), which originated in the US in the 1960s with the Women's Liberation Movement. Radical feminism does not have a single or unified theoretical or political doctrine, however it does take a consistent stance towards men. Radical feminists identify *patriarchy as the principal and universal cause of women's oppression via its control of women's reproductive capacity, sexuality and—perhaps most importantly, though much less obviously—via the ideology of *femininity. Some radical feminists, such as Shulamith *Firestone, argue that it is precisely because of women's reproductive capacity that they are vulnerable to subordination by men because pregnancy and childrearing makes them dependent on men for support, at least in humanity's prehistorical beginnings. Therefore control of reproduction via such means as the contraceptive pill is seen as a crucial political step. Similarly the control of women's sexuality is resisted by redefining sex in such a way that it is no longer seen in terms of satisfying male desires and needs (as exemplified by pornography and prostitution). One solution, advocated by at least some radical separatists, is to opt out of the heterosexual matrix altogether and adopt a lesbian lifestyle. The more widely adopted solution, which was advocated by the likes of Germaine *Greer, is for women to set aside the restrictions of the cultural expectations of chastity until marriage and self-denial within marriage and actively pursue their own pleasure needs. Many *post-feminists have in recent times written off this strategy as a pyrrhic victory at best, describing its outcomes as melancholy sex without commitment or love. Probably the greatest changes, though, have been made with regard to the ideology of femininity, which radical feminists sought to overturn. Radical feminism, via the work of people like Mary *Daly, has constructed a women's epistemology, that is, a way of knowing the world from a woman-centric perspective.

Rancière, Jacques (1940–) French philosopher. Born in Algeria, Rancière completed his undergraduate studies in Paris at the prestigious finishing school, École Normale Supérieure (ENS). There Rancière, along with fellow students Étienne *Balibar, Pierre *Macherey, and Michel *Pêcheux, worked very closely with Louis *Althusser. They all collaborated on a major re-reading of *Marx, which culminated in the publication of *Lire le capital* (1968), translated as *Reading Capital* (1970). However, almost as soon as the book was published the group fell out with Althusser over his failure to respond to the events of *May '68, and in subsequent editions the contributions of everyone except Balibar were excised. Rancière settles his account with Althusser in the rather stern critique *La Leçon d'Althusser* (The Lesson of Althusser, 1974). A highly prolific author, Rancière's many publications have focused on three main areas of interest—aesthetics, politics, and pedagogy and explored the interrelationships between the three.

Further Reading: N. Hewlett *Badiou, Balibar, Rancière: Re-thinking Emancipation* (2007).

T. May *The Political Thought of Jacques Rancière: Creating Equality* (2008).

rational choice theory A framework for modelling economic behaviour which assumes that people will always seek to optimize their own situation by maximizing wealth and minimizing costs and will only choose to act in favour of others if there is also a clear benefit to themselves. Economists do not claim that rational choice theory is an exhaustive description of human society, only that it is a workable assumption.

rationality In philosophy, the ability to use reason to make decisions regarding possible actions and determine the optimal choice. Philosophy tends to privilege rationality over the *instinctual, the passional, and the willed, arguing that it is only by exercising reason that humans can be free. In some cases, it is argued that rationality only obtains in mathematics and the physical sciences and that all the other disciplines are too tainted by irrational elements. Some philosophers also hold that rationality is unique to humans, but this view has been seriously challenged in recent times. In contrast, the *Frankfurt School is critical of rationality precisely because they see it as inhuman because it favours the smooth-running of systems (such as the economy) over the inconsistency of individual humans.

Rawls, John (1921–2002) American political philosopher best known for his work on fairness. Born in Baltimore, Rawls went to school in Baltimore and Connecticut. He did his undergraduate degree at Princeton, graduating in 1943. He then joined the army and saw active service as an infantryman in New Guinea, the Philippines, and Japan, where he witnessed the aftermath of the atomic bombing of Hiroshima. After the war he returned to Princeton to complete a doctorate in moral philosophy. He did post-doctoral work at Oxford University in the early 1950s, where he was influenced by Isaiah Berlin. He worked then at Cornell and MIT (Massachusetts Institute of Technology) before obtaining a position at Harvard in 1962, where he was to remain for the next 40 years. Rawls is best known for his 1971 magnum opus, *A Theory of Justice*. One of the most cited humanities books in history, *A Theory of Justice* focuses on the problem of *distributive justice and introduces two principles which have since become famous: the principle of liberty and the principle of difference. The first principle, which Rawls regards as inviolable, holds that all people must enjoy freedom of speech, assembly, worship, and so on in order for society to be just; the second principle, which is more complicated, holds that the economy must be arranged in such a way that it is of the greatest benefit to the least well-off and that the opportunity for social advancement is made open to everyone. *A Theory of Justice* is a much debated work, but it has in many ways set the agenda for debate about social justice in political science since its publication nearly four decades ago. His subsequent publications, particularly *Political Liberalism* (1993) and *The Law of Peoples* (1999) extended these principles to international politics.

Further Reading: C. Audard *John Rawls* (2006).
P. Lehning *John Rawls: An Introduction* (2009).
T. Pogge and M. Kosch *John Rawls: His Life and Theory of Justice* (2007).

reaction-formation (*Reaktionsbildung*) In *psychoanalysis, a psychological attitude that is the direct opposite of the *repressed wish. So an outgoing and exhibitionist person might act bashful and coy. The reaction-formation is a counter-*cathexis, a conscious outlet for *desire that is equivalent to or stronger than the usual *unconscious pathways. Reaction-formations are regarded as pathological or symptomatic only when they take on an obsessive character, or the actual results are in themselves undesirable (e.g. a shy person suddenly becoming overly exhibitionist).

readerly and writerly (*lisible* and *scriptible*) French literary theorist Roland *Barthes proposed these terms in *S/Z* (1970), translated as *S/Z* (1974) to distinguish between literary works that because of their specific formal qualities either constrain the reader to adhere closely to the text with little or no room for interpretive manoeuvre (readerly), or, demand that the reader work hard to make sense of the text and effectively contribute to its very writing (writerly). The first kind of text renders the reader passive, while the latter variety forces the reader to become active. Barthes classifies so-called classical or realist texts, such as George Eliot's *Middlemarch* (1871–2) and Honoré de Balzac's *Eugénie Grandet* (1833), as readerly because there is a central organizing plot (usually in the form of an enigma—either something has happened or is about to happen, but it isn't immediately known what this is) around which the story develops in a very structured fashion—it is always known who is speaking, who they are speaking to and what they are doing and why. In contrast, a writerly text, and for Barthes this generally means the *modernist works of experimental authors like James Joyce and Samuel Beckett, offers the reader no such clarity of attribution. It is, therefore, a more plural text in Barthes's view, implying that it gives the reader greater freedom to construct meanings for themselves. As Fredric *Jameson argues in *The Modernist Papers* (2007), there is an undisclosed 'cold war' ideology and politics behind this concept which wants to equate the readerly text with so-called 'closed' or totalitarian societies and the writerly text with 'open' or democratic societies (the terms open and closed are adapted from Umberto *Eco's famous 1962 essay, 'The Poetics of the Open Work'). This distinction has fallen into a state of relative disuse, undoubtedly in part because its politics are no longer relevant, but also because it is formally untenable: as several detractors of modernists works have argued, it is just as plausible to say that writerly texts are tyrannical because they deny the reader the comfort of a bit of sense. *See also* WORK AND TEXT.

Further Reading: C. Belsey *Critical Practice* (1980).

r

reader-response criticism A mode of literary criticism that prioritizes the role of the reader (rather than the author's intentions or the text's actual structure) in both establishing the meaning of a text and evaluating its critical worth. It grew out of a dissatisfaction with *New Criticism and *Practical Criticism (which operate on the assumption that it is only the text that matters), and the recognition that all writers respond to what readers say about their work and modify their future writing accordingly. The theoretical core of this mode is derived from both Hans Robert *Jauss's *Reception Aesthetics and Wolfgang *Iser's *Reception Theory. Hence reader-response criticism also starts from the ontological premise that the text does not have full existence until it is read and that as a consequence its meaning cannot be deduced in isolation from a community of readers. It differs from Reception Aesthetics and Reception Theory in that it gives much greater emphasis to the difference between actual readers. It is much more politically aware in this sense, in that it recognizes that factors like *gender, *race, *class, and ethnicity have a necessary influence on the way readers respond to texts.
See also INTEPRETIVE COMMUNITY.

Further Reading: J. Tompkins (ed.) *Reader-response Criticism: From Formalism to Post-structuralism* (1980).

real (*réel*) One of the three 'orders' structuring human existence, according to French *psychoanalyst Jacques *Lacan (the other two are the *imaginary and the *symbolic). The real is that which resists *representation absolutely. It is in this sense impossible to imagine for itself (if we could imagine it, we could represent it). As such, it is impossible to integrate into the symbolic order, which means—somewhat paradoxically—that the real is in fact opposed to reality. Therefore our encounter with the real is always traumatic.

realism **1.** In the arts, particularly literature and the visual arts, it refers to the 19th-century movement that was the precursor to *modernism. It called itself realism because it broke with the artistic conventions of the times and challenged the accepted view of what art should be, namely the pursuit of the beautiful, the moral, and the improving, and instead claimed that it should try to record and, where necessary, indict what is. In art this was achieved by means of heightened *verisimilitude in *representation, while in literature it was achieved by exploring the inner motivations of characters, who were drawn from *everyday life.

2. In philosophy, the position that the only acceptable argument, idea, or theorem, is one that can be verified independently of a subjective observer. It is premised on the view that the world exists and is not an artefact of the mind (as an extreme *relativist might argue), nor simply an effect of language. Its goal is to describe the world as accurately as possible in objective terms. It tends to align itself very closely with mathematics and the physical sciences. Since not all phenomena are verifiable by mind-independent means, this position is ultimately very limited in what it can deal with.

reality-effect (*effet de réel*) The small details of person, place, and action that while contributing little or nothing to the narrative, give the story its atmosphere, making it feel real. It does not add to the plot to know that the character James Bond wears Egyptian cotton shirts, but it clearly does add considerably to our understanding of him. By the same token, knowing that he buys his food from Fortnum and Mason makes him more real. Thus, as Roland *Barthes argues in his essay introducing this concept, 'The Reality Effect' (1968, reprinted in *The Rustle of Language* 1984) no analysis of a text can be considered complete if it does not take these seemingly insignificant details into account.

reality principle (*Realitätsprinzip*) The counterbalance to the *pleasure principle in Sigmund *Freud's early account of mental functioning. It regulates and restricts the *subject's search for the immediate satisfaction of their *desire, postponing gratification according to the conditions imposed by external reality. The reality principle emerges after the pleasure principle and only takes formation when the psychical apparatus has undergone significant development (i.e. when the rational processes of judgement gain ascendancy in the conscious). The reality principle never attains absolute mastery over the pleasure principle, particularly where the sexual *instincts are concerned, so it must constantly reassert itself.

reality-testing (*Realitätsprüfung*) The process by which we discriminate between external and internal stimuli, that is to say between perceptions of actual objects in the world and hallucinations of non-real or virtual objects. It operates in the conscious part of the psychical apparatus. It is not, however, foolproof—e.g. someone in the grip of *psychosis is incapable of reality-testing.

Reception Aesthetics (*Rezeptionsästhetik*) German literary theorist Hans Robert *Jauss's term for his theory that the history of literature can only be fully understood as a *dialectical relationship between the production of texts and their reception by readers. It is readers, Jauss argues, that determine the aesthetic value of a work and it is the accumulated responses of readers across time that constitutes the aesthetic itself. Jauss was particularly interested in the influence of readers on writers and the more or less unspoken interaction between the two which transforms history into aesthetics. Influenced by *Russian Formalism as well as *phenomenological critics like Hans-Georg *Gadamer, Jauss uses the notion of 'horizon of expectation' (*Erwartungshorizont*) to characterize the status quo in literature and suggests that readers respond most favourably to works whose novelty (which he defines in terms very similar to **ostranenie*) challenges that status quo and thereby creates a new horizon of expectation. The rapid evolution of *magical realism offers an excellent and recent case in point: the publication of Gabriel García Márquez's novel, *Cien años de soledad* (1967), translated as *One Hundred Years of Solitude* (1970), created the possibility for Salman Rushdie's *Midnight's Children* (1981), which in turn led to a popular appetite for literature of this type. *See also* READER-RESPONSE CRITICISM; RECEPTION THEORY.

Further Reading: R. Holub *Reception Theory: A Critical Introduction* (1984).

Reception Theory (*Wirkungstheorie*) German literary theorist Wolfgang *Iser's term for his theory of the reader's construction of texts. As Iser points out in his seminal work, *Der Akt des Lesens: Theorie ästhetischer Wirkung* (1976), translated as *The Act of Reading* (1978), Reception Theory is interested in trying to understand the actual process of reading itself, in contrast to *Jauss's *Reception Aesthetics, which is interested in how existing texts are read and responded to. Its key ontological assumption is that the text does not properly exist until it is read, which is to say it exists only in the moment of reading. It is this productive moment that Reception Theory tries to understand and articulate by drawing on and adapting the conceptual resources of *phenomenology. Its key question is: how and under what conditions is a text meaningful to a reader? Iser's answer is that as readers we passively synthesize images on the basis of what we read—this means we form images in our minds as they come to us, not as a deliberate, intentional, or conscious act. We constantly adjust these images as new information comes to hand. In doing so, we must push to the background our own thoughts and memories and thus allow what we are reading to occupy the foreground. This process has the effect of alienating our own thoughts, thereby putting them into a fresh perspective. According to Iser, then, this is what makes reading 'improving' in a moral and ethical sense. It is worth adding the following caution: *Wirkungstheorie* is sometimes translated as reader-response theory (indeed, Iser himself suggests response as the most viable translation of *Wirkung*), but in spite of similarities it is not the same thing. *See also* READER-RESPONSE CRITICISM; RECEPTION AESTHETICS.

Further Reading: R. Holub *Reception Theory: A Critical Introduction* (1984).

recovered memory Repressed memory, usually of a traumatic event, recalled during psychoanalytic therapy. The concept was developed by Sigmund *Freud in the early stages of his thinking about *psychoanalysis, when he assumed that *Oedipal desires must have some basis in fact, but because the events were disturbing to the individual the memory of them was buried in a place beyond recall (this is his so-called seduction theory). Freud quickly abandoned this theory when he realized that oedipal thoughts could be just as potent if they were imagined. The concept of recovered memory is controversial because there is significant evidence to suggest that in the majority of cases the so-called memories that are recalled are in fact phantasms of events that took place only in the unconscious.

referent The real object in the world referred to by a *sign. The referent of an image of a tree is an actual tree. The referent should not be confused with the signified, which is a concept not a thing. Not all signs have a referent. Indeed, for a great many signs it is simply another sign that stands in the place of the referent.

Reich, Wilhelm (1897–1957) Austrian *psychoanalyst whose combination of *Marxism and psychoanalysis influenced a generation of political activists and writers in Europe and the US. In later life, he became an extremely controversial figure because of his rather eccentric views. He was prosecuted by the Food and Drug Administration (FDA) in the US and died in prison.

Reich was born in Dobrzanica, which is now in the Ukraine but was then an outer satellite of the Austro-Hungarian empire. His family were wealthy farmers (a fact that he would later credit with sparking his interest in the study of sex), and although of Jewish descent they disavowed their cultural heritage. Reich was home-schooled by a private tutor until he was 12, when his mother committed suicide. He was then sent to a boys' school. After the outbreak of World War I, when the Russians invaded in 1915 Reich and his brother fled to Vienna, losing everything. He joined the army in 1915 and served until the end of the war. He then studied medicine at the University of Vienna, where he met Sigmund *Freud who invited him to join his Psychoanalytic Association while he was still a student.

He set up private practice as an analyst in 1922. Over the next few years he wrote what is probably his best known and arguably his most important work, *Die Funktion des Orgasmus: Zur Psychopathologie und zur Soziologie des Geschlechslebens* (1929), translated as *The Function of the Orgasm: Sex-Economic Problems of Biological Energy* (1968). It was this work, perhaps not surprisingly, that caught the attention of writers like William Burroughs and Norman Mailer who, in their turn, popularized Reich's work for the counter-culture generation.

In 1930 he moved to Berlin and joined the Communist Party of Germany (KPD). He was witness to the rise of Nazism in Germany, which he theorized in *Die Massenpsychologie des Faschismus* (1933), translated as *The Mass Psychology of Fascism* (1980), by asking the question: why did the masses turn towards an authoritarian party even though it was manifestly not in their interest to do so? His somewhat simplistic, but nevertheless suggestive answer was that sexual suppression in childhood prepared people for authoritarian rule in later life. Reich was expelled from the KPD for this book, as a liability to their cause, and when the Nazis came into power it was immediately banned and he was forced to flee the country. He moved to Scandinavia, but was forced to move again, this time to the US, when World War II broke out.

In the US he extended the work begun in Norway, namely his search for the origins of life. He claimed to discover an observable energy he called 'orgone', which he said was the source of life itself. Although his scientific methods and procedures were questioned in his lifetime by scientists as eminent as Albert Einstein, Reich was unshakeable in his conviction that he had discovered the beginnings of life itself. He created 'orgone accumulators' designed to collect and concentrate this 'cosmic' energy so that it could be used to such beneficial ends as healing the sick. Unfortunately for him, Reich sold 'orgone accumulators' to mail-order customers and this attracted the attention of the FDA. An injunction was taken out in 1954 to prevent him from shipping his apparatuses across state lines, but he refused to comply with the order. And though he sent the judge presiding over his case copies of his books, he was found to be in contempt and given a two-year sentence.

Further Reading: R. Corrington *Wilhelm Reich: Psychoanalyst and Radical Naturalist* (2003).

reification The transformation of intangible human qualities, such as thoughts, ideas, and values, into physical objects. According to Karl *Marx all of the key elements of capitalism involve a greater or lesser degree of reification. For instance, capitalist production subordinates the lives of millions of people to its regime of making and selling things. This fact is obscured by what Marx called *commodity fetishism, the process whereby the socially produced *value of things is mistaken for natural value. Reification is a crucial concept for Hungarian Marxist literary critic György *Lukács, particularly in his 1923 book *History and Class Consciousness*. Lukács argues that the priority given to the needs of business (an outlook Max Weber usefully termed economic rationalism) is a form of reification because it obscures the social origins of production and privileges the needs of the system.

relativism In philosophy, the position that all value judgements (e.g. ethics, morality, and truth) are relative to the standpoint of the beholder. To put it another way, relativism does not accept that there is an absolute ground or reference point that could provide an objective guarantee that things are not necessarily the same as they are perceived to be by a given subject. If one is neither religious nor a hard-headed *realist, then some version of relativism is unavoidable, which creates a great many difficulties for philosophers in this situation because it is easy (though not necessarily accurate or just) to turn this into an accusation. *Postmodernism has been taken to task on numerous occasions for precisely this reason: it challenges the plausibility and possibility of an absolute ground. As a consequence it has been charged with being apolitical, ahistorical, unethical, and so on, because all these things—politics, history, ethics, etc.—are said to require a ground to function properly. As Jean-François *Lyotard shows, the problem with relativism is that it enables historical *revisionists such as Holocaust-deniers to claim that their position is as valid as any other. His solution, only partially successful, is to focus on what he calls truth-regimes. Alain *Badiou offers a slightly different solution to the same problem via a retooling of Jean-Paul *Sartre's concept of the project. Badiou's project is that which attracts political conviction, i.e. a belief equal in strength to religious belief. *See also* ANTI-FOUNDATIONALISM.

representamen One of the three key components of American philosopher Charles Sanders *Peirce's tripartite concept of the *sign (the other two being the *interpretant and the *object). The representamen is the image of a sign created in the mind of an observer. It is in this sense a sign of a sign. However, it cannot be considered in isolation from the other two components of the sign.

representation The image of an idea or thing. At its most basic, representation means two things: (i) creating something that can stand for another thing—this is the sense in which a *metaphor, to give only one example, is a form of representation; but it also applies to representative politics in which an elected person stands for their electorate in a particular political forum; (ii) creating something that is in at least some sense equivalent to another thing, most often because it resembles that other thing. For example, a photograph is a representation because its image closely resembles the actual object on a two-dimensional plane, but it is also (obviously, but this point is often forgotten) not the same as that other thing. *Critical theory, particularly the *post-structuralist modulation, has taken a keen interest in representation because of the central problem of the relationship between the thing and its representation. *Cultural Studies has also taken a keen interest in the problem of representation, recognizing that it is central to the kinds of political questions surrounding *identity it is concerned with.

repression (*Verdrängung*) In *psychoanalysis, the process whereby the conscious defends itself against unwelcome thoughts, impulses, and ideations rising up from the *unconscious. These thoughts are unwelcome because they are representatives of one or other of the *instincts, and as such they strike the conscious's governing body, namely the *superego, as being both uncivilized and vulgar. Repression is not, however, a single-shot act like closing the door; it is rather, a constant process akin perhaps to force exerted by a dam wall to hold back the flow of water behind it. Sigmund *Freud conceived of the idea of repression in trying to explain *parapraxis (better known as 'Freudian slips'), which he reasoned are evidence of two things: first, that these slips of the tongue and so on indicate that there is a part of the mind not accessible to conscious thought or inspection, which he called the *unconscious; and second, that these unconscious processes are constantly bombarding and being repelled by the conscious mind. Freud also came to think that both *hysterical and *neurotic symptoms are a product of repressed thoughts which have been subjected to either *condensation or *displacement and thereby rendered acceptable to the conscious (they are also known as 'compromise-formations' for obvious reasons). In their newly disguised state these thoughts are no longer recognizable to the conscious, and although it had previously repressed them, it now allows them to pass through without further censorship. Now, however, repression takes on a new form because it must repress those thoughts and associations which would betray the true identity of the disguised thoughts and trigger what Freud called a return of the repressed. Freud referred to these two moments or types of repression as primal repression and repression proper.

repressive desublimation *See* DESUBLIMATION.

r

repressive hypothesis Michel *Foucault's term for the perception, which he demonstrates is historically false, that the Victorian era was silent on the issue of sex and sexuality. The era that was famously so morbidly fearful of the merest hint of sex that it covered the legs of pianos lest they call to mind naked human legs was as this very example illustrates obsessively concerned with sex. As Foucault argues in *La Volonté de savoir* (1976), translated as *The History of Sexuality: An Introduction* (1978), under the guise of repression sex became an object, or even more strongly, an incitement to knowledge in the Victorian era.

Repressive State Apparatus (RSA) French *Marxist philosopher Louis *Althusser's concept for what is known in contemporary political discourse as 'hard power', i.e. a form of power that operates by means of violence. It is usually accompanied by what Althusser termed the *Ideological State Apparatus, which is a 'soft power' concept. The Repressive State Apparatus consists of the army, the police, the judiciary, and the prison system. It operates primarily by means of mental and physical coercion and violence (latent and actual).

Further Reading: L. Althusser *Lenin and Philosophy* (1971).

repressive tolerance The passive acceptance of social and governmental practices, policies and actions which restrict freedom in an absolute sense. The *Frankfurt School theorist Herbert *Marcuse coined the term in an essay of that title for a book co-written with Robert Wolff and Barrington Moore, *Critique of Pure Tolerance* (1965). Repressive tolerance, Marcuse argues, takes two main forms: (i) the unthinking acceptance of entrenched attitudes and ideas, even when these are obviously damaging to other people, or indeed the environment (the painfully slow response to warnings about climate change and environmental degradation might be seen as an example of this); and (ii) the vocal endorsement of actions that are manifestly aggressive towards other people (the popular support in the US and the UK in the aftermath of 9/11 and 7/7 for the respective government's attempts to override or limit *habeas corpus* is a clear example of this). Genuine tolerance, Marcuse argues, can only exist in a situation of intolerance for these limits on real freedom. Slavoj *Žižek's books *Violence* (2008) and *In Defence of Lost Causes* (2008) continue and update this line of thought.

resistance A general term in critical and cultural theory for any non-violent act of cultural or social defiance of *hegemonic power. The term is most widely used in *Cultural Studies, which—somewhat over-optimistically, it has to be said—in some cases is prepared to see even so simple an act as wearing jeans to work or school as resistive because it defies certain social conventions (now largely outmoded as a consequence). But this view of what resistance means is also criticized within Cultural Studies for being naive about the ease with which such acts of resistance are recuperated from by power—in this case, it simply created a much larger market for jeans than previously existed. Consequently, resistance is probably better treated as a *problematic than a social fact: 'what counts as resistance?' is a useful question to ask.

ressentiment A vengeful, petty-minded state of being that does not so much want what others have (although that is partly it) as want others to not have what they have. The term, which might be translated as 'resentment', though in most places it is generally left in the original French, is usually associated with German philosopher Friedrich *Nietzsche, who defined it as a slave morality. Nietzsche sees *ressentiment* as the core of Christian and Judaic thought and, consequently, the central facet of western thought more generally. In this context, *ressentiment* is more fully defined as the desire to live a pious existence and thereby position oneself to judge others, apportion blame, and determine responsibility. Nietzsche did not invent the concept of *ressentiment*, it was a term that was very much 'in the air' in his lifetime (the late 19th century), as Fredric *Jameson points out in his sharp critique of the concept in *The Political Unconscious* (1981). Jameson's quarrel with *ressentiment*, or more particularly Nietzsche's deployment of it, is that the latter fails to consider the ideological weight the term carried in its own time; thus, in Jameson's view Nietzsche fails to see that it is a category deployed by the ruling bourgeoisie elite to simultaneously justify their privileges and rationalize the denial of those same privileges to the poorer classes (on this view of things, the masses revolt not because their cause is just, but because they resent the rich).

Further Reading: G. Deleuze *Nietzsche and Philosophy* (1983).

revisionism A general term that can be used with both positive and negative connotations for any scholarly practice dedicated to revising an established position. In *Marxism, revisionism is used in a pejorative sense to describe any deviation from the central tenets of Marx's thought (e.g. his theory that the transition to socialism will require a revolution). It is also used by communist leaders as a general term of political abuse in arguments between communist countries (e.g. Mao accused Khrushchev of being a revisionist for his de-Stalinization policies, while Albanian General Secretary Enver Hoxha accused the Maoists of being revisionists for normalizing relations with the US). In history, revisionism is generally reserved for those historians who seek to deny that major historical events such as genocides actually took place. The so-called Holocaust-deniers are one example, but there are many others. On a positive note, however, historians who seek to overturn the bias and exceptionalism of certain national histories are also known as revisionists, but they plainly serve an important purpose. In former colonial countries like the Americas and Australia, revisionist historians have played an crucial role in challenging popular misconceptions about indigenous peoples.

rhetoric The art of persuasive speaking and writing. It has been the subject of scholarly study since at least the 4th century BC. It was a central component of Classical learning alongside logic and grammar in both Athens and Rome, where it was divided into three categories: judicial, deliberative, and epideictic. While Classical scholars considered rhetorical skill essential to the good conduct of both politics and philosophy, and as a consequence eminent scholars of the time like Aristotle wrote treatises on the subject, over time, but especially in the Romantic period, rhetoric has come under suspicion for emphasizing persuasiveness over truthfulness. Rhetoric in some contexts, particularly the political arena, has become a codeword for empty or insubstantial discourse. In literary studies, rhetoric is treated as a sub-category of style.

rhizome Term adapted from plant biology by Gilles *Deleuze and Félix *Guattari to conceptualize *non-linear relations in both the realm of pure thought and the concrete and the *everyday. Appearing for the first time in a short pamphlet entitled *Rhizome* (1976), which was subsequently republished as the introduction to *Mille Plateaux* (1980), translated as *A Thousand Plateaus* (1987), the concept of the rhizome is presented in binary opposition to what Deleuze and Guattari refer to as the arboreal or tree-like, by which they mean linear or hierarchical relations. Arboreal is effectively Deleuze and Guattari's codephrase for the three main targets of their *schizoanalytic project: (i) structuralist linguistics; (ii) *Althusserian Marxism, or indeed any determinate form of history; (iii) *psychoanalysis.

The rhizome is Deleuze and Guattari's figure for thinking multiplicity as a substantive. One arrives at the rhizomatic or the multiple only by subtracting the power or quality of the unique from the equation (Deleuze and Guattari use the matheme n-1 to express the rhizome). The standard example of what they mean by this is the notion of the crowd—a crowd comes into being only when the various individuals that compose it cease to think of themselves *as* individuals and become part of the collective entity itself, moving and acting according to its dictates rather than their own *desire. For Deleuze and Guattari, the rhizome is synonymous with the swarm and the pack. Deleuze and Guattari are clear, however, that no pure form of the rhizome or indeed the arboreal actually exists; rather, these two forms are best seen as tendencies present to a greater or lesser degree in all processes.

Deleuze and Guattari identify 6 key principles underpinning the operation of the rhizome: (i) connection—any point of the rhizome can be connected to anything other, there is no prescribed pathway for connections; (ii) heterogeneity—the rhizome not simply connects *signifier to *signified, as in *structuralist linguistics, but entire semiotic chains to regimes of power and specific historical circumstances; (iii) multiplicity—the rhizome is always as complete as it can be, it doesn't *lack anything, so there are no supplementary or hidden dimensions that can be mobilized to overcode it; (iv) a signifying rupture—the rhizome can be broken at a certain point, but it will always restart elsewhere (what they mean is that ideas can mutate, so that even if we break with something as being fascistic, for example, there is no guarantee that it won't return again under a different guise); (v) cartography—the rhizome can be mapped, but not traced or copied [*calqué* in the original French] (maps refer to *performance in Deleuze and Guattari's view, whereas tracings refer to *competence); (vi) decalcomania—the rhizome can incorporate tracings, meaning any pre-existing programme of thought, by plugging them into its own heterogeneous process, thereby changing their function (in other words, one doesn't necessarily need to reject psychoanalysis outright, its insights can be used as starting points).

Further Reading: K. Ansell Pearson *Germinal Life: The Difference and Repetition of Deleuze* (1999).
I. Buchanan *Deleuzism: A Metacommentary* (2000).

Richard, Jean-Pierre (1922–) French literary critic in the *phenomenological tradition of the *Geneva School. His best known work is *Littérature et Sensation* (1954). He also wrote important works on Marcel Proust and Gustave Flaubert. His work is relatively little known in the Anglophone academy.

Richards, Ivor Armstrong (1893–1979) British literary critic, leading exponent of *Practical Criticism, born in Sandbach in Cheshire. Richards's parents were, as Terry *Eagleton puts it in his surprisingly affirmative essay 'The Rise of English' (chapter one of

Literary Theory: An Introduction, 1983), 'provincial petty bourgeoisie', meaning that he belonged to a social class that had hitherto been excluded from university. He was educated at Clifton College in Bristol and at Cambridge University. He lectured and tutored in English and the Moral Sciences at Cambridge from 1922 until 1929, when he took a year off to take up a fellowship in Beijing. In 1931 he accepted a visiting position at Harvard. In due course his position there was made permanent and he spent the remainder of his career in the US.

When Richards started teaching at Cambridge in the early 1920s, English Literature did not exist as a scholarly discipline and its study was viewed with suspicion. Yet within a decade it had become a vital part of the university and has only grown in strength since then. Richards, along with his former student F. R. *Leavis, was instrumental in this development. In large part, this was because Richards and Leavis transformed the study of literature from a question of mere taste (i.e. what one likes and doesn't like) into a question of moral education and judgement (i.e. whether or not a text can teach us something important about how we should conduct our lives). As Eagleton puts it, English Literature became the arena in which the fundamental questions of human existence were thrown into relief and put under intense examination via a process that became known as 'close reading'. Literature was to pick up where religion left off and provide moral order in the midst of chaos. Despite writing prolifically on the subject of what counts as good literature and why it is important, Richards did not really establish an aesthetic that could be emulated. He treated poetry, in particular, as transparent windows into the *psyches of poets, yet did so in such a way that one would have to be him to see it as he does. Yet as Eagleton points out, the true achievement of Richards and Leavis is not the methods they created, which have been superseded anyway, but the transformation of literature into a scholarly object. Richards's most important books are: *The Meaning of Meaning* (1923), which he co-authored with C.K. Ogden; *The Principles of Literary Criticism* (1924); and *Practical Criticism* (1929). Interestingly, Richards's work proved more enduringly influential in the US (where he is credited as one of the fathers of *New Criticism) than in his native country.

Further Reading: J. Russo *I. A. Richards: His Life and Work* (1989).
J. Schiller *I. A. Richards's Theory of Literature* (1969).

Ricoeur, Paul (1913–2005) French religious philosopher and hermeneuticist. Born in Valence, Ricoeur was orphaned at two (his father was killed in World War I at the Battle of the Marne and his mother died shortly after his birth), and raised by his devoutly Protestant paternal grandparents in Rennes. He completed his preliminary training at the University of Rennes, having failed the entrance exam to the illustrious École Normale Supérieure. Graduating in 1935, Ricoeur moved to Paris to undertake doctoral work at the Sorbonne. There, he participated in weekly study sessions at the home of Gabriel Marcel, who introduced him to *existentialist philosophy and theology. He also collaborated with Emmanuel Mounier, founder of the left-wing Christian journal *Esprit*.

The irruption of World War II interrupted his studies. Ricoeur was drafted into the infantry in 1939 and flung into the fray almost immediately. His unit was captured by the invading German army in 1940 and he spent the remainder of the war in a prison camp. It was not especially arduous in the camp, it gave him time to read and think and there were a number of other intellectuals there with whom he could converse (indeed the camp was accredited as a degree-granting body by the Vichy government). He also began his translation of Edmund *Husserl's *Ideen 1* (Ideas 1) there, which he would subsequently submit as his minor thesis. He also collaborated with Mikel Dufrenne on a study of the German existentialist Karl *Jaspers, which was published after the war as *Karl Jaspers et la philosophie de l'existence* (Karl Jaspers and the philosophy of existence, 1947).

After the war Ricoeur taught at the Collège Cévenol until 1948 when he succeeded Jean Hyppolite as Chair in the History of Philosophy at the University of Strasbourg. In 1950 he submitted his major thesis, *Philosophie de la volonté: Le Volontaire et l'involuntaire* (The Philosophy of the Will: The Voluntary and Involuntary), which would prove to be the first part of a trilogy. In 1956 he moved to the Sorbonne, where he remained for a decade before taking up a senior administrative position in the newly established and so-called experimental university at Nanterre (among its faculty members were Alain *Badiou, Gilles *Deleuze, and Michel *Foucault), but this experience proved a disappointment. He was assaulted by students during the events of *May '68 and derided by them for being out of touch. This was in complete contrast to his experience in the 1950s when as an outspoken critic of France's war in Algeria, his students had saved him from internment. Disenchanted with French academic life, Ricoeur left France, first for Belgium and then definitively to the University of Chicago in the US.

Ricoeur is best known for his critique of Freud, *De l'interprétation. Essai sur Freud* (1965), translated as *Freud and Philosophy: An Essay on Interpretation* (1970), his study of metaphor, *La métaphore vive* (1975), translated as *The Rule of Metaphor* (1977), and the immense three-volume work on narrative, *Temps et Récit* (1983–85), translated as *Time and Narrative* (1984–88). Always acknowledged as important, Ricoeur's work has never enjoyed fashionability, but in a way that is precisely what is important about it: he was never taken in completely by fashionable ways of thinking such as existentialism or *structuralism and his work always offered a powerful alternative viewpoint.

Further Reading: F. Dosse *Paul Ricoeur: Les Sens d'une Vie* (1997).
D. Kaplan *Ricoeur's Critical Theory* (2003).
R. Kearney *On Paul Ricoeur: The Owl of Minerva* (2004).
K. Simms *Paul Ricoeur* (2002).

risk society (*Risikogesellschaft*) German sociologist Ulrich *Beck's term for the present situation (which in Beck's view began to take shape in the aftermath of World War II), which in his view is defined by the expansion of uncontrollable risks, i.e. risks which have no straightforward or direct cause and therefore no obvious or easy means of attenuation (climate change is the best-known example of such a risk). Beck is particularly concerned with new types of risk that have arisen—or may arise in the future—as a consequence of human action. The issue is not so much that the world has become inherently more dangerous than it used to be, although that is in fact one of the implications of Beck's thesis, but rather that the nature of the threats we face now has changed—they have become, in Beck's terms, 'de-bounded' in spatial, temporal, and social terms: risks are no longer bound by regional or even national boundaries, but are frequently global in scope; risks may have long latency periods such that the actual cause of particular threats may lie in the distant past or as is the case with nuclear material may stay with us for thousands of years; and because of these spatial and temporal unboundings it has become difficult to assign responsibility in a legally relevant fashion. Although global in scope, risks plainly do not affect everyone and every part of the world equally—e.g. as catastrophic as Hurricane Katrina was for New Orleans in 2005, it caused nowhere near as much misery as hurricanes routinely cause in much poorer countries like Haiti, which lack the resources to defend against natural disaster, and what damage it did cause was the fault of failed human-made structures rather than nature. As the case of Hurricane Katrina made abundantly clear, the real problem with respect to risk is that decisions affecting the types of threat we face and the possible responses that might be made to address them have become 'sub-political', consigned to the essentially unaccountable realms of bureaucracy and business where the people most affected by these decisions are unable to have any direct input.

Further Reading: U. Beck *Risikogesellschaft: Auf dem Weg in eine andere Moderne* (1986), translated as *Risk Society: Towards a New Modernity* (1992).

Ritzer, George (1940–) American sociologist best known for his *McDonaldization thesis. Ritzer was born and raised in New York City and his parents were in his own words 'upper lower class' Jews: his father drove a taxi and his mother was a secretary. Ritzer's first degree, from City College of New York, was in psychology; he followed this up with an MBA from the University of Michigan. He then took a position in human resources at Ford, where he worked until 1968, when he completed a PhD in organizational behaviour from Cornell. He then held jobs at the Universities of Tulane and Kansas, before being appointed Professor of Sociology at the University of Maryland in 1974, where he has remained ever since. Ritzer is a prolific author, but it was his rather pessimistic thesis that the whole world was steadily being transformed into a mirror image of McDonald's, which first appeared in *The McDonaldization of Society* (1993), that brought him international attention and turned him into an academic superstar. He is primarily a critic of what Jean *Baudrillard termed 'consumer society', but resists attributing the cause of the changes he decries to *late capitalism and instead makes consumption seem like a character flaw.

romance A literary genre dating back to the early Middle Ages that has evolved considerably over time. The term itself derives from the fact that the first examples were written in the so-called Romance languages, that is to say, in the local vernacular rather than Latin as most other books were at that time. Also known as courtly tales, these stories were largely adventure and quest narratives focusing on the lives of medieval kings and queens. Thematically, most of these tales concentrate on chivalric issues to do with courage, love, honour, manners, and fidelity, both to one's betrothed, but also (and indeed more importantly) to one's realm. The most studied examples of such texts are the tales of King Arthur, which have known several permutations. The first modern novel, namely *Don Quixote* (1604) by Miguel de Cervantes, is a parody of courtly romances that at once undermines the genre and at the same time frees it to evolve in new directions. Romance today refers to what is essentially a sub-genre of the novel whose thematic focus is love—Jane Austen's *Pride and Prejudice* (1813) is often taken as the starting point for this modulation of the romance genre, which extends all the way to the popular romances of the variety Mills & Boon publish. This version of the romance genre tends to be shorn of the more adventurous elements, and told from the point of view of the female protagonist.

But the romance novel is not the only form in which the genre survives: it continues too in the fantasy novel, such as J.R.R. Tolkien's 'Ring Trilogy'.

Further Reading: B. Fuchs *Romance* (2004).

Rorty, Richard (1931–2007) American philosopher, often (though wrongly) associated with *postmodernism because of his focus on language and its inherent ambiguity and his concomitant rejection of the idea that there is anything other than language by means of which thought can express itself. Rorty is probably best thought of as a *pragmatist, albeit one of a very peculiar stripe (his claim to this title has been challenged by a number of critics, particularly Susan Haack), because he treats concepts as mere tools of expression, which can only be evaluated in terms of their specific usefulness in a given context and in relation to a specific problem. He might also be referred to as an *anti-foundationalist because he rejects the argument that there must be some concepts that are self-justifying (the usual examples of such concepts are history, memory, and society). Similarly, he rejects the notion of an objective reality that can be called upon to explain existence in the last instance. Rorty is one of the most cited philosophers of the 20th century, and a vast body of secondary literature devoted to his work has accumulated in the past two decades ensuring that his work will continue to be discussed for years to come.

The child of two so-called 'New York intellectuals' James Rorty and Winifred Raushenbush, whose politics were left-of-centre but fervidly anti-communist, Rorty grew up in an intensely intellectual environment in rural New Jersey where his parents bought a house as a deliberate retreat from city life. At 15, he went to Hutchins College at the University of Chicago, completing both his BA and MA there, focusing on philosophy. He then went to Yale to complete a PhD under the direction of metaphysician Paul Weiss. His first academic post was at Wellesley College, but he soon moved to Princeton, where he remained for more than two decades. In 1982, riding high on the critical success of *Philosophy and the Mirror of Nature* (1979), undoubtedly his best known and most influential work, Rorty took the radical step of moving to the English Department at the University of Virginia, giving himself leave to teach a wider variety of subjects than philosophy departments permitted. He retired in 1998 and took up an Emeritus position at Stanford, where he remained until he succumbed to pancreatic cancer.

Further Reading: N. Gross *Richard Rorty: The Making of An American Philosopher* (2008).

RSA *See* REPRESSIVE STATE APPARATUS.

Russian Formalism One of the most influential literary critical movements of the 20th century. Speaking very generally, Russian Formalism as a critical movement was interested in identifying the specific quality of language use that separated the literary text from the non-literary text. Their approach was scientific inasmuch as they thought it was possible to establish what it is precisely that distinguishes ordinary usages of language from the poetic. Unlike the later *post-structuralists, the Russian Formalists treated poetry as an autonomous form of discourse that was distinct from all other forms of discourse. They referred to this difference in qualitative terms as **literaturnost* (literariness) and sought to quantify (i.e. formalize) it by means of their theory of **ostranenie* (estrangement), which simply put is the process of making the already familiar seem unfamiliar or strange, thereby awakening in us a heightened state of perception.

Russian Formalism is a generic term that covers the work of at least two major groups of researchers based in Russia in the early part of the 20th century. The first group, based in St Petersburg, was known by the acronym **Opoyaz* (*Obschevesto po izucheniyu poeticheskogo yazyka* (Society for the Study of Poetic Language)). Formed in 1916 by a small gathering of students and professors working in language studies, it was chaired by the poet Osip Brik. The original membership included Victor *Shklovsky, Boris Eichenbaum, and Roman *Jakobson. The group folded in 1923, not the least because many of its core members fled into exile to escape either the First World War or the Russian Revolution or both. The remnants of this group merged with the second of Russian Formalism's constitutive groups, namely the Moscow Linguistic Circle founded by an *Opoyaz* exile Roman Jakobson. Established for the purpose of investigating the poetic function of language, its membership included such figures as Victor Shklovsky and Yuri Tynyanov, who would both play a major part in advancing the theoretical development of Russian Formalism. The group sought to connect poetics and linguistics so as to show that you could not properly understand one in the absence of the other.

Further Reading: T. Bennett, *Formalism and Marxism* (1979).
V. Erlich *Russian Formalism: History—Doctrine* (1955).
F. Jameson *The Prison-House of Language* (1972).

Said, Edward (1935–2003) US-based Palestinian literary critic and theorist and one of the founding figures of *Postcolonial Studies. An accomplished pianist, Said also wrote extensively on music. Outside of the academy, Said was a member of the Palestinian National Council (PNC) from 1977 until 1991 (for which the FBI opened a file on him and kept him under surveillance).

Said was born in Jerusalem, then part of the British Mandate of Palestine. His family were solidly middle class, and at that time actually lived in Cairo. His father was a businessman with American citizenship and his mother a Nazarene Christian. Although primarily based in Cairo, the family maintained a home in Talbiyah in West Jerusalem until 1947, and Said lived 'between worlds'. Talbiyah was incorporated into the State of Israel following the Arab-Israeli War in 1948.

In 1951 said was sent to boarding school in the US. Thereafter he completed a BA and MA at Princeton, followed by a PhD on Joseph Conrad at Harvard, which was published in 1966 as *Joseph Conrad and the Fiction of Autobiography.* A year before he completed his PhD, he was appointed to a position in English and Comparative Literature at Columbia University, where he remained for the rest of his life. His main theoretical inspirations were Theodor *Adorno (particularly with respect to music), Antonio *Gramsci, and Michel *Foucault.

Said's second book, *Beginnings: Intention and Method* (1975) established him as part of the new wave of literary critics (e.g. Paul de Man, J. Hillis *Miller, and Gayatri *Spivak) who advanced beyond, without necessarily leaving behind, the established critical practice of 'close reading', and became known as practitioners of *theory. This was in many respects a transitional work for Said, for it was not until his third book *Orientalism: Western Conceptions of the Orient* (1978) that he really found his true metier and with it worldwide fame as one of the originators of postcolonial theory. *Orientalism as Said conceives it is almost the complete opposite of the traditional meaning of the term.

Orientalism in the strictest sense simply means any study of or fascination with the Orient, which roughly speaking encompasses

North Africa, Turkey, the Middle East, Pakistan, Afghanistan, and the Northern Tip of India. Said's argument is that Orientalism's study of the Orient conceives it as a monolithic, undifferentiated region; but, more problematically, its conception of the Orient is utterly phantasmal. As he points out, many of the most famous Orientalist scholars never travelled to the Orient and those that did arrived and departed with their all their preconceptions and prejudices intact. He cites several purple passages from Gustave Flaubert's Egyptian memoirs in support of his thesis. Unsurprisingly, this thesis has its critics (notably Ernest *Gellner, Bernard Lewis, and Aijaz Ahmad), and it even divides opinion among those who basically support it. Nonetheless as a way of thinking about the relation between culture and power it has been enormously influential. *Culture and Imperialism* (1993) furnishes the sequel to *Orientalism*, extending its claims to literatures the other work did not consider.

In the years following the publication of *Orientalism*, Said immersed himself in Palestinian politics and wrote a series of articles and books describing the situation of the Palestinian people and decrying the politics that had put them in that situation: *The Question of Palestine* (1979), *Covering Islam: How the Media and Experts Determine how We See the Rest of the World* (1981), and an edited collection entitled *Blaming the Victims: Spurious Scholarship and the Palestinian Question* (1988). Said favoured a two-state solution and he resigned from the PNC in 1991 when it became clear in the lead up to the Oslo accords that this was not the agenda. After 1991, he wrote several more books on Palestine, including *The Politics of Dispossession* (1994), *Peace and its Discontents* (1996), and *From Oslo to Iraq and the Road Map* (2003).

In 1993, Said used the occasion of the prestigious Reith Lectures on BBC Radio to reflect on his situation as literary critic, cultural commentator, and political activist in a series of talks he titled *Representations of the Exile* (1994). He develops this theme further in his marvellous memoir *Out of Place* (1999), written between treatments for the leukaemia that would claim his life at the early age of 67. Perhaps aware of his limited time, Said granted several book-length interviews in this period, which offer terrific insights into his life and work. He also devoted time to his other great passion, music. He wrote a column for *The Nation* (a selection of these pieces has been published as *Music at the Limits* (2007)), and gave the Wellek Library lectures on this topic as well, published as *Musical Elaborations* (1991). More concretely, he collaborated with Daniel Barenboim to create the West-Eastern Divan Workshop. His last, unfinished book, fittingly enough, was *On Late Style: Music and Literature against the Grain* (2006). 'Late style' is Said's term for the aesthetic that develops when an artist knows they have made it career-wise, that their reputation is secure and they can relax enough to permit themselves to experiment.

Further Reading: B. Ashcroft *Edward Said* (2001).
H. Bhabha and W. J. T. Mitchell (eds.) *Edward Said: Continuing the Conversation* (2005).
A. Hussein *Edward Said: Criticism and Society* (2004).
B. Moore-Gilbert *Postcolonial Theory: Contexts, Practices, Politics* (1997).
I. Warraq *Defending the West: A Critique of Edward Said's Orientalism* (2007).

Sapir-Whorf Hypothesis A now discredited theory of language which holds that linguistic competence determines cognitive capacity. Developed by American linguist Edmund Sapir and his student Benjamin Whorf, using a study of Native American languages as its baseline, this theory holds that the relative complexity of a language—what it is able to say—determines the limit of what those language speakers are able to know. Moreover, each language is born of a different world-view, so it is impossible for speakers from different language groups to ever properly come to know one another. In effect it makes an absolute of the idea of cultural relativism widely embraced by both *Cultural Studies and *Postcolonial Studies.

Sartre, Jean-Paul (1905–80) See overleaf.

Saussure, Ferdinand de (1857–1913) Swiss linguist, one of the founders of *semiotics and a crucial influence on the development of *structuralism. Born in Geneva, Saussure studied in Leipzig, Berlin, and Geneva. He taught in Paris for several years, before taking the chair of linguistics at the University of Geneva. He only published one work in his lifetime, a massive study of the vowel system in Indo-European languages, which appeared in 1878. However, it is the lecture courses he gave between 1906 and 1911, assembled from student notes by his former students and published posthumously as *Cours de linguistique générale* (1916), translated as *Course in General Linguistics* (1959), which brought him lasting fame. Saussure and his students are sometimes referred to as the *Geneva School. Although trained as a philologist, Saussure realized that the history or etymology of particular words does not explain either their actual origin or their contemporary meaning. This observation gave rise to two crucial hypotheses: first, that the association of a particular sound and a particular word and its meaning is arbitrary (there is no intrinsic reason that the word for the object we call a bat should either be bat or sound like 'bat'); second, these arbitrary choices are governed by a general system of meaning-making that is universal

SARTRE, JEAN-PAUL (1905–80)

French *Marxist philosopher best known as an exponent of *existentialism. He was one of the most influential intellectuals of his generation. He was awarded the Nobel Prize for literature in 1964 in recognition of his plays, novels, and philosophical works, but he declined it, saying that a writer must not allow themselves to be transformed into an institution.

Sartre was born in Thiviers in the Dordogne region of France, to middle-class parents. His father was a naval officer, but died when Sartre was only 15 months old. His mother moved back to Paris to live with her parents, who effectively raised him. Sartre recalls his childhood very fondly in his autobiography *Les Mots* (1963), translated as *The Words* (1964), as a bookish paradise. His grandfather, Charles Schweitzer, a relative of the Nobel prize-winning medical missionary Albert Schweitzer, was a German teacher and author of works of cultural criticism.

Sartre studied at the prestigious lycées Henri-IV and Louis-le-Grand, before gaining entry to the École Normale Supérieure (ENS). His was an illustrious class—his classmates included Raymond Aron, Simone de *Beauvoir, Georges *Canguilhem, Daniel Lagache, and Paul Nizan. At the ENS he studied psychology and the history of philosophy as well as sociology and physics. He failed on his first attempt at *agrégation*—according to legend it was because he tried to present his own ideas rather than those the examiners expected him to recite—but passed on his second attempt, attaining the highest score in France for that year (Beauvoir came second).

Legend also has it that Sartre became interested in *phenomenology, which served as the precursor to his own existentialist theories, when his friend Raymond Aron returned from a year's study in Berlin and told him that phenomenology meant that one could philosophize a glass of beer. He was so inspired by this idea that on the way home from the pub he stopped at a bookshop and purchased a book by *Levinas on *Husserl. In 1933, following his compulsory military service, he made his own study trip to Germany, which is where he first read *Heidegger, and though he could not have failed to see the rise of Nazism it made little impression on him at the time. When he returned to France, he took a teaching position at lycées in Le Havre, Laon, and Neuilly.

Sartre's first and probably best-known novel, *La Nausée* (Nausea) appeared in 1938. It was well received critically, but was not an immediate commercial success and Sartre privately worried that he was going to be a failure. At the outbreak of World War II he was immediately recalled into military service and was captured in 1940, but fortunately for him was released when the armistice between France and Germany was signed. As his posthumously published notebooks from this period, *Les Carnets de la Drôle de Guerre: Novembre 1939–Mars 1940* (1983), translated as *War Diaries: Notebooks from Phoney War November 1939–March 1940* (1984), make clear, his time in service and particularly in prison focused his mind on the question of freedom, which would become the central problematic of his thinking for the rest of his life.

War seemed to galvanize Sartre as a writer. The period between 1940 and 1945 was a highly productive one. He started to write for the theatre, using his plays as opportunities to criticize the German occupiers, but also to explore his concept of existentialism. Probably his most famous line, 'hell is other people', was coined in this period, occurring in the play *Huis Clos* (1944), translated as *No Exit* (1990). He also wrote a trilogy of novels about the war published under the collective title *Chemins de la liberté* (1945), translated as *The Roads to Freedom* (1990). But if Sartre emerged from the war as one of the most prominent intellectuals in France (and in the years to follow he became one of the most prominent intellectuals in the world) it was because of *L'Être et le Néant* (1943), translated as *Being and Nothingness* (1958), which in its evocation of freedom as a kind of intolerable burden resonated perfectly with the tenor of the times. It became a bestseller, thus giving Sartre financial independence, allowing him the freedom to become a writer without the necessity of also having to hold down a university post.

Being and Nothingness introduced the world to the notion of *mauvaise foi* or *bad faith, which Sartre opposes to the *psychoanalytic notion of consciousness. As the title suggests, the book constructs a *dialectical opposition between Being (the objects of consciousness) and Nothingness (the consciousness itself, which has no Being). In apprehending objects, though, consciousness has being-for-itself, while objects only have being-in-themselves. This distinction is important to Sartre because he wants to argue that it is *how* we think about the world that is crucial, not the sheer fact of the world itself. This becomes problematical when we factor in what it means to be looked at by another person (to fall under their *gaze, in other words)—in that situation we are simultaneously a consciousness of something and an object of a consciousness. Our being-for-itself is in a sense degraded by this state of affairs and turned into what Sartre rather bleakly calls being-for-others. Sartre developed this problematic further in the long delayed follow-up work, *Critique de la Raison Dialectique* (1960), translated as *Critique of Dialectical Reason* (1976).

In 1947, beginning as a series of articles in the journal he co-founded with Beauvoir and *Merleau-Ponty, *Les temps moderne*, then re-published as the book *Qu'est-ce que la littérature?* Sartre introduced the notion of *littérature engagé* or *committed writing, which was to define what writing meant for at least the next decade or so. Its influence can perhaps be seen most clearly in Roland *Barthes's attempt to move beyond its somewhat dogmatic structures in *Le Degré Zéro de L'Écriture* (1953), translated as *Writing Degree Zero* (1967). Sartre rejected an aesthetics of 'pure writing' for its own sake and argued that the writer had a responsibility to explore and interrogate universal values of freedom. Ironically, none of the writers Sartre would subsequently write about at such length, particularly not Flaubert, to whom he devoted over 3,000 pages of close analysis in *L'idiot de la famille* (1971–72), translated as *The Family Idiot* (1993), but not Genet or Mallarmé either, engaged in this particular task.

If the 1950s belonged to Sartre (as Fredric *Jameson once put it), then the 1960s belonged to *structuralism, and the influence of his work fell into decline, though he personally was still much in demand as a political activist and voice. He championed Third World writers such as Frantz *Fanon, for whose *Les Damnés de la terre* (1961), translated as *The Wretched of the Earth* (1965) he provided a famous preface in which he provocatively declared that the earth numbers 'two thousand million inhabitants: five hundred million men, and one thousand five hundred million natives. The former had the Word; the others had the use of it.' Sartre's legacy is perhaps less a specific body of work, which today has few followers, and more an attitude, that of the 'engaged' or 'committed' intellectual and writer. This is how the generation that followed him, Gilles *Deleuze and Michel *Foucault, among others, thought of him. He was a 'breath of fresh air' Deleuze said.

Further Reading: H. Barnes *Sartre* (1974).
R. Bernasconi, *How to Read Sartre* (2006).
G. Cox *Sartre: A Guide for the Perplexed* (2006).
N. Levy *Sartre* (2002).
F. Jameson *Sartre: The Origins of a Style* (1961).

SEE WEB LINKS

- A range of biographical and bibliographical information and online resources regarding Jean-Paul Sartre.

(i.e. common to every language). This distinction between language as it is used (*parole*) and its rules of use (*langue*) underpins the entire so-called structuralist revolution. Taking this **langue/parole* distinction a step further, Saussure argued that the spoken word has to be considered a *sign comprising two elements—*signifier and signified—which, in a famous phrase, he said were like opposite sides of a single sheet of paper. The signifier is the actual acoustic sound, e.g. 'bat', which must be distinguishable from other sounds and repeatable, while the signified is the concept we arbitrarily associate with that sound (bearing in mind that different languages can associate different concepts with ostensibly the same sounds). What is important to note here is that Saussure does not define the signifier as pointing to a thing in the world (*referent). Structuralism was born from the intuitive leap made by people like Claude *Lévi-Strauss (in anthropology) and Jacques *Lacan (in *psychoanalysis) that other human constructed systems—kinship, the *unconscious, films, and so on—could be seen to behave 'like a language' in this respect.

Further Reading: J. Culler *Ferdinand de Saussure* (1986).

-scapes A suffix (or word ending) adapted by Arjun *Appadurai from the word 'landscape' in his account of what he calls the cultural economy of *globalization. In *Modernity at Large* (1996), he proposes that there are five different -scapes that, taken together, comprise the 'imagined world' (a notion he adapts from Benedict *Anderson's concept of *imagined community) of the present as we understand it from a cultural perspective. These are (i) ethnoscapes (the mobility of people—tourists, workers, migrants, refugees); (ii) mediascapes (the global media and the representations of the world they collectively create); (iii) technoscapes (the mobility of manufacturing); (iv) financescapes (global capital flows); and (v) ideoscapes (the movement and traction of ideas). In order to think about the transition or movement within these different -scapes, Appadurai borrows Gilles *Deleuze and Félix *Guattari's concept of *deterritorialization.

schizoanalysis Gilles *Deleuze and Félix *Guattari's term for their project of re-engineering *psychoanalysis by (i) repolarizing it around *psychosis rather than *neurosis and (ii) aligning it with *Marxism by finding a true point of commonality between the respective *discourses. The word first appears in Deleuze and Guattari's first collaborative effort, *L'Anti-Oedipe* (1972), translated as *Anti-Oedipus* (1977), and recurs in their subsequent books, *Kafka: Pour une littérature mineure* (1975), translated as *Kafka: Towards* *a Minor Literature* (1986), and *Mille Plateaux* (1980), translated as *A Thousand Plateaus* (1987), but, interestingly enough, does not appear in their final collaborative work *Qu'est-ce que la philosophie?* (1991), translated as *What is Philosophy?* (1994). In *Anti-Oedipus* Deleuze and Guattari specify that the project of creating schizoanalysis involves three tasks—one negative and two positive. The negative task is the setting aside of those aspects of psychoanalysis which in their view do not work—this is not as straightforward as simply jettisoning the concepts of the *id, *ego, and *superego because Deleuze and Guattari are prepared to say that psychoanalysis works perfectly insofar as it is only a matter of dealing with neuroses, but the problem is that neuroses are a second order problem, meaning that—contrary to *Freud—they do not tell us anything essential about the operation of the *unconscious. Deleuze and Guattari argue that the unconscious is schizophrenic at its core but machine-like in its processes, which they refer to as *desiring-production, and that in its day-to-day operations it creates *desiring-machines which combine with one another to produce the assemblage known as the *subject. The two positive tasks are: first, discover in a subject the nature, formation, and function of their desiring-machines; second, separate the psychic investments of desire from the psychic investments of interest. These three tasks are predicated on the following four theses: (i) every libidinal investment of the unconscious is social (not personal) and therefore bears upon a historical field; (ii) there are two types of unconscious libidinal investment—desire and interest; (iii) the non-familial (or psychotic) unconscious libidinal investments have priority over the familial (or neurotic) investments; (iv) the unconscious libidinal investments of desire have two modes—paranoid and utopian. Schizoanalysis cannot be considered a completed project: it must continue to adapt and change to keep in step with the changing times.

Further Reading: I. Buchanan *Deleuze and Guattari's Anti-Oedipus* (2008).

scopophilia A *psychoanalytic concept created by Sigmund *Freud to describe the pleasure in looking, or what is more usually known as voyeurism. It is widely used in film studies, for obvious reasons, particularly by feminist scholars, to describe cinema's popularity as an artistic medium. The best known articulation of this concept is undoubtedly Laura Mulvey's account of it in her famous 1975 essay, 'Visual Pleasure and Narrative Cinema'. Mulvey argues that the act of viewing cinema can usefully be compared to the developmental moment Jacques *Lacan referred to as the *mirror stage inasmuch that the sense of 'escape' we feel while watching a movie is reminiscent of the *imaginary 'world' of a child whose *ego has not yet formed, while the heroic figures seen on screen offer us plenty of examples of *ego-ideals to identify with. But, she argues, perception is gendered, meaning that men and women view things differently, or more precisely are positioned differently by the things they view. Men see their *fantasy projected on screen, while women see themselves depicted as the sexual objects of men's fantasy—Mulvey argues that it does not alter things if it is in fact a male body women are gazing at because in doing so they are still inhabiting the male heterosexual fantasy space.

Further Reading: T. De Lauretis *Alice Doesn't: Feminism, Semiotics, Cinema* (1984).

screen memory (*Deckerinnerung*) A childhood memory that is paradoxically vivid and inconsequential. Because of the apparent banality of these memories there does not seem to be any reason for them to be preserved in the memory, a fact that *psychoanalysis latches on to as an important clue to their deeper importance. Sigmund *Freud theorized that such memories are compromise formations, or symptoms, like *parapraxes, meaning they function to disguise or conceal a trauma of some kind, usually of a sexual nature.

Searle, John Rogers (1932–) American analytic philosopher, best known for his work on *speech act theory, but also well known for his work on the philosophy of mind. Born in Colorado, Searle completed his undergraduate degree in philosophy at the University of Wisconsin. He then went to Oxford as a Rhodes Scholar to complete his DPhil. He worked briefly as a tutor at Oxford before returning to the US to take a position at the University of California, Berkeley, where he has been ever since. Searle's reputation is based on his extension of J.L. *Austin's idea in *How to Do Things with Words* (1962) that sentences can perform actions as well as state facts and express truths. In *Speech Acts: An Essay in the Philosophy of Language* (1969), Searle develops the idea of an indirect, or illocutionary speech act, listing five different varieties: assertives (true or false), directives (obliging an action), commissives (promise of action), expressives (revealing of speaker's psychological state), and declaratives (which cause something to happen). This work has proved useful in the development of artificial intelligence. Searle became widely known outside of the closed ranks of analytic philosophy when he got involved in a very public debate with French philosopher Jacques *Derrida, over a short critique the latter wrote of Austin's theory in *Marges de la philosophie* (1962), translated as *Margins of Philosophy*

(1982). Searle wrote a sharp defence of Austin, which prompted a book-length rebuke from Derrida.

Second Wave feminism A shorthand reference for the politically active form of *feminism that emerged in the US and elsewhere in the 1960s. It was neither a unified nor a homogeneous movement, but it did of course have a common goal, however disparately this was conceived, namely the equality of the sexes. It was born of the recognition that in spite of the considerable advances of the retrospectively christened *First Wave of feminism, women had still not achieved genuine equality with men in every facet of life. Its starting point, in the US, was Betty *Friedan's *The Feminine Mystique* (1963), which argues that women are trapped in a system that denies them self-identity as women and demands they find fulfilment through their husbands and children. Later writers, particularly those identifying as *radical feminists, would use the term *patriarchy as a shorthand for this systemic subordination of women at the level of *culture itself, rather than individual men.

In 1966, the National Organization for Women (NOW) was formed, as a civil rights organization for women, and in many respects it became the driving force of Second Wave feminism, particularly on the political front. NOW lobbied the US government to adopt the Equal Rights Amendment (ERA), but while it had many victories at State level, it remained without ultimate success at Federal level.

In 1970, a NOW committee member Kate *Millett published her PhD dissertation *Sexual Politics*, arguing that there is in effect a patriarchal and a non-patriarchal way of writing, with D. H. Lawrence, Normal Mailer, and Henry Miller falling into the former category and Jean Genet into the latter. The book sparked a huge debate and was attacked quite savagely by Norman Mailer; it is frequently held up as an example of what is wrong with *political correctness. Nonetheless, Millett's work offered an early and powerful critique of the patriarchal values in art and literature. Australian critic Germaine *Greer's *The Female Eunuch* (1970) was published in the same year, causing a similar stir by suggesting that the way to fight patriarchy is through women taking charge of their own sexuality.

The extent to which sex is a neglected problem of violence and exploitation was brought to light by Susan Brownmiller's angry exposé, *Against Our Will* (1975). Brownmiller's book divided feminism into two separate and opposed camps: those like Greer who advocate sexual promiscuity as a political weapon and those like Brownmiller who see this as simply catering to a male-dominated view of *desire. Second Wave feminism came to an end in the early

1980s. In part, it was a victim of its own success because there was a powerful backlash against political correctness, even among women, who found some of its messages 'over the top'. But the far bigger problem was the profoundly unfavourable political conditions that materialized in the 1980s: both Ronald Reagan in the US and Margaret Thatcher in the UK were anti-ERA in their outlook and policy-making. Second Wave feminism has since been succeeded by *Third Wave feminism on the one hand and *post-feminism on the other.

seduction theory In the development phase of *psychoanalysis, Sigmund *Freud initially thought that all *neuroses were the product of sexual abuse in childhood. He soon realized that not everything his patients reported referred to actual events. Psychoanalysis effectively begins from the moment Freud abandons this theory and starts to think more closely about the role of *fantasy and the *imaginary in shaping the *unconscious. In 1984, the director of the Freud archives, Jeffrey Moussaieff Masson, published *The Assault on Truth*, which controversially charged that Freud abandoned his seduction theory in order to cover up the fact that so many of his patients had been abused. According to Masson Freud was worried that it would discredit his theory and harm his professional standing. Debate on this topic continues, but without any clear conclusion. Janet Malcom's *In the Freud Archives* (1984) provides an account of how Masson was transformed from archivist to anti-psychoanalysis activist, but rather disappointingly does not clear Freud of this charge, or show that the charge is without foundation.

semanalysis Julia *Kristeva's attempt in *The Revolution in Poetic Language* (1984) to fuse *semiotics and *psychoanalysis so as to produce a method of analysis capable of simultaneously comprehending the process of the formation of texts and the process of deciphering texts. It was intended to transcend the limitations of the Hegelian *dialectic and provide a method that was genuinely materialist and at the same time able to deal with what she would term *abjection, the unrepresentable excess semiotics overlooks. Although a rich synthesis of *post-structuralist methodologies and ideas, semanalysis was in many respects a failed experiment and Kristeva soon abandoned it herself. Her later work does not use the term at all. However, out of the project of developing semanalysis arose the concept of *intertextuality, which has become a bedrock concept in *critical theory.

semantic field A group of words that are interrelated because of their common point of reference. For example, 'object', 'desire', 'drive', and 'lack', are all words belonging to the semantic field of *Lacanian *psychoanalysis.

semiotics The science of *signs, as one of the founders of the field Swiss linguist Ferdinand de *Saussure famously put it. There are two main schools of semiotics, Saussurean and Peircean, the latter referring to the work of American *pragmatist philosopher Charles Sanders *Peirce. The two semiotic models, which were constructed independently of one another, differ in one important respect: whereas Saussure's model of the sign is binary, Peirce's is triple. As a result there has been little cross-fertilization between the two schools of thought. Saussure's key insight, on which semiotics as a whole is built, is that the sound of a word is arbitrary with respect to both its meaning and the thing to which it ultimately refers: there is no intrinsic reason, for example, that a cow should be called a 'cow' and that the word should be sounded in the way it is (that different languages have different words for the same thing may be taken as proof of this latter point). On Saussure's view of things, the word 'cow' is more usefully understood as a sign consisting of a signifier (the sound of the word) and a signified (the concept we associate with that sound) and he extends this idea to the whole of language. More than five decades after Saussure died, in the 1950s and 1960s, particularly (but not exclusively) in France, linguists, literary theorists, cultural critics, and psychoanalysts, like Roland *Barthes, Claude *Lévi-Strauss, Christian *Metz, and Jacques *Lacan, began to experiment with Saussure's notion of the sign and found that it could be extended to a great range of meaning-making activities, including the non-linguistic realms of *everyday life. This led to a veritable explosion of interest in semiotics and for a number of years it was the dominant mode of analysis in the humanities, particularly in *Cultural Studies which saw semiotics as a means of theorizing how *ideology works. The pioneer in this respect was Roland Barthes, whose work on *myth, showed that even the most ordinary of objects, such as soap bubbles, convey significance beyond mere utility (they can be a sign of purity, joy, cleanliness, childhood fun, and so on). As critics have since pointed out, however, the price of this has been to treat every cultural activity as being 'like a language' and while this has been a powerfully effective model to follow it does have drawbacks, inasmuch that not every cultural activity performs like a language. Since its heyday in the 1960s, semiotics has become a specialist and highly sophisticated area of study which has found a new audience amongst artificial intelligence researchers.

Further Reading: J. Culler *The Pursuit of Signs* (1981).
U. Eco *A Theory of Semiotics* (1978).

W. Nöth *Handbook of Semiotics* (1990).
H. Ruthrof *Pandora and Occam: On the Limits of Language and Literature* (1992).

semiotic square A graphic figure used by the Paris-based Lithuanian linguist Algirdas Julien *Greimas to map out the deep structure of meaning, and more especially meaning-production. Premised on the principle of difference established by Swiss linguist Ferdinand de *Saussure that something means what it does by power of its ability to simultaneously differentiate itself from and negate what it doesn't mean, the semiotic square is built from a combination of simple opposition and complex negation. The four corners of the 'square' designated S1, S2, S1′ and S2′ respectively, represent different positions in the production of meaning. The resulting graphic should be read from left to right as well as vertically and transversally.

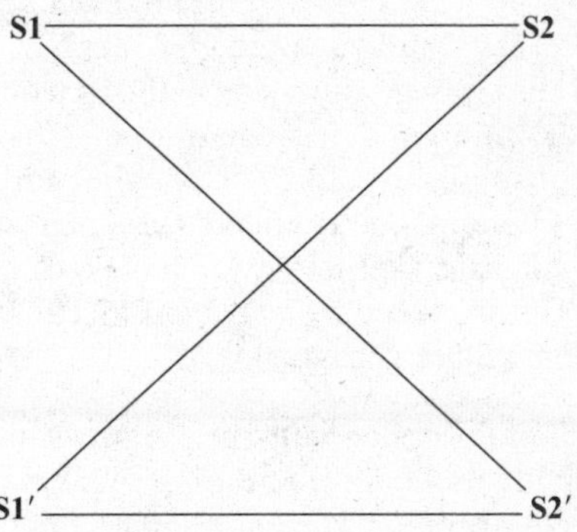

As Fredric *Jameson puts it in his foreword to the translation of Greimas's *On Meaning* (1987), a compilation of his writings on the theme of meaning, it takes a lot of 'working out' to establish exactly how these terms should be distributed. For example, take the term 'freedom' if we place that in the S1 position then we can say that its simple opposite S2 is 'unfreedom', whereas its negation S2′ might be something like 'enslaved', suggesting that the final term S1′, normally reserved for the negation of the negation should be 'liberation'. By juxtaposing freedom and liberation the semiotic square compels us to think through the 'gap' or 'distance' between these two terms, thus asking what is at stake in choosing one over the other. It is for this reason that Jameson suggests that the semiotic square (as is amply evidenced by his own use of the device) can be utilized to develop a *dialectical reading of texts.

S

Further Reading: F. Dosse *History of Structuralism* (1997).
F. Jameson *The Prison-House of Language* (1972).
R. Schleifer *A.J. Greimas: Linguistics, Semiotics and Discourse Theory* (1987).

Senghor, Léopold (1906–2001) Senegalese poet and politician. Regarded by many as one of the most important intellectuals in Africa in the 20th century, Senghor was the first president of Senegal, following its independence from France. Prior to that he was, like his friend Aimé *Césaire (who represented Martinique in the same period) Senegal's representative in the National Assembly in France. Senghor met Césaire as a student in Paris. The two of them, along with fellow student Léon Damas, from French Guiana, founded the literary review *L'Étudiant Noir* (The Black Student), which was one of the first serials to give critical attention to black writers. It was in the third issue of this journal that the word with which his name would become most closely associated, namely **négritude* (blackness), was used. Coined by Césaire, but rapidly adopted by Senghor, *négritude* is an early example of the strategy gay rights activists would later deploy to good effect, the adoption of a negative or derogatory term and its transformation into a positive. In 1948, Senghor compiled and edited a volume of Francophone poetry called *Anthologie de la nouvelle poésie nègre et malgache*, (Anthology of New Black and Malagasy Poetry) which was introduced by Jean-Paul *Sartre's now famous essay 'Orphée Noir' (Black Orpheus).

seriality French philosopher Jean-Paul *Sartre's term for an ensemble of individuals who have nothing more in common than what they are presently doing, such as people standing in line to go to a cinema. The opposite of a group, the individuals in a series are *alienated from one another. A crucial concept in his magnum opus *Critique de la Raison Dialectique* (1960), translated as *Critique of Dialectical Reason* (1976), seriality designates a state of affairs that politics ought to try to overcome.

Serres, Michel (1930–) French philosopher of science. Born in Agen, in south-western France, Serres studied at naval college and the École Normale Supérieure. Following his agrégation in 1955, he did his compulsory military service in the national maritime service. In 1968 he gained a doctorate for a thesis on the mathematical work of the German philosopher Leibniz. During the 1960s he taught at Clermont-Ferrand and Vincennes, before being given a post at the Sorbonne where he remained for the rest of his career. Operating at the extreme edge of *structuralism, Serres's research seeks a common point between mathematics and mythology, a *paradigm of knowledge consisting of pure forms purged of all their content. His position is that poetry, mythology, philosophy, and science are all systems and are in that respect comparable. His interest, then, is to discover what is central to each type of system, including that which the system purposefully excludes (e.g. disorder, noise, and turbulence). He calls this approach logoanalysis.

sexism The assumption that a person is inferior because of their sex, regardless of any other attribute, effectively reducing them to the status of an *object. *Feminist theory uses the term sexism to classify political and cultural *practices or works that denigrate women, or exclude them (most often by omission).

shifter A class of words whose meaning can only be fully determined in the context of a specific message between a sender and a receiver. Also known as *deictics, shifters are words like 'I' or 'this' whose meaning varies according to context because their principal function is connective rather than semantic. The Russian linguist Roman *Jakobson was the first person to use the concept of shifter.

Shklovsky, Viktor (1893–1984) Russian literary theorist and founder of **Opoyaz*, one of the two groups (the other was the *Moscow Linguistic Circle) which combined to give rise to *Russian Formalism. Born in St Petersburg, he attended St Petersburg University, and then entered the army. He fought in World War I, recording his experiences in a memoir, *Sentimental'noe puteshestvie, vospominaniia* (1923), translated as *A Sentimental Journey: Memoirs, 1917–22* (1970). A prolific author, Shklovsky wrote studies of Laurence Sterne, Maxim Gorky, and Leo Tolstoy, as well as several semi-autobiographical works. He is best known though for his invention of the concept of **ostranenie* ('defamiliarization' or 'estrangement'), central to so much of the work of the Russian Formalists. A neologism, it implies two kinds of actions: making strange, and pushing aside. Shklovsky's best-known work, which is also one of the best accounts of **ostranenie* available, is *O teorii prozy* (1929), translated as *Theory of Prose* (1990). Sections of it, especially the key essay 'Art as device', were translated in the 1970s, and circulated very widely.

Further Reading: T. Bennett *Formalism and Marxism* (1979).
V. Erlich *Russian Formalism: History—Doctrine* (1955).

sign The basic unit of interest for *semiotics. It is perhaps best apprehended as a unit of meaning whose principal point of distinction is the fact that it is not meaningful in itself, but is only ever a sign of (or pointer to) a theoretically 'full' meaning that lies elsewhere. Although the two principal 'fathers' of semiotics, Ferdinand de *Saussure and Charles Sanders *Peirce, did not agree on whether the sign is a binary or tertiary construct, their independently arrived at conceptions of the sign nonetheless share a number of key features. The sign is composed of two or three inter-related and interactive parts which are distinct from one another but inseparable. For Saussure, the sign consists of a signifier and a signified—the former is the distinctive acoustic image (the 'c' sound in 'cat', for instance, which sounds very different from the 't' sound in the same word), while the latter is the mental concept we arbitrarily associate with that sound (i.e. not an actual cat, but the idea of a cat). For Peirce, the sign consists of the *representamen, the *interpretant, and the *object—the representamen is the perceptible object (or what is also known as the sign vehicle), the interpretant is the meaning or the effect of the sign, while the object is that which the sign represents. In both cases, too, the sign is greater than its constituent material vehicle (e.g. the colour red in a traffic light is only one part of the semiotic signal drivers use to know when to stop); it is not identical with its material vehicle (i.e. the colour red is not in and of itself a sign); nor is it identical with its elements (i.e. the colour red is only one part of the sign).

Simmel, Georg (1858–1918) German philosopher and one of the founding figures of social research and *critical theory. Although his works are relatively little known in English, Simmel was a prolific author of more than 25 books, and a direct and indirect influence on one of the most important schools of thought of the 20th century, namely the *Frankfurt School. He was born in Berlin, and the city was a touchstone for much of his writing, particularly his most famous essay 'Die Groβstädte und das Geistesleben' (1903), translated as 'The Metropolis and Mental Life' (1948). In spite of an illustrious group of friends and correspondents—Stefan George, Rainer Maria Rilke, Auguste Rodin, Edmund *Husserl, and Max Weber—Simmel was for most of his professional life an isolated figure occupying the very position of marginality his work illuminated so brilliantly.

Simmel commenced his studies at Berlin University in 1876, first in history, then psychology (where he was taught by Moritz Lazarus, who also taught Wilhelm *Dilthey) and finally philosophy. His first attempt at his habilitation, a psychological and ethnographic study of music, which included a chapter on yodelling, failed. He succeeded second time round with a more traditional dissertation on *Kant. In 1885 he was duly given a post at Berlin University, which he held until 1900. His academic career in no way reflected his brilliance. He remained untenured for 15 years, partly because of his Jewishness, partly because he failed to secure the support needed from powerful colleagues to advance, but mostly because sociology did not then have the recognition and legitimacy it does today. Simmel was, however, very popular with students (among them Ernst *Bloch) and was one of the first to admit women into his classes (long before this became officially possible in 1908). After being rejected for several professorships, Simmel finally succeeded in obtaining a chair in philosophy at Strasbourg University shortly before the outbreak of World War I in 1914. He remained there until his death in 1918.

At first glance Simmel's work appears to cover an utterly eclectic range of topics, but underpinning it there is a clear focus on three main lines of inquiry. He was interested in: (i) the origins of cultural forms such as music, painting, drama, philosophy, religion, and even science; (ii) the nature and structural properties of social forms; (iii) personality types such as the outsider. Simmel's work hinges on the distinction he develops between form and content in a cultural setting. For Simmel, content is essentially unavailable to us except through the lens of forms, which are the functional equivalent of Immanuel Kant's categories. Forms give content a determinate and determining existence. For instance, music is a cultural form that has evolved from an actual set of practices into a virtual entity by which we judge sound to be either sheer noise or something aesthetically interesting. Simmel approached the problem of personality types in the same way.

The four basic principles underpinning Simmel's method are: (i) the world consists of a bewildering variety of contents given shape by a limited number of forms; (ii) the meaning of events and objects only emerges through their interaction with other events and objects; (iii) the properties of forms and the meanings of objects are a function of the distance we are able to interpose between ourselves and the respective forms and objects; (iv) the world is best understood as a series of conflicts between contrasting categories. These principles are vividly evident in Simmel's best-known and arguably most important work *Philosophie des Geldes* (1900), translated as *The Philosophy of Money* (1978). This work divided his contemporaries: it was greatly admired by György *Lukács and roundly criticized by Émile *Durkheim. Siegfried *Kracauer wrote (but never published in full) an appreciative study of it after Simmel's death.

Further Reading: D. Frisby *Georg Simmel* (1984).
D. Frisby *Fragments of Modernity* (1985).

simulacrum Although the term has been around since Plato's time, it is really only in the 20th century that it has acquired the significance it has today. The two most important names that have come to be associated with this concept are Jean *Baudrillard and Gilles *Deleuze.

Baudrillard tends to use the words *simulation and simulacrum interchangeably, and offers not so much a new theory of the simulacrum as a new history of the present viewed through the conceptual lens of the simulacrum. For Baudrillard, the simulacrum is essentially the copy of a copy, that is to say, the copy of something that is not itself an original, and is hence an utterly degraded form. At its limit, as in certain accounts of *postmodernism, the simulacrum is used to deny the possibility of anything being the singular source or origin of either an idea or a thing. On this view of things, anything deemed to be an original idea or object is in fact a mirage, an optical illusion of the same order as back-projection in cinema. Another way of putting this would be to say that a simulacrum is only ever an effect and never a cause.

In contrast, Deleuze uses the concept of the simulacrum against that of the simulation, to create an *immanent theory of *representation. The simulacrum is not a concept Deleuze wrote much about, indeed he only addresses it directly in two essays (on Plato and Lucretius) attached as appendices to *Logique du Sens* (1969), translated as *Logic of Sense* (1990), but his contribution has been decisive. His argument is that the copy or simulation is an image *with* resemblance (by definition, the copy resembles the thing copied), whereas the simulacrum is an image *without* resemblance (man is made in the image of God, according to catechism, but since the fall—i.e. because of his sin—he no longer resembles Him). The simulacrum is not just a degraded copy, Deleuze argues, it has its own positive power, which interrupts the relation between original and copy. His example of this is Pop Art, which in his view pushed the copy so far it became a simulacrum, an image without resemblance (e.g. Andy Warhol's famous Campbell's Soup prints).

S

simulation A general term for the aesthetic, cultural, and philosophical problem of the relation between original and copy. Walter *Benjamin, writing about the mass production of cultural commodities in latter part of the 19th century, was one of the first to draw attention to its significance. His concept of *aura was conceived to articulate his thesis that multiplying the number of copies of a thing tended to degrade the symbolic potency of the original. Several decades later, Umberto *Eco reached basically the same conclusion writing about what he called the *hyperreality of contemporary or *postmodern life, especially in the US. Mystified by the apparent passion in the US for replicas of European icons such as one sees par excellence in Las Vegas, Eco theorized that simulation is an attempt to produce something more real than the real itself and in that way compensate for its absence or impossibility. For Baudrillard, who is undoubtedly the theorist most well known for his interest in simulation, it is the generation by models of a real without origin or reality, or what he also calls a hyperreal. As he explains in *Simulacres et simulation* (1981), translated as *Simulacra and Simulation* (1994), in such circumstances the usual order of things is reversed: the copy no longer follows the original, it now precedes it. But more than that, simulation threatens to erode the distinction between real and copy, true and false, imaginary and real, and so on, and that is why postmodernism, which according to Baudrillard is defined by the presence of simulation at every level, is so alarming. His example of this process is the famous cave drawings in the caves at Lascaux. Because they are so old and fragile the caves are sealed off from visitors, apart from a tiny peephole; but so as to satisfy the tourists' desire to see them at close hand a full-scale replica has been constructed nearby. Thus, Baudrillard says, the duplicate renders the original artificial: it is not the 'real' that visitors carry away in their memories. It is not difficult to extrapolate from this line of argument that film, TV, and especially the Internet, also perform a similar function, on a much bigger scale.

singularity The critical threshold or division between two states of being, e.g. between boiling and not boiling. At such a point it is impossible to decide whether the object is in one state of being or another—thus, one would have to say it is neither boiling nor not-boiling and in this precise sense it is properly referred to as undecidable. Both Alain *Badiou and Gilles *Deleuze define the event in terms of singularity, substituting it for *essence, which they both dismiss as overly Platonic.

singular universal French philosopher Jean-Paul *Sartre's term for what it is that sets apart great writers like Gustave Flaubert—they are the singular instance of that which is universal. Sartre develops this concept in his five-volume work on Flaubert *L'Idiot de la famille: Gustave Flaubert de 1821 á 1857* (1971), translated as *The Family Idiot: Gustave Flaubert 1821–57* (1981), which begins with the question: what can we know about a person? He argues that every detail about a person's life, from the most mundane to the most momentous, is at some deep level profoundly homogenous, which is to say all are parts of a greater whole. Every person is a product of their history, Sartre argues, and at the same time a producer of their own history; as a result, the universal is always singular and the singular always universal.

situation A term introduced by Jean-Paul *Sartre in *L'Être et le Néant* (1943), translated as *Being and Nothingness* (1958), to describe the *existential environment in which every subject is immersed. The situation is the complex set of circumstances that taken together form the condition of possibility in which the subject must choose to act or not. *Cultural Studies has adopted this term, jettisoning its existential dimension, and used it to distinguish between the opportunities and challenges faced by people in different parts of the world, taking into account factors such as *class, *gender, *race, and *sexuality.

Situationism A small, influential and highly politicized artistic movement founded in 1957, from the remnants of two previous *Avant-garde groups, the Movement for an Imaginist Bauhaus (led by Asger Jorn, who had also been involved in *COBRA) and the Lettrist International (founded in 1946 by Isidore Isou, an early influence on Guy *Debord). After an illustrious but tumultuous decade and a half it dissolved in 1972. *Internationale Situationniste*, the group's journal and principal means of disseminating its ideas, published the first of its twelve issues in 1958 and its last in 1969. Long out of print, the full run is now available in English translation on the Internet.

The name of the group as well as the philosophy underpinning it derives from Jean-Paul *Sartre's concept of the *situation read as an answer to Henri *Lefebvre's injunction in his critiques of *everyday life that change can only be radical if it is engineered at a grassroots level. Creating new and surprising situations through art was its means of challenging the orthodoxy of everyday life and countering its *alienations (in *Marx's sense of the word). The principal thesis of Situationism was that art prefigures or anticipates what is possible in the social. This idea, which owes an obvious debt to *Surrealism, appealed to a wide range of activist groups throughout the 1960s, especially the so-called 'soixante-huitards' who participated in the events of *May '68, and still today influence protest movements of all types, but especially adbusters and culturejammers.

Although they were orthodox Marxists, the Situationists did not favour state-led communism or Stalinism (to give it its other name), and therefore their relations with the Left were always quite fraught, which was one of the main reasons why the group was so fractious and expulsions so frequent. Their critique of everyday life hinged on the concept of *spectacle developed by Debord in *La Société du spectacle* (1967), translated as *Society of the Spectacle* (1970). Debord's thesis is that capitalist society compensates for the fragmentation of daily life with a numbing image of false unity he calls the spectacle, which alienated workers of all types unknowingly consume and accept as real life. Breaking people out of this ideological slumber and enabling them to access authentic life is the chief purpose behind Situationism's three key practices or methods: **dérive*, **détournement*, and *psychogeography.

The other major theorist associated with Situationism was Belgian scholar Raoul *Vaneigem, author of *Traité de savoir-vivre á l'usage des jeunes générations* (1967), translated as *The Revolution of Everyday Life* (1983), a kind of user's guide to the late 20th century for the younger generation (which is what the French title might be if it were more literally rendered). Vaneigem's thesis, inspired by Wilhelm *Reich and Herbert *Marcuse, is that capitalism immiserates not by depriving people of their desires, but fulfilling them, or at least appearing to. Thus abundance is the most politically disabling state of all. The problem for Vaneigem is that this type of society relies on passivity and **ressentiment* or what Peter *Sloterdijk calls *cynical reason rather than conscious affirmation.

The spectacle or inauthentic *hyperreality of late 20th century existence the Situationists deplored and hoped could be transfigured by means of *dérive* and *détournement* is precisely the *simulacral universe Jean *Baudrillard argues we are condemned to. And though Baudrillard would chide Debord and others for their seeming nostalgia for authenticity, his own work, especially the later pieces, exhibits much the same longing. More importantly, the Situationists were *utopians, always looking to the future, and their practices were intended to hasten its arrival not transport them back in time to some mythical past.

Further Reading: M. Gardiner *Critiques of Everyday Life* (2000).

K. Knabb (ed.) *Situationist International Anthology* (2007).

S. Plant *The Most Radical Gesture: The Situationist International and After* (1992).

P. Wollen *Raiding the Icebox: Reflections on Twentieth-Century Culture* (1993).

P Wollen et al. *On the Passage of a Few People through a Rather Brief Moment in Time* (1991).

SEE WEB LINKS

- A comprehensive archive of Situationist publications.
- An archive and bibliography of key Situationist thinkers.

Sloterdijk, Peter (1947–) German cultural critic and philosopher. Born in Karlsruhe, he studied philosophy at the University of Munich, and completed a PhD at the University of Hamburg in 1975. He came into prominence with the publication of *Kritik der zynischen Vernunft* (1983), translated as *The Critique of Cynical Reason* (1987), which was a surprise bestseller, retailing over 40,000 copies in just a few months (for an academic book, this is virtually unheard of). His thesis, buried beneath five hundred odd pages about Weimar Germany, is that we have reached the end of the period in which understanding or *Enlightenment can prompt social action. This rather provocative idea struck a chord with academics, social critics, and activists alike, who similarly were discouraged by the failure of various social change projects. Since then he has published prolifically on a wide range of subjects. His main work, though, has been his trilogy *Sphären* (Spheres) (1998–2004), which tries to present a kind of unified field theory of the co-existence of humans with all other things on the planet. In 2002 he became co-host of the German cultural affairs TV programme *Das Philosophische Quartett.*

social formation A term used by *structuralist *Marxist scholars like Louis *Althusser to differentiate between different types of *societies in terms of their operation and structure, or more specifically their *mode of production.

Socialism or Barbarism (Socialisme ou Barbarie) A political group so-called because of the journal they established of the same name, which ran for 40 issues. Formed in response to Tito's break with Stalin in 1948 by a breakaway group from the Trotskyist Parti Communiste Internationaliste which included Cornelius *Castoriadis, Guy *Debord, Claude Lefort, and Jean-François *Lyotard, Socialism or Barbarism was essentially *Marxist in its outlook yet, paradoxically, broke with virtually every major tenet of Marxism in the course of its nearly two decades of effective life. The group's name was taken from a line by Rosa Luxembourg and reflected the conviction that a Third World War was inevitable, and following that the choice would be between socialism or barbarism, and that it was necessary to begin preparing for that moment. The group folded in 1965 because internal tensions reached such a high point it became impossible to continue. During its lifespan the membership of the group never rose above 100, but its influence was felt more widely than that number suggests. The group's two main theorists were Castoriadis and Lefort, both of whom also wrote under pseudonyms (Pierre Chaulieu and Claude Montal respectively). Anti-Stalinist in its outlook, the group was against all forms of bureaucracy and favoured worker-led councils instead. It agitated in factories, particularly the Renault factory in Billancourt which would be at the centre of the events of *May '68, although it never had more than a few members who were actually blue-collar workers. Its peak period was in the early 1950s following Stalin's death when both the Korean War and the war in Algeria gave fresh impetus to the group's aims. Interestingly, although Castoriadis tried to revive the group following May '68 it proved impossible. Influential in its time, the group has faded from view, largely because its economic prognoses have not panned out.

socialist feminism A synthesis of *radical feminism and *Marxism (particularly its New Left inflection) that challenges *feminism's neglect of *class and the Left's neglect of *gender. Socialist feminism rejects radical feminism's central claim that *patriarchy is the sole and universal source of the oppression of women, just as it rejects Marxism's claim that *class and *class struggle are the only determining factors in understanding the present *situation. Socialist feminism argues that class and gender are mutually reinforcing systems of oppression (later critics of socialist feminism would add the reminder that *race must also be taken into account). This is clear in the phrase 'women's work' which designates a type of work that only women can or should do and at the same time justifies the lowly pay scale assigned to it. Socialist feminism does not share, therefore, Simone de *Beauvoir's foundational claim in *Le Deuxième Sexe* (1949), translated as *The Second Sex* (1952), that the transition to socialism predicted by *historical materialism would in and of itself free women from their subordination to men.

Further Reading: J. Mitchell *Women: The Longest Revolution* (1984).

socialist realism The official, mandated style for all art and literature in the Soviet Union from 1934 until its collapse in 1991. In Stalin's time, there was a high degree of scrutiny of all artworks, and artists could be imprisoned or exiled to Siberia for deviating from the prescribed style. The level of scrutiny diminished dramatically after his death, but it was not until the advent of *glasnost* that artists could begin to operate without being concerned about the opinion of the state. Socialist realism was born of the idea that the creation of the Soviet Union as not only a new state, but a new kind of state, required art that would advance its *ideological cause and contribute to its human re-engineering programme (what the Chinese would later call the 'Cultural Revolution'). Art should, in other words, help to define and create the so-called 'New Soviet Man'. To this end, then, it must describe and celebrate the people's historical struggle to create socialism. Moreover, its subject matter and manner of construction must be both relevant and comprehensible to the proletariat; it should focus on aspects of daily life familiar to the proletariat; it should be realistic in a representational sense; and, most importantly, it should support the aims of the state. In 1948, this doctrine was laid out explicitly by Andrei Zhdanov, a senior bureaucrat in the Soviet government, and as a consequence socialist realism is sometimes referred to as *Zhdanovism. Pre-revolutionary art was regarded with suspicion since it was produced under a bourgeois regime, whose values were at odds with those fostered by the Soviet Union. Therefore artistic styles that emerged before the 1917 revolutions were discouraged, particularly non-representational forms (such as abstract art), which were thought too difficult for the proletariat to comprehend. Socialist realism is derided in the west for being programmatic—artistic inspiration, it is usually said by western critics, cannot be willed on command or made to work to rule—and while that is true to some extent, it nonetheless gave rise to some magnificent artworks celebrating the *everyday life of the working people. Socialist realism was the official art of the Soviet Union, but it was not confined to the Soviet Union or its satellites—authors all over the world (e.g. Louis Aragon, Johannes Becher, Jaroslav Hasek, and Pablo Neruda) contributed to its development. The principal exponent of socialist realism in critical theory is the Marxist literary scholar György *Lukács.

social movement A contemporary term for a politicized group of people united by a common purpose. The term was introduced by German sociologist Lorenz von Stein in 1850 in a book on the political history of post-revolutionary France. He adopted the notion from *Marx and *Engels's *Communist Manifesto* published two years previously. Charles Tilly, in his authoritative history, *Social Movements 1768–2004* (2004), argues that social movements emerged as a synthesis of three different elements: (i) public campaigns directed at specific government bodies with a view to either preventing them from taking an action (such as building a road through a nature reserve) or compelling them into taking an action (such as increasing funding for healthcare); (ii) special purpose coalitions (e.g. vigils, rallies, marches, petition drives, media stunts, and so on); (iii) public representations of WUNC—worthiness, unity, numbers, and commitment (e.g. signing petitions, attending marches, showing solidarity by wearing badges and so forth). Social movements employ all these *tactics, but they do so in a more sustained and intense manner. The term entered the popular vernacular in the late 1990s with the appearance of the so-called anti-globalization movement, which rose in response to the formation of the World Trade Organization. *See also* GROUP-IN-FUSION.

society An abstract term for the complex set of beliefs, *practices, rules, and traditions groups of people adhere to. Society is always greater than a single individual, and as such it is often defined in the negative as the opposite of the individual, or as that which constrains the individual and prevents him or her from living out their *desires. But it is also used in more affirmative terms to classify the ensemble of institutions, organizations, and relationships that give support to the individual. It is often contrasted with *culture, with the implication that society is the form to culture's content—it is organized and organizing, whereas culture is not. To put it another way, society speaks in the imperative, whereas culture uses the interrogative.

society of the spectacle A *zeitgeist or *periodizing term proposed by French *Marxist critic and activist Guy *Debord as the appropriate designation for the latter half of the 20th century in which the process of *alienation had achieved its nadir. Whereas earlier Marxists had been concerned that the process of commodification had brought about a generalized shift in social *ontology away from being towards having, Debord argues that things had in fact gone still further, so that having has been replaced by appearing. What is at stake here is of a higher order than the problem of image saturation which Susan *Sontag thought might be curable by going on an image diet. The image, Debord famously proposed in *La société du spectacle* (1967), translated as *Society of the Spectacle* (1970), is the final form of the commodity. In other words, it is not producing things, or even owning things, that drives society forward in the era of *late capitalism; it is, rather, how things appear, or more precisely, how they make us appear to ourselves, that matters. Importantly, for Debord, this is not a simple case of vanity. Image consciousness is what we are condemned to in a society which has substituted the spectacle for God. The spectacle is the illusion that our fragmented, alienated life is in fact whole, true, and authentic; the spectacle is what we believe when all our beliefs have been devalued by the market; the spectacle is the idea that the market is sufficient unto itself, no longer a means to an end but an end in its own right. *See also* CONSUMER SOCIETY.

Further Reading: A. Jappe *Guy Debord* (1999).

sociobiology A study of human and animal behaviour premised on the idea that specific behaviours can and must confer evolutionary advantage, or else they would not exist or persist. Behaviour can therefore be understood in terms of natural selection. Sociobiology makes use of Dutch *ethologist Nikolaas Tinbergen's four categories of analysis: it analyses the function of certain behaviours in an evolutionary sense; it asks how those behaviours evolved; it specifies how these behaviours contribute to the development of the individual; and finally it tries to determine the proximate mechanism (anatomy, hormones, etc.). To the sociobiologist, the protective feeling most parents have towards their children can be explained logically as the necessary behaviour needed by the species to sustain itself (human children being comparatively weak and vulnerable, compared to other animals which are much more able to fend for themselves); by the same token, the vulnerability of the human child is seen as an advantage because the longer nurturing time allows for greater levels of learning to be passed on by parent to child. The principal champion of the field is Edward O. Wilson, whose bestselling book *Sociobiology: The New Synthesis* (1975) brought international attention to the concept. The science, as well as the political implications of sociobiology, is criticized by the science writers Stephen Jay Gould and Steven Rose, but defended by Steven Pinker.

Soja, Edward (1941–) American *Marxist geographer. Soja obtained a PhD from Syracuse University for a thesis on urban planning in Kenya. His early work focused on Africa. However, it is for his later work on Los Angeles that he is most widely known, starting with *Postmodern Geographies: The Reassertion of Space in Critical Social Theory* (1989), which along with the work of David *Harvey introduced *postmodernism as a new kind of *problematic that geographers should take note of. Utilizing the work of Henri *Lefebvre, Soja expanded on *Postmodern Geographies* with two further works also devoted to Los Angeles, *Thirdspace: Journeys to Real-and-Imagined-Places* (1996) and *Postmetropolis: Critical Studies of Cities and Regions* (2000). Soja's work is distinctive for the way he factors the imagination into his geography: he argues persuasively that a city like Los Angeles, which is so consciously invested in image-production of all types, cannot be adequately engaged with if the imagination is not taken into account.

solipsism The extreme thesis that only the self exists. It arises from the view that only the self can be known with any certainty. On this view of things, it can be acknowledged that other consciousnesses may exist, but since those consciousnesses cannot be known their existence must remain speculative. Because of its *anti-foundational stance, *postmodern philosophy is frequently accused of solipsism, as were many of the key *poststructuralist figures like Jacques *Derrida and Michel *Foucault.

Sollers, Philippe (1936–) French writer and editor. Born in Bordeaux to a middle-class family of factory owners, he was educated at the Jesuits' École Sainte-Geneviève, but was expelled. He pretended to have schizophrenia to escape compulsory military service in Algeria. He adopted the nom de plume Sollers (his real name is Joyaux) in the early 1950s. His first novel *Une curieuse solitude* (A Strange Solitude), which he would later disavow, was published in 1958. It received high praise from Louis Aragon and François Mauriac, prompting Sollers to quip that his career had been launched with the help of both the Kremlin and the Vatican. Sollers experimented with the style of the so-called **nouveau roman* (new novel) pioneered by Alain Robbe-Grillet and Claude Simon, but later dismissed it as overly academic. A devotee of the work of James Joyce—he collaborated with Stephen Heath to translate *Finnegans Wake* (1939) into French and famously pronounced that novel to be the most formidably anti-fascist work produced between the two World Wars—Sollers's work displays a similar interest in language's prodigious capacity for meaning. He created the journal *Tel Quel* in 1960 and it rapidly overtook *Les Temps moderne* as the leading intellectual publication of its time. For a period of over 20 years, *Tel Quel* set the international benchmark for new and innovative thinking and writing by publishing figures such as Roland *Barthes, Jacques *Derrida, Michel *Foucault, and Julia *Kristeva. Many of them, Barthes and Derrida in particular, repaid the compliment by writing fine studies of Sollers's own work. Through the 1960s Sollers was an avid Maoist and together with Barthes and Kristeva made study trips to China to witness the Cultural Revolution at first hand. The journal folded in the early 1980s, at least in part because of disagreements within its editorial board about how to respond to Maoism. In 1983 Sollers launched a new journal, *L'Infini*, which much as its predecessor did, continues to publish cutting-edge work in *critical theory and creative writing.

Sontag, Susan (1933–2004) American literary and cultural critic. Born in New York City, but raised in Tuscon and Los Angeles, Sontag gained a BA from the University of Chicago. She did graduate work at Harvard, Oxford, and the Sorbonne, but never completed a higher degree. She taught briefly at Columbia University, but for most of her life she lived by her writing. Her essay 'Notes on Camp' (1964), which first appeared in *The New York Review of Books* and was later included in her landmark collection *Against Interpretation* (1966), caused a sensation, propelling her into literary stardom and the role of public intellectual. For many, this essay defined the sensibility of the 1960s. Similarly, the title essay of *Against Interpretation* resonated strongly with the literary critical *zeitgeist, which was then moving rapidly towards *postmodernism. Sontag's essay celebrated what art could not say, its silences, as the highest form of what art could achieve; she also insisted that art should primarily be thought of as an experience, and that this was beyond interpretation. For this reason, Sontag championed a number of European writers, such as Walter *Benjamin, Roland *Barthes, and Antonin *Artaud, bringing their work to the attention of Anglophone readers. Like Barthes, Sontag had a profound interest in the visual image, particularly the photograph. Her book-length essay *On Photography* (1977) is still a touchstone for media studies today. In the 1970s, Sontag was diagnosed with breast cancer. Chronicling the way cancer changes how the sufferer is perceived by society, Sontag wrote two powerful books on the cultural construction of disease, *Illness as Metaphor* (1978) and *AIDS and its Metaphors* (1988). Combining her interest in illness and photography, she wrote an affecting response to 9/11 and the march to war that followed entitled *Regarding the Pain of Others* (2003). In her final years, she lived with celebrity photographer Annie Leibovitz, who chronicled her illness and even her death in pictures. She died in 2004 shortly after the massive Indian Ocean tsunami which killed more than a quarter of a million people, effectively denying her the front-page farewell she might well have otherwise had, but also in a way proving her thesis about the power of images. She was buried in Montparnasse Cemetery in Paris.

sovereignty A form of *authority. Its principal characteristic is that it is the supreme or final authority, meaning that there is no other form of authority surpassing it. Sovereignty has taken a number of different forms throughout history, ranging from the tribal chief to feudal king and democratically elected president. The key political and theoretical problem it raises is the question of legitimacy: sovereignty is never purely intrinsic, or naturally occurring, it must be embedded in a social structure that serves as its condition of possibility. For instance, feudal kings ruled by virtue of their lineage and divine right. Ultimately, sovereignty can be seen as an issue of who has the right to rule and how that right is vested.

space At once the container of *everyday life (i.e. where we live) and an active agent in it (a social-acting force). An incredibly wide-reaching term, with complex and even contradictory points of reference, it can refer to either the physical environment (built and natural) on its own or the physical environment as it is inhabited by defined groups of people, or both. Similarly, it can range in scale from the personal to the planetary. It is conceived differently by several different disciplines, each one emphasizing one or more of its facets—e.g. architecture, *Cultural Studies, geography, history, sociology, planning, and urbanism—thus lending itself to an interdisciplinary approach.

French *Marxist sociologist Henri *Lefebvre is undoubtedly the most influential theorist of space in the 20th century. His distinction between perceived space, conceived space, and lived space—i.e. space as we see it (but also touch it, feel it, and so on), space as we design and build it, and space as something we relate to in an emotional and affective way—captures the principal ways in which space has been thought about in the past century. Visual artists have tended to foreground perceived space, architects and urbanists have tended to focus on conceived space, with cultural studies, geography, and sociology claiming lived space as their own. But as Lefebvre insists, these three types of space can only be separated in the abstract and the real task of spatial thinking is to try to think of the three facets of space together. American geographer Ed *Soja refers to this process as trialectics and his work offers several interesting examples of how this can be made to work.

The other major theorists of space in the 20th century who have had a major influence on the field are: Gaston *Bachelard, Maurice *Blanchot, Maurice *Merleau-Ponty, Michel de *Certeau and Marc *Augé. Michel de Certeau opposed space to place, defining the latter as what space becomes through the investment of power. By implication, space is the preserve of the powerless according to Certeau; those who dwell in space rather than place are forced to use *tactics against *strategy. Drawing on Certeau's work, Marc Augé created the concept of the *non-place, which he also opposed to place: the non-place is a place invested by power that does not confer any of the benefits of place (such as belonging or locatedness)—his examples include subway systems, airports, and so on.

In his highly influential synopsis of *postmodernism, Fredric *Jameson argues that in the post World War II era there has been a mutation in the spatial environment. Drawing on Lefebvre, he foregrounds the fact that since 1945 there has been a massive demographic shift away from the country to the city, with the result that by the end of the century for the first time in human history more people live in cities than the country. But he also observes that in the West at least there has been a move towards creating structures that are self-contained, that seem to want to stand apart from the rest of the city, as though they were mini-worlds. His case in point, the Bonaventure Hotel in downtown Los Angeles, has become since his discussion of it a key *topos of postmodernity.

Further Reading: M. Doel *Poststructuralist Geographies* (1999).
D. Gregory *Geographical Imaginations* (1994).
N. Thrift *Spatial Formations* (1996).

speciesism A prejudice or exceptionalism exhibited by one species (typically humans) with regard to another species (typically animals in general). The term was first used by British psychologist Richard Ryder in 1973 and has since been adopted by a large number of critics, most notably animal rights campaigner Peter Singer. Generally speaking, the charge of speciesism is made wherever and whenever the rights humans enjoy are not extended to other species—in particular, this implies the right of animals not to be kept in captivity, eaten, or experimented upon. The key issue is whether or not humans are morally and ethically justified in regarding themselves as a superior species with a sovereign right to treat all other earthly creatures as resources. As one might expect, opinion is divided quite sharply on this issue.

spectacle *See* SOCIETY OF THE SPECTACLE.

speech act *See* PERFORMATIVE.

Spivak, Gayatri (1942–) Indian-born *postcolonial, *post-structuralist, *Marxist literary critic and theorist. The daughter of middle-class parents, she was born in Calcutta at a time when India was still part of the British Empire. Borrowing money, she moved to the US to attend graduate school at Cornell, where she did comparative literature because that was the only school to offer her a scholarship. She wrote her PhD on William Butler Yeats, under the direction of Paul de Man. Her first job was at the University of Iowa, which she started a full two years before her dissertation was defended in 1967.

Around the same time she happened to read about a certain book by Jacques *Derrida, whom she had not at that time heard of, and was so struck by it she decided to translate it. That book was *De la grammatologie* (1967); her translation of it as *Of Grammatology* (1974) literally changed her life. She was suddenly propelled into the spotlight right at the moment when *deconstruction was the height of intellectual fashion. Although she uses deconstructive ideas and motifs in her work, Spivak is not a Derridean. Her work is diverse in its outlook but concentrates on a handful of key problematics underpinning what, in her magnum opus *A Critique of Postcolonial Reason* (1999), she terms postcolonial reason, particularly agency, identity, and subjectivity.

These three themes are brought together to stunning effect in what is undoubtedly Spivak's best-known work, the 1988 essay 'Can the Subaltern Speak?' (incorporated into *A Critique of Postcolonial Reason*), which offers a powerful meditation on and theorization of the practice of *sati* (the ritual immolation of widows). Spivak's answer to this vexed question is quite straightforward: the *subaltern cannot speak insofar as he/she remains a subaltern—by definition the subaltern is politically mute, unable to voice their perspective on the way things are and expect to be heard. But in true deconstructive fashion, she also questions the possibility of the 'pure' voice of the subaltern. It is in this context that she has argued that it is sometimes necessary to adopt a stance she calls *strategic essentialism, as a means of finding a speaking voice. In later works, she has admitted that this essay is largely autobiographical; she has also amended her position with regard to *Deleuze and *Foucault and softened her often misdirected critiques of their work.

Not one to pull punches, Spivak has also written blistering critiques of so-called French feminism, especially of Julia *Kristeva, for the blithe way it treats non-European others, placing it in a long line of western appropriations of the East (the honourable exception in her view is Hélène *Cixous). Mindful of her comparatively privileged position and the necessary complicity with the global capitalist system it entails, Spivak has used status to set up foundations in India to support literacy campaigns for indigenous women. She has also translated a series of works by Indian novelist Mahasweta Devi.

Further Reading: B. Moore-Gilbert *Postcolonial Theory: Contexts, Practices, Politics* (1997).
M. Sanders *Gayatri Chakravorty Spivak: Live Theory* (2006).

Stanislavsky, Konstantin Sergeyevich (1863–1938) Russian theatre director, best known as the 'father' of so-called 'method acting' (Hollywood devotees include Marlon Brando, James Dean, and Paul Newman). Born to a very wealthy family, Stanislavsky had a very privileged upbringing. Incredibly, given his bourgeois background, Stanislavsky survived both the revolutions of 1917 and Stalin's purges. Although his family disapproved of acting as an occupation for their son, it being considered too low class, they were wealthy enough to have their own private theatre in which he could experiment. His access to family money enabled him to establish first the Moscow Society for Literature and then, more importantly, the Moscow Art Theatre, whose touring performances to Europe and America were the real source of his global influence. The Moscow Art Theatre staged works by many of the leading lights of Russian literature, e.g. Isaac Babel, Mikhail Bulgakov, Anton Chekhov, and Maxim Gorky. It is however for his contribution to acting methodology that Stanislavsky is best known. Several of his works are available in English, for example: *An Actor Prepares* (1936), *Building a Character*, *Creating a Role* (1961), and the autobiography *My Life in Art* (1925). Stanislavsky's 'method' or 'system', as it is variously known, teaches actors to 'live' their parts either by calling on their own memories and experiences, or by 'inhabiting' the imagined world of their character. Stanislavsky famously used to ask his actors to perform theatrical exercises and games designed to estrange them as individual actors from their selves, to better enable them to 'become' their characters. This naturalistic style was explicitly rejected by Bertolt *Brecht, but it is virtually the standard mode in contemporary cinema. There is probably no more influential theorist of theatre in the 20th century.

Further Reading: J. Benedetti *Stanislavski: An Introduction.* (1982).
J. Benedetti *Stanislavski: His Life and Art* (1998).

statement (*énoncé*) French historian Michel *Foucault's term for the most elementary unit of *discourse. It does not correlate to a sentence, word, or even a proposition. It does not have the same kind of existence as either language or an object, though in fact it can be constituted by both. Foucault's most famous example of a statement is undoubtedly his claim that the keyboard of a typewriter is not a statement, but when it is reproduced in a typing manual it is. It is a statement about the construction of typewriter keyboards in a particular country. This is a statement because it refers to a set of laws of possibility or rules of existence—the shape and organization of the keyboard, the need to master it, and so on.

Further Reading: M. Foucault *L'Archéologie du savoir* (1969), translated as *The Archaeology of Knowledge* (1972).

Stiegler, Bernard (1952–) French philosopher. Before becoming a philosopher, Stiegler led a colourful life, which included a period of incarceration for armed robbery between 1978 and 1983. As he recounts in his autobiography, *Passer à l'acte* (2003), translated as *Acting Out* (2009), it was during this period that he became interested in philosophy. He went on to complete a PhD at the École des Hautes Études en Sciences Sociales (EHESS) in 1992. Since then his career has taken off. Presently he is the cultural development department director at the Centre Georges-Pompidou, but he also holds a teaching appointment at EHESS. An incredibly prolific author, Stiegler has written many books, the best known of which are: *La Technique et le temps* (three volumes, 1994–2001), *De la misère symbolique* (two volumes, 2004–2005), and *Échographies de la télévision* (with Jacques Derrida, 1996). He is best known for his development of the concept of *technics, which has become a key term in philosophical investigations of the ontology of new technology.

story and plot *See* FABULA AND *SJUŽET*.

strategic essentialism The political practice of overlooking the fact that from a *post-structuralist perspective *essences (in a philosophical sense) are difficult to sustain both *ontologically and *epistemologically. For example, few *feminist theorists would agree that there is a set of definable attributes essential to the idea, the concept, or the actuality of woman. Yet the more one pushes this *deconstructive line of thinking, the harder it becomes to establish common ground, or more especially common cause, sufficient to the needs of political action. If all women are irreducibly different, then why should they act together? The same problem besets all political groups defined by their *identity (e.g. *race, *class, ethnicity, sexual orientation). For that reason, US-based Indian critic Gayatri *Spivak proposes the notion of a strategic essentialism which simultaneously recognizes the impossibility of any essentialism and the necessity of some kind of essentialism for the sake of political action. French *feminist critic Luce *Irigaray has taken up this term in her work for precisely the same reason.

strategy and tactics Michel de *Certeau proposed that these terms (which he adapted from the work of the German war theorist Karl von Clausewitz) could be used to analyse what he termed the *practices of *everyday life. Strategy and tactics are defined as different types of calculations: strategy is the kind of calculation one can make when one is in control of all the variables, whereas tactics is the kind of calculation one must make when one is not in control of all the variables. For Certeau, the *panopticon is the most fully realized example of strategy, but contra Michel *Foucault he did not regard its power to control the behaviour of inmates to be absolute. Indeed, he praised the inventiveness of inmates in circumventing surveillance and maintaining a semblance of autonomy and used the term tactics to describe their various subterfuges. Tactics, then, is what one can do in spite of the fact that one lacks the power to control one's environment. It is an ambivalent term and though it has been used to describe *resistance to power (by John Fiske, among others), it is more accurately seen as an accommodation to a situation that cannot easily be changed.

Further Reading: I. Buchanan *Michel de Certeau: Cultural Theorist* (2000).

M. de Certeau *L'Invention du quotidien 1. arts dę faire* (1980), translated as *The Practice of Everyday Life* (1984).

J. Fiske *Understanding Popular Culture* (1989).

J. Frow *Cultural Studies and Cultural Value* (1995).

B. Highmore *Michel de Certeau* (2006).

Strauss, Leo (1899–1973) German-born Jewish-American political philosopher, generally regarded as the 'father' of neo-conservative thinking. He completed his PhD at the University of Hamburg under the direction of Ernst Cassirer in 1921. He also took classes at Freiburg, where his teachers included Edmund *Husserl and Martin *Heidegger. He was active in the Zionist movement in Germany and intellectually engaged with several of its key figures, such as Franz Rosenzweig and Gershom Scholem. He left Germany in 1932 to go to the US on a Rockefeller Fellowship, but because of the rise of Nazism chose not to return to Germany at the fellowship's conclusion. Instead he went to Paris, and then Cambridge, before resolving finally to relocate to the US, which he did in 1937. After several years of precarious living on short-term contracts at a variety of universities, he finally attained a tenured position at the University of Chicago, which is where he really made his mark with several books that offered both a rereading of the history of philosophy from Plato to *Nietzsche and a coherent political doctrine. It was the latter aspect (reinforced by the first) that was to prove the most influential. Strauss's principal themes were, according to Perry *Anderson's incisive critique in *Spectrum* (2005), that a just order must be based on the demands of natural right and that nature is inherently unequal. The best political regime, he reasoned, is one that takes human inequality into account and is led by a select elite. It is not difficult to see why this appeals to neo-conservatives. Strauss tends to be better remembered for who his students were, rather than for specific books or ideas: his students included Allan *Bloom, Paul Wolfowitz (a key figure in George W. Bush's administration), and Susan *Sontag. He is also cited as an important influence by Francis *Fukuyama.

stream of consciousness A continuous flow of sense-data (perceptions, thoughts, memories, and sensations) produced in the mind without either self-censorship or self-reflection. The concept was conceived by the American psychologist William James (brother of the writers Henry and Alice James), but is widely used in literary studies to describe a style of writing that tries to emulate this particular state of mind. The key examples are James Joyce's *Ulysses* (1922) and Virginia Woolf's *To the Lighthouse* (1927). Ideally, writing of this type should give the reader the impression they are witnessing thoughts as they are born, as though they were somehow able to jack directly into another consciousness.

structural causality Derived from Baruch Spinoza's conception of God as the immanent cause of all things, Louis *Althusser used this term to characterize the causal relationship between abstract entities like the social totality and concrete entities such as economic, political, and ideological institutions (e.g. banks, political parties, and schools). The structure is thus said to be immanent in its effects, which means it only exists in its effects and therefore cannot be separated from its effects. It is for this reason also defined as an absent cause because it is nowhere present in and of itself as an actual element. The most straightforward example of this is the notion of the universe: it is literally everywhere, but can in no way be separated out as a singular entity. Similarly, one can say we live in society, but the abstract entity 'society' is nowhere in evidence. Applied to God, as in Spinoza's thought, this notion was seen as heretical by Spinoza's peers because it denied the idea of a transcendental God distinct from His creation. In *The Political Unconscious* (1981), Fredric *Jameson shows that the idea of structural causality can be mobilized to develop political readings of cultural texts by treating the economy in the fullest sense of the word as an absent cause. *See also* IDEOLOGICAL STATE APPARATUS; INTERPELLATION.

Further Reading: L. Althusser *Lire le capital* (1968), translated as *Reading Capital* (1970).

G. Elliott *Althusser: The Detour of Theory* (1987).

STRUCTURALISM

One of the most important and wide-reaching intellectual movements of the 20th century. It is often referred to as a 'linguistic turn' because the origin of the method is the insight, derived from the work of Swiss linguist Ferdinand de *Saussure, that virtually all human creations can be understood as though they were structured like language. Indeed, French psychoanalyst Jacques *Lacan went so far as to pronounce that the *unconscious is structured like a language. The crucial implication of Lacan's claim, often missed, is that what this means is that the unconscious is a system, just as language is a system, and that they are both structured in the same way. For the same reason, it is also described as an anti-humanist method because it neither prioritizes nor privileges the human subject or individual conscious.

Interestingly, in *Cours de linguistique générale* (1916), translated as *Course in General Linguistics* (1959), to which the origins of structuralism are generally traced, Saussure never used the word 'structure', his preference was for the term 'system', which was in fact the more apt choice. What Saussure set out to discover was the universal system of language itself, that which is common to all languages. He wanted to know *how* language means, not *what* its meanings are. To do this, he had to change the way linguistics looked at language. Saussure made three crucial moves, which taken together add up to the basic methodological matrix of structuralism.

First, he shifted attention from the temporal to the spatial dimension of language. Until then, linguistics (still a branch of philology and not yet the science it has since become) focused on the history or evolution of specific languages, charting changes in pronunciation, spelling, vocabulary, grammar, and so on across time. Saussure referred to this trajectory of analysis as the *diachronic axis and while he conceded its importance he argued that it left unanswered the question of what language is. He focused instead on what he called the *synchronic axis, which is language as it is right now, and his way in was to think about the intriguing problem of why different languages have different words for the same thing, or similar words with different meanings.

The second move, namely his conclusion to the foregoing problem, which after several decades of delay revolutionized the human sciences, was that the relation between a particular sound and its meaning is *arbitrary*. Saussure had thus to make a further distinction between the concrete fact of a language as it is spoken in the present (which he referred to as **parole*) and the underlying system of combination enabling language to function as a mode of communication (which he referred to as **langue*). *Langue* and *parole* are inseparable, but while *parole* must, of necessity, have a concrete presence, *langue* does not. *Parole* is an imperfect and partial realization or instantiation of *langue* and Saussure's genius was to use it to triangulate what the 'whole' system must look like. *Langue* as Saussure understood it is a social fact, that is to say a greater conceptual entity than a single individual can grasp, regardless of how many languages they may have mastered.

Finally, Saussure proposed that linguistics should change the object of its analysis from words to what he called *signs. Signs, which are the concrete instantiations of *parole*, whose meaningfulness is made possible by *langue*, are composed of two elements, a *signifier (*signifiant*) and a signified (*signifié*). The former is the sound of a particular word, which must be both distinguishable from other sounds and reproducible (it is these twin attributes that separate phonetics from sheer noise). The latter is the concept we generally associate with that sound. The relationship is not that of a word and a thing (*referent), which would reduce language to a naming system. The sign is not self-sufficient, as a symbol is, but relies on a system of inter-relating differences for its meaning.

Structuralism became a global intellectual movement when its methodology was adopted by other disciplines and adapted to suit their own specific objectives and problematics. The first discipline to do so was anthropology, led by Claude *Lévi-Strauss, who was introduced to Saussure's work by Roman *Jakobson in New York, where they were both exiled during World War II (the two co-published a number of short explorations of what a structuralist method might look like outside of linguistics). In philosophy, it was Maurice *Merleau-Ponty who took the initiative, while in literary studies it was Roland *Barthes who paved the way forward, and film studies (Christian *Metz), psychoanalysis (Jacques *Lacan), and Marxism (Louis *Althusser) followed suit.

The advantage of structuralism over other methods was, as later critics came to realize, also its inherent disadvantage. Nevertheless, its advantages are considerable, as can be seen in popular fiction studies, where its power of comparative analysis continues to be useful. Umberto *Eco's analysis of James Bond novels and films in *The Role of the Reader: Explorations in the Semiotics of Texts* (1979) is exemplary in this respect. Eco reads the entire Bond catalogue and extracts a series of features in common to them all at the level of the organization of the narrative. In this way, he is able to show how the Bond 'machine' functions to create stories that are consistent, similar in their essentials, yet different enough to satisfy readers, and thus open a window into the *unconscious of author and reader. A similar approach has been used by Janice Radway in her analysis of popular romances, *Reading the Romance* (1991) and Will Wright in his study of westerns, *Sixguns and Society* (1992). The most sophisticated analysis of this type is undoubtedly A. J. *Greimas's *semiotic squares.

The disadvantages of structuralism are twofold: first, as Marxist critics like Fredric *Jameson have pointed out, structuralism is ahistorical (deliberately so, since it was the refusal of the diachronic that enabled the focus on the synchronic), which is a problem because although it is able to identify the various models and machines operative in culture, it cannot explain how they were created, nor why they persist; second, as Jacques *Derrida has pointed out, the signified does not supply the signifier with a meaning because it itself is undecided. Almost any example will prove this point—if the concept of redness is the signified of the signifier 'red', then what gives 'redness' its meaning? Derrida thus argues the whole system is based on an illusion of 'presence', that is the presence of a definitive meaning. Derrida is generally credited with bringing the structuralist era to a close at a conference in Baltimore which, ironically enough, was intended to showcase structuralism to American scholars.

Further Reading: F. Jameson *The Prison-House of Language: A Critical Account of Structuralism and Russian Formalism* (1972).
J. Sturrock *Structuralism* (1986).

structure of feeling Raymond *Williams coined this phrase in *Preface to Film* (1954) to discuss the relationship between dramatic conventions and written texts. What concerned Williams was the social acceptability of particular conventions—think of the theme of mistaken identity which is rife in Shakespeare's plays which without the benefit of special effects relies on convention for its plausibility. In later works, particularly *The Long Revolution* (1961), Williams would develop this concept further, using it to problematize (though not refute) Antonio *Gramsci's concept of *hegemony. Hegemony, which can be thought of as either 'common sense' or the dominant way of thinking in a particular time and place, can never be total, Williams argued, there must always be an inner dynamic by means of which new formations of thought emerge. Structure of feeling refers to the different ways of thinking vying to emerge at any one time in history. It appears in the gap between the official discourse of policy and regulations, the popular response to official discourse and its appropriation in literary and other cultural texts. Williams uses the term feeling rather than thought to signal that what is at stake may not yet be articulated in a fully worked-out form, but has rather to be inferred by reading between the lines. If the term is vague it is because it is used to name something that can really only be regarded as a trajectory. It is this later formulation that is most widely known.

Further Reading: A. O'Connor *Raymond Williams: Writing, Culture, Politics* (1989).

subaltern A term conceived by the Italian Marxist Antonio *Gramsci, who because he was in prison and his writings subject to censorship used it as a codeword for any class of people (but especially peasants and workers) subject to the *hegemony of another more powerful class. The term has been adopted by a group of *Postcolonial Studies scholars, thus forming a sub-discipline within the field known as Subaltern Studies. The group was founded by South East Asian historian, Ranajit Guha and over time it has included such scholars as Homi *Bhabha, Gayatri *Spivak, Partha Chatterjee, and Dipesh Chakrabarty. Its aim, following Gramsci's precepts, is to examine the formation of subaltern classes in a variety of settings in South East Asia, but principally India and its near neighbours, with the aim of providing a kind of counter-history, to address the imbalances of 'official' histories, which tend to focus exclusively on the affairs of the state and the ruling class. Spivak's famous essay 'Can the Subaltern Speak?' (incorporated into *A Critique of Postcolonial Reason* (1999)), problematizes the key premise of Subaltern Studies, namely that the heterogeneous group of peoples classified as subaltern can in fact have sufficient unity such that 'they' can speak. Her answer to her own question is a resolute no. The term has also been used in Latin American studies to similar purpose, though there it is given a slightly different slant: it also refers to the habit or mindset of servitude and subservience that needs to be overcome in order to bring about political change.

Further Reading: D. Chakrabarty and H. Bhabha (eds.) *Habitations of Modernity: Essays in the Wake of Subaltern Studies* (2002).

R. Guha and G. Spivak (eds.) *Selected Subaltern Studies* (1988).

W. Mignolo *Local Histories/Global Designs: Coloniality, Subaltern Knowledges, and Border Thinking* (2000).

subculture A group of people who consciously define themselves as different to or apart from the culture to which they officially belong. The study of subcultures was important to *Cultural Studies in the early part of its history, particularly in the formative Birmingham period, because it seemed to offer an antidote to the pessimistic outlook of the *culture industry thesis, which was dominant in the 1950s and 1960s. The best known example of this line of thinking is Dick Hebdige's bestseller *Subculture: the Meaning of Style* (1979), which argues that subcultures use style as a means of creating an *identity (what Stephen *Greenblatt would in different context call self-fashioning). Identity in this context amounts to a form of *resistance because it is created in opposition to the *hegemonic norms of the day.

Further Reading: K. Gelder *Subcultures: Cultural Histories and Social Practice* (2007).

subject A generic term widely used in *critical theory to designate what used to be termed the individual or the self. The shift in language is intended to signal the fact that in the face of the arguments by critical theory, *Marxism, and *psychoanalysis, the idea of an autonomous individual able to think and act wholly according to their own reason is insupportable. On the one hand, as psychoanalysis shows, the fact of the *unconscious means that no agent is fully conscious of all their acts, while on the other hand Marxism shows that no agent is capable of determining the course of history. The key implication of this, which is central to *Cultural Studies, is that the subject is the product of the conjunction of history and the unconscious, and not a naturally occurring or ready-made entity.

sublimation The transformation of the sexual instincts towards non-sexual ends. Sigmund *Freud proposes this concept as an explanation for how it is possible for all human activity to be driven by the libido and for there to be a wide range of activities not obviously sexual in nature. Indeed, Freud will go so far as to say that civilization itself is a steady process of the sublimation of the sexual instincts. His principle example of sublimation is art: art, Freud argues, is a result of the sublimation of the artist's libidinal energy. What Freud does not properly explain, however, is the mechanism by which this process of sublimation takes place. For this reason, although the concept is widely referred to by Freud, in contemporary *psychoanalysis it is usually treated with scepticism. Jacques *Lacan uses the concept of sublimation in his work only in a highly modified form.

sublime A quality a concept, object, or experience may be said to have if it is breath-taking, unique, incomparable, and beyond words. As several 17th and 18th century travellers noted, the Alps are sublime in this sense because nothing at ground level prepares one for the view from their austere peaks, where earth and sky seem to meet (e.g., Caspar David Friedrich's famous painting, *Wanderer above the Sea of Fog* (1817)). Western aesthetics has been interested in the concept of the sublime since at least the first century, when the Greek scholar of *rhetoric Longinus wrote his treatise *On the Sublime.* But it was not until the publication of Edmund Burke's *A Philosophical Inquiry into the Origin of Our Ideas of the Sublime and Beautiful* (1756) that it became a topic of philosophical interest. Burke's opposition between beauty as that which is well-formed and pleasing and sublime as that which is ugly, fearful and desirable all at once continues to inform thinking on this subject still. In effect, Burke's distinction is between that which we perceive with simple *pleasure (the beautiful) and that which truly moves us (sublime). German philosopher, Immanuel *Kant adopts Burke's opposition and uses it to discuss the limits of the imagination and the senses in contrast to the power of reason. In the *postmodern era, French philosopher Jean-François *Lyotard has utilized the concept of the sublime to describe his vision of what political art should do. For Lyotard the sublime is the presence of the necessarily failed attempt to say the unsayable, to bring forth and articulate the wrong inherent in a *differend. It is this kind of sublime that Daniel Libeskind was no doubt aiming for in his design for the extension to the Jewish Museum in Berlin.

Further Reading: P. Shaw *Sublime* (2005).

superego (*Über-Ich*) The *unconscious personification of the conscience in the tripartite psychical apparatus Sigmund *Freud constructed. It is constituted by the internalization of the prohibitions and demands parents make on their children and its role is to emulate them and act as an internal judge and censor the *ego. The *subject is not necessarily conscious of the superego's operation, but its presence is keenly felt as guilt in pathological cases of mourning and melancholia. As Freud theorizes it in his second *topography, the superego is formed via a process of gradual separation from the ego when the child stops trying to satisfy their *Oedipal desires and transforms his or her *cathexis with them into an identification. In contrast, Melanie *Klein holds that the superego is present from the earliest stages and forms as a result of the *introjection of good and bad *objects.

supermodernity (*surmodernité*) French anthropologist Marc *Augé's term for the present historical conjuncture as outlined in a series of four books commencing with: *Non-Lieux, Introduction à une anthropologie de la surmodernité* (1992), translated as *Non-Places: Introduction to an Anthropology of Supermodernity* (1995); *Le Sens des autres: Actualité de l'anthropologie* (1994), translated as *A Sense for the Other: The Timeliness and Relevance of Anthropology* (1998); *Pour une anthropologie des mondes contemporains* (1994), translated as *An Anthropology for Contemporaneous Worlds* (1998); and *Le Guerre des rêves: exercises d'ethno-fiction* (1997), translated as *The War of Dreams: Exercises in Ethno-Fiction* (1999). The present times, as Augé sees things, are not so much 'post' modern, in the sense of spelling the end of something, as being in excess of the modern, meaning the present age is not yet different in kind from what we refer to as 'modernity', but in the extremeness of its difference in degree it is rapidly approaching that point. Another way of putting this is to note that three symptoms of modernity have, for their own different historical reasons, come to define the present in a way that was not previously true. The three excesses he speaks of are: (i) time; (ii) space; (iii) individuality.

By an excess of time, Augé means our sense of contemporaneity is stretched past its limit by the welter of events we are expected to register at any one time. The exemplary image of this is, as Jameson has suggested, the gaunt figure of David Bowie in *The Man Who Fell to Earth* (director, Roeg 1976), helplessly watching some 50 televisions at once. The excess of space, which goes hand in hand with the excess of time, and obviously exacerbates it, too, is the paradoxical result of the so-called shrinking of the planet—air travel puts even the remotest regions of the globe within reach, satellite technology allows us to view the world from our living rooms and watch events unfold in real time. The excess of individuality is the paradoxical result of the enforced solitudes of modern life—long commutes to work, the lonely hours in front of the computer, and so on. Our ego expands to fill the vacuum of the shattered collectivities that in more traditional times coordinated daily life. There is an obvious element of nostalgia in Augé's analyses, but there is also a serious and interesting attempt to fabricate a new way of thinking about and doing anthropology. *See also* POSTMODERNITY.

Further Reading: I. Buchanan 'Non-Places: Space in the Age of Supermodernity' in R. Barcan, and I. Buchanan (eds.) *Imagining Australian Space* (1999).
J. Frow *Time and Commodity Culture* (1997).

superstructure *See* BASE AND SUPERSTRUCTURE.

Surrealism Artistic movement dating from the last days of World War I and ending in 1966 (some like Maurice Nadeau, the movement's semi-official historian, would say it is alive still) with the death of André *Breton, the unofficial Pope of Surrealism. Its peak period was the two decades between the two World Wars, the tumultuous years which saw the stock market crash in 1929 and fascism take power in Italy, Spain, and Germany. It was also a period of hope for the international Left, with whom Surrealism sympathized.

Although it began as a literary movement, it is doubtless better known for its striking visuals—none more so than the excruciatingly vivid, eye-slicing scene in Salvador Dalí and Luis Buñuel's 1929 film *Un Chien andalou* (An Andalusian Dog) which was Dalí's debut on the Parisian scene. The movement's playful aesthetic is captured in Comte de Lautréamont's definition of beauty in *Chants de Maldoror* (1868), which became a kind of Surrealist slogan or watchword: 'the chance meeting of a sewing machine and an umbrella on an operating table'.

The word 'Surrealism' was coined by Guillaume Apollinaire in 1917, but it was Breton who gave the term the meaning we recognize today in the first *Surrealist Manifesto* (1924). Surrealism, he said, is pure psychic automatism, which through writing or any other artistic means, expresses the true functioning of thought, by which he meant thought unconstrained by reason, or by moral, ethical, or aesthetic considerations. Influenced by Sigmund *Freud's *Zur Psychopathologie des Alltagslebens* (1901), translated as *The Psychopathology of Everyday Life* (1914), Surrealism wanted to get in touch with the untutored creativity of the unconscious itself and dissolve the dividing line between art and life. Interestingly, Freud himself was unimpressed by Surrealism, and did not warm to Breton when the two met in Vienna in 1921.

Surrealism adapted Freud's therapeutic technique of *free association to develop its two signature artistic procedures: automatic writing (a *stream of consciousness flow of words, thoughts, and ideas written down without regard for syntax or sense) and collage (random combinations of images and materials). German cultural critic, Walter *Benjamin, writing in 1929, described the often quite provocative results of these techniques as inspiring a 'profane illumination'. Virtually every medium of art experimented with Surrealist techniques during the movement's heyday, leading to the production of several memorable works, with the exception of music which never found a way of accommodating itself to its emphasis on chance and randomness.

In literature, Surrealism yielded Louis Aragon's *Paris Peasant* (1924) and André Breton's *Nadja* (1928); in cinema it was the aforementioned Buñuel who led the way, but even Alfred Hitchcock experimented with Surrealism (he hired Dalí to design a dream sequence for his 1945 Ingrid Bergman and Gregory Peck feature, *Spellbound*); in photography it was Man Ray, Lee Miller (Man Ray's model and muse), Eugène Atget, and Max Ernst who set the standard; in the visual arts it was undoubtedly Dalí who captured the limelight, but no less important were René Magritte, André Masson, Joan Miró, and Yves Tanguy; in the plastic arts, it was Marcel Duchamp who created the best-known works; while in theatre it was undoubtedly Antonin *Artaud who was the most notorious, though he later denounced Surrealism (itself a very Surrealist thing to do, judging by the frequency of the denunciations and expulsions the group experienced).

Surrealism was a direct influence on three major figures in critical theory: Georges *Bataille, Henri *Lefebvre, and Jacques *Lacan; and a distant, but not insignificant influence on Jean *Baudrillard and Guy *Debord.

Further Reading: W. Benjamin 'Surrealism' in *Reflections* (1978).
M. Gale *Dada and Surrealism* (1997).
D. Hopkins *Dada and Surrealism: A Very Short Introduction* (2004);.
M. Nadeau *Histoire du Surréalism* (1964), translated as *The History of Surrealism* (1968).

SEE WEB LINKS

- A brief overview of the Surrealist movement, and short biographies of famous Surrealists.
- A history of Surrealism, and Surreal art, as well as information about famous Surrealists.
- http://www.surrealismcentre.ac.uk

suture A term used in both *psychoanalysis and film studies, where its use is in any case adapted from psychoanalysis, to refer to the way like and unlike can be 'stitched' together. French psychoanalyst Jacques *Lacan used the term to signify the relationship between the conscious and the *unconscious. However, it is really film studies, initiated by a 1977 essay in *Screen* by Jean-Pierre Oudart, which has given the most attention to this concept. Oudart suggested that cinema deploys a number of techniques to suture its audience to what is happening on screen, and more particularly to enable them to understand a narrative composed of images not words. The best known of these is the shot/reverse shot typical of TV interviews and practically any emotional encounter on screen: first we see the face of the speaker, then we see the face of the listener, enabling us to see their reaction to the other person's words. This change in perspective gives the spectator the feeling that they are in fact standing in the—now off screen—position of the speaker, thus suturing them into the action on screen by making their own position outside of the screen seem like a part of the greater totality of the action. The term has fallen out of use in recent years, but it remains significant for stimulating debate about the relationship between film and its audience.

symbol **1.** A specific type of *representamen in Charles Sanders *Peirce's *semiotic model, which he contrasts with the *icon and the *index. Peirce defines the symbol as conventional because the relation between it and its object is governed by an external law (e.g. the word 'give' has only a conventional connection to the actions it describes).

2. Swiss analytical psychologist Carl *Jung used the concept of symbol to denote an intuitive idea unable to be formulated in words. As such, symbols generally appear as an impediment in therapy, as a moment when it feels as though there is more to be said but somehow the words are missing. They are effectively unconscious answers to conscious questions. Symbols step in to articulate what cannot otherwise be verbalized. The content of symbols—e.g. the rose as a symbol of love—should not be viewed as fixed; rather it changes according to the requirements of a particular idea. In doing so, however, it draws on and reworks existing imagery. Symbols captivate the imagination and compel us to attend to alternative perspectives. They are indistinct, enigmatic, even metaphoric, presentations of our own psychic reality.

3. In aesthetics, including literary studies, a symbol is a conventional image or *trope (e.g. the use of the rose motif to signify love, or the cross to signify sacrifice). Ernest Cassirer and Northrop *Frye are the main names associated with this branch of aesthetics.

symbolic (*symbolique*) One of the three 'orders' (the others are the *imaginary and the *real) which, according to Jacques *Lacan, structure human existence. Lacan adapted the concept from the work of French anthropologist Claude *Lévi-Strauss, who, in turn, took his model from the work of Swiss linguist Ferdinand de *Saussure. Taking Saussure's idea that the *signifier is arbitrary in its relation to the signified, that there is in effect no necessary link between a representation and its meaning, Lévi-Strauss extended this principle to all cultural phenomena and argued that what had to be understood was the symbolic system that gives all phenomena their specific meanings. Lacan adopts this argument and adds two important implications of his own: first, that the unconscious must be structured like a language for it to have produced such a system and to be able to exist within it; second, that the *subject is born into the symbolic system which they have to learn to use and this experience is *alienating. For Lacan the maturation of the *ego occurs when the child is inducted into the symbolic order. *Psychosis, for Lacan, is the state of being one falls into if this process of induction into the symbolic fails and the subject is left stranded in the illusory world of the imaginary.

symbolic exchange Jean *Baudrillard's theory for a model of exchange which existed prior to capitalism in which goods and actions that have no intrinsic *value are exchanged for purely symbolic reasons. It is like a *performative, in this respect, because it is the fact of the exchange being made that is socially significant in symbolic exchange, not the nature of substance of what is exchanged. In so-called 'primitive' societies, exchanges had to be made in a way that did not obligate the receiver to reciprocate and thus incur a debt. The perfect gift was therefore a 'useless' or purely symbolic gift. When the gift is symbolic in itself, or useful, then symbolic exchange is extinguished and the twin motors of capitalism—exchange-value and use-value—take its place.

symbolic violence Pierre *Bourdieu's term for the process whereby the dominant social class impose their *ideology on the dominated classes. To put it another way, it theorizes the form *hegemony takes when it is achieved. The dominant class legitimizes its own class interests in the eyes of the dominated classes by giving them the appearance of the naturally right.

symptomatic reading A mode of reading literary and historical works proposed by French Marxist Louis *Althusser which focuses on the text's underlying presuppositions. In particular it tries to determine what a particular text is unable to say or represses because of its *ideological conviction. For example, one might compare the frontier literature of Australia and America, both of which countries are the product of colonial conquest, and inquire why their respective literary traditions are so different: America produced the western, whereas Australia created stories of lost children and isolated battlers.

synchronic and diachronic A binary pair introduced by Ferdinand de *Saussure to define the two available temporal axes for the analysis of language, which can logically be extended to encompass virtually all forms of human activity. Linguistics, in Saussure's time, approached the problem of the multiplicity of languages by trying to trace each of them back to a handful of common sources (in much the same way as evolutionary biologists approach the problem of the multiplicity of species). This approach was deemed diachronic by Saussure because it looks for the production of difference across time. But for Saussure this ignored the (to him, more interesting and important) problem of how to account for the existence and operation of language itself. To get a handle on this, he insisted that it was necessary to take a snapshot of language at a particular time and effectively produce a freeze-frame of it. This approach he referred to as synchronic. By freezing time, or better ignoring its effects, Saussure thought it would be easier to see that which was eternal and universal.

Further Reading: F. Jameson *The Prison-House of Language: A Critical Account of Structuralism and Russian Formalism* (1972).
J. Sturrock *Structuralism* (1986).

syncretism Used in cultural anthropology and *Cultural Studies to describe the synthetic cultural productions that result from the coming together of *diasporic cultures (e.g. bhangra and reggae). Syncretism differs from *hybridity in that its synthesis can occur across class as well as race barriers.

synecdoche A standard form in *rhetoric in which either a part can be made to stand in for a whole, or a whole can stand in for a part. For example, in the phrase 'Washington said...' commonly heard on TV news, Washington is a whole standing in for the actual individuals who work in the US federal government; but it is also a part of the US standing in for the whole of the country.

syntagm Used in both linguistics and *semiotics to theorize the possible (i.e. meaningful) combinations of *paradigmatic elements. The syntagm is the deep structure of a sentence or phrase which remains unchanged even if its specific elements are changed. For example, there is no difference at the level of the syntagm between 'the boy went to the shop' and 'the girl went to the shop' because in both cases the structure 'a person went somewhere' is preserved. The syntagm is in effect the horizontal axis of communication, while the paradigm is the vertical axis.

tactics *See* STRATEGY AND TACTICS.

talking cure Josef Breuer's patient Fräulein Anna O (later identified as Bertha van Pappenheim), whose case is analysed in the book Breuer co-authored with Sigmund *Freud, *Studien über Hysterie* (1895), translated as *Studies on Hysteria* (1955), famously described her treatment this way because her therapy consisted largely of talking about herself and her childhood, usually under hypnosis. It has become a standard codephrase for *psychoanalysis.

Taussig, Michael (1940–) *Marxist cultural anthropologist. Born in Papua New Guinea and educated in Australia and the UK, Taussig studied medicine at undergraduate level but did not pursue a career as a general practitioner. Instead he completed a PhD in medical anthropology. He is best known, however, for his accounts of magical beliefs in South America, particularly his seminal work *The Devil and Commodity Fetishism in South America* (1980). Based on extensive fieldwork amongst tin-miners in Columbia, Taussig showed the way pagan beliefs adapt to accommodate changes in society, such as the advent of capitalism. A highly prolific author, Taussig has written several important books: *Shamanism, Colonialism, and the Wild Man: A Study in Terror and Healing* (1987), *Mimesis and Alterity: A Particular History of the Senses* (1993), and *Law in a Lawless Land: Diary of a Limpieza in Colombia* (2003).

TAZ *See* TEMPORARY AUTONOMOUS ZONE.

technics American philosopher Lewis Mumford's term for the transformation of human existence via the invention of machines, from the simplest levers through to complex cities. French philosopher Bernard *Stiegler also uses this term for his theory of the interrelatedness of humans and technology developed at length in his three-volume work *La technique et le temps* (1994–2001). Drawing on the work of Martin *Heidegger, André Leroi-Gourhan, Gilbert Simondon, and Bertrand Gille, Stiegler argues that temporality depends upon technology, that without the technological means to measure time, the sense of passing time would not be possible.

Therefore insofar as temporality is intrinsic to what it means to be human, the human is inseparable from the technological. To put it another way, there is nothing essential to the human; the human always requires a technological prosthesis to support it.

teleology The study of, and the implicit assumption that everything has, a final purpose. Derived from the Greek word 'telos' meaning end, teleology is a philosophical position premised on the idea that human action has a purpose. This purpose is sometimes considered divine, where teleology is equated with God's design, and may be compared to fatalism. But there is also a secular version in which teleology and history are equated. On this view of things, which is often described as a social Darwinist perspective, all human society is constantly evolving towards some as yet unknown, but certainly higher and more sophisticated form.

Tel quel A French literary and philosophical journal published between 1960 and 1983. Edited by Philippe *Sollers, the journal published work by many of the leading figures of what would become known as *post-structuralism, or simply as *theory, and so played a major part in both disseminating and popularizing theory. Roland *Barthes, Jacques *Derrida, Michel *Foucault, and Julia *Kristeva all published with the journal—they all also broke with the journal at some point for philosophical and more especially political reasons. The journal was distinctive for its pugnacious stance: it overtly championed political causes such as Maoism, and defended the **nouveau roman* against criticism, but also attacked it for not being experimental enough, and favoured *psychoanalysis and *Marxism when these things were out of fashion. It was undoubtedly one of the most influential academic journals of its time.

Further Reading: P. ffrench *The Time of Theory: A History of* Tel Quel, *1960–83* (1995).

Temporary Autonomous Zone (TAZ) Anarchist poet and social activist Hakim Bey's radical proposal for a concept of *utopia suited to the historical conditions of *late capitalism. Conceived in the late 1980s when the Cold War still dominated geopolitical thought and the Internet was in its infancy, the temporary autonomous zone proposed to deploy the resources of the latter in order to offer an alternative political model to the capitalism/socialism binary underpinning the former. Arguing that the all or nothing rhetoric of revolution paralyses politics, because the sheer scale of the task of trying to change the world inevitably overwhelms even the hardiest of activists, Bey instead suggests that activism should look to insurrection as its model. Rather than take power, as revolution demands, the TAZ looks simply to create a space or enclave for an alternative to power. Inspired by *Deleuze and *Guattari's concept of *nomadism, though it derives its historical precedents from sea-going pirates rather than desert tribes, its logic anticipates the anti-WTO (World Trade Organization) slogans that circulated in the late 1990s, e.g. 'one world with many worlds in it' and 'another world is possible', in that it is not concerned with seizing territory, but simply wants to mobilize any thing it can find to hand—art, ideas, slogans, festivals, theatre—to open up a space for new ways of thinking and living. He refers to this process as either 'ontological anarchy' or 'poetic terrorism'. But it is also more radical than the anti-WTO movement in that it wants to break with existing social structures, such as that of the family, and it eschews permanence in favour of transience. Bey insists that the TAZ is not a political doctrine and offers no programme for creating it, claiming instead that as a kind of psycho-spiritual or existentialist state it is always already being created (in this regard it also anticipates *Hardt and *Negri's concept of the *multitude and could usefully be compared to Deleuze and Guattari's notion of the *rhizome).

Further Reading: H. Bey *T.A.Z.: Temporary Autonomous Zone, Ontological Anarchy, Poetic Terrorism* (1985).

Theatre of Cruelty French poet and dramatist Antonin *Artaud's proposal—put forward in two short manifestos published together in *The Theatre and its Double* (1970)—for the recovery of theatre's specific powers of action and its own language. Theatre had to break with its subjugation to the text, he argued, and find its own way of expressing itself, which he thought would lie somewhere between gesture and thought. He didn't want to dispense with spoken words altogether, but he argued that rather than use words from known languages, theatre should use the language of things, which would consist of vocalizations he called 'breath sounds'. He also advocated the use of lighting and music as part of the performance and not merely as an adjunct to it. The aim was to create a theatre that was not focused around the psychological states of specific characters and therefore beholden to an old-fashioned notion of what theatre can be. Artaud was vehemently opposed to *realism in the theatre for this reason. Like Bertolt *Brecht, he insisted that the way the actors moved themselves on stage had to be changed, so as to break with the conventions of *realism. By cruelty, then, Artaud meant not sadism or horror as such, but a concentrated discipline, attentiveness to every detail of the performance and a constant vigilance against backsliding into the old way of doing things. For Artaud cruelty is synonymous with lucidity. Although most theatre critics and practitioners consider Artaud's proposals impossible to stage in full—they are like the impossible-to-build designs of conceptual architecture in this regard —this has in no way diminished their importance or influence, particularly with radical and experimental directors like Peter Brook and Richard Schechner whose work was pushing the boundaries of the possible in any case.

Further Reading: S. Barber *Antonin Artaud: Blows and Bombs* (1993).

Theatre of the Absurd An anti-political form of theatre that emerged in Europe in the 1950s, largely as a rejection of Bertolt *Brecht's *Epic Theatre. Inspired by Alfred *Jarry's *'pataphysics, Franz Kafka's bleak stories, *Dada, and *Surrealism, the Theatre of the Absurd is *nihilist in its outlook. In this respect, it is congruent with *Absurdism's *solipsistic view of the world. It is typified by clever language play, which pushes language to the point of non-meaning and nonsense, thereby exposing language's capacity to betray its users. There was no coherent group of practitioners who identified themselves with this garve, but the term is generally applied to the following directors and playwrights: Samuel Beckett, Eugène Ionesco, Jean Genet, and Harold Pinter.

Further Reading: M. Esslin *The Theatre of the Absurd* (1968).

theory A generic term for the interdisciplinary combination of philosophy, literary criticism, and sociology produced by scholars like Roland *Barthes, Michel *Foucault, Jacques *Derrida, and Gilles *Deleuze. It is difficult to define theory in an exhaustive manner because it is by nature an inclusive mode of discourse, though its detractors never seem to have any such difficulties. It is perhaps best defined in terms of what it is not: it is not philosophy because it rejects the possibility of one philosophical system being capable of explaining everything; it is not literary criticism because it is not interested in the meaning of specific texts, but rather in the more general problem of how texts are meaningful; it is not sociology either because it is mistrustful of generalizations and does not accept that human behaviour can be quantified. In many respects, however, the term is obsolete because its real purpose was always to stake out the claim for a new way of conceiving both the object and the subject of research in the humanities, and now that purpose has been served, the term has lost its edge. Even so, it is still possible to find people who say they 'don't do theory', but they are getting rarer and rarer.

thick description In cultural anthropology thick description is the analysis not just of a particular statement or gesture, but the background and context needed to understand the full meaning of that statement or gesture. The concept was conceived by English analytic philosopher Gilbert Ryle, but its influence in anthropology is due to its uptake by Clifford *Geertz in the programme essay 'Thick Description: Toward an Interpretive Theory of Culture' which introduces his widely read book, *The Interpretation of Cultures: Selected Essays* (1973). Geertz extrapolates from Ryle's rather forced example of the complexity of determining the meaning of a wink—is it a wink? a twitch? is it intended as a wink? or was it meant to be the burlesque version of a wink?—the general hypothesis that *culture itself is a form of ongoing interpretive practice. So, he argues, to understand another culture what one has to first of all grasp is the manifold array of codes and rules for making and interpreting meaning in that culture. His implication is that one cannot understand another culture through remote observation alone; one has to find the means of seeing it from the perspective of those who belong to that culture. Only then will one be in a position to know when an eye twitch is a wink and whether that wink implies collusion.

Third Space A creative space that lies between the discourse or position of the ruling subject and the discourse or position of the *subaltern subject. This, according to the term's originator Homi *Bhabha, is inscribed within the communicative situation itself. He explains that this never self-sufficient because there is always a gap between the statement and its expression (this formulation draws on a variety of *post-structuralist accounts of language, but principally that of Jacques *Derrida and his concept of **différance*). The 'I' who speaks and the 'I' who is spoken about never coincide. Once we understand this, Bhabha argues, we cannot but realize that all claims concerning the purity or originality of cultures are untenable by definition. Urban geographer, Edward *Soja has adopted this term as a means of articulating the problematic space of contemporary Los Angeles, which, as his researches make plain, is neither as fully American nor as fully First World as its boosters make it out to be, because of the huge number of migrants living there as well as the presence of sweatshops in the inner city. Soja takes it a step further and considers the gap between Los Angeles as the producer of cinematic representations and its representation in images, arguing that the fantasy images of film feed into the way in which the city sees itself and lives are lived there. Third Space has become an important term in *Postcolonial Studies for thinking about geographical *hybridity.

Further Reading: H. Bhabha *The Location of Culture* (1994).
M. Doel *Poststructuralist Geographies* (1999).
E. Soja *Thirdspace: Journeys to Los Angeles and Other Real-And-Imagined Places* (1996).

Third Wave feminism A movement for the renewal of *feminism's original project—i.e. equality between the sexes—expanded to incorporate those women, particularly women of colour, and women from the *Third World, who felt excluded from *Second Wave feminism. Often conflated with so-called *post-feminism, although it is not the same thing at all, Third Wave feminism has its roots in the disappointments and conflicts which brought the Second Wave to a halt. Writers like Gloria *Anzaldúa and bell *hooks argued for a new conception of feminist subjectivity that took account of *race as well as *class and *gender. In the public sphere, feminism fought to retain the gains it had made, in the face of an anti-equal rights onslaught by the Reagan and Thatcher administrations in the US and UK respectively. The tipping point, so to speak, was the way Anita Hill's allegations of sexual harassment against Supreme Court nominee Clarence Thomas were handled in 1991. In spite of Hill's testimony, Thomas was nonetheless confirmed as a Supreme Court judge, sparking Rebecca Walker (daughter of Alice Walker, the author of *The Colour Purple* (1982)) to write a stirring riposte for *Ms.* magazine entitled 'I am the Third Wave' thus giving the movement a name.

Further Reading: S. Gillis, G. Howie, and R. Munford *Third Wave Feminism: A Critical Exploration* (2007).

Third World Alternative phrase in common use for the developing or underdeveloped parts of the world. It was coined by French economist Alfred Sauvy in an article published in *Observateur* in 1952 which compared the politically non-aligned countries (i.e. countries that had not taken a side in the Cold War) to the Third Estate (i.e. peasants and commoners) in France during the Revolution. His point was that like the peasants, the people of the Third World had very little material wealth, but had begun to assert their right to and desire for a better share of global resources. This became manifest as the process of *decolonization began in earnest following the end of World War II. At the Bandung conference in 1955, at which the leaders of countries from Africa and Asia met to discuss their collective future, and possible forms of cooperation and collaboration between the 29 participating countries, the notion of the Third World became a rallying cry of solidarity. It was used to signal common cause and as an indictment on the First World (i.e. the former colonial powers, the present-day G8 countries). In more recent times, *Postcolonial Studies has rejected the use of the term Third World for being both too generalizing and too demeaning. The argument against its use usually points out that countries in the First World have sections in them that are as poor as anywhere in the Third World (such as the garment district, or skid row, in downtown Los Angeles), and Third World countries like India have sections in them every bit as wealthy as First World cities (e.g. Mumbai).

Further Reading: M. Denning *Culture in the Age of Three Worlds* (2004).

Thompson, Edward Palmer (1924–93) British *Marxist cultural historian and nuclear disarmament activist. Born in Oxford to parents who were Methodist missionaries, he went to high school in Bath and university at Corpus Christi College, Cambridge. During World War II he served in a tank corps in Italy. At Cambridge he joined the Communist Party and in 1946 together with Christopher Hill, Eric *Hobsbawm, and Rodney Hilton, formed the Communist Party Historians Group, which established its own highly influential journal *Past and Present*. It was the publication in 1963 of *The Making of the English Working Class* that brought Thompson widespread recognition as one of the key intellectuals of the time. Like Richard *Hoggart's *The Uses of Literacy* (1957) and Raymond *Williams's *Culture and Society* (1958), *The Making of the English Working Class* set aside the old model of culture which ignored the daily lives of the labouring classes in favour of the pronouncements and peccadilloes of the aristocracy, as though to say it is only kings and queens who have culture and make history. It was for this reason, despite its focus on 17th century Britain, that Thompson's work proved to be of enduring interest to *Cultural Studies, which is similarly interested in *everyday life. In the 1970s, having moved from Cambridge to Warwick, from which he famously resigned in protest at what he saw as its commercialization, Thompson made his living as a freelance writer, producing short works on a wide variety of historical and contemporary topics. He found true notoriety in 1978 with the publication of *The Poverty of Theory*, a blistering, albeit misdirected and intemperate, attack on *theory, and particularly on its then leading exponent Louis *Althusser. Perry *Anderson wrote an equally scathing reply, *Arguments within English Marxism* (1980), demolishing virtually every one of Thompson's points. From 1980 on, Thompson devoted his attention and energy to the nuclear disarmament movement, writing countless polemical pieces attacking the militarist ideology.

Todorov, Tzvetan (1939–) Bulgarian literary theorist and one of the key disseminators of *Russian Formalism. Born in Sofia, Todorov completed his undergraduate degree there and then like Julia *Kristeva he moved to Paris to undertake postgraduate work. In spite of an initially frosty reception at the Sorbonne, where he was told literary theory was not done, he persevered and eventually met Roland *Barthes and in him found a receptive master. He completed his doctorate under Barthes at the École des Hautes Études en Sciences Sociales in 1966. Todorov's principal interest in his early work was in the formal properties of narrative (his work is in this regard congruent to that of *Genette and *Greimas), specifically its syntax, or the rules of combination. He distinguished between propositions and sequences, showing that for every proposition (an action performed by an agent, e.g. the hero goes on a quest) there is a limited number of things that can happen (either the hero succeeds or he doesn't). These propositions are the basic building blocks of all narrative, as most creative writing schools now instruct. Todorov utilized this insight to great effect in his book on uncanny literature, Translated as *The Fantastic: A Structural Approach to a Literary Genre* (1973), which is still used as the standard point of reference in genre studies. In contrast to his colleague Genette, for instance, Todorov's work continued to progress and develop beyond its structuralist beginnings and engage topics other than the purely formalist. He has tackled the ethical and moral issues arising from colonialism (*The Conquest of America: The Question of the Other* (1982)), racism (*On Human Diversity: Nationalism, Racism and Exoticism in French Thought* (1989)), and the Holocaust (*Facing the Extreme: Moral Life in the Concentration Camps* (1999)).

Tönnies, Ferdinand (1855–1936) German sociologist best known for the formative distinction he drew between *Gemeinschaft* and *Gesellschaft* (community and society), for which he is widely considered one of the 'fathers' of sociology (along with *Durkheim, *Simmel, and Weber). Born in Nordfriesland in Schleswig-Holstein, then under Danish rule but now part of Germany, Tönnies's family were wealthy farmers. His family's money enabled him to remain aloof from the academic world and consequently his professional career progressed rather slowly. He didn't attain a full professorship until three years before his retirement in 1913. He continued as a professor emeritus at the University of Kiel until 1933 when the Nazi government forced him out because of his earlier criticisms of them. A relatively prolific author, Tönnies is nonetheless remembered for only one work, his first book: the seminal *Gemeinschaft und*

Gesellschaft (1887), translated as *Community and Society* (1957), still an essential cornerstone of any introductory course on sociology. The distinction between community and society, which Tönnies treated as ideal types or tendencies rather than actually existing entities, distinguishes between social groups which are held together by mutual bonds of filiation and friendship (community) and those which are bound by mutual self-interest (society). The two types of social group are approximations of village or country life (community) and town or city life (society). Tönnies thought of these two types of social groups as tendencies, which are present to a greater or lesser degree in actual towns or cities. These tendencies were, according to Tönnies, manifest in the way a particular social group oriented itself towards social action. That is to say, is the glue holding the social group together the product of 'natural' inclination, or 'strategic' calculation.

topography In *Die Traumdeutung* (1900), translated as *The Interpretation of Dreams* (1953), Sigmund *Freud borrows this term from geography (where it refers to a type of map that distinguishes between features such as mountains and lakes and specifies their exact height or depth), to describe his conception of the psychical apparatus as consisting of three distinct regions: the *unconscious, the preconscious, and the conscious. Freud did not intend this to be a form of anatomical localization, to specify one part of the brain as being unconscious and another conscious, which is why he is careful to use the term psychical apparatus to describe what he is talking about. He adopted the notion of topography because his analysis of patients suggested very strongly to him that the kinds of impulses, thoughts, and wishes he associated with the unconscious occur on a different stage to those of the conscious. This hypothesis is effectively the starting premise of *psychoanalysis: the unconscious is a different kind of psychical mechanism to the conscious and its productions can only pass into the conscious if they are distorted and transformed by the primary processes (i.e. the *dreamwork). Except for the occasional, unwelcome intrusions, which Freud termed *parapraxes (better known as 'Freudian slips'), the conscious is generally unaware of what is happening in the unconscious, but the constant pressure of the *repression it has to apply to remain ignorant takes its toll. Freud produced a second topography late in his career replacing the terms unconscious, preconscious, and conscious with the terms *id, *ego, and *superego, but retaining the idea of their spatial separation. The main difference, though, between the two topographies is that in the second, Freud allowed that certain psychical impulses may occur in two or more regions simultaneously, whereas previously he had thought they originated in the unconscious and migrated to the conscious.

topos The Greek word for place. It is used in *rhetoric to denote common motifs, such as the idea that a flower can signify both the beauty and the brevity of life. It is also used in *Cultural Studies to refer to places emblematic of particular movements—e.g. the Bonaventure Hotel in Los Angeles has been described as a topos of *postmodernism because of Fredric *Jameson's discussion of it.

Touraine, Alain (1925–) French post-Marxist sociologist with a strong interest in social movements and the possibility of people-led politics. Born in the wealthy seaside resort town of Hermanville-sur-Mer in Basse-Normandie ('Sword' beach in the D-Day landings in 1944) to a long line of medical practitioners, Touraine broke the family mould, first by not studying medicine, and second by not immediately pursuing further studies upon graduation from École Normale Supérieure. Instead he took a job in a coalmine. This experience awakened his desire to study and sharpened his focus on sociology. He took a research position with Georges Friedman at the Centre National de la Recherche Scientifique in 1950. But then in 1952, again breaking the expected pattern, he went to the US to undertake graduate work with the giants of American sociology Talcott Parsons and Paul Lazarsfeld. He returned to France in 1960 and completed his doctorate at the École des Hautes Études en Sciences Sociales, where he has remained ever since. True to his coalmining inspiration to do sociology in the first place, Touraine's early works were close empirical studies of workers in factories and the fields. But in contrast to his *Marxist colleagues, he did not view this in terms of revolutionary potential. Indeed, in his unselfconsciously prophetic 1969 book translated as *The Post-Industrial Society. Tomorrow's Social History: Classes, Conflicts and Culture in the Programmed Society* (1971), he would come to think of the 1960s as the start of the so-called *post-industrial period (a term generally associated with Daniel *Bell, though it was in fact Touraine who coined the phrase) in which the central axis of the economy, in the West at least, shifts from manufacturing to information, leaving union labour behind. He wrote a rapid response to the events of *May '68, an experience which seemed to spark his interest in social movements, giving rise to a series of works, including case studies on the anti-nuclear movement in France as well as the Solidarity movement in Poland. The overall trajectory of his work, then, is towards a theory of the subject as a rational actor capable of bringing about change in spite of the weight of history.

transcoding American cultural critic Fredric *Jameson's term for his comparative analysis of what he calls theoretical discourses or codes, such as *deconstruction, *structuralism, *post-structuralism, and so on. He suggests that the key issue to be decided is what kinds of thoughts and ideas are possible in one theoretical code and not another and what the relative advantages and disadvantages of each code are in consequence. By the same token, this comparative viewpoint itself implies still another code that is itself 'untranscendable' to use Jameson's famous description of *Marxism from *The Political Unconscious: Narrative as a Socially Symbolic Act* (1981). *See also* METACOMMENTARY.

transcultural The movement of ideas, influences, practices, and beliefs between cultures and the fusions that result when the ideas, influences, practices, and beliefs of different cultures come together in a specific place, text, or *contact zone. The movement of cultures is not always reciprocal or voluntary—indeed, a large majority of what is deemed transcultural is the product of colonization, *diaspora of different types, and exile. Some examples are the product of the necessary compromises subjugated cultures make in order to survive, as was the uptake of Catholicism by indigenous peoples in South America. As Michael Taussig demonstrates in *The Devil and Commodity Fetishism* (1983), the indigenous peoples could adopt Catholicism without having to give up completely on their own animistic beliefs because of the focus on spirit in Catholicism and the figure of the devil, which they could imbue with pantheistic traits. Other examples are more directly the result of *globalization, which has brought about a widespread taste for the 'cultural', as for instance films like *Bride and Prejudice* (director Gurinder Chadha, 2005), which fuses Bollywood and Hollywood. The unequalness of the transcultural is exemplified by singer Paul Simon's borrowing of African music styles in the production of his bestselling album *Graceland* (1986)—the people he borrowed from received nothing for their contributions or their original ideas.

transference (*Übertragung*) Initially used by Sigmund *Freud as an alternative word to *displacement for describing the process of the transfer of libidinal energy between one ideation of an *unconscious thought or wish and another. However, he also used it to denote what occurs in the relationship between analyst and analysand and it is this sense of the term that has become dominant, not the least because of the influence of Jacques *Lacan, who insists that the analytic relationship is the defining nucleus of *psychoanalysis. Transference of this latter type refers to the process whereby the analysand *projects onto the analyst the affectionate (positive transference) or the hostile (negative transference) feelings aroused by the analysis. In effect, the *analysand acts towards the analyst as though he or she were the embodiment of the figure important to them from childhood (e.g. father, mother, uncle, etc.). Freud noticed that this often occurred when the analysand seemed most reluctant to reveal something, so he counted it among the defences of the *unconscious, describing it as a form of resistance. But inasmuch as the analysand is thereby repeating or rehearsing the essentials of the relationship they once had with their father, etc., the transference could also be made to serve a positive therapeutic purpose because it afforded the opportunity of working through in the immediacy of the present the issues from the past.

trope A figure of speech, or mode of *rhetoric, which changes the meaning of words. The main varieties of trope are *metaphor, *metonymy, *synecdoche, and *irony. Tropes may also take an extended form as Hayden *White demonstrates in *Tropics of Discourse* (1978). White uses the concept of trope to account for the way historians give meaning to the historical record. For White, all narratives are in effect tropes inasmuch that at a macro-structural level they shape the meaning of all words.

uncanny (*unheimlich*) That which is unfamiliar—or more literally, un-homely—in the familiar or homely. In a famous essay, 'Das Unheimliche' (1919), Freud argued that the uncanny is the feeling we get when an experience that occurred by chance suddenly feels fateful and inescapable. His own quite humorous example of this is an anecdote about an afternoon walk he took in a small provincial Italian town in which he happened upon the brothel district and though he hurriedly exited the area the continuation of his walk somehow brought him back there, twice, a discomforting fact that he felt was noticed by the locals. He traces the uncanny feeling this provokes in him back to infantile psychology because it clearly evidences a *compulsion to repeat and argues that anything that reminds of this aspect of our childhood will be perceived as uncanny. Literature then is able to create the same feeling by evoking situations in which a character acts without reason, or, more particularly, returns when they are thought to be gone—the archetype of this is the ghost or the zombie. The uncanny is not a new thing; it is always an old, and usually repressed, thing that recurs in the place where it is not expected. Russian literary critics Tzvetan *Todorov uses the concept of the uncanny in the development of his theory of fantastic literature in *The Fantastic: A Structural Approach to a Literary Genre* (1970).

unconscious An adjective for thought processes not present—or not visible—in the field of consciousness at a given moment in time. When Sigmund *Freud adopted the term, at a very early stage in his development of *psychoanalysis, he transformed it from an adjective into a noun designating one of the three operative systems in the psychical apparatus (the other two being the preconscious and the conscious), as he refers to it in *Die Traumdeutung* (1900), translated as *The Interpretation of Dreams* (1953). As Freud conceives it, the unconscious is both a dynamic and a *topographic system: it is dynamic in the sense that the *libidinal energy and *cathexes that are active within it are ceaseless—they apply a constant pressure on the preconscious and the conscious and are met in turn by an equally constant pressure (*repression); it is topographical in that its processes and contents are only accessible to the conscious mind under very specific conditions, as though there were some kind of wall separating the different regions of the psychical apparatus.

In his later years, Freud would modify his view slightly, but he basically held fast to the idea that the three different parts of the psychical apparatus are topographically distinct from one another and that contents of one region cannot pass directly into the next, but must undergo some kind of distortion or transformation as he details in his account of the *dreamwork. Dreams, Freud famously said, are the royal road to the unconscious because they reveal its primary processes: *condensation, *displacement, and symbolization (a general term referring to the fact that the unconscious is the place where the *instincts are given representational form). As a system, the unconscious is characterized by four main features: (i) the presence of these primary processes, and the corresponding flexibility and mobility of *desire that goes with them; (ii) the absence of any kind of negation (there is no 'no' in the unconscious, according to Freud); (iii) an indifference to reality (anything and everything is possible in the unconscious); and (iv) subordination to the *pleasure principle. In the 1950s, at the height of *structuralism, one of Freud's most important interpreters, the French psychoanalyst Jacques *Lacan, developed the thesis that the unconscious is structured like a language. His rationale for this is the fact that, as Freud defines it, we can only grasp the processes of the unconscious when they take a linguistic form, but for them to be able to do this the unconscious has to already be structured like a language. Lacan also described the unconscious as the *discourse of the *Other, by which is meant the discourse of radical *alterity—it is that which we cannot witness in full and that which transforms us insofar as we come into contact with it. Lacan's account of the unconscious has been criticized for being overly linguistic, particularly by Gilles *Deleuze and Félix *Guattari who argue that the unconscious is better understood as a factory or machine.

unreliable narrator American literary theorist Wayne Booth's term for a narrator who cannot be relied on either to tell the truth or in the case of self-reflexive narrators to know the truth. For example Humbert Humbert, the narrator of Vladimir Nabokov's *Lolita* (1955), is obviously extremely biased in his view of things, constantly shifting blame for his actions onto the teenaged Lolita; but, he also seems to deceive himself as to the true nature of what he is doing. A major part of the dramatic interest of the novel stems from the need to try to sort out these two different kinds of deception. Similarly, narrators can be considered unreliable if they are found not to be in full possession of all the relevant facts. Henry James's *Turn of the Screw* (1898) is a well-known example of this type.

utopia The title of a book written in 1516 by Sir Thomas More, who was beheaded by King Henry VIII for his refusal to sign the Act of Supremacy. Derived from the Greek for 'good place', More's *Utopia* imagines an island cut of from the rest of the world, in which a quite different set of customs and laws than those of his own day are devised. Over time, utopia became a kind of codeword for any attempt to deliberately construct a world that was better than the existing world out of which it was produced. It also tended to be overcoded as idealist, impossible, and unrealistic, making utopia into a pejorative, at least in political discourse. But this misconstrues More's purpose and misunderstands what utopia is: it is not the end result, the perfect place, that is crucial, but rather the process of imagining what it would take to make the present world different than it is. Utopia resides not in the ideal dream of global equality, for example, but in the practical problems associated with achieving that dream. Utopia means being prepared to alter the status quo and refusing to accept the dogma that 'there is no alternative'.

Further Reading: F. Jameson *Archaeologies of the Future* (2004).

value A measure for distinguishing the absolute and relative worth of a thing (an object or a service) both to its owner and to others. Intrinsically hierarchical, value is used in a number of different disciplines. It is theorized in two main ways, as an ethical problem and as an economic problem (recent work in sustainability studies tries to combine these two problems so that the ethical choice and the economic choice are one and the same thing).

Ethics uses value as a means of determining the difference between the various ideas and concepts impacting on *everyday life, such as the notions of freedom and life which come into conflict over issues like the right to life of the unborn foetus versus the right to decide of the mother, or equally problematically the right to die of terminally ill patients versus the medical profession's commitment to life. As both Michel *Foucault and Giorgio *Agamben have pointed out, however, placing a value on life in this way has given rise to a new form of *governmentality that they both describe as *biopower.

In economics, it is Karl *Marx, above all others, who has devoted the most effort to thinking through what value means. But his theory builds on a long line of philosophical inquiry, beginning with Aristotle who first observed that there is a difference between the use-value of a thing (what a thing is worth to a person who actually uses it) and the exchange-value of a thing (what another person would be willing to trade for a particular thing). In use-value it is the intrinsic physical properties of the thing itself which are determinant (e.g. one axe can chop wood better than another because it is made from better materials); while exchange-value is a social construction and varies constantly according to the whims and tastes of a particular society (e.g. fashion).

Aristotle saw as aberrant the fact that (putting it in contemporary terms) a car could have a higher value than a house, when the latter is obviously of far greater use to its owner than the car. Marx saw this state of affairs as normal in capitalism and set out to explain it, basing his theory of value, the so-called 'labour theory of value', on classical economist David Ricardo's famous work *Principles of Political Economy and Taxation* (1817). Marx defined value relative to the 'socially necessary abstract labour' embodied (or stored) in a given commodity. If a table takes 10 hours to produce and a car 10,000 hours to produce then the car is more valuable than the table. This fact is obscured by the way that money (which for Marx is a *commodity) standardizes the exchange-value of all things.

Vaneigem, Raoul (1934–) Belgian anarchist philosopher who, along with Guy *Debord, was one of the key theorists of *Situationism. Born in Lessines, Belgium, he studied at the Free University of Brussels before moving to Paris. In 1960 he sent samples of his poetry to Henri *Lefebvre who in turn passed them along to his student Guy Debord, thus facilitating their meeting and future collaborations. Vaneigem's most famous book, *Traité de savoir-vivre á l'usage des jeunes générations* (1967), translated as *The Revolution of Everyday Life* (1983), was published shortly before the irruption of student protest in *May '68 and many of the slogans the students graffitied on walls were lifted from this text. A prolific writer and principal contributor to *Internationale Situationniste*, Vaneigem used pseudonyms for his more polemical texts. Consistent with the Situationist outlook, but also showing the influence of Wilhelm *Reich, Vaneigem's thesis was that only creative, poetic activity can rescue us from the inauthenticity of everyday life in the capitalist world. This theme is continued in recent works such as *Le Mouvement du libre-esprit* (1986), translated as *The Movement of the Free Spirit* (1994).

Vattimo, Gianni (1936–) Italian philosopher. Born in Turin, Vattimo studied philosophy at the University of Turin, graduating in 1959. He then went to Heidelberg to complete his doctoral studies under the supervision of renowned hermeneuticists Karl Löwith and Hans-Georg *Gadamer. He returned to Turin in 1964 to take up a position at his alma mater, a link he has maintained for his entire career. In 1999, Vattimo was elected to the European Parliament on the Party of Italian Communists ticket. He remained there until 2004, when he resigned from the party. He has since then worked as a journalist, but remains active in European politics. Although openly gay, Vattimo is not a *queer theorist as such. He is a Catholic and several of his works, including a collaboration with Jacques *Derrida, *Religion* (1998), deal with religious and theological issues. Vattimo is best known as an exponent of *weak thought, or weak *ontology, which takes the view that since there is no strong link between language and reality there are only interpretations; the task of philosophy under such conditions is to develop better and more rigorous interpretations. Consequently, *hermeneutics is in Vattimo's view the principal mode of doing philosophy today. Vattimo is in this respect usefully thought of as a *postmodern philosopher, albeit one closer in his thinking to Richard *Rorty than Jean-François *Lyotard. His best-known works are *La fine della modernità* (1985), translated as *The End of Modernity: Nihilism and Hermeneutics in Post-modern Culture* (1991) and *La società trasparente* (1989), translated as *The Transparent Society* (1994).

Veblen, Thorstein (1857–1929) Norwegian-American sociologist and pioneering cultural theorist. His best known work, *The Theory of the Leisure Class* (1899), spawned the well known phrase 'conspicuous consumption', which so aptly describes the antics of the super wealthy. Veblen was born in Wisconsin. His well-to-do parents were recent immigrants from Norway who spoke Norwegian at home. He obtained a BA in economics from Carleton College in Minnesota. He then did graduate work, first at Johns Hopkins University, under the founder of American *pragmatism Charles Sanders *Peirce, and then at Yale, where he completed a PhD in 1884. In 1891 he was appointed professor of economics at the newly created University of Chicago. He taught there until 1906, when he moved to Stanford. He was to remain at Stanford only a short time, moving to the University of Missouri in 1911. In 1919 he moved to New York, taking a position as an editor for *The Dial* (then in its heyday as the audacious publisher of *modernist works by T.S. Eliot, William Butler Yeats, and Ezra Pound, among others). During this period he collaborated with Charles Beard, James Harvey Robinson, and John Dewey to establish the New School for Social Research. If Veblen's work is still a standard feature of introductory sociology courses it is because of *The Theory of the Leisure Class*, which is at once a biting satire and a keen analysis of the social use of wealth in the early part of the 20th century. What intrigued (and disgusted) Veblen was the way money was spent uselessly by the scions of the so-called 'Gilded Age' merely to demonstrate that they could afford it. He also analysed the way the wealthy classes adopt certain fashions, emulating one another so as to reassure themselves of their belonging together.

Further Reading: J. Diggins *Thorstein Veblen* (1999).

verisimilitude The state of appearing to be a 'true' likeness—the term is derived from Latin 'verum' meaning truth and 'similis' meaning like. For example, the dust and grime on the robots and spaceships in the *Star Wars* cycle of films has the effect of making them seem 'more real', as it were, than if they were shiny and new like toys fresh out of their boxes. In this respect, verisimilitude is clearly the goal of the techniques Roland *Barthes analyses in his account of the *reality-effect. It is often also used as a measure of the comparative achievement of works of either *realism or naturalism (the greater the degree of verisimilitude the better the works). Verisimilitude might be regarded as the ultimate form of *mimesis. In philosophy, verisimilitude is used to describe the degree to which a certain hypothesis approaches the truth; it was first used in this sense by Karl *Popper.

Vienna Circle (*der Wiener Kreis*) A group of philosophers, mathematicians, and scientists who met in Vienna in the 1920s and 1930s whose work became known as *logical positivism. The meetings were initiated and chaired by Moritz Schlick, a physicist from Berlin appointed to a chair in theoretical physics at Vienna University in 1922. Membership of the circle included such luminaries as Rudolf Carnap, Kurt Gödel, Otto Neurath, and Hans Hahn. The group was disbanded when Schlick was murdered by an anti-Jewish former student on the steps of his university building in 1936. Schlick was not in fact Jewish, but many of the other members of the circle were and they fled the country (mostly to America) before the Anschluss with Nazi Germany was announced in March 1938. The group produced a manifesto stipulating the core beliefs of their scientific world-conception: first, that knowledge only comes from experience (effectively a flat rejection of *metaphysics); second, that the world can only be properly known by the application of logical analysis, which separates those statements which can be reduced to simpler statements referring to an empirical reality, and those which cannot and therefore contain logical errors or confusions. The ultimate goal of the Vienna Circle was a unified science, but it was never finally realized.

Virilio, Paul (1932–) French architectural theorist. Best known for his essays on speed and war Virilio ranks alongside Jean *Baudrillard as one of the most provocative and counter-intuitive essayists on the impact of technology in the *postmodern era.

Virilio was born in Paris in 1932. He grew up in the northern coastal region of Brittany. When the Germans invaded, his hometown was subjected to heavy attack and then prolonged military occupation. It was also bombed by the Allies because it was used as a military port by the Germans. In later life, Virilio would often say that the war was his university. His choice of subject matter for his research certainly bears this out.

Virilio's path into academia was circuitous. Initially he studied at the École des Métiers d' Art, specializing in working with stained glass.

He then worked alongside the great French artist Henri Matisse helping to restore churches. In 1950 he converted to Catholicism. His compulsory military service came at a time when France was fighting against Algeria in its War of Independence, so Virilio was sent there for his tour of duty. After completing military service Virilio went to the Sorbonne to study philosophy. His teachers there included Maurice *Merleau-Ponty, who sparked his interest in *phenomenology.

In 1958 Virilio conducted a phenomenological analysis of the 'Atlantic Wall', the fortifications network the Germans constructed on the French coastline (near where Virilio grew up) with a view to repelling the Allied invasion. Consisting of over 15,000 concrete bunkers, these defences nevertheless failed because the Allies were able to use their superior weaponry, principally the Air Force, to neutralise it. To Virilio, who published his study under the title *Bunker archéologie* (1975) translated as *Bunker Archaeology* (1994), this demonstrates not only the importance of speed in modern warfare, but the multiple ways in which the landscape of the battlefield must be viewed. As Virilio theorises with his concept of the 'fleet in being' (which *Deleuze and *Guattari adopt in their account of the *war machine), controlling a space no longer requires its constant occupation—now it is enough to be able to move rapidly to interdict a possible attack.

The subject of several of his books, speed is a key interest for Virilio. In 1977 he published *Vitesse et Politique,* which was translated into English in 1986 as *Speed and Politics.* The first of his works to be translated into English, this was the entry point for Anglophone readers and though Virilio has written on a great many topics besides speed, he is generally thought of as a theorist of speed or as he himself terms it 'dromology'. Virilio is ambivalent about speed. In contrast to the *Futurists, he does not regard it as intrinsically liberating; indeed, many of his works show that speed can be an utterly repressive force. In later work, Virilio connects speed to the development of digital technology, particularly surveillance technology, and argues that cinema itself is a kind of weapon. His most provocative thesis in this respect is undoubtedly his claim in *Guerre et cinéma* (1984), translated as *War and Cinema* (1989) that Adolf Hitler conceived of World War Two as a kind of movie.

Digital technology, Virilio argues, has so transformed the contemporary world in terms of speed of communications it has resulted in a kind of inertia—we no longer need to move, as we once did, in order to communicate across vast distances. And this inertia, which is the subject of his short book *L'inertie polaire* (1990), translated as *Polar Inertia* (1999), has resulted in the paradoxical disappearance of the local. Although we no longer need to move, we are nonetheless nodal points in a vast network of communications, such that a virus released in one part of the world will in a very short space of time come to infect the entire world, or at least put the entire world at risk of infection.

Virilio is a provocative writer, but he is more of an essayist than a theorist or historian. And though his pronouncements are (or at least can be) thought-provoking, they can also be frustratingly gnomic and unsubstantiated.

Further Reading: I. James *Paul Virilio* (2007).
S. Redhead *Paul Virilio: Theorist for an Accelerated Culture* (2004).

virtual *See* ACTUAL AND VIRTUAL.

vitalism In philosophy, the position that life in all its forms cannot be explained adequately or completely in either chemical or physical terms. It assumes there must be some 'higher' or 'other' dimension as well, such as the 'soul' or Henri *Bergson's notion of the *élan vital*. Vitalist principles have been at the heart of medical thinking since at least the time of the ancient Egyptians, but in the latter half of the 20th century fell into decline as scientists came to believe that the chemical and physical accounts of life were sufficient and anything beyond that was an unnecessary abstraction, or worse, obfuscation.

Wallerstein, Immanuel (1930–) American historian and sociologist, best known for the elaboration of the world-systems theory. Born and raised in New York City, Wallerstein gained his BA and PhD from Columbia University. He worked there from 1959 to 1971; he then went to McGill for five years, before settling at Binghampton, where he was head of the Fernand Braudel Centre. His initial training was in the economic development of post-colonial Africa, but in the early 1970s he started to take a broader, more global view of economic development in recognition of the fact that the situation in Africa could not be accounted for satisfactorily without taking into account factors that are now associated with the process known as *globalization. The first instalment of his three part magnum opus *The Modern World-System* appeared in 1974, with the next two following in 1980 and 1989. Drawing on Karl *Marx's conviction that the underlying economic factors have a determining effect on cultural and ideological matters, as well as Fernand *Braudel's historical research on the creation of economic networks, Wallerstein offered a revised form of *dependency theory as a riposte to the then fashionable Three Worlds model of the global economy. He argued that economically and historically there is only *one* world, consisting of very complex networks of relations. He overlays this model with a distinction between core and periphery, arguing that it is the movement between the two that functions as the true 'motor' of history. Consistent with his own economic theory, Wallerstein predicts the end of America's reign as the 'lone superpower' in *The Decline of American Power* (2003), a book written on the eve of the invasion of Iraq. Obviously it is too soon to tell if that prediction will prove accurate, but it shows a perhaps *utopian conviction that the future must be different from the present.

waning of affect A feature of the new depthlessness in art attributed to the cultural transformation known as *postmodernism as described in Fredric Jameson's essay 'Postmodernism, or, the Cultural Logic of Late Capitalism' (1984). According to Jameson, by the 1960s a new character type had emerged both in fiction and in reality (in the form of the celebrity artist), which because of its complexity could no longer be thought in terms of such categories as the *ego, or indeed the various pathologies of the ego enumerated by Sigmund *Freud such as *anxiety and *hysteria. Jameson illustrates his point by comparing Vincent Van Gogh's 'A Pair of Boots' (1887) with Andy Warhol's 'Diamond Dust Shoes' (1980). He argues that it is possible to imagine the *situation that yielded the former picture because it readily conjures an image of a tired peasant flinging their boots against the wall at the end of a hard day's toiling in the field, but we cannot do the same for the latter which offers only a random collection of dead objects. For this reason, Jameson argues, its impact on us has to be thought in terms of *intensity rather than *affect because we cannot reconstruct the individual life or life-world which could serve as its point of reference, or our anchor in the real. As a result, it has no depth, by which Jameson means, there is nothing behind or beyond the picture that we can use to decode it. Its surface and its meaning are one and the same.

Further Reading: I. Buchanan *Fredric Jameson: Live Theory* (2006).

war machine A term introduced in Gilles *Deleuze and Félix *Guattari's account of *nomadology in *Mille Plateaux* (1980), translated as *A Thousand Plateaus* (1987), to name and theorize artistic and political dissidence and creativity. It is, however, a highly ambiguous concept. Deleuze and Guattari introduce it as a historical concept, but then develop it into an aesthetic concept and it is not always clear how one gets from the former to the latter. As a historical concept, the derivation of the war machine is the counter-intuitive, but anthropologically plausible, argument that the war machine is not the property of the state, but was in fact formed in direct opposition to the state. The war machine is not the same thing as a standing army, which is the province of the state, and its primary object is not war. But the war machine is also vulnerable to capture, and the marauding hordes that sweep in from the desert are taken into the state and their objective changed. As an aesthetic concept, the war machine is the line of deviation inherent in every form that enables it to be transformed—it is, in effect, the pure potential for change.

Watkins, Gloria *See* HOOKS, BELL.

weak thought (*pensiero debole*) A label applied to the work of Italian philosopher Gianni *Vattimo. Although Vattimo adopted this description of his thought, his own term for what he is trying to do in his work is in fact 'weak ontology'. He derives the idea of a weak *ontology from his reading of Martin *Heidegger and Heidegger's student Hans-Georg *Gadamer, whose key work he translated into Italian. On Vattimo's reading of Heidegger there is a profound separation between language and reality; language on this view can at best convey an interpretation of reality, but never the thing itself. Hence it is a 'weak' not 'strong' ontology. But in contrast to a number of other philosophers in the *postmodern *anti-foundation tradition, Vattimo does not interpret this state of being as a crisis for *metaphysics. He sees it rather as a challenge to develop a more rigorous process of interpretation.

Weiss, Peter (1916–82) German author, artist, and activist. Born near Berlin to a Hungarian Jewish father and Christian mother, he lived in Bremen and Berlin as a child, then moved to London to study photography, and after that to Prague until Germany annexed the Sudetenland in 1938. He fled, first to Switzerland and then to Sweden, where he remained for the rest of his life. In the 1940s and 1950s, Weiss divided his time between teaching art, making experimental films, and writing prose and drama in both Swedish and German. His first play *Der Turm* (The Tower) was premiered in 1950, but it was not until the production of *Marat/Sade* in Berlin in 1964 that Weiss gained a large international audience. The internationally renowned director Peter Brook staged *Marat/Sade* in New York the following year and Weiss's reputation as an innovative, highly political playwright was made. Set in Charenton Asylum, where de Sade was incarcerated, the play revolves around the attempt by the inmates to stage a play about the assassination of Jean-Paul Marat (a leading figure in the French Revolution) under the direction of the Marquis himself. Exhibiting the influence of both Antonin *Artaud and Bertolt *Brecht, the play quickly became a classic and was subsequently and successfully transposed to cinema with Peter Brook directing. For many though, Weiss's true masterpiece is his three-volume historical novel *Die Ästhetik des Widerstands* (1975–81), partially translated as *The Aesthetics of Resistance* (2005), which explores the rise of Nazism in a more overtly political fashion than Thomas Mann's allegorical *Doktor Faustus* (1947), translated as *Doctor Faustus* (1948), and also takes in the Spanish Civil War.

Further Reading: R. Cohen *Understanding Peter Weiss* (1993).
F. Jameson *The Modernist Papers* (2008).

Wellek, René (1903–95) Czech-American literary critic and comparativist. Born and raised in Vienna, speaking both Czech and German at home, Wellek studied linguistics and literature at the

Charles University in Prague. After graduation, with the aid of several fellowships, he was able to pursue studies in the US and UK, developing his appreciation of English literature until a lectureship became available at the Charles University in 1930. He taught there for 5 years, becoming an active participant in the meetings of the *Prague Circle, before accepting a post at what is now part of University College London teaching Slavonic language and literature. Funded by the Czech government, this position was terminated when the Nazis invaded Czechoslovakia. Wellek chose to immigrate to the US rather than return to Europe. He was found a job in Iowa by his contacts in the US, where he worked for a few years before moving to Yale. Wellek's reputation rests on the massive surveys of literature and literary theory he compiled: *History of Modern Criticism* (1955–91) and *Theory of Literature* (1949), which he co-authored with Austin Warren. The latter work argued for a systematic approach to the study of literature along the lines recommended by the *New Critics. In his later work, Wellek defended New Criticism against the critiques of *theory in both its *structuralist and *post-structuralist guises. It is perhaps ironic then that he is memorialized today by a lecture series at the University of California Irvine which is hosted by the Institute for Critical Theory and is widely regarded as one of the most prestigious lecture series for the promulgation of theory.

Western Marxism A general category describing a sea change that occurred in the development of *Marxism following the Russian Revolution in 1917. Scholars in Russia were expected to toe the party line and focus their energies on ensuring the success of the revolution at home. Meanwhile, scholars in the West found themselves cut off from developments in Russia and perplexed by the failure of their own countries to replicate events in the East. The failure was all the more perplexing because of the fact that according to Marxist doctrine, the socialist revolution should have occurred in the more highly industrialized countries of the West rather than the largely agrarian and still quite feudal Russia. Marx's faith in the inevitability of the socialist revolution had to be abandoned in the face of this defeat and that meant Marxism had to shift its focus and give thought to why the expected revolutions failed to occur. By the end of the Second World War, Western Marxism had become the almost exclusive preserve of the academy—whereas figures like Antonio *Gramsci and György *Lukàcs had been active in government, scholars like Walter *Benjamin, and more especially Theodor *Adorno and Max *Horkheimer were strictly academic. It also started to focus more on cultural rather than economic problems and it is for this reason also known as cultural Marxism. Today, the principal organ of Western Marxism is the British journal *New Left Review*; among its contributors are many of the most prominent figures in the field such as Perry *Anderson, Terry *Eagleton, and Fredric *Jameson.

Further Reading: P. Anderson *Considerations on Western Marxism* (1976).

White, Hayden (1928–) American historian best known for his *post-structuralist approach and his emphasis on the importance of *tropes in *historiography. Educated at Wayne State University and the University of Michigan, graduating from the latter with a PhD in 1956, White worked at the University of Rochester, UCLA (University of California Los Angeles), and for the bulk of his career at the University of California Santa Cruz. White became internationally renowned with the publication of *Metahistory: The Historical Imagination in Nineteenth-Century Europe* (1973), a magisterial work that changed the shape of historiography in the latter part of the 20th century. Discussing the work of the great historians of the 19th century, Jacob Burkhardt, Benedetto Croce, G.W.F *Hegel, Jules Michelet, Friedrich *Nietzsche, and Leopold von Ranke, White argues that the writing of history is influenced by the choice of narrative type (e.g. comedy, farce, romance, tragedy, etc.) and that this choice reflects *ideological conviction. White developed this line of thinking further in the *Tropics of Discourse* (1978), coining the term 'tropology' to delineate his topic.

Further Reading: F. Ankersmit, E. Domanska, and H. Kellner *Re-figuring Hayden White* (2009).

whiteness A polemical rubric for analysing the way in which the white peoples of Europe constructed and perpetuate a discourse which uses skin pigmentation as a political marker and privileges their own skin colour above all others. It is a polemical term in the sense that although the term *race has been around for centuries, it was rarely if ever applied to white peoples, as though to say only people of colour have race. As is also obvious, the very notion of people of colour implies that being white is somehow the standard against which skin pigmentation should be measured and judged. But by the same token, it is the existence of those racialized others that gives whiteness its meaning. Critical analysis of whiteness seeks to expose the falseness of its position as the 'natural', 'normal', or 'given' term in any debate about skin colour. Whiteness studies is a sub-branch of *Postcolonial Studies.

Further Reading: R. Dyer *White: Essays on Race and Culture* (1997).
S. Garner *Whiteness: An Introduction* (2007).
G. Hage *White Nation: Fantasies of White Supremacy in a Multicultural Society* (1997).
R. Mohanram *Imperial White: Race, Diaspora, and the British Empire* (2007).
R. Young *White Mythologies: Writing History and the West* (1990).

Williams, Raymond (1921–88) Welsh *Marxist literary and cultural critic who, through the elaboration of what he called *Cultural Materialism had an enormous influence on *Cultural Studies and *New Historicism.

Williams was born near the small railway and market town of Abergavenny on the Welsh-English border. Although this was not a Welsh-speaking region, Williams nonetheless identified very strongly with his Welsh heritage, writing several novels on the theme in later life. He began his undergraduate degree at Trinity College, Cambridge, where he also joined the Communist Party and met people like Eric *Hobsbawm, but interrupted his studies in 1941 to join the army. He saw active service in Europe during the Second World War as a tank commander, returning to Cambridge in 1946 and completing his BA and MA. He then took a job at Oxford as an adult education tutor, a position he held until 1961 when he was invited back to Cambridge as a lecturer. He remained there until his retirement in 1983, having been appointed professor in 1974. Among his most notable students were Terry *Eagleton and Stephen *Greenblatt.

His first books were on drama and criticism, but his reputation as a critic of rare insight and distinction was made in 1958 with the publication of *Culture and Society*. In it Williams explores the changes in meaning of the idea of 'culture' from 1780 to 1950, arguing that such changes record and reflect the changed conditions of everyday life. He distances himself from the Leavisite model of *Practical Criticism, which took pains to avoid any direct reference to society or what Williams describes as 'lived experience'. Eagleton's famous description of him as a 'Left-Leavisite' was perhaps a calculated insult. He followed this book with *The Long Revolution* (1961), which theorizes in detail the relationship between social relations, cultural institutions, and subjectivity, with the aim of showing how progressive political ideas emerge and become established as the norm. He expands the concepts of *structure of feeling (introduced in the early work, *Preface to Film* (1954)) and of dominant, residual, and emergent to explain the kinds of cultural mood shifts required for ideological change to occur. This is developed further in *Marxism and Literature* (1977).

In the early 1970s, Williams wrote several books that were to have a formative and lasting impact on the incipient field of Cultural Studies: *Communications* (1962), *Television* (1974), and *Keywords* (1976). However his most influential book from this period was undoubtedly the *Country and the City* (1973). A prolific author and an engaged public intellectual, Williams was a towering influence on Anglophone literary and cultural studies throughout the 1970s and 1980s.

Further Reading: J. Higgins *Raymond Williams* (1999).
F. Inglis *Raymond Williams* (1995).
P. Jones *Raymond Williams' Sociology of Culture* (2003).
D. Smith *Raymond Williams: A Warrior's Tale* (2008).

Winnicott, Donald Woods (1896–1971) English psychoanalyst, key member of the *object relations school, and probably the most influential theorist of child *psychoanalysis. Winnicott was born in Plymouth, UK to a comfortably middle-class family. He went to boarding school in Cambridge, and entered university there as well with the intention of studying medicine. His plans were interrupted by the outbreak of World War I in 1914. He worked as a medical trainee for a number of years in Cambridge; then he joined the navy as a medical officer in 1917, recommencing his medical training shortly thereafter. In 1923 he obtained a paediatrics post at the Paddington Green Children's Hospital in London, where he worked for the next 40 years. It is for his work as a child psychoanalyst that Winnicott is best known, particularly for his theory of the 'transitional object' (better known in popular discourse as the 'security blanket'). This object enables the child to move between what Winnicott calls the subjective world of the 'me' and the objective world of the 'not-me', by trailing a little piece of the former into the alienating arena of the latter. Winnicott's child development theories are built on the idea that the parent—he emphasizes the mother—should only be 'good enough', by which he means they should provide a safe environment for the child and satisfy their needs, but not smother the child by never allowing them to take a risk or compelling them to do something for themselves. The 'perfect' mother, he argues, stifles the child. Winnicott is a major influence on the popular Welsh psychoanalyst Adam Phillips.

Further Reading: R. Rodman *Winnicott: Life and Work* (2003).

wish-fulfilment (*Wunscherfüllung*) The essential premise of Sigmund *Freud's theory of dream-interpretation. All dreams, he postulates, are the symbolic fulfilment of wishes. He later extended this thesis to the interpretation of *symptoms. The interpretation of dreams in *psychoanalysis turns, then, on uncovering the wish (which isn't always obvious) underpinning a particular dream. French psychoanalyst Jacques *Lacan offers a striking defence of this thesis in one of his early seminars: he asks his audience to consider how dreaming of a friend who had recently died could stem from a wish-fulfilment? Everything would seem to point in the opposite direction inasmuch that the last thing one would wish concerning a friend is their death. Yet Lacan argues that the dream does fulfil the wish of not wanting to forget that friend. Gilles *Deleuze and Félix *Guattari argue that the dreams and more particularly the delusions of schizophrenia are exceptions to this thesis.

Wittgenstein, Ludwig (1889–1951) Austrian philosopher, generally regarded as one of the most important of the 20th century, not the least because his work bridged the usually insuperable divide between *analytic philosophy (particularly the branch known as *logical positivism) and continental philosophy. His notion of *language games played a very important role in this regard. Wittgenstein's work was predominantly concerned with the theory of meaning. An eccentric figure, his life story has been the subject of film—*Wittgenstein* (1993), scripted by Terry *Eagleton and directed by Derek Jarman—as well as several speculative novels. Biographers have had a field day with his life. Ray Monk's excellent biography presents him as a tormented genius, while Kimberley Cornish's more fanciful effort claims him as a Soviet spy linked to the so-called Cambridge Five.

He was born in Vienna into a family of assimilated Jews. The children were all baptized as Roman Catholics. Wittgenstein's father was one of the wealthiest men in Europe. He made his fortune in iron and steel, then at a quite young age consolidated his wealth into real estate and retired from active involvement in his company so as to devote time to the arts. He commissioned paintings by Klimt and sculptures by Rodin and music from Mahler and Brahms. All the Wittgenstein children were talented. His elder brother Paul was an internationally renowned pianist, who even managed to continue on the concert circuit after losing an arm in World War I. In such a household, Ludwig felt like something of a failure. It was evidently an unhappy household, too, as three of his brothers committed suicide, and all of them including Ludwig suffered from depression.

Philosophy was something that Wittgenstein only became aware of when he entered university. Initially he was interested in engineering, particularly aeronautics, and this is what he studied, first in Berlin, then in Manchester. While he was in England he started reading work on the foundation of mathematics by Alfred North

Whitehead, Bertrand Russell, and Gottlob *Frege. He visited the latter, who advised him to study with Russell, so in 1911 he went to Cambridge to do precisely that. Russell was immediately impressed by his intelligence and encouraged his work. But to write and think properly, Wittgenstein needed solitude, so in 1913 he took himself to an isolated hut in Norway and there wrote what was effectively the first draft of *Tractatus Logico-Philosophicus* (1921). Further work on it was delayed by the outbreak of World War I. Wittgenstein returned to his native country and volunteered for the army, and served in the artillery on both the Russian and Italian fronts, winning several decorations for valour.

On leave from the front, late in the summer of 1918, Wittgenstein received the sad news that one of his closest friends had been killed in an air crash. Almost suicidal with grief, Wittgenstein retreated to his Uncle Paul's house, and there completed the final manuscript of *Tractatus Logico-Philosophicus*. In spite of its later reputation as one of the most important works of philosophy of the 20th century, it was initially very difficult to find a publisher willing to take it on, and in all probability would not have been published without the assistance of Bertrand Russell.

In Wittgenstein's own mind, the *Tractatus* had solved all the basic problems of philosophy that interested him, so he decided there was no point in pursuing a career as a philosopher. He opted to become a primary school teacher instead. He also wanted to unburden himself of his family legacy, so he gave his not inconsiderable inheritance to his brothers and sisters and returned to Austria. But as perhaps might have been expected, Wittgenstein was not well suited to the task of teaching young children and he was forced to resign in 1926. In somewhat of a slump and feeling a failure as a teacher, Wittgenstein worked for a time as a gardener in a monastery and contemplated taking orders. He was woken out of his mental and spiritual torpor by the offer from his sister to design her new house. He leapt at the chance and designed a house of such austere beauty that his other sister described it as being fit only for gods, not humans. Wittgenstein slaved over every detail, right down to the design of the window latches. The house still stands today and is used as a cultural centre.

Moritz Schlick, the leading figure in the *Vienna Circle, contacted Wittgenstein as he was completing work on the house and persuaded him to meet with him and some of his colleagues, who were admirers of the *Tractatus*. These meetings, which Wittgenstein often found very frustrating, stimulated him into thinking he had more to give philosophically speaking, and more importantly, started him thinking that perhaps the *Tractatus* contained grave errors that needed to be remedied. So in 1929 he returned to Cambridge. Reflecting on the occasion, his friend John Maynard Keynes famously wrote to his wife: 'Well, God has arrived. I met him on the 5.15 train.'

At Russell's suggestion the *Tractatus* was submitted as a PhD so that Wittgenstein could obtain the requisite qualification to teach at Cambridge (at that point he did not even have an undergraduate degree). With extended sabbaticals in Russia, Norway, and Ireland, as well as a long stint working as a medical orderly in Newcastle and London during World War II, Wittgenstein worked at Cambridge until 1947. He resigned his post then in order to concentrate on writing, which he found himself unable to do in what he perceived to be the stifling atmosphere of Cambridge. For the next three years, before he succumbed to cancer, he led a peripatetic existence travelling and writing. Although the *Tractatus* was the only work of philosophy published in his own lifetime, he left behind hundreds of pages of manuscript that have since been shaped into books and published, the most important of which is undoubtedly *Philosophische Untersuchungen* (1953), translated as *Philosophical Investigations* (1953).

It is customary to divide Wittgenstein's career into two parts—the first part is determined by the abstract formalism of the *Tractatus*, which rejects even its own meaningfulness because its meaning has to be constructed on the basis of context; the second part is determined by *Philosophical Investigations*, or the PI as it is usually known, which does a complete turnaround and argues that it is only by dealing with context that meaning is possible, and introduces the idea of the language game to try to deal with it.

Further Reading: A.C. Grayling *Wittgenstein: A Very Short Introduction* (2001).
R. Monk *Ludwig Wittgenstein: The Duty of Genius* (1990).
R. Monk *How to Read Wittgenstein* (2005).

Wittig, Monique (1935–2003) French *feminist critic and author, and a self-described radical lesbian. Wittig's work argues that the concept of 'woman' is a heterosexual construct. Thus, a lesbian is not a woman, she claims, because her position outside of the heterosexual matrix means she is no longer defined by the heterosexual norm. Therefore that construction of both her gender and her sexuality does not apply. Her best-known works are *Le Corps Lesbien* (1973), translated as *The Lesbian Body* (1975) and *The Straight Mind and Other Essays* (1992). Wittig left France in 1976 and moved to the US and started writing in English.

Further Reading: N. Shaktini *On Monique Wittig* (2005).

Wölfflin, Heinrich (1864–1945) Swiss art historian best known for his so-called 'principles of art', which continue to inform art criticism to this day. He argued that art history should be studied in terms of changes in styles and the emergence of new forms, rather than in terms of the biographies and oeuvres of individual artists. Wölfflin studied art and history at Basel under the great historian Jacob Burckhardt, philosophy at Berlin University, and art history at Munich, where his father was a professor. His doctoral thesis *Prolegomena zu einer Psychologie der Architektur* (1886) applied the nascent science of psychology to architecture, setting a pattern for his future works, which similarly tried to understand the effect as well as the affect of artistic works. Following his graduation in 1886, Wölfflin undertook a two-year study tour of Italy, after which he wrote *Renaissance und Barock* (1888), which, inspired by *Nietsche's *Die Geburt der Tragödie* (1870–71), The Birth of Tragedy, went a long way towards rehabilitating the Baroque as an artistic style. He taught at Basel, Berlin, and Munich. His best known books are *Die Klassische Kunst* (1898), translated as *Classic Art. An Introduction to the Italian Renaissance* (1948), and *Kunstgeschichtliche Grundbegriffe* (1915), translated as *Principles of Art History. The Problem of the Development of Style in Later Art* (1929).

work and text (*oeuvre* and *texte*) French literary critic Roland *Barthes proposed this distinction in the essay 'De l'oeuvre au texte' (1971), translated as 'From Work to Text' (1977), which together with Jacques *Derrida's 'La structure, le signe et le jeu dans le discoursdes sciences humaines' (1966), translated as 'Structure, Sign and Play in the Discourse of Human Sciences' (1978), is generally regarded as one of the inaugural texts of *post-structuralism, representing a sea change within Barthes's own thinking. Referring to the way Einstein's theory of relativity has necessitated that scientists take into account the relativity of their frame of reference, with the implication that there are no longer any absolutes in science (in their place are undecidable limit points), Barthes proposes that *psychoanalysis, *Marxism, and *semiotics combined necessitate a similar kind of rethinking of the cultural object. This newly relativized cultural object—in which he includes the relations between readers, writers and critics—is what he wants to call text (he sometimes writes it as Text to underline the fact that it is an ontological distinction he is trying to make). In contrast, work refers to an older, Newtonian, conception of the cultural object, which is self-contained, singular and closed. He compares the distinction to the one Jacques *Lacan makes between reality and the *real: the work belongs to the order of reality inasmuch as it can be held in the hand, so to speak, whereas the text is of the same order as the real, which is to say it is a problematic or experimental field and not a concrete object. It is rather the limit through which a work must pass if it wants to attain what *modernist critics praised as the new. The distinction between work and text restates and complicates the distinction Barthes previously made between the readerly (work) and writerly (text). *See also* READERLY AND WRITERLY.

Further Reading: M. Moriarty *Roland Barthes* (1991).

world-system theory An explanation of human history that focuses on the development of large-scale social systems such as banking, international trade, geopolitical alliances, and technological advancement. It emerged in the 1970s via the work of the *Marxist economists and historians, Samir Amin, André Gunder Frank, and Immanuel *Wallerstein. Influenced by the **Annales* School of history, its perspective is rigorously **longue durée*, always taking things back to the point of emergence of a particular type of system (thus it tends to dismiss *globalization for failing to observe that economic systems like capitalism have been global since their inception). Moreover, it is rigorously international in its geographical perspective (but is, nevertheless, mindful of the kinds of geospatial iniquities *dependency theory emphasizes).

Further Reading: C. Chase-Dunn *Global Formation* (1998).
T. Shannon *Introduction to the World-Systems Perspective* (1996).

Wright, Eric Olin (1947–) American *Marxist sociologist. Born in Kansas, Wright did undergraduate studies at Harvard and Oxford. He completed a PhD in sociology at Berkeley in 1976. He then took a position at the University of Wisconsin, where he has remained ever since. As is clear from the list of his principal publications, for most of his career Wright's research has focused on the classical Marxist problematic of *class—e.g. *Class, Crisis and the State* (1978), *Classes* (1985), *Class Counts* (2000), and *Approaches to Class Analysis* (2009)—but late in his career he expanded his view to take in the question of *utopia. Wright's work tries to resolve the two key problems in Marxism: (i) the apparently anomalous existence of a middle class who are neither owners of the means of production, nor completely at the mercy of the owners of the means of production; (ii) the conflict between *class struggle and technological determinism as the principle factors driving history. Wright resolves the first problem by treating the middle class as a contradictory class and the latter by arguing that technological innovation gives impetus to history, but doesn't drive it because ultimately technology has to be adopted by humans for it to be effective.

Further Reading: A. Milner *Class* (1999).

writerly *See* READERLY AND WRITERLY.

Yale School of Deconstruction A shorthand way of referring to a moment in the 1970s when the work of Jacques *Derrida was taken up and experimented with by four prominent literary critics in the Department of English at Yale: Paul de Man, J. Hillis *Miller, Geoffrey Hartmann, and Harold *Bloom. While it is true that these authors drew inspiration from Derrida's work, it has to be said that their brand of *deconstruction bears very little resemblance to Derrida's (we could also say, to adapt a phrase from Fredric *Jameson—himself sometimes mistakenly included in this school because he happened to be at Yale then—that the two versions of deconstruction have much in common, indeed everything save the essentials). The Yale form of deconstruction tends to be a highly playful and erudite form of close reading, with very little interest in making either a philosophical or political point, whereas Derrida is precisely concerned with the latter.

Further Reading: J. Arac et al. (eds.) *The Yale Critics: Deconstruction in America* (1983).

H. Bloom (ed.) *Deconstruction and Criticism* (1979).

Zeitgeist A German word that translates literally as 'spirit of the time'. It is used to describe social, cultural, and intellectual trends, but it also implies that there is some kind of superhuman 'force' at work influencing the actions and decisions of entire peoples. While such a phantasmal force is difficult to document empirically, the fact that something like it must exist can be seen in the various fads that every historical period seems to know. Why people en masse did one thing rather than another at a certain point in time is very often accounted for in terms of *zeitgeist.*

zeugma Literally meaning 'yoking', it is a figure in *rhetoric in which one word in a sentence is used to refer to two others in the same sentence. For example, 'the children like to run and sing'.

Zhdanovism A shorthand term for the doctrine governing all aesthetic production in the Soviet Union laid down in 1948 by Andrei Zhdanov, a senior bureaucrat. It is in effect a code word for any form of artistic prescription.

Žižek, Slavoj (1949–) Slovenian *Marxist philosopher and *psychoanalyst. Known for his uncanny ability to connect *critical theory and popular culture in a way that is both humorous and thought-provoking, Žižek is one of the most high profile intellectuals in the world. An incredibly prolific and wide-ranging author, his work is much in demand and he writes for a variety of publications, from newspapers like *The Guardian* (UK) and *London Review of Books*, to blogs and academic journals. Working in several languages, it is one of Žižek's great gifts that he is almost always able to give near instantaneous counter-intuitive critical responses to world events. Having made the perverse counter-claim into something of a personal trademark, he can be relied on to say the opposite of what everyone else is saying. Žižek is not without his critics or his faults, but is widely regarded as an essential voice of dissidence.

Žižek was born in Ljubljana in what was Communist Yugoslavia but is now the capital of Slovenia, into a middle-class family. He studied philosophy and sociology at the University of Ljubljana and in 1971 gained a position there as an assistant researcher. Although Yugoslavia was comparatively liberal for a socialist country, it still had its hard-line elements and Žižek was fired in 1973 because his MA dissertation was deemed to be 'non-Marxist'. He spent the next four years in the Yugoslav national army, completing his obligatory national service. In the late 1970s he was hired as a researcher at the Institute of Sociology at the University of Ljubljana, enabling him to complete a PhD on German idealism in 1981. He then studied psychoanalysis in Paris with Jacques *Lacan's son-in-law, Jacques-Alain Miller, and completed his habilitation thesis (on Lacan, *Hegel, and Marx). Outside of academia, Žižek co-founded the Slovenian Liberal Democratic Party and in 1990 stood for a seat in the four-member collective Slovenian presidency and only narrowly missed gaining office.

The publication of *The Sublime Object of Ideology* in 1989, Žižek's first work in English, was the major launching point of his career. It set the pattern for his numerous future publications by applying a mixture of Lacan and Hegel to a basically Marxist problematic: what is *ideology and how does it work? Žižek defines ideology as the set of beliefs which glue society together—these beliefs are often false, inconsistent and irrational, but no less necessary for being so. For example, money requires our belief in its value—it is literally a promissory note—to function, in spite of the fact that our senses tell us it is intrinsically worthless. The point is, even though we know better, even though we know the truth, we act as though the truth were otherwise, and this leads Žižek to propose the provocative thesis that it is *fantasy that supports reality (and not the other way round). Fantasy is a conscious disavowal of a known truth coupled with an *unconscious (and therefore stronger) belief in an alternate truth. Fantasy is faced constantly by the threat of dissolution should it come into contact with the *real, therefore *culture must find ways of staving off that eventuality. Žižek's best work details how this process works and fails at the same time.

Further Reading: R. Butler *Slavoj Žižek: Live Theory* (2004).
S. Kay *Žižek: A Critical Introduction* (2003).
T. Myers *Slavoj Žižek* (2003).
M. Sharpe *Slavoj Žižek: A Little Piece of the Real* (2004).

SEE WEB LINKS

- A site detailing regular updates of Slavoj Žižek's frequent publications and speaking appearances.

Recommended web links

SEE WEB LINKS

This is a web-linked dictionary. To access the websites, go to the dictionary's web page at www.oup.com/uk/reference/resources/criticaltheory, click on Web links in the Resources section and click straight through to the relevant websites.

Film Theory

- A range of links to film theory and review websites.

Literary Theory

- A listing of theorists and a brief overview of their work. It has a list of other helpful URLS.

Philosophy

- The Stanford Encyclopaedia of Philosophy is a comprehensive and academically rigorous website of philosophical terms and an excellent site for biographical details of major philosophers.
- A peer-reviewed Internet encyclopaedia of philosophy.
- A variety of resources about philosophy, politics, and the human condition.
- A dictionary of terms, overviews of the major figures, and a survey of major western philosophical developments.

Popular Culture

- A popular culture website that explores the relationships between media and identities.

Theatre Studies and Theory

- Biographical details of theatre figures as well as a range of theatre resources sorted chronologically and alphabetically.

Oxford Paperback Reference

The Kings of Queens of Britain
John Cannon and Anne Hargreaves

A detailed, fully-illustrated history ranging from mythical and pre-conquest rulers to the present House of Windsor, featuring regional maps and genealogies.

A Dictionary of World History

Over 4,000 entries on everything from prehistory to recent changes in world affairs. An excellent overview of world history.

A Dictionary of British History
Edited by John Cannon

An invaluable source of information covering the history of Britain over the past two millennia. Over 3,000 entries written by more than 100 specialist contributors.

Review of the parent volume
'the range is impressive ... truly (almost) all of human life is here'
Kenneth Morgan, *Observer*

Oxford Paperback Reference

A Dictionary of Sociology
John Scott and Gordon Marshall

The most wide-ranging and authoritative dictionary of its kind.

'Readers and especially beginning readers of sociology can scarcely do better . . . there is no better single volume compilation for an up-to-date, readable, and authoritative source of definitions, summaries and references in contemporary Sociology.'

A. H. Halsey, *Emeritus Professor, Nuffield College, University of Oxford*

The Concise Oxford Dictionary of Politics
Iain McLean and Alistair McMillan

The bestselling A-Z of politics with over 1,700 detailed entries

'A first class work of reference . . . probably the most complete as well as the best work of its type available . . . Every politics student should have one'

Political Studies Association

A Dictionary of Environment and Conservation
Chris Park

An essential guide to all aspects of the environment and conservation containing over 8,500 entries.

'from *aa* to *zygote*, choices are sound and definitions are unspun'

New Scientist